To Cecil,

The Erotic Arts

Many, many thanks.

Love,

Drew

Nov. 78.

The Erotic Arts

Peter Webb

Secker & Warburg

London

In memory of my mother,
Enid Ida Webb

First published in England 1975 by
Martin Secker & Warburg Limited
14 Carlisle Street, London W1V 6NN

SBN: 436 56550 1

Printed and bound in Great Britain by
Morrison & Gibb Ltd, London and Edinburgh

Table of Contents

List of Illustrations

Acknowledgements

No one could write a book of this scope on his own, and my first debt of gratitude is for all the co-operation I have received from Hornsey College of Art, now the Faculty of Art and Design of the Middlesex Polytechnic, and in particular from my colleagues John Field, Barry Curtis, and David Cheshire, whose help and encouragement has extended far beyond their contributions to the text of the book; also from Ted Sebley, Bobby de Joia, Anne Whitehead and Olive Warner. My researches at the British Museum were greatly helped by Bentley Bridgewater, Edward Croft-Murray, Reginald Williams, Kenneth Gardner, and Richard Camber; and at the Victoria and Albert Museum by John Harthan, Brian Reade, John Irwin and Mrs Edgington. I have also received assistance from Robert Short, John Gauge, and Eric Fernie of the University of East Anglia; Philip Rawson of the Gulbenkian Museum of Oriental Art, University of Durham; Michael Kitson of the Courtauld Institute, University of London; Simon Wilson of the Tate Gallery; and Graham Pilkington of the Piccadilly Gallery, London. Special thanks are due to Andrew Bradford, Barry Burman, Nick Callow, Louis Dunand, Peter Fryer, Neil Hornick, Phyllis and Eberhardt Kronhausen, Andrew Lloyd-Eley, Richard Neville, Graham Ovenden, Celia Quicke, Jeffrey Rund, Ronald Serlin, Christine Taylor, Nicholas Webb, and Sylvia Wright. To all these people, to all my contributors, and to all who have allowed me to reproduce works in their collections, I should like to take this opportunity of expressing my gratitude.

Peter Webb
January 1974

Picture Credits

Philadelphia Museum of Art (Louise and Walter Arensberg Collection), cover and number 5; Mansell Collection, London, 1, 71, 72, 74–77, 79, 86, 88, 96, 97, 103, 120, 122–24, 133; Philip Rawson, Durham, 3, 47, 48; C. M. Dixon, London, 7, 8, 27, 38, 45, 46, 67; Trustees of the British Museum, 9, 26, 29, 32, 33, 36, 37, 39, 40, 42, 45, 46, 59–65, 78, 80–84, 93, 99, 105–7, 113, 114, 117, 129, 166, 173, 244–48; Boris de Rachewiltz, Milan, 10, 15 (from *Black Eros*, 1964); Aerofilms, London, 12; Fabrizio Mori, Rome, 13; Cambridge University Press, 14; Hamlyn Group, London, 16; Axel Poignant, London, 17; Museum of Primitive Art, New York, 18; Museum für Völkerkunde, Berlin, 19; Museum für Völkerkunde, Hamburg, 20, 21; National Gallery, Washington, D.C., 22; Bodleian Library, Oxford, 23; Institute for Sex Research, Indiana University, 24, 25; Louvre Museum, Paris, 28; Ephesus Museum, Greece, 30; Staatliche Museen, Berlin, 31, 34; G. Lo Duca, Paris, 35, 68, 92, 98, 121, 147, 171; Naples Museum, 41, 43, 44, 73; Victor Lownes, London, 49, 50, 56, 57, 168–70, 189; Victoria and Albert Museum, London, 51, 52, 109, 110, 174; Bibliothèque Nationale, Paris, 53, 115; Museum of Turkish and Islamic Art, Istanbul, 54, 55; Jeff Rund, New York, 58, 179, 268, 269; Museum of Fine Arts, Boston, 66; University of East Anglia (Fine Arts Department), Norwich, 69; Officine Grafiche Poligrafici, Bologna, 70; National Gallery, London, 85, 94; Bayerische Staatsgemäldesammlungen, Munich, 87, 95; Minneapolis Institute of Arts, 89; Galerie Weltz, Salzburg, 90; Cary von Karwath, Vienna, 101, 102 (from *Die Erotik in der Kunst*, 1908); Wolverhampton Art Gallery, 104; Edward Croft-Murray, London, 108, 111, 112; Musée Ingres, Montauban, 118, 119; Lefèvre Gallery, London, 125; Tate Gallery, London, 126, 132, 144, 145, 172; Musée Toulouse-Lautrec, Albi, 127; Vincent van Gogh Museum, Amsterdam, 128; Simon Wilson, London, 131, 137; Piccadilly Gallery, London, 134–36; Studio Vista, London, 138, 139, 140, 161; Newark Museum, 141; *Playboy* Magazine, New York, 142; Lady Lever Gallery, Port Sunlight, Cheshire, 146; Graham Ovenden, Cornwall, 150–56, 158, 182, 186; *Penthouse* Magazine, London, 157, 258; Radio Times Hulton Picture Library, London, 162–64; Musée Rodin, Paris, 165; Fischer Fine Art, London, 167; Private Collection, Australia, 175; Peyton Skipwith, London, 176; Athletic Model Guild, Los Angeles, 178; Robert Crumb, California, 180, 265; Acoris Gallery, London, 181; Peter Widdison,

Coventry, 183; Barry Burman, Leamington, 187; Cordier and Ekstrom Gallery, New York, 188, 190; London Arts, London, 191; Norman Lundin, Washington, D.C., 192; Knut Andreassen, Lund, 193; Stedelijk Museum, Amsterdam, 194; Peggy Guggenheim, Venice, 195; Roger Jean Segelat, Paris, 197, 203; George Melly, London (Photo: John Webb), 198; Robert Descharnes, Paris, 199; P. Molinier, Paris, 200; Galerie Louise Leiris, Paris, 201; F. Labisse, Paris (SPADEM), 202; Contemporary Films, 204; Slavia Prague, 205; 20th-Century Fox, 206, 209, 211; Cinema International Corporation, 207, 210; Metro-Goldwyn-Mayer, 208; Cinerama (Fox-Rank), 212, 215; United Artists, 213, 214, 216, 217, 224; Miracle Films, 218; Commonwealth United Films, 219; Twenty-four Frames, 220; Vaughan Films, 221, 222, 254; Fair Enterprises, London, 223; Mander and Mitchison Theatre Collection, London, 225, 226, 227; Paul Raymond, London, 228, 256; Richard Buckle, London, 230; Anthony Crickmay, London, 231, 236; Houston Rogers, London, 232; Keystone Press Agency, London, 233, 234; Michael Peto, London, 235; *News of the World*, London, 239; Friedman-Abeles, New York, 238, 239; Laurie Asprey, London, 240–42; Jaime Andrews, New York, 243; Hans Bellmer, Paris, 249, 250; Marlborough Fine Art, London, 251; John Kasmin, London, 252; Henry Moore, Much Hadham, 253; Columbia-Warner, 255; Jean Straker, Sussex, 260; *Sun and Health*, Harrow, 261, 262; *Scorpio* Magazine, London, 263; *Oz* Magazine, London, 266; P.W. Publications, Pennsylvania, 271; Atomage, London, 272; Scandinavian Picture, Copenhagen, 273; International Male Studio, Copenhagen, 274, 275; Bernard Hancock, London, 276; Author, 2, 6, 91, 100, 116, 130, 143, 148, 149, 159, 160, 177, 184, 185, 196, 229, 257, 259, 264, 267, 270.

Preface

This book is something new, an art book with a difference. It is about art, but also about sociology, history, and law. It is about events and about people. It is essentially about attitudes—a record of the attitudes of various people at various times and in various places to the uses of sexual imagery, whether in paintings, sculpture, films, plays, novels, or music. To my knowledge it is the first book to tackle this subject in such a far-ranging manner, but I am sure it will not be the last. Although my contributors and I have attempted to produce an authoritative text, certain of our interpretations must be taken as tentative, and the reader will find a degree of scepticism a healthy asset. In spite of the present climate of liberality, we are still not sufficiently advanced in the new study of eroticism to come to many definitive conclusions. But I have attempted to provide a framework for further discussion which will lead to controversy, and without controversy progress is impossible.

My interest in the subject of the Erotic Arts goes back to 1968, when some of my students at Coventry College of Art asked me to discuss the difference between Art and Pornography at a seminar class. The more I thought about it the more intrigued I became, but the further I researched into the problem, the more difficult I found it to obtain material. It became quickly apparent that research would be obstructed by the blind prejudice which the subject incurs and that this would be difficult to counteract by rational argument.

My interest in the subject led me into what became almost a personal campaign, as I found myself invited to lecture on 'Art and Pornography' and 'Censorship in the Arts' at various universities, colleges, and even grammar schools. What had started as a side-line was rapidly becoming a full-time occupation, and my concern for freedom and honesty in discussion of sexual topics was confirmed by the attention I received from the police. Twice my home was raided by detectives who suggested I might be able to 'help with their inquiries'. Subsequently, I found myself being treated as dangerous to the point of flattery. My Head of Department at Coventry College of Art tried to have me dismissed for 'corrupting the minds of young people'. The Proctors of Cambridge University banned a scheduled lecture (which I gave nevertheless after signing a legal document accepting responsibility for the consequences). Other universities and colleges made feeble efforts to protect their young from my 'evil' influence.

[xxi]

After being appointed Senior Lecturer in the History of Art at Hornsey College of Art in 1970, I was invited to give an optional course of lectures which I chose to call 'The Erotic Arts'. I received nothing but co-operation from the college, and the result inspired great interest and enthusiasm in those students who enrolled for what was in 1971 the first course of this kind ever held in this country. Harassment for my work has now diminished considerably, though various local ratepayers and other self-appointed guardians of morality have found occasion to complain about the course to the college. In order to clear up misunderstandings, a press conference was held, and although the tabloids managed to sensationalise the story out of all proportion (for example, the *Sun*'s headline was 'Homework: nudes and sexy undies'), the serious press treated the matter very fairly indeed.

The present book is based largely on my course, and I was very pleased to be invited to write it by Fredric Warburg of the London publishers, Secker & Warburg, for he contributed to the fight for artistic freedom by standing trial for publishing Stanley Kauffman's *The Philanderer* in 1954. The present book posed something of a dilemma for me, because I make no claims to having expert knowledge and insight relating to every subject covered by my course, and for this reason I had invited outside contributors to join certain of my seminar classes. The choice lay between a survey of the whole subject of eroticism in the arts written solely by myself, which would certainly have been uneven in places, and a compendium of articles by different authors, which would have had little unity or cohesiveness. The result is, I hope, a satisfactory compromise: a study of historical and contemporary celebrations of love, written largely by myself, but including contributions from researchers in particular fields relevant to a survey of eroticism in the arts.

The book begins with an introduction to the study of eroticism which attempts to put the subject into some form of brief historical perspective related in particular to the contemporary debate regarding sexual freedom. Chapter 1 explores the essential differences between erotic art and pornography, and searches for satisfactory definitions of these and other emotionally loaded terms. The following five chapters examine in some detail the incidence and relative importance of erotic art works in various ancient and modern civilisations, from the prehistoric world to Greece and Rome and from the Orient to Western Europe. The emphasis is on the West, with special consideration being given to the nineteenth and twentieth centuries, and in these periods certain crucial topics are singled out for more extensive treatment. These include Decadent Art, Victorian Art and Literature, and Surrealism.

In contrast to the historical approach of these chapters, the second half of the book tends to present a more critical and thematic method in discussions of the novel, the play, and the film. Other topics such as poetry and photography are treated in different contexts. The book ends with a critical bibliography and appendices which include a discussion of restricted collections in London museums, the Aretino sonnets, the range of pornography available today, and also interviews with selected artists: Hans Bellmer, David Hockney, Allen Jones, and Henry Moore. Like all new projects, the book is likely to contain mistakes, and I hope that any reader who finds factual errors will not hesitate to inform me.

The main objection to my work is given on moral grounds. The history of crimes committed in the name of 'morality' need not be elaborated here. Morality is defined in the *Oxford English Dictionary* as 'good moral conduct', and 'moral' means 'concerned with right and wrong conduct to one's neighbour'. Therefore, to behave morally is to behave rightly as regards one's neighbour. Whether making people aware of sexual attitudes is less right than teaching them to make money at the expense of others or to kill in order to defend what is theirs must be a matter of personal opinion. But the idea that anything to do with sex is immoral is a dangerous one, and should be attacked by everyone concerned about freedom.

The weapons to use in the fight against prejudice are knowledge and honesty, and these will prove invincible—and I would like to feel that this book is a small signpost on the way to freedom.

Completed January 1973
Revised January 1974
Peter Webb

Introduction

'Erotic' means 'pertaining to the passion of love', and it is natural that the passion of love should have inspired some of the world's greatest art—paintings, sculpture, literature, theatre, dance, films, and music. The degree of freedom achieved by the artist in recent years is large compared with that of the previous hundred and fifty or so years, but in wider terms it is less impressive. In the East, the artist has traditionally been encouraged to use sexual imagery in his work, and eroticism has been openly celebrated for hundreds of years. Primitive societies have always concentrated on depicting sexual themes, and still do today. In the great civilisations of Greece and Rome, erotic art had a religious significance and was considered a major part of the full life. In the Judao-Christian world a sense of guilt has become associated with anything to do with sex, and the post-Renaissance period has seen the institution of numerous laws to inhibit the open expression of erotic feelings. And so today there exists a tragic dichotomy between those who welcome a growing openness and honesty in the discussion and depiction of sexual matters and those who see life as being progressively cheapened by what they call an unhealthy obsession with sex.

It is sad that, for the majority of people, open discussion of sexual matters is impossible without acute embarrassment. In his study on *Sexual Deviation*, Dr Anthony Storr wrote: 'Many people would like to dissociate their erotic behaviour from the rest of their life and, in attempting to do so, treat sex as a fundamentally unimportant part of their existence. . . . Sex is so important, so pervasive, and so intimately connected with every aspect of personality that it cannot be separated from the person as a whole without impoverishing even superficial relationships. . . . Sexual intercourse . . . is one of the most natural, and certainly the most reward-ing and the most life-enhancing of all human experiences.'[1] Although almost everyone now recognises that sex plays a vital part in his life, many people still associate it with guilt and shame. This, of course, results from pre-conditioning and repression in the formative years, and we only have to look at the Victorian period to see how disastrous the repression of sexual instincts can be. The prejudices that ruled then are still not dead, as anyone in the advance-party of those seeking new freedom in the arts will know to his cost. In *The Mechanical Bride*, Marshall McLuhan wrote: 'Freedom, like taste, is an activity of perception and judgement

[xxv]

based on a great range of particular acts and experiences. Whatever fosters mere passivity and submission is the enemy of this vital activity.'[2] Yet it is still considered reasonable that adults should be told what films they may and may not see in a public cinema. It is still believed that society needs protection from certain books and photographs, in spite of the clear expert opinion of the British Arts Council's Report on Obscenity and President Nixon's Committee on Pornography that this is not so.

Many of our 'censors' still think it unnecessary to distinguish between pornography and erotic art. But this distinction is important, and the confusion of terms matters in two ways in particular. Artists concerned with eroticism are not pornographers, an assumption which does them a great disservice as well as making appreciation of their works more difficult. At the same time, the confusion betrays a prejudice against sexual material in general, and pornography in particular, which merits serious examination.*

It has recently become clear that the anti-pornography lobby in various parts of the world is strongly motivated by political considerations. Most of its supporters are markedly right-wing, and of the older generation, e.g. Mr Angus Maude, Conservative MP for Stratford-upon-Avon: 'Campaigners for sexual freedom are among the new revolutionaries who must be stopped.'[3] It is of interest to note in passing that it always seems to be totalitarian regimes that take a firm stand against sexual freedom, pornography, erotic art and literature, etc., cf. Hitler's Germany, Franco's Spain, Vorster's South Africa. In Russia, free love and an end to censorship of sexual literature were openly preached by the revolutionaries in 1917; the Soviets, however, soon instituted a forceful puritanism when they realised that individual freedom of that sort constituted a threat to the state.

In the summer of 1971, British newspapers were full of editorials and correspondence which pointed to the fact that the severe prison sentences (later reversed on appeal) in the *Oz* magazine obscenity trial were out of all proportion to the crime and therefore a political move: a word of warning to the 'alternative society'. Mr John Mortimer, QC, the defending counsel, stated: 'This is a trial about the right to dissent,' and it was clear to many people that the Obscene Publications Acts were being misused. This is, of course, the sort of legislation that is prone to such manipulation, especially in view of the provocative use of explicit sexuality by the 'underground movement'. Obscenity on its own does not threaten the fabric of a nation, but used in conjunction with political argument, it can become an ideological weapon, as the underground press has found in England (*Oz*), America (*Screw*), and Holland (*Suck*). The intention of all these publications is not titillation for its own sake, but sexual awareness leading to a freer and happier society. They are worlds away from the pornographic magazines, yet the law treats them in the same way, if not more harshly.

In using sex as a revolutionary weapon in the fight for a free society, the underground press follows on from those writers from Freud onwards who have seen the

* This question is discussed in detail in Chapter 1 of the present work.

power of eroticism to revolutionise society. Wilhelm Reich in the late '20s propounded his genital theory of the neuroses in *Die Funktion des Orgasmus*, in which he underlined the importance of the orgasm and pointed to the desperate need of modern man for an unrepressed sexuality.[4] He pointed to sexual repression as one of the principal mechanisms of political domination, an idea pursued in the '50s by Herbert Marcuse in his historical analysis of sexual repression, *Eros and Civilization*.[5] Marcuse argued that the repression of pregenital sexuality was brought about by the economic needs of capitalist society, and that the libido had become deliberately concentrated on the genital areas so that the rest of the body might be transformed into an instrument of labour; at the same time, since society was based upon labour, pleasure was of necessity devalued. Norman Brown in his book *Life Against Death*[6] took further Marcuse's idea that a truly non-repressive civilisation would be allowed to reassume its 'polymorphous perversity' of sexual behaviour which had been repressed since infancy. Inspired by Geza Roheim,[7] he suggested that in such a civilisation, the male–female differentiation would be unimportant and bisexuality would prevail.

At the time of the *Oz* trial, Richard Neville, one of the defendants, wrote: 'A sexual ethic designed by the superstitious to be imposed on the ignorant has not the mildest relevance in the seventies. If you have no wish to preserve the inheritance of property, why preserve the family? If you have no wish to preserve the family, of what use is even lip service monogamy? If aggression has outlived its usefulness, what better substitute than exhilarating exploration of our sexuality in word, deed and fantasy?'[8] While not suggesting that a sex revolution alone can change the face of society, the underground movement is committed to the idea that sexual awareness and the ending of repression will lead in the direction of a freer and happier world. Pornography is a transient phenomenon which, though it tends to dehumanise women to an extent, nevertheless helps the sexual lives of many people who at present suffer from the repressions of society.

Perhaps the greatest charge to be laid against pornography is that of exploitation: in a simplistic and often degrading way it often exploits human beings at their most vulnerable point. This book is about celebration, which, as we shall see, is diametrically in opposition to any form of exploitation. There are many books, plays, and films in existence today masquerading as art and yet which are no more than the exploitation of sexual needs. Pornography, at least, makes no pretence to be art, and fulfils a need for many people. In some ways, a far worse and more subtle form of exploitation is found in advertising.

During the last forty or fifty years the advertising industry has grown immensely, owing to the rapid growth of industry and trade. The most noticeable feature of this growth has been the increasing use of a psychological method of approach: the ad-man often seems to be less a trained designer than a psychologist, and he is not averse to using the psychology of sex to hit us literally—below the belt. Dr Johnson discerned this tendency as early as 1761 when he wrote about the moral question of 'whether they do not sometimes play too wantonly with our passions'.[9]

The post-Freudian world has learned to accept the fact that a good deal of what a person does can be interpreted as having a sexual motivation. The advertising world was slow to see the full implications, but once advertisers had recognised the potential of this remarkable fact they began to exploit it to the full. The inclusion in an advertisement of the words 'free' or 'new' used to pay the best dividends; nowadays the most successful theme is sex, and the manner most often employed is overt or covert exploitation of unconscious sexual motivations.

Nudity became commonplace in advertising in the late '60s: the first naked breasts in a British advertisement appeared when Enkasheer tights took the risk in 1969 and got away with it.[10] Since then, the shock of nudity has worn off, and more subtle approaches are used. A recent example shows a photograph of a nude girl superimposed on a round canister of Kiku bath salts with the words: 'Every body needs love. Fabergé made love and called it Kiku.' Toiletries are, of course, an obvious product for such treatment, but alcohol also tends to be sold by its connection with sexual pleasure. The classic example is the caption to a Grants' whisky advertisement in America: 'Is yours as good as Grants'?' Such an approach is very common in Great Britain today. A car is, of course, one of the most potent of all sexual symbols, sometimes seen as a speeding phallus and at other times a comfortable womb or an inviting vagina. One does not have to be a student of Freud to understand the reasons for this. A car is a status symbol for men, and most magazine advertisements for cars manage to include a sexy girl.[11] Television plays the same game: Cadbury's have their young lady with her oral-genital chocolate Flake, and Manikin display the manifold bodily delights of the beautiful girl with a penchant for horse-riding and swimming and some vague connection with phallic cigars.

A comparatively recent development in advertising is the phallic image, an added sophistication after the shock of nudity had worn off. Cigarettes lend themselves to this treatment, as in the Silver Thins advertisements, which show a girl's face in close-up with a cigarette hanging out of her mouth at the perpendicular. The pioneer in this esoteric world was Gala, who produced an advertisement in 1968 showing upright giant lipsticks, around one of which a grinning girl was clasping her legs and arms. The by-line read: 'I love cool colours with a sizzle.' The follow-up showed a girl's mouth in close-up descending on an upright lipstick. The wording ran 'The big news is the way it looks and feels.' In 1969 Fabergé caused a minor sensation with their Aphrodisia advertisement, which showed a woman's hand pointing a stick perfume into an ambiguous anatomical area (presumably meant to represent the inside of her knee, but looking suspiciously vaginal) with the legend: 'Aphrodisia says what most perfumes daren't even whisper—a fragrant breach of the rules.'[12]

At present, many people are subconsciously brainwashed by such advertisements because of the sublimation that their sexual instincts have undergone. The freer our sexual attitudes become, the less persuasive these sexually motivated advertisements will be.

Society is moving inexorably towards the goal of individual freedom. Recent pointers in Britain—unimportant in themselves—are the passing of *Trash, Last Tango in Paris* and *Emmanuelle* for public showing, the refusal of High Court judges to ban a television documentary on Warhol, and the 'not guilty' verdict on editors of a collection of American underground 'comix' entitled *Nasty Tales* after an Old Bailey obscenity trial. But the day is not won, for there are signs, too, that the pendulum may soon begin to swing the other way: in the U.S.A. six Supreme Court decisions declared that the First Amendment to the Constitution could no longer be used to protect films or books declared by certain states to be prurient by community standards. In Britain, the Home Secretary showed an intention to tighten the Obscene Publications Acts by means of a Cinematograph and Indecent Displays Bill which would give him wide-ranging powers, and the Film Censor warned that he would in future have to pay more attention to the growing demand for stricter censorship of films.

How long will it be before we can recognise the essential fact that the unhealthy element in sex cannot thrive in the free atmosphere of open discussion, where there is no place for the snigger and the sly wink? Let us hope that the 1970s will see the end of the prejudice which still restricts open discussion and portrayal of sexual matters and inhibits the creation and appreciation of erotic art, a true celebration of love.

Chapter 1
Art and Pornography

In the various chapters of this book we will mainly be concerned with a discussion of the use of erotic themes in the arts of all times and civilisations. We will frequently find it necessary to use the word 'pornography' to describe in a pejorative manner the sexual explicitness in a painting, sculpture, photograph, or novel. The present obsession with sex which Western societies are experiencing has ensured for the word a widely distributed, but often counterfeit, usage. Not since the Victorian period has the word been bandied about so unscrupulously, and the emotional and irrational reactions which it inspires today recall the Victorian Achilles heel of false prudery at its worst. A large number of paintings, sculptures, novels, and poems have been labelled pornographic by people whose prejudices have vitiated their ability to appreciate a work of art. The words of Sainte-Beuve are apposite: 'Prudishness is a dismal thing . . . up to the point of obscenity, art consecrates and purifies all it touches.'

In their book *To the Pure* (1929), Ernst and Seagle wrote: 'Pornography is any matter or thing exhibiting or visually representing persons or animals performing the sexual act, whether normal or abnormal.'[1] Few would agree with this narrow view today. But a satisfactory definition of pornography is hard to find. Like beauty, although here the comparison ends, pornography is in the eye of the beholder, or perhaps more aptly, in the 'groin of the beholder'.[2] Pornography has been described as 'books you read with one hand',[3] also as 'writing or art whose whole purpose is to make one feel randy'.[4] The Oxford Dictionary definition of pornography is: 'the expression or suggestion of obscene or unchaste subjects in literature or art', a definition which depends on the meaning one gives to the word 'obscene'. This according to the Dictionary is 'offensive to modesty or decency; lewd, indecent, bawdy'. Such definitions depend on so many subjective interpretations as to be of little value in the present discussion. The law demands more precision: in the courts of Great Britain, obscene means 'tending to deprave or corrupt' and in America, 'utterly without redeeming social value'. Yet neither of these definitions is satisfactory, as is witnessed by the numerous complicated trials to which they have given rise.

My own definition of pornography is 'the representation, without aesthetic or sociological justification, of sexual acts with an intrusive vividness, which offends commonly accepted standards of decency'. Clearly, 'commonly accepted standards of decency' needs amplifying, and 'aesthetic or sociological justification' leaves room for discussion. By 'commonly accepted standards of decency' I mean the average person's opinion of what is and what is not offensive, but by 'aesthetic or sociological justification' I mean the justification on aesthetic or sociological grounds by a cross-section of expert testimony. Thus the sex act can be pornographic in a Danish sex magazine, but aesthetically justified in a painting by Boucher and sociologically justified in a sex-instruction film. I do not claim that this definition will be universal; it is certainly open to criticism by those who consider that art can be pornographic. But for the purpose of this discussion I think it will prove helpful, for it makes what I consider to be a clear distinction between art and pornography. The subject-matter in any given case is unimportant; what matters are the intention and the treatment.

One thing my definition does make clear: pornography is related to obscenity rather than eroticism, and this is a vital distinction. Although some people may find a pornographic picture erotic, most people associate eroticism with love, rather than with sex alone, and love has little or no part to play in pornography. That love is at the basis of eroticism the etymology makes clear. Pornography originally meant 'the writing of harlots', and is derived from *porne*, Greek for harlot. The *pornai* were the lowest class of prostitutes and performed purely for money, as opposed to the *hetairai* (companions) and *auletriades* (entertainers), who were respectable women in Greek society and performed a function similar to that of Geisha girls in Japan. On the other hand, eroticism is derived from *eros*, Greek for love, the human concept of love for another person as opposed to *agape*, or spiritual, unselfish love for a god. Eroticism, therefore, has none of the pejorative associations of pornography; it concerns something vital to all of us, the passion of love. Erotic art is art on a sexual theme related specifically to emotions rather than merely actions, and sexual depictions which are justifiable on aesthetic grounds. The difference between eroticism and pornography is the difference between celebratory and masturbatory sex.

The subject-matter of erotic art has often been sexually explicit to the point where it could be confused with pornography, depending on individual interpretations of the word. Many of the most intelligent people have fallen into the trap of seeing no more than the subject-matter and ignoring intention. But there is a clear dividing line between art and pornography which the enlightened world of the 1970s should be able to distinguish. There is today no excuse for describing as pornographic the Roman frescoes at Pompeii, the Greek phallic idols at Delos, the Indian temple sculptures of Khajuraho, the ceramics of ancient Peru, or the *shunga* prints of Japan, any more than it would be reasonable to judge as pornographic Michelangelo's *David*, Giulio Romano's frescoes at Mantua, Boucher's *Mlle O'Murphy*, Beardsley's *Lysistrata* illustrations, or Brancusi's *Princess X*

Also, strictly speaking, eroticism is a meaningless term to apply to Oriental and Primitive art, for the word implies recognition of the idea that there is something special and also something slightly wicked in sexuality, whereas sex was just a part of life—albeit an important one—for Orientals and Primitives. Georges Bataille has suggested that eroticism distinguishes man from the animals because it is a self-conscious activity, a consciously intellectualised feeling, that is only possible in a context where sexuality is repressed.[5]

The difference between art and pornography is largely one of intention, although this is to over-simplify the issue. But the point must be made that there is an essential difference. For some writers, the difference is simply found. For instance, James Joyce believed that art was an aesthetic experience and that pornography aroused disturbing emotions. Since an aesthetic experience precluded disturbing emotions, art and pornography were for him at opposite poles. D. H. Lawrence wrote: 'You can recognize [pornography] by the insult it offers, invariably, to sex and to the human spirit'.[6] For him, pornography leads to masturbation, which in turn leads to 'mob self-consciousness', whereas sexual art redirects one from mob self-conscious-ness to 'true individuality'. Steven Marcus writes that art is largely concerned with 'the relations of human beings among themselves', whereas pornography 'is not interested in persons but in organs . . . sex in pornography is sex without the emotions'.[7] But the question is not so easy for others.

In his interesting book on the relationship between art and pornography, Dr Morse Peckham writes: 'There is available no definition of pornography which would make it possible to investigate the relation between the category "pornog-raphy" and the category "art".' His reason for believing this he gives thus: 'Defini-tions of pornography are controlled by the interests of the definer . . . All definers are controlled by the interest in asserting that what pornography directs us to do, whether in covert or overt behaviour, is something that we ought not to do.'[8] The definitions of Joyce, Lawrence, and Marcus quoted above would therefore be un-satisfactory for Dr Peckham because they betray a pejorative attitude to pornography, but since almost any definition is bound to reflect the interest of the definer, this argument would seem to be self-defeating.

Dr Peckham would appear to suffer from masochistic tendencies if his means of argument are to be taken literally. Having rightly dismissed the legal definitions of pornography as unusable in this context, since their purpose is to regulate behaviour, he goes on to say: 'One can no longer create a tenable definition by defining pornography as that which has sexual content.'[9] He is led to believe this because of the influence of Freud's teachings on today's intelligent man. Freud said that any impulse originating in the body which reaches the mind is sexual, whether it is unconscious or not, and also that most of man's instincts are basically sexual. Since almost any behaviour can nowadays be categorised as sexual, the association of pornography with sex is to Dr Peckham meaningless.

For the vast majority of people, pornography is very closely associated with sex, and this provides a useful distinction between pornography and obscenity. There is no reason why obscenity should concern sex. Obscenity can be considered that which one finds objectionable, and so a film of a man being hanged or a photograph of a starving child is as likely, and as reasonably, to be termed obscene as the depiction of explicit sexual activities. A wide knowledge of Freud's teachings has resulted in articulate people thinking seriously about sexuality and forming their own opinions about it. This is why pornography has been given such diverse definitions.

Dr Peckham defines pornography as 'the presentation in verbal or visual signs of human sexual organs in a condition of stimulation'.[10] He is at great pains not to allow any pejorative impression to colour his definition, and the reason he gives is that in this way 'the response continuum is eliminated', though this is surely not the case, given that post-Freud man is very aware of the importance that sexuality has for him and so responds in spite of himself. But it is curious that Dr Peckham here associates pornography with sex, in view of his own affirmation that such an association is now meaningless.

The difficulty arising from Dr Peckham's carefully unprovocative definition is that it makes any distinction between art and pornography impossible. And yet it appears by some paradox that this is exactly what he wants. Other definers have concentrated on the unacceptability of pornography, which has led them to declare that it could not be art. Dr Peckham, in fact, believes that pornography is not only acceptable but can play a functional role in the individual's life. He is therefore as interested as any of the other definers: he is just cleverer at hiding his interest. He can now go on to say that pornography can be art, for this is where all his semantics have been leading. It is not original to suggest that pornography can play a functional role, and it does not follow from this premise that pornography can be art.

Whether one uses the term 'erotic art' or the Kronhausens' description 'sexual realism',[11] there is a field of representation where sexual activities are depicted in such a manner, and with such an intention, as to differentiate them from the phenomenon of pornography. In all modesty, I would suggest that the definition of pornography that illuminates its relation to art, and which Dr Peckham says does not exist, could be mine quoted above: 'the representation, without aesthetic or sociological justification, of sexual acts with an intrusive vividness which offends commonly accepted standards of decency'. This, it must be admitted, is an 'interested' definition like any other, but it is not a pejorative one. I too recognise that pornography can have a beneficial effect, and I see no reason why it should not offend people.

Dr Peckham chooses to dismiss the question of aesthetic merit in art, and so aesthetic justification would be meaningless to him. And yet it seems strange that a man who writes of those 'foolish enough to subject themselves to the propanganda of aestheticians' should be tackling such a subject as art and pornography in the first place. It is due to this blindness—for such it is—that he can describe a Boucher painting of a couple having intercourse as both pornography and art. He fails to allow for the fact that Boucher's great talents and abilities as an artist make of his painting far more than merely the depiction of sexual intercourse. The subject-matter could be pornographic, but in Boucher's hands it is transformed into art through its aesthetic justification. My definition distinguishes between art and pornography; Dr Peckham's merely confuses them both.

The hysterical reaction to pornography which results in a general tendency to attempt to define it in a pejorative sense is the long-lasting result of the Christian Church's association of sex with guilt. Although clearly not pornographic, Michelangelo's *David* (1504; Accademia, Florence; see illustration 1) is a provocatively sexual portrayal of idealised male beauty; a short time after its completion, it was provided with a fig-leaf (see illustration 2), much to the artist's disgust. In 1970, a bookseller in Sydney, Australia, was arrested for displaying a poster of the nude *David*, and the same happened in South Africa in 1973. This reflects a prejudice which is seemingly immune to the effects of all the expert evidence pointing to the harmlessness—and occasional benefits—of pornography. St Paul's admonition: 'To be carnally minded is death' (Romans) is still flung at people concerned with expressing the totality of human experience in the arts, witness Lord Longford and

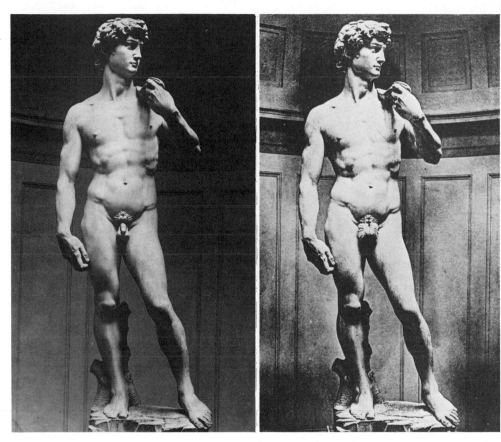

1   Michelangelo, *David*   2   Michelangelo, *David* (with fig leaf)

his crusade against pornography, or Malcolm Muggeridge and the 'Festival of Light', an attempt to mobilise popular opinion to halt 'permissiveness' through the medium of the Bible. To these people, any explicit representation or discussion of sexual matters is dangerous, and evidence of an unhealthy obsession. Sadly, it is these people who are obsessed. The vast majority of sexually explicit works of art are produced as part of an overall desire to express the totality of human experience: very few artists have made sex their only motivation. The exceptions (a recent example is the German artist Hans Bellmer) are truly obsessed with sex and make of their obsessions something of value to us all. But this in no way excuses the application of the word 'pornographic' to their work; at the same time it must be pointed out that this pejorative use of the word in such a context betrays an unfortunate prejudice.

Pornography is illegal in Great Britain and America because of its 'tendency to deprave and corrupt' those into whose hands it may fall. Yet the fact is that no one has been able to prove that pornography can deprave or corrupt; all the careful scientific studies that have been made clearly indicate the exact opposite,[12] and informed medical opinion on the Freudian concept of sexual guilt is united in placing the causes of depravity and corruption elsewhere. Daydreams or fantasies can be of great value in maintaining a form of stability. Pornography provides an escape into fantasy, which for some is merely a diversion, but for others can be an essential part of life, as will be discussed in Appendix V. There are clear benefits to be gained from the open availability of pornography, but that does not mean that one needs to associate it with true erotic expression. It cannot be denied that pornography often degrades women, and the charge of exploitation can be levelled at most pornographers. True eroticism is literally a world apart from the emotionless cavortings of the average pornographic magazine, such a pathetic target for an obsessional campaign of self-righteousness.

As we shall see, the contemporary obsession with sex—whether desiring more of it or none of it—is in marked contrast to the traditional attitudes of the East, where sex was treated as a very important and very beautiful part of life. The Indian temple sculptures at Khajuraho celebrate the glory of sex as an essential part of religion and there is no sense of shame or guilt involved in depicting the pleasures of sexual activity in a place of worship. Yet these same sculptures have often been classed as pornographic by Western observers, and the Indians themselves were made to feel ashamed of them by our Victorian empire-builders.

The inability to distinguish between sexually explicit sculptures such as those at Khajuraho and sexually explicit photographs in pornographic magazines is rarer today. The sexual revolution in the West is underway and nothing can stop it. Yet the forces of reaction still confuse freedom with licence, and still sincerely believe that personal freedom has to be severely limited. In a curious way, these people are at one with Dr Peckham in confusing art and pornography, in failing to distinguish between intention and subject-matter.

The clear ground for asserting that the Khajuraho sculptures are not pornographic is to be found in comparing an example with a pornographic photograph (see illustrations 3 and 4). The effect is totally different. The sculpture does not have the shock stimulus of the photograph: this is to be expected, since the photograph only exists to stimulate sexual appetite. The photograph can be taken in immediately, whereas the sculpture requires, and repays, more leisurely consideration. The photograph has nothing to offer after the initial reaction; the sculpture can be appreciated on various levels as the eye explores the forms and notes the flowing line that describes the volumes. The power of imagination and the high level of creativity that the sculpture exhibits continue to impress and excite us long after we have

3 *Sexual Intercourse with Apsarases*, Kaula Cult, Vishvanatha Temple, Khajuraho, India, *c.* 1000

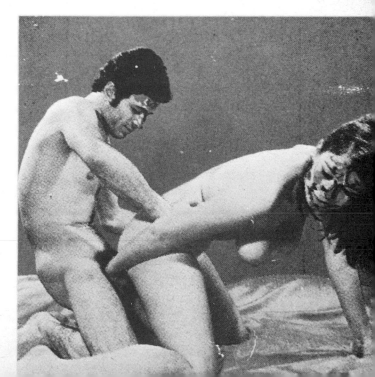

4 *Danish pornographic photograph, c.* 1967

become bored with the photograph. And in the long run it is the sculpture which leaves its sensuous mark on us.

We have seen that 'pornography' originally meant descriptions of matters relating to harlots. Prostitution has, in fact, been the subject of many works of art, from the Pompeian murals of the first century A.D. through the works of Carpaccio, Hans Baldung Grien, Goltzius, Jan Steen, Hogarth, Rowlandson, Ingres, Rops, Lautrec, Degas, and Manet to Picasso's *Demoiselles d'Avignon* of 1907. In the twentieth century, artists as diverse as Rouault, Pascin, Grosz, Otto Dix, Pechstein, Corinth, Bellmer, Jones, Lindner, and Kienholz have been fascinated by the subject, but it was the nineteenth century that really suffered from an obsession with prostitution, and this is as obvious from the writings of 'Walter' and Baudelaire as it is from the art of the time. In the 1850s, Charles Baudelaire found inspiration in the world of prostitutes for some of his most fascinating poetry: his *Fleurs du Mal* showed great insight into this area of human sexual behaviour, without in any way pandering to a desire for simple titillation. Yet in 1857, he was found guilty of an offence against public morality and six of the poems were banned. Edouard Manet came under attack eight years later for his *Olympia* (Louvre; see illustration 123), which depicted a Parisian prostitute as a modern version of Titian's *Venus of Urbino*, and by the end of the century, the total honesty of Toulouse-Lautrec's brothel scenes (see illustration 126) had earned him a great deal of abuse and criticism.

The irrationality and unfairness of prejudice of this sort is an underlying theme

5 Constantin Brancusi,
Princess X, 1916

of this book. Lautrec, Baudelaire, and Manet are only three of many hundreds of artists who have suffered at its hands. Another was the Rumanian sculptor Constantin Brancusi, whose work often expressed the deep sexual motivations that lie behind surface appearances. His *Princess X* of 1916 (Philadelphia Museum of Art; see illustration 5) has deliberate phallic connotations in the beautifully harmonious forms of the bronze which seem to invite the spectator's caresses. The undoubted aesthetic value of the sculpture did not prevent it from being banned from exhibition as soon as it was completed, and many people still find it objectionable, yet one can openly buy cheap postcards such as the one of the girl pointing to a lighthouse rising from two rounded rocks with the message 'This reminds me of my boyfriend' (see illustration 6) which uses similar imagery in a much less sophisticated and more

6 *English post-card, c.* 1960

titillating manner, but which gains acceptance through providing the safety-valve of laughter.

We have discussed examples of erotic art that have at times been mislabelled pornographic in the modern pejorative sense of the word. And we have seen that the distinction between art and pornography is a clear one involving intention and merit rather than merely subject matter. We can now move on to detailed considerations of the uses of erotic themes in various branches of the arts at all times and in many civilisations.

Chapter 2

Sexual Themes in Ancient and Primitive Art

a: Ancient and Primitive Cultures

by

JOHN H. FIELD[1]

Human sexuality, although primarily manifest in love-making and procreation, has many other ramifications. In all ancient and 'primitive' cultures people have humanised and sexualised their universe by 'projecting' their emotions and activities onto the spiritual powers thought to control nature. A basic concern of most religions has been the ritual promotion of fertility in humanity and its food supply. Sexual magic has also been widely used as a defence against malignant forces. Socially unacceptable erotic impulses are 'projected' and personified as sexual demons and are vicariously gratified in the outrageous behaviour of clowns and 'trickster' heroes. Cultures define in various ways the male and female 'sex roles'. Subjugation of the weak by the strong often involves sexual aggression in culturally patterned manifestations. Sexuality permeates the beliefs and rites marking the human cycle of birth, sexual maturation, marriage, child-rearing, death, and hopes for an afterlife or rebirth. Such diverse cultural activities as hunting, fighting, head-hunting, fire-making, irrigation, land-tillage, metallurgy, and other craft processes, often involve sexual symbolism. Thus the myths, rituals, and arts of ancient and 'primitive' cultures express a wide variety of sexual themes.

The Paleolithic Hunters and Food-gatherers
Erotic images are among the earliest surviving indications of human culture in the Paleolithic Period between *c.* 30,000 and 10,000 B.C. It is generally assumed that the art, which is sometimes found deep within the 'cave-womb' of the earth, reflects magico-religious beliefs of hunting and fertility magic and totemism.[2] Images in which human and animal characteristics merge express the feeling of kinship between hunters and their prey which is common in hunting cultures. Possibly the early hunters' intense observations of the seasonal periods of animal rutting and

birthing, when the prey are especially vulnerable, first suggested to men the causal connection between their own erotic impulses and the mystery of childbirth.

Recent interpretations of Paleolithic art emphasise pervasive sexual symbolism. Alleged phallic and female symbols range from relative naturalism to extremely ambiguous abstraction.[3] It has been conjectured that the two most commonly depicted species of animal, the horse and the bison, *regardless of the sex of individual animals*, may have symbolised the polarities of the 'male principle' and the 'female principle' in the 'sexualised universe'.[4] The hunt may have been associated with sexuality as in some surviving 'primitive' tribes. 'Taken as symbols of sexual union and death, the spear and the wound would then be integrated into the cycle of life's renewal, the actors in which would form two parallel and complementary series: man—horse—spear and woman—bison—wound.'[5]

Although some of these controversial interpretations strain credulity, many unmistakably sexual images are found in Paleolithic art. Isolated emblems of the human vulva were found in the cave of La Ferassie and elsewhere.[6] On a cave wall at Angles-sur-l'Anglin is a relief of three women, or rather three vulva triangles with adjacent hips and thighs, for the rest of their anatomy has significantly been omitted. Below is engraved a bison with its tail raised, perhaps indicating a state of rut linking human and animal sexuality.[7] In a cave at La Magdaleine it was the carefully delineated pubic triangle that led to the discernment of two naturalistic reliefs of reclining nude women. Below one woman was carved a bison and near the other is depicted a horse.[8]

Natural rock formations in the mysterious caves may have been interpreted by Paleolithic humanity as magical images of fecundity. In the cave of Le Combel stalactites suggest pendulous breasts and a stalagmite column near the entrance resembles a phallus.[9] A natural protuberance on the cave wall at Le Portel was incorporated as a phallus in a figure crudely outlined in red.[10] Pierced staffs carved from bone or antler are sometimes phallic, *e.g.* a single phallus from Farincourt[11] and a double one from La Madeleine.[12] A bone shaft from the latter site is engraved with a vulva, testicles, and a penis juxtaposed with a bear's head with a protruding tongue, possibly licking the tip of the penis.[13] The various carvings found in a rock-shelter at Laussel hint at erotic rites: one stone represents an ithyphallic man; another is engraved with an enigmatic image variously interpreted as representing a copulating couple, or a woman giving birth, or a primal hermaphrodite, or merely an unfinished image of a woman.[14] Most impressive are the reliefs of a naked woman holding a crescent-curved horn. Throughout the world in ancient and 'primitive' cultures the horn has been revered as a symbol of vital power and fertility.

The Paleolithic 'Venus' statuettes are probably emblems of the veneration of female sexuality, child-bearing, and nurture. The faces and extremities of these Paleolithic 'sex-objects' are only cursorily represented, focusing attention on the enormous breasts hanging heavily above the swelling belly and forming with the hips, buttocks, and thighs a symphony of feminine rotundities[15] (see illustration 7). Siberian hunting tribes still carve female figurines which represent the progenitress

7 *Venus of Willendorf*,
Austria, *c.* 30,000 B.C.

and protectress of the family, to whom are addressed prayers for the safety of the
hearth and home, for success in the hunt and in the pursuit of happiness.[16]

The Neolithic Farmers

After the end of the Ice Age the hunting and food-gathering life continued, while in
the Near East, between *c.* 9000 and 7000 B.C. there was a gradual but momentous
transition to the agricultural economy of the Neolithic culture-stage. Perhaps the
earliest image of human copulation is a carved stone from Ain Sakri in the Judean
Desert from the transitional Mesolithic Natufian culture.[17]

By the seventh millennium Neolithic agriculture was established at many sites
in the 'Fertile Crescent' of the Near East. Characteristic artifacts at Neolithic sites
are little clay figurines of women, usually obese and naked with the vulva emphasised,
often associated with images of bulls and other horned animals, which probably

[12]

represented the 'male principle', for with the advent of stock-breeding the male role in procreation must have been well understood and highly valued.

Among the oldest, most impressive, and varied Neolithic images of the fertility cult are those excavated at the sites of Çatal Hüyük and Hacilar on the Anatolian plateau of Turkey. The 'female principle' seems to have predominated,[18] personified in images of nubile young women, authoritative mothers of obese maturity and old women associated with death, perhaps all aspects of one Great Goddess. A terracotta group, found in a grain bin at Çatal Hüyük, portrays 'fat momma' apparently giving birth, majestically enthroned between a pair of heraldic leopards.[19] She was probably 'Mother of Beasts' as well as of humanity. On the walls of shrines were modelled rows of breasts containing skulls of animals. The male principle was represented by murals of great bulls and stags and by numerous clay heads incorporating real horns of bulls and rams, probably sacrificial offerings. Anthropomorphic male deities are less common, but one statuette from Çatal Hüyük represents a bearded man riding a bull and thus identified with the bull's mighty power and fecundity. In later Near Eastern fertility cults bull-men were associated with mountain-tops, thunder, lightning, and the rain which fertilises Mother Earth. The Mother Goddess was often represented with her little son, who may have become her lover-consort. One image from Hacilar has been interpreted as showing the adolescent son making love to his mother,[20] a theme documented in later literate periods. A high-relief schist plaque from Çatal Hüyük apparently shows a couple in sexual embrace beside a mother and child, as though indicating cause and effect. This may be a prefiguration of the 'Sacred Marriage', a ritual copulation to promote the fertility of humanity, animals, and all nature.

After a cultural time-lag agriculture reached Britain c. 4000–3500 B.C. Figurines of the Great Goddess are scarce and crudely abstract, but various artifacts identified as phalluses have been found at several Neolithic sites in Britain. At 'Maumbury Rings', Dorchester, forty-four deep tapered shafts were sunk in the bottom of a circular ditch in the late Neolithic or Early Bronze Age. The infill of these ritual shafts included antler picks, flint scrapers and balls, and chalk phalluses[21] (see illustration 8). In Neolithic flint-mines at 'Grime's Graves', Norfolk, a unique ritual deposit was discovered in Pit 15, which had apparently produced poor quality flint-nodules. On an altar of chalk blocks was seated a small chalk statuette of an

8 *Carved chalk phallus*,
Maumbury Rings,
Dorset, England,
c. 2000 B.C.

obese woman, associated with a chalk phallus, balls, a chalk cup, and antler-picks. It is thought that a fertility ritual was performed in the hope of stimulating Mother Earth to produce better flint-nodules in her chthonic (underground) womb.[22]

Egypt

By *c.* 3000 B.C. the great Bronze Age civilisations of Egypt and Mesopotamia had evolved from Neolithic village cultures. Whereas the interpretation of earlier art can only be a matter of conjecture, the written texts of these ancient civilisations illuminate the religious symbolism of their art, and sexual themes abound.

An Egyptian creation myth relates that the sun god Atum-Re had existed alone in the primal watery chaos until he created the first couple Shu and Tefnut by masturbation.[23] The sun god was 'Lord of the Phallus' and a drop of semen fell into the waters and solidified into the *Benben* stone, the first solid land, symbolised in art by a gilded pyramidion atop a 'phallic' obelisk.[24] Two deities came into being from drops of Ra's blood when he mutilated his phallus, perhaps a reference to the sacrificial blood-offering of circumcision.[25]

Shu, the god of air, and Tefnut, the goddess of moisture, mated incestuously as did many Egyptian mortals, members of the royal family as well as commoners. Tefnut gave birth to Geb, the earth god, and Nut, the sky goddess, a curious inversion of the usual pair Earth Mother and Sky Father. In Egypt vegetative nature was masculine and fertility imagery stressed the phallic element. Geb and Nut united in continuous love-making until they were wrenched apart by their father Shu, who raised Nut up to become the starry vault of heaven. A papyrus in the British Museum illustrates their sexual frustration by Geb's long phallus thrusting skyward in a vain attempt to reunite with his beloved sister-wife (see illustration 9). Each night Nut swallowed, or was impregnated by, a sun-disk which was reborn each morning from between her legs. Thus the lovely nude body of Nut was often depicted in full-frontality on the interior of coffin-lids as a promise of rebirth after death.

9   From Papyrus of Tameniu, Egypt, twenty-first Dynasty, 1102–952 B.C.

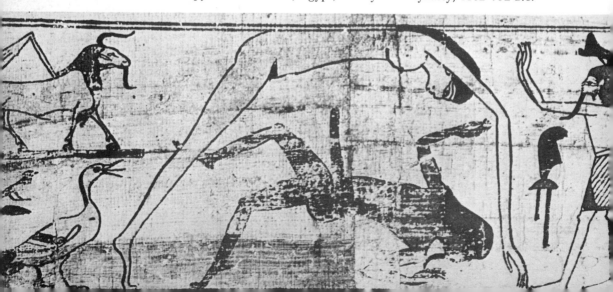

Neolithic peasant cults survived in the Egyptian worship of rams, bulls, cows, and other beasts and anthropomorphic deities with animal attributes. In the classical period the cult of Banebdetet, the ram god of Mendes, was notorious because a woman actually copulated with a ram as part of the sacred rites.[26] At Memphis the Apis bull was associated with the moon and the fertilising Nile, and women who wished to have babies would expose their genitals before the bull's magic fertilising power. Isis addressed Osiris: 'O Great Bull, Lord of Passion! Lie with thy sister Isis!'[27] Hathor, the maternal love goddess, was represented either as a cow or as a beautiful woman with a horned head-dress. Hathor's annual festival at Denderah included her mating as a cow with a bull in a 'Sacred Marriage' to promote the fertility of nature. Her worshippers enthusiastically joined in a drunken and amorous orgy to celebrate and magically reinforce the love goddess's power. In her shrine at Deir el-Bahri numerous votive wooden phalluses were found.[28]

Min of Coptos was an ithyphallic god in human form with bull-man attributes. He was the god of male procreativity who brought sexual pleasure into the world. At Coptos three large statues of Min were unearthed which probably date from c. 3000 B.C. and may be the earliest-known large-scale statues.[29] These stiff archaic idols clasped their phalluses in a gesture which was perpetuated in later statues and reliefs of Min (see illustration 10). As the personification of the fertility of his kingdom the Pharaoh was identified with Min. Reliefs on the mortuary temple of Ramses III (twelfth century B.C.) show the Pharaoh accompanying the ithyphallic image of Min with his aphrodisiac lettuces[30] and his sacred white bull in the Harvest procession. After Pharaoh ceremonially reaped the 'first fruits' of corn, Min, as

10   *Pharaoh Sesostris I before the ithyphallic god Min*, stone relief from shrine of Amon-Ra, Karnak, Egypt, twelfth Dynasty, c. 1950 B.C.

Kamutef ('The Bull of his Mother'), was invoked: 'Hail to thee Min, who impregnates his mother! How mysterious is that which thou hast done to her in the darkness!'[31] Pharaoh may then have performed ritual coitus with his queen for their heir was supposed to be conceived at the harvest festival, thus linking the continuity of kingship with the fertility of crops, herds, and humanity.

Unlike the worship of Min, the cult of Osiris involved dramatic myths of great emotional appeal. Osiris and Seth and their sister-wives Isis and Nepthys were the children of Nut and Geb. According to Plutarch,[32] Osiris and Isis were already lovers in their mother's womb. As the villain of the piece, Seth was the antithesis of Osiris and personified disorder, destruction, and sterility.[33] Jealously he murdered Osiris, dismembered his corpse and strewed the fragments throughout the land. The mourning sisters retrieved and reassembled Osiris's body. Their attempts to reanimate it were only partially successful, but Osiris's phallus rose up, enabling Isis to conceive his posthumous son and avenger, Horus. In the temple of Seti I (*c.* 1300 B.C.) at Abydos is a relief showing Isis as a sparrowhawk hovering upon the tip of the living phallus of the recumbent corpse of Osiris to receive his impregnating seed.[34] Isis raised her son in secrecy until he was old enough to avenge his father. In one version Horus battled with his bull-like uncle Seth and tore off his testicles and grafted them onto himself. A later bawdy burlesque text[35] relates how Horus and Seth combined physical battle with legal litigation. Seth attempted a homosexual assault on Horus to humiliate him and disqualify him from kingship,[36] but Isis tricked Seth into inadvertently swallowing Horus's semen when he ate his favourite salad of aphrodisiacal lettuces, and so it was Seth who was discredited. The dead pharaoh was identified with Osiris and his successor with Horus, the model son. Horus is said to have raped, or dutifully copulated with, his mother and Isis returned his passion.[37] Thus Horus was identified with Min 'The Bull of his mother', and a late amulet depicts Horus as a boy with a huge penis.[38]

Plutarch, writing in the second century A.D., said that the only portion of Osiris's anatomy which Isis was unable to recover was his phallus, which had been swallowed by a fish. Therefore, Isis had to fabricate a magical simulacrum. There is some support for this late tradition in the discovery at Sakkara of male mummies of the Second Dynasty furnished with phallic simulacra made of linen and resin.[39] In the Middle Kingdom period the dead man's mummified penis was sometimes separately encased in an obelisk-shaped casket.[40] Clearly the phallus had a particular importance as a symbol of resurrection and a necessity for blissful after-life. Originally only the dead Pharaoh was identified with Osiris but later every Egyptian could aspire to become an Osiris after death by means of magical rituals which transmuted his every bodily organ into that of Osiris. Thus in the New Kingdom period the magical 'Book of the Dead' provided for the deceased scribe Ani it is written: 'The phallus of Osiris-Ani, triumphant, is the phallus of Osiris!'[41] It was the fervent hope of Everyman to become like Osiris 'Lord of the Phallus and Ravisher of Women for ever',[42] and lovely little images of naked girls were often supplied for the erotic pleasure of the dead man along with other necessaries for a happy eternity.

As in many 'primitive' cultures the Egyptian cult of the dead was linked with the agricultural fertility cult, for the dead ancestors sent the good crops with their eternal vital energy. Osiris was both King of the Dead and a symbol of the chthonic energy of the germinating corn which sprouts from beneath the ground like Osiris's phallus rising triumphant over death when energised by the sun.[43] The annual flooding of the Nile bringing fertilising water and silt to the fields was identified with Osiris's gushing semen, and in this aspect Osiris was hailed as the 'Triumphant Ravisher of men's wives'.[44] Herodotus described a festival of Osiris, in which women carried in procession images whose virile members were moved with strings.

Another deity associated with sexuality was the bearded dwarf Bes. Portrayed naked, with a lion's tail dangling between his legs, Bes was not usually ithyphallic until the Late Period when he merged syncretistically with Amon-Ra-Min and other deities.[45] Bes was the patron of the female musicians and dancers who also supplied erotic services in the ancient world. His image adorned beds and the cosmetic utensils of the boudoir essential for feminine erotic wiles. He may also have presided over the sexual initiation of adolescents and he was invoked in erotic magic. Polychrome high-reliefs of Bes accompanied by naked women were discovered in Ptolomaic 'Bes chambers' at Sakkara,[46] and in the Hellenistic-Roman period he was associated with grotesque terracottas including gigantic phalluses and compliant naked girls.[47] Bes was a very popular deity and his cult spread throughout the Mediterranean area (see illustration 30).

Egyptian amulets for love magic, fertility, and protection from malign supernatural forces included the cowrie shell, a vulva symbol throughout the world, but phallic amulets were not common until the Græco-Roman period.[48] Several of the most sacred amuletic symbols are thought to have a sexual significance. The *Ankh*, the symbol of the Life-Force worn by many young people today could symbolise the male and female sexual organs conjoined. Similar in shape is the red *Tjet* emblem which represents the genital organs of Isis, whose blood was sacred and of great magic power.

Several papyrus collections of secular love poetry have survived from the New Kingdom period.[49] Many of the erotic metaphors which have echoed down the centuries were already themes: the beloved as a delectable fruit, nipples like stars, woman's body as a palace with an open gate, a tender trap in which the penis is caught like a bird or a fish. The earthy copulatory imagery of farming and stock-breeding was replaced by the delicate language of courtly lovers in which feminine erotic sensibility finds expression. The girl speaks: 'Can anything be sweeter than this hour when I am with you and my heart soars? For when you visit me do we not embrace and fondle each other and surrender ourselves to delight? If you desire to caress my thigh I will offer you my breast as well . . .,' and: 'How sweet it is to enter the lotus pond to do as you desire, to plunge into the water and bathe before you, to let you admire my beauty with my dress of sheerest royal linen all wet and clinging and perfumed with balsam. I join you in the water and catch a red fish which lies quivering and splendid in my fingers . . .'

[17]

It is curious that despite the explicit phallicism of the images of Min and Osiris anthropomorphic copulation was *not* depicted in official art. The curious asexual convention employed in the reliefs of Queen Hatshepsut's temple to depict the impregnation of her mother by the god Amon is in marked contrast with the passionate and sensual eroticism of the adjacent hieroglyphic text describing the same event.[50] A single exception to this polite omission of coition in monumental art seems to have occurred in an Eleventh or Twelfth Dynasty tomb mural at Beni Hassan, where lovers coupling on a couch to the accompaniment of a harpist were observed and sketched by Champollion, but this mural has since been deliberately erased.[51] Although representations of human copulation were apparently barred from 'Establishment' art several erotic graffiti have survived drawn on New Kingdom potsherds, and some of these sketches were clearly done by trained artists.[52] In a similar vein are the bawdy illustrations in a Twentieth Dynasty papyrus at Turin.[53] The text is apparently a satirical account of the coupling of a young priest with a sacred prostitute in at least nine imaginative and acrobatic positions. One scene shows the man carried away in erotic exhaustion, his long penis dangling limply, and another portrays the aloof but insatiable woman sexually impaling herself on a conical object while she absent-mindedly repairs her makeup.

Mesopotamia

During the fourth millennium B.C. the civilisation of the Sumerian city-states arose in southern Mesopotamia and was assimilated and elaborated by their Semitic neighbours in the successive empires of Akkad, Babylonia, and Assyria. Sexual themes often occur in Mesopotamian myths: Enlil, the Sumerian god of the life-bringing rains, lusted after the virgin grain goddess Ninlil when he spied her bathing. Despite her protest: 'My vagina is too small; it knows not how to copulate! My lips are too small; they know not how to kiss!', he raped her and impregnated her with the moon god.[54] In another Sumerian myth fresh water, vital for irrigation, gushed from the phallus of the god Enki, and he vigorously impregnated a succession of vegetation goddesses.[55] Tilling the soil was also related to sexuality. The Sumerian fertility goddess Inanna (Semitic: Ishtar) sang an erotic song to her lover: 'I, the Maid, ask who will be my plowman? For my vulva is moist soil.' Dumuzi (Semitic: Tammuz) responded: 'Lady, . . . Dumuzi the king will plow it for you!' She responded: 'Plow my vulva, my sweetheart!'[56]

The Great Goddess and her 'Sacred Marriage' were main subjects of Meso-potamian erotic poetry and art. The 'Eternal Feminine' principle was worshipped under a variety of names, titles, and aspects. As Inanna-Ishtar she was the goddess of female sexuality and, by extension, of fertility throughout nature.[57]

Her most famous consort was Dumuzi-Tammuz ('Quickener of the Child in the Womb'), who was her son, lover, and husband, representing the indwelling vital forces in grain, beer, milk, date-palms, and the vegetation of the brief-flowering Mesopotamian springtime. Although he was sometimes referred to as a Wild Bull, he more often embodied a feminine ideal of youthful male grace and charm. He was vulnerable, strangely passive, a male 'love-object' for female adoration and doting desire. His loss caused ecstasies of grief and tender yearning laments among women, and his annual reappearance and 'Sacred Marriage' were occasions of joyous raptures and erotic celebrations.[58]

At the beginning of the new year the mortal ruler, impersonating his god, was conducted to the 'House of Life' to consummate the 'Sacred Marriage' with the fertility goddess, represented by her high priestess. The 'goddess' greeted him with an erotic rhapsody: 'You have captivated me; let me stand trembling before you Bridegroom. I would be taken by you to the bedchamber . . . Bridegroom, let me caress you; my precious caress is more delicious than honey. In the bedchamber, honey-filled, let us enjoy your goodly beauty. Lion, let me caress you . . .'[59] In another Sacred Marriage lyric the girl compares the sweetness of her lips and vulva with date wine.[60] As Sacred Bridegroom, the ruler was the fecundator of his land's fertility: 'With the exalted rising of the king's loins, rose at the same time the flax, rose at the same time the barley, did the desert fill with gracious gardens. . . .'[61] The fertility goddess's sexual appetite was voracious, and in a Sumerian text Inanna croons voluptuously: 'My beloved met me, took his pleasure of me, rejoiced together with me. My brother brought me to his house, made me lie on its honey-bed. My precious sweet, having lain by my heart, in unison the "tongue-making" . . . made fifty times. . . .' Her paramour replies in amorous exhaustion: 'Set me free, my sister, set me free!'[62]

'Sacred prostitution' was part of the worship of Inanna-Ishtar. According to Herodotus every Babylonian woman had a religious duty to prostitute herself, at least once, to a stranger within the temple precincts as an offering to Ishtar.[63] Professional 'hierodules', votaries with duties of 'sacred prostitution', ministered in temples, and common prostitutes, who plied their trade in streets and brothels, were also considered her votaries. The goddess was referred to as 'Hierodule of the gods', and Assyrian ivory icons depict her face framed by a window, like a harlot soliciting customers.

The heroic demi-god Gilgamesh was a legendary king of Uruk, one of Inanna's main cult-centres. He was the antithesis of the passive, subordinate Dumuzi. He was a bull-like deflowerer of virgins whose subjects complained: 'Gilgamesh leaves not the maid to her mother, the warrior's daughter, the noble's spouse!'[64] So excessively virile was he that a male rival, the shaggy wild bull-man Enkidu, was created to divert his libidinous energy. A 'noble savage' living with animals in the wild, Enkidu was tamed by means of a harlot-votary of the love goddess: 'The lass freed her breasts, bared her bosoms. She was not bashful as she welcomed his ardour. She laid aside her clothes and he rested upon her. She taught him, the savage, a woman's art, and his love was drawn into her. For six days and seven nights Enkidu came forth mating with the lass. . . .' Having lost his animal innocence and been 'made a man' by the harlot, Enkidu was led to meet Gilgamesh, who was on his way to an erotic assignation. They fought, measuring each other's might and then embraced to become loving comrades. They ventured forth to slay a giant, and on their triumphant return Inanna-Ishtar invited Gilgamesh to be her partner in the 'Sacred Marriage' rite. In an unprecedented spirit of masculine protest the hero rejected the goddess, brutally taunting her for her voracious promiscuity and reminding her of the sad fate of her previous lovers.[65] With the vengeful fury of a woman scorned and the bitter knowledge that Gilgamesh preferred the virile companionship of his beloved Enkidu, the goddess caused the latter to sicken and die,[66] whereupon Gilgamesh mourned Enkidu 'like a bride'. Freudians detect a homosexual component in the phallic ultra-masculinity of Gilgamesh and Enkidu.[67]

There are many sexual images in Mesopotamian art. In the Protoliterate Period before *c.* 3000 B.C. naked women are pictured with a bull, from whose mouth water flows,[68] and with scorpions, the emblem of the 'Mistress of Life'.[69] Astrology began in Mesopotamia and the zodiacal Scorpio controls the genital organs. Fully-frontal nude images depict Inanna-Ishtar and her votaries on cylinder-seals and moulded terracotta plaques. Sometimes the goddess is partially clothed, but lifting her skirt to exhibit her sacred vulva.[70] Other mass-produced terracotta reliefs showing a naked woman on a bed, sometimes with a baby or a man,[71] probably commemorate temple-service or prayers for success in love or procreation. Prayer-texts refer to votive offerings to the goddess of a lapis lazuli vulva and a golden star,[72] and small images of penises and vulva-symbols were excavated near her temple at Assur.[73] At the same site were found small lead reliefs depicting orgiastic rites with music, dancing, and sexual intercourse. A 'sacred prostitute' is shown lying on an altar in coitus, sometimes pleasuring more than one man at a time. Homosexual priests, 'whose virility Ishtar has changed to femininity' were represented in all-male embraces.[74]

Archaic seal-impressions and terracotta plaques of the Babylonian period illustrate copulation in various positions.[75] A recurrent theme is standing rear-entry coitus. On the moulded plaques and late Achaemenid seals[76] the passive partner drinks from a vase through a tube (see illustration 11). The sex of this figure is not always clear,[77] and it is uncertain whether vaginal or anal intercourse is depicted. Anal coitus, both homosexual and heterosexual was and *is* popular in the Near East and may also have had a ritual significance.[78]

Several cylinder-seals showing a reclining couple probably illustrate the 'Sacred Marriage' ceremony. In one example a scorpion [79] is beneath the nuptial couch and nearby is a large vessel with drinking tubes for the sacramental imbibing of the 'Water of Life'.[80] On two specimens a pair of bystanders also appear to be copulating 'a posteriori'.[81]

A unique cylinder-seal shows a naked woman squatting above a supine man, apparently in copulation, while a bystander grasps her wrist and brandishes what may be a weapon.[82] Although other interpretations have been made,[83] it is possible that this scene alludes to the spectre of woman as succubus as in a much later Hellenistic Greek relief which shows a beautiful nude siren, with bird's wings and feet, crouching astride a sleeping man whose penis is erect.[84] Mesopotamian images depict a similar winged female divinity, associated with wild animals and nocturnal

11   *Terracotta relief depicting copulation from behind*, Mesopotamia, Babylonian period, *c.* 2000 B.C.

screech-owls.[85] She may be the Babylonian 'Maid of Desolation' (*ardat lili*), who once inhabited the 'Tree of Life' in Inanna-Ishtar's garden paradise but was evicted by Gilgamesh and moved to the desert wilds. She reappears in the Bible and the Talmud as Lilith, who was created with Adam, before Eve, but refused to acknowledge male supremacy; she would not accept the supine position in coitus but aspired to ride on top. Cast out of Eden, Lilith lurked in the wilderness, a predatory nocturnal succubus who caused erotic dreams by copulating atop sleeping men, draining their sacred seed to spawn demons.[86]

Syria-Palestine
Syria-Palestine was a cultural crossroad between Egypt, Mesopotamia, Asia Minor,

and the Mediterranean. The majority of the population were western Semitic Canaanites, called Phoenicians on the coast. Texts dating from *c.* 1300 B.C. from the Syrian port of Ugarit reveal the pagan Canaanite background of Judaism. The Creator was the elderly remote high god El. Although titled 'Bull', he was 'getting a bit past it' in the Sacred Marriage, and his potency was a subject of bawdy jests.[87] The more virile active fertility god was his son Baal-Hadad, a deity associated with thunder, lightning, rain and vegetation, who had bull attributes. A Canaanite-Phoenecian terracotta bust of a bull has an erect human penis and testicles modelled in relief between its horns.[88] In Ugaritic texts Baal copulates with a heifer, an aspect of his mate and sister-protector, the young warrior-goddess Anath.[89] Asherah-of-the-Sea was the wife of El and mother of the gods in Ugaritic texts, but was later displaced by Astarte-Ishtar as the main goddess of female sexuality and fertility. Male and female 'sacred prostitution' was a prominent feature of the Canaanite fertility cult and an almost irresistible attraction to back-sliding Israelites. At every important archaeological site in Syria-Palestine were found images of the naked 'Holy Hierodule' with her genitals emphasised.[90] Various artifacts have been interpreted as phallic symbols, but with little certainty.[91] The fertility goddess was associated with a wooden pole, called an *asherah* in the Bible, which was probably a stylised 'Tree of Life'. In the precincts of Canaanite temples and on mountain-tops standing stones called 'massaboth' were erected. Some of those on the 'High Place' of Gezer were thought to be phallic.[92] Probably most *baetyls* were essentially aniconic foci of spiritual power commemorating manifestations of divinity or potent ancestors.

The Old Testament stresses the generative fertility of the patriarchs and the sacredness of their genitals.[93] Virile potency generating fertility throughout nature was as much a characteristic of the Hebrew Yahweh as of his Canaanite rivals. It was a hard struggle for monotheistic Jewish reformers to make their stiff-necked people forsake the 'abominations' of the Canaanite fertility cult. Even the family of Moses worshipped the 'Golden Calf', the young bull of the fertility cult, which was re-established by the Israelite king Jeraboam and his Aaronite priesthood *c.* 920 B.C.[94] Solomon's many foreign wives and the notorious Phoenician princess Jezebel promoted the pagan cults of Baal and Astarte and other deities among the Jews. Solomon's great temple in Jerusalem, built for him by Phoenicians, had to be purged of the emblems and votaries of Baal and Astarte *c.* 600 B.C.[95] Solomon's 'Song of Songs' is typical of the genre of Sacred Marriage rhapsodies. To appeal to his corrupted flock the prophet Hosea had to adapt the traditional imagery of the Sacred Marriage to the union of Yahweh with his promiscuous harlot of a wife, Israel.[96] The Jews resisted Jeremiah's jeremiads against their idolatry, claiming that the pagan fertility cult brought better crops and herds.[97] Images of the 'Naked goddess' are so common at Israelite sites that if the Bible and the Judeo-Christian tradition had not survived, archaeological artifacts alone would suggest that the main deity of the Jews was the fertility goddess, there being no images of iconoclastic Yahweh.[98] The effacement of the mother goddess from Judaism was never complete, and she re-emerged as the Virgin Mary and as the Talmudic female personifications of the Torah and the Synagogue as the 'brides' of Yahweh.[99] Kabbalistic Jewish mysticism frequently used the sexual imagery of the union of male and female principles.

In the hellenised Roman period a text ascribed to Lucian of Samosta[100] described the paramount temple of the great Syrian goddess Atargatis at Hierapolis-Bambyce. In front were two enormous free-standing columns, comparable in scale with Nelson's column, one of which was inscribed: 'Dionysus erected these phalluses to Hera his mother-protectress'. Lucian noted a phallic bronze figure in the portico and inside the temple were numerous votive phalluses with little figurines perched upon them. Beside the idol of the Great Goddess was her consort, a late syncretistic version of Baal-Hadad.

In the same period flourished the Syrian cult of Adonis (Semitic: *adon*: lord, master) a deity akin to both Dumuzi-Tammuz and Osiris. Adonis was a beautiful boy born from the incestuous union of a king and his daughter. He was loved by two goddesses: the love goddess and the queen of the underworld. He died from a wound in his genitals inflicted by a wild boar, and thereafter each spring he returned with the blooming flowers from the Land of the Dead for a brief season of passionate love with Astarte-Aphrodite. Women joined in the goddess's lamentations for his annual death and at Alexandria and among the Greeks and Romans his return, like the 'phallic resurrection' of Osiris-Dionysus was celebrated with phallophoric processions.[101] These Syrian fertility cults were notorious in the Roman period because of orgiastic 'sacred prostitution', male and female, and the frenzied excesses of votaries who slashed their limbs to make blood-offerings. Sometimes as a supreme act of devotion to the Great Goddess men emasculated themselves.[102]

Minoan Crete

The religion of the splendid Bronze Age civilisation of the Cretan palaces, which flourished in the second millennium B.C., seems to have been a sophisticated elaboration of the primitive Neolithic fertility cult. The Great Goddess in various aspects apparently dominated. Caves probably symbolised the womb of the Earth Mother; a cave near Amnisos was sacred to a goddess of childbirth from the Neolithic Period into Christian times and an aniconic stalagmite was probably venerated as a manifestation of fertility as at Çatal Hüyük.[103] The birth of a male god was celebrated in various Cretan caves. A gracile youth depicted in Minoan art may represent the son and lover of the Great Goddess, and there are indications that he died and was mourned by women in the same way as Dumuzi-Tammuz, Adonis, and Attis in neighbouring lands. The forceful, impregnating male principle seems to have been represented by the bull and, perhaps, by the 'labrys' or double-axe emblem, which elsewhere represented the fertilising thunderbolt. Some scholars see the 'labrys' as the emblem of the Great Goddess herself, perhaps used to sacrifice the virile bull.[104] Others have interpreted the axe-head, penetrated by the vertical shaft, as a symbol of male and female in sexual union like the Egyptian *Ankh* and the Indian *Lingam-*

[23]

Yoni. In Minoan Art of the Palace Period, nudity and the exhibition of the genitals' characteristic in contemporary fertility cults, are strangely absent,[105] and it has been denied that there are *any* unequivocal images of the phallus in Crete.[106] However, one sensitive lady archaeologist dissented, asserting that 'sex symbols are everywhere' and seeing bulls, 'horns of consecration', mountain peaks, stalagmites, and pillars all as symbols of 'phallic power'. She also observed that in their poetry women often symbolise their femininity with plants, flowers, and birds, characteristic subjects of Minoan art.[107] The clothing of fashion-conscious Minoans was certainly erotic: women were elaborately clothed, but their naked breasts were prominently displayed; men wore little more that a wasp-waisted loincloth with a sheath which held the penis in a vertical 'erection'. On the Cretan island of the Great Goddess there was a curious feminine blend of diffuse and dainty 'Rococo' eroticism with a lack of sexual explicitness.

Indoeuropean Bronze Age Europe

Around 2000 B.C. aggressive Indoeuropean warrior-herdsmen were spreading over Europe, imposing their rule and patriarchal ideology upon the indigenous Neolithic peasantry. Their chieftains, priests, and warrior aristocracy worshipped the supreme Sky Father; Earth Mother was made subordinate, but retained her vital importance among the mixed populations of farmers.[108] Sun symbols appear everywhere in Bronze Age European art, and the ethos of the warrior rulers is abundantly illustrated by the rock-engravings of Sweden and southern Europe. One engraving in the Val Camonica, in the Italian Alps, shows a warrior brandishing a spear while his penis touches a sun-wheel,[109] perhaps indicating the sun as the source of virile power. In southern Sweden sun-disks are associated with depictions of copulation, which may represent 'Sacred Marriages', and ithyphallic men plow with bulls.[110] A curious feature of Bronze Age rock-art is the prevalence of men with erect penises, apparently not stimulated by women. The phallus may have symbolised the bellicose power of virile 'afflatus', or supernatural inspiration, as among the Maori warriors of New Zealand. A Danish psychoanalyst has discussed the role of phallic aggression in hierarchical male relationships which involve dominance and submission, characteristic of various warrior societies.[111]

Stonehenge, on Salisbury Plain, was elaborated into a great cult-site by Bronze Age chieftains, probably for the worship of the sun and other astral luminaries. One hypothesis interprets Stonehenge in terms of the sexual symbolism of the 'Sacred Marriage': the single standing stones are allegedly phallic symbols, the 'trilithons' with their slit-like openings being complementary female symbols. At sunrise on the summer solstice the fertilising rays of the sun penetrate the 'trilithon' group, whose horseshoe-shaped plan may have symbolised the uterus of the Earth Mother.[112]

The Earth Mother was too indispensable to be eclipsed by the sun, and her power gradually reasserted itself in the later Bronze Age and early Iron Age.[113] She dominates the naked group on the bronze cart from Strettweg in Austria.[114] Tacitus, in the first century A.D., described the worship of Nerthus (Mother Earth) among the tribes of northern Germany and Denmark, where the goddess toured the land in a wagon pulled by cows, bringing peace and fertility.[115] Some of the corpses preserved in the peatbogs of that region may have been her sacrificial victims. In a bog at Broddenbjerg, Denmark, was found an image of a grossly ithyphallic fertility god, rough-hewn from a tree-fork. A tree-trunk phallus and several rustic images of goddesses were found in other peat-bogs.[116]

The Celts

Ireland preserved many archaic Celtic traditions. According to legendary history 'The People of the Goddess Danu' ruled Ireland before the coming of the Gaels, perhaps a misty folk-memory of the Megalithic cult of the Great Goddess which had spread from the Mediterranean in the Neolithic period. Versed in magic, they had four potent talismans, one of which was the 'Stone of Fal', a large stone phallus which shrieked out beneath the rightful High King on Tara Hill.[117] Irish kings derived their authority from their Sacred Marriages with the proprietary goddess of the locality. In his inauguration ritual the king of Ulster apparently impersonated a stallion to mate with a white mare.[118] The Dagda ('The Good God') was a larger than life personification of the Celtic chieftain: immensely wise and strong, he was also a heroic glutton and lover. Having devoured an enormous feast, despite his uncomfortably distended belly he was still able to copulate with the daughter of an enemy to her full satisfaction, thereby winning her to his cause.[119]

Irish goddesses were a formidable lot. They were fatal viragos in war, like many Near-eastern fertility goddesses. They could assume at will terrifyingly haggish appearances; one ghastly apparition had a huge mouth and her pudenda hung down to her knees.[120] Alternatively, they could appear as passionate and youthful beauties. There was no one special love goddess, for most Irish goddesses had equally voracious sexual appetites, which they gratified with numerous paramours among the gods and heroes. The regal goddess Medb had as one of her lovers the hero Fergus ('virility'), who had the strength of seven hundred men. His penis was the length of seven fingers and his scrotum was as big as a flour-sack.[121] The 'Stone of Fal' was popularly known as 'Fergus's Penis'. When deprived of the erotic solace of Medb and his wife Flidais, who ruled the wild beasts of the forests, Fergus required seven women to appease his sexual ardour.

The battle-frenzy of Irish heroes was of terrifying intensity. When Cu Chulainn returned after his first kills with his features grotesquely distorted with bloodlust,[122] his frightened king ordered the queen and her ladies to meet him naked. While he was thus distracted he was plunged into three successive vats of icy water to cool his ardour. Like later witches, British women performed certain rituals naked,[123] apparently because nudity is thought to enhance spiritual power. Probably this was the reason that some Celtic warriors battled in the nude. Cu Chulainn's 'initiation' into his vocation as a warrior hero entailed several battles with women, whom he conquered with violence and sexual aggression.

A category of Irish tales describes the poignant conflict between adulterous passion

[25]

and duty. Diarmuid's elopement with the seductive lady Grainne prefigures the guilty passion of Lancelot and Guinevere. These stories seem to express the romantic fantasies of unhappily married women, for the lovers embody a gentle, feminine ideal. Diarmuid had a musical voice, the gifts of sweet words and irresistible charm; he was 'the best lover of women and of maidens in the world'.[124] Irish stories often have tragic endings, and often sexuality was linked with death: Cu Chulainn, like Gilgamesh, provoked the fatal wrath of a goddess he spurned because he wanted to make war, not love. Fergus was killed while he swam with Medb's legs amorously entwined around him, and his foeman, Ailill, was slain during the annual Maytime orgy, while busy in the bushes with a woman.

Sexual motifs are not very common in surviving Celtic art. A few examples occur among the miniature bronze figurines from Central Europe: a tiny figure of an ithyphallic warrior holding a trumpet, comparable with Bronze Age rock-engravings, was found in the Celtic fort near Stradonice, Czechoslovakia.[125] A pair of finger-rings from Stuttgart-Uhlbach, Germany, are adorned with minute figures of a naked man and woman respectively, which interlock in sexual embrace.[126] A fibula brooch from Niederschönhausen, Germany, is decorated with a little naked man whose genitals merge with the muzzle of a ram's head, suggesting that his penis is in the ram's mouth.[127].

The broken stone pillar from Pfalzfeld, Germany, originally had a stylised head at the top, and some scholars regard the rounded base as phalloid, combining the two most potent symbols of vital power, fertility and protective magic: the severed head and the phallus. Another example which may express this idea is the 'Serpent Stone' from Maryport, Cumberland.[128] Phallic, or phalloid, stones adorned tombs in Asia Minor, Greece, and Etruria,[129] perhaps as a symbol of resurrection and immortal life-force. This motif seems to have reached the Celts in northern Europe, for similar phalloid stones were found at Irlich-Neuwied, Germany,[130] and Düno, Sweden,[131] and many Iron Age sites in Brittany,[132] Scandinavia, and Ireland, where the Turoe Stone, County Galway, probably relates to the phallic 'Fal' stone of Tara.[133]

One of the most remarkable antiquities of Britain is the Cerne Abbas Giant in Dorset (see illustration 12). This ithyphallic hillside figure has been faithfully maintained ever since Roman times and, according to local folklore, a woman wishing to have a child should spend the night upon the giant's phallus. The figure probably represents the Roman-British deity Hercules-Ogmios.[134] In style the figure is Celtic and is in the spirit of the Irish Dagda, whose magic club, perhaps a phallic symbol, could deal death with one end and life with the other. Similarly, the grotesque sexual aspects of lusty Irish goddesses survived in the enigmatic *Shelah-na-Gig* sculptures of Britain and Ireland (see Chapter 4a).

The Vikings
The gods of the Viking warriors were the Indoeuropean Aesir, headed by Odin and Thor, who had warred with another group of deities, the Vanir, who gave 'hostages'

12 *Romano–British cult figure*, Cerne Abbas, Dorset, England, third part, second century A.D.

to live among the Aesir: the god Njörd, his son Frey ('Lord'), and his daughter Freyja ('Lady'). Njörd was a deity of fertility and seasonal growth, apparently linked with Nerthus, the Earth Mother of earlier Nordic religion. Together with Odin's passive wife Frigg,[135] Freya had apparently superseded Nerthus. In the thirteenth century A.D. Snorri Sturleson wrote that Freyja was the only pagan deity to survive in his day. Fertility cults die hard among conservative peasants.

Freyja was a beautiful and seductive goddess of sexual passion. Like Hathor and Ishtar she had a talismanic necklace which worked powerful erotic magic. The malicious bisexual 'trickster' Loki jeered that Freyja had paid the four dwarfs who made her magic necklace by sleeping with each in turn. He also accused her of incest. She had a reputation for wide-ranging promiscuity and was described as roaming the night like a she-goat in rut among bucks. As a perennial ritual 'bride', her fiery-eyed eagerness for the nuptial bed was a matter of bawdy jest among gods and men. The unromantic Viking rulers actually forbade the singing of love-songs in their scorn and fear of feminine erotic power.[136] Freyja had a dark side associated with death and the ancient witchcraft called *seidr*, which could kindle erotic passion or blast fertility and kill. Its male practitioners were notorious for homosexuality.[137] The greatest insult to a Viking warrior was the allegation that he was *agr* ('effeminate') and had submitted to the passive 'female' role in anal sodomy. On the other hand, for a hero to dominate and sodomise another man was a proof of aggressive virility.[138] Red-bearded Thor's virile thunder-hammer was traditionally laid on the lap of brides.[139] In order to recover his hammer from the giants Thor allowed Loki to disguise him as a bride, but he had qualms that he might be accused of being *agr*.

Though of Vanir stock, Frey was one of the most important Norse gods, especially in Sweden where paganism survived longest intact. The German monk Adam of Bremen, writing about the time of the Norman conquest of Britain, described the main temple of pagan Sweden at Gamla Uppsala. Within were images of the three major gods including Odin and Thor. 'The third is Frey who gives to mankind peace and sensuous pleasures. His idol therefore, they endow with a mighty phallus.'[140] A small bronze figure with an erect penis, found at Rallinge, Sweden, probably represents Frey.[141] Animal and human sacrifices were offered to this Viking trinity at Uppsala. Obscene songs were sung and dramatic acts were publicly performed, which may have included the ritual copulation of the Sacred Marriage.[142] Nerthus had been accompanied on her travels by a priest who may have represented her consort. In the Viking Period a thousand years later the ithyphallic image of Frey was similarly paraded on a wagon, bringing peace and the warmth and abundance of springtime and a priestess, who was his wife, travelled with him.

At the end of the tenth century the Norwegian king Olaf Tryggvesson waged a vigorous campaign to christianise his domain. One of his chieftains, Gunnar Helming, suspected of murder, fled to pagan Sweden where he encountered a band of Frey's votaries. The priestess-wife in charge of Frey's wagon allowed the fugitive to join their troupe, saying 'The people like you, so I think it will be best if you stay the winter and take part with Frey and me in the festival when Frey ensures for the countryfolk a fruitful year. But Frey does not like you at all.' Crossing the mountains they were caught in a storm and the servants ran off leaving spring-bringing Frey stuck in a snow-drift. Left alone with the comely priestess and the antagonistic image of Frey, Gunnar decided 'three's a crowd' and, calling on Christ's help, expelled the pagan 'devil' and smashed the ithyphallic heathen idol. Opportunistically he took Frey's place in the wagon and as the consort of the priestess in the Sacred Marriage they continued their sacred tour, everywhere feted by the devout pagan peasants, who were delighted when Frey's wife eventually showed signs of pregnancy.[143]

Boars and spirited stallions were sacred to Frey, and King Olaf deliberately committed the iconoclastic sacrilege of riding a sacrificial stallion into a Norwegian temple and dragging Frey's image out tied to its tail. Early in the eleventh century another Christian king, Olaf Haraldsson, ruthlessly completed the conversion of the Norwegians. At a remote pagan farmstead the farmer's wife preserved a stallion's penis which would do her bidding in 'seidr' magic. One evening as the farmer's family were ceremoniously passing this magical phallus from hand to hand with appropriate prayers, the royal Saint Olaf arrived and wrathfully seizing the sacred fetish, threw it to the dog to devour.[144]

Africa

The Sahara Desert was once fertile grassland, and pictures on its rocks vividly portray the lives of ancient hunters and herdsmen. In the Fezzan there are images of a semi-human creature with an enormous penis and canine head and tail, sometimes shown copulating with a woman (see illustration 13).[145] The meaning of these ancient erotic images is lost, but they may portray a totemic spirit or a sexual demon associated with initiation ceremonies or fertility rites. An explorer has luridly described rites of the 'Dog People' of western Ethiopia, who impersonate jackals and hyenas in moonlit sex orgies.[146]

The Dogon tribe of the western Sudan revere the lubricious jackal as a sacred 'trickster', the only creature cunning enough to deceive Amma, their Supreme Deity. Transcendental Amma embodies both the male and female principles. The emblem of Amma's maleness is the phallic column; Amma as Earth Mother is

13 *Semi-human sexual demon*, rock engraving, Ti-n-Lalan, Libyan Fezzan, *c.* 5000 B.C.

represented on Dogon altars by a bowl. Offerings of the blood of sacrificial animals are poured into the bowl and onto wooden statuettes of a man, a woman, and a hermaphrodite. A Dogon holy man explained: 'Rain and sun fertilise the earth, seeds fall and are fertilised in the earth's womb, just as the seed of the man fertilises the woman. It is all the manifestation of Amma, the giver of life. There is only one good, for the field or for a tree or for a man or a woman: fertility, fruitfulness, fecundity, life. There is only one evil . . . sterility, barrenness, death. So Amma is life, and the religion of Amma is the religion of life.'[147]

A Dogon myth tells of the first coitus of Amma-Sky-Father with Amma-Earth-Mother, whose phallic clitoris, a termite column, got in the way so that from this defective union the jackal was born. This mischievous and libidinous 'trickster' incestuously defiled Mother Earth to steal her magic skirt containing the secret of words. This theft has enabled the jackal to reveal Amma's secret intentions to Dogon diviners.[148]

The Dogon commemorate the primal sexual embrace of Sky Father and Earth Mother in the architectural symbolism of their houses, and the plan of a Dogon village symbolises the primal hermaphrodite whose penis is the phallic foundation altar, while the oil-grinding stones symbolise the female genitals.[149] All Dogon men and women have spirit-twins of the opposite sex, and during their puberty initiations the boy's 'vaginal' foreskin and the girl's 'penile' clitoris are cut away to transform them from immature bisexuals into true men and women.

Another Dogon myth relates that a woman found the Earth Mother's fibre skirt stained with her sacred menstrual blood. Wearing it, she queened over the men until they seized the sacred skirt and established male domination. Other tribes have stories which credit women with the discovery of the sacred masks which were then appropriated by the men.[150] Male envy of the 'female mysteries' of menstruation and childbirth is exemplified in a grotesque custom of the Chaga tribesmen of the Congo, who justify their ascendancy over women by claiming that they are able to refrain from defecation. They allege that at the secret manhood initiation the anus of the novice is 'stopped up'. To maintain this 'male mystery' the men must furtively hide from the women when they empty their bowels.[151]

In southern Ethiopia there are an estimated 10,000 phallic stone columns, some as tall as twenty feet.[152] The provenance of these ancient erections is unknown, but the area has since been occupied by Hamitic warrior-pastoralists who also venerate the phallus. Ethiopian tribesmen customarily emasculate defeated enemies, living or dead, as is portrayed in Ethiopian paintings. Some Italian soldiers were mutilated in this manner during the battle of Adowa in 1896. A recent study of the Konso tribe, the Cushitic negro farmers of south-western Ethiopia, characterised them as obsessed with the phallus as the symbol of male power. Their dignitaries wear a metal phallus as a head-dress of rank. Phallic clay roof-pinnacles adorn the houses of priests, elders, and the communal Bachelor House, whither Konson husbands sometimes seek refuge from the depleting sexual demands of their wives, for phallic vitality and power are sapped by sexual intercourse.[153]

Many African tribes believe that the Supreme Creator is remote and indifferent to humanity, having delegated authority to his children such as the ithyphallic god Legba, who is worshipped by the Ewe peoples of West Africa. It is said that an erect penis has no conscience, and Legba is cruelly capricious. Every man has his own personal Legba as a sort of guardian angel-devil, and beside each front door is a vaguely humanoid mound of clay from which protrudes a large phallus, which must be constantly anointed in pious placation of Legba. More elaborate and realistic images of the god apotropaically guard the entrances to the village, crossroads, and public places (see illustration 14). Legba's secret rites include ritual coitus and public dances in which men furnished with exaggerated phalluses mime copulation with the earth, crops, trees, and even houses.[154] The neighbouring Yoruba worship him as Elegba or Eshu. A Yoruba statue portrays the god wearing a phallic head-dress, and at Oyo there is a phallus about three feet high, which must be constantly anointed to avert calamity.[155] The slave trade brought Legba-Eshu to the New World where Voodoo worshippers still honour 'Papa Legba' and another phallic 'trickster' named Ghede, Lord of Life and Death.[156]

The Yoruba *Gelede* men's society performs masked dances to celebrate fertility and deter malignant witchcraft with phallic images. One *Gelede* mask has on its superstructure wooden statuettes of a woman and a man, whose outsized penis is manipulated with strings to simulate desire and couplation.[157] Such African customs are analogous with the ancient phallophric processions Osiris-Dionysus. The female principle is personified by Onile, the goddess of the *Ogbuni* society, who is portrayed in a fine Yoruba bronze kneeling with her vulva prominently displayed (see illustration 15). A cleft in a cliff near Igbetti, Nigeria, is worshipped

14 *Phallic God Legba*, clay, Dahomey, mid-twentieth century

15 *Earth-Mother Onile*, Yoruba, Nigeria, *c.* eighteenth century

16 *Djanggawul sisters giving birth*,
bark painting by Mawalan,
Arnhem Land, Australia, mid-twentieth
century

as the vulva of the Earth Mother, and her clay altars are stylised representations of the female genitalia.[158]

Among the Ibo of southern Nigeria Ala, the Earth Mother, is supreme as bountiful giver of children, yams, life, and death. As an act of worship the Ibo of the Owerri district build and decorate *mbari* houses filled with gaily painted mud sculptures. Ala is shown majestically enthroned, accompanied by her children and her consort. Amadioha, the fertilising god of thunder, lightning, and rain. Dozens of other mud figures portray all aspects of Ibo life and fantasy incorporating the acquired blessings of European technology represented in traditional style. In one *mbari* house a tableau shows an Ibo woman giving birth in a modern maternity clinic attended by a white doctor and uniformed nurses.[159] Like many people the Ibo are ambivalent about sex. Because it is holy it is surrounded with taboos. Lovers meeting in the bush make love standing up because to copulate on the ground offends Mother Earth. For a husband to peek at his wife's genitals is sufficient grounds for divorce.[160] Yet the sculptures of the *mbari* houses deliberately flout these prudish conventions: 'A variety of openly sexual imagery from myth and legend greets the Owerri villager to whom even a veiled discussion of sex is impolite if not forbidden. Women brazenly display their private parts, and scenes of copulation include sodomy between mythological man-beasts. . . . Erotic scenes, among others, are strong magnets in *mbari* amusing and entertaining the public. . . . As one *mbari* artist said: "When we want to play tricks we put figures in poses which excite laughter. Wherever the bad things are in *mbari* that is where the people flock. They even call them the most beautiful!" '[161]

Australia

Hunters and foodgatherers, the Australian Aborigines live life as the ritual re-enaction of myths of the primeval 'Dreamtime'. In Arnhem Land, northern Australia, a cycle of hundreds of songs and rituals celebrate the creative acts of the

Djanggawul,[162] two sisters and their brother, children of the vaginal sun, who came from the east over the sea. Being creative fertility spirits their genitals were extra-ordinary: the clitorises of the sisters were so long that they dragged on the ground, and the brother wore his penis wrapped around his neck to save wear and tear. In a woven mat representing the sisters' wombs they carried magic *rangga*, pro-creative instruments of germination. During their 'walkabout' the Djanggawul poked the phallic *rangga* into the ground, causing vaginal waterholes to gush forth. Throughout Australia caves, waterholes and ritual pits symbolise vagina-uterus spirit repositories and abstract designs of concentric circles often are their symbols. The Djanggawul brother repeatedly copulated with his sisters, from whose ever-fertile wombs whole populations came forth (see illustration 16). One day, while the sisters were gathering food, the brother and other men stole their magic instruments of creation. The sisters accepted this male usurpation philoso-phically, being preoccupied with sexual reproduction and 'life-support' activities. Next the brother cut his sisters' clitorises down to present size and also shortened his own penis—but not as much. The fragments of the Djanggawul's abbreviated genitals became more magic *rangga*. Discovering that young men were copulating with their own sisters, the Djanggawul brother punished them with circumcision.

The Wawilak sisters, daughters of the Djanggawul, roamed in exile because of their incest and camped by a sacred waterhole. One sister had just given birth to a son and the other was menstruating. Blood from her vagina dripped into the water-hole arousing Yurlungur, the great totemic water snake, who slithered out of the hole causing rain to fall. Frantically the women yelled and danced to keep the monster at bay, but each time vaginal blood dripped it advanced. Swallowing the sisters and the boy, the giant serpent rose erect stretching from the waterhole up to the rainclouds, and then crashed down spewing out the Wawilak sisters, who turned into stones. They appeared to men in dreams and instructed them in the puberty rituals of circumcision and initiation into manhood. In this secret male ceremony the boys are said to be swallowed by the python, dying as children to be reborn as mature men ripe for marriage and procreation.[163] This is the artificial equivalent to the physiological 'coming of age' of girls at the onset of menstruation. Commenting on these rites, a native man admitted, 'We have been stealing what belongs to them (the women). . . . Men have nothing to do really, except copulate. . . . All that belonging to the Wawilak, the baby, the blood, the yelling, their dancing, all that concerns the women. . . . We have to trick them. . . . In the beginning we had nothing. . . . We took these things from the women.'[164] Barred from the male initiation mysteries a woman dismissed them contemptuously as 'men's rubbish', and added: 'Men make secret ceremonies; women make babies!'[165]

In addition to circumcision men voluntarily undergo a more drastic mutilation of the penis: subincision, a slit cut into the urethra on the underside of the penis, varying in dimension from half an inch to the full length of the penis. This wound, which is kept open, is sometimes referred to as a vulva, and on important ritual occasions the slit is made to bleed, for subincision blood has a sacred power superior to menstrual fluid. The Dieri tribe of central Australia had long conical stone *tjurungas*, magic repositories of tribal procreative essences derived from the totem ancestors of the 'Dreamtime'. After his subincision a Dieri tribesman carried one of these heavy phallic stones until he dropped from exhaustion, an ordeal which infused great potency.[166]

Men assert their supremacy by aggressive phallic ostentation. In central Australia Malpunga, the totem hero of the Aranda men, was represented in rituals with an enormous and ever erect phallus-tjurunga.[167] At Wintjara in western Australia, a site sacred to the Yiwara tribe, a crack in a cliff is said to have been caused by the rampant phallus of Yula, the penis totem, when he lunged for a fleeing woman and missed. Water dripping in a nearby cave is really Yula's semen.[168]

Aboriginal artists often depict grossly ithyphallic beings. At Djilgu in north-western Australia a rock engraving depicts the wild-yam spirit Ungamin, who stole the biggest yams from the Warulu people (see illustration 17). They punished him by pulling his penis until it was like the longest yams.[169] Phallic lightning spirits are also pictured.[170] The Aranda call lightning 'water-penis', and their medicine men cause lightning and rain by a dance in which they make their phalluses sway up and down.[171]

Aranda men also make irresistible love magic with a phallic 'bull-roarer', a wooden plaque on the end of a string which makes a rhythmic whirring that arouses sexual desire in coveted women. The love-object is magically drawn by an erotic vision of the lover surrounded by phallic lightning.[172] Women also make love magic, sometimes using a snake because of its resemblance to a long penis. They also know a dread spell to deter unwelcome sexual advances by causing detumescence.[173] In Arnhem Land paintings of copulating couples are sometimes made as a magical means of procuring the reality. A vengeful cuckold can punish his erring woman and her paramour by depicting them painfully pierced by sting-ray spines.[174]

Sometimes around the men's campfire they sociably indulge in mutual mastur-

17 *Ithyphallic spirit*, rock painting, Australia,
    probably twentieth century

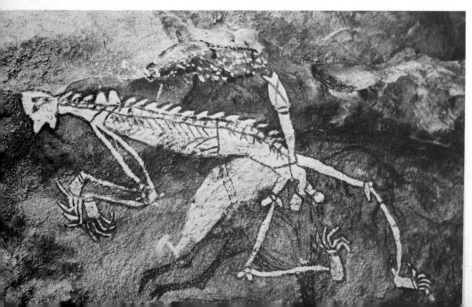

bation accompanied by polite and reassuring comments of admiration:

'You have a big one!'
'No, yours is big; you might kill her when you copulate!'
'Mine is little; yours is big. . . .'
'No, yours is big, like a devil!'
'The subincision hole is as big as a spear-thrower!'
'Yours is big as a Water Serpent!'
'When you copulate yours will be so big it will burst!'[175]

New Guinea

A myth of the Iatmul tribe of the middle Sepik River area tells that in the beginning a woman named Shotkaman-Agwi gave birth to two totems: a bird and a reptile, either a lizard or a great snake. After many adventures a phallic 'trickster' named Betman-Gambi died. Shotkaman-Agwi spread herself upon his corpse while her reptile entered his body restoring him to life. In a ritual re-enacting this event a wooden image of Betman-Gambi is set up. It has a large hole in its abdomen through which a large pole is inserted to the accompaniment of bawdy songs. On one end of the phallic pole is carved the woman Shotkaman-Agwi and on the other the bird perches on the head of the serpent.[176] Both myth and ritual seem to embody a curious inversion of the sexual act with a 'uterine man' penetrated by a 'phallic woman'.

Elaborately carved hooks suspended from the ceiling protect valuables in the men's Ceremonial House. Shotkaman-Agwi may be represented on a Iatmul hook which shows a naked woman displaying her vulva squatting upon a crescent form (see illustration 18). Phalloid shapes, possibly yams, grow on either side of her, and one appears to enter her vagina. On a similar hook the woman's body merges with the crescent which is a serpent. Her head is a real human skull overmodelled and adorned with hair, and more human hair fringes her gaping vulva.[177] Headhunting, sexuality, and the fertility of nature are linked. In order to prove himself a 'real man' fit for marriage and procreation, a young warrior had to take an enemy head.

18 *Wooden suspension hook* from Iatmul, New Guinea, Middle Sepik River, early twentieth century

This was a means of obtaining more of the spiritual life-force believed to reside in the head, thus increasing the tribe's power and fertility at the enemy's expense.[178]

A long nose is considered a mark of virile beauty with phallic associations. Masks often have exaggeratedly long noses which may take the form of a down-curved bird's bill or a pendulous snake. In some statues the proboscis actually connects the head to the penis linking the two main power centres.[179]

Phallic male pride and aggression are closely linked in the Iatmul stereotype of the male role. A man is supposed to be competitive and hot-tempered and he adopts histrionic mannerisms: swaggering, shouting, scowling, and making menacing gestures. In contrast, the women are cheerful, co-operative realists, caring for the children and the home, gardening, and generally making a larger economic contribution than their vain spouses. Man's life is largely devoted to theatrical public ceremonials and centres on the village Men's House, which is barred to women and children. In addition to organising exciting hunts and war parties, the men monopolise the religious ceremonies of the ancestral cult of power and fertility. The essence of the 'male mysteries' is the covert playing of the long flutes which are said to be the voices of the ancestors conveying male authority from the spirit world. When, in an attempt to debunk traditional religion, Christian missionaries ordered their converts to play the secret flutes in front of the women, the latter were as embarrassed and disconcerted as the men, for while accepting their humble 'feminine role', they had vicariously shared the aggressive achievements and dramatic ceremonials of phallic pride.[180]

It is a common pattern in boys' initiation ceremonies for the novices to be 'swallowed' by a dragon-like creature, apparently a 'mother figure'. The Iatmul Men's House is considered to be a monstrous woman, the secret interior is termed her 'belly' and her apotropaic head appears at the top of the façade, her tongue protruding fiercely. The same symbolism applies in the ceremonial houses of the Abelam tribe, a related people inhabiting the foothills of the Prince Alexander Mountains. The phallic-aggression of warrior pride is combined with the symbolism of the Dragon-Mother. The ridgepole is a sort of phallus-spear and more spears project aggressively from the top of the façade. From the ridgepole hangs a tassel containing two enemy skulls and referred to as the 'testicles'. Sometimes a protuberance of the ridgepole called its 'nose' rests in a grooved post with which it is said to copulate.[181]

In addition to identifying the penis with aggression, it is also regarded as a nutritive organ like the female breast. The ancestor statues which live in the Men's House often have a drop of white semen painted on the tip of their penises. A totemic bird or a pig are represented sniffing the semen, which is regarded as a beneficial nutrient fostering the growth of pigs and long yams.[182] This belief recurs in other parts of New Guinea: in orgiastic rites the Papuans of Kiwai Island collect semen for use in sympathetic magic to cause initiated boys and girls and sago palms to grow.[183] The Marind-anim of West Irian use sperm as a magic fertiliser to make plants grow, and it is rubbed on girls' bodies to foster the growth of their breasts and feminine curves. Semen reinforces the magic power of totemic stones, and applied to the forehead acts as apotropaic protection against evil spirits.[184] The Arapesh believe that after conception frequent copulation, producing quantities of semen, is required to make the foetus grow.[185]

Now that the white rulers have banned headhunting and war, the main basis of male prestige among the Abelam is the competitive growing of a species of yam which can attain lengths up to fifteen feet. Prize yams are adorned with long-nosed masks and named after clan ancestors, whose spiritual force they manifest. During the yam-growing season the proud 'father' of the 'yam-child' must refrain from sexual intercourse, having first purified himself from the weakening female pollution of past coition by making his penis bleed.[186] Thereafter all his sexual energy is 'sublimated' into reinforcing the vital power of his growing yams. There is said to be a very close identification between a man and his yam. Like the spear, the long nose, and the sacred long flutes, the long yam can be considered a phallic symbol, although the phallus might equally be considered a 'yam symbol', for these are all cognate emblems of the aggressive male 'ethos'.[187]

In their role of exaggerated masculinity contemptuous of feminine passivity, men constantly use the imagery of phallic attack in their speech: An Iatmul man disdainfully referred to the women: 'Yes, we fuck them but they never retaliate.'[188] To protect themselves from the phallic aggression of their rivals Iatmul men walk about with a small stool protecting their buttocks. Weaker males from outside the tribe are targets of homosexual assault as a demonstration of superiority, but passive homosexuality is unthinkable. So rigid is their proud male ethos that on occasions when they wish to express warm affection to their nephews Iatmul men must resort to grotesque and obscene transvestite parody of femininity as in the *Naven* ceremony.[189]

The natives of Mount Hagen exhibit a similar radical polarisation of masculinity and femininity which is displayed in their main art form, self-adornment. Men are supposed to be aggressive and monopolise the ancestral fertility cult. Therefore they tend to decorate themselves with dark colours associated with warlike hostility and the supporting presence of spectral ancestors. Semen is associated with pig grease, and so men also wear some white or bright shiny materials and an oily sheen associated with fecundity and wealth. Men are weakened by sexual contact with their womenfolk and are especially threatened by the pollution of female genital blood. Bright red body-paint is associated with women but regarded with ambivalence by men, probably because of their fear of sexual pollution and effeminate identification of themselves with the loving passivity of women. Nevertheless, on special occasions when they wish to express receptive friendliness to neighbours or to exert an erotic appeal to women, men adopt in their self-adornment a discreet amount of the red, usually associated with the female principle as though momentarily signalling their desire to 'make love not war'.[190]

Male fear of women is 'projected' in the widespread belief in 'phallic-aggressive' female witches. These deadly monsters fly through the air emitting fire from their vaginas. They also have inside their bodies, like eggs, female witch testicles which can cause elephantiasis.[191] A controversial interpretation of the traditional image on

Trobriand Island war shields suggested that they represent a phallic witch displaying her dreaded vulva, analogous with the apotropaic Medusa of the ancient Greeks.[192] Another instance of the spectre of female sexual aggression is the tradition, recorded by Bronislaw Malinowski, that the women of a certain Trobriand Island village have the customary right to insult, batter, and 'mass-rape' any 'foreign' man who strays into their gardens. The anthropologist did not venture to verify the authenticity of this tradition by trespassing.[193]

Micronesia

The Palau Islands of western Micronesia were rich in erotic art which adorned the *bai*, the sacred club-houses of the unmarried men's fraternities.[194] The main façade of a *bai* was profusely decorated with images of cosmic fertility. The main feature was the *dilukai*, an apotropaic wooden statue of a naked woman with her legs widespread, exhibiting her tattooed vulva (see illustration 19). On the horizontal

19   *Wooden Dilikai figure from Men's House*, Palau Islands, Micronesia, *c.* 1900

plank to which this figure was attached were engraved processions of ithyphallic men carrying toward her fish, fowl, and sun symbols. The men nearest her have enormously long phalluses with barbed glans which point toward the *dilukai* like spears. The young warriors of the *bai* were identified with the male sun. The *dilukai* woman probably symbolised the earth opening herself to the sun's fertilising rays.[195] Before marriage, sexually 'ripe' girls were sent to the *bai* of another village to cohabit with the young bachelors. Couples paired off, and when she left for home the girl was given a gift of money in recognition of her erotic favours. Like the *dilukai* figure the *bai* girls embodied the female fertility principle, and their religious role is comparable with the 'sacred prostitute' duty of all women in the temples of ancient Babylon.

On the rafters inside the club house were illustrations of myths and legends carved in low-relief and painted in black, white, red, and yellow. One illustrated story tells of the creator Jagad-re-ngel, who made a number of phalluses while, on another island, his sister made a similar quantity of vulvas. When he visited her the phalluses and vulvas became sexually excited and, despite the sister's efforts to ward them off, the phalluses succeeded in uniting with the vulvas. From these happy unions descended the various families of the tribe.[196] In the illustration the vulvas are black because on reaching sexual maturity a girl's genitals were depilated and tattooed with a black pubic triangle. From infancy her labia minora had been systematically stretched by pulling and sucking, a chore relegated to impotent old men.[197] Another *bai* scene illustrates a tale of a man whose phallus was so long that he had to stand on another island to make love to his wife.[198] A bawdy image depicts a man who accompanied a *bai* girl into the woods. She seductively removed her skirt and lay on her back with her legs spread. Instead of making love to her, the fool tried to talk to her vulva, mistaking it for a face because it had 'hair', a 'nose', and a 'mouth'.[199] The aggressive phallic boasting and ribaldry of these illustrations are comparable with the locker-room bawdy of our own men's clubs.

Phallic aggression is manifest in a large wooden phallus which proudly adorns the kingpost of the chief house of Rauau on Ifaluk Atoll in the Caroline Islands. This commemorates the phallus of the conquering hero Maur. He had married a woman on the island of Woleai, and jealous local men beat him up and left him for dead. He revived when a woman accidentally urinated on him in the dark. He escaped to his native Ifaluk and roused his people for vengeance and conquest saying, 'I will not waste words. I will take off my loincloth. If my penis points toward Woleai, that will be a sign to you to go there and kill all the people!' It did and they did.[200]

The women of Ifaluk perform for their beloved men erotic songs and dances similar to the Hawaiian *hula-hula* dances. Like the 'bumps' and 'grinds' of modern American 'strippers' their rhythmic pelvic movements mime copulation. The words of the serenades composed by the women combine tender loving sentiments and explicit sexuality: 'I am his sweetheart; he is my true love. . . . He sees beneath my skirt, what I call my devil, but he thinks it very nice. It is a place reserved for him.'[201] And, 'His penis wakes up whenever I take off my skirt. . . . He hugs me tight, our noses touch. I am as happy as he is. We put our tongues in each other's mouths. He lies on my breast; he tells me how happy he is.'[202] A wife sings of her husband, 'He goes and searches for a moonlit clearing; he sits down to rest, takes off his loincloth. I come and lie upon him. Broad is his chest, covered with tattooing with rich designs. . . . I will never leave him; his tattooing is a bed for me. I make the soot for the designs. I am fixed as firmly as they; I would like to go about with him, inside the tattooing. . . . Let other women keep away!'[203] Another song tells of token resistance to an adulterous lover: 'He took off my skirt and said, "Give me your body . . . you are fair as the sands on the beach!" "Wait," I said to him, "after a while". But he said, "Now!" I told him, "You mustn't see me naked! You have a very nice wife, beautiful as the morning. I can't give you my body!" But after a while: "Well, all right; whatever you like." His loving was furious; he darted about like a fish. Till at last I said, "That's enough!" . . .'[204]

Polynesia

Before Christian missionaries triumphed, Polynesia was pervaded with exuberant eroticism. Within the rules of rank and social decorum children freely gratified their burgeoning sexuality. Adolescent *Ka'ioi* groups performed dances and sexual exhibitions at public feasts exemplified by a song from the Tuamotu Archipelago: 'Tight-stretched hymen, take it by force! The clitoris stands; the woman parts with her fingers the cleft portal below! It is the War God Tu-of-the-Long-Blade who has thrown her down! His blade plies in and out; a sudden flow escapes! Slappety-slappety-slap!'[205] Inspired by the lascivious goddess Lono, Hawaiian *Hula* dancers vied to produce maximum erotic stimulation. In the Society Islands the *Arioi* cult, led by men and women of the highest rank, toured the islands presenting performances of myths and legends featuring erotic themes intended to promote fertility.

Maori myths relate that in the beginning Sky-Father Rangi lay upon Earth-Mother Papa in continuous coition until their sons, led by Tane, rebelled and forced them apart. Tane was the male procreative principle who mated with various female forces to procreate birds, animals, trees, etc. He formed from earth Hina, the first woman, and by means of Tiki, his personified phallus, he impregnated her with a succession of daughters, with whom he also copulated. Realising with shame that her 'husband' was also her incestuous father, one daughter retreated to the underworld as Hine-nui-te-po, goddess of death.

Other Polynesian stories tell of the seduction of Hina by the Polynesian equivalent of the phallic serpent: 'One day while she was bathing, an eel (tuna) of great size came from its place beneath the rocks and startled Hina by its pleasing touch; that eel went sliding under Hina in the place where pleasure is. And the eel was wicked and the same thing happened many times and Hina permitted it. That eel gave Hina pleasure with its tail.'[206]

Throughout the Polynesian universe there was a basic polarity between the 'male principle': positive, active, associated with the transcendent upper regions of light, air, and the 'divine spark' conveyed in semen, and the 'female principle': negative, the passive receptive uterus embodying the lower material regions of the earth and the womb-tomb of the underworld, associated with night, darkness, and death. The phallus and the vulva contain powerful *mana* (vital, effective, supernatural power), but are circumscribed with taboos, for *mana*, like electricity, can be dangerous, and the genitals can be destructive as well as procreative.

The phallus is often compared with a weapon, as in a love-song from central Polynesia in which a woman compares her lover's penis with his spear.[207] Erection of the penis was a sign of virile *mana* or 'afflatus', and it was a good omen if the leader of a Maori war-party awoke with an erection on the day of battle. In their war-dance Maori warriors taunted their enemies: 'When will your penis become enraged? When will your penis become erect?'[208] The aggressive warrior in his defiant stance with his tongue stuck out and his penis prominent or erect was frequently carved on Maori houses or stockades.[209] The phallus is a weapon of defence in a Maori incantation against sorcery: 'Attack the penis! Death weaken and pass by! Let what you attack be my penis!'[210] A bawdy tale from the Tuamotu Islands described the phallic combat between the 'trickster' hero Maui and the eel-god Tuna. As Tuna brandished his mighty phallus, as big as a whale's, a terrifying tidal wave arose, but when Maui displayed his virile member, with its distinctive bent end, the wave subsided, leaving his enemies helplessly stranded.[211] In the Austral Islands the highest chiefs were titled *uretu* (erect penis), and wore necklaces adorned with testicle symbols.[212]

The Maori sometimes termed the vulva *whare o aitua* (house of misfortune or death), for therein the phallus loses its strength and 'dies'. A Maori legend tells of Maui's last quest for immortality for humanity, which could only be gained by his entering the toothed vagina of the sleeping goddess of death, cutting out her heart and emerging from her mouth. Unfortunately, as Maui stuck his head into her vulva, one of his friends could not suppress a loud laugh and the dreaded goddess awoke and crunched our hero to death[213] (see illustration 20). The powerful negative *mana* of the vulva could harm male *mana*, and so men needing the full force of their supernatural power to make sculptures, carve a canoe, or go to war were careful to avoid women. In the Marquesas a woman could halt a war-party by declaring: 'This road I name after my genitals!' Any warrior rash enough to pass that way would surely die.[214] When an elaborately carved Maori ceremonial house was completed the powerful male *mana* activated for its construction had to be safely neutralised by having a woman of high rank ritually straddle the doorsill exposing it to the negative *mana* emanating from her genitals.[215] An apotropaic image of a woman with her vulva prominently displayed was sometimes carved above the door, and sculptors of the Taranaki district sometimes added an extra vulva on the out-thrust tongue to increase the power of the image.[216] The Maori also carved images of copulating ancestors on their houses (see illustration 21) and on the lids of wooden boxes in which sacred feathers were kept. Phallic symbolism occurs on many carved objects, including flutes and various knobbed handles.[217]

The dramatisation of the Sacred Marriages of the Creator Tangaroa opened performances of the *Arioi* cult. A remarkable image of that deity from Rurutu in the Austral Islands is in the Museum of Mankind (British Museum), London. The idol's phallus projected horizontally forward before it was truncated, apparently by prudish missionaries.[218] Numerous Maori images have also been 'bowdlerised'[219] and the offending phallus of 'Staff Gods' from Raratonga have often been sawn off. These images, up to eight or nine feet long, have at one end a flat, stylised profile of the ancestral god and at the other end his progenerative phallus. Around the centre is wrapped a roll of bark cloth, the vehicle for the indwelling *mana* of the image, perhaps symbolising the 'female principle' penetrated by the phallic staff to procreate the generations of little figures on the shaft, some of which are also ithyphallic.[220]

20 *Maui and Hine-nui-te-po*, from Maori ceremonial house, Polynesia, nineteenth century

21 *Copulating ancestors*, from Maori ceremonial house, Polynesia, nineteenth century

From infancy a Polynesian boy's penis was pulled to lengthen it and stimulate his phallic power as a future warrior. At puberty his penis was superincised; that is, the foreskin was slit on the upper surface. Like the Micronesians the Polynesians depilated body hair. In the Marquesas the overall body-tattooing of eminent men extended painfully to their penises, and the genitals of Maori women were tattooed with a triangular pattern of spiralling lines.[221] The girl's clitoris and labia minora were artificially lengthened. A fully 'stretched' clitoris was described as 'a mast in a boat' or 'a bird in its nest'. The inturned phallic handle of Maori canoe-bailers may represent such a clitoris, for the erotic goddess Hina sometimes took the form of a bailer.[222] Wooden figurines from Easter Island portray squatting women with grossly elongated genitalia.[223] Ceremonial inspection and public exhibition of a

[42]

girl's 'improved' genitals took place when she reached marriageable age.[224] Virginity was almost unknown after early childhood except among the sheltered daughters of the élite. In Samoa the defloration before marriage of such prestigious virgins also took place in a public ceremony.[225]

Atop a hill on Molokai in the Hawaiian Islands was discovered a basalt phallus about the height of a man, known to the natives as the penis of the god Nanahoa.[226] Lava carvings of a phallus and a vulva were found in a stream on the island of Maui.[227]

Eroticism seems to have dominated the social and religious life of pagan Ra'ivavae in the Austral Islands. The *marae*, temple enclosures with stone platforms, contained phallic stones representing the virility of gods and ancestors and statues of pregnant women. One statue portrayed 'a woman in the ecstasy of being implanted by a huge penis'.[228] Ceremonial copulation and other sexual acts were performed in public on the altars to stimulate fertility in humanity and throughout nature. Semen was smeared on the priests' faces, bringing together the most vital powers of head and phallus. Rapturous hymns accompanied these sexual rites: 'O Primordial Rod of Life, tattooed like a mighty pillar, carved with erotic symbols, bounding up like a startled bird! O Divine Phallus of the vast ejaculation! O Divine Phallus of the first awakening of desire, ardently impenetrating there below the Primeval Vulva! O Primordial Clitoris together with the Womb, source of human progeny! Our First Progenitress, of whom it is said: "Thou art the Origin, the Divine Vulva, plying with quickening ardour!" . . .'[229]

On remote Easter Island the main deity was the Creator Makemake, whose cult was associated with migratory seabirds, their eggs, and the sacred 'birdman' of the year. Girls' elongated genitals were inspected at the clifftop cult centre of Orongo where petroglyphs include at least forty-nine *komari* vulva symbols.[230] These female symbols were also tattooed on men's bodies,[231] engraved on ancestral skulls, statues, and 'pillow-stones' which fostered fertility and good fortune.[232] After Peruvian slavers kidnapped the last pagan priests in 1864 the traditional religion disintegrated, though it still survives in the use of the old fertility fetishes to promote the fecundity of fowl in henhouses.

Mexico

Maize was cultivated *c.* 5000 B.C., and by *c.* 2000 B.C. village farmers were producing clay statuettes of nude women comparable with those of the Old World Neolithic fertility cults. In the cave of Agua Bendita (Blessed Water), Guerrero, the male fertility principle, is symbolised by a stalactite formation shaped like a pendant penis. During the rainy season water drips from the tip into a concavity in the top of an altar-like stalagmite beneath, on which are engraved vulva symbols.[233] Today the Mixtec Indians of the region continue this phallic rainwater fertility cult.[234] Late in the second millennium B.C. Olmec civilisation developed theocratic ceremonial centres with temple mounds and monumental stone sculpture. Carved on a mountainside near Chalcacingo, Morelos, are a group of Olmecoid reliefs depicting a fertility cult involving caves, rain symbols, serpents and sprouting maize. one relief shows a bearded figure with an erect penis, reclining with his wrists bound and confronted by figures with grotesque beaked and fanged faces.[235] This enigmatic relief may relate to traditions of the Huastec and Maya Indians who share a deity called Mam ('grandfather'), who is associated with chthonic caves, mountain-tops, thunder and lightning, rain, serpents, vegetation, and sexuality. The highland Maya say that Mam is tied up in the interior of the earth and rumblings at the start of the rainy season are his voice proclaiming that he wants to come out. In one post-Christian tradition, his wife is said to be a prostitute and the Huastec remember orgiastic sexual rites in caves.[236] Mayan rainwater deities called Chacs are beaked and serpent-fanged and sometimes cause rain by urination.[237] Two buildings at Toltec-Mayan Uxmal, Yucatan, have phallic rainwater spouts.

The Mayan 'Dresden Codex' of the Classic Period depicts a seated copulatory embrace between an elderly god, probably Mam, and the youthful goddess of love and procreation, Ix Chel, who was notorious for her promiscuous amours.[238] This amorous couple was often represented on contemporary terracottas from the island of Jaina.[239] The goddess was also 'Lady of the Beasts' and the codex and terracottas show her cuddling various animals.[240] Among the Maya and Aztec, sexuality was usually symbolised by flowers[241] and animals such as the naughty monkey, who represents playful, irresponsible eroticism. On a fragment of a Mayan bowl a nude woman resembling Ix Chel reclines while a monkey fondles her breast.[242]

In contrast to this discreet eroticism are a group of grossly ithyphallic ceramic statuettes from the western states of Colima and Michoacan.[243] Such blatant sexuality was a notorious characteristic of the Huastec culture of the Gulf coast. About 1521 an anonymous member of Cortes's expedition wrote of the Huastec: '. . . they adored the member that men carry between their legs, and they have it in temples, and similarly placed in squares, together with images in relief of all manners of pleasure which can be executed between man and woman, and have them depicted with the legs up in different ways. In the province of Panuco the men are great sodomites and very lazy and drunkards. . . .'[244] Few traces of Huastec sexual imagery have survived the iconoclastic zeal of the Spanish clergy, but three monumental stone phalluses were discovered at Yahualica, Hildago.[245]

During the Classic and Post-classic periods the dominant civilisations of the Mexican highlands were relatively puritanical. They believed that fertility resulted from blood sacrifices rather than from sexual magic. Worshippers pierced their ears, tongues, and penises to offer blood to their deities, and major rites invariably entailed human sacrifices. A typical Aztec earth-goddess was the dragon-like Coatlicue ('Snake-skirt'), the antithesis of erotic with her ghastly attributes of human sacrifice and death. However, the Aztec borrowed deities of sexuality from their neighbours: Xochiquetzal ('Flower-Quetzal-Plume', or 'Precious Flower') was a beautiful goddess of erotic delight worshipped in orgiastic festivities during which female votaries, usually prostitutes, were sacrificed. Her consort was ithyphallic Xochipilli ('Flower Prince'), god of festive gaiety and sensuous pleasure and another associate was the 'trickster' Ueucoyotl ('Old Coyote'), a deity of music and dance and a notorious copulator.

A more sinister divinity of sexuality was Tlazolteotl, goddess of dirt. She too was an Earth Mother and a patroness of childbirth. A magnificent Aztec statuette of a naked crouching woman in childbirth is thought to portray Tlazolteotl bearing the young maize god, Cinteotl.[246] According to the angle of light the face seems to express pain or exaltation (see illustration 22). As goddess of the 'female mysteries', Tlazolteotl was the patroness of healers and witches and in the 'Codex Fejervary-Mayer' she is shown naked astride a broomstick with the red serpent Tlapaplcoatl, the symbol of the dark forces of blood and libido.[247] As the instigator of sinful lust she had the power to absolve sexual guilt once in a lifetime following the sinner's confession and penance. In this role she was called Tlaequani ('Eater of excrement').[248] Like Ix Chel she was associated with the moon as well as the earth, and the 'Codex Laud' portrays her in her various phases. In one picture she crouches naked, exhibiting her vulva to Quetzalcoatl-Ehecatl as an ocean wave curls up behind her[249] (see illustrations 23). Tlazolteotl had been imported from the Huasteca. The 'Codex Borbonicus' illustrates rites at the harvest festival, where a female votary impersonated the maize goddess and was decapitated and flayed. Dressed in her skin, a priest mimed copulation with the sun and then gave birth to Cinteotl, the young maize god. Folio 30 shows the skin-clad priest gorgeously apparelled as the maize goddess, flanked by Tlazolteotl's priestesses. Seated on the ground Tlazolteotl received the homage of a priest who leads a procession of Huastec votaries each supporting an enormous phallus and holding a bundle of sticks, probably drenched in sacrificial blood drawn from their penises. A Spanish inscription says 'These are the sodomite priests'.[250]

The most fascinating and enigmatic figure in Toltec-Aztec culture was Quetzalcoatl ('Quetzal-plumed Serpent', or 'Precious Twin'). In one of his aspects he was Ehecatl, the personification of the wind, who brings the fertilising rain, and as an aerial rain-serpent he probably had a phallic significance.[251] The myths of the god are mixed with traditions of priestly rulers who bore his name such as Quetzalcoatl-

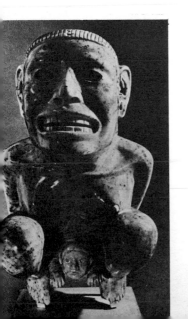

22 *Tlazolteotl giving birth to Cinteotl,*
Aztec, Mexico, fifteenth century

23 *Tlazolteotl displaying herself*, Codex Laud, Mexico, fifteenth century

Topiltzin, who came from the Huasteca to rule the Toltecs at Tula. He lived in saintly chastity and holiness until he was seduced by black magicians into incestuous debauchery and the Toltec Empire declined and fell amid sexual corruption.[252] The exiled Quetzalcoatl and his followers eventually emigrated to the Yucatan penninsula. This legend roughly corresponds to the historic seizure of power by rulers who imposed Toltec culture on the decadent Post-classic Maya. Ruling from ceremonial centres such as Chichen Itza and Uxmal they introduced the cult of the 'Feathered Serpent' Quetzalcoatl-Kukulkan and profuse phallic imagery, which suggests influences from the Huasteca and Gulf Coast.[253] A building at Chichen Itza is called 'The House of the Phalluses' because those images protrude from the walls of its rooms[254] and many large stone phalluses 'stand about like toadstools to shock or amuse visitors'[255] beside the causeway from Uxmal to Chichen Itza.

Although nudity was rare in the Toltec homeland and among the Maya of the Classic Period, it occurs in Post-classic Toltec-Maya imagery and may relate to the phallic cult. At Chichen Itza warriors are shown without the usually obligatory loincloth in a state of ritual nudity.[256] Among their Mayan subjects the foreign rulers had a bad reputation for lechery, including homosexuality.[257] Ithyphallic images of naked men with ropes or snakes around their necks suggest a connection between human sacrifice and sexuality, for hanging is said to produce paroxysmic erection of the penis.[258] In one form of sacrifice the victim was tied to a stake, his genitals were made to bleed and he was shot full of arrows.[259] A relief at Chichen Itza apparently shows a priestly ruler with the splendid quetzal-plume headdress of the 'Feathered Serpent' cult, cutting his own penis before a phallic altar.[260] Terracotta figurines from Santa Rita, British Honduras, portray men cutting their penises, and a realistic model of a penis has slits cut into the glans.[261] The most valiant Indians of Guatemala split the whole length of their penises.[262]

The Spanish conquerers obsessively commented on the widespread practice of sodomy among the Indians. An explorer of the Pacific coast of Mexico described houses adorned with paintings '. . . especially men joined with women and men with men . . .'.[263] A pious Spaniard proudly recorded his personal satisfaction in smashing a gold jewel from Santa Marta, Columbia, which portrayed '. . . a man mounted upon another in that diabolic and nefarious act of Sodom, made in gold relief . . .'.[264]

Peru

In the fertile river valleys of the arid Pacific coast, agriculture was developed at an early date, and the desert fringes are dotted with tombs from a succession of cultures. From these graves thousands of figurative pots have been recovered, including an extraordinary corpus of erotic art.[265] In the Formative Period pots of the Vicus culture sometimes have double phallic spouts or phallic tripod 'legs'.[266] An amusing pot from the Salinar culture is adorned with a kneeling, naked couple; the woman gleefully reaches for the man's genitals while displaying her own.[267] A Classic period polychrome Nazca pot represents a solemn pair coupling face-to-face like fat, shiny beetles.[268] Also in the Classic Period, the Mochica civilisation was by far the most prolific and varied in its ceramic production and it has been estimated that approximately one per cent of these works portrayed erotic subjects.[269]

Like the Olmec in Mexico, the early Peruvians worshipped a fanged deity with the combined attributes of jaguar, reptile, and bird. A few moulded reliefs on Mochica pots show the fanged god copulating with a woman in a house or under a tree, assisted by various animal-headed acolytes. This was probably a 'Sacred Marriage' to ensure fertility.[270] Most other Mochica erotica are modelled fully 'in-the-round', and apparently reflect non-religious sexuality.

Pots with stirrup-shaped spout-handles represent the human genitals. The penis appears either flaccid,[271] or more often, erect as a phallic spout. Some otherwise naturalistic phalluses have a human face below the glans; on one specimen the phallus-homunculus holds his nose as though commenting on the sexual odour of the vulva surrounding the base of the male genitals.[272] Various vessels represent the female genitals, and there are several examples of a type of false-bottomed bowl which has, moulded on its interior, a woman lying on her back with her legs flexed and her vulva a gaping aperture, through which liquid would gush forth from the concealed cavity beneath if the bowl were tipped.[273]

Another popular motif is a seated man holding his enormous phallus. The main opening is in the top of his head-dress, but liquid would dribble from the perforations below the rim if one tried to drink from there, and instead one would be forced to suck from the small hole in the glans of the phallus-spout. Although most of the faces on Mochica pots are stolidly impassive in the throes of their sexual acts, one of these ithyphallic Toby-jugs proudly offers his huge phallus with an expression of exuberant glee, as though relishing the rude joke of compelling the drinker to perform fellatio on him (see illustration 24). Representations of heterosexual fellatio are quite common. In some examples the man sits majestically on a throne-like seat while the woman kneels before him mouthing his exaggerated organ as though in obeisance to phallic male power (see illustration 25). Sometimes the female figure is

24 *Ceramic Vessel*, Mochica Culture, Peru, *c.* A.D. 500

25 *Ceramic Vessel*, Mochica Culture, Peru, *c.* A.D. 500

larger than the male and might depict a goddess[274] of voracious sexual appetite. Many pots show men masturbating or being manipulated by women.

Copulation is depicted in a variety of positions: reclining face-to-face, or with the man kneeling, or with both partners seated, or with the man penetrating from behind a kneeling or prone woman. In a surprisingly large number of cases the man's phallus is undeniably in the woman's anus.[275] The puritanical, imperialistic Inca waged bloody, punitive campaigns to wipe out this popular custom prevalent among their subject peoples, for they considered sodomy a sinful waste of sacred semen. Spanish missionaries concurred and described the stubborn persistence of the 'nefarious sin' among the coastal peoples[276] although homosexuality is rarely depicted among Peruvian erotica. As among many devout Catholic peasants today, anal intercourse may have been a means of birth-control.

Bestiality is rarely shown: one pot shows a man copulating with a large mammal, but there is no confirmation of the folkloric tradition that syphilis originated from the coition of Peruvian men with their llamas.[277] Women are portrayed in suggestive postures or in sexual intercourse with cormorants, dogs and a jaguar, the latter suggests mythic rather than mortal perversion.[278]

These pots from the tombs held alcoholic beverages for the comfort of the dead in their after-life. Spanish sources relate that when important men died their favourite women were often interred with them to be their companions in death. The most bizarre erotic subjects on Mochica pots are those which illustrate the sex-after-life of the dead. The erect penis of semi skeletal corpses continues to manifest desire, but the living-dead seem to have enjoyed only a sexual half-life, for although dead men are shown masturbating or being embraced and masturbated by women, they are never shown in copulation.[279] In many cultures confrontation with death and bereavement evokes impassioned erotic reassertions of the life-force.

North America

Maize cultivation spread northward from Mexico, and for many centuries the Hopi tribe and other Pueblo Indians have peacefully farmed in the arid southwestern United States. Their elaborate ritual cycle is largely concerned with bringing rain to make their crops grow. They are assisted by hundreds of *Katchina* spirits, who are impersonated in masked dances.

At ancient, abandoned sites petroglyphs include the totemic image of the ithyphallic 'Hump-backed Flute Player', the Kokopelli insect.[280] He carried seeds and other gifts in his hump and his long proboscis is his flute with which he performs fertility magic. The insect has the reputation of being a copulator who 'just won't quit'. A Hopi story tells that once upon a time there was a vain, beautiful girl who rejected all suitors. Kokopelli is not handsome, but he is ingenious and persistent. He observed that every day after lunch the girl withdrew to a secluded spot to relieve herself. Kokopelli dug a trench from his house to that place and buried in it a long tube. Next noon, as his love object squatted, she felt a strange but pleasant sensation in her genitals. Remaining at home Kokopelli had inserted his extensible phallus through the subterranean tube into her vagina! This mutual pleasure was repeated each day until the girl gave birth to a baby. Eventually the son recognised his sire and they lived happily ever after.[281]

A fragment of an early seventeenth-century mural in the abandoned Hopi pueblo of Awatobi shows a humpback wearing an artificial phallus seizing a naked girl whose thighs are parted for coitus[282] and a similar erotic scene is depicted on a bowl from the ancient site of Sikyatki.[283] Hopi women's religious societies initiate girls into their magic fertility roles. A girl's thighs are painted with vertical stripes at the onset of menstruation. A petroglyph near Old Oribai pueblo shows a maiden '. . . wearing her distinctive headdress and leg markings, legs outspread, her huge vulva exposed ready for copulation and fertilisation'.[284]

Inside a bowl from a priest's grave at Awatobi[285] (see illustration 26) is a unique

26   *Bowl showing Hopi Indian fertility rite,* from Awatobi, North America, *c.* seventeenth century

illustration of an ancient Hopi fertility rite: above a file of dancers with enormous phalluses is a heraldic figure of a maiden, probably the Maize Maid, flanked by a pair of ithyphallic men wringing drops of water from their hair, doubtless 'imitative magic' to make the rain fall.[286] Although they no longer wear the artificial phallus, analogous rain-making ceremonies are still performed. Hopi men's societies dance with their bare bodies painted with abstract phallic symbols, holding ears of maize and vulva images cut from melon rind. Leering, they sing erotic songs and shout obscene insults at women of their 'sister' societies, who, from the rooftops, pour down onto the men dirty water and putrid urine.[287] Fertility is stimulated by the generation of sexual excitement and the poured liquid magically brings rainfall. Such ceremonies also provide a socially integrated outlet for antagonism between the sexes.

Similar rituals are performed at Zuni pueblos, the recipients of the drenching being 'Mudhead' clowns. Clowns provide comic relief between the solemn *Katchina*

[49]

dances, but they are highly sacred and play vital roles in maintaining cosmic fertility. The 'Mudheads' have round heads with bumps containing seeds and are covered with the slimy mud of holy Katchina springs. They often mime copulation, and they possess potent love-magic. But the 'Mudheads' drums also contain a butterfly which causes erotic madness. Products of incest, 'Mudheads' are pre-human and asexual like embryos. They seem to personify the mindless, amoral, prodigal fertility of non-human nature.[288]

Other clowns specialise in gluttony, gobbling quantities of food, including disgusting and 'inedible' matter such as raw offal, wood, bits of blankets, urine, and faeces. The Zuni 'Galaxy' clowns have a curative function but are feared because their excessive 'cures' verge on insanity.[289] In a typical example of Hopi erotic clowning the clowns were drenched with water and sprinkled the spectators with urine, which they also drank exclaiming: 'Good medicine!' Loinclothes were snatched off and clowns were roughly tugged about by their penises and whipped. Grotesque male clowns enacted a parody of a wedding: An 'Old Woman' stripped the ragged mantles from the 'Wedding Guests' exposing their large false penises made from the necks of gourds. She assaulted them, rubbing filth on their genitals and stamping on the 'penis' of one 'Guest', who moaned, wept, and 'died' but was revived by 'Glutton' clowns who pretended to suck his anus. The 'Bride' and 'Groom' simulated copulation beneath an old blanket, which was snatched away to expose the false 'vulva' and 'phallus' of the newlyweds to the ribald cheers of the onlookers. After more copulation the groom rolled over exhausted and the 'Bride' and the 'Female Guests' were carried about kicking their legs about to expose their 'vulvas', which the 'Gluttons' pretended to suck.[290]

The ambiguous distinction between obscenity and holy fertility magic is exemplified in a Hopi Indian's account of playing the role of a sacred clown. He and the other clowns thought up deliberately naughty and shocking sexual 'turns', mindful of past punishments meted out by censorious white government agents. After his erotic clowning the Indian scolded a prurient white spectator: 'Well, whiteman, you want to see what goes on, don't you? You have spoiled our prayers, and it may not rain. You think this business is vulgar, but it means something sacred to us. This old Katchina is impersonating the Maize Maiden; therefore we must have intercourse with her so that our maize will increase and our people will live in plenty. If this were evil we would not be doing it.'[291] The whiteman's persecution has had two results: some sacred phallic rituals, formerly held in public, have literally 'gone underground', to be performed secretly in the subterranean ceremonial *kivas*; simultaneously, the sexual clowning in public has become self-conscious and inhibited, or, in defiant outbursts, clowns go out of their way to shock and embarrass white tourists with aggressive obscenity.[292]

Traditionally these 'transcendental buffoons' stimulated erotic excitement to promote fertility by 'sympathetic magic'. Their grotesque and shocking antics taught morality by 'horrible example'[293] while providing a vicarious safety valve for infantile, asocial, and forbidden 'polymorphous perverse' impulses.

Further north among the Plains Indian tribes the Sun Dance is a central ritual for the creation of life, world renewal, thanksgiving, and communion with the Great Spirit. A tree, ritually killed like an enemy, is set up and from it are hung various symbols, formerly including buffalo-hide silhouettes of a grossly ithyphallic man and a bull bison with a prominent pizzle,[294] representing the life-force of the human and animal prey of warriors and hunters. The lodge surrounding the tree is open to the east so that it is fertilised by the heavenly bodies passing over it. The sponsor of the ceremony is called 'Reproducer' or 'Multiplier'. He and his wife must abstain from sexual activity after he makes his vow until at a dramatic climax of the rites the priest and the sponsor's wife leave the lodge alone and, after offering the woman's body to the gods, they perform the 'Sacred Marriage' coitus to 'grow the earth'.[295]

The Pawnee myth of Creation relates that the warrior Morning Star conquered the female Evening Star and, after knocking out her vaginal teeth, copulated with her to procreate the first woman. In return, the Pawnee customarily sacrificed a captive maiden to the Morning Star. As in the ancient Mexican rite, the victim was tied to a scaffold and, after cosmic rituals, shot full of arrows and her blood soaked into the earth as an offering. The sacrifice was followed by an orgy of special sexual licence to promote fertility.[296]

The bison was the mainstay of Plains Indian life, and the Buffalo Dance linked success in the hunt and animal increase with human sexuality. Women were required to maintain strict sexual discipline, for the buffalo were attracted by virtuous women but repelled by erotic laxity. The Mandan Buffalo Dance culminated with the terrifying apparition of the ithyphallic demon Okihide,[297] a 'Spirit of the Wild' from the plains. His mortal impersonator was masked and painted black, with white astral emblems symbolising his cosmic power.[298] He wore a buffalo tail behind and in front a long black phallus tipped with a bright red glans, made to move by an invisible sinew attached to a wand terminating in a knob symbolising an enemy's head with a scalp attached. The demon dashed wildly among the crowd frightening the women and children. Placated with gifts Okihide signalled the sun to come closer. Further rampaging was halted by the Sacred Pipe and the spirit turned his libidinous attention to the eight Buffalo Dancers with whom he realistically mimed copulation like a rutting bull, to the great delight of the crowd. At last, exhausted, he was surrounded by women who mocked him with a licentious dance of sexual invitation. However, Okihide could no longer rise to the occasion. His wand was broken and he was driven back onto the open plains, where he was assaulted by the women and children, who tore off his great phallus and bore it triumphantly back to the village. Okihide was a complex and ambivalent figure. He was credited with founding the magic 'medicine' ceremonies but was also feared. He seems to have been the embodiment of sexual 'libido', amoral, asocial and dangerous, but vital for fertility. Through ceremonial drama libido was symbolically subdued by society.

When asked by an explorer how he cured the sick, a Brazilian witchdoctor stuck out his tongue and, leering, pointed at his genitals. He drew a circle in the sand and, inside it, a phallus, saying: 'All sorcery comes from hate and rut and with these we cure, too!'[299]

b: The Classical World

During the eighteenth century, interest in the world of Classical Antiquity began to grow rapidly, helped by archaeologists and writers. The ruins of Pompeii and Herculaneum were at last excavated, and engravings of art-objects from these and other sites were widely published. Most important of all, the German art historian Winckelmann wrote learned books on the art of the Classical world.[1] But during this and the following century, many discoveries were kept secret for reasons of decorum,[2] and Winckelmann's description of Classical art as the embodiment of 'a noble simplicity and a calm grandeur', with its implications of frigid perfection and detachment from reality, has only comparatively recently been shown to be far from the whole truth. In fact, the art of the Classical world was a passionate expression of the life of the Classical world, a life in which spiritual and physical needs and pleasures went hand in hand.

In Classical religion and mythology, the love stories of the gods were vitally important, both as powerfully erotic inspiration and as the symbolic representation of fertility in nature. Sex, religion, and magic were closely interwoven; art-objects, from lamps and vases to paintings and sculptures, show explicit sexual activities in a completely open manner, with no intimations of guilt, for the close connection between sex and shame had yet to be invented. Jupiter or Zeus, King of Mount Olympus, whose exploits were later to be the subject of so many erotic works by Renaissance artists (see Chapter 4 a), is the divine hero of many Classical legends, and his amorous conquests are depicted on many Greek vases and Roman lamps and cameos. Especially popular was the story of his love-making, in the form of a swan, with Leda, the wife of King Tyndarus of Sparta. A beautiful marble relief of *Leda and the Swan* in the Museum of Heracleion, dating from the Graeco-Roman period in Crete (see illustration 27), shows the nude figure of Leda helping

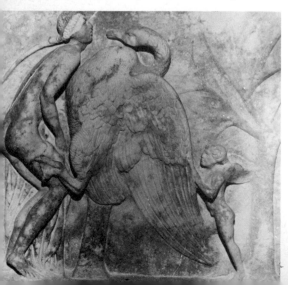

27 *Leda and the Swan*, Græco-Roman marble relief, Crete, *c.* second century A.D.

the swan to penetrate her, encouraged by a naked cupid. The same incident is depicted on another relief in the National Museum of Athens, and the theme was taken up again and again on Roman cameos and in the designs on lamps from Crete, Delos, Herculaneum, Pompeii, and elsewhere.

Jupiter was king of the gods, but from the earliest times, Eros was the most popular deity and was invested with great power. In *Antigone*, Sophocles writes: 'Invincible Eros, you swoop down on our flocks and watch, ever alert, over the fresh faces of our maidens; you float above the waves and across the countryside where the wild beasts lie. Among the gods themselves, and among mortals, no one can escape you. Whoever touches you is at once thrown into delirium.' Eros, as the personification of love, was seen as a fundamental principle of all life, extending his sway over the whole of creation. The *Theogony* of Hesiod states that Eros was born when only Chaos and Earth existed, and the *Danaides* of Æschylus suggests that Eros brought about the union of the Sky and the Earth. Eros fell in love with Psyche, and the two became symbols of the fulfilment of love; as such, they were depicted in many marble groups from the fourth century B.C. onwards, right up to the famous Roman version in the Capitol Museum in Rome. These erotic groups relate to earlier examples which show Demeter, who lay with Iasion in a ploughed field and conceived Pluto, spreader of abundance. Such figurines of embracing couples were used as talismans to ensure a fruitful harvest, and later ones were worn to promote human fertility.

To the Greeks, beauty was of paramount importance, and essential for immortality; ugliness is avoided in their works of art. Eros was often claimed to be the son of Aphrodite, goddess of beauty, and these two figures were personifications of the ideals of male and female beauty in Greek art of the first Classical era. In Hellenistic and Roman art, Eros becomes a chubby infant, but earlier artists show him as a beautiful young man with a slim and perfectly proportioned body. He became both the ideal and the exemplar of athletes, and his altars were set up at the entrances to gymnasiums, where Greek men would go to admire the beauty of nude youths. Thus he became the patron of many of the homosexual unions that flourished in Greece, where such love was considered not only normal but one of the highest forms of affection. This, in turn, was reflected in the way Eros was depicted, as can be seen in the increasingly seductive figures by Praxiteles during the fourth century B.C.

Nude images of Aphrodite were equally popular, and she was usually shown with one hand lowered towards her vulva to emphasise her femininity. The *Aphrodite of Cnidus* by Praxiteles was placed in an open shrine dedicated to the goddess, and became famous for its perfect beauty. It is related that one young man fell in love with it, and made love to it under cover of night. Unfortunately he left visible marks of his passion and was discovered, though not punished. Another work by Praxiteles, the *Aphrodite of Delphi*, had claims to notoriety since the model was Phryne of Thespiae, one of the most beautiful of *hetaerae* or high-class courtesans. Phryne was the star of a famous trial at which she was accused of corrupting the youth of

Athens. Her counsel secured her acquittal by tearing off her robe and revealing the beauty of her naked body to the courtroom. 'Phryne was more beautiful in the unseen parts' comments the gossip-writer Athenaeus who witnessed the scene.[3]

The *hetaerae* were often attached to temples as *hierodoules* or sacred prostitutes in the Hindu sense, and Phryne won her acquittal because her judges considered such beauty in a 'Priestess of Aphrodite' could only be divine. It was considered perfectly acceptable for a temple to provide pilgrims with sexual gratification, for the activity thus became a rite of homage to the deity. The Temple of Aphrodite at Corinth was, according to Strabo, 'so wealthy that it acquired more than a thousand sacred prostitutes, many of whom were offered to the service of the goddess by private individuals, both men and women'.[4] Courtesans and temple prostitutes performed an honourable and indeed important function in Greek life. Demosthenes in his oration *Against Neaera* of 340 B.C. said, 'We keep courtesans as mistresses for pleasure, prostitutes for daily service, and wives for legitimate childbearing and looking after our homes.' Love and its sexual expression were vitally important to the Greeks and did not involve feelings of shame. In Plato's *Symposium*, Socrates is quoted as saying: 'Union between man and woman is a creative act and has something divine about it . . . the object of love is a creative union with beauty on both the spiritual and physical levels.' And this creative union was likely to be most satisfactory with a courtesan, with the result that a whole genre of literature—pornography in its original meaning, 'writings about the life and manners of prostitutes' grew up about this class of woman. Especially famous are the *Letters of Alciphron*, the *Deipnosophists* of Athenaeus, and, above all, the *Dialogues* of Lucian. In the Sixth Dialogue, Crobyla instructs her daughter Corinna on how to make a good living from prostitution so as to be able to provide for her mother in her declining years: 'Well, Corinna, you can see now that it's not such a terrible misfortune as you imagined to lose your virginity and live with a nice young man, whose first payment I shall use to buy you a pretty necklace . . . To earn a lot of money without any trouble, you must not restrict yourself to younger men, but be equally pleasant to all men, especially those who are not so good-looking, not so strong, not so well-built. . . . These are the ones you should sleep with above all, for they pay the best.' Not all courtesans and prostitutes were as outstanding as Phryne, or as Lais of Hyecara, who was discovered and painted by the artist Apelles and who counted among her lovers Demosthenes and Diogenes. But the *hetaerae* inspired many a poet and playwright, and they were usually the models for the sculptors and vase-painters.

Vases, dishes, bowls, and cups were the most common gifts in Greece. They were usually black or red with figures painted on them in red or white. The figures were often painted to order, so that the donor could choose an activity appropriate to the occasion. Since many were gifts to courtesans, explicit scenes of love-making are common on such objects, although museums do not usually exhibit these examples.[5] A cup in the Louvre attributed to Skythes (see illustration 28) shows scenes of a wild orgy with various types of intercourse depicted in vivid detail. Such a cup

28 *Orgy scene*, Attic cup, Greece, attributed to Skythes

would be a welcome gift, and the activities it shows would form the climax to many a religious festival in honour of fertility and sexual pleasure. Often, a vase will show men paying court to *hetaerae* on one side and making love to boys on the other, for as we have seen, homosexuality and pederasty were common in Greece and accepted as normal and indeed desirable, playing an important part in mythology in the loves of Jupiter for Ganymede and Apollo for Hyacinthus. Sophocles and Plato were well known for their predilection for boys, and Herodotus and Xenophon wrote admiringly about pederasty. In *The Birds*, Aristophanes wrote: 'I'd like to know a town where the father of a handsome lad would come up to me and reproach me as follows: "You're a fine one, you meet my son coming out of the gymnasium, all bathed, you don't kiss him, you don't say a word to him, you don't embrace or tickle him, and you call yourself a friend of the family".' And Lucian concludes his *Dialogue of Love* thus: 'The need to perpetuate the human race has driven man to marriage, but pederastic love alone exercises its noble sway over the philosopher's heart.'

For the Greeks, religion justified all varieties of sexual love, and erotic excitement was endowed with a sacred character largely because of its association with the cult of Dionysus. The characteristics of Eros were to a large extent taken over by Dionysus in the later period, and whereas Eros had been the god of love-making,

[55]

29 *Dionysiac ritual*, Attic bowl, Greece

Dionysus was associated with fertility as well as with pleasure and sexual stimulation. There are numerous vases and bowls decorated with erotic scenes of Dionysiac dances and rituals; a bowl in the British Museum (see illustration 29) shows Dionysus holding vine-branches, a symbol of fertility and renewal, flanked on either side by an ithyphallic seilenos, a half-human and half-animal follower of the god, dancing between maenads, the god's priestesses. Seileni and satyrs were known for the lewdness of their behaviour, and representations of their sexual exploits were considered to be magic talismans of a joyful renewal of life. Such scenes were especially popular with Roman artists.

The age-old belief in magic was a powerful force in the worship of Dionysus, and was characterised by the cult of the phallus. Phallic worship had been an important part of many religions for a very long time, and the Greeks probably took it over from the Egyptian phallic deity, Min (see Chapter 2 a). It found expression in the crude figures of Hermes and Priapus—often merely a head surmounting a tall base, from which protruded an erect phallus—which were popular with the common folk as fertility symbols in the fields or as magic talismans to ward off the evil eye in houses or on tombstones. Minor deities were often depicted with enormously exaggerated phalluses, for example *Bes* (Ephesus Museum; see illustration 30). Each Dionysiac temple had its own phallic image, sometimes an image of the god

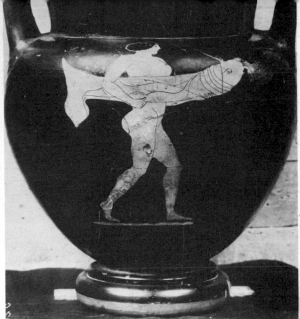

30 *Greek Deity (Bes?),*
     Hellenistic

31 *Naked woman carrying*
     giant phallus, Attic vase,
     Greece, by the Painter
     of Pan

with enlarged phallus, sometimes a bird with a phallic head or a lamp in the form of a phallus. At Delos, the choregic monument erected by Karystios at the beginning of the Hellenistic era contains giant erect phalluses on bases decorated with sacred birds with phallic heads. Characteristic of Dionysiac rites were processions in which giant phalluses made of wood were carried through the streets to the temple. Aristophanes describes such a procession in *The Archanians*, and many vases and plates show such a scene. A black-figure vase in the Museum of Antiquities in Florence depicts a colossal phallus being carried by a group of ithyphallic figures, and such ceremonies are known to have taken place in Athens and Attica. At Delos, the phallus was elaborately carved and painted so as to resemble a monstrous bird. From a description by Athenaeus, we know of a memorable procession that took place at Alexandria in the reign of Ptolemy II Philadelphos which included ten enormous sacred chariots bearing phalluses, one being 'a golden phallus one hundred and twenty cubits long, all covered with engravings and hung with gilded streamers, with a golden star six cubits in circumference at the end'.[6] At such ceremonies, nude women would often straddle the phallus to ensure fertility (and no doubt for more immediate pleasure), and would appear in the procession carrying large phalluses dedicated to the god, as is represented on an Attic vase by the Painter of Pan in the Berlin Museum of Archaeology (see illustration 31).

Greek drama owes its initial inspiration and development to these religious celebrations. Satyrs, seileni, and maenads were shown acting out stories of the gods and singing obscene songs in the early Greek dramas, with actors wearing giant phalluses and their faces smeared with wine-dregs, and this was the popular entertainment of the day. Although Plato disapproved, Sophocles, Euripides, and Aristophanes all incorporated such ribaldry into their plays. A bowl in the British Museum shows

[57]

32 *Scene from the Iris of Archaios*, Attic bowl, Greece

scenes from the *Iris* of Archaios (see illustration 32). Dionysus stands by his altar while his priestess Iris is grabbed by ithyphallic seileni. A vase in the same museum shows revelling seileni, one of whom is balancing on the tip of his penis a wine-jar into which another is pouring wine (see illustration 33). The exploits of the seileni were very popular on the stage and in pottery decoration: a vase in the Berlin Museum of Archaeology shows a seilenos manipulating his enormous erect penis (see illustration 34).

The bawdiness of early Greek drama is reflected in Aristophanes' comedy *Lysistrata* of 411 B.C. The lady of the title leads the women of Athens to seize the state treasury and pledge themselves to abstain from intercourse with their warrior husbands until the war with Sparta is ended: 'Let us wait at home with our faces made up and then advance to greet our husbands with nothing on but our little tunics... Then, when they are panting with desire, if we slip away instead of yielding, they'll soon conclude an armistice, I can tell you ... So no more legs in the air, and no more playing at the lioness on the cheese-grater.' Ample opportunities are thus provided for ribald jokes, such as when Myrrhine tantalises her husband Kinesias: 'Get up.' 'But I am up.' 'So you are!' The jokes involving the erections of the frustrated men, which so fascinated Beardsley many centuries later (see illustration 161), continue to the end, when the Spartan envoys arrive in Athens to discuss peace terms, since their women are playing the same game. The sight of the

[58]

33   *Revelling Seileni*, Attic vase, Greece

obviously sex-starved Spartans on the stage, while the Athenians pretend to believe they are hiding spears under their clothing, must have brought the house down.

The Romans inherited many ideas and customs from the Greeks, but the highly civilised attitude towards sexuality manifested by the Greeks in art and life did not find a parallel in Rome, where a form of lustful brutality tended to become char-

34 *Ithyphallic Seilenos,*
Attic vase, Greece

35 *Fresco,* Tomb of the
Bulls, Tarquinia,
c. 550–20 B.C.

acteristic of sex relations as the years passed. Greek literature had a stronger
influence, and Roman erotic literature tended towards the lighthearted and amusing.
There was no philosophy behind the expressions of eroticism in Roman art to equal
that of Greece (or India), but nevertheless the Romans created their own brand of
mystery and poetry in the realm of erotic art.

The cult of the phallus was an important part of Roman religion, and although
the Greek influence was obviously an important factor, phallus-worship had been
practised centuries earlier by the Etruscans, who placed phallic emblems on tombs
from the pre-Hellenic period onwards. This seems to have been a practice related to the
idea of the phallus as a symbol of life renewed through death via the infinite fertility
of the Earth Mother, for the Etruscans took great pains to decorate the inside of
tombs with brightly-coloured paintings full of life and vitality with no hint of
sadness. Very often, highly suggestive scenes were included, and the Etruscans seem
to have associated death with a renewal of sexual powers. This connection between
eroticism and death is most obvious in the *Tomb of the Bulls* at Tarquinia, dating
from the sixth century B.C.: on the back wall of the first chamber, two scenes of
sexual intercourse are depicted. On the left a nude woman lies on the back of a
crouching nude man with an erection, with her legs over the shoulders of a standing
nude man who is copulating with her. On the right (see illustration 35), a nude
man is having anal intercourse with a nude woman.

The Romans were intensely superstitious, and their cult of the phallus led them
to see it as a powerful talisman against the evil eye. In the ruins of Pompeii were

36 *Roman phallic amulets*, Pompeii, Italy, first century A.D.

37 *Roman phallic charm*, Pompeii, Italy, first century A.D.

found many evidences of such beliefs. On the wall of a baker's shop, a stone carving of an erect penis (now in the Naples Museum) was inscribed with the words: *Hic Habitat Felicitas*, meaning that happiness came from the protection which the emblem afforded, rather than from the pleasure of the sex act. In the Restricted Collection of the British Museum are many amulets and good-luck charms from Pompeii (see illustration 36), some being in the form of phalluses with wings and hind legs, and with bells attached to them.[7] These would have been worn round the neck or hanging from a belt. One unusual charm (see illustration 37) is in the form of a helmeted warrior with bells hanging from either hand and from the end of his enormous, erect penis. In the homes, lamps had phallus-shaped pendants, and tables were supported by carved ithyphallic figures. Mosaic floors often depicted a phallus —an example is at Ostia (see illustration 38), and a very unusual figure in the British

38 *Roman floor mosaic*, Ostia, Italy, *c.* second century A.D.

39 *Roman phallic figure*,
    Pompeii, Italy, first
    century A.D.

40 *Roman phallic figure* (top
    removed), Pompeii,
    Italy, first century A.D.

Museum is a depiction of a man whose top half can be lifted off to reveal a large phallus (see illustrations 39 and 40). In the House of the Vettii at Pompeii is a fresco of a deity weighing his enormous phallus with a pair of scales; no doubt it had the double value of a talisman against evil and an emblem of fertility.

A large number of the objects found at Pompeii are now in the Naples Museum, not all of them being available to the public. Amongst them is a small stone object depicting an erect phallus set in a temple façade (see illustration 41). This is probably a cult object which would perform the function of a private altar, and is evidence of the cult of the phallus so popular in Ancient Greece. The god concerned was, no doubt, Priapus, who was worshipped by the Romans as Mutinus. Temples dedicated to this phallic deity were often decorated with scenes of humans and animals in sexual congress, drawing a parallel between human and animal sexuality. The Greeks often depicted satyrs and seileni taking part in Dionysiac rites, and such scenes were also popular with the Romans. Many sculptures found at Pompeii and Herculaneum showed bestial activities, one of the most famous being *Pan and the Goat* (Naples Museum). The English sculptor Joseph Nollekens was inspired by this marble group to execute a fine terracotta copy while living in Italy in the 1760s, and his hitherto unrecorded version is now in the Restricted Collection of the British Museum (see illustration 42).

The Romans took over the close association of sex and religion from the Greeks, but were also influenced by the Etruscans and the Egyptians. The importance of sexual symbolism in Egypt is seen in the cult of Isis, the goddess of reproduction,

41 *Roman phallic shrine*,
Pompeii, Italy, first
century A.D.

who searched for the torn fragments of the body of her husband and brother, Osiris,
until she discovered his penis which still retained its potency, and built a shrine in
its honour. An alternative legend suggests that the shrine was built because the penis
had been eaten by fish in the River Nile. The temple of Isis in Rome was staffed by

42 Nollekens, *Pan and the Goat*, 1760s, copy of Roman original

male attendants, and women devotees took part in activities which recall the Hindu temple-rites of India. Female deities such as Isis and Cybele were served in a sexual manner by their priests, as Frazer describes in *The Golden Bough*: 'These feminine deities required to receive from their male ministers, who personated the divine lovers, the means of discharging their beneficent functions: they themselves had to be impregnated by the life-giving energy before they could transmit it to the world.'[8] These were the activities that so disturbed the early Christians such as St Augustine, and which also provided inspiration for sculptors, vase-painters, and cameo-designers who paralleled them in their works with scenes of the loves of the gods.

The Romans followed the Greeks in linking sexuality and the cult of fertility gods. Their favourite among these was Liber, patron of growth and of wine, whose festival—the Liberalia—was held on March 17. On this occasion, a chariot carrying a huge phallus would be drawn through the fields and into the town where a matron would crown it with a garland of flowers. Sexual orgies would follow and so fertility for man, beast, and nature would be assured for another year. St Augustine wrote of such occasions: 'Liber's sacrifices were kept with such licence in the highways of Italy, that they adored men's privities in his honour: their beastliness exulting, and scorning any more secrecy.'[9] There are many artistic depictions of such scenes: an engraving after Francesco Salviati in the Restricted Collection of the British Museum shows a sacred phallus being carried towards a representation of a vulva. The most notorious of these festivals was the Bacchanalia held in honour of Bacchus who replaced Dionysus for many Romans. These were opportunities for orgies of incredible debauchery and licentiousness, and were described at length by Livy in his *History of Rome*. Eventually they were stopped by order of the Senate. Another festival was the Lupercalia in honour of Pan, the protector of flocks and shepherds, though the activities were more related to human fertility as they included naked men running around beating women with thongs made from the skin of a newly sacrificed goat. Women so struck were supposedly rendered fertile (*cf.* Shakespeare's *Julius Caesar*), and the festivals usually developed into wild orgies.

The degree of sexual licence displayed at these religious ceremonies was no doubt partly responsible for the extremely repressive attitude of the early Christian Church towards sexuality. But, in fact, many pagan festivals have survived or been incorporated into Christianity in Italy and elsewhere. An interesting account of one instance is given in a letter written by Sir William Hamilton in 1781 when he was British Ambassador at the court of the King of Naples, in which he describes a celebration of the feast of St Cosmo and St Damian in Isernia: 'In the city, and at the fair, votive objects of wax, representing the male parts of generation, of various dimensions, some even of the length of a palm, are publicly offered for sale. The "vows" are chiefly presented by the female sex, and the person who was at this fête in 1780 told me that he heard a woman say, at the time she presented her "vow" in church, "blessed St Cosmo, let it be like this".'[10] Richard Payne Knight, a Fellow of the Royal Society, Member of Parliament, and learned antiquary, published this letter as a preface to his important but unpopular book, *An Account of the Remains of the Worship of Priapus*, which appeared in London in 1786. His contemporaries were not happy to read such remarks as: 'In an age when no prejudices of artificial decency existed, what more just and natural image could they find, by which to express the beneficent power of the great creator, than that organ which endowed them with the power of procreation and made them partakers, not only of the fertility of the Deity, but of his great characteristic attribute, that of multiplying his own image, communicating his blessings, and extending them to generations yet unborn?' One critic described the book as 'one of the most unbecoming and indecent treatises which ever disgraced the pen of a man who would be considered as a scholar and a philosopher'.[11] Knight left his collection of phallic objects to the British Museum, and they have lain hidden in the Restricted Collection ever since (see Appendix II).

One of the most intriguing and little-known aspects of Classical religion is the initiation rite. We know that the Mysteries of Eleusis, held in honour of Demeter and originating in the fourteenth century B.C., included both a purification ceremony and a sacred rite in which the initiate was 'admitted into the inmost recesses of the temple and made acquainted with the first principles of religion, the knowledge of the god of nature'.[12] St Gregory and St Chrysostom suggest that perverted sexual practices took place, but one of the features of the Mysteries was that initiates were forbidden to discuss them on pain of death. One of the greatest finds in the buried ruins of Pompeii came in 1909 when the Villa of Mysteries was uncovered. Around the walls of one room, twenty-nine superbly painted life-size figures are depicted on a rich red background, enacting what are believed to be the secret initiation rites of the cult of Dionysus (see illustration 43). In one scene, the god is shown tenderly caressing Ariadne, but the rest of the frieze depicts anything but tenderness. Seileni and satyrs play musical instruments and drink wine as they watch a lightly clad woman unveil a mysterious basket containing an enormous phallus which has just been anointed with oil. In front of her, a half-nude female with enormous black wings wields a long thin whip with which she is about to lash the naked back of a young girl who is supporting herself on the knees of another girl. Nearby, a nude dancer whirls about, clashing cymbals above her head. The seileni, satyrs, and winged tormentor are the actual figures in the mystery of the god, and the unveiling of the sacred and anointed phallus takes place as the naked maiden is painfully yet excitedly initiated into the secret rites of the cult, rites which will doubtless develop into a frenzy of sexual abandon. All is depicted with magnificent realism and a superb command of figure composition. After nineteen centuries of burial in volcanic lava, the modelling of the naked bodies still elicits a sensuous response. A recent critic has commented: 'Who could fail to be fascinated by the voluptuous bodies of the woman brandishing the whip, the suffering girl, and the dancer, by the proudly out-thrust breasts, the trembling delicate shoulders, and the harmonious movement of the hips—three hallmarks of feminine grace, all magnificently depicted. There is no doubt that the paintings in the Villa of Mysteries occupy a special place in the history of erotic art.'[13]

Another intriguing discovery at Pompeii was the brothel excavated in 1860. Situated at the corner of two streets in Zone VIII, the building had a phallus above the door, and contained a series of small rooms opening onto a vestibule. Here, as in every Roman town, the prostitutes entertained their visitors. Their Greek counterparts were *hetaerae* (literally 'companions') and were often priestesses in a cult of love; very different were these Roman *meretrices* ('sellers') so familiar from the writings of Juvenal and Apuleius. In the *Satyricon*, Petronius describes them as insatiable, vicious and sex-mad; some are especially fond of corrupting children: 'Pannychis is only seven or eight years old? But what does that matter?' 'May Juno strike me dead,' Quartilla says, 'if I can ever remember being a virgin. When I was

43 *Dionysiac celebration*, fresco in Villa of Mysteries, Pompeii, Italy, first century
A.D.

a little girl, I played ducks and drakes with the little boys: as I got bigger, I applied myself to bigger boys, until I reached my present age, whence I think the proverb arose, she'll bear the bull that bore the calf.' She is excited by Giton's youth. 'Tomorrow,' she laughs, 'this will make a fine antipasta for my lechery. But today's entrée stuffed me so full, I couldn't swallow even this little titbit now.' The brothel at Pompeii is decorated with very explicit scenes of love-making (see illustration 44) which a winking guide will take visitors to see for extra payment. This sly and covert attitude which is so typical of our age would have been out of place in first-century Pompeii where love-making was a vital part of life and therefore to be depicted openly and erotically. The frescoes show intercourse of all possible types

[67]

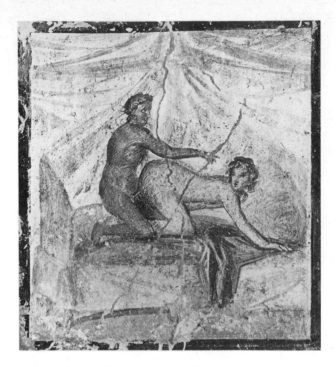

44 *Brothel scene*, Pompeii,
Italy, first century A.D.

and in all possible positions, illustrating the activities provided by the building.[14] Although not in as good condition as the paintings in the Villa of Mysteries, many of these scenes display a real command of form and a poetic sensitivity that relate them to Greek art, and they may well have been executed by artists from Greece.[15] Despite their seeming obscenity, they derive from a great tradition, although the religious interpretation of sexuality has been replaced by a dignified philosophy of human love. A recent commentator[16] has compared these depictions of sexual acts with those found on bronze lamps and ceramics, and has concluded that they all share an inter-related iconography derived from Hellenistic illustrated manuals or treatises on modes of copulation in the manner of the *Kama Sutra*. None of these has survived, but one of the earliest is thought to have been the *Dodekatechon* of Paxamos; section three of Ovid's *Art of Love* includes what appears to be an imitation of such a manual. The paintings are art rather than mere pornography: the degrading antics of the brothel are transmuted into the art of love. To quote Jean Marcadé, they are 'less scandalous and degraded than they might seem . . . their subject is not the sordid intercourse of prostitutes and their clients, but men and women, in the enchantment of their beauty and the instinctive freedom of the senses, mutually sharing the intoxication of the gods'.[17]

These paintings are now unique, but many other such series existed in early times. The walls of the Imperial Banqueting Hall in Nero's Golden Palace were decorated by the finest artists in Rome with scenes of couples making love. The Emperor Tiberius had his palace on Capri hung with erotic pictures, and when offered an explicit scene of *Atlanta and Meleager* by Parrhasius, hung it in his bedroom.[18] We have no idea of the quality of these pictures, but the brothel frescoes from Pompeii are certainly concerned more with love than mere sex, and could almost be illustrations to Ovid's famous volume of poems, *The Art of Love*. These elegant masterpieces comprise a manual of seduction in which the emphasis is laid on psychology: how a man should win a mistress; how he should hold on to her; and how a woman should satisfy the sensual desires of a man. The advice does not relate to money or force, but rather aims to achieve complete possession, the conquest of the soul as well as of the body. With delicacy, elegance, and real aesthetic sense, and no note of coarseness, Ovid presents his philosophy of love as pleasure shared in the intimacy of the bedroom, as is well captured in Dryden's translation:

> *The bashful virgin, though appearing coy,*
> *Detains your hand, and hugs the proffer'd joy.*
> *Then view her eyes with humid lustre bright,*
> *Sparkling with rage, and trembling with delight:*
> *Her kind complaints, her melting accents hear,*
> *The eye she charms, and wounds the list'ning ear.*
> *Desert not then the clasping nymph's embrace,*
> *But with her love maintain an equal pace:*
> *Raise to her heights the transports of your soul,*
> *And fly united to the happy goal.*

But Ovid's advocacy of free, light-hearted love was not welcome in the atmosphere of moral reform that characterised the reign of the Emperor Augustus, and he was exiled (for political reasons as well) in A.D. 8.

Roman love-poetry tends towards this light-hearted vein. Poets show the objects of their love to be wayward, mercenary, tormenting yet delightful creatures, whether it be Catullus writing of Lesbia, Tibullus of Delia, or Propertius of Cynthia. The prime example is Horace, who wrote passionate verses to at least eight different women, usually ending the affair with recrimination or self-pity before starting off on a new amorous adventure. Very different was the love-hate attitude towards women in Martial's *Epigrams*[19] and Juvenal's *Satires*.[20]

The bawdiness of Imperial Rome is best captured in the two classics, *The Golden Ass* by Apuleius and the *Satyricon* of Petronius. *The Golden Ass* is a picaresque narrative about Lucius, who is transformed into an ass and finds himself in various interesting situations, including that of being sexually attacked by a woman. At one point, the narrator describes an evening's entertainment: 'She climbed into bed, flung one leg over me as I lay on my back, and crouching down like a wrestler, assaulted me with rapid plungings of her thighs and passionate wrigglings of her supple hips. My head swam. It was as though the apple-bough of love had bent down over me and I was gorging myself with the fruit until I could gorge no more; and at last with overpowered senses and dripping limbs, Fotis and I fell into a simultaneous clinch, gasping out our lives.' The *Satyricon* is largely a sardonic caricature of a society seeking an escape from boredom in debauchery. In part it is a comic account of the revenge of Priapus on some dissolute homosexuals who have

[69]

stumbled into a secret celebration of his rites. At one point, the narrator is attacked by a high priestess of the temple who inserts a dildo smeared with oil and ground pepper into his rectum and then whips his naked body with stinging nettles. But the incomplete manuscript also includes incidental stories, such as the famous 'Matron of Ephesus', which originated in China, was imported into Greece from Syria, was used a century after Petronius by Apuleius in *The Golden Ass*, was later retold by La Fontaine and then Voltaire (in *Zadig*), and even appeared in a popular book of piety in 1651, Bishop Jeremy Taylor's *Rule and Exercises of Holy Dying*. The story tells of how a beautiful and virtuous widow who insisted on keeping vigil in her husband's tomb was seduced by a young soldier who was guarding the crucified bodies of some criminals nearby. Taking advantage of the situation, relatives of one of the crucified men steal his body for burial, and the soldier, who now faces execution for neglecting his duties, prepares to kill himself. But the virtuous lady prevents him: 'Heaven forbid I should have to look at one and the same time at the corpses of the two men I love; I would rather hang up the dead man than cause the death of the living one.' The soldier then fixes the husband's body to the cross and returns to the tomb for further love-making.

The later years of the Roman Empire were characterised by an increasing debauchery and licentiousness, particularly during the reigns of Tiberius, Caligula, Nero, and Domitian. This is the period criticised in the *Satyricon* of Petronius, the *Epigrams* of Martial and the *Satires* of Juvenal; it is also described in some detail in the *Lives of the Caesars* by Suetonius. From him, we learn about the above-mentioned Emperor Tiberius in his erotically-decorated palace on Capri, where 'he had taught young boys, whom he called little fishes, to play with him and kiss him between the legs when he was swimming; older boys he had taught to suck his penis at the same time'. We learn also about Caligula's sexual relations with his sister and also a famous actor; the visits of Messalina, wife of Claudius, to a brothel disguised as a prostitute; and Nero's abduction of Vestal Virgins, his sexual relations with his mother Agrippina, and his public marriage to a boy. The picture is a lurid one, and is added to by a French author, Hancarville, who published three volumes of stories about the Emperors in the late eighteenth century.[21] These books are now very rare, copies of each being in the British Museum's Restricted Collection, and they are especially notorious because the author reproduced many engravings of highly erotic subjects, which he claimed were from Roman cameos jealously guarded in private collections in Italy. These included mythological scenes and also incidents from the lives of the more degenerate emperors: thus Jupiter raping Ganymede is followed by Tiberius ministered to by three naked prostitutes. The quality of the engravings is not high, and the original cameos were never produced, but from extant cameos, seals and medals (many are in the British Museum Reserved Collection) we know that very explicit scenes of the sexual life of the later Roman period were not uncommon.

The Romans rarely displayed the highly civilised feelings that characterised the Greek view of sexuality. In the later years, debauchery seems to have become wide-

[70]

spread, and this has led moralists to see the eventual break-up of the Empire as being the direct result of the Romans' free attitude towards sexual matters. This view conveniently ignores the fact that such debauchery was merely symptomatic of the political and economic chaos that brought the Roman Empire to an end. The Classical world celebrated the joys of love-making as a vital, guilt-free, and often sacred activity, and to this end they devoted much of their finest literature, painting, sculpture, and decorative art.

Chapter 3

Eroticism in Oriental Art and Religion

a: Introduction

The Orient, in particular India, China and Japan, has produced a great wealth of erotic art, most of which is little known in the West. The civilisations of the East have, without exception, recognised the vital importance of sex in human life; the Hindu, Islamic, and Taoist philosophies all accept basic human sexual relations as natural, admirable and beautiful, and therefore make no provision for the repression of sexual instincts. Since Oriental religions contain no doctrine of original sin, their adherents tend not to suffer from the sexual phobias that beset the Judao-Christian world.

The creation of the world is seen by an important body of Oriental thought as resulting from a process analogous to human sexual activity, with the Deity manifesting the dual role. The original male sexual energy of the Deity is reflected in the female mirror, which is the world. Thus icons of a male and female nature—representations of phalluses and vulvas—are worshipped as embodiments of aspects of the Deity, as in Ancient Greece and Rome, and sexual activities can be considered religious activities. Sexual juices are vital to human well-being, and are themselves proof of the presence of creative divinity in the individual. As such, they may benefit from frequent stimulation. Having sexual relations is therefore a very important activity, and not one to be treated lightly; it is, in fact, an end in itself, not merely the means of procreation. For many sects, it can form part of the way to enlightenment, and in some Hindu and Islamic philosophies, sexuality is seen as intrinsically divine.

Orientals were always far more aware than Europeans of the special joy that can result from prolonged sexual relations; and since such happiness was one of their principal aims in life, sex had to be carefully cultivated. For them, sex was a ritualistic activity which had to be learned, as the numerous sex manuals and illustrations of sexual positions show. But this must not be confused with pleasure for pleasure's sake, as in enlightened Western thinking; to the Orientals, the physical and the metaphysical were inseparable. As Philip Rawson writes in *The Erotic Art of the East*, 'To every Oriental mind, mere orgasm is never the goal of love.'[1]

The original function of both art and religion was to express man's spiritual needs: self-management, self-reconciliation, self-understanding. But Western religion has tried desperately to compete with the new god of science, and in the process has alienated many of its potential adherents, through its concern with material historicism. Oriental philosophies, of which Hinduism is the prime example, have continued to concentrate on concepts which relate the ego to a living world. Hinduism has been described by the medical authority Dr Alex Comfort as 'a comprehensive shorthand for almost all that we now know discursively about the unconscious mind', and he adds, 'its versatility as an emotional tool-kit is staggering'.[2] It is therefore easy to understand why so many Westerners have in recent years turned to the East for religious fulfilment, finding a philosophy of life based on the needs and instincts of the individual preferable to one centred around worship of a paternal and largely prohibitive God, in which sexual instincts have to be repressed. Seen in this light, Oriental erotic art acquires a relevance and an importance that may not be immediately appreciable.

In India, temple-paintings and sculptures, like sex-instruction pictures and illustrations to novels and poetry, sometimes show extremely explicit sexual activities. The drama and excitement of sexual energy is consecrated in these images, which can be tender and sensuous and often extremely beautiful. They have been criticised as being pornographic (and therefore not worthy of attention) or over-emotional (*i.e.* the feeling predominates over strictly artistic qualities, so that the result is not art at all). Both criticisms are sadly typical of an uninformed Western attitude to depictions of sexuality, and neither would be even remotely comprehensible to an Oriental.

---

b: India

Edited by Peter Webb from a lecture given by

PHILIP RAWSON[1]

That sexual force, or libido, is the basic driving energy of mankind, is a belief which lies behind practically all the imagery we find in Indian art. The Hindu religion makes it clear that the sexual act is a sanctified act, and its adherents consider that religion should be pleasurable. In this way, Indians bear witness to the cultural heritage they share with Greece. Like the Greeks, the Indians see the creation of the world in terms of human procreation. This is represented in metaphorical terms as the 'lingam in the womb-house', the designation for the phallic emblems set up in the inner cells of Indian temples. And it explains the traditional manner of depicting the deity as a male with a female sitting on his lap, he with an erection showing that he is inflated with sexual energy and desire, and she holding a mirror. A good example is *Shiva and the Goddess as Prakasha and Vimarsha*, a stone sculpture dating from the twelfth century at Kiching near Orissa.[2] The significance of the mirror relates to the belief that the creation of the world is a reflection of the god's own sexual energy back to himself, so that he experiences his own sexual urge as bliss. This recalls St Bonaventure, the thirteenth-century Italian Franciscan writer, who saw the glory of God as reflected back upon his central being from the created world.

The Indians took their conviction that sexuality is divine, and that creation was a sexual process, from the most sacred literature of Hinduism, the *Upanishads*. The earliest of these, the *Brihadaranyaka Upanishad*, dating from the early first millennium B.C., says: 'In the beginning this world was the Self alone in the form of a Person. Looking around he saw nothing else than himself . . . Verily he had no delight. He desired for a second. He was indeed as large as a man and a woman closely embraced. He caused that self to fall into two pieces. Therefrom arose husband and wife . . . He copulated with her. Therefrom human beings were produced.'[3]

This quotation from the *Upanishads* makes clear that there is no concept of original sin in Hinduism and no equation of sex with guilt, unlike Christianity. In India, the human being became the expression of artists' vision of the life force, and so Mithuna, or loving couples, abound in Indian art, especially on temple walls, as consecrations of the drama of sexual energy (see illustration 45). Most Indian temples contain as

45 *Temple sculpture depicting Mithuna couple*, Candulla, India, late-tenth century A.D.

46 *Lingam figure*, Kashmir, India, seventh to eighth century A.D.

their centre of worship a phallic icon enclosed in a shrine (see illustration 46). These are sacred manifestations of the seminal energy which flows throughout the world, and all these *lingams* are like crocuses poking up through the ground in spring, concrete evidence of hidden sacred energy.

The *lingams* are, therefore, metaphors for the root of the world, and perfect objects for worship. Since creation involves a female aspect as well as a male aspect, one can revere the female emblem as well as the male. There are many icons representing the vulva (called *yoni*), but the most common of such images is the combined form of *lingam* and *yoni*, as a round-topped cylinder standing in a shallow circular basin with a spout to one side. It is the custom to pour on to the *lingam* an offering of melted butter or coconut oil, which then gathers in the basin. In this way, the worshipper empathises with the sexual emblem, thus identifying his own sexual energy with the energy of the world. For the Hindu, worship of the source of creation is a sure way to enlightenment.

The *yoni* is also important on sculptured figures once found near the entrances to Indian temples. Visitors habitually lick a finger and touch the genitals for luck, and over the centuries this has caused deep holes to develop. A good example is at Aurangabad, Deccan, dating from the eighth century, and another example is in the Victoria and Albert Museum in London. This symbolic act of intercourse with a female divinity recalls the horseshoe luck-symbol, which is derived from Celtic *Shelah-na-Gig* figures (see Chapter 4). Like the horseshoe, the touching of the *yoni* is thought to bring luck.

The belief that sexual energy is the driving force in the world has led members of a strict Brahmin sect to see the need to conserve this energy in themselves. This has become a cult of sexual miserliness which demands that sexual juices be bottled up inside and not on any account be lost in orgasms or wet dreams. In this way, sexual juices can be agitated, shaken up like a bottle of soda, so developing in the individual an enormous inner head of steam, a divine afflatus, which is a sacred possession and makes one radiant with a kind of *tejas* or sacred power. This belief that a person can only be a true servant of the divine if he conserves his juices, lies behind the Western idea of priestly celibacy. It also finds echoes in Chinese Taoist philosophy.

Indian temples usually contain sculptures depicting beautiful women in a variety of sexual postures. These represent the promise of heaven, and the promise was meant quite literally for those who died gloriously, as, for example, soldiers in battle. Occasional frescoes survive, such as those at Sihagiri, a six-hundred-foot-high rock in Ceylon. The pictures date from *c.* A.D. 489 and represent *apsarases*, the girls who populate heaven, bringing offerings to the king, whose palace was built on the top of the rock. Visitors have been well aware that these were the inhabitants of heaven, as the graffiti that one sees there today show: 'Now that I have seen you, death has no fears for me' and 'Hurry on death, I long for your embraces'. The style of these frescoes is very close to the contemporary Buddhist wall-paintings in the Ajanta caves, with their depictions of beautiful girls and lovers in pavilions. Erotic wall-paintings were very common in Indian houses many years ago, but the severe climate has since destroyed nearly all of them.

The Heavenly girls in Indian temples perform the same function as pin-ups, though of a very serious kind. They were meant to excite the appetites of pilgrims. These *apsarases* have their earthly counterparts in the *devadases*, temple women whose job was to entertain the visitors. These slaves of the god represent a parallel in this world for what lies in the next, and their official function was to dance in front of the sacred *lingam* three times a day. Their other duties involved sexual activities: they were literally married to the god, and so intercourse with them assimilated the pilgrim and the god. Thus they were sacred prostitutes, as honourably considered as their counterparts in Ancient Greece, and their children were dedicated to temple service. They were renowned for their gymnastic ability, and would often entertain two men at once. Tavernier, an early French traveller in India, reported seeing a temple girl pick up a coin from the ground in her lips while bending over backwards. It is not surprising therefore that the temple sculptures show a great variety of sexual combinations. The girls depicted are both *apsarases* and *devadases*, metaphysical and physical at once, for the Indians do not recognise a dividing line between the two.

Two of the most famous of all Indian temples are at Khajuraho: the tenth-century Lakshmana Temple and the Vishvanatha Temple from the eleventh century.[4] The temples are conceived as symbols of the cosmic mountain, Mount Meru, which lies

47 *Ritual orgy of a Kaula sect*, Lakshmana Temple, Khajuraho, India, late-tenth century A.D.

48 *Ritual orgy of a Kaula sect*, Lakshmana Temple, Khajuraho, India, late-tenth
century A.D.

at the centre of the world, and the sculptures are in bands which are draped around
it, standing for the whole cosmos garlanding the world's central column (see
illustrations 47 and 48). Each temple's base rests upon earth, the goddess Prithivi,
the eternal mother of all. By climbing the steps up to the portico one literally enters
heaven, walking past the sculptured *apsarases* until one reaches the *lingam* in the
womb-house, the male principle penetrating into the realm of physical reality. The
whole temple is conceived as an enormous outward-facing sculpture: it effloresces
outwards as a symbol of the entire creation. The sculptured figures are carved with
great sensitivity and are totally convincing in spite of the fact that they follow not a
Western, but an Indian, canon of proportion. They are treated as a series of convex
forms, with hardly any concavities at all, as is fitting for beings who are full of the
divine afflatus or sexual energy (see illustration 3). And they form a marvellous
rhythm in their multiplicity of sexual congresses, a divine rhythm which is echoed
in the architecture and in the music that would be played in the temple. As well as
figures, one often finds sculptured vegetation and foliage in such temples, and this
too is full of the sap, the heavenly juices that flow throughout the building and, by
analogy, throughout the world. The Sanskrit word for juice is *rasa*, which also means
erotic feeling, and so human beings and plants are intertwined and sexual energy
flows through everything in a musical rhythm. The temple was often the scene for

[77]

music and dancing, activities which, for the Hindus, were all deeply interwoven with art and sex; the energies aroused by sexual activities were the same as those aroused by any aesthetic response.

There are other temples that bear witness to the high peak of artistic ability that one finds at Khajuraho. One is the Raja Rani Temple at Bhubaneswar near Orissa, of about A.D. 1000. Perhaps the greatest of all is the partly ruined Temple of Love or Black Pagoda at Konarak, dating from the thirteenth century. The whole of this fantastic building is covered with erotic sculptures depicting soldiers with lion head-dresses and Brahmins with turbans engaged in an endless variety of sexual activities with the heavenly *apsarases*. These women are also shown coupled with animals, a perfectly acceptable idea since the Hindu belief was that the goddess had to be fertilised by all the beasts in order to produce the various species of the animal kingdom. A famous album miniature of about 1780 from Rajasthan, *The Nayika as the embodiment of the love of all creatures*,[5] shows the goddess coupled with a bird, an elephant, a bear, a goat, a monkey, a stallion, and so on, and then shows each species mating with itself. On land-boundary stones the goddess is shown with a male elephant: a symbol in Indian poetry and art for monsoon clouds (represented by the elephant) fertilising the earth (represented by the lady). The idea of the goddess of love coupling with animals to create the species is a very old one, shared by the Greeks, which dates from the Paleolithic age.

The beautiful *apsarases* in the temple sculptures perform fantastic sexual feats with the lucky men who have reached heaven, and it is important to bear in mind that sex is a ritualistic and immensely serious activity in India, a true art that has to be perfected through practice. No Indian temple sculptures can be understood without a knowledge of the *Kama Sutra* of Vatsyayana, the classic text on proper behaviour in all areas of life, especially as regards sex, which Sir Richard Burton translated in the nineteenth century. The *Kama Sutra* treats sex as a vitally important activity which must be performed according to certain definite rules and rituals. Its chapter headings show the detailed instruction offered: 'On Kissing; On Pressing or Marking with the Nail; On Biting; On the various ways of Striking, and the sounds appropriate to them.' This latter chapter suggests the use of: 'words such as "mother" and "father"; sounds like those of the dove, the cuckoo, the green pigeon, the parrot, the bee, the sparrow, the flamingo, the duck and the quail; also sighing, weeping, and thundering sounds. Blows with the fist should be given on the back of the woman, while she should give blows in return, abusing the man as if she were angry, and making the cooing and the weeping sounds.'[6] The book describes sixty-four ways of making love; some of the suggestions are certainly exotic and quite unbelievable to a Westerner, although from Tavernier's accounts, it would seem that Indian *devadases* could perform amazingly athletic feats. One method of sexual intercourse described in the *Kama Sutra* is this: 'When a man supports himself against a wall, and the woman, sitting on his hands joined together and held underneath her, throws her arms around his neck and putting her thighs alongside his waist, moves herself by her feet, which are touching the wall against which the man is leaning, it is called "the suspended congress".[7] The author adds thoughtfully: 'This is learnt by practice only.' The *devadases* clearly had plenty of practice, and the temple sculptures at Khajuraho and Konarak show the degree of perfection they achieved.

This ritualistic and sacred nature of sexual intercourse is also manifest in the album miniatures that reached such a height of artistic ability in the courts of India, often showing Princes and their ladies in acrobatic varieties of intercourse (see illustrations 49 and 50). Many show the god Krishna, a very important deity, whose cult is based entirely on love. Krishna devotees abandon the world and devote themselves to an intense feeling of love for Krishna. The deity is always shown in human terms as a blue male (Krishna means 'the Dark One') making love to Radha, a girl who represents us and the whole world. All souls are considered feminine (as in Christianity) and all give themselves to the god in sexual intercourse. So Krishna and his beloved provide the pattern for human couples in works such as *Krishna and Radha dancing in an embrace*, a thirteenth-century bronze from East India, and *Krishna and Radha make love in the flowering forest*, an album miniature in the Kangra style from about 1780.[8]

The aspect of Indian religion that has attracted most interest in the West is Tantricism, which holds that sexual activities constitute a way of inflating one's inner sexual energy which can then be used for religious purposes. Tantra is a cult of ecstasy, focused on a vision of cosmic sexuality, sex as philosophy and philosophy as sex. It is a special yoga, and requires careful preparation through yantras, rituals, mantras, and meditation. It is concerned with the ritualistic excitation through sexual intercourse of the afflatus, which is then turned back inward into the roots of the

49 *Lovers*, Ganges Valley, India, mid-nineteenth century

50 *Lovers*, Jaipur, India, late Bundi-Kotah style, mid-nineteenth century

organism and transmitted through the central nervous system into the brain. This produces an all-pervading sensation of heavenly bliss, which is the goal of all followers of Tantricism. But it would be quite wrong to suppose that the purpose of Tantrik ritual is carnal indulgence. Millions of people seek pleasure and ecstasy and make nothing of them, leaving them lying as dead and sterile experiences in their past, but Tantrikas treat their senses and emotions as assets to be turned to a special kind of account, in order to propel the consciousness towards blissful enlightenment. Many paintings, sculptures, and temple ornaments relate to the Tantrik cult of ecstasy,[9] and some of the most exciting of such images are to be found in the brightly coloured wooden carvings and wall-paintings in the temples of Tibet and Nepal, where Tantra has flourished from early times.[10] These depict a wide variety of sexual couplings and also the strange many-armed Tantrik divinities such as Durgu and Samvara in ritualistic sexual congresses.

The many erotic album paintings of India and Nepal often refer to Tantrik practices in their depictions of the act of intercourse, treated as it is with ritualistic precision as both sex-instruction manual and paradigm for the divine sex act or symbol of divine bliss. Famous examples include *Lovers on a Terrace*, Nepal, from the late eighteenth century and under Pahari influence, and *Prince and Lady prolonging intercourse with a cup of tea* of about the same date in the Kangra Style, from India (see illustrations 51 and 52; both are in the Victoria and Albert Museum, London). These are earthly manifestations of heavenly activities, depicted in a beautifully poetic manner evidencing a highly developed sense of design. They are like images in a torch beam. In following the beam back to its source, one reaches the primal sex act of creation. Sex was a serious and carefully prepared activity, and one that brooked no interference. A famous album miniature of the eighteenth century is entitled *Man shooting tiger in the forest without interrupting his intercourse.*

51 *Lovers on a Terrace*, Nepal, eighteenth century

52 *Prince and Lady prolonging intercourse with a cup of tea*, India, eighteenth century

By the end of the eighteenth century, the strictly puritan Brahmin sect was becoming very strong, and when the Empire-builders from Great Britain arrived in the nineteenth century, they gave strong encouragement to this sect while persecuting other Hindus and closing the erotic temples. Their imposition of Victorian moral standards had a disastrous effect on Indians. Modern Brahmin apologists have gone so far as to declare that there is no reference to the penis involved in the *lingam*, and many temple-maiden sculptures have had their *yoni*-holes cemented over (*cf.* the Kailashanatha temple at Ellora). India is today still experiencing the effects of the wave of puritanism that swept over the country during the nineteenth century.

c: Islam

Although Islam is a religion with strict moral codes of behaviour, the Arab world has produced an enormous amount of erotic poetry and also, as far as we can tell from the few surviving examples, a great deal of erotic art of a high standard. Much has been destroyed by waves of puritanism, and the inherent dislike of many Moslems for representational art has told against sexually explicit pictures. But, to quote a leading authority on the subject, 'were examples more readily accessible, we should probably find that erotic work formed a major part of medieval Arab and Persian painting, just as it did of poetry.'[1]

The Islamic religion decreed severe punishment for adultery, in keeping with the teachings of Mohammed, but it is important to keep in mind the very low position that women held in Moslem society. An Arab medical book of the medieval period declares: 'Breaking a maiden's seal is one of the best antidotes for one's ills; cudgelling her unceasingly, until she swoons away, is a mighty remedy for man's depression. It cures all impotence.'[2] Orthodox morality was often circumvented, and punishments for sexual misdemeanours were in practice not usually severe. In any case, each qualified male could have four wives, and his slaves were also available to him. Islamic society accepted sex as a natural and necessary part of human activity, and had none of the medieval Christian belief in the evil in man's nature. Illicit extra-marital intercourse was condemned because it could lead to the disruption of the Islamic community, not because it was sinful. Sex manuals were welcome and popular because they brought about harmony and satisfaction in marriage, ensuring the stability of the home. Arab art and literature reflected this unrepressive attitude, an attitude summed up, on a less elevated level, in an Arab saying: 'Naked about the genitals, and perfume well applied beneath them: thus

53 *Lesbian scene*, from
Islamic treatise on
physical love, translat[ion]
of Indian Koka Shast[ra]
Mogul period,
seventeenth century

eat, drink and copulate and let the world go to ruin.'[3]

The earliest examples of Islamic erotic art seem to have been wall-decorations, painted or in ceramic tiles, in the widespread bath houses. Early examples are known only from descriptions: Mahmad of Ghazna's son had a pavilion whose walls were covered with erotic paintings from a sex manual in the eleventh century, and in the thirteenth century, Sharaf Ad-din Harum of Baghdad had a bathroom decorated with scenes of sexual intercourse. No doubt this custom was borrowed from the Greeks.

Islamic manuscripts are the main sources of erotic art; whether they were poems and romances or manuals of sexual positions, they were often enlivened with erotic miniatures (see illustration 53). Sex manuals were very popular right up until the nineteenth century, of which *The Perfumed Garden* by Sheikh Nefzawi, translated by Sir Richard Burton, is the best known example.[4] The book lists all the most satisfactory methods of making love, and sets the art of love in its socio- logical and ritual context; it is thus the Islamic counterpart of the *Kama Sutra*, and brought as much righteous indignation down on Burton's head as had his earlier, more famous translation of the Hindu classic.[5] A recent commentator has written: 'The erotic atmosphere of the *Perfumed Garden* is . . . that of *The Song of Solomon*—or even that of "The Ecstasy" of Donne. It is the pure, free, non- obsessional, non-guilt-laden eroticism of the Greeks or the Elizabethans.'[6] The book discusses human sexual activity in a poetic and colourful manner, presenting it as a natural and necessary part of the whole life. Chapters have such titles as: 'Concerning the causes of enjoyment in the act of generation' and 'Prescriptions for increasing the dimensions of small members, and for making them splendid'. Chapter 6, 'Concerning everything that is favourable to the act of coition', begins: 'Know O Vizir (God be good to you!), if you would have pleasant coition, which ought to give an equal share of happiness to the two combatants and be satisfactory to both, you must first of all toy with the woman, excite her with kisses, by nibbling and sucking her lips, by caressing her neck and cheeks . . . when you observe the lips of the woman to tremble and get red, and her eyes to become languishing, and her sighs to become quicker, know that she is hot for coition; then get between her thighs, so that your member can enter into her vagina. If you follow my advice, you will enjoy a pleasant embrace, which will give you great satisfaction, and leave with you a delicious remembrance.'[7] As in the *Kama Sutra*, positions of intercourse are given descriptive names, such as 'the screw of Archimedes', 'the tail of the ostrich', 'driving the peg home', 'the reciprocal sight of the posteriors'. The second manner listed is called 'El modefeda' (or frog-fashion): 'Place the woman on her back and arrange her thighs so that they touch the heels, which latter are thus coming close to the buttocks; then down you sit in this kind of merry thought, facing the vulva, in which you insert your member; you then place her knees under your arm-pits; and taking firm hold of the upper part of her arms, you draw her towards you at the crisis.' There were many of these sex manuals and very often they were Islamic interpretations of the *Kama Sutra* or the *Anangaranga*. Few of the illustrated ones have survived, although we know that Turkey in particular produced many examples.

One of the chapters of *The Perfumed Garden* discusses homosexuality, which, as Herodotus said, was a common activity in the Arab world and in no way despised. In the famous *Book of Counsel* by the Emir Kai-Ka'us ibn Iskander of the mid-eleventh century, Chapter 15, 'Of the Pleasures of Love', ends: 'In summer devote thyself to boys, and in winter to women.' Numerous miniatures from the sixteenth century onwards glorify homosexual relations (see illustration 54), as do poems by

54 *Homosexual scene*, from the Khamsa (five poems) of Ata'î, Turkey, nineteenth century

most of the finest poets, and there are many references to such activities in the *Arabian Nights*. In a society where the sexes were strictly segregated, where adultery was so strongly condemned, and where women were considered low and unclean, it was natural for homosexuality to flourish.

One of the finest, and most often illustrated, of the Arab story-books is *The Book of One Thousand Nights and a Night* or the *Arabian Nights*, first translated by Sir Richard Burton in the 1880s. This is a real treasure-house of Islamic manners and behaviour, showing clearly how the Arabs treated sex as a natural part of the full life: 'In the *Arabian Nights*, sex is very much on the surface, not submerged as in many contemporary Western medieval works, and is treated as a natural part of human behaviour, neither ignored nor appearing as a disproportionate obsession with the writers of the *Nights*.'[8] The language of the book is a sort of exquisite and exotic poetry, which Sir Richard Burton's translation manages to capture: 'She hath breasts like two globes of ivory, like golden pomegranates, beautifully upright, arched and rounded, firm as stone to the touch, with nipples erect and outward jutting. She hath thighs like unto pillars of alabaster, and between them, there vaunts a secret place, a sachet of musk, that swells, that throbs, that is moist and avid.'[9]

At the same time, certain of the Arabian legends express a concept of romantic idealism, a love of two people for each other in God. This love was usually un-requited or unfulfilled, as in the story of Majnun and Leila, Islamic counterparts to our Tristram and Iseult. Majnun loved Leila but was unable to have any contact with her as she belonged to an enemy tribe. He therefore went mad and wandered into the desert, singing to the animals. In many of the Arabian and Persian poems with a strong erotic flavour, the central theme is love transcending the pleasures of the flesh and becoming a means of philosophical perception and mystical fulfil-ment. Thus the act of love is endowed with a metaphysical significance. For the followers of the teachings of Zoroaster, sexual intercourse, if performed with due holiness, made its own contribution to the equilibrium of the world. The Sufi sect of religious mystics often used love poems to generate the state of ecstasy necessary for their sought-after union with the Deity. Love was seen by them as the means of elevating the human soul by sublimating fleshly desire to a desire for this mystical union:

> *When I contemplate thy cheek,*
> *Formed in the image of the moon,*
> *O my love,*
> *It is in truth the effect of divine grace*
> *That I am contemplating.*[10]

One of the most famous expressions of such religious passion is the long *Divan* by the thirteenth-century poet, Jalal al-Din Rumi, the founder of the order of Whirling Dervishes:

The soul that has not experienced true love,
T'were better never born. Its existence is but shame
Be drunk with love, for love is all.
Outside the pleasures of love there is no way to God.[11]

Probably the best known of such poems in the West is the *Rubaiyat* of Omar Khayyam, the twelfth-century Persian poet, which was translated by Edward Fitzgerald in 1859. This poem is characterised by its philosophic questioning of the purpose of life and its resignation to the inevitable passing of all the joys and happiness resulting from love:

The Moving Finger writes, and having writ,
Moves on: nor all thy Piety nor Wit
Shall lure it back to cancel half a Line,
Nor all thy tears wash out a word of it.[12]

The Indian concern with erotic imagery was an important stimulus to the Moslems, and Islamic erotic illustrations owe a great deal to India in their flattening of perspective, elimination of shadows, and concern with overall design. The restraints imposed by Islam discouraged the study of human anatomy, and nudity is very rare in the illustrations under consideration. Sex manuals were often enhanced with explicit depictions of the activities described, but the finest examples of Islamic erotic pictures are to be found illustrating poetry (see illustration 55). These brightly coloured miniatures reflect the abundant use of erotic metaphors in the text. In the poems, the cypress is the tree of life, the sacred tree of Zoroaster, and in its erect

55 *Khusrau and Shîrîn's Wedding Night,*
from the Khamsa (five poems) of
Nîzamî, Islamic, Safavid period,
early-sixteenth century

position it has clear sexual implications. Similarly, ruby lips represent the joy of intoxication, and the pearls of the teeth are 'the inviolate object which is to be pierced, and, more fundamentally, the primal pearl, which, in the most venerable theogonies of the East, burst open to give birth to the world'.[13] Thus we find in the erotic illustrations the inclusion of symbolic plants, animals, and objects, which at first sight seem to be entirely free from sexual associations. The early-seventeenth-century miniatures which illustrate the *Khamsa* (or Five Poems) of the Persian poet Nizami[14] include scenes of intercourse in luxuriant gardens where trees seem to embrace each other and all the plants are in full bloom, signs that sex and fertility are both natural parts of the divine order of the universe. Numerous manuscript pages in the style of the Persian master Riza 'Abbasi dating from the sixteenth and seventeenth centuries[15] show couples in intercourse with little more depicted than a flagon of wine and a dish of fruit. Wine stood for the Dionysiac energy expended in sexual intercourse and fruit was a poetic symbol of pleasure. Neither were the extremely obvious phallic-shaped wine-flagons coincidental.

Amongst the finest examples of Persian erotic art are the illuminated pages of the love poems of Sa 'adi. This famous thirteenth-century poet has been quoted above, and he wrote poems in the vein of the romantic ideal of love, as well as others that breathe a passionate sexuality. In a volume of these latter poems dating from the seventeenth century,[16] the beautiful calligraphy of the text is incorporated in the design of the page which includes brightly coloured scenes of amorous couples. Very often, other people are shown watching the love-makers, an indication that there was nothing about the sex act that had to be hidden. One of the finest examples of such a page is made to look like the cross-section of a palace, with figures in various rooms and on a balcony, household utensils, phallic wine-flagons, decorative tiles, and the calligraphy, all contributing to the beautiful design of the page. Erotic art of this variety is, however, a thing of the past, for the modern Islamic world has adopted many Western habits and taboos.

d: China

The Chinese have always regarded sex as constituting a perfectly normal, and essential, part of life. Chinese religion does not see flesh and spirit as irreconcilable opposites, in the manner of Christianity, and the Chinese are suspicious of celibacy since it denies the vital importance of sex. For the Chinese, sex is integrated into religion, and eroticism in Chinese art is often religiously inspired.

Since the second century B.C. the official religion of China has been Confucianism, but most Chinese have in fact been disciples of Taoism. Confucius was a deeply religious man with puritanical leanings, and the religion bearing his name was really a common-sense method of ordering the individual's private life in relation to his duties to the state, so as to provide a discipline for a vast country. Confucius never said that sex was wrong, and certainly would never have wanted to associate it with feelings of guilt. He strongly disapproved of chastity and taught that a man was bound by honour to visit each of his concubines once every five days until he was seventy, as explained in *Li Chi*, the text of the rituals of Confucianism. But he disapproved of frivolity, whether in sexual relations or in erotic pictures, and under this influence China has experienced successive waves of censorship.

The Chinese have produced two different types of sexually-inspired art. For the uneducated, there were pictures of sexual positions which made no pretence at aesthetic merit, and also illustrations to erotic novels, such as *Chin P'ing Mei* (*Metal Vase Plum Blossom*), which showed little of the imaginative power of Indian or Japanese erotic art. Under the influence of Confucianism, this variety was often censored, and we know of practically none at all from periods previous to the Ming dynasty of the sixteenth century. More important is the erotic art aimed at the educated classes. This was allusive, philosophical, to a large extent religiously inspired, and of a much more subtle variety. The main influence behind such art was the Taoist philosophy.

Taoism lies behind the Chinese concern with sexuality, and it is summed up in the saying: 'i yin i yang she wei tao' ('a period of yin, a period of yang, such is the Tao, or order of the world'). The *yin* and the *yang* are the female and male elements in life that lie at the root of all being. The coming together of the *yin* and the *yang* in sexual intercourse provides contact with the cosmic force of the Tao. For the Chinese, a correlation exists between the organs. This is the basis of the fundamental text of Chinese religion, the *I Ching* or *Book of Changes*, which dates from about the twelfth century B.C. and was known and revered by Confucius. This contains sixty-four hexagrams made up of *yin* and *yang* symbols illustrating essays on moral themes. The hexagrams represent the operations of the natural world, and are followed by philosophical divinations which refer to the harmonious interaction of the natural and spiritual worlds. All changes in any sphere are interpreted as combinations of the two forces, *yin* and *yang*, the *yin* being dark, weak, and feminine, and the *yang* being bright, vigorous, and masculine. The message of *I Ching* is summed up in the saying: 'Sexual union of man and woman gives life to all things.'[1]

The ancient Taoist books on love-making are only known by their texts now, for their illustrations have all been destroyed. They give careful details of how to achieve maximum pleasure in postures with names such as 'the fluttering of butterflies', 'the union of kingfishers', 'the galloping charger', 'wailing monkey embracing a tree', and 'cat and mouse in the same hole'. But the philosophical meaning of the act is always stressed. 'Man is the most sublime of all creatures born of Heaven. Of all that appertains to man, nothing can be compared with sexual union; reflecting the harmony of Heaven and Earth, it regularises the *yin* and governs the *yang*. Those

[87]

who understand its true meaning can nourish their being and prolong their life; those who do not will do themselves harm and shorten their days.'[2]

The reference to prolonging life is important, for the Chinese worshipped long life and immortality. The patron of longevity is Shou Lou, and he is usually shown in sculptured images as a very old man with a dragon staff (*yang* symbol) in one hand and a peach (*yin* symbol) in the other.[3] Shou Lou has a grossly enlarged skull which is full of *yin* and *yang*, and that is how he has achieved immortality. The Taoist doctrine was that a man needed to collect a lot of *yin* and to conserve his own *yang*. *Yin* was obtained in sexual intercourse from the orgasm of the woman, but the man endeavoured to avoid reaching orgasm so as not to lose any precious *yang*. The stimulation of sexual intercourse could cause the man's *yang* to travel up his spinal column to his head, together with the woman's captured *yin*, and deep meditation after intercourse would assure that this would happen. The more *yin* and *yang* a man could store in his head, the nearer he would be to immortality (the Yellow Emperor is said to have become immortal as a result of having intercourse with twelve hundred women). This is the theme of many of the ancient books of love-making: 'the art of sexual relationships with women consists in remaining master of oneself so as to avoid ejaculation, in order that the sperm may rise to the brain and strengthen it. Those who are able to perform the sexual act many times a day without emission of sperm will cure their maladies and live to a great age.'[4]

The allusive symbolism that makes images of Shou Lou into examples of erotic art is such as would probably be missed by people unfamiliar with Chinese religious philosophy. *Yin* and *yang* symbols abound, and the dragon is probably the most important. He is usually shown as violent and horned in his male manifestation (*yang*), and in this form appears on the robes of emperors and their families and ministers of state. He is also found on imperial porcelain and even turns up as decoration on belt buckles. The celestial dragon, the imperial emblem of authority, represents heaven, and is believed to have mated with the earth, represented by the female dragon (*yin*), a less ferocious animal, usually shown with the *ling-chih* fungus in her mouth. The intercourse is manifested in the rain, the essential juice of heaven, falling to earth from the clouds. Thus clouds and rain are an image of sexual intercourse in Chinese literature and painting.

Jade, the most precious stone to the Chinese, is interpreted as the petrified semen of the celestial dragon. This precious stone plays a very important part in Chinese symbolic language. The popular expression for having sexual intercourse is 'drinking at the fountain of jade'. The female genitals are known as the 'gateway of jade', and the penis is called the 'flute of jade' (on which a woman can play with her fingers and her lips). Other common expressions include 'wine from the grape' (*yin* juice); 'field of cinnabar' (woman's genitals); 'doorway of destroying' (prostate); 'gateways of life' (testes); 'fluid of the peach blossom' (menstrual discharge). Metaphors for the male organ include a stallion and a tree; for the female organ, a deer, clouds, the *ling-chih* fungus, a lemon, and most common of all, a peach. The Chinese peach has a deep cleft and produces an abundance of sweet juice; the metaphor for the vulva and its

[88]

yin-juice is obvious. Richly succulent peaches are often depicted on Chinese porcelain vases and other receptacles, objects which are themselves visual representations of the female genitals. The Gulbenkian Museum at Durham University possesses a good example of such symbolism: a hardstone carving from the seventeenth century which shows a goddess holding a vase (female emblem) out of which flows *yin*-juice in the shape of the *ling-chih* fungus. At her feet is the animal *Kylin* representing the male *yang*.[5] Often one finds porcelain cups (*yin*) with painted or plastically modelled dragons (*yang*). Other decorative emblems for the female genitals include the pomegranate, the lotus, and the peony; these and many other such metaphors are often found on ink-pots, brush-washers, and paper-weights.

A knowledge of the rich variety of sexual metaphors in Chinese art is essential for a real appreciation of such objects as these, although many people may be surprised, to say the least, to learn the meaning behind these beautiful works of art. Similarly, Chinese poetry is rich in metaphors:

> *The Beauty of Wu offers wine.*
> *The Beauty of Wu is fifteen years old, and her hair floats in the breeze;*
> *Her cup of jade invites the guest to savour the wine from the grape.*[6]

The works of art mentioned above are religious by implication only; for overtly religious erotic art one has to look to works resulting from the influence of the imported Tantrik Buddhism. Taoism and Tantra had a great deal in common, of course, and the Buddhist shrine at Tun-Luang dating from the late thirteenth or early fourteenth century recalls Indian temple art at its finest. Erotic couples are painted on the walls, symbolising the mystical union of male and female at the centre of the wheel of creation. It is known that Tantrik sculptures were used in China to instruct young members of the Royal Household in the refinements of the art of love, in the same way as handbooks of sexual techniques had done earlier.[7]

Of the erotic illustrations provided for the less educated Chinese, there are none surviving from periods earlier than the Ming dynasty, for reasons mentioned earlier. However, many examples survive from the Ming period, the sixteenth and seventeenth centuries, and these were intended to provide pleasure as well as education. A set of watercolours of the seventeenth century called *Ladies' Occupations* shows amorous couples in a variety of positions of intercourse inside a house (using chairs specially designed for the purpose) and in a garden (on ornate rugs with carefully placed cushions). The colours are delicate and attractive, but the anatomy tends to be rather lifeless and the figures have little expression.[8] Another series of twenty-four scenes called *Intimate Scenes of Leisurely Love* by the Ming artist Chiu Ying of *c.* 1550 shows rather statuesque ladies and gentlemen dallying in austere houses and decorative gardens.[9] These may be taken as typical of this kind of picture, and they all show a sad lack of imagination.

There are also some illustrations to erotic novels which survive from the Ming period and later. *Jou P'u-Tuan* (The Prayer-Mat of Flesh) gives a picture of the delights of sex with full instructions, but the tale ends with a strong Buddhist moral; the twenty-four illustrations to this famous novel are only known through censored nineteenth-century photographs. One set of seventeenth-century erotic illustrations that has survived intact shows a man and a woman performing amazing feats of copulation on the back of a rather startled horse going at full gallop.[10] The knowledge of anatomy evidenced here is perfunctory in the extreme. It is clear that Chinese artists never worked out aesthetic conceptions of the nude based on knowledge of proportion in the manner of European or Indian artists, and their work is the poorer for this. Even erotic album paintings of the eighteenth and nineteenth centuries suffer from this lack of imagination and inability to construct convincing anatomy (see illustrations 56 and 57), although they often have a lyrical charm of their own. An unusual variation is a set of six carved-relief plaques in ivory, jade, and mother-of-pearl dating from the mid-nineteenth century (see illustration 58), which depict figures in different positions of intercourse. These exhibit a great degree of craftsmanship, even though the aesthetic level could be somewhat higher.

Very different are Chinese landscape paintings, perhaps the highest form of Chinese art. Many of these are endowed with deep sexual meaning in the true Taoist sense. Mountains represent bright, strong *yang*, and misty valleys are *yin*. From one to the other flow the fertilising waters of heaven, and the cosmic dragon's semen falls to the earth in the rain. A mountain-man or sage is often shown in these landscapes, and like his urban counterpart he accumulates *yin* and *yang*, though in his case it is through his closeness to the whole cosmic sexual process. At their best these pictures breathe the real atmosphere of the open air; the delicacy, tenderness, and magic of such paintings are unsurpassed in Chinese art.

The rise of Communism brought with it another wave of censorship, and it is difficult to know how much erotic art has survived in China today. The Communists feel they are transforming the Taoist superfluity of sexual energy into social energy. But fortunately, enough early Chinese porcelain and landscape and erotic art exists

56 *Trio in a garden*, China, eighteenth century

57 *Couple in a garden*, China, eighteenth century

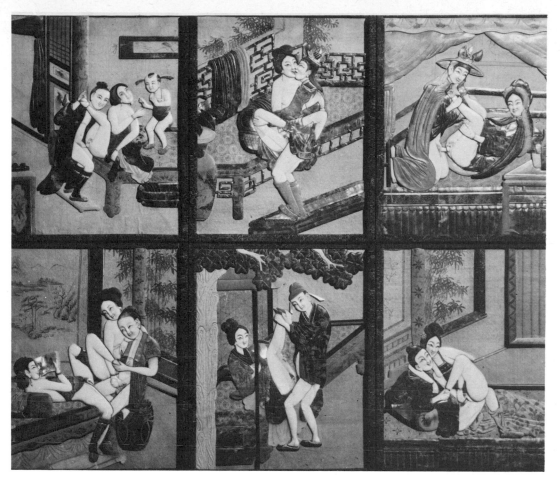

58   *Carved-relief plaques*, ivory, jade, and mother-of-pearl, China, *c.* 1850–80

abroad; and its value can be appreciated, together with the religious philosophy that inspired it.

e: Japan

To the Japanese, sex has always been something wonderful, to be enjoyed whenever possible. And Japanese art and literature have, from earliest times, concerned themselves with the act of love. The male is, of course, dominant in Japanese society, and his sexual needs have traditionally been met by the easy availability of women trained in the art of love-making. There was no social stigma attached to such women: they provided an essential service, as in Ancient Greece and Rome, and many attained high social rank. A large number of the coloured prints of the *Ukiyo-e* type, the greatest flowering of Japanese art, are devoted to these women performing their skills. The attendant ceremony involved and the elaborate costumes they wore are carefully depicted. These erotic prints, or *shunga*, are beautiful glorifications of sexual pleasure with no hint of wrong-doing, yet they are little known in the West, where our knowledge of Japanese art is confined to landscape scenes and portraits of actors. Such *shunga* albums as have appeared in the West have usually been retouched, sometimes by means of newly-carved wood-blocks, or censored, so that only the few 'presentable' prints in the series are ever exhibited or reproduced.

A noticeable feature of Japanese erotic art is the absence of nudity. Unlike the Greeks, the Japanese have little interest in the nude, and couples engaged in sexual intercourse are rarely depicted without at least a little clothing. The fact that the Japanese shun nudity in art is not however due to any Victorian concept of shame relating to the human body. In fact, the universality of communal bathing in Japan has divested nudity of any erotic implications. On the other hand, clothes can be sexually stimulating, and beautiful garments in the very latest fashion, when lovingly depicted in a *shunga*, conjure up a voluptuousness that nudity could never inspire. The many folds in the material and the various openings in the loose-hanging garments all serve the same purpose for the Japanese as the mini-skirt and the tight sweater do for us in the West.

Japanese art is essentially linear, and this is ideal for portraying the excitement suggested by Japanese clothing. This linearism has its own convention of reproducing reality: Japanese artists do not use the Western method of single-point perspective, but suggest space by means of atmosphere. This is a great advantage as far as erotic art is concerned, for the artist can organise his images in two dimensions as long as he observes the linear logic, and thus he can show the genitals in intercourse in ways that a Western artist would find impossible. Line was especially important for the *Ukiyo-e* artist, for he had to provide the means for an engraver to transfer a design onto a block and then cut it out of wood. At first one block was used and prints were hand-coloured, but later a series of blocks was used, each one registering a different colour. These prints tended to be more garish, but they fascinated Van Gogh, Gauguin, Lautrec, and Degas.

Shunga are truly sex pictures, and show sex as neither a romantic ideal of love, nor a means of religious worship. They concentrate on showing the pleasure that results from sexual union, and they imply that this is one of man's greatest pleasures. However, there was sexually explicit art in Japan before the period of the *Ukiyo-e*.

The original religion of old Japan was Shinto, and this was based largely on ancient beliefs such as those related in the *Kojiki*, a book of legends dating from A.D. 712. This tells of how Izangi ('The Inviting Male') and Izanami ('The Inviting Female') created the first land on earth and erected the August Celestial Pillar, where they made love and thus gave birth to the human race. Creation is therefore sexual to Shintoists, and it is also fundamentally good, comprising no sin, only misdemeanours which society curbs. Love and sexuality are good, and this explains the large number of erotic amulets, wall-carvings, Mother Goddess figures, and grave-figures that date from prehistoric times onwards, mostly with prominent sex organs and sometimes depicting figures in sexual intercourse.

The backbone of the Shinto religion was phallic worship, and this had an entirely innocent character. The August Celestial Pillar was known as the Phallus of Heaven, and giant phalluses were carried in Shinto processions, exactly as in the cult of Dionysus in Ancient Greece and Rome (see Chapter 2 b). There was a phallic deity whose name was Konsei-Mijo-jin, and this was the god invoked traditionally by courtesans. Phallic fertility symbols were very common, and phallic talismans were kept for good luck, as at Pompeii. The arrival of Buddhism in the sixth century saw a temporary lull in such overt sexuality, but Buddhism did not wipe out the deeply-held Shinto beliefs. These, in fact, became absorbed into the newly imported religion, just as Confucianism absorbed Taoism in China. Today, every Buddhist temple in Japan has an associated Shinto shrine. Shingon, a Tantrik sect of Buddhism, had special favour with Shintoists. This sect taught that passion was sacred because it led through self-sublimation to enlightenment; their god of love, Aizen Myoo, therefore encouraged passionate and erotic behaviour. Another of their deities was Kangiten, who is always shown as a male and female pair in a standing position of intercourse, with human bodies but the heads of elephants. The most famous example is at Matsuchiyama.

The Japanese have an erotic reaction to religion, and this can be seen in novels and plays as well as in pictorial art. Examples include the *Tales of Ise* dating from the ninth century, illustrated in a highly erotic vein by Shonso in the eighteenth century; the *Tale of Genji* of the eleventh century; and *Ugetsa Monogatari* written in the eighteenth century by Ueda Akinari, a collection of love stories in which ghosts often appear, these being usually kind but sometimes evil beings who wander on earth for a very long time. Ghosts and spirits form an important part of Japanese legend, and they often appear in art. Shuncho produced an album in the late eighteenth century entitled *The 100 Tales of Love*, and this depicted penis-headed monsters and giant phalluses. Utamaro designed many prints based on these old legends. One (see illustration 59) shows two water spirits, or *kappas*, ravishing an Awabi fishergirl under water, while a naked girl watches from a nearby rock, 'languidly ready to yield to temptation' (Edmond de Goncourt). This print is distinguished by the remarkable colour-effect of a restricted range of greens set off by the bright red of the watching girl's clothing, and also by the superbly lecherous expressions on the faces of the water-spirits.

For the Japanese, the pleasures of the flesh are natural and normal, and this goes for homosexual as well as heterosexual relations. Pillow-books (scrolls of erotic prints) were produced at a very early date (a famous one was presented to the Emperor in 1288, but they were already common by the eighth century), and they were specifically designed as manuals of sexual knowledge to be kept inside the pillow-boxes. In this respect, Japan was well ahead of the West. Early examples

59 Utamaro, *Awabi fishergirl ravished by water-spirits*, from *The Song of the Pillow*, 1788

of erotic prints include two scrolls dating from the twelfth century. One known only through copies, depicts *The Phallic Contest*, with lusty males from all over Japan displaying their phallic splendours to be measures by the judges at the Imperial Court. The other, preserved in the Temple of Emman-In at Lake Biwa, shows *The Fart-Battle*, with two groups of Imperial Courtiers taking part in this unusual form of contest. The Rabelaisian humour of these early examples is characteristic of the light-hearted Japanese, and large numbers of amusing novels, story-books, plays, and albums of prints have been produced from the medieval period onwards. Typical of this love of humour are the *Kyogen*, the hilarious interludes that always appear in *Noh* dramas. Similarly, many *shunga* artists liked to add humorous touches to their works, for example Harunobu's *Couple engaged in intercourse* (see illustration 60), where two cats are shown on the veranda mimicking the couple in the house.

At the end of the seventeenth century, a new form of Japanese art came into being. This became known as *Ukiyo-e*, 'pictures of the floating world', and the artists were concerned with depicting the everyday world of pleasure. The philosophy behind their works held that the art of living entailed being absorbed in the present moment, floating along without effort, looking for beauty in the moon's crescent or in flowering cherry-trees, drinking, singing, and making love, as described in *Asai Ryoi*, stories of the shifting world, written in Kyoto in *c.* 1661. The most

60   Harunobu, *Couple engaged in intercourse*, late 1760s

famous *Ukiyo-e* works are coloured prints from the Edo School (the old name for Tokyo), and they depict the pleasures of life in the city, concentrating on the famous courtesans of Yoshiwara. A high proportion of these prints are *shunga*, literally 'spring pictures', which for the Japanese means sex pictures, and these are, as mentioned above, glorifications of sexual pleasure with no hint of wrong-doing. They combine the tasks of fashion plate, publicity for the courtesan, and pillow-book. Some of the earliest were actually commissioned by brothel-keepers, such as *The Yoshiwara Pillow Pictures* of 1660 by the Kambun Master, which is almost a guide to the pleasures of sex in forty-eight positions.[1]

An art based on extolling the virtues of prostitution sounds suspect to our Western minds, but to a Japanese there would be no need for suspicion. Courtesans and geishas were two distinct classes of Japanese women who offered their favours to men, and no social stigma was attached to either. Geishas were cultured and artistic women who often took part in political intrigues. They were highly respectable, and many married into the top levels of society. Love was only part of their service, and geishas never lived in red-light districts or appeared in the famous Green Houses. In this way they differed from courtesans, whose lives were devoted to the art of love-making and who lived in the red-light district of every major town. The most famous of these districts were Shimabara in Kyoto and Yoshiwara in Edo (Tokyo).[2]

One of the most famous volumes of *shunga* is the *Album of the Green Houses* by Utamaro of *c.* 1800, which was much admired by Edmond de Goncourt. Typical of this album is *Yoshiwara courtesan and her lover*,[3] which shows the two figures about to engage in sexual intercourse, with a minimum of the setting details included. Utamaro shows his brilliance in the way he concentrates attention on the rhythmic outlines of the two figures, on the way they relate to each other on the flat surface of the print, and on the beautiful colours and designs of their clothing. The whole picture is a harmony of red, blue, and orange, and the design is completed by the inclusion of carefully placed calligraphy relating to the participants in the scene. The elaborate kimono and *obi* (sash) of the woman are used to enhance the erotic effect, in the manner mentioned above, and we can be sure that these were the latest fashion, for courtesans were famous for setting the fashion in Japanese society. Especially noticeable are the genital organs, which are enlarged and elaborated by the artist. Of course, the genitals are the normal focus of sensation and interest in erotic experience, and it is not unusual to draw attention to them in art of a sexual nature. But since they are such familiar objects in Japan, it is the custom for Japanese artists to exaggerate them in a manner that may appear to us grotesque, but which is in line with the lavishly depicted garments and ensures the intended dramatic and extravagant effect.

Utamaro's *Album of the Green Houses* has a text by Jippensha Ikku which lists the types of courtesans at Yoshiwara and discusses their special skills in love-making: 'On important occasions, outdo your rivals and make yourself loved by the employees by offering them tips from time to time. As soon as you are favoured and well known in the house, you can do anything and all pleasures await you.'[4]

These Yoshiwara courtesans, who dreamed of real love and happy marriage, are the heroines of many novels and also of some of the most popular *Kabuki* plays, for example, *Suicide Pact at Amajima* by Chikamatsu Monzaemon, a tragic love story of a courtesan and a rich merchant, and *The Lovers' Nightmare at Yoshiwara*, a tale of a beautiful courtesan's love for a brave and handsome brigand. Charles Grosbois writes of 'the extraordinary prestige of the courtesan. Subject to the law like any other Japanese woman, practising a profession that was not recognised but tolerated, she was not only a sex symbol; she was also the symbol of free love and of an advanced and refined civilisation.'[5]

The first great master of *shunga* was the late seventeenth-century artist Moronobu. In twenty years he produced about one hundred and fifty separate sets of book illustrations, and about one-fifth of these were erotic, reflecting the new hedonism of his generation, the Genroku Period. In his prefaces, Moronobu pioneers the attitudes of later *shunga* artists by declaring that the purpose of sex is pleasure and that his books will ensure the full enjoyment of such pleasure. In the *Stylish Yoshiwara Pillow Book* of *c.* 1683 he shows real psychological insight and emotional expression with great economy of means, and foreshadows future artists in his use of clothing for decorative effect. Followers of Moronobu include Kiyonobu, son of a *Kibuki* actor, who specialised in erotic scenes reflecting the free-love world of the theatre (see illustration 61), and Masanobu, a pioneer of colour-block printing, who

61   Kiyonobu, *Couple engaged in intercourse*, early 1700s

produced brightly coloured albums depicting the exploits of the Yoshiwara courtesans. Prints were cheap, and so found a market among the middle classes,

[97]

but all these artists also produced a few hand-painted *shunga* scrolls for more affluent connoisseurs.

In 1722 the Confucian Tokugawa Government issued edicts curbing erotic literature and art, and although the short-lived laws were seldom enforced, they gave rise to a new form of print, *abuna-e* ('dangerous pictures'). These were semi-nude pictures which did not show pubic hair or sex organs, and their effect was close to that of a titillating pin-up, concentrating less on the balanced harmony of nude or semi-nude forms than on erotic interest in the pubic regions. Certain artists such as Toyonobu specialised in *abuna-e*, but these soon gave way to the straight-forward *shunga* artists, of whom Harunobu was the greatest example in the eighteenth century.

Harunobu's career was cut short by his early death in 1770, but he brought about a revolution in *shunga*. He helped to develop the four-colour block-printing technique, and his work is characterised by the bold use of strong yet delicate tonally related colours to create a whole mood and atmosphere for the incidents he depicts. He conjures up a dream-like world in scenes like *A fantasy* (see illustration 62), in which a young girl masturbates while day-dreaming about her lover, with whom she is shown in intercourse in a 'thought bubble' at the top of the print, and *Two people on the terrace*, which shows a man feeling under a woman's dress as

62   Harunobu, *A fantasy*, late 1760s

she plays a mandolin, in a setting surrounded by flowering bushes with a river winding into the distance, the whole scene being shown in a range of warm reds and mauves contrasting with areas of brown and grey.[6] This warm richness of colour is characteristic of Harunobu, as is the gentle rhythm of the figures, and his innovation was to give real importance to the background setting of his couples.

Utamaro was probably the greatest *shunga* artist. He was widely known in his own lifetime, and his prints were exported to Europe. He was much admired by Edmond de Goncourt and is probably the best-known Oriental artist in the Western world. His finest album of *shunga* was *The Song of the Pillow* of 1788, which shows his fascination for the grotesque in scenes such as the rape of the fishergirl by water-spirits mentioned above (see illustration 59), with its brilliant colour-effect and superbly lecherous rapists, and another scene of a hairy monster with a young girl (see illustration 63). But the album also includes delicate scenes of intercourse with glimpses of genital organs amongst sumptuous clothes (see illustration 64). One of the finest is *Two people on a veranda*,[7] in which a woman is seen from behind, her head hiding the man's face, and except for a glimpse of the woman's buttocks, almost the whole print is taken up by the inter-relation of the colours and designs of the figures' clothing, a harmony of blacks and greys with touches of red.

We have already discussed Utamaro's print *Yoshiwara courtesan and her lover* from his famous series, *Album of the Green Houses*, another supreme example of his

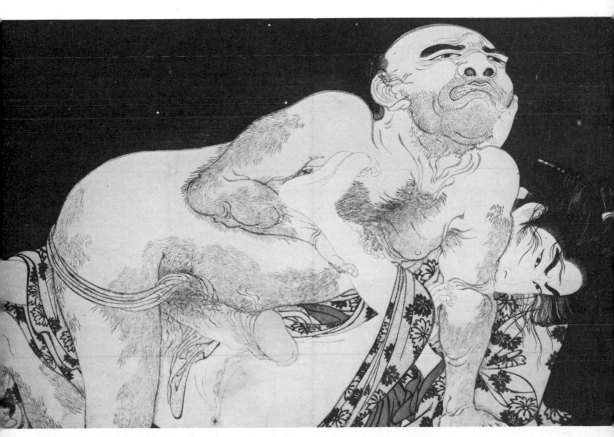

63   Utamaro, *Young girl ravished by a hairy monster*, 1788

64   Utamaro, *Couple engaged in intercourse*, 1788

65   Hokusai, *The Dream of the Fisherman's Wife, c.* 1820

compositional and colouristic skill and a print that shows the characteristic elaboration of the genitals. Utamaro's art is very frankly sexual, in a way that Harunobu's
is not, and also very direct, resulting no doubt from his habit of working from models
which was not the usual practice in Japan. But the high level of taste which is
characteristic of Utamaro, together with his very well developed sense of design,
make his works the finest of all Japanese *shunga*.

In writing about Utamaro, Edmond de Goncourt referred to 'the fiery passions of
the copulations he depicted . . . those swooning women, their heads uptilted on the
ground, their faces death-like, their eyes closed beneath painted eye-lids; that
strength and power of delineation that make the drawing of a penis equal to that of
a hand in the Louvre Museum attributed to Michelangelo'.[8] Utamaro certainly
liked drama, and depicted many scenes of rape and also of the extremes of physical
passion. Of all the masters of *Ukiyo-e* art, he best understood the psychology of the
courtesan and her sexual attractiveness, and he produced some of the most beautiful
of all Yoshiwara prints.

Utamaro's art was the high point of *Ukiyo-e* print-making. The nineteenth
century that followed was instead the great age of landscape prints, but it had one
last great figurative artist, Hokusai. He was a great draughtsman, and his work
includes every subject and inspired a host of followers. His best-known album is
Models of Loving Couples[9] of *c.* 1810, prints of brilliant colour and design which walk
a tight-rope between beauty and crudity and achieve a very powerful if rather
insensitive effect. His most exciting print is probably the most sensational of all

66   Kunisada, *Rape*, from *The Scenery of the Four Seasons*, 1829

Japanese *shunga*, *The dream of the fisherman's wife* of *c.* 1820 (see illustration 65). This is a fantastic scene of a nude woman in the tentacles of two octopuses. She is swooning with pleasure on rocks covered with green seaweed as an enormous octopus with terrifying eyes sucks greedily at her vulva, and a smaller octopus embraces her mouth. This is the descendant of Utamaro's print of water-spirits raping the fishergirl, which it surpasses in power of design and sheer frightening drama, although the colour is surprisingly delicate and restrained.

During the nineteenth century the figure-print declined as Japan suffered the long-term effects of isolation, as can be seen from the violent erotic prints of Kunisada (see illustration 66). After the opening up of Japan by the Americans in 1853, a process of Westernisation began which saw the end of the sexually explicit *shunga*. Japan adopted the morals and customs of Victorian culture, and officially banned *shunga* and nudes in art, condemning both as pornographic. It was a sad end to perhaps the greatest school of erotic art of all time.

Chapter 4

Eroticism in Western Art

a: Middle Ages to 1700

The pioneer of studies in erotic art was Eduard Fuchs, a German professor who published a series of learned books on the subject in Munich in the early years of this century, surviving various prosecutions in the process. He summed up his thesis in these words: 'Art has treated erotic themes at almost all periods, because eroticism lies at the root of all human life.'[1] The obvious reasonableness of this statement took time to gain universal acceptance; the English philosopher S. Alexander was voicing a widely-held view when he wrote in 1933: 'If the nude is so treated that it raises in the spectator ideas or desires appropriate to the material subject, it is false art, and bad morals.'[2] Kenneth Clark put the subject into correct perspective in 1956 when he wrote in his book *The Nude*: 'All good nude painting and sculpture is sexually stimulating . . . No nude, however abstract, should fail to arouse in the spectator some vestige of erotic feeling, even although it be only the faintest shadow—and if it does not do so, it is bad art or false morals.'[3]

The nude is the prime erotic image, and every culture and period in the history of art would be represented in a survey of the treatment of the nude. The female nude seems to be the core of erotic painting in the West, no doubt because almost all painting is done by men. Very rarely is the nude painted dispassionately, for by its very nature it arouses the senses. But the power of the attraction of sex has of course led it to be feared, and the resulting censorship of explicit sexuality in art has resulted in works whose eroticism is deliberately veiled, and whose erotic power is often thereby greatly increased. In fact, Georges Bataille, one of the most interesting and perspicacious of writers on the subject, sees eroticism as self-conscious activity—a consciously intellectualised feeling, which is only possible in a context where sexuality is repressed.[4] On the other hand, Lo Duca, who has written widely on erotic art, puts forward an explanation of eroticism that results from a marrying of the ideas of Freud and Jung. For him, erotic art springs from the subconscious world of dreams and myths.[5] It arises out of the artist's own sexual instincts and is controlled by his complexes, but its real root lies in the collective unconscious of sexual myths and fantasies. For Lo Duca eroticism is a sublimation of instinctive sexual emotions. But Freud had gone further than this: he was convinced that erotic stimulation had an important function, that of reopening the sources of pleasure that had been closed by inhibitions.

Auguste Renoir, whose favourite subject of painting was the nude, once said: 'The female nude rises from the sea or from her bed: she is called *Venus* or *Nini*. One can imagine nothing beyond that.'[6] This well categorises the two main types of nudes in art: the perfection of eternal beauty personified by the Classical goddess and therefore providing the artist with the respectable cover of mythology; and the fascination of real feminity as portrayed in the painter's response to the body of his lover or his model. As we have already seen in Chapter 2 b, the beauty of Venus was celebrated by both the Greeks and the Romans in painting and sculpture, as was the delight in the reality of a beautiful body. Greek pottery-decorations, Etruscan frescoes, and Græco-Roman wall-paintings all attest to the open and guilt-free worship of sex that characterised the Ancient World.

Eroticism is rare in the art of the Early Christian period and the Middle Ages. Pagan monuments were often overtly sexual, but Christian art shunned the world of physical love and concentrated instead on spiritual upliftment. Christianity was a non-sexual religion (*cf*. the doctrine of the virgin birth; the teachings of St Paul about celibacy; the lack of sex in the life of Jesus compared with Buddha and Mohammad), whereas other world religions regarded sexual pleasure as an important part of worship, and treated the sexual adventures of gods and goddesses as sacred texts. Jesus was sympathetic towards women and the state of matrimony, but Paul's antipathy towards the union of the sexes became the stronger influence. Since the Church was the main patron of the arts in the West, this process had a deep affect on painting and sculpture, and drove a wedge between Primitive, Oriental, and Classical art on the one hand, and Western art on the other.

By the eighth century, the Christian Church had formulated a rigid code of sexual behaviour which dominated the Middle Ages and still has many adherents today. This was the Greek concept of *nomos* or ceremonial and unquestioned law, but applied to the individual's most private behaviour. This strict Church law resulted from an obsession with sex. Everyone was considered to be born sinful as a result of the original sin of Adam and Eve, and therefore sexual practices were associated with guilt. Sin was propagated through sexual intercourse, so sex was sinful. Baptism would wash away the sin as long as sexual intercourse was used only for procreation. Thus masturbation, pre-marital intercourse, and homosexual love were decreed to be sinful, as were any sexual activities that did not involve coital inter-course. The concept of *nomos* decreed celibacy for clerics and monks, two very important bodies of the Christian Church, and the Canon Law also had great control over the marriage and sexual life of the laity, a control exercised especially through the confessional.[7] The importance of these developments in the present context cannot be overestimated; the whole concept of eroticism in Western art is coloured by this background of sexual taboos.

Representations of erotic scenes in the medieval period are mainly confined to articles of value owned by the rich: jewellery, decorated furniture, manuscripts, etc. Examples include a set of silver plates in the Leningrad Hermitage, a ninth-century ivory casket from Veroli in the Victoria and Albert Museum, London, and a thirteenth-century gilt mirror in the Frankfurt Städelinstitut decorated with scenes of love-making. Most large libraries and print-rooms possess erotic miniatures or illustrated manuscripts from the period relating to Chaucer and Boccaccio. Ivories and miniatures depicting allegories such as the Fountain of Youth or of Life and the Garden of Love or of Earthly Delights appear throughout the period, famous examples being the *Douce Manuscript* from the fifteenth century in the Bodleian Library, Oxford, and the *Très Riches Heures du Duc de Berry* (*c.* 1485) in the Musée Condé at Chantilly. They precede the later and more explicit versions of such themes by Lucas Cranach and Hieronymous Bosch, and usually display more spiritualised hedonism than overt eroticism. Of course, there are exceptions, such as the Bayeux Tapestry from the latter part of the eleventh century, which shows in one early scene a nude couple, the man having an erection and stretching his arms out to the woman.[8]

One seeming anomaly of the Early Christian period is that in spite of Christianity's sexual taboos, churches all over Europe were provided with erotic images of various sorts, though admittedly they were few and far between. Most obvious are the *Shelah-na-Gig* fertility figures of nude women exposing their vulvas which are found on English and especially Irish Saxon and Norman churches.[9] These were usually taken from pagan places of worship and incorporated into the fabric of Christian churches, a result of the Pope's directive to St Augustine not to destroy the idols of the heathen. Good English examples are to be found in the twelfth-century church at Kilpeck in Herefordshire (see illustration 67) and on Oaksey church near Cirencester; many Irish examples are now in the Museum of the Society of Antiquaries of Dublin. An unusual variant over a window of the church at

67 *Shelah-na-Gig*, Kilpeck Church,
Herefordshire, England, early Medieval

Whittlesford in Cambridgeshire shows a *Shelah-na-Gig* one side and an ithyphallic man opposite her; a similar male figure can be seen on the wall of the church at Abson near Bristol. Depictions similar to *Shelah-na-Gigs* can be found on churches elsewhere in Europe, such as the capitals in the Romanesque Cathedral of Piacenza in Italy, and striking resemblances can be found in heraldic female figures in the art of primitive peoples such as those of the Sepik River area of New Guinea (see Chapter 2 a). These pagan fertility figures are related in conception to the famous *Giant of Cerne Abbas* in Dorset, a male figure with an enormous erection which was cut in the chalk of the hillside in the Romano-British period (see illustration 12).

Explicit erotic depictions are found on the capitals and misericords of Romanesque and Gothic churches all over Europe. Some are clearly meant to represent Adam and Eve (as in a capital in the twelfth-century church of St-Saveur at Dinan in France), while others refer to later famous couples (Heloise and Abelard on a capital in the thirteenth-century Conciergerie in Paris). A fourteenth-century misericord in Chichester Cathedral shows a violinist kissing a dancer, and more explicitly sexual depictions are to be found on misericords in the fifteenth-century Choir School of the Chateau Montreuil at Bellay in France (see illustration 68); in the Cathedral of Burgos in Spain; in Metz Cathedral, France; and in Sherborne Abbey and Ely Cathedral. A boss at Hereford Cathedral depicts a devil with a large erection, and one in the cloister of Norwich Cathedral shows a man defecating (see illustration 69). In Italy nudes are depicted in a provocative manner on the south façade of Modena Cathedral and in the fourteenth-century church of Santa Maria near Giulianova. Couples performing intercourse or in the 'sixty-nine' position are to be found on capitals in Toledo Cathedral and the Church of San Gregorio at Valladolid in Spain and on doorways in the Church of Saint Martin at Isle-Adam in France. At the Cathedral of Ciudad Rodrigo near Salamanca in Spain, a large phallus is carved in wood on one of the choir-stalls. The façade of Fidenza Cathedral in Italy shows a

68 *Misericord*, France, fifteenth century

69 *Boss*, Norwich Cathedral, England, Gothic

70 *Façade Frieze*, Fidenza Cathedral, Italy, early Gothic

couple engaged in sexual dalliance (see illustration 70). The Cathedral at Freiburg-im-Breisgau in Germany and the Church of St Lo at Rouen in France have various gargoyles in human form which drain the water through the anus, the penis, or the vagina. These scattered erotica are not so much proof of the Church's liberality as of the wily artfulness of the craftsmen it employed.

The new humanism of the Renaissance in Italy during the fifteenth century, with its renewal of interest in the world of Classical Antiquity, brought about dramatic changes in the progress of the arts. The shameful connotations associated with nudity *per se* began to disappear, and with the rise of enlightened secular patronage, the hold of the Church over the arts weakened. This new enlightenment is perfectly expressed in Francesco del Cossa's frescoes in the Palazzo Schifanoia at Ferrara which he completed in 1470. These were commissioned by Duke Borso d'Este to illustrate the pleasures of life at his court, and are beautifully lighthearted without being at all trite. One scene depicts *The Triumph of Love*, and in the centre, a very contemporary Venus sits enthroned on a decorated barge drawn by two white swans, with a knight in armour kneeling before her. On the left, courtiers walk in the countryside, and one kisses a lady who has been playing a mandolin. The right-hand section (see illustration 71) shows the three Graces, naked and unashamed, with a party of courtiers in the foreground talking and making music together. One girl is wearing a flower garland, while nearby, a youth kisses another

[107]

71 Francesco del Cossa, *The Triumph of Love* (detail), 1470

girl and puts his hand inside her dress between her legs. There is no sense of shame here; instead, there is an atmosphere of relaxation and happiness where love is openly celebrated.

The rebirth of Classical Antiquity was also the rebirth of Venus, and erotic images of the goddess of love are characteristic of Renaissance art. One of the

72 Botticelli, *Birth of Venus*, 1484–90

finest is Botticelli's *Birth of Venus* of 1484–90 (Uffizi Gallery, Florence; see illustration 72). A recent critic wrote of this figure: 'The quintessence of the design . . . dispels all carnal desire from it. . . . If it stimulates the sense of touch it is only in the manner of a sculpture . . . the blood which flows through the veins of [Botticelli's] Venus has not the warmth of human blood.'[10] Although clearly inspired by Classical sculpture and even more by Gothic ivories, this Venus is surely flesh and blood: not the Virgin Venus of certain art-historians' imaginations, but the personification of sexual beauty. As Kenneth Clark wrote in *The Nude*, 'We can feel how [Botticelli's] hand quickens or hesitates as he follows with his eye those inflections of the body which awaken desire.'

Unlike the comparable depiction of *The Birth of Venus* at Pompeii (in the Villa of Venus, first century A.D.; see illustration 73), Botticelli's goddess attempts to hide her sex, while an inviting smile hovers around her mouth, and in doing so she merely succeeds in drawing attention to her own sexuality. While bowing to a convention that required modesty in the depiction of Venus, Botticelli must also have been aware of the enhanced eroticism he was thus able to achieve. This subterfuge in eroticism, so notably lacking in Pompeii, looks forward to the coyness of much erotic imagery, although it does not undermine Botticelli's brilliant achievement. He was a man of his time, and one essential characteristic of the Renaissance was the urge to be seen to be civilised. Thus a code of behaviour was worked out which involved strictly defined precepts and taboos. This, of course, had the very real distinction of being the foundation of our present concept of social education, but at the same time it also slowed the process of enlightenment by encouraging a sort of prudery that was out of keeping with the freedom that characterised the Classical world it sought to emulate. It was, after all, the Renaissance that found a new use for the fig-leaf, which soon sprouted on many Greek and Roman sculptures, not to mention Michelangelo's *David* (see illustration 2).

Later Renaissance painting reached greater peaks of eroticism than Botticelli's *Venus*: the depictions of the Goddess of Beauty by Giorgione and Titian may be

73 *Birth of Venus*, Pompeii, first century A.D.

74　Giorgione, *Sleeping Venus, c.* 1505–10

taken as examples. But it is noteworthy that they are both called Venus. It will be a long time before the female nude can be depicted for its own sake. The *Sleeping Venus* of about 1505–10 by Giorgione (Dresden; see illustration 74) breathes a refined voluptuousness as this prototype of the reclining nude lies seductively in the open air of an idyllic landscape, bathed in the golden light of a warm Italian summer afternoon, supporting her head on one arm while the other modestly hides her sex. Titian's *Venus of Urbino* of *c.* 1538 (Uffizi Gallery, Florence; see illustration 75) echoes the pose almost exactly, except that the head is now raised and the eyes are open and aware of our presence. No longer is the viewer spying on an un-suspecting maiden: here he is the welcome guest, perhaps the lover, for Titian's *Venus* makes no pretence to that title as she reclines on her couch with her Italian lap-dog at her feet and her sixteenth-century servants busying themselves in the room beyond. She is, in fact, Renoir's Nini, a sixteenth-century pin-up for some aristocratic patron, and she personifies the typical beauty of the day. Titian was by all accounts a passionate man, and we know he painted many Venuses for wealthy private patrons who may or may not have been inspired by love of Ancient Greece. Many, like the *Venus with Organ-Player* (a portrait of Prince Ottavio Farnese) of 1433–35 (Prado, Madrid), are private celebrations of contemporary sexual relation-

75　Titian, *Venus of Urbino, c.* 1538

ships. In this painting, the Prince is seated at the organ and is looking over his shoulder at his companion's *mons veneris*. But none of Titian's works can match the warm and gentle eroticism of his *Venus of Urbino*.

When Edouard Manet's *Olympia* (Louvre, Paris; see illustration 123) was exhibited at the 1865 Salon in Paris, it provoked a storm of indignation and had to be protected from the outraged visitors by means of a rail and two policemen. And yet this most famous of all nineteenth-century nudes was Manet's attempt to bring up to date Titian's painting, which he had copied in 1856. It had, therefore, an impeccable pedigree which stretched back through Giorgione to the *Hypnerotomachia Polifili* of 1499 and thence to antique sarcophagi. Manet had no desire to enrage anyone; he had painted what was to him an 'academic' picture in the sense that the original by Titian was 'academic' and admired by everyone. The pose of the model was very similar as were the arrangements of curtains, bedclothes, and pillows. But there were subtle changes. Titian's model could well have been a high-class Venetian courtesan, but this is not explicit in the painting; Manet deliberately painted a typical Parisian prostitute, wearing nothing but a flower in her hair, a black neck-band and high-heeled shoes. A negro servant girl is delivering a bouquet from her 'protector', and at the foot of the bed, a Baudelairean black cat replaces Titian's lap-dog. It was the obviousness of the woman's profession that so outraged Parisians. The public preferred the antiseptic and dishonest nudity of 'Classical' subjects such as *The Birth of Venus* by the academically respectable painter Alexandre Cabanel of 1865 (see illustration 124), a provocatively posed and badly painted nude reclining on a rock, attended by flying cupids blowing into seashells.

The hypocrisy of the nineteenth century in France—and England—was not unknown in sixteenth-century Italy. But while the nineteenth-century academic painter could titillate and excite his audience without jeopardising their sense of decent respectability, the sixteenth-century artist had to observe a convention which made nude paintings *per se* unthinkable. As a result, the hot-blooded Titian produced a veritable army of Venuses, not one of whom could have spoken a word of Greek. Although the sensualism of Venetian painting was less common in the art of central Italy, where neo-Platonism and the idealistic abstraction of the fifteenth century did not favour such overt expressions of eroticism, figures from Greek mythology rivalled saints and biblical characters in Renaissance painting, providing endless opportunities for erotic portrayals. Of these, Jupiter was the most popular, and there were countless depictions of the exploits of the King of Mount Olympus, whose appetite for love was notoriously inexhaustible, and the imagination he put into his courting inspired almost every major painter.

An example is the story, already mentioned, of *Leda and the Swan*. Leda was the wife of King Tyndarus of Sparta, and when Jupiter saw her bathing in a river, he changed himself into a swan and threw himself into her arms as if for protection from an eagle. The result of this precipitous mating was the birth of Castor and Pollux. This incident was painted during the sixteenth century by Lorenzo di Credi, Perino del Vaga, Bronzino, Correggio, Titian, the Carracci, Veronese, and Sodoma, as well as being the subject of famous works by Michelangelo, Raphael and Leonardo da Vinci. Later artists who turned to this story include Poussin, Rubens, Rowlandson, Boucher, Gericault, Barye, Moreau, Renoir, Cézanne, Bayros, Beardsley, Maillol, Van Dongen, Dali, Delvaux, Paul Wunderlich, and Sidney Nolan. Raphael executed a beautiful drawing of *Leda and the Swan* (Royal Collection, Windsor Castle) as a study after a now lost work by Leonardo which was painted for Giuliano de Medici in about 1505. Leonardo wrote of it in his *Treatise on Painting*: 'I executed the painting . . . for a lover. He wished to see the features of his goddess mirrored so that he might kiss them without arousing suspicion.' After his marriage, the Prince found it expeditious to return the painting to the artist. It later passed to King Francis I of France and is now only known through copies in the Borghese and Spiridon collections in Rome. Leonardo chose to show Leda standing in a flowery meadow embracing the swan, who enfolds her with his wing. She is shown completely nude, looking affectionately at her twins.[11] Michelangelo painted *Leda and the Swan* for Duke Alfonso of Ferrara in 1529, and the picture later passed to the collections of King Francis I and then King Louis XIII of France, one of whose ministers burnt it as a dangerous obscenity.

As with Leonardo's version, we fortunately possess clues as to the character of the lost original. The Royal Academy in London has a contemporary copy after Michelangelo's lost cartoon (see illustration 76) which in spite of the weakness of the drawing gives some idea of the powerful eroticism of the original, as does a painted copy by Rosso Fiorentino of 1530 in the National Gallery, London, and

76 After Michelangelo, *Leda and the Swan*, sixteenth century

one by Rubens in Dresden. Leda herself is modelled on Michelangelo's nude figure of *Night* in the Medici Chapel in Florence, and the swan is shown between her legs after the act of intercourse, its neck between her breasts and its beak touching her lips. One wing flutters in the air, while Leda sinks into her pillows in post-coital exhaustion. The original must have been one of the most explicit and powerful of all depictions of the legend. A related work is the marble sculpture of 1536 by Bartolommeo Ammanati in the Museo Nazionale in Florence (see illustration 77). He does not show the fluttering wing of the swan, and Leda's head is raised so that the feeling of exhaustion is less effective. But the overall impression is still powerfully erotic. In later life, Ammanati regretted the freedom of many of his works, and in a letter to the Art Academy of Florence he confessed to having fallen into a 'horrible vice. . . . It is a grave sin to create nude statues . . . laying bare those parts which should be covered, and which one cannot contemplate without shame. . . . I have gravely offended society and God.'[12] His confession is a sad example of the type of Renaissance prudery that foreshadowed the nineteenth century's obsession with the evils of nudity.

Leonardo da Vinci declared that 'l'arte è cosa mentale', and intellect was paramount in High Renaissance painting. But Leonardo's idealised women in such paintings as the *Mona Lisa*, the *Virgin of the Rocks* and the *Virgin and Child with St Anne* seem to embody strong erotic forces. When Walter Pater saw in the *Mona Lisa* 'the animalism of Greece, the lust of Rome, the mysticism of the middle age with its spiritual ambition and imaginative loves, the return of the pagan world,

77 Ammanati, *Leda and the Swan*, sixteenth century

the sins of the Borgias', [13] he was reacting to a sexually provocative image that has fascinated or repulsed people since the early sixteenth century. And although widely rejected nowadays as pure fantasy, Sigmund Freud's interpretation of the holy ladies in Leonardo's paintings as objects of a homosexual mother-fixation (as revealed in Leonardo's memoir of his childhood) is further proof of the powerful appeal of the understated eroticism in Leonardo's works.[14]

Michelangelo's turbulent love-life has often been explored by writers looking for insights into the sexual motivations for his art, and it is not difficult to see the erotic force of the male nudes in the Sistine Chapel ceiling and the marble *Slaves* as resulting from his now recognised homosexuality. His *Last Judgement* fresco in the Sistine Chapel shows a great interest in various forms of physical love, including those classed as perverted, and also an obsession with nudity which caused Pietro Aretino (of all people) to denounce it in an open letter of 1545 as 'fit for a brothel wall'. When the Pope wanted to destroy the fresco, Michelangelo said: 'The Pope has merely to change the world and I will paint the new one.' Nonetheless, his pupil, Daniele da Volterra, was employed in veiling the naked bodies, for which service he was christened *Il Braghettone*, 'the trouser-maker'.

Leo Steinberg[15] recently discussed the definite erotic appeal of Michelangelo's marble *Pietà* groups, in which he sees the artist as being concerned to show the Virgin as the Bride of Christ rather than the Mother, recalling the preaching of Savonarola. This makes the *Pietà* in St Peter's, Rome, of 1498 a formal equivalent to the lament of Venus for the dead Adonis, and the *Pietà* in Florence Cathedral of 1547–56 a symbol of sexual union (the now missing left leg of Christ was originally slung over the Virgin's thigh). Steinberg concludes his fascinating argument, 'Much of Michelangelo's idiom is unintelligible so long as its indwelling sexuality remains unexplored. His bodies, in action or immobilized, are possessed by their sex.' Viewed in this light, the nude *David* of 1501–4 in the Accademia, Florence (see illustration 1), which is one of the most historically and aesthetically important sculptures of the Renaissance, can be seen to embody the epitome of male sexual attraction and excitement. It is, therefore, perhaps the more understandable, if no less regrettable, that in order to hide the figure's powerful maleness a fig-leaf was added within a short time of the sculpture's completion, much to Michelangelo's horror. The offence was not rectified until the early years of the twentieth century (see illustration 2).

Raphael, the other member of the trio of high Renaissance Italian Masters, was the only heterosexual of the group. His amorous affairs made him notorious,[16] and some of his designs for frescoes in the Loggie of the Vatican, for example *Isaac and Rebecca spied on by Abimelech*, show a keen interest in physical love, as do his frescoes of mythological scenes in the Farnesina in Rome of *c*. 1518. A drawing in the British Museum for the *Disputà* fresco in the Vatican Stanze of 1509–11 shows him in a very human light, for while working on the intensely religious subject, he broke off to scribble a poem in the margin: 'Love has enchained me to a beautiful face, fresh as a rose and white as snow, with sparkling eyes whose brightness gladdens my heart. . . . No river nor sea could put out the fire that consumes me, but I am not complaining.' Many engravings after lost subjects by Raphael show highly erotic scenes: a series of *Loves of Cupid and Psyche* engraved by the Master of the Thimble and a print of *Venus and Cupid with three couples* by Bonasone show explicit scenes of intercourse,[17] and an engraving of *Tarquin and Lucretia* by Enea Vico in the Bibliothèque Nationale in Paris after a lost drawing of about 1505 shows the nude figure of Tarquin about to stab Lucretia lying nude on a bed, with two dogs copulating on the floor. One of the most famous of all sixteenth-century Italian engravings is *The Judgement of Paris* by Marcantonio Raimondi after Raphael, which shows numerous nude figures in an extensive landscape (see illustration 78). The loss of the original work by Raphael is one of the greatest tragedies of Renaissance art.

The most notorious of Raphael's erotic works are his frescoes for Cardinal Bibbiena's bathroom in the Vatican. Guidebooks to the Vatican to this day do not mention this room, and enquiries from prospective visitors are met by a refusal to acknowledge its existence. Cardinal Bernardo Bibbiena, secretary to Pope Leo X, was an author of somewhat improper plays, and lived permanently in the Vatican Palace. When his bathroom was damaged by fire in 1515, he asked Raphael to design him a new one in the Antique style on the theme of the *History of Venus*. Most of the work was done under Raphael's supervision by his pupils, and included scenes representing *The Birth of Venus*, *Venus and Cupid on Dolphins*, *Venus complaining to Cupid of the wounds of Love*, *Venus and Adonis*, and *The Castration of Uranus* (Uranus was castrated in order to provide the foam from which Venus arose in a seashell). During the eighteenth century the room was made into a kitchen, and by the nineteenth century, when it was open to the public for a short period, the frescoes were described as being already in a poor condition. Since then, access to the room has been almost impossible even for scholars, although Bernard Berenson once saw the frescoes and praised them highly. In 1931, after the *Venus of Cnidos* by Praxiteles in the Vatican Museum (depicting the courtesan Phryne) had been divested of its fig-leaf, permission was given to E. Rodocanachi to visit the room in connection with his book on the pontificate of Leo X. He related that many of the frescoes had been whitewashed, and the photographs he reproduced in his book[18] were uninformative. In 1972, colour reproductions of three scenes from the series appeared in a London magazine.[19] The condition was too bad for any aesthetic judgment to be made; only one, a scene representing *Pallas attacked by Vulcan*, seemed at all erotic, and this was clearly painted by a pupil. It is to be hoped that the room will soon be open to inspection, so that this episode in Raphael's work can be properly evaluated.

One of the most celebrated of all the artistic scandals in sixteenth-century Italy involved Raphael's most gifted pupil, Giulio Romano. This was the publication in about 1527 of *Aretino's Sonnets* or *Postures*, a book consisting of engravings by Marcantonio Raimondi after drawings by Giulio with accompanying sonnets in bawdy language by Pietro Aretino* (see illustrations 244 and 245). Each picture

---

* These are discussed in detail in Appendix I.

78   Marcantonio Raimondi (after Raphael), *Judgement of Paris, c.* 1520s

showed a man and a woman in a different position of sexual intercourse. All copies of the original publication seem to have been destroyed, as have Giulio's drawings, but these must have related to the many known erotic works by him, such as the painting of a *Nude Couple on à Bed* in the Dahlem Museum, Berlin. As a result of the scandal caused by the book, Giulio fled to Mantua, where he worked for Duke Federico Gonzaga II. In the Palazzo del Te he produced some of the most sexually provocative of all mythological paintings of the Renaissance, including *Jupiter and Olympia*, where the King of the Gods is shown as an ithyphallic sea-serpent about to have intercourse with the nude Olympia (see illustration 79). This and a scene of *Parsiphae concealing herself in the statue of a cow made by Daedalus in order to receive the love of the bull* are in the Sala di Psyche; in the nearby Camerino are frescoes of ithyphallic satyrs taunted by naked nymphs.

The above-mentioned missing erotic drawings by Giulio were probably a sct of *Loves of the Gods*; these were common in sixteenth-century Italy, and most are only known to us today through the occasional surviving print by another artist. A set by Perino del Vaga and Rosso Fiorentino of 1527, which included scenes of Jupiter having intercourse with Semele, Io, and Mnemosyne, is known through prints by Caraglio and Réné Boyvin. Sets are known by Primaticcio (engraved by Georges Ghisi) and Titian (engraved by John Smith), and there are also series of erotic prints

79   Giulio Romano, *Jupiter and Olympia*, 1525–35

by Giulio Bonasone, Pietro Buonacorsi and Baviera. Giulio Romano appears to have produced a large number of erotic drawings: besides the remaining Marcantonio prints relating to the Aretino volume, there is an engraving after Giulio by Marco da Ravenna of *Jupiter and Semele* which shows Jupiter playing with Semele's vulva while she manipulates his erect penis[20] and an anonymous engraving of a nude woman trying to escape from the grasp of a nude man with an erection.[21]

However, the most prolific creator of erotic imagery at this time was Agostino Carracci, who made many engravings after his own and other artists' works. His four paintings on the theme of *Love in the Golden Age* of 1588–89 (Kunsthistorisches Museum, Vienna)[22] show various nude couples making love in extensive landscapes, but his most famous erotic works are a series of engravings known as the *Lascivie* (1584–87). Adam Bartsch in his *Peintre-Graveur* catalogues mentions thirteen prints as belonging to this series, and describes them as very rare;[23] examples are hidden in the Restricted Collections of the British Museum, the Bibliothèque Nationale, and the Musée de Lyon. One print which is owned by the British Museum (see illustration 80) depicts a satyr having intercourse with a nymph against the trunk of a tree.[24] The nymph is nude and the sexual act is shown in detail. It is a spirited piece of etching showing a very strong and well-developed grasp of form; like the others in the series, it displays Carracci's great ability to depict the nude in positions of physical exertion. Other *Lascivie* in the British Museum include a scene where an old man pays a nude courtesan lying on her bed, while a cupid breaks his bow beside her;[25] a nude nymph having her toe-nails cut by a cupid while a young ithyphallic satyr plays with her vulva;[26] and a nude nymph reclining on her bed while an ithyphallic satyr wearing a brief apron holds a plumb-line over her vulva.[27] Others in different collections show a masturbating satyr watching a nude nymph asleep under a tent; a satyr whipping a nude nymph tied to a tree; and a nude nymph chained to a rock being approached by a sea-monster.[28] Further subjects of the series include *Suzanna and the Elders*, *The Three Graces*, *Orpheus and Eurydice*, and *Lot Committing Incest with his Daughters*. The whole series shows Carracci's debt to Tintoretto, but the prints are evidence of a very real talent, and from the examples still in existence it is obvious that the *Lascivie* formed one of the most beautiful of all projects in the history of erotic engravings.

The more usual subject for such series of prints was as we have seen the *Loves of the Gods*; indeed, Agostino Carracci executed such a set later in his career, known only through later copies by a pupil of Goltzius. Another artist who executed such a series was Francesco Parmigianino. Only one scene is now known, and this shows *Venus and Mars at the Forge of Vulcan*, engraved by Enea Vico in 1543. The British Museum possesses a copy of the very rare first state (see illustration 81), in which Venus and Mars are nude on a bed in the act of intercourse while Vulcan works busily at his forge in the foreground.[29] The eroticism of the scene is very explicit, with the gods openly celebrating their love, although the draughtsmanship of the engraver leaves a lot to be desired. In the more common second state, the figures on the bed have been effaced and Venus is shown asleep.

80   Agostino Carraci, *Satyr copulating with a Nymph*, 1584–87

81　Enea Vico (after Parmigianino), *Venus and Mars at the Forge of Vulcan*, 1543

Parmigianino was one of the earliest artists to use the medium of etching to make works of art of his own. The British Museum owns an uncatalogued engraving which is signed by him, and shows a *Witches' Sabbath* (see illustration 82) with a hooded witch holding a broomstick and sitting astride a giant phallus, surrounded by owls, devils, and other disturbing apparitions.[30] The sheer bravura of the print is astonishing, and in its freedom of technique it looks on to Goya, whose *Sleep of Reason Produces Monsters* of 1799 it partly resembles. Detailed information about this print will probably never be known, but it is of interest to note that Vasari describes Parmigianino in the last years of his life, the late 1530s, as 'having his thoughts filled with alchemy, as happens to all those who have once given themselves to running after its phantoms; and having changed from the delicate, amiable and elegant person that he was, to a bearded, long-haired, neglected, and almost savage, or wild man', so that he 'became at length strange and melancholy'.[31] The quality of the engraving is very high, and one can presume that it is an autograph work, reflecting the nightmare visions of Parmigianino's last years.

There are two other interesting Italian engravings in the British Museum which are relevant in this connection. *Priapus and Lotis* (see illustration 83) is by an unknown monogrammist of the Bolognese School, I.B., sometimes identified as Giovanni Battista del Porto,[32] and no fewer than eight other impressions are extant in European museums including those in Paris, Berlin, Vienna, and Munich. Priapus is shown

82   Francesco Parmigianino, *Witches' Sabbath*, 1530s

83   Giovanni Battista del Porto (?), *Priapus and Lotis, c.* 1520s

with his erection peeping out from under his clothing; he is removing the coverings from Lotis who lies asleep on a grassy bank in front of a castle in an extensive landscape. In the foreground, two nude nymphs lie asleep. This talented but not outstanding artist is also known to have produced many other engravings of an erotic variety. The second print in the British Museum is *The Profane Parnassus* by

[122]

an unknown monogrammist, H. E., probably after a drawing by Jacopo de Barbari[33] (see illustration 84). This is the very rare first state, and shows a couple on the lefthand side leaving a scene of sexual orgy in which nude men and women engage in various explicitly sexual activities, while animals copulate and even trees are shown with genital organs in acts of sexual intercourse. The print is of a high standard of execution and on a very large scale, and the engraver was probably a student or follower of Marcantonio Raimondi. In the second and more common state, all sexual organs, whether human, animal, or arboreal, are eliminated.

We have seen how the frequently underlying sexual impetus in Italian art came more into the open as the sixteenth century progressed. This reflected the growing importance of enlightened private patronage. In addition to works already mentioned, one can cite Francesco Albani's very explicit *Salamacis raped by Hermaphroditus* (Turin Pinacoteca); the beautiful bronze sculpture of a copulating couple by Andrea Riccio in the Louvre; Primaticcio's very free mythological scenes painted for the Palace of Fontainebleau[34] and engraved by Leon Davent; the erotic works collected by the Austrian Archdukes and now in the Vienna Kunsthistorisches Museum, including Tintoretto's *Susanna at the Bath*, Titian's *Diana and Callisto*, and Veronese's *Venus and Adonis*.

Onc of the most celebrated, and notorious, of erotic paintings of the period is Bronzino's *Venus, Cupid, Folly and Time* of *c.* 1545 in the National Gallery, London

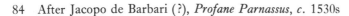

84   After Jacopo de Barbari (?), *Profane Parnassus, c.* 1530s

85 Bronzino, *Venus, Cupid,
Folly and Time, c.* 1545

(see illustration 85), which was commissioned by Cosimo de Medici for the French
King Francis I. A recent art historian has described it as 'of a frigid and passionless
perfection',[35] but the brilliant colour and incredible brushwork and modelling give
it a strong tactile sense which is exciting and stimulating and far from passionless.
Later generations found its explicit nudity and erotic overtones unacceptable, and
until comparatively recently, overpainted veils covered the pubis of Venus and the
buttocks of Cupid. Erwin Panofsky[36] has shown that the painting was conceived as
an allegory demonstrating the futility and transience of the pleasures of love. Cupid
and Venus embrace in a far from maternal way in the centre, while Pleasure scatters
roses over them, but Jealousy appears at the left, and Deceit with her scaly serpent's
body threatens from the right. Nevertheless, it is the beautiful nude bodies of Venus,
Cupid, and Pleasure which catch the eye and hold the interest.

In spite of the increasing demand for erotic art from private patrons, the Church
continued to be a major source of patronage for artists, and so religious subject-
matter is predominant in the paintings of the period. Yet even here, erotic themes or
undertones are frequently present. Certain Old Testament stories were ideal for
erotic treatment, such as *Susanna at her bath spied upon by the Elders* (painted by
Tintoretto, Domenichino, Annibale Carracci, Guido Reni, Palma Vecchio, etc.),
Joseph tempted by Potiphar's Wife (Tintoretto, Paris Bordone, Guercino, Titian,
Veronese, etc.), *Lot Committing Incest with his Daughters* (Agostino Carracci, Raphael,
Francesco Furini, etc.). Perhaps the most powerfully erotic is the story of Judith,

[124]

who seduced Holofernes, the enemy commander, and then cut off his head while he was recovering from the physical exertions of intercourse.[37] This was a favourite subject of Northern artists such as Lucas Cranach and Hans Baldung Grien, but in Italy it was painted by Giulio Romano, Mantegna, Giorgione, Titian, Pellegrino Tibaldi, and many others. The version by Artemisia Gentileschi in the Uffizi Gallery in Florence shows the loosely dressed Judith in the act of cutting through the neck of the half-nude Holofernes, who struggles with her as his blood spurts over her. This is one of the earliest erotic paintings by a female artist, and its motivation can clearly be interpreted in Freudian terms. A similarly effective treatment is Tintoretto's painting in the Prado: the erotic undertones of violent death are here superbly displayed, and relate to the parallels of violence and orgasm characterised by Georges Bataille as *la petite mort* in *Les Larmes d'Eros*.[38]

The New Testament also offers many opportunities for erotic interpretations. We have already seen how certain of Michelangelo's *Pietà* sculptures were deliberate expressions of a sexual relationship, and also how erotic connotations have been read into Leonardo's *Holy Family* paintings. Many Madonna and Child depictions seem to cater to an erotic interest: paintings by such artists as Giovanni Boltraffio and Bernardino Luini seem to draw attention to the exposed breast of the mother feeding her child, a theme especially popular in Northern art. But more explicit are two works by the already discussed Parmigianino, *Madonna with a Rose* (Dresden Gallery) and *Madonna and Child* (Pitti Palace, Florence), in which the Madonna is shown with breasts lightly covered by thin, clinging draperies, as she caresses a well-developed and nearly adolescent boy.[39] But the most obvious figure for erotic portrayal in the New Testament is the reformed adulteress Mary Magdalene, and she was very popular with artists.[40] Francesco Furini portrayed her (National Gallery of Ireland, Dublin) as a full-length frontal nude in a state of excitement, clutching a crucifix and stroking a skull. More usually, she is shown as a half-length figure, with her hands clasped over her naked breasts and a look of ecstasy on her features, as in works by Tintoretto, Guercino, Renieri, Pedrini, and Agostino Carracci. A painting by Sirani (Musée de Besançon) shows her clutching a whip to her naked breasts, thus adding an extra dimension to the eroticism of the subject. And in Titian's famous portrayal of 1554 (Pitti Palace, Florence; see illustration 86), she is shown gazing rapturously up to heaven as she clutches her long silky tresses to her body, leaving her full breasts provocatively exposed. Similarly erotic depictions would later be painted by Van Dyck and Rubens (see illustration 87), and perhaps the ultimate version, Rodin's marble (see illustration 165), shows her in the nude embracing the body of Christ on the cross, a further extension of Bronzino's suggestive *Noli Me Tangere* in the Louvre.

Martyrdom scenes also provided subjects for artists concerned in giving expression to erotic interests. The *Martyrdom of St Sebastian* by Sodoma (Pitti Palace, Florence) shows a beautifully idealised male nude transfixed by arrows and struggling to free himself as he gazes upward with an expression that mingles agony with ecstasy. In the version by Guido Reni (Capitoline Museum, Rome), the saint could almost be

87 Peter Paul Rubens, *Christ with Mary Magdalene, c.* 1620

86 Titian, *Mary Magdalene,* 1554

posing for a male pin-up photograph. Nuvolone's painting of *St Ursula* (Karlsruhe Gallery) shows the saint in an ecstatic fit with an arrow penetrating her body between the breasts. St Agatha underwent various unmentionable tortures; a portrayal of her by Sebastiano del Piombo (Pitti Palace, Florence) of 1520 shows two men attacking her breasts with tongs, and in paintings by Guido Reni, Zurbaran, and Lorenzo Lippi she holds her severed breasts on a plate. Veronese painted her for King Philip II in 1593 (Prado) clutching her dress in an unsuccessful attempt to conceal her mutilated body. And like Saints Barbara, Christine, Catherine, and Margaret, she was often painted in the nude being whipped by excited torturers.

It was, however, the Classical themes that offered themselves as the best alibi for sensual pictures, and as the sixteenth century progressed, the sexual under-current came more into the open. This is especially clear in the works of Correggio, who managed to express a really convincing depth of passion, rather than mere physical beauty. His mythological scenes are characterised by the voluptuousness of the females beloved by Jupiter. *The Sleep of Antiope* (1523, Louvre), which was commissioned by the same Duke of Mantua who employed Giulio in the Palazzo del Te, and was later owned by King Charles I of England and King Louis XIV of France, shows the beautiful daughter of Nycteus, King of Thebes, about to be ravished by Jupiter disguised as a faun, a scene later painted by Titian, Rembrandt, Van Dyck, Jordaens, Fragonard, etc. Antiope lies asleep on a grassy bank, and her nude body seems to irradiate a golden *sfumato* which gives it a languorous fascination and makes it one of the most enticing nudes ever painted. Correggio also painted *Jupiter and Io* for the Duke of Mantua (1532, Dahlem Museum, Berlin). In this scene, the daughter of the river-god Inachos is carried off on a cloud, yet another

[126]

88   Titian, *Danae and the Shower of Gold, c.* 1553

of the love-sick Jupiter's disguises. Io is depicted nude in a state of heightened ecstasy as she is caressed by the cloud.

Another of Correggio's erotic mythologies painted for the Duke of Mantua was *Danae and the Shower of Gold* (1531, Borghese Gallery, Rome). This illustrates the story of the daughter of Acrisius, King of Argos, who was incarcerated in a bronze tower by her father, who had been warned by an oracle that his daughter would bear a son who would kill him. Here she was seen by none other than Jupiter, who descended in a shower of gold which she caught between her legs. The result of this strange mating was Perseus, who fulfilled the words of the oracle. This legend was second only to *Leda and the Swan* in popularity with artists, and was painted by Titian, Mabuse, Tintoretto, Veronese, Rembrandt, Rubens, Van Dyck, Tiepolo, Girodet, Klimt, and many others. Correggio shows Danae catching in her lap what could well be drops of golden semen falling from a cloud. Titian, who was as we have seen the supreme master of erotic painting in sixteenth-century Italy,[41] painted at least four versions of the story for various private patrons (see illustration 88), all showing a provocatively posed and expectant nude Danae with one hand between her legs while a shower of gold coins pours from the sky. An eighteenth-century version by Tiepolo (Stockholm University) shows a nude and very excited Jupiter sitting on a cloud, tossing gold coins down to a sultry-looking, nude Danae reclining on her bed. A fascinating variant on the theme is *Mlle Lange as Danae Offering Herself to the Shower of Gold* by Girodet (1799, Minneapolis Institute of Arts; see illustration 89), which shows a beautiful nude woman in an exotic setting catching gold coins in a cloth, helped by a nude cupid whom she is fondling, the whole bathed in a strangely unreal atmosphere.[42] A later version, and

[127]

89   Girodet, *Mlle. Lange as Danae*, 1799

the most erotic, is *Myth of Danae* by Gustav Klimt (*c*. 1905, Private Collection, Graz, Austria; see illustration 90) in which a nude girl is curled up in a foetal position with gold coins streaming down from the sky and disappearing between her legs. In this connection a 1971 *Children's Advent Calendar* from Germany (see illustration 91) is of interest. It shows a little girl catching in her dress a shower of

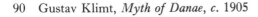

90   Gustav Klimt, *Myth of Danae, c.* 1905

91   *German advent calendar, c.* 1971

gold coins falling from a star in the sky, while excited little gnomes watch from behind trees and bushes. Consciously or subconsciously, the illustrator was making reference to the erotic Danae legend.

In northern Europe during the Renaissance, artists were, of course, far less aware of the erotic potential of the mythologies of the Classical world. Instead, biblically inspired paintings became at times vehicles for the expression of erotic interests. Very often the content of the work seems highly puritanical. Thus Grünewald's painting of *The Lovers* (*c.* 1490s, Strasburg Museum) shows a nude couple in agony, suffering the torture of writhing snakes and various unpleasant insects, with a toad crouching over the woman's vulva. This allegory relates to themes found in medieval church carvings such as those at Moissac in France of the twelfth century. In the same way, altar-pieces by Hieronymus Bosch point out the wages of sin. In *The Temptation of St Anthony* (*c.* 1500, Lisbon Museum), the hermit looks away from a nude woman revealed to him when a toad pulls back a curtain. In *The Garden of Earthly Delights* (*c.* 1510, Prado), the central panel shows a Golden Age where the carefree, naked population surrender to quite open erotic pleasures, but this is seen in the context of side-panels representing earthly paradise with the fall of man and the origin of sin (on the left), and a terrifying hell where sinners are punished by horrific and obscene tortures. Both artists were working in a religious tradition, but it is very likely that they obtained some vicarious pleasure from the subject-matter they chose to paint.

Some northern artists visited Italy in the sixteenth century and so became aware of the Classical traditions at first hand. Thus Jan Gossart, known as Mabuse, introduced Classical subject painting with nude-figure compositions to Flanders after his visit in 1508, and produced his version of *Danae and the Shower of Gold* (1527, Munich Pinakothek). But his favourite subject was Adam and Eve. He painted at least four versions of the nude couple, and there are also many drawings on the theme. One in the Kunsthistorisches Museum, Vienna, is a very overtly sexual interpretation, where the figures are full-frontal nudes in an embrace; another now at the Rhode Island School of Design in America, is dated 1523 and also shows full-frontal nudes, with Adam fondling Eve as she picks an apple with one hand and reaches for his penis with the other.

Dürer was a similar link between Germany and Italy; he produced the painting of *Lucretia* (Munich Pinakothek) in which the nude girl stabs herself between the breasts. There are drawings by Dürer of nude girls in the Vienna Albertina collection, and also one dated 1510 of *Adam and Eve* showing the nude couple embracing passionately. The same subject was often depicted by Hans Baldung Grien in a very erotic manner, the most extreme example being a painting of 1519 (Budapest Museum of Fine Art) which shows the nude couple looking at each other in a very knowing way as each covers their sex with their hands. There is a very explicit scene of *Lot Committing Incest with His Daughters* by Grien in the Kunsthistorisches Museum, Vienna, and the Karlsruhe and Munich Print Rooms have a series of drawings by him of 1514–15 which show brothel scenes and witches' orgies (see illustration 92).

Another German artist who specialised in erotic subjects was Lucas Cranach the

92 Hans Baldung Grien, *Witches' Orgy*, 1514

Elder; apart from paintings of nude girls either standing or reclining, with transparent veils across their sexual areas, whom he called sometimes *Venus* and sometimes *Eve*, his favourite subjects were the sado-masochistic stories of *Lucretia*, *Judith with the Head of Holofernes*, and *Salome with the Head of John the Baptist*. Cranach was a close friend of Luther, and the naturalness and earthiness of the women in his pictures, especially his religious works, which are really only differentiated by their titles from his secular works, reflect an iconoclastic reaction against the sentimental piety of Italy which he shared with many of his fellow artists.

One area of northern Europe that was more closely in touch with Italy in the sixteenth century was France. King Francis I knew Italy at first hand, and invited various artists including Leonardo, Primaticcio, and Rosso to work for him in France. He at one time owned famous paintings of *Leda and the Swan* by both Michelangelo (later destroyed) and Leonardo (now lost). His love of erotic paintings was paralleled by his fondness for beautiful mistresses: collections of both were kept at his Palace of Fontainebleau.[43] He and his successor, Henry IV, were great patrons of French painters, and the so-called School of Fontainebleau produced a wealth of pictures which reflected an awareness of Italian Mannerist art as well as the atmosphere of court life, and parallel the contemporary erotic miniatures produced in the courts of India (see Chapter 3 b). Paintings such as *Venus at the Mirror* (Louvre) and *Diana at the Bath* (Tours Museum) with their thinly veiled nudes reflect a beautifully refined sensualism; more explicit are *Mars and Venus* (Louvre), which shows a man fondling the breasts of a nude woman seated on his lap, and *Ceres and Vulcan* (Wildenstein Collection, New York), which, as we know from a print by Caraglio, originally depicted a fully frontal nude couple kissing and embracing, although the man's penis is now covered by a piece of drapery.

The Classical titles of such pictures were merely a bow to convention, as is clear from *A Court Lady as Flora* and *A Court Lady as an Allegory of Peace* (Aix Museum); certain of these works have been identified as depictions of Diane de Poitiers, Francis I's most famous mistress, including half-length nude portraits in the Dijon Museum and the Musée Condé at Chantilly, and the full-length frontal nude of *Diane de Poitiers as Diana the Huntress* in the Louvre. A curious painting of *c.* 1594 in the Louvre, *Two Court Ladies in the Bath*, has been identified as depicting the Duchesse de Villars with her sister Gabrielle d'Estrées, Henry IV's most famous mistress and mother of several of his children. Gabrielle is shown feeling one of the Duchess's nipples.

Like Titian's many Venuses, these paintings were highly erotic and presumably highly effective pin-ups for the rich and powerful. This gallantry in French art did not, of course, die out with the decline of the School of Fontainebleau at the end of the sixteenth century. Boucher and Fragonard were their heirs a hundred and fifty years later, but Poussin in the seventeenth century depicted for his patron, the erotic poet Giambattista Marino, many Classical scenes that gave him opportunities for creating sexual images. Examples include *Satyr uncovering the sleeping Venus* (National Gallery, London), a very nude *Sleeping Venus* (Dresden) and an extremely explicit version of *Leda and the Swan* (Musée Condé, Chantilly). This last museum also possesses a drawing which shows an ithyphallic satyr caressing a nude nymph, and the Bayonne Museum contains a drawing of a sexual orgy entitled *The Triumph of Bacchus*. One of Poussin's most erotic works is a wash drawing in the Louvre entitled *Acis and Galatea*, which shows a nude man watching from behind a rock while a nude couple have intercourse.

In the Netherlands, too, erotic themes became more common in the sixteenth century. An early example is Lucas van Leyden's etching of *Lot and his Daughters* (1530, Rijksmuseum, Amsterdam), a very explicit scene with Lot kissing and fondling one of the nude girls. Later on, Goltzius specialised in erotic subjects, and produced a series of *Loves of the Gods*, now known only through engravings by J. Matham. He also did a series of drawings relating to brothel life, and a painting of *Leda and the Swan* (1560, Valenciennes Museum). Other subjects included *Susanna and the Elders*, *Eve tempting Adam*, and *Neptune and Galatea*. At the end of the century, Hans van Aachen produced a famous depiction of *Jupiter and Callisto* (*c.* 1600, destroyed in Dresden in 1944) known today through a copy in Berlin and a print by Caraglio. Callisto is shown lying down with her legs open, while Jupiter as a faun with an enormous erection prepares to have intercourse with her. Other such works by van Aachen are now in the Kunsthistorisches Museum, Vienna, which also houses erotic paintings by Bartholomaus Spranger, including *Venus and Adonis*.

The trend towards particularised naturalism rather than generalised idealisation in the Eves and Venuses of Dürer, Cranach, and Grien is continued in the work of Rembrandt in the seventeenth century. Rembrandt was very aware of the Italian Classical tradition and painted many religious and mythological subject pictures, but his version of *Danae and the Shower of Gold* (1636, Leningrad Hermitage) seems more like an intimate glimpse of his private life than a scene from Classical mythology. The beautiful young girl rising from her bed, her nude body caressed by the soft golden rays of dawn, is in fact his wife Saskia, and the painting has a quality of tenderness about it that makes the spectator feel he is intruding. The artist seems to have successfully merged the two females of Renoir's imagination, Venus and Nini. The same can be said of *Bathsheba* (1654, Louvre), for whom Hendrickje Stöffels posed; the nude holding David's letter is a real woman in a real situation, not an idealised figure without a personality. Rembrandt felt free to celebrate love in its open enjoyment in some of his drawings and engravings, including *Jupiter and Antiope* (where the god is shown with an erection approaching the sleeping nude nymph), *Monk in a Cornfield* (where the monk is shown having intercourse), *Sleeping Shepherd* (where a couple are making love while the shepherd sleeps) and the best known, *Ledakant* or *The French Bed* of *c.* 1646 (see illustration 93). This print shows a couple having intercourse on a large bed, and is believed to represent the artist and his mistress, Hendrickje Stöffels; the private, unfinished nature of the work is shown by the experimentation in the treatment of the female figure who appears to have three arms, since the left one is drawn in two positions. The print has all the

93 Rembrandt, *Ledakant*, *c.* 1646

characteristics of Rembrandt's brilliant graphic style, and is evidence of the importance to him of the right of the artist to concern himself without shame with the
most private aspects of life. Similar subjects can be found in the drawings of contemporaries of Rembrandt such as Jan Steen, Isaac Ostade, and David Teniers the
Elder.[44]

Rubens was probably the first artist who dared to paint an erotic portrayal of the
woman he loved, without concealing it behind a biblical or mythological story.
Helène Fourment in a Fur Cloak (1630–31, Kunsthistorisches Museum, Vienna)
shows his amply endowed wife in the nude, clutching a fur cloak around her
shoulders, perhaps having just got out of bed, but this private portrait is a rarity.
More usually, Rubens painted Helène in disguise, as in *The Toilet of Venus, Diana
and her Nymphs surprised by Satyrs*, and *Mars, Venus and Love.* Helène typified the
sort of buxom, earthy women whom Rubens loved, and whom he painted in his
powerfully sensual technique, and his obsession with the charms of such women is
very evident in works such as *The Rape of the Daughters of Leukippos* (Munich
Pinakothek), with its crowd of nude girls being attacked by excited men, and *Pan and
Syrinx* (Buckingham Palace, London), which shows a nude woman being chased by
a satyr. His painting of *Christ with Mary Magdalene* (Munich Pinakothek, see
illustration 87) is similar to works by Titian, Tintoretto, and other Italian artists, in
the way in which a religious subject is used to express a highly erotic sentiment. Mary
Magdalene is depicted in a state of ecstasy as she kneels before the almost nude
figure of Christ, herself half naked and clutching her breasts in her hands. Similarly
erotic scenes can be found in the work of Rubens's pupil Jacob Jordaens, examples
being *King Candaules and his wife* (Stockholm Museum), an etching of *Diana and her
Nymphs receiving Silenus*, and *The Martyrdom of St Appoline* (Petit Palais, Paris),

[133]

which shows a torturer applying a pair of tongs to the tongue of a nude woman.

Italian art of the Baroque period includes many swooning and ecstatic saints in works which are further evidence of repressed sexuality; the best example is perhaps Bernini's life-size, coloured-marble sculpture of *St Theresa in Ecstasy* (1645–52) in the Church of Santa Maria della Vittoria in Rome, in which the saint appears to be in the throes of orgasm.[45] At the beginning of the seventeenth century, the most notorious Italian artist was Caravaggio, whose brawls and drunken rages brought him an early death. Many of his religious commissions were found unacceptable on the grounds of indecorum, for his rejection of idealisation and his love of vivid realism led him to interpret many religious scenes too literally. The nakedness of his altar pieces for Santa Maria del Popolo (1600–1601) was bitterly criticised, as was the bloated figure of the Virgin in *The Death of the Virgin*, said to have been painted from a drowned prostitute fished out of the Tiber. Caravaggio's work was an extension of his life,[46] and many of his paintings of nude male saints and mythological figures suggest a degree of homosexual involvement similar to that found in works by Michelangelo.

Spanish painting seems to reflect a stronger inhibition against nudity than the art of Italy or northern Europe, and yet Spain has produced two of the most famous of all depictions of the female nude. Velazquez painted the *Rokeby Venus* in about 1655 (National Gallery, London; see illustration 94), and the goddess seems a very contemporary example of Spanish beauty as she presents her rear view to our gaze and looks at us via a mirror held by a naked Cupid. André Malraux once described her as 'the first goddess become woman, and therefore of an outstanding historical importance',[47] thereby ignoring the deities painted by Titian, the School of Fontainebleau, Rembrandt, and Rubens; more correctly, the *Venus* of Velazquez is of

94   Velazquez, *Rokeby Venus*, c. 1655

singular aesthetic importance; for its choice of colours, handling of paint, and balance of composition go to make it one of the most beautiful of all paintings of the nude. In particular, the eroticism of the painting is enhanced by the handling of the paint on the back and buttocks of the woman and by the titillation provided by her rear view, although the effect is less obvious here than in Boucher's *Mademoiselle O'Murphy* (see illustration 95).

95   François Boucher, *Mlle. O'Murphy*, 1755

The second masterpiece of Spanish nude painting, Goya's *Naked Maja* of 1800–1805 (Prado; see illustration 96) is a complete contrast to the first. Malraux described her as 'erotic without being voluptuous'[48] and certainly compared with the *Rokeby Venus*, the eroticism is greatly muted. The courtesan[49] is shown completely nude in a fully frontal position, reclining on a sumptiously furnished couch, but the tight handling of the brushwork on her body and the slight awkwardness of her anatomy create a far less sympathetic and desirable result. The companion painting in the Prado in which she is shown clothed is a more beautiful and sensitive work (see illustration 97). There are other works believed to be by Goya which show erotic scenes: a drawing of a clothed woman lifting up her dress to reveal her naked buttocks is in the Cardeiera collection in Madrid,[50] and another of a couple making love in the 'sixty-nine' position is in a private collection in Bordeaux (see illustration 98).

[135]

96   Francisco de Goya, *Nude Maja*, 1800–1805

Many of Goya's etchings show erotic scenes of a very particular variety: his *Capriccios* of 1799 include horrifyingly violent sexual incidents. Cut off from the world by deafness, he parallels the physically imprisoned Marquis de Sade, whose imagination also conjured up intolerable scenes of sexual aberration. At the same time, Fuseli in England was portraying his terrifying nightmares. The end of the eighteenth century saw the return of that sadistic fascination we have seen in the works of earlier artists, but it was preceded by a period when, for the first time, eroticism was sure of itself.

b: Eighteenth and Nineteenth Centuries

French painting of the eighteenth century reflects the amoral, fun-loving atmosphere of court life; the joys of love-making are celebrated with official approval, and the resulting art is the heir to the productions of the sixteenth-century School of Fontainebleau. The Royal patrons of the earlier period, Francis I and Henry IV, with their succession of captivating mistresses, were emulated by that lover of beautiful women and beautiful objects, Louis XV. The King was five years old when he succeeded to the throne on the death of his great-grandfather Louis XIV in 1715. He had no immediate family, and was brought up by his grand uncle, the Duke of Orleans, the intelligent and kindly Regent of France, whose life had been dedicated to the pleasure provided by women and by general dissipation. The new King grew up to be a charming man and an intelligent and much admired ruler, and not surprisingly he shared his guardian's hedonistic interests. At the age of fifteen he was

[136]

97   Francisco de Goya, *Clothed Maja*, 1800–1805

betrothed to the King of Poland's daughter. He fell in love with her at once, and is reported to have proved his love to her nine times on their wedding night. By the time he was twenty-seven he had ten children and was already spending a lot of time with prostitutes. The Queen was exceedingly nice, but, unfortunately, also exceedingly boring, and made no attempt to remain attractive to her husband, who was seven years her junior, or to entertain his friends. She was in the habit of denying her husband access to her bed on Saints' Days, and as her list of saints grew longer and longer, so the King's attentions were more widely distributed. And so began the reigns of his mistresses, of whom the most famous were Madame de Pompadour and Madame du Barry.

When the French court moved from Versailles to Paris at the death of Louis XIV, there was a great demand for artists to decorate apartments in a new style, and the heaviness of the Baroque decorative approach was replaced by the light-hearted

98   Francisco de Goya (?),
     Sixty-nine, c. 1790s

eroticism of the Rococo, while the Rubens style was ousted by that of Watteau. As the Goncourt brothers described it: 'There was everywhere diffused a refined elegance, a delicate voluptuousness, what the epoch itself specified as the quintessence of the agreeable, the complexion of grace and charm, the adornments of pleasure and love . . . Love is the light of this world; love impregnates and permeates it, is its youth and its sincerity; and when you have passed the lakes and the fountains, then the Paradise of Watteau opens before you.'[1]

Watteau was a tragic figure, a semi-permanent invalid, who seems to have foreseen his early death. When he paints the pleasures of love, there is always a note of wistful poetry, as in his masterpiece *The Embarkation from Cythera* (1717, Louvre), which shows a procession of elegant ladies and gentlemen leaving the Island of Love, where they have garlanded a statue of Venus with flowers. This beautiful allegory is well conjured up by the Goncourts: 'It is Love; but it is poetic Love, the Love that contemplates and dreams, modern Love with its aspirations and its coronal of melancholy.'[2] Watteau was a compulsive figure sketcher, and his many notebooks are full of quick but brilliant red-chalk drawings, many being of nudes. Certain of them show a great lack of inhibition, such as one entitled *Le Curieux*, which shows a man looking up a woman's skirt.[3] In the Louvre is a painting of *The Judgement of Paris*, in which the nude Grace is transposed to Watteau's own poetic Cythera, the scene of so many 'galant' trysts: an example is *Le Faux Pas* (Louvre) in which a young woman tries to free herself from the embraces of an amorous young man.

Watteau's Cythera, the Island of Love, lies at the beginning of French eighteenth-century painting, and love remains the paramount subject until the Revolution. The Duke of Orleans, Regent of France, was a great admirer of such paintings: he was, in fact, present when Watteau's *Embarkation* was received by the French Academy as his Diploma work. The Orleans collection was later dispersed, but an album of watercolours in the Restricted Collection of the British Museum has the family coat of arms emblazoned on every page, and may have belonged to the Regent, although the style suggests a slightly later date.[4] The sixty-eight watercolours of this *Histoire Universelle* show explicitly erotic scenes from biblical history and mythological legend. From the Bible, we see Adam and Eve making love, Judith with the head of Holofernes, and Delilah shaving Samson's pubic hair. From mythology there are depictions of Bacchus practising cunnilingus on Ariadne, Jupiter carrying off Ganymede, Neptune violating Medusa, scenes of intimate love-making between Cupid and Psyche, Rinaldo and Armida, and Hercules and Omphale, as well as Jupiter with Callisto, Antiope and Leda. The drawing of *Leda and the Swan* (see illustration 99) is unusual in that it shows Leda in the embraces of the swan, with Jupiter in human form also present, and in the act of copulation. The colouring is rich and expressive, but the draughtsmanship here, as in the rest of the album, is somewhat deficient.

Artists who produced erotic pictures in the period following Watteau's death in 1721 included Pater and Lancret; also J.-F. Schall, three of whose paintings in a Paris private collection show excited nude girls on beds, one manipulating her

99   Antoine Coypel (?), *Jupiter with Leda and the Swan*, from *Histoire Universelle*,
c. 1750

breasts, another playing with a cat between her legs. Engravings were easily obtained
and very popular. Artists who specialised in engravings of erotic subjects included
Lavreince, Eisen, Binet, and Baudouin (see illustration 100). Towards the end of the
century, Louis Boilly was the author of numerous erotic prints at the same time as
he was producing works celebrating the glories of the Revolution.

In 1765, François Boucher was officially made first Court painter to Louis XV,
but he had already been the King's favourite painter for many years, as well as being
the friend and teacher of Madame de Pompadour. Boucher was the archetypal
eighteenth-century French painter, embodying and expressing the tastes and preoccupations of his age. He was passionately devoted to the beauties of the female
figure, and thousands of nude drawings attest to this, as well as hundreds of paintings.
It was the pagan world that he loved to paint, for mythology gave him opportunities
for erotic pictures that the Church would have denied him, and after stories of
Venus, his favourite subject was *Danae and the Shower of Gold*. In 1755, he executed
seven tapestry designs for the King on the subject of *Loves of the Gods*, a favourite
theme since the sixteenth century, as we have seen, and Jupiter was, of course, the
hero. But Boucher's personal deity was Venus, and many of the models who posed
as the Goddess of Love were actually his mistresses. He painted Venus again and
again: *Venus Asleep*; *Venus at the Bath*; *Venus and Mars at the Forge of Vulcan*;
Venus, Mercury and Cupid; and his Venus was a living and passionate deity. The
Goncourts once more capture the right spirit: 'Voluptuousness is the essence of
Boucher's ideal; the spirit of his art is compact of it. And even in his handling of the
conventional nudities of mythology, what a light and skilful hand is his, how fresh
his imagination even when its theme is indecent and how harmonious his gift of

100   P. P. Chossard after Louis Baudouin,
Surprise Visit, 1782

composition, naturally adapted, it might seem, to the arrangement of lovely bodies upon clouds rounded like the necks of swans . . . The flesh he paints has a kind of inviting effrontery; his divinities, nymphs, nereids, all his female nudities are women who have undressed; but who knew better how to undress them? The Venus of whom Boucher dreamt and whom he painted was only the physical Venus; but he knew her by heart.'[5] When Boucher died in 1770, it was in his studio, seated alone in front of an unfinished painting of Venus.

Madame de Pompadour was a beautiful and intelligent woman, an actress and an artist, and she was the King's mistress for fourteen years. Boucher was her favourite artist as well as her confidant, and his painting of *Venus and Mars at the Forge of Vulcan* was one of her first gifts to the King. She employed him to paint decorations for her Chateau at Belleville in 1750, and at the Salon of 1753 she bought his masterpieces, *The Rising of the Sun* and *The Setting of the Sun* (Wallace Collection, London), with their crowds of beautiful nudes. She also commissioned from him a set of four *Loves of Venus* in 1754, extremely erotic compositions by which she hoped, so it is said, to inspire the King, whose affections were beginning to be placed elsewhere. These were later thrown out by the King's son, Louis XVI, who was rather a prudish man—although his wife Marie Antoinette had fruit bowls moulded from her breasts. The paintings were bought by the Marquis of Hertford and are now in the Wallace Collection in London. Another commission was a rustic scene entitled *The Love-Sick God* (now lost) which was said to represent the King and his mistress. Madame de Pompadour was an able draughtswoman, and a book entitled *Mes Loisirs*, which was published in Paris in 1764 with illustrations 'after F.B.' is believed to be her own work.[6] The engravings were described by Portalis in 1877 as very erotic, able if a little unassured, and probably by Madame de Pompadour.[7] It is known that reading was one of Madame de Pompadour's greatest pleasures: in the inventory of her effects listed after her death are over three thousand volumes, which included *Tom Jones*, *Roderick Random*, and *Moll Flanders*. All were sold at public auction except one, a report on prostitution in Paris, which was withdrawn. One of Madame de Pompadour's favourite books was *Histoire de Dom D., Portier des Chartreux*, a highly indecent story of a gardener in a convent.[8] She had it printed on parchment and illustrated with twenty-eight miniatures. Another famous reader, Restif de la Bretonne, reported that after reading the book he ran out and seduced the first two women he met.

Boucher is known to have painted many overtly erotic pictures, an example being *Venus, Mercury and Cupid* (Berlin, Dahlem Museum), where Mercury is shown with an erection. But the most famous of such works were six rustic scenes, commissioned by the King, all of which are believed to have been destroyed in the Tuileries fire in 1871, but not before they were photographed—without the permission of their owner, the Emperor Napoleon III. A recent book[9] suggests that they were originally painted as educational pictures for the rather slow-witted Dauphin, the future Louis XVI, but the explanation offered by both Fuchs and Karwath, that they were a present for Madame de Pompadour's boudoir, seems more likely.[10]

[141]

The scenes included two of nude couples copulating on a bed; a girl buying a winged phallus from a man and playing with her vulva; a man taking a nude woman from behind; a man about to have intercourse with a partly unclothed woman in a seated position while he kisses her exposed breasts (see illustration 101); and a clothed couple playing with one another, the girl's hand on the boy's erect penis, beside a sleeping girl (see illustration 102). Four of the scenes take place out of doors, with sheep and birds in attendance. From the old photographs, the quality appears to have been high. The loss of this decorative scheme is a serious one to the sum total of Western erotic art.

The art historian Michael Kitson wrote in a recent publication: 'With Boucher the cloud of Olympus became the pillows and sheets of an eighteenth-century bed, and Venus and Diana were made into sex symbols of greater accessibility than ever before.'[11] Of none of Boucher's paintings is this more true than of *Mademoiselle O'Murphy* (1755, Munich, Alte Pinakothek; see illustration 95). In his later years, Louis XV kept a succession of common prostitutes in a villa in the town of Versailles, and this beautiful Irish girl was its first and best-known occupant. Louise O'Murphy's father was a cobbler, and all her five sisters were prostitutes. She went to Paris to make her fortune and was immediately noticed by Boucher. When the King saw the painting, he called for the model, and she remained his mistress for several years. When the cobbler heard the news, he is said to have remarked: 'Ah me, among all my girls not one is virtuous.'[12] Louise brought about the end of her relationship with the King by asking him one day: 'What terms are you on now with the old lady?', referring to Madame de Pompadour. She lived for

101 François Boucher, *Pastoral Scene*, c. 1750s

102 François Boucher, *Pastoral Scene*, c. 1750s

another fifty years, but Boucher's painting captures her in the prime of her life at the age of eighteen, lying provocatively nude on her stomach and thus hiding her sexual charms. There is no coyness in the blatant titillation of her superb body as she sinks into the silks and satins that cover the beautifully upholstered chaise-longue, her enticing buttocks demanding to be stroked and fondled. The depiction of her skin is one of the most erotic passages in the history of oil-painting; in fact, under the magic of Boucher's brush, even the draperies and cushions seem to take on that tactile quality that attracts and excites. As Kenneth Clark wrote: 'Freshness of desire has seldom been more delicately expressed than by Miss O'Murphy's round young limbs, as they sprawl with undisguised satisfaction on the cushions of her sofa'.[13] Only a handful of artists have ever been able to create such a powerful and unashamedly erotic effect in paintings of the nude.

When Madame de Pompadour died in 1764, the King mourned her deeply; nevertheless, her place was soon taken by Madame du Barry, who surpassed her in beauty, but was otherwise entirely commonplace. Madame de Pompadour liked intelligent company and was often painted reading a book or looking at a sculpture; Madame du Barry was illiterate and liked artists to depict her in the nude. Allegrain made various nude sculptures of her beautiful figure, and Fragonard painted her as the nude *Queen of Hearts* crowned by Cupid. Madame du Barry was the daughter of a monk and was discovered by the King working in a milliner's shop; as Boucher was to Madame de Pompadour, so was Fragonard to her. Like Boucher, Fragonard reflected his times, but he was a more lightweight painter. The Goncourts called him 'the Cherubino of erotic painting', and his favourite subjects had such titles as *Cupid Stealing a Nightgown* and *The Stolen Kiss*. Madame du Barry bought four paintings including *Love Enflaming the Universe* and *Venus and Cupid* in 1770, and then commissioned him to execute decorations for her chateau at Louvieciennes. The paintings, which are now in the Frick Collection in New York, show the awakening and progress of love in scenes such as *The Lover Crowned* and *Storming the Citadel*, where a young couple frolic and gambol in a park scattered with statues of *Venus and Cupid*.

Fragonard made his reputation with *The Swing* (1767, Wallace Collection, London). This beautiful picture of a pretty girl in a pink dress kicking up her legs as she rides on a swing originated in a commission to another artist, Doyen, who was asked to paint a man's mistress 'sitting on a swing being pushed by a bishop. As for me, I should like to appear somewhere in the composition so that I am in a position to observe the legs of this charming creature, and I should be even better pleased, if you should feel like enlivening the picture still farther.'[14] The commission was passed on to Fragonard, and he created his most successful work. The lady is clothed in yards of pink and blue silk, suspended in mid-air on her swing, kicking up her legs and revealing her satin stockings to an excited young man lying amongst some roses in the foreground. All the delicacy, charm, and light-hearted eroticism of the period is summed up in the picture.

Fragonard specialised in bedroom scenes, many of which were destroyed in the nineteenth century as indecent, though sketches and prints remain to show us his fascination with this subject. An oil sketch entitled *The Longed-for Moment* (Picard Collection, Paris) shows a nude girl on a bed in the arms of her lover; an ink sketch in the Musée Cognacq-Jay in Paris depicts a rustic scene of a couple making love in the straw of a stable watched by the cattle. Other such scenes include *The Useless Resistance* (National Museum, Stockholm) and *The Orgy* (Boymans Museum, Rotterdam). In the Louvre there are two oval oil sketches on this theme: *Cupid Stealing a Nightgown*, which shows Cupid removing the gown from the body of a nude girl on a bed who makes little attempt to stop him, and *All Ablaze*, in which naked *putti* uncover the nude body of a sleeping girl, while another holds up a torch to illuminate her naked beauty. These little boudoir scenes breathe a special sort of poetic eroticism. Less successful are the more contrived bedroom scenes related to fire, such as *My Nightgown is Alight* and *Aquatic Sports*, now known only through engravings. In the latter,[15] three almost-nude girls are pretending to be frightened by an unseen fire and at the same time are fascinated by jets of water spurting out of phallic nozzles appearing through a trap door and aimed right between their legs. The engraver has added a little poem full of very obvious *doubles-entendres*.[16]

As the century progressed, voices were raised that questioned the morality of an art based solely on sexual pleasure. One of the loudest was the critic and author, Denis Diderot. In reviewing a Salon Exhibition of 1767, he wrote of Baudouin's *Wedding Night*: 'All that preaches depravity is made to be destroyed, and all the more so if the work is especially perfect.' Boucher was his main enemy: 'What

103　Jean Baptiste Greuze, *The Broken Pitcher*, 1773

imagination can a man have who has passed his life in the study of mythological prostitution? . . . His paintings are nothing but beauty spots, rouge, gew-gaws. . . . They betray the imagination of a man who spends his time with prostitutes of the lowest grade.'[17] Diderot wanted art to be morally uplifting, and he knew who could do it: 'Greuze is an artist after my own heart; his style satisfies me; it is moral picture-making. The brush has been too long used to reproduce debauchery and vice, it is well to see it join hands with dramatic poetry, to arouse in our hearts hatred of vice and a love of virtue.'[18] Greuze was the author of such works as *Filial Piety* and *The Fruits of a Good Education*, but he also showed a great fondness for domestic tragedies such as *The Broken Pitcher* (Louvre, see illustration 103), *The Dead Bird*, and *The Broken Mirror* (both Wallace Collection, London), which always concentrated on pubescent girls with loose clothing which revealed their ripening breasts, and which contained clear allusions to loss of virginity. Yet if these could be described by some stretch of the imagination as studies in virtue, the same could certainly not be said of *The Sisters* (1788, Louvre) which shows two sugary girls with bare breasts fondling each other and embracing, or of *Ariane* (Wallace Collection, London), a study of a girl in a state of ecstasy with eyes cast heavenwards as she clasps her hand to her bodice and reveals her well-developed breasts like a teenage Mary Magdalene. The coy titillation and simpering sentimentality of these pictures is quite nauseating, and it is sad to find Diderot pretending that these are healthier than the works of Boucher with their honest sexuality.

Diderot's professed morality is called into question by an erotic novelette which he wrote in 1748, entitled *Les Bijoux Indiscrètes* (*The Indiscreet Jewels*). This is the tale of a magic ring which has the power of making women's vaginas (the 'jewels' of the title) tell their life-stories. In Chapter 47, the speaker belongs to a courtesan said to be a satirical portrait of Madame de Pompadour: 'This noble Lord was succeeded by a couple of Privateer Commanders lately returned from cruising. Being intimate friends, they fucked me as they had sailed, in company, endeavouring who should show most vigour and serve the readiest fire. Whilst the one was riding at anchor, I towed the other by his tarse, and prepared him for a fresh try. Upon a modest computation, I reckoned in about eight days I received a hundred and eighty shot.'[19]

The taste for erotica which was so amply satisfied by French artists in the eighteenth century was also catered for in England at the same period, and many artifacts were decorated with erotic themes (see illustration 104). Vice and its punishment had been the theme of popular prints for a very long time, and in eighteenth-century England William Hogarth made this his speciality. He called his engravings 'modern moral subjects', for he was presenting a clear moral argument in a series like *A Harlot's Progress* of 1732, which told the story of a young girl who takes up prostitution and dies within the year in Bridewell Prison. This series, however, was inspired by an oil sketch that he proudly exhibited in his studio of a 'common harlot . . . just rising about noon out of her bed', and the prints show a clear interest in the erotic, coupled with a knowledge that such a subject would

104 *Copulating Couple*,
concealed inside lid of
snuff-box, Birmingham,
England, *c.* 1765

produce a big demand. This knowledge had enabled him to sell large numbers of his print of *The Beggar's Opera* of 1728, helped of course by the scandal caused by the elopement of the star, Lavinia Fenton, with the Duke of Bolton. Hogarth's fascination for sexual matters is very clearly reflected in the two series of paintings named *Before* and *After* (1730–31), which relate to the violation of a young girl. The interior scenes are said to have been painted for 'a certain vicious nobleman', apparently the Duke of Montagu. The resulting prints are full of symbols, such as a broken mirror and a page of a book with the words 'all agreed she did not die a maid'. And in the second scene of the outdoor pair (in the Fitzwilliam Museum, Cambridge), the man's sexual organs are partly visible as his breeches are not yet buttoned up. These works seem to arise out of direct experience, and are unlike the voluptuous fantasies of Boucher or Fragonard. Professor Lawrence Gowing has said of them: 'Hogarth's imagination remains intensely erotic.'[20] Certainly they are evidence of a clear desire to moralise, but the erotic interest is strong. This was recognised by Hogarth's contemporaries, and as a result of *The Harlot's Progress*, a promised royal commission was cancelled. It is interesting to note, however, that the Royal Collection at Windsor Castle contains a Hogarth drawing entitled *Boys Peeping at Nature* (1731), which shows a boy looking under the skirt that has been put round a statue of a nude woman.[21]

Hogarth's greatest ambition was to achieve fame as a history painter, and one of his most brilliant works in this vein was *Satan, Sin and Death* (1735–40, Tate Gallery, London), derived from Milton's *Paradise Lost*.[22] This is a dramatic and powerful proto-Romantic work and includes a sensual nude woman representing sin. Later in the century it inspired the caricaturist James Gillray to produce his own version, with Queen Charlotte, the wife of King George III, as Sin (1792). Gillray was the author of many prints which attacked the sexual adventures of figures in high society, such as *The Fall of Phaeton* (1788), which depicts the Prince Regent falling out of his carriage, preceded by Mrs Fitzherbert his mistress, whose naked behind he is managing to observe very closely. Perhaps the most famous of these prints is *Fashionable Contrasts* (1792), subtitled *The Duchess's little Shoe yielding to the Magnitude of the Duke's Foot*, a satirical view of the Duchess of York which shows a pair of legs with female shoes in a horizontal position with a male pair between them. This was Gillray's reaction to the infatuation of contemporary journalists with the none-too-pretty new wife of George III's favourite son, a woman whose principal asset was said to have been the smallness of her feet.[23] One of Gillray's political engravings is *Presentation of the Mahometan Credentials or The final resource of French Atheists* (1793), a caricature on Fox's sympathies for the French Revolution, which shows the new ambassador holding a gigantic scroll in a phallic position, with two seals hanging below in the position of testicles.

The same Hogarth history painting was also copied by Thomas Rowlandson, who can claim to be England's greatest erotic artist. Trained at the Royal Academy and also in Paris, where he studied the works of Boucher and Fragonard, Rowlandson became a brilliant draughtsman who specialised in depicting the everyday trials of the common man in drawings and engravings that bear witness to a marvellous sense of the ridiculous. His works are in the tradition of Hogarth, but without the moral overtones, and also without the bitterness of Gillray. His interests were the ordinary pleasures of life, eating, drinking, gambling (his great passion), and making love, and all these are depicted in his prints. He was a friend of the fast-living Prince Regent, and for him produced a series of drawings 'notoriously of free tendency as regards subject' which are in the Royal Collection at Windsor Castle. In 1810 he issued a set of ten erotic prints with descriptive poems for his friends; these were published posthumously as *Pretty Little Games for Young Ladies and Gentlemen; With Pictures of Good Old English Sports and Pastimes* in c. 1872.[24] These included *The Country Squire New Mounted* (and it is certainly not a horse that he has mounted), *Rural Felicity or Love in a Chaise* (a couple having most uncomfortable intercourse in a carriage), *New Feats of Horsemanship* (a couple having quite unbelievable intercourse on horseback) and *The Wanton Frolic* (a girl revealing herself to a man holding his large and erect penis, see illustration 105). This last print was accompanied with the following mock-serious comment: 'We object—strongly object—to the absurd form of the taper which the gentleman holds in his hand. It looks more like a carrot than the genuine article. It burns brightly enough, but the shape is monstrously unreal—as any fair devotee will know.'

Rowlandson's erotic prints form a small but important part of his total output.[25] His most recent biographer has called his work 'an indispensable commentary on the manners and events of the period in which he lived',[26] and his erotic prints are an integral part of that commentary. Yet ever since his death, these erotica have been divorced from the rest of his work and either ignored or condemned. Even today, the large collections of Rowlandson's erotic prints in the British Museum and the Victoria and Albert Museum, London, remain uncatalogued and hidden in the Reserved Collections, where they can only be seen if applicants have special reasons. The first major study on Rowlandson was by Joseph Grigo at the height of the Victorian period in 1880, and he virtually omits all reference to erotic works except for *Exhibition Stare Case* (1811), a jumble of women falling down the stairs at the Royal Academy galleries and exhibiting their nudity under their disturbed dresses.

[147]

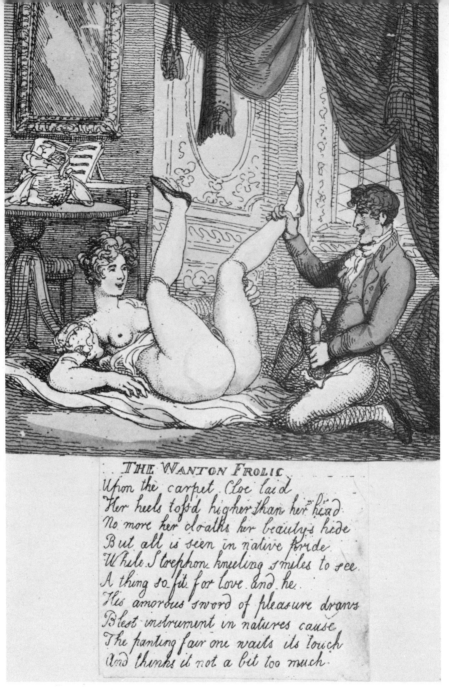

THE WANTON FROLIC

Upon the carpet Cloe laid
Her heels toss'd higher than her head.
No more her cloaths her beauty's hide
But all is seen in native pride.
While Strephon kneeling smiles to see.
A thing so fit for love. and he.
His amorous sword of pleasure draws
Blest instrument in natures cause
The panting fair one waits its touch
And thinks it not a bit too much.

105   Thomas Rowlandson, *The Wanton Frolic*, 1810

This print he feels he has to excuse: 'The Editor acknowledges the situation is
treated with a license which, perhaps, may be held to verge on the inadmissable. . . .
If the subject is treated with more freedom than is desirable according to the luster
ideas of our generation, at least its humours are innoxious, and, we trust, guiltless of
offence'.[27] More recently, A. L. Oppé wrote: 'In his indecency, he is utterly without
passion, presenting or dragging in the fact, in his earlier and lighter efforts, merely

[148]

for the sake of producing an effect like that of speaking a naughty word. His later abscondita are mere accumulations of pictured filth, incredible elaborations of things chalked by gutter-snipes on street walls or worse.'[28] This attitude was foreshadowed by a remark made late in life by George Cruikshank, the caricaturist who had been as boisterous a character as Rowlandson, but who later turned to lecturing on the evils of alcohol: 'Rowlandson suffered himself to be led away from the exercise of his legitimate subjects to produce works of a reprehensible tendency.'[29]

Rowlandson showed a particular interest in erotic subjects very early in his career, when he copied nude paintings by Titian, Francesco Albano, Rubens, and Boucher. A beautiful early composition is *The Discovery* of 1799, a scene of two reclining nymphs surprised in the forest by a young shepherd. It has the rustic charm of the French School of the eighteenth century, and is truly erotic without being at all explicit. More characteristic are prints which give candid expression to his feelings about sexual life, usually without great emotional involvement, but with gentle amusement and a lack of salaciousness. The degree of explicitness varies. *Searching the Philosopher's Stone* shows an old man busily at work in his laboratory while his young wife enjoys the kisses of her lover in a further room. *The Star Gazer* shows an old man looking through his telescope in his study while his young wife has intercourse with her young lover in the next room. Both are equally valid examples of the artist's work.

Rowlandson shared his contemporaries' fascination for the exotic East which William Beckford described in *Vathek* (1782) as a world of debauchery and sensual indulgence, and which inspired the voluptuous nudes of Ingres and Delacroix and the fantastic architecture of John Nash's Brighton Pavilion built for the Prince Regent. *The Pasha* shows an oriental potentate in a state of sexual excitement, surrounded by attentive nude slaves. In *The Harem* a similarly excited caliph watches a parade of nude harem girls. According to a recent commentator, this second print is very revealing; 'Expressionless like dolls, lined up in almost identical attitudes . . . these imaginery houris differ only in their perimeters: the schematism of the design as well as the pedantry with which the sexes are inscribed into their clean shaved bellies, are all characteristic of the imaginative technique of the masturbation-fantasist.'[30]

It is known that these and most of Rowlandson's other erotic prints date from his later years, when his vitality had waned considerably. Whether or not one accepts a strictly Freudian interpretation of the work, there is certainly a voyeuristic element, which finds parallels in the recent erotic prints by Pablo Picasso of an elderly artist watching young couples having intercourse, and these late works by both artists can be seen in terms of the fantasies of wish fulfilment. Works in this vein by Rowlandson include *The Observers* (two old men in uniform watch a young couple having intercourse on a sofa), *The Happy Teacher* (an old teacher with a girl on his lap is watched by two colleagues through the window), *The Curious Parson* (an old parson examines a nude girl), *The Congregation* (a group of men gaze at a nude girl with her legs apart on a raised dais), and *Susanna and the Elders* (two old men ogle a nude girl).

[149]

Among Rowlandson's other erotic subjects are *The Empress Catherine of Russia receiving her Brave Guard* which shows the men lining up to enjoy a little intercourse with their notorious Empress, and one in the process of doing so,[31] and *Departure of the Husband* (see illustration 106), a scene in a tavern with a woman having intercourse with a sailor while she waves a handkerchief out of the window to a departing ship. Another print called *Meditations among the Tombs* (see illustration 107) shows a young couple having sexual relations leaning against a church wall, with a funeral service in progress nearby, and surrounded by tombstones with such legends as 'Here lies intombed beneath these bricks the scabbard of ten thousand pricks.' And one of the most amusing is *Les Lunettes*, an illustration to a story by La Fontaine about a nun who becomes pregnant in a convent. The nuns, one of whom is a man in disguise, are parading in front of the abbess with their robes lifted; the culprit has become so excited at the moment of his inspection that his penis knocks the abbess's glasses off her nose.

An important contemporary of Rowlandson was also producing erotic works of art in London at this time. This was the Swiss artist Henry Fuseli. His erotica, however, was in the form of drawings, and they were strictly not for publication. Fuseli was

106   Thomas Rowlandson, *Departure of the Husband, c.* 1815

107　Thomas Rowlandson, *Meditations among the Tombs, c.* 1815–20

born and brought up in Zurich in a strict Lutheran household. His father refused to allow him to develop his artistic ability, and forced him to become ordained as a minister. Fuseli's wit already showed in the text he chose for his probationary sermon: 'What will this babbler say?'[32] He soon had to flee Zurich as a result of an inflammatory article he had written; and he made his way to London, where he began his artistic career.

An early writer on Fuseli described him as 'always very susceptible of the passion of love'.[33] Another commentator wrote that the artist lay on his back to admire the Michelangelo frescoes of the Sistine Ceiling on his visit to Rome in a position 'necessary for a body fatigued like his with the pleasant gratifications of a luxurious city'.[34] We know that Aretino was one of his favourite authors, and that his speech and behaviour shocked many of his contemporaries. He had a rather prosaic wife whom he was continually trying to persuade to use swear-words, and he had various affairs, of which the best documented was with Mary Wollstonecraft in 1790. He produced many hundreds of erotic drawings, some of which verged on the obscene, which are very revealing of an artist with a repressed childhood. They are certainly not the work of an oversexed libertine, however; they express the obsessions of a man who was painfully aware of his lack of sex appeal owing to his diminutive height and unattractive disposition.[35]

Most of Fuseli's erotic drawings date from the second half of the 1790s, and show elegantly dressed courtesans with exotic hairstyles, for example, *The Debutante* (Tate Gallery, London), which includes three grotesquely attired women watching a young girl sewing. They are full of irrational details which grow out of the artist's own erotic dream world, but they also owe something to the erotic atmosphere of sixteenth-century Mannerism, for example the works of Parmigianino, Bandinelli, and Bellange whom Fuseli much admired. They also recall his fervent devotion to Rousseau, whose *Confessions* contain an expression of a personal erotic attitude. Basically, however, these erotic drawings express Fuseli's life-long obsession with 'lascivious, haughty, almost bestial women'[36] and they reveal his fetishistic interest in hair. They give expression to his hidden wishes and private dreams, and thus relate to his better-known works on the theme of the *Incubus* and the *Succubus*,[37] the visitation of the devil in the form of a horse or, more commonly, a male or female to people asleep in their beds in order to have sexual relations with them. These literal night-mares were an obsession he shared in public, through drawings and paintings, but the courtesan drawings were essentially private productions, shared only with a very few personal friends. A good example is *The Toilet* (Brinsley Ford Collection, London), which shows a woman with naked breasts wearing a strange wig crowned with long trailing feathers, seated at a dressing-table and attended by two similarly grotesque women, the whole breathing an atmosphere of disturbing eroticism. A more decorous version of this work was used in engraved form with the title *Folly and Innocence* to illustrate the 1806 edition of Cowper's poems.[38] These courtesan drawings form an important part of Fuseli's work; Sacheverell Sitwell has compared them to Goya's *Capriccios* in the degree to which they express the disturbing illogicality of the artist's dream-world.[39]

The eroticism of Fuseli's work is, however, not confined to such private works. A painting of 1799 in the Kunsthaus, Zurich, shows a nude woman in chains being embraced by a shadowy phantom. His illustrations to Shakespeare are filled with erotic imagery, especially those for *Much Ado About Nothing*. In a sketchbook in the British Museum is a drawing for *Timon of Athens* which shows Timon in a cave in the background with two alluring and provocative women in the foreground. For this, the artist had chosen the only scene in the play where these women appear, and in the published version of the illustration he thought it prudent to leave the women out. Erotic scenes appear among Fuseli's later work as well, for instance *Woman seen from the back* (Kunsthaus, Zurich) of 1817, which shows a tall fantastic woman with elaborate head-dress wearing a long clinging dress. A related drawing (Edward Croft-Murray Collection, London; see illustration 108) shows a woman seen from the back, standing in front of a fireplace and looking in a mirror. The lower part of her dress is open, revealing naked buttocks and legs. The perverse humour of the artist takes the eroticism further: the woman's exotic head-dress is coiffured to resemble a flaccid penis hanging down her back between two testicles, and the supports

[152]

108 Henry Fuseli, *Woman by a Fireplace,*
c. 1817

on either side of the chimney-breast in front of her are in the form of enormous erect
phalluses. Other late drawings include *The Embrace* (*c.* 1815, Kunstsammlung,
Basle), which shows two nude figures entwined; and *The Kiss* (1819, Kunsthaus,
Zurich) in which a nude man passionately kisses a woman seated at a spinet.[40]

Fuseli also executed a number of explicitly sexual drawings which verge on the
obscene. Although rarely seen, these were known about soon after the artist's death.
In his diary, Benjamin Robert Haydon, a pupil of Fuseli, recorded a meeting with
John Flaxman on 13 July, 1826: 'Flaxman said "He has left, I understand, behind
him some drawings, shockingly indelicate." "Has he, Sir," I replied. "Yes, Mr
Haydon. Poor wretch!" said Flaxman, looking ineffably modest.'[41] Another observer
wrote in 1829: 'Fire, however, fell amongst most of these obscene drawings when he
died—nor do I blame the hand of his widow who kindled it.'[42] It is not known how
many obscene drawings Mrs Fuseli consigned to her kitchen stove, but certainly
some have survived. In 1943, Sacheverell Sitwell described some he had seen as
being too obscene ever to be published.[43] Three years later, Ruthven Todd in his
interesting book on eighteenth-century art and science entitled *Tracks in the Snow*
described six such drawings which he had recently owned as 'among the finest of
(Fuseli's) works. . . . They possess an extra-ordinary atmosphere, where the faces

[153]

109   Henry Fuseli, *Bedroom Scene, c.* 1820s

110   Theodore Mattias Von Holst, *Bedroom Scene, c.* 1820s

of the actors are quite unmoved by the strange actions which they perform', and went on to say: 'My only regret is that I am unable, under our present dubious legal system, to reproduce several of them here in their entirety; all that I can do is to give some details.'[44] The details he reproduces are from four drawings now in the Victoria and Albert Museum, London. Only one of these is definitely from Fuseli's hand (see illustration 109). This is an unfinished pencil and wash drawing in Fuseli's characteristic style, showing three nude girls on a bed servicing a nude man. The girls all have exotic hairstyles, and the drawing is of high quality. A second water-colour drawing (see illustration 110) is much more highly finished, and shows two girls on a bed playing with a nude boy who has an erection. The girls have very elaborate hairstyles, and the style of the drawing is very tight and precise. It is probably by Fuseli's pupil Theodore Mattias von Holst, who is remembered for having married a wildly jealous woman who kept a knife in her bodice to use on her husband if necessary. The other two drawings are weaker, and are probably by another of Fuseli's pupils, Thomas Wainewright, famous in his day as a forger and poisoner. One shows an old woman inspecting a young girl's vulva, and the other depicts a half-undressed couple having intercourse on a dressing-table while an old

[155]

woman walks past, taking no interest in the proceedings. Although these drawings are not from Fuseli's hand, they clearly owe a lot to him in both style and subject-matter.

There are two other erotic drawings by Fuseli in Edward Croft-Murray's collection. One is in ink over pencil (see illustration 111) and shows two elegantly coiffured

111   Henry Fuseli, *Lesbian Couple, c.* 1815–20

girls in a lesbian activity. One half-undressed girl sits in front of a mirror which stands on a dressing-table; with her right hand she plays with the clitoris of a nude girl who sits on her lap, watching in the mirror, and she also kisses the girl's right breast. It is a quick sketch which shows Fuseil's remarkable abilities as a draughts-man, and it breathes a beautifully tender atmosphere of eroticism. The other drawing is in ink with a grey wash, and shows a man and a woman standing at opposite ends of a small table, on which stands a lamp (see illustration 112). The woman is clothed

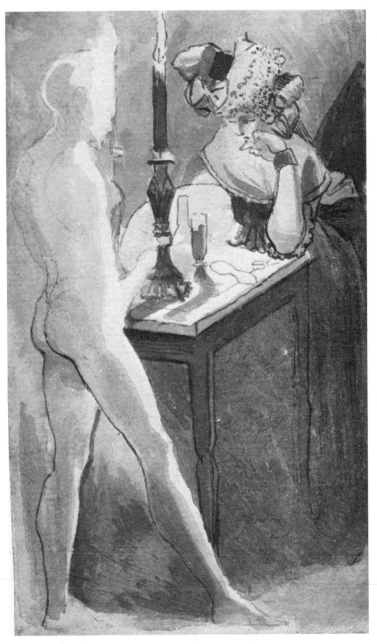

112   Henry Fuseli, *Couple by Candlelight*, c. 1815–20

and has an elaborate head-dress; she is looking at the man who is nude and is displaying a large erection. The man's figure is only sketched in outline, but the work is a strong piece of drawing and the domesticity of the scene suggests it may depict Fuseli and his wife.

Fuseli's erotic drawings were intensely private productions, expressions of his personal fantasies and obsessions. They relate to his more public works, but tell us a lot about himself. They also include some of his finest drawings. Professor Ganz is surely quite wrong to apologise for these works as expressing the contempt and moral indignation of the satirist.[45] Eudo Mason is nearer the mark when he writes: 'His obscenity was certainly not that of the naïve sensualist but of the disappointed sentimentalist.'[46] Such works need no apology. They are among Fuseli's finest and most important productions.

Erotic works played an important part in the careers of Rowlandson and Fuseli, but for many artists, they are merely a normal part of artistic development. Such is the case with another member of the English School, J. M. W. Turner. It is known that after Turner's death, the critic John Ruskin, one of his executors, destroyed certain of his drawings which he considered objectionable.[47] This should cause no surprise when one bears in mind Ruskin's intense prudery and Turner's sexual licence. Turner never married, but he had a strong sexual appetite. Throughout his life he had numerous affairs, beginning with a musician's widow named Mrs Danby, by whom he had three children, and culminating towards the end of his life in his clandestine relationship with the good-natured and intelligent Mrs Booth of Chelsea, in whose house he used to stay under the name of Admiral Booth. He is known to have frequented the London brothels in early life, and Ruskin must have been well aware of this aspect of the artist's life, for he told the journalist Walter Thornbury, who was planning a biography, that one of the main facets of Turner's personality was sensuality. He added somewhat surprisingly, 'Don't try to mask the dark side,' words which Thornbury took at their face value since his subsequent book[48] caused a sensation with its account of an artistic genius who was also a drunkard, a womaniser, a begetter of bastards, and a week-end frequenter of low-sailors' haunts in Wapping, where he would 'wallow until Monday morning'. It turned out that, in fact, Turner's visits to Wapping were to collect rents on some property bequeathed to him by an aunt, but Thornbury's picture was not entirely untrue.[49]

Traces of sexual interest are not obvious in Turner's work, but they certainly exist. Among the many landscapes in the Turner Bequest at the Tate Gallery in London are two oil paintings of nude couples making love, one of which is entitled *Venus and Psyche*.[50] It has been suggested that some of the rather indistinct landscapes of his later period take on the appearance of nude women when turned on their side, and Adrian Stokes sees his numerous tunnels and tree-glades and silhouetted towers and hills as psychological vaginas and penises.[51]

The British Museum possesses a large collection of Turner's sketchbooks dating from all periods of his career, and at least nine of these contain erotic drawings. It is surprising that these escaped Ruskin's bonfire, but in all probability he did not realise what they represented. In the *Swiss Figures Sketch Book* of 1802, for instance, there is a drawing of two nude girls on a bed.[52] It has all the characteristics of an actual event, and is very probably autobiographical. *The Lowther Sketch Book* of 1809–10 includes many carefully-drawn female nudes which are described in the official catalogue of the collection[53] as *academic studies*, yet the poses of the models would never have been permitted in the studios. They are in fact private works showing full frontal nudes reclining on beds, the viewpoint often being straight up the legs.[54] It is interesting to notice that the book also includes an almost illegible poem on an erotic theme, one line of which reads: 'as a jewel guarding her breast'. The *Woodcock Shooting Sketch Book* of 1810–12 includes a drawing described in the official catalogue as *life study*, which shows a female nude in a full-frontal pose kneeling on the side of a bed, holding one breast: a very unacademic work.[55] The *Petworth Sketch Book* of 1830 contains some of Turner's most beautiful watercolours: one shows a nude woman lying on a bed, and in another, a nude woman is sitting in front of a dressing table.[56]

Other sketchbooks at the British Museum show very explicit erotic scenes. Two books of colour studies dating from 1834 include numerous pencil and watercolour sketches which show a nude couple on a bed engaging in all varieties of sexual intercourse including fellatio and cunnilingus.[57] One of the most interesting is the *Academy Auditing Sketch Book* of 1824 which is inscribed in Ruskin's handwriting: 'They are kept as evidence of the failure of mind only.' The catalogue gives the drawings such titles as *Group*, *Figures wrestling*, *Satyrs at play*, *Nymphs and satyrs*, and *Mercury and Argus*, titles which disguise very sketchy but explicit scenes of sexual activity.[58] Numerous men with erections are shown copulating with women or fondling them; on one page, a nude man with an enormous erection is grabbing a nude woman (see illustration 113). These drawings are not of high artistic quality;

113   J. M. W. Turner, *Nymph and Satyr*, 1824

114 J. M. W. Turner, *Sheet of Sexual Drawings, c.* 1820s

rather they are the sort of quick sketch that anyone with a sexual imagination could produce, and they make no pretensions to be anything else. But quite different is an uncatalogued and unpublished sheet of drawings in the Restricted Collection of the British Museum, which was originally also part of the Turner Bequest.[59] On the back, among a mass of very faint pencil lines, a clear sketch shows a woman performing fellatio on a man. On the front (see illustration 114) at the right-hand side is a pen and ink close-up view of a man's penis entering the vulva of a woman whose legs are over his shoulders. The revelation is on the left-hand side, where a reasonably well-finished watercolour sketch shows a nude man kneeling beside a nude woman whom he is kissing, while he very clearly manipulates her vulva with his fingers. This drawing is undoubtedly by Turner, and is far more painstaking and accomplished than any of his other erotic sketches. It is, in fact, an outstanding example of Turner's highly uneven figurative work, and would appear to be a Classical study since the male figure has the pointed ears and twisting tail of a seilenos. These erotic studies do not play an important part in Turner's work, but they add considerably to our understanding of the artist's strong sexual appetite.

With Turner we are well into the nineteenth century, which proved to be a period more obsessed with sex than any that had gone before. Sexual undercurrents in Victorian art will be discussed in Chapter 5, and Rossetti and Beardsley are also considered in the essay on Decadent Art, section c of the present chapter. As far as France was concerned, sex lay behind a great deal of nineteenth-century art, especially that sanctioned by the official Academy, but the freest liberties were taken by illustrators. We have already seen how eighteenth-century engravers such as Eisen and Baudouin produced a wealth of erotic subjects; during the following century, there was a great vogue for erotic prints, such as the series by Tony Johannot depicting *Les Amours des Grands Hommes*. *Napoleon et Madame de Georges* (1804; see illustration 115) shows the Emperor sporting a large erection, with his nude mistress in his bedroom, the pair being surprised by Josephine; in *Louis XVIII et Madame Cayla*, the King is picking snuff off the naked posterior of a lady who is

115 Tony Johannot,
*Napoleon and Madame
de Georges*, 1804

lying across his legs on a bed. Other prints depict the intrigues of Louis XIV and Louis XV. Similar portrayals of famous people include a series of Napoleon's marshalls by Etienne Bericourt, and *Lamartine et Elvire* by Nicholas Maurin. Other illustrators who specialised in erotic prints include Gavarni, Deveria, Gravelot, and Le Poitevin, and a favourite subject was the sexual profligacy of members of the Church (see illustration 116). Books with erotic illustrations became very popular; early in the century, works by Bernard appeared with prints after drawings by Prud'hon, and in the 1830s, many erotic prints were produced by Henry Monnier, the pupil of Girodet and Gros and friend of Balzac, whose works were later much admired by Edmond de Goncourt[60] (see illustration 117). Among the finest erotic prints of the nineteenth century are the illustrations to novels drawn by Martin van Maele, Jules-Adolphe Chauvet, and Louis Legrand.[61] These have a delicacy and refinement that relate them to the best illustrations of the previous century.

Neo-classical sculpture can appear to be cold and passionless, hardly relevant to a discussion of celebrations of love. But close examination shows this to be an inaccurate generalisation. Flaubert admitted to actually kissing Psyche in Canova's *Eros and Psyche* in his excitement, and Wordsworth was deeply shocked by the same group. Writing of Canova, Mario Praz declared: 'for the refined and nerveless sensuality, for voluptuousness and repressed eroticism . . . the Neo-classic doctrine offered itself not as a check, but as a supremely appropriate and felicitous medium.'[62] Neo-classicism was mainly a male orientated movement, owing much to the personal tastes of the homosexual historian Winckelmann, whose androgynous ideal was 'the incorporation of the forms of prolonged youth in the female sex with the masculine forms of a beautiful young man', as he explained in his *History of Ancient Art*. This ideal was personified in Cipriani's canvases for Lansdowne House in London (1775, Heim Gallery, London) illustrating *The Education of Achilles* and also many of Sergel's delightful sculptures such as *The Faun* (1770–74, Stockholm National Museum). And Thorvaldsen's marble reliefs, for example *Cupid Received by*

116 *Monk with Girl*, French, early-
     nineteenth century

117 Henry Monnier, *Man with Three
     Girls*, 1830s

Anacreon (1823–4, Thorvaldsen Museum, Copenhagen), often contain very clear homo-erotic implications.

When the nineteenth century began, French painting was dominated by the austere Neo-classicism of the school of David, soon to be challenged by the passionate Romanticism of Delacroix. But passion was not lacking in the works of some of David's followers: we have already mentioned the erotic illustrations by Prud'hon and the references to mythological love-stories such as Girodet's *Mlle Lange as Danae with the Shower of Gold* (see illustration 89). The best example of the passion underlying Neo-classical painting is provided by Ingres, greatest pupil of David and arch-enemy of Delacroix. Ingres painted the female nude throughout his life, and subjects such as *The Venus of Valpinçon* (1808, Paris, Louvre) and *La Grande Odalisque* (1814, Paris, Louvre), though chastely seen from behind, betray through their brilliant control of draughtsmanship not just an admiration for the female body but an obsession with the sexual attraction of the nude. This is especially clear in his hundreds of sketches and detailed drawings of the female nude, which seem to bear witness to a repressed sensuality. Ingres is known to have had strong sexual appetites, and Robert Baldick has described how the artist used to become so excited by the dancers at the Opéra or in the cabarets that he would cry 'Back to our carriage Madame Ingres' and copulate all the way home.[63] In the Louvre there are drawings by Ingres of nude couples embracing,[64] and amongst the works he bequeathed to the museum in his home town of Montauban are a series of careful copies of erotic sixteenth-century Italian prints by Marco da Ravenna, Rosso, Bonasone, etc.[65] Many of these drawings remain unpublished, and subjects include

118 J. A. D. Ingres, *Copy of sixteenth-century Italian erotic print*

119 J. A. D. Ingres, *Copy of sixteenth-century Italian erotic print*

Mars and Venus (see illustration 118), in which the nude couple embrace each other while Mars puts his hand between Venus's legs; *Venus and Cupid* (see illustration 119), which shows Cupid playing with Venus's vulva; and scenes of a young man throwing a nude woman onto a bed and a man seated on a bed pulling towards him a woman who is undressing. These drawings are finely executed, although they are hardly major works; rather, they are proofs of Ingres's interest in erotic subjects and his admiration of Italian engravings, and they show where he obtained many of the characteristic poses of the figures in his paintings.

At the end of his life, when he was over eighty, Ingres painted one of his most erotic subjects, *Le Bain Turc* (1863, Louvre). This circular painting is a mass of nude female bodies, many seen frontally and some fondly caressing their companions. Buttocks, legs, arms, and breasts intertwine in a vision of the lustful yearnings of an old, but by no means decrepit, man, and the painting seems a harem of objects awaiting the master's pleasure. The hothouse atmosphere of the bath and the obvious borrowings from Persian miniatures and Hindu temple sculptures reinforce the Oriental feeling of the painting. It was a common practice of Ingres to disguise the reality of desire in an Oriental context, in deference to both his own, and the public's moral scruples. This interest in the East linked him to his rival, Delacroix, although Ingres's knowledge of the Orient was derived through engravings. The Romantic painter, on the other hand, travelled in North Africa, and in works such as *Women of Algiers* (1834, Louvre) tried to evoke the mystery and excitement of Oriental women. Delacroix is less concerned than Ingres with personal obsessions, and his works are less rich in Freudian potential. His concern is with atmosphere and colour effects captured by loose brushwork, and his imaginative and colourful nudes (*e.g. Woman with Parrot*, 1827, Musée de Lyon) tend to be less erotic in their effect than the more prosaic examples by Ingres.

The Romantic idea of eroticism tended, however, to differ from Ingres's conception: for Delacroix, violence added an essential ingredient. Baudelaire discerned a theme of sadism running through Delacroix's work, and certainly details of paintings such as *The Massacre at Chios* (1824, Louvre) bear witness to this. Géricault shared such a fascination for sexual violence: his bedroom scenes of nude couples such as *The Lovers* (1815–16, Dubaut Collection, Paris) and *The Kiss* (1822, private collection, America) are sensual but also disquieting, owing to their dramatic use of light and shade, a feature more obvious still in *Nude Being Tortured* (c. 1817, Musée Bonnat, Bayonne). Géricault's major work, *The Raft of the Medusa* (1819, Louvre) and the related studies of severed heads and limbs show what amounts to an abnormal obsession with the extremes of violence, and in his only known sculptures, two versions of *Nymph Attacked by a Satyr* (c. 1818, Rollin Collection, Paris; and c. 1819, Albright-Knox Art Gallery, Buffalo, New York), he portrayed startling representations of a violent rape, an idea he had worked out in numerous drawings. This Romantic fascination for the violent aspects of sexuality is also characteristic of the literature of the period, and is well summed up in the statement by Charles Baudelaire in *Fusées*, his intimate journal written in about 1851: 'The unique and supreme pleasure in love lies in the certainty of doing evil. Both man and woman know from birth that evil lies at the root of all pleasure.'[66]

At the same time, Baudelaire was a great admirer of Courbet, whose paintings were a direct reaction against the excesses of Romanticism. Courbet tried to paint only what he knew from first-hand experience, without any embellishment, and his taste for buxom women led him to paint a series of nudes that shocked many people through their ugliness and their outspokenness. These included *Woman with Parrot* (1866, Metropolitan Museum, New York) which had clear sexual overtones; *Nude in the Waves* (1868, Metropolitan Museum, New York) with its Freudian image of water lapping around the woman's breasts; and *Woman with White Stockings* (1861, Barnes Foundation, Merion, Pennsylvania) in which the viewer looks directly at the woman's crotch. When *Women Bathing* (1853, Musée Fabre, Montpelier) was exhibited at the Salon, Napoleon III struck it with his riding crop and his wife was appalled by the picture's directness. One critic commented on 'this Hottentot Venus with the monstrous backside', and another described the bathers as 'so ugly that not even a crocodile would want to eat them'. The scandals provoked by Courbet's nudes were, as usual, the result of feelings of moral outrage, but it is interesting that the objections were by this time often couched in terms of criticism of the artist's conception of beauty and eroticism.

Another of Courbet's notorious paintings was *Venus and Psyche* of 1864 (Kunstmuseum, Bern) which has as little to do with ancient mythology as so many of the sixteenth-century Italian versions mentioned above. It caught the eye of Khalil Bey, former Turkish ambassador to St Petersburg, who then commissioned Courbet to paint his two most scandalous and least seen paintings. The first was *Sleeping Women* of 1866 (Petit Palais, Paris; see illustration 120), which actually shows two entwined nude women relaxing on a bed after making love. Courbet's own title was *Laziness and Sensuality*, and it is one of the few major works of western art on the theme of lesbianism. The amazing fluency of the limbs of the two bodies owes a great deal to Courbet's study of the nudes of Titian and Correggio, but the firm brushwork and direct modelling are his own. Although the subject-matter is explicit rather than disguised, the moment depicted is not the sensational climax to a bout

120   Gustave Courbet,
Laziness and Sensuality,
1866

of love-making but the quietness that follows, and Courbet has succeeded in portraying the tenderness and intimacy of a true celebration of love.

The second of Khalil Bey's commissions was Courbet's most outspoken work, *Origin of the World* of *c.* 1867 (present whereabouts unknown[67]), which was a painting of the torso of a nude woman with legs apart, concentrating on the sexual area (see illustration 121). This painting has rarely been seen or even heard of, and judgement of its quality is difficult from the blurred photograph that remains. However, it was seen soon after it was painted by Maxime du Camp, who wrote: 'The front view of a naked woman extraordinarily convulsed with emotion, painted in a remarkable style and handled *con amore* as the Italians say, which represents the very last word in realism. However, by some astonishing oversight the painter, who executed it from life, has forgotten to show the feet, legs, thighs, abdomen, hips, chest, hands, arms, shoulder, neck and head.'[68] Twenty years later, Edmond de Goncourt wrote in his journal on 29 June 1889: 'I feel obliged to make a full apology—it is as beautiful as the flesh of a Correggio.' The painting was last heard of in Budapest in 1945.

Various of Courbet's French contemporaries produced erotic works of art; these include Corot's rather bold nudes reclining in landscapes; *Woman Masturbating Before a Statue of Priapus* (1860) and *Woman Embraced by a Goat* (1865) by Diaz; and a series of crayon drawings of nudes masturbating and making love by Millet. All these were reproduced in the early part of this century by Fuchs in his pioneering books on eroticism. But the most important artist in the context of eroticism at this time was Manet. Courbet had been the victim of prejudice, but his frontal attacks on convention had invited a reaction. Manet, on the other hand, considered himself conventional, yet he produced two paintings that brought him the undesired reputation of a pornographer. In 1863 his *Déjeuner sur l'Herbe* (Louvre; see illustration 122) provoked a violent outcry because it showed naked women with clothed men.[69] Such an idea had excellent precedents, for instance Giorgione's *Rustic*

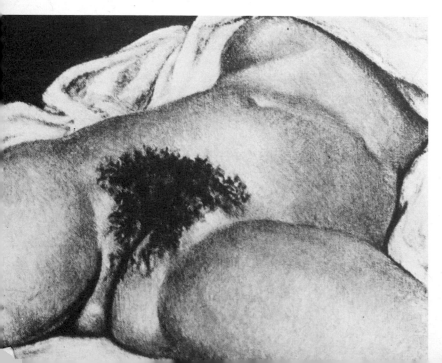

121 Gustave Courbet, *Origin of the World*, *c.* 1867

122　Edouard Manet,
Déjeuner sur l'herbe,
1863

Concert of *c*. 1510 (Louvre) which had in fact provided Manet with his inspiration, just as Marcantonio Raimondi's print of Raphael's lost *Judgement of Paris* (see illustration 78) had served as model for the composition. But these were sanctified by the context of history and mythology; Manet had brought the scene up to date, and in a contemporary setting it became obscene. The same was true of his *Olympia* of 1865 (Louvre; see illustration 123), a reclining nude based on Titian's *Venus of Urbino* of *c*. 1538 (Uffizi, Florence; see illustration 75 and section a of this chapter).

The star of the 1865 Salon was not Manet's *Olympia* but *The Birth of Venus* by the highly respected Alexandre Cabanel (see illustration 124). This titillating pin-up with the artfully posed legs was protected by its mythological title and conventional technique from any criticisms of impropriety, and Napoleon III, who had violently attacked Courbet's *Women Bathing* in 1853 and Manet's *Déjeuner* ten years later, had no hesitation in buying the picture. Cabanel was only one of many admired artists in Paris and London who catered for the enormous interest in acceptable

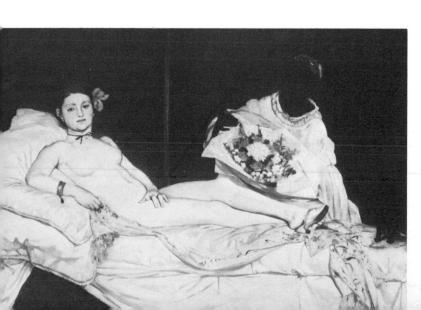

123　Edouard Manet,
Olympia, 1865

124 Alexandre Cabanel,
Birth of Venus, 1865

nudes. The Royal Academy and the Salon regularly exhibited reclining nymphs in landscapes and graceful maidens by marble baths. William Bouguereau painted practically nothing else; his long and distinguished career was crowned with *Les Oréades* of 1902 (see illustration 147), in which excited satyrs watch a swarm of nude nymphs flying through the air. Alma-Tadema's *In the Tepidarium* of 1881 (Lady Lever Art Gallery, Port Sunlight, Cheshire; see illustration 146) includes a few archaeological accessories, but is really a finely painted nude girl holding a well-placed ostrich feather and lying on a bear-skin rug. Examples may be found by these and many others including Gérôme, Henner, Lord Leighton, and Albert Moore: the artistic level is uneven, but many are well painted and extremely erotic. They provided the aspiring middle classes with an entry into a cultural dreamland that was sexual yet respectable.

The immense popularity of these academic painters was disturbing, not merely because it was won at the expense of much greater artists, but because it was to an extent based on dishonesty and hypocrisy. Courbet and Manet, like other great artists of the second half of the nineteenth century, were totally honest in their art, and while the future lay with them, they received little thanks from their contemporaries. But the academic nude painters gave expression to repressed feelings, and this fulfilled a great need felt by millions of English and French men and women who had learnt to be afraid of sex.[70] These painters invoked the great heritage of Classicism and mythology, and so the attendant eroticism could be considered safe. When artists like Courbet and Manet defied that heritage, then the resulting works could only be outrageous.

The painters of safe nudes concentrated on producing pretty pictures with little effort at gaining insight into the nature of sexuality. But Toulouse-Lautrec and Degas were at this time exploring the world of prostitutes. Edgar Degas was fascinated by the race-course and the ballet; his series of monotypes of brothel scenes are inevitably less well known but were no less important to him. He executed about one hundred of these, working in thick ink on copper plates in such a way that only one copy of the print was obtainable. About seventy were destroyed by his brother after the artist's death, but Ambroise Vollard saved the rest and used them to illustrate Maupassant's *La Maison Tellier* and Lucian's *Mimes des Courtisanes*.[71] Renoir wrote of this series: 'Lorsqu'on touche à de pareils sujets, c'est souvent pornografique, mais toujours d'une tristesse désespérante. Il fallait être Degas pour donner à la *Fête à la Patronne* un air de rejouissance en même temps que la grandeur d'un bas-relief égyptien.'[72] These small, dark, smudgy prints show the prostitutes caught unawares in their off-duty moments, and are the real examples of what Degas once referred to as his 'key-hole art'. *Fête à la Patronne* (see illustration 125) is a beautiful example: a marvellously lucid, vividly compassionate study revealing a complete mastery of graphic art. Others are more explicitly sexual: *Deux Femmes* (Boston Museum of Fine Arts) and *Sur le Lit* (Pablo Picasso Collection, Mougins); both depict lesbian activities.

Henri de Toulouse-Lautrec shared Degas's fascination for the world of the prostitute, and he painted at least fifty brothel scenes (including one of his greatest masterpieces), as well as producing numerous drawings and a set of lithographs which were published under the title *Elles* in 1896. Lautrec was a cripple with a stunted body, the result of two accidents when he was a boy, and he left his aristocratic home in the South of France because he felt himself somehow a failure. In Montmartre he joined the world of cabaret artists and circus performers where he felt at home and at ease, and here he was always a welcome visitor. During the 1890s he spent long periods in the *maisons closes* in the Rue d'Amboise and the Rue des Moulins, and in the rooms put at his disposal he would entertain visitors and friends such as Yvette Guilbert and Paul Durand-Ruel. He would preside over dinner insisting that conversation should be kept on an elevated level, and on the girls' days off, he would accompany them to the races or to the theatre.

The physical appearance of these brothels fascinated Lautrec almost as much as did the prostitutes. Architecture was usually of the heavy Louis XIV style, with Louis XV décor of an incredible richness that bordered on the vulgar, giving the

125 Edgar Degas,
Madame's Birthday Party, c. 1879

clients the illusion of being treated like princes in a royal palace. Some *maisons closes* had luxurious rooms known as 'The Egyptian', 'The Roman', 'The Persian', 'The Arabian', etc., and there were some rooms with swaying beds for those who liked the feeling of travelling in a ship, or projected slides in movement to suggest a train journey. Torture rooms with every conceivable device for masochistic and sadistic pleasure were also provided. The Madame of the Rue d'Amboise establishment commissioned Lautrec to redecorate her salon in the *style Pompadour* in 1892, and he executed sixteen panels including portraits of various of the prostitutes. Unfortunately, most of these have not survived.

Yvette Guilbert recalls Lautrec once saying to her: 'Everywhere and always ugliness has its beautiful aspects; it is thrilling to discover them where nobody else has noticed them.'[73] The works that resulted from Lautrec's visits to the Parisian brothels are a perfect illustration of this belief. He records what he sees frankly and honestly, with no ulterior motives and no attempt to moralise, and he uses a wit and an elegance which is lacking in the stark realism of Degas's monotypes. There is no bitterness and no hint of mockery in his views of prostitutes in bed, or making their beds, or playing cards, or washing themselves. One painting (*Rue des Moulins: The Inspection*, 1894, Chester Dale Collection, New York) shows prostitutes parading for a medical inspection, an unpleasing subject which is treated dispassionately and without any hint of salaciousness. This ability to record what he sees without comment, and at the same time to create a work of art out of seemingly unpromising subject-matter, is characteristic of Lautrec.

During his periods in the *maisons closes*, Lautrec became fascinated by lesbianism, for many of the girls developed passionate relationships for each other as a form of

126   Henri de Toulouse-
Lautrec, *The Two
Friends*, 1894

solace for the endless bitterness that resulted from selling their bodies to men. *The Kiss* (1892, Dortu Collection, Paris) and *Two Friends* of 1894 (Tate Gallery, London; see illustration 126), show the same dispassionate curiosity as the other brothel studies. One of the finest is *Friends* (1895, Schins Collection, Zurich), where Lautrec's expressive brushwork and restrained use of colour create a beautiful and serene composition in which the erotic element is in no way exaggerated.

The masterpiece among Lautrec's brothel pictures is *Au Salon: Rue des Moulins* of 1895 (Museum of Albi; see illustration 127), a large work which was painted in his studio from numerous studies made on the spot. The picture shows some of Lautrec's favourite prostitutes in the exotic salon of the brothel, languidly awaiting clients under the watchful eye of the Madame, who sits primly erect, covered up to her neck in a pink gown with her hair piled up on her head. Lautrec has used a daring compositional device learnt from the study of photographs and Japanese prints, with raked perspective, one figure cut in half by the frame, and a great empty space in the left foreground. In the hands of a lesser painter this could have been disastrous. The colour harmonies are also extraordinary: a carefully modulated range of mauves, pinks, reds, and blues which build up a claustrophobic hot-house atmosphere evocative of the brothel itself. There is no repugnance, no condemnation, yet there

127   *Toulouse-Lautrec and model photographed with* Au Salon, 1895

is no glorification either, merely a sympathetic and masterly reportage. Like Goya, Lautrec used the motto 'I saw this'. Brothels were a part of the life around him—to Lautrec, a particularly fascinating one—and so they have their part in his depiction of life. And in the prostitutes he painted, he found a naturalness and an uninhibited grace which no professional models could match.

Very few of these brothel pictures were exhibited in Lautrec's lifetime. Usually they would be kept in the back room of the gallery to be seen only by 'serious students of art', much to Lautrec's disgust. And this was an age when French academic painting abounded in the 'innocent maidens' of Paul Chabas, the mythological nudes of Bouguereau, and the languorous red-headed beauties of Henner. Lautrec's fault was shared by Baudelaire, Manet, and Degas: a total honesty in showing real life, an acceptance of the realities of prostitution without an accompanying expression of moral condemnation. Lautrec's *Elles* find their echo in Baudelaire's *Fleurs du Mal*:

> *Vous que dans votre enfer mon âme a poursuivies*
> *Pauvres soeurs je vous aime autant que je vous plains*
> *Pour vos mornes douleurs vos soifs inassouvies*
> *Et les urnes d'amour dont vos grands coeurs sont pleins.*[74]

This total honesty and lack of deliberate titillation is also evident in the beautiful nudes of Gauguin and the bathing scenes and Classical subjects such as *Leda and the Swan* by Renoir and Cézanne. Renoir was, of course, one of the greatest painters of the nude; his portrayals of young women's bodies in sunny landscapes are celebrations of female beauty rather than exploitations of women as sex-objects for men.

Vincent van Gogh, too, considered that titillation was not enough for serious art on a sexual theme. His early drawing of a prostitute with whom he lived in the Hague in 1882 is entitled *Sorrow* (London, Lady Epstein Collection), and shows the nude girl sitting with her head buried in her arms; the drawing expresses great affection and yet deep compassion. In Paris, a few years later, Van Gogh produced three paintings of a certain nude girl reclining on a bed. These are usually considered to be studio studies and are unique in his work.[75] The preparatory drawing for one of them (1887, Amsterdam, Vincent van Gogh Foundation; see illustration 128) shows a woman wearing stockings, and neither her pose nor her figure suggests a Parisian studio. The drawing is more likely a painstaking attempt to portray the no longer beautiful body of a woman who has had to earn her living by selling herself, the sort of person who would attract the sympathy of this intensely human painter. Van Gogh's letters from Arles to Emile Bernard speak continually of prostitutes and visits to brothels (in the company, for a while, of Gauguin), and it is clear from them that he planned a major painting of a brothel interior, although he never produced more than a few studies.[76] He had had three disastrous love-affairs in early life but had never married, and prostitutes must have been vitally important

128   Vincent Van Gogh,
      Reclining Nude, 1887

sources of affection in what became a very lonely life. His few drawings and paintings
of prostitutes are among his most moving works.

   Besides the repressed painters of titillating nudes and the serious explorers of
sexuality there were also during the nineteenth century a few well-known artists
whose works were intended purely as straightforward sexual entertainment. Some,
like the Austrian Court painter Peter Fendi, produced erotic works as a sideline.
Fendi's series of watercolours, showing every conceivable setting for human
coupling, from a bath-tub to during an acrobat's stage-act, are light-hearted and
charming though essentially minor works.[77] A similar artist was Mihály Zichy,
Court painter to Tsar Alexander II, who produced over many years a set of forty
prints entitled *Love*, which trace the sexual life of an artist from infancy to fatherhood
(see illustration 129). These delicate and finely drawn prints show the child ex-

129   Mihály Zichy, *Bons Souvenirs*, from
      Love, *c*. 1875–80

130 Mihály Zichy, *Woman Undressing,*
c. 1875

perimenting alone, being initiated into sex by an aunt, practising with a kitchen
maid, trying out various sophisticated techniques and positions, and finally making
love to his wife while she suckles their baby.[78] As well as his Court commissions
Zichy found time to produce more private watercolours (see illustration 130).

Others devoted their whole time to producing erotic works. Foremost among these
was the Marquis von Bayros, who illustrated many classics of erotic literature, from
Fanny Hill to *The Arabian Nights*. He was fascinated by women and depicted them
as all-powerful manipulators of men, in skilful drawings that reflected fin-de-siècle
extravagance and showed a great debt to Aubrey Beardsley (see illustration 131).

131 Marquis Von Bayros, *Salome with
the Head of John the Baptist, c.* 1900

He conjured up a world of guiltless sex, a carefree world of sexual pleasure only occasionally marred by harsher realities.[79] Besides Beardsley, Bayros's work also has traces of the influence of Rops, but he was in fact a minor artist compared to these two vital figures of Decadent Art, the movement which brought the nineteenth century to a close.

---

c: Decadent Art

by

SIMON WILSON[1]

Our social realities are so ugly if seen in the light of exiled truth, and beauty is almost no longer possible if it is not a lie. What is to be done? We who are still half alive, living in the often fibrillating heartland of a senescent capitalism—can we do more than reflect the decay around and within us? Can we do more than sing our sad and bitter songs of disillusion and defeat?
—R. D. Laing, *The Politics of Experience*

'. . . Death is coitus and coitus is death.'
—Geza Roheim, *Animism, Magic and the Divine King*

'Death *is* orgasm *is* rebirth *is* death in orgasm.'
William Burroughs, *The Ticket that Exploded*

In Western Europe, and especially in France, the second half of the nineteenth century was marked by a progressive alienation of the artist from society. The symptoms of this alienation were various. Some artists turned to an increasingly hermetic formalism which culminated in abstract art. These do not concern us here. Some turned to traditional types of subject-matter which could be adapted to express their sense of apartness: historical events, ancient myths, and religion (especially extreme mystical forms). Some turned to relatively new kinds of subject-matter: to the primitive and to dreams and private fantasies. And some, and these are the artists we call 'Decadent', produced art which, while it often falls into one or other of the above categories, is characterised by a special emphasis on sexuality and death.

[175]

Before looking at their work, we must try to answer in more detail the question of why they chose to deal with these subjects. The Decadents were revolted by the kind of society that had evolved since the Industrial Revolution. In the eyes of the artists the values of this society were grossly materialistic and therefore inimical to art. Art is a spiritual activity, and the artist thus found himself representing a system of values totally at variance with the system by which the society he lived in was increasingly being governed. If the making of art is a positive assertion of spiritual values, there is a sense in which all art can be said to be subversive in a well-disciplined industrial system: as Oscar Wilde said, 'All art is perfectly useless,' and useless objects which nevertheless have a mysterious importance to many people are a threat to such a system. However, although the relationship of the artist to society is an uneasy one, which not infrequently breaks down altogether (*e.g.* the suicide of Van Gogh or, more recently, that of Mark Rothko), the new and unfamiliar forms which art has taken since 1848 have, after an initial period of hostility, been quite quickly assimilated. The Decadent artists sought to preserve their apartness, to prevent or at least postpone the process of assimilation. The problem was, how? What they seem to have done is to utilise the notion (later developed by Freud and others) that industrial societies are based partly on sexual repression.[2] (The degree of such repression and its ramifications and effects in the nineteenth century and in our own time has been discussed in a number of recent studies.[3])

In general, sexually repressed people cannot tolerate any public and overt expression of sexuality. Thus any work of art having a strong sexual content is bound to be unacceptable to the mass of conforming members of society and also, and perhaps more importantly, to the authoritarian controllers of society. Herbert Marcuse, in particular, has emphasised the revolutionary potential of sexuality: 'The unsublimated, unrationalised release of sexual relations would mean the most emphatic release of pleasure as such and the total devaluation of work for work's sake. The tension between the innate value of work and the freedom of pleasure could not be tolerated by the individual: the hopelessness and injustice of working conditions would strikingly penetrate the consciousness of individuals and render impossible their peaceable regimentation (*Einordnung*) in the social system of the bourgeois world.'[4] Erotic art can thus be seen to have a positive subversive potential.

The work of art can be made even more unacceptable if the sexual content is 'perverse': that is if it concerns sexual activity undertaken exclusively for its own sake. Perverse sexuality in this sense should more strictly be called eroticism if we accept Georges Bataille's definition: '*Eroticism, unlike simple sexual activity, is a psychological quest independent of the natural goal of reproduction and the desire for children . . . Eroticism is assenting to life even up to the point of death.*'[5] It is interesting to compare this with John Cage's statement that, in art: 'Our intention is *to affirm this life*, not to bring order out of a chaos or to suggest improvements in creation, *but simply to wake up to the very life we are living.*'[6] From this point of view art and eroticism can be seen to be very similar activities.

The Decadents' obsession with death is a natural corollary of their obsession with the erotic. Sexuality and death are what Salvador Dali once called 'the great vital constants' of human life: 'The subconscious has a symbolic language that is truly a universal language, for it does not depend on special habitude or state of culture or intelligence, but speaks with the vocabulary of the great vital constants, sexual instinct, feeling of death, physical notion of the enigma of space—these vital constants are universally echoed in every human being.'[7] It is worth noting too that Freud eventually came to believe in the existence of a death instinct (*Thanatos*) playing a role of equal importance to the life instinct (*Eros*), which he had previously considered to be the sole major drive in human life.[8] Like sex, death is the subject of taboos, and social attitudes to it are similarly extremely evasive. The preoccupation with death may also be a reflection of the despair felt by these men—the feeling that the world was submitting to Mammon, that civilisation was coming to an end—the feeling, in fact, of *fin-de-siècle*.

In Decadent art the subject-matter is typically projected through an image of woman seen as a fascinating and mysterious goddess. She may be passive or active, but she is no longer a victim, as she had been in the art of the Romantics. She is an independent creature using her sexuality to dominate men. She has about her an aura of the grave: she appears as Proserpine, handmaiden of Pluto and queen of the dead; she appears as Salome, the vengeful harlot; she appears as Beatrice, actually dead but still exercising her fascination from beyond the grave; or she appears as the sphinx, half-woman, half-beast, a devourer of men. She appears as a creature of Satan—as his instrument of subversion in the world, and she appears as the modern city prostitute, a bearer of syphilitic death.

Surprisingly, perhaps, this image of woman makes its first appearance in England, in D. G. Rossetti's *Beata Beatrix* of c. 1863 (Tate Gallery). This painting of the death of Dante's Beatrice is in reality a posthumous portrait of Rossetti's wife, Elizabeth Siddall (died 10 February, 1862), and a monument both to her and to the obsessive love Rossetti bore her. Significantly, she does not have the appearance of death: her lips are parted and her expression is ecstatic (Rossetti described her as being '*rapt* from the Earth to Heaven').[9] A malignant red bird hovers near her folded hands bearing in its beak a poppy, the source of opium, an overdose of which was the cause of her death. She had been a muse to Rossetti as well as mistress and wife, and it was some time before he found a woman who could fill her place. Towards the end of the 1860s, however, he refocussed his obsession on Mrs William Morris—Jane Burden. Jane Burden, with her long columnar neck, her superabundant crinkly hair, her thick, but finely modelled cupid's bow lips and her withdrawn expression of dormant sexuality was the archetype of the *fin-de-siècle* woman. In his paintings of her, Rossetti blended all these qualities into a series of images of haunting eroticism. Outstanding among them is *Proserpine* of 1874 (Tate Gallery, see illustration 132). Here Jane is seen in Hades, bearing in her left hand the fatal pomegranate (because she had eaten one seed she was forced to remain as Pluto's queen for six months of the year), from which she has peeled a thin strip of skin revealing the pulpy pink flesh within; the pomegranate is also a vulva.

[177]

132 Dante Gabriel Rossetti, *Proserpine*, 1874

133 Gustave Moreau, *The Apparition*, c. 1874–76

Rossetti's innovatory work in England in the 1860s and '70s was paralleled by that of Gustave Moreau in France during the same period. Moreau embodied his vision of woman in the historical character of Salome, and she appears in those two extraordinary works *Salome Dancing* and *The Apparition*. The French writer, J. K. Huysmans, made these paintings famous by describing them in that major literary monument of Decadence, his novel *A Rebours* (*Against Nature*) of 1884: 'With a withdrawn, solemn almost august expression on her face, she begins the lascivious dance which is to rouse the aged Herod's dormant senses: her breasts rise and fall, the nipples hardening at the touch of her whirling necklaces; the strings of diamonds glitter against her moist flesh; her bracelets, her belts, her rings all spit out fiery sparks . . . Here she was no longer just the dancing girl who extorts a cry of lust and lechery from an old man by the lascivious movements of her loins . . . She had become, as it were, the symbolic incarnation of undying Lust, the Goddess of Immortal Hysteria, the accursed Beauty exalted above all other beauties . . .'[10] Huymans continues to develop this theme of the savage goddess in his description of the second painting, in which Moreau shows Salome contemplating the severed head of the Baptist, which gazes at her in horror, suspended supernaturally in space (see illustration 133). Here the blend of the morbid and the erotic is particularly

[178]

strong: 'She is almost naked; in the heat of the dance her veils have fallen away . . . a wondrous jewel sparkles and flashes in the cleft between her breasts; . . . where the body shows bare between gorgerin and girdle the belly bulges out, dimpled by a navel which resembles a graven seal of onyx with its milky hues and rosy finger-nail tints. . . . The dreadful head glows eerily bleeding all the while, so that clots of dark red form at the ends of hair and beard . . . Here she was a true harlot, obedient to her passionate and cruel female temperament. . . . Here she roused the sleeping senses of the male more powerfully, subjugating his will more surely to her charms—the charms of a great venereal flower, grown in a bed of sacrilege, reared in a hot-house of impiety.'[11]

A similar vision of woman was simultaneously being elaborated in the graphic work of one of the most misunderstood of all the pioneers of Decadent art: the Belgian etcher Felicien Rops. Rops emerges as a significant figure remarkably early on; in 1865 at the age of thirty-two he met Baudelaire and through him the brothers Goncourt—all key Decadent writers. Rops excited their immediate admiration; Baudelaire commissioned a frontispiece for his volume of banned poems *Les Epaves*, published 'underground' in Amsterdam in 1866, and wrote a sonnet in which he compared Rops to the pyramid of Cheops. But it was the Goncourt brothers who inspired Rops's first major Decadent work: in 1867 he made a magnificent drawing of the prostitute heroine of the Goncourts' novel *Manette Salomon* and presented it to the authors. They later wrote in their journal: 'Rops is truly eloquent in depicting the appearance of cruelty taken on by the contemporary woman, her look of steel, her ill-will towards men which is neither hidden nor dissimulated but shown in her whole appearance.'[12] The drawing of Manette Salomon marks the first appearance in Rops's work of this type of the contemporary woman, and in later versions her 'look of ill-will' becomes explicitly a look of death: woman becomes death. The most striking of these later versions and one of Rops's finest etchings is *Mors Syphilitica*, but *La Mort qui Danse* runs it very close.

In 1883 Rops executed a remarkable series of etchings illustrating Jules Barbey D'Aurevilly's celebrated book of short stories *Les Diaboliques* (The Possessed). These stories of Second Empire society constitute a vicious (and entirely humourless) satire on a grotesquely corrupt ruling class. One of their main themes is that of woman as representative of the Devil on earth, as the author explains with heavy irony in his Preface: '. . . as for the women in these stories, why should they not be *The Possessed*? Haven't they enough of the devil in them to merit this name? *The Possessed*! there is not a single one . . . who is pure, innocent, virtuous!' He also reveals the Decadent's characteristic contempt for the contemporary world: '. . . *The Possessed* are real stories of this era of progress, of this civilization of ours which is so delicious, and so divine that when one tries to write about it the devil always seems to be dictating.'[13] It is worth pointing out that for the Decadents, as for William Blake earlier in the century, the Devil represented freedom from, and opposition to, the restrictions and controls placed on man by the Christian God and reflected in the institutions of Christian countries: hence the Decadents' addiction to blasphemy and diabolism as well as eroticism and death.

Rops's illustrations to *The Possessed* are a perfect complement to the text: the frontispiece shows a naked woman lasciviously embracing a sphinx. She is apparently oblivious of the presence of the Devil gloating possessively over her. Rops here identifies woman with the destructive sphinx and establishes her as the Devil's creature.

The main story in *The Possessed* is 'Happiness in Crime' ('Le Bonheur dans le Crime'). This tale concerns a beautiful woman who murders the wife of an enormously wealthy and handsome aristocrat in order to marry him. In defiance of all normal rules, they live blissfully ever after. Rops's etching shows symbolically the couple's situation: they are naked, enshrined on a pedestal, locked in a passionate embrace, and from them streams an intense radiance; this energy, derived from the realisation of their desires and their refusal to accept guilt for their crime kills the serpent of Envy which is stretched dead on the ground and even makes them invulnerable to Death itself, which is seen clawing unsuccessfully at the foot of the pedestal.

In another story, 'At an Atheists' Dinner' ('A un dîner d'athées') a guest tells how the mistress of a vicious, drunken cavalry officer conceives a child by another man which dies young. The officer believes it to be his and, grief stricken, has the child's heart preserved in a glass casket. Years later in the course of a quarrel she reveals the truth. He smashes the casket, hurls the child's heart full in her face, then half strips her, and in revenge seals her vagina with hot sealing-wax. At this moment he is transfixed by a sword thrust by a brother officer (the narrator) who has observed the scene. The focal point of Rops's etching for this story is the naked woman lying across a table, her head hanging over the edge. With one hand she is clutching at her mutilated vulva. But the image is intentionally ambiguous: the gesture of her hand also indicates masturbation, the expression on her face could as well be ecstasy as agony. The series ends with two compositions, showing respectively Prostitution and Crime and Prostitution and Folly dominating the world; they have no direct connection with the stories but are a kind of summing up. And indeed they effectively express the disillusioned, despairing *Weltanschauung* of the Decadent artists.

The following year Rops etched *Les Sataniques* ('The Possessed of Satan'). This series has no literary source; it is a fantasy in which Rops imagines a woman carried off to Hell, where she has sexual intercourse first with an ithyphallic statue of Satan (see illustration 134) and then on an altar with Satan himself in the form of a giant, snake-like penis (see illustration 135). The final plate of this series is a startling image of eroticism and death; it is also obscenely blasphemous: Satan, parodying Christ, is nailed to a cross. He has an enormous erection. Between his legs stands the woman: she is being strangled with her own hair (see illustration 136) and her expression indicates that she is dying in orgasm. Rops also made two beautiful soft-ground etchings in which he followed up the theme of obscene blasphemy (see illustration 137). The subject of both these plates is Mary Magdalene, a favourite biblical figure with the Decadents because she was a 'sinner' and because it could be

134   Felicien Rops, *Les Sataniques I*, 1884

135   Felicien Rops, *Les Sataniques II*, 1884

136   Felicien Rops, *Les Sataniques III*, 1884

137 Felicien Rops, *Mary Magdalene, c.* 1885

implied that her relationship with Christ was a sexual one. This is the line that Rops takes in these works. The first quite explicitly shows the Magdalene masturbating at the foot of a cross—nailed to it is not the full figure of Christ but simply a large phallus. In the second plate the woman is relaxed and the phallus hangs limply.

In 1893, when Rops was sixty, worn out by overwork and with only a few years to live, a new and brilliant Decadent talent appeared. In April of that year, the first issue of *The Studio*, a new art magazine, was published in London. It contained, among other things, a long and copiously illustrated article about a then still unknown young artist, Aubrey Beardsley. This article helped to make Beardsley famous, and it marks the start of his short but glittering career.

It is entirely characteristic of Beardsley's relations with his publishers that his design for the cover of that first issue of the *The Studio* was censored by the editor, and a suspiciously ithyphallic looking faun removed from the woodland scene Beardsley had depicted: right from the beginning he made clear his intention to provoke.

Beardsley knew the work of both Moreau and Rops, but his art is primarily rooted in the English tradition of Rossetti and his follower, Burne-Jones, although he was also strongly influenced by Whistler, an artist who had chosen the path of formal research in his reaction against materialism. In Beardsley, indeed, the two streams, the pursuit of Decadence and the search for new forms in art, 'art for art's sake', are momentarily and sensationally linked. It is this which gives Beardsley's art its unique power.

A variety of Decadent themes appear in Beardsley's work: he developed his own version of the Decadent woman, a more sinister, even satanic, sister to Rops's sexy, pug-faced Paris prostitutes, and he created a male counterpart to the woman, an androgynous but highly sexualised dandy. An obsessive phallicism runs right through

[182]

his *oeuvre*; he is frequently blasphemous (his blasphemies were given a retrospective edge by his reception into the Catholic Church in 1897), and his view of eroticism as a goal in itself is pointed up by the recurring motif of a malignant dwarf (sometimes a foetus-like creature), which Beardsley once described as '*not* an infant but an unstrangled abortion'.[14]

In 1893 Beardsley read Oscar Wilde's play *Salome*, published in Paris early that year, and almost immediately put down its central image in a remarkable drawing '*J'ai baisé ta bouche, Iokanaan, J'ai baisé ta bouche*' ('I have kissed your mouth, Jonathan, I have kissed your mouth'). In his play, Wilde gave a new, and from the Decadent point of view, crucial twist to the legend of Salome: here she falls in love with the Baptist, he rejects her advances and she plots his death *not* in revenge, but so that she can consummate her lust for him in death as she could not in life. Beardsley's drawing is a striking representation of this necrophiliac theme; the triumphant Salome floats in space gloating over the head of John, still dripping blood, which she holds before her. As the title of the drawing indicates, she has just kissed it full on the mouth. This idea was taken further and made more explicit by a German follower of Beardsley, Franz von Bayros. In his drawing of Salome the severed head of the Baptist is shown sucking her nipple (see illustration 131).

On the strength of '*J'ai baisé ta bouche*' Beardsley was commissioned to illustrate the English edition of *Salome*, which was published in 1894 with eleven of his drawings. All of them have a strong erotic atmosphere and it is Beardsley's great achievement that this quality is inherent in the very manner of the drawings, in what used to be called his 'line'. D. H. Lawrence introduced the Salome drawings into his novel *The White Peacock* of 1911, where the following remarkable lines of dialogue occur between George Saxton and Cyril Beardsall. The girl under discussion is Lettic Beardsall: 'I want her more than anything—and the more I look at these naked lines, the more I want her. It's a sort of fine, sharp feeling, like these curved lines. I don't know what I'm saying—but do you think she would have me? Has she seen these pictures?' 'No.' 'If she did, perhaps she'd want me—I mean she'd feel it clear and sharp coming through her.'

But some of the Salome drawings were sufficiently explicit to run into censorship problems: Beardsley's omnipresent phalluses both erect and flaccid (and even in a state of rest they retain a rivetingly erotic quality) were the usual problem. His publisher, John Lane, insisted on the removal of the genitals from the two figures on the title page, and one drawing, *The Toilet of Salome* (see illustration 138), was suppressed altogether because the beautiful young man seated on the Japanese tabouret has a delicate but noticeable tuft of pubic hair, because his penis can just be seen to be erect, and because the all-over suggestion (intended, of course, by Beardsley) is that he is masturbating. Furthermore, as far as can be told from his marvellous, dreamy, heavy-lidded gaze (most of Beardsley's figures have this look) the source of his stimulation is not the body of Salome (who from her expression, the tilt of her head, and the position of her left hand is engaged in the same activity as the seated boy) but that of the effeminate page-boy beside her. After this it seems

[183]

almost superfluous to draw attention to the gesture of the musician's hand on the long stem of the instrument he is playing, to the foetus on the dressing table, to the provocative titles of the books on the shelf (Baudelaire's *Fleurs du Mal* among them), or to the fact that the edge of the Pierrot's skirt forms an enlarged outline of Salome's breasts.

In two of the Salome series, however, Beardsley managed to defeat Lane's censorship; the musician who accompanies Salome in *The Stomach Dance* displays unequivocal, if cunningly hidden, evidence of her erotic impact on him, and in *Enter Herodias* (see illustration 139), two of the candlesticks are unmistakably and fatly phallic, the foetal figure accompanying Herodias has a barely concealed erection and the page-boy is eye-catchingly naked. This last Lane *did* notice, and he demanded a fig-leaf. Fortunately for posterity, Beardsley flatly refused to alter the original drawing, using instead a proof of the line-block engraving which had already been made. On the proof, he ironically drew a fig-leaf so prominent, so incongruously attached (with a neat little bow), so obviously an addition, that the spectator's attention is inevitably drawn to it, to the act of censorship, and, of course, to the censored object itself. Having done this Beardsley sent a proof to Frank Harris with the following inscription:

> *Because one figure was undressed*
> *This little drawing was suppressed*
> *It was unkind—*
> *But never mind*
> *Perhaps it all was for the best*

Beardsley's phallic obsession reached its peak in his now famous illustrations for

138 Aubrey Beardsley,
Toilet of Salome (first
version), 1893

139 Aubrey Beardsley,
Enter Herodias (first
version), 1893

140   Aubrey Beardsley,
Toilet of Lampito,
from *Lysistrata,* 1896

Aristophanes' *Lysistrata.* By the time he executed these works, Beardsley, largely as a result of the Wilde scandal of 1895, had been forced out of the respectable public domain and into the arms of an 'underground' publisher, the much-maligned Leonard Smithers, and *Lysistrata* appeared in a strictly limited, under-the-counter edition, in 1896. In the *Toilet of Lampito* (see illustration 140), which is certainly the most explicitly erotic of all Beardsley's drawings, the main effect comes from Beardsley's perverse transformation of Cupid from the usual plump *putto* into a slim pubescent boy, caressing his erection with one hand while he powders Lampito's bottom with the other. And in *The Lacedaemonian Ambassadors* (see illustration 161), the hugely exaggerated phalluses are grotesque and perverse in themselves, but in the central figure Beardsley also plays tellingly on the contrast between the youth's self-evident and superb virility and the effeminacy indicated by his delicate features, his elaborately coiffured shoulder-length hair, his no less elaborately curled pubic and axial hair, and his lace-trimmed boots.

Aubrey Beardsley died on 16 March, 1898; Gustave Moreau on 18 April, 1898, and Felicien Rops on 23 August, 1898; it was the end of an era. But today many young artists are looking again to the Decadents and their art as a valid historical precedent, and they continue their exploration of eroticism and death. It is in the nature of things that they have not gained fame, but their work appears in the publications of the underground press. A relevant example is Jim Leon's beautiful drawing 'Lot and his Daughters' which appeared in *Oz* 31 (1970), since it splendidly illustrates Georges Bataille's dictum that 'Eroticism is assenting to life even up to the point of death.' In this version of the Old Testament story Lot and his daughters are seen making love while in the background atomic war destroys the corrupt world they have left behind them.

[185]

Chapter 5

Sexual Attitudes in Victorian Art and Literature

a: Erotic Themes in Victorian Art and Photography

We can now see the Victorian period in its true light. Recent studies by Steven Marcus,[1] Alex Comfort,[2] Peter Fryer,[3] and Ronald Pearsall[4] have shown a non-permissive age in which, however, pornography flourished underground, brothels catering for every extreme proliferated, and child-prostitution was commonplace. It was an age of sexual repression, in which hypocrisy seems to have characterised the sexual attitudes of the majority, and nowhere is this more clearly reflected than in the art of the day. Most English art-lovers shared the views of Napoleon III, who condemned Manet's *Olympia* (see illustration 123) as obscene in the 1860s while being quite happy to purchase Cabanel's provocative *Birth of Venus* (see illustration 124). Nudes from stories of mythology and Oriental or Classical nudes being sold into slavery or tortured or perhaps just taking a bath filled the Royal Academy's annual exhibitions, allowing the visitor the pleasure of vicarious involvement in their activities, without seriously compromising his respectable position as a connoisseur of beauty.

Visitors to the Academy were not just lovers of art but buyers. Patronage of the arts was no longer in the hands of the cultivated gentry, for this was the age of the common man whose aesthetic taste was unlikely to be of the highest order. Art enjoyed enormous prestige among the wealthy, self-made middle class, and Classical art was looked upon as a civilising influence, offering as it did an escape from vulgar reality into a sort of cultural dreamland. The beauty of the naked form was the basis of the Classical ideal, as had been recognised by Ingres, Canova, Flaxman, and the other Neo-classicists. As the nineteenth century progressed, their ideal became processed for the mass-market. Thus the American sculptor Hiram Powers gained instant fame when his *Greek Slave* (Newark Museum, New Jersey; see illustration 141) was exhibited at the Great Exhibition in London in 1851, although it bore little relation to the nude sculptures of Ancient Greece, and the same was true of John Gibson's *Tinted Venus*,[5] which was the sensation of the Universal Exhibition of 1862. Ostensibly these sculptures were appreciated as modern counterparts of their Greek prototypes, but their real appeal lay elsewhere. The Gibson is life-size

141 Hiram Powers,
     The Greek Slave, 1847

and flesh-coloured (for which there were many Greek precedents) and the impression
created by the girl clutching a sheet with one hand and an apple with the other as
she gazes upwards with her mouth slightly open is highly suggestive. The implications of Powers's work seem distinctly Freudian to the modern spectator: the girl
averting her face as she covers her vulva with one manacled hand and pats an
extremely phallic post with the other bears close comparison with any number of
today's pin-up photographs of a sado-masochistic variety (see illustration 142).

142 *Pin-up photograph,*
     Playboy magazine,
     New York, 1969

Admiration for such works as these was by no means universal, and whether or not their deeper attractions were recognised by the critics, both these sculptures were attacked as being offences against propriety. Of course, to some Victorians the nude body was indecent *per se*, and nude art indefensible. Art schools where life drawing was encouraged were continually under fire; in 1860, Lord Haddo tried unsuccessfully to introduce into Parliament a bill which would withdraw subsidies from schools where nude female models were provided. The most famous of such places was the Royal Academy Life School, where the early-Victorian painter William Etty used to sit among the students almost until the end of his life, painting nudes that at their best recall the voluptuousness of Rubens, good examples being *Sleeping Nymph with Satyrs* (1828; Royal Academy, London) and *A Bivouac of Cupid and his Company* (1838; Museum of Fine Arts, Montreal). Clearly, such activities met a real need for the outwardly gentle and retiring Etty, but he had to put up with a great deal of criticism. His painting of *The Sirens and Ulysses* was described as 'a disgusting combination of voluptuousness and loathsome putridity' (*The Spectator*) and 'entirely too luscious (we might with great propriety use a harsher term) for the public eye' (*The Times*).

American art schools found it equally dangerous to encourage life drawing from the nude model. A recent book[6] has, in fact, suggested that prudery was far more deeply entrenched in America at the time than in England. Thomas Eakins, America's greatest figure painter of his time, studied at Pennsylvania Academy of Fine Arts in the early 1860s, and recorded that on the rare occasions when nude models were provided, they wore masks to conceal their identities.[7] When studying under Gérôme in Paris in 1866, he found plenty of nude models provided, but was horrified to see that Salon painters could only produce affected and artificial nudes. Back in America, his four versions of *William Rush carving his allegorical figure of the Schuylkill River* (especially those of 1877 in Philadelphia Museum of Art and of 1908 in the Honolulu Academy of Arts) included a nude model, seen from the front in the last version, and these brought him an immense amount of harsh criticism, which partially caused his resignation as head of Pennsylvania Academy. His most notorious, yet perhaps finest, painting was *The Agnew Clinic* (1889; University of Pennsylvania School of Medicine), which was rejected by the Pennsylvania Academy Exhibition of 1891, because it showed a woman being operated on for breast cancer, revealing the naked upper half of her body.

If few art schools in London managed to provide nude models without provoking an outcry, established painters had no such troubles. Leighton, Alma-Tadema, and Burne-Jones worked frequently from models they employed in their own studios; by preference they chose Italians who, they considered, posed more gracefully than English models, and many villagers from the Naples area thus made their fortunes in London. Especially popular were Antonia Cura, a favourite of Leighton and Burne-Jones; Alessandro di Marco,[8] painted by Alma-Tadema, Walter Crane, and Leighton; and Gaetano Meo, discovered playing music in Gower Street by Simeon Solomon and thereafter painted by Rossetti, Burne-Jones, and Leighton. The thinly

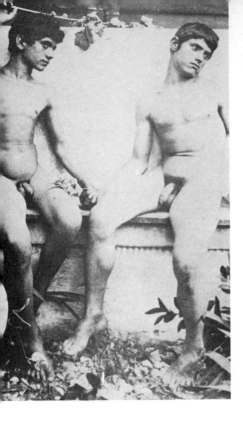

143   Baron Van Gloeden, *Sicilian Youths*, photograph, 1880s

veiled homosexuality of the 'Classical' nude youths photographed in Sicily by Baron van Gloeden in the 1880s (see illustration 143) and illustrated in the first number of *The Studio* (1893) on pages 103–9 also had a strong appeal for artists such as Leighton. Watts and Moore preferred the home-grown models, but made sure they wore loose-fitting, Classical robes when not posing nude, for they objected strongly to the modern fashion for corsets. Watts was a member of the Anti-Tight-Lacing Society; his painting *Orpheus and Eurydice* (Aberdeen Art Gallery) shows a nude Orpheus catching the expiring Eurydice, whose body is clearly visible under her loose transparent robe.

Albert Moore was a Yorkshireman who specialised in painting Grecian scenes of pretty girls, with titles such as *The Dreamers* or *Reading Aloud. Summer Night* (1890; Walker Art Gallery, Liverpool) shows a group of nude girls preparing for bed, painted in a meticulously photographic technique that goes beyond the merely decorative, in spite of the wealth of detail in the wall-hangings and furniture; the overall effect is certainly erotic, and that must surely have been the artist's intention. His painting *The Marble Seat* was shown at the Royal Academy in 1865, the year that Manet's *Olympia* caused a sensation at the Paris Salon, and one would have thought that a painting which showed a nude boy, his genitals precisely depicted, pouring wine for three girls wearing transparent robes, would have caused an equal sensation, although the Grecian setting presumably gave it respectability.

From the 1870s onwards, titillating scenes of the ancient world such as these were commonplace in the Academy's annual exhibitions. Sir Edward Poynter presented the down-to-earth Victorians with a playful dreamland in works such as *Water*

[189]

Babies of 1900,[9] in which one nude girl bathes in a pool while another, portrayed frontally, pours water over her from a fountain. It seems incredible that such pictures could be openly enjoyed in public by people who would object to a lady showing her ankles. More often, these pictures at least had the excuse of Classical subjects: Poynter's *A Visit to Aesculapius* (1880; Tate Gallery, London; see illustration 144) shows a completely nude Venus, attended by three nude maidens, extending her foot to the physician, while Lord Leighton's masterpiece, *The Daphnephoria* (1876)[10] depicts a procession in honour of Apollo, and shows many nude boys and bare-breasted girls. Leighton, peer of the realm and President of the Royal Academy, lived in splendour in his Classical mansion in Kensington, basking in the glory his Grecian scenes brought him. Many of his paintings, however, had only the most tenuous connection with Greece, examples being *Flaming June* (1895; Museo del Arte, Ponce, Puerto Rico), a study of a girl in a transparent robe curled up in a foetal position resembling Klimt's *Danae* (see illustration 90), and *The Bath of Psyche* (1890; Tate Gallery, London; see illustration 145), in which a life-size maiden poses provocatively at the side of a pool, gazing at the reflection of her nude body in the water. One of his biographers described this picture rather naïvely as 'a sauve conception informed with a spirit of perfect chastity, through its inimitable purity of feeling and classic refinement'.[11] Similar eulogies greeted Burne-Jones's daring, yet curiously cold and unsympathetic, *Pygmalion* series (Birmingham City Art Gallery).

One of the most talented of these late-Victorian Classical painters was Sir Lawrence Alma-Tadema, a Dutchman who became naturalised in 1873. He

144 Edward Poynter, *A Visit to Aesculapius*, 1880

145 Lord Leighton,
The Bath of Psyche,
1890

specialised in bath-scenes of Ancient Rome, which were planned with archaeological exactness, and painted with an attractive and incredibly skilled technique. Many are anecdotal and suggest nineteenth-century girls playing at being Romans; these include *An Apodyterium* (1886; Jerdein Collection, London) and *The Frigidarium* (1890; present whereabouts unknown), which show women in various states of dress and undress at the baths, and also *A Favourite Custom* (1909; Leighton House, London) in which two nude girls play in the water together. These were painted from Italian models posed in the luxurious settings of his Classical villa in St John's Wood, a rival to that of Lord Leighton in Kensington, and here Alma-Tadema lived a blameless life with his wife, who painted sentimental pictures with titles such as *Hush-A-Bye* and *The Pain of Parting.*

From time to time, however, Alma-Tadema would produce a powerfully erotic study such as *In the Tepidarium* of 1881 (Lady Lever Art Gallery, Port Sunlight, Cheshire; see illustration 146) which shows a nude girl lying on a bear-skin rug, holding in one hand a tactfully placed ostrich feather, and in the other an instrument for cleaning the skin after a bath. The painting is executed with a meticulous technique which gives the woman's body, and the bear-skin rug, a marvellously tactile quality; this adds greatly to the erotic effect of the subject and almost enables one to experience the luxurious ecstasy of the delicate skin cradled in the soft rug. And the eroticism works at other levels, for the ostrich feather draws attention to the vulva it so carefully hides (in the best tradition of the titillating pin-up), and the cleaning instrument has strongly phallic connotations. Whether the artist was consciously aware of the levels of erotic attraction in his painting is open to question, but he must have known that its popularity owed little to a love of Ancient Rome. What is sad is the apparent need to be arch in this way, although in this painting the result is nevertheless a stunning work of art.

In the Tepidarium is exceptional in Alma-Tadema's work; far more characteristic are the purely anecdotal scenes of Roman life, scenes which were 'high art' in the eyes of the painter and his admirers. His artistic credo, as reported by an admiring biographer, was 'Art must be beautiful because Art must elevate',[12] and he would certainly have considered his art to be elevating, although in an honest moment he would surely have admitted that much of its popularity lay in the opportunities it offered the Victorian gentleman to see pictures of nude women. The hypocrisy of

[191]

146   Lawrence Alma-Tadema, *In the Tepidarium*, 1881

such 'high art' appalled Morris and Whistler, who could see through the shallow sentimentality and fancy-dress Classicism of Leighton, Poynter, and the rest of them, but it was to be many years before the hypocrisy was generally recognised as such.

In France the situation was very similar. Zola, Manet, and the Impressionists saw equally clearly through the *grandes machines mythologiques* of academic painters such as Bouguereau (see illustration 147) and Cabanel (see illustration 124) which were hung at the Salon each year. These titillating nudes performed the same function for the French bourgeoisie as their Royal Academy counterparts in England. Numerous albums of nude photographs 'for artists' were issued between 1890 and 1910, with such titles as *La Grâce Féminine* (by Meyer) and *Le Nu Esthétique* (by Bayard). The latter had a preface by Gérôme of the Institute, and was dedicated to 'my venerated master and friend William Bouguereau of the Institute'. The text included the statement: 'the nude is chaste when it is beautiful', but the title page bore the warning: 'These photographs must not be put on public display.' Besides paintings and photographs, respectable titillation could also be obtained from *poses plastiques* (these are discussed in Chapter 9): in 1898, a ball at the Moulin Rouge organised and staged by students from the studios of Gérôme, Cormon, and Dalou included cameos representing 'nude captives of Tamerlan, as painted by Cormon;

147 William Bouguereau,
Les Oréades, 1902

nude adulterers roughly paraded through the streets of mediaeval towns, their mournful breasts expressing the voluptuousness of suffering flesh; slim fettered nudes at the mercy of savage Huns or church inquisitors'. The spectator who has left this description of the scene added 'no obscenity came to mind in front of so much female flesh'.[13]

Photography, of course, had a deep effect on art during the nineteenth century, especially as regards the nude. It was much easier to obtain nude photographs than to find a nude model, and many of the albums must indeed have been of great value to artists. But as soon as the first daguerrotypes of nudes were produced in about 1840, the wider possibilities of nude photography were recognised, and although photographers used poses derived from Classical statues or those of Michelangelo (see illustrations 148 and 149), the results were more likely to be enjoyed by repressed titillation-seekers than art students. Serious artists like Toulouse-Lautrec and Degas often used photographs for works relating to the nude, and Alphonse Mucha took many beautiful photographs to serve as studies for his posters, an example being a studio photograph of 1899 (see illustration 150) showing a nude child, which he used for his poster advertising the play *Medée*.[14]

Probably the finest photographer of children in the Victorian period was Lewis Carroll, more famous for his children's stories such as *Alice in Wonderland*. Carroll was a highly respected bachelor don at Oxford University, who obtained great pleasure from the company of little girls. He would invite them to tea, tell them stories, and sometimes photograph them. On very special occasions he would

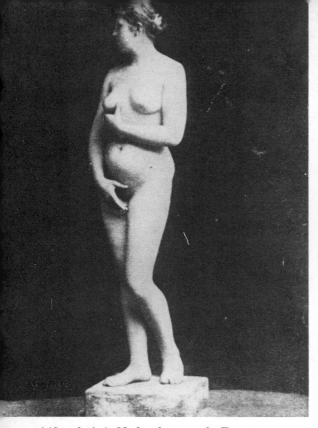

148 *Artistic Nude*, photograph, France, 1890s

149 *Artistic Nude*, photograph, France, 1890s

photograph them in the nude or semi-nude. There was no hint of impropriety here; indeed, he always sought their parents' permission, and often invited them to be present. In his will he asked that all such photographs be returned to the girls' parents, and the only one generally known is *Alice Liddell as Beggar Child*, reproduced in Stuart Dodgson Collingwood's biography in 1898.[15] In this example the girl is

150 Alphonse Mucha, *Studio photograph*, 1899

mainly covered. Writing of the nude photographs in 1949, Helmut Gernsheim concluded: 'as far as I know, none have survived',[16] but recently examples have come to light, some being in America (Parish Collection, Princeton University and Rosenbach Foundation, Philadelphia) and a few in England (Graham Ovenden Collection).[17] One of the latter (see illustration 151) is a beautiful photograph with dramatic lighting, showing a well-developed young girl with draperies covering her lap. The undeniable power of this picture results from the photographer's undisguised emotional involvement with his model, and others in the series are equally touched with erotic feeling.

From Carroll's letters and diaries we can form a good idea of the psychological, as well as aesthetic, importance that such photographs held for him. In a letter to Harry Furniss, Carroll wrote: 'Naked children are so perfectly pure and lovely . . . I confess I do *not* admire naked boys. They always seem to me to need clothes—whereas one hardly sees why the lovely forms of girls should *ever* be covered up.'[18] Carroll's diaries for May 1858 to May 1862 were destroyed by his nephew and biographer Stuart Dodgson Collingwood, who wished to suppress all knowledge of the nude photographs,[19] but from other diary entries we know that Carroll was tortured by guilt as a result of his sexual impulses, and at night would need to read the Bible in order to still lustful thoughts. On days when he had photographed a girl in the nude he would write: 'This is a day to be marked with a white stone' (a

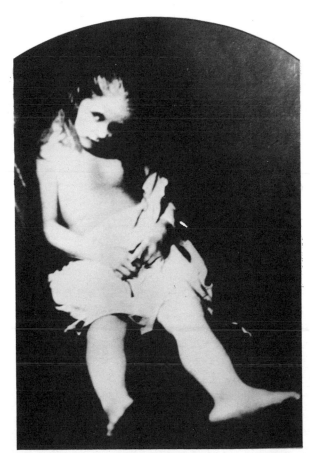

151 Lewis Carroll, *Maud
Constance Mealbury as a
Beggar Girl*,
photograph, 1860

Roman sign for good fortune). Clearly the repressed don's sexual impulses were fixated on little girls, and his sex-life must have been characterised by the agony of perpetual frustration; it has recently become known that he had proposed marriage to the young Alice Liddell, but had been rejected by her parents.[20] One of the tragedies of Lewis Carroll's life is that girls ceased to attract him after they had reached puberty, for then they threatened the repressed structure he had built up in his mind. Another is that he gave up photography in 1880, after a scandal in Oxford concerning his photographing a nude girl.

There are examples of Victorian nude photographs which show a real attempt at artistic creation (see illustration 152), but far more common are the straightforward pin-up photographs, often crowded with exotic paraphernalia (see illustrations 153 and 154), some of which are, however, far more beautiful and imaginative than most of the pin-ups of the following period (see illustration 155), the twenties (see illustration 156), or the present day (see illustration 157). Of course, exceptions can be found (see illustration 158).

Today, pin-up magazines proliferate, but the phenomenon was not unknown in Victorian times. *The Exquisite* ('a choice selection of Pictorial and Literary Beauties') was on sale as early as 1842, and offered its readers pictures of nude girls and scantily dressed actresses; issue number 59 featured a full-frontal nude kneeling in a river, with the caption 'Who wants me?'.[21] During the 1860s *The Day's Doings* and *Here and There* were full of girls in bathing costumes, or else in long skirts blown by the wind so that a saucy knee was revealed. By the 1890s a wide selection of such magazines was available, including the famous *Photo Bits*.

At the same time, stronger material was circulating underground. Victorian pornography (see illustrations 159 and 160) catered for every taste, and in its essentials it was little different from the products of Denmark and Sweden today, apart from

152   *Victorian photograph,*
1890

153 *Victorian pin-up photograph*, 1890s

154 *Pin-up photograph,*
France, 1900s

155 *Pin-up photograph,*
France, *c.* 1915

156 *Pin-up photograph,*
English ?, *c.* 1925

157 *Pin-up photograph,*
Penthouse magazine,
London, 1969

its general lack of sophistication. The main suppliers were Charles Carrington and Charles Hirsch in Paris and Leonard Smithers in London. In an album of catalogues in the British Museum Library is a list of 'strictly confidential' items imported from Paris, including *The Belle of Castillane*: 'a most befitting girl, whose coquetry is most tempting. Her beautiful knickers with lace insertion and embroidery excites alone men's admiration, revealing still prettier scenes underneath. She is seen in lusty indulgences with a young gentleman, a debauchery is going on, and at the very moment when both their sperm is fired off, she indicates her sweet enjoyment by frantically beating a Tambourine. Twenty cabinets for thirty shillings, or seven

158 *Pin-up photograph,*
France, 1920s

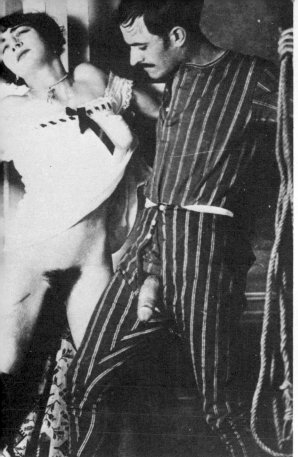

159 *Victorian pornographic photograph,*
    c. 1890s

160 *Victorian pornographic photograph,*
    c. 1890s

dollars.'[22] Another set is entitled *In the Nunnery*: 'the nun is well shaped, its forms are standing out prominently, the secret charms of an irreproachable freshness, the eyes blazing with unsatiable desires. Add to this a sexton who knows how to handle the holy-water sprinkler and to ring the bell during the divine service.'

In the same album are catalogues of books and magazines. One issued by Charles Carrington in 1901 ('rare, curious and voluptuous reading') includes *Teleny or the Reverse of the Medal* ('most powerful and celebrated written erotica'), the homo-sexual novel said to be the work of Oscar Wilde, and certainly one of the most interesting and well-written of all Victorian underground publications.[23] Also listed are such famous books as *Gynecocracy* ('the adventures and psychological experiences of Julian Robinson, Viscount Ladywood, under petticoat rule, written by himself'); *My Secret Life or The Modern Casanova* by 'Walter'; *The Horn Book* ('a girl's guide to the knowledge of Good and Evil, or modern studies in the science of stroking'); *The Romance of Lust; Venus School-mistress, or Birchen Sports*; and *The Pearl, a Journal of Facetiae and Voluptuous Reading* ('the best and grandest erotic work in the English language'). Many of these works are quoted at length by Henry Spencer Ashbee in his three-volume bibliography of erotica written in the 1870s and 1880s, which is discussed in Appendix II of the present work.[24]

[199]

The Pearl, which has recently been reprinted in America,[25] made its debut in London in July 1879 and ran to eighteen issues before vanishing mysteriously in December 1880. Like *The Exquisite* it contained blue jokes and anecdotes, gossip of the day and stories of a sexual nature. A special feature was a parody of *The Merry Muses* by Robert Burns, entitled *The Joys of Coming Together*. The stories were standard examples of the pornographic novels of the day, with titles such as *Lady Pokingham, Or They All Do It* and *Miss Cootes' Confession, or the Voluptuous Experiences of an Old Maid*. They contained no feelings or emotional commitments; women were shown being used by men as sex objects, and the stories merely catered for the fantasies of their usually male readers.

Another catalogue offers an item called *Raped on the Railway* ('the true story of the extraordinary adventures that befell a Lady who was first Ravished and then severely Beaten on the Scotch Express. 1894, Society of Bibliophiles. N.B. When ordering it will be sufficient to write: "Please send a Railway Guide".') It is interesting to compare this with an American book called *Raped on the Elevated Railway* ('a true story of a lady who was first ravished, then flagellated on the Uptown Express, illustrating the perils of travel in the new Machine Age'). There was an enormous market for pornography in America at this time, and little home-produced material, and so English books would often be adapted for the American market. But America could boast one major work in this vein: Mark Twain's *1601*, written in 1876. This is a fictitious conversation between Queen Elizabeth and various of her courtiers about farting, fucking, and similar subjects. The language is extremely free: Twain wrote to a Cleveland librarian: 'If there is a decent word findable in it, it is because I overlooked it.'[26] Later American works of pornography include *Dolly Morton*, set in the slave plantations of the Deep South, and *Sodom in Union Square, or Revelations of the Doings in 14th Street* ('by an Ex-Police Captain of New York').

The abundance of pornography and pin-ups in Victorian England met a need felt by a large proportion of the population, mainly male, which could not be satisfied solely by respectable titillation in the form of Classical nudes painted by Leighton, Poynter, Alma-Tadema, etc. But the dual standard employed consciously or subconsciously by these Academicians was not characteristic of all Victorian art. We have already seen that Rossetti and Beardsley were at the same time producing works of art whose eroticism was genuine and central to their whole purpose. Rossetti's *Beata Beatrix* of 1863 and *Proserpine* of 1874 (see illustration 132) were the direct outcome of his relations with two remarkable women, and their eroticism is made mysterious rather than polite.

Aubrey Beardsley was a prolific artist during his short career, as well as the author of *Venus and Tannhäuser* (or *Under the Hill*),[27] one of the most elegant examples of erotica ever written. Sexually provocative drawings do not occupy a large proportion of his work, but they were certainly of great importance to him. His most startling works in this vein are his illustrations to Juvenal's Sixth Satire and the *Lysistrata* of Aristophanes, both of 1896. In a letter to Smithers he wrote: 'The *Lysistrata* drawings are going very well . . . surely it is the occasion for a little prayer and praise',[28] and to Andre Raffalovich: 'I have just completed a set of illustrations to *Lysistrata*, I think they are in a way the best things I have done.'[29] These drawings, which were too extreme for Eduard Fuchs,[30] constitute a clear and strong expression of Beardsley's phallic obsession and castration complex, with their enormous and lovingly delineated erect penises (see illustration 161). Beardsley was a lonely man, who remained from childhood very close to his mother and sister Mabel. Both appear frequently in his work, taking on the figurative roles of the Madonna and the Magdalene. Recent books by Brian Reade[31] and Malcolm Easton[32] have suggested that he was a transvestite, a clothes fetishist, a homosexual or a trans-sexual, and that he had incestuous relations with Mabel; certainly his cult of Wagner was largely due to his fascination with the brother–sister incest theme of *The Ring*. He was a pre-cocious child who remained one for the rest of his short life, dying at the age of twenty-five in 1898. Much of his behaviour as a man was that of a child, and in his drawings, his tall long-necked women seem like a child's view of its mother. 'The genius of Beardsley's eroticism is precisely the quality Freud ascribed to the sexuality of children: polymorphous perversity', writes Brigid Brophy in her fascinating book on Beardsley,[33] and one does not have to subscribe literally to her description of him as 'the most intensely and electrically erotic artist in the world'[34] to see that her analysis of his eroticism is correct. Beardsley's work encompasses the whole spectrum of sex, from hermaphroditism (*Salome*) and transvestism (*Mlle de Maupin* and *Mrs Pinchwife*) to bestiality (*Venus and Tannhäuser*) and flagellation (*Earl Lavender* and *Juvenal's Satire*). Fetishism appears frequently, especially as regards shoes and hair; 'his imagination seems to be at the actual infantile origin of

161   Aubrey Beardsley, *The Lacedaemonian Ambassadors*, from *Lysistrata*, 1896

fetishism . . . everything is a jewel and everything is a sex organ.'[35]

Beardsley once alluded to himself as a eunuch, and his work betrays a castration complex which is not uncommon in sexually repressed individuals; in his case, it was heightened by his awareness of his approaching death from consumption. The giant erect phalluses of the late *Lysistrata* illustrations (see illustration 161), drawn with such tender care yet aching with sexual frustration, constitute an unequivocal and moving testimony to this castration complex, and along with the *Salome* drawings they contribute to the art of the Victorian era some of its few examples of genuine and honest eroticism.

---

b: Erotic Themes in Victorian Literature

by

BARRY CURTIS[1]

Shortly after the beginning of the nineteenth century, a new and stricter morality began to impose itself on English Society. The transition from the relatively open-minded 'Age of Reason' to the narrow morality of Victorian England was fostered by the rise of Evangelicalism, the insular attitudes adopted during the Napoleonic Wars, and by a new domestication, a withdrawal from the exigencies of commercialism into larger family-units, which acted as cradles for new moral and religious attitudes.

Bowdler's censored edition of Shakespeare indicates the shift in opinions. It made its first appearance in 1804 as a children's book, but the review of the 1820 edition was prophetic of what was to become a familiar attitude to matters of 'indelicacy' in literature: 'It is better every way that what cannot be spoken and ought not to have been written should not be written.'[2] Nevertheless, a large number of Victorians did not subscribe to the strict demands of 'Propriety', and many who did so outwardly, in fact, pursued life-styles essentially unchanged from that of earlier and laxer generations. Even those who conformed totally to Victorian standards of morality might be suspect in terms of our own sophisticated awareness of 'deviations'.[3] Energies which might now be devoted to personal relationships were often channelled by the rigid concentration of the period into matters of social concern, but the reluctance to explore problems of sexuality in both public and private realms of life often led to a terrible neglect.

Victorian writers were primarily concerned with the social context. Carlyle, Ruskin, Arnold, Tennyson, Eliot, and Dickens felt the necessity of commenting on achievements and shortcomings, and weighed their age against previous ages, often unfavourably. Insights derived from the interactions of social compromise and 'that lost pulse of feeling', inspired passages of discontent and despair which often explored the boundaries of moral permissiveness. Some of the most popular authors whose work has scarcely survived in critical terms: Coventry Patmore and Martin Tupper (whose *Proverbial Philosophy* sold one and a half million copies in fifty editions) were content to versify maxims of conventional behaviour and to celebrate the new domestic mythology, avoiding areas of discussion which might be considered taboo. The more adventurous authors were sometimes taken to task: George Eliot was rebuked in the *Saturday Review* for writing about pregnancy in *Adam Bede* and Tennyson was accused of 'amatory tenderness' by *The Times* when he synthesised his bereavement with intellectual consolation in *In Memoriam*, a long poem suffused with a strong element of homosexual love.[4] Tennyson's ability to evoke sensual beauty in early poems like 'The Lotus Eaters' had led to accusations of 'aestheticism', and his involvement with 'questionable' subject-matter in 'Maud' drew the following comment: 'If an author pipe of adultery, fornication, murder and suicide, set him down as a practiser of those crimes.'[5]

Few writers were prepared to rebel against the morality so carefully guarded by the critics; but even before the 'Aesthetic Movement', which through its amoral concern for the propagation of beauty and its associations with French Decadence, violated the conventions; artistic heterodoxy had occasionally been associated with moral revolution. Shelley had written in his Introduction to *Queen Mab*: 'Not even the intercourse of the sexes is exempt from the despotism of positive institution.' Swinburne offered his pagan alternatives to: 'the supreme evil—god'. Rossetti endorsed Keats's toast: 'Confusion to Newton', and the general refusal of avant-garde Romantic artists to: 'stand in the foremost files of time'[6] suggested an alternative to the puritan capitalist ethos of progress. The defenders of morality could find confirmation of what they must have felt—that unconstrained sexuality was radically opposed to the existing structure of society—from socialist theorists like Robert Owen at one extreme and from *My Secret Life* at another, where Walter testifies: 'To talk of fucking with a woman is to remove all social distinction.'[7] Interestingly, the Romantic rebel, driven to disaffection from society by the demands of the spirit, invites comparison with that figure of Victorian medical fantasy—the self-loving masturbator:

> *Silent, pensive, idle, restless, slow—*
> *His, like all deep grief, plunged in solitude.*
> —Lord Byron, *Don Juan*.

Such behaviour was far from what was to be expected from the 'normal healthy buy'. William Acton, a leading authority on sexual matters, pointed out that those most given to that 'dangerous' form of sexual introversion were likely to be: 'the puny exotic', whose 'intellectual development has been fostered at the expense of his physical development'.[8] Warnings against sexual activity became explicit and even those writers who avoided the conspiracy of silence seem to have been caught, like the medical science of the time, in an equation of sexuality with loss, waste, and pain. The Malthusian view of semen as an asset to be 'spent', or, in default, as a waste-product, spills over into Victorian pornography, where it is treated with Micawber-like denials. The cynical Walter even saw modesty in economic terms as the means of conserving an asset in order to sell later at a higher price. The features of Aesthetic beauty with their suggestion of over indulgence and enervation called forth quasi-medical diagnoses; Octave Mirbeau commented on Burne-Jones's figures: 'The rings under the eyes are unique in the whole history of art; it is impossible to tell whether they are the result of masturbation, lesbianism, normal love making or tuberculosis.'[9]

Of the writers with Aesthetic tendencies Dante Gabriel Rossetti was singled out by Thomas Maitland in 1871 to bear the brunt of a not entirely unreasonable attack on the 'Fleshly School of Poetry', which was published in the *Contemporary Review* under the pseudonym 'Robert Buchanan'.[10] Maitland came to admit that the article was 'irresponsible', but it seems that his opinions were shared to some extent by Browning and Tennyson.[11] In retrospect, Rossetti's poems seem more concerned with the spirit than with carnal aspects of love, as Yeats noted: 'He listens to the cry of the flesh until it becomes proud and passes beyond the world, where some immense desire that the intellect cannot understand mixes with the desire for a body's warmth and softness.'[12] But his is a confused spirituality which maintains an uneasy balance between ideal and worldly love: the ethereal 'Blessed Damosel' is sufficiently material to impart warmth:

> And still she bowed herself and stooped
> Out of the circling charm
> Until her bosom must have made
> The bar she leaned on warm.

Perhaps the poem which most successfully balances physical desire and spiritual attainment is 'Nuptial Sleep', which was excluded from some editions of his poems. The title had been changed by Rossetti from 'Placate Venere' to 'help it stand fire', but Tennyson is said to have found it: 'the filthiest thing he had ever read',[13] and Maitland singled it out for detailed attention, finding in it: 'the most secret mysteries of sexual connection and that with so sickening a desire to reproduce the sensual mood, so careful a choice of epithet to convey mere animal sensations that we merely shudder at the shameless nakedness'.[14]

Another controversial poem by Rossetti, 'Jenny' took for its subject the contemporary issue of prostitution; the tone was didactic and he himself considered it: 'a sermon, nothing less'.[15] It contained some justifiable moralising on: 'the hatefulness of man' and speculations on social mutability, which could not have been welcome in this context, mingled with passages of *fin-de-siècle* eroticism:

> *Your silk ungirdled and unlaced*
> *And warm sweets open to the waist*
> *All golden in the lamplights gleam.*

Having experienced Ruskin's reluctance to submit this poem to Thackeray for publication, Rossetti withheld publication for ten years. Maitland seized upon it and found it: 'Full of coarseness from the first line to the last . . . no extract can fitly convey the unwholesomeness and indecency.'[16] His more general criticisms point up the Aesthetic element, the 'unnaturalness' which was to be a major consideration in later attacks on 'immorality': '. . . such an excess of affection is not in Nature'.[17] Rossetti's contribution, particularly to Symbolist thought, included a feeling for a unity of the arts, which he recognised as analogous to sexual union: 'Picture and poem must bear the same relation to each other as Beauty in man and woman: the point of meeting where the two are most identical is the supreme perfection.'[18]

In England, Swinburne was the poet most concerned with erotic themes and the defence of his right to be so. About his much-criticised *Poems and Ballads* of 1865, he wrote: 'I have striven here to express that transient state of spirit through which a man may be supposed to pass foiled in love and weary of loving, but not yet in sight of rest, in those violent delights which have violent ends in free and frank sensualities, which at least profess to be no more than they are.'[19] In spite of the modesty of his professions, the 'libidinous laureate of a pack of satyrs', as one critic saw him, did suggest an alternative to Victorian puritanism, fragmentarily based on a Dionysiac Hellenistic ideal of the: 'noble and nude and antique'. Many critics would argue that all of Swinburne's poetry, especially the erotic element, professes to be more than it is. T. S. Eliot has denied that there is any erotic content in his work, because, he claims, eroticism can only attach itself to an object, and Swinburne's language is so far removed from the object as to be non-referential.[20] Buchanan's contemporary criticism, published in the *Athenaeum* suggests a similar view: 'The strong pulse of true passion beats in none of them.'

Those who approved and those who attacked Swinburne's early poems found in them a celebration of animal passion not to be found elsewhere in English literature of the period. Most of the criticism levelled against him showed an awareness that he was conversant with French models which were themselves looked upon with great indignation. Maitland pointed out that *Anactoria* was about, 'that branch of crime', the Sapphic passion, and that Swinburne was trying to emulate Baudelaire's *Femmes Damnées*. Later poets turned to French models as an alternative to sentiment and composure, and, eventually, to purge the rhetoric of Swinburne himself.

Swinburne's attitude to the female protagonists of his own poetry seems to express an extreme reaction to the polarity of the sexes in Victorian England. The refusal to allow women any participation in matters of intellect fostered both contempt and an eagerness to consider the feminine principle as an expression of

[205]

the life-force, an Earth Mother or nature goddess. However, the poet's masochism contained an active perversity which favoured the 'roses and raptures of vice' over the 'lilies and languors of virtue', and suggested an antipathy to passive 'aestheticism' with its chivalric worship of a feminine ideal.

Dolores, with its enumerated but unspecified sins, and *Faustine*:

> *Ah beautiful, passionate body*
> *That never has ached with a heart!*
> *On thy mouth though the kisses are bloody,*
> *Though they sting till it shudder and smart*
> *More kind than the love we adore is*
> *They hurt not the heart nor the brain*
> *Oh bitter and tender Dolores*
> *Our Lady of Pain,*

with its indefinite, incomplete actions of half-enjoyed pain, are characteristic of a number of poems. In *Hermaphroditus*, the poet explores the permutations of male and female sexuality with the thoroughness of de Sade, whose writings were a profound influence.

The 'punishment' which Swinburne apparently received from hired women in St John's Wood is a rare example of active deviation in his own life, though his obsessions with flogging manifest themselves in his work, especially in the novel *Lesbia Brandon*: 'Deeply he desired to die by her if that could be, to destroy her; scourge her into swooning and absorb her blood with kisses,' and in the limited edition of *The Whippingham Papers* of 1887 he made some extravagant claims for the pastime, in the same self-confident tones we encounter in Acton and other highly regarded Victorian sexual theorists: 'No propensity to which human nature is addicted, or lech to which it is prone, holds firmer root than Flaggelation.' Elsewhere, he wrote of the flogging of schoolboys in terms of heroic literature: 'There can be no subject fuller of incident, character, interest; realistic, modern, dramatic, intense and vividly pictorial.'[21] He even discussed the frequent critical onslaughts on his own poetry in terms of birching: 'Twice I have been swished in private and twice in public before the whole school for irreverence. My skin has the marks of the birch still on it.' *The Whippingham Papers* includes poems; birchings in dramatic form; and *Hints on Flogging*, where the dominating female figure reasserts itself: 'One of the great charms of birching lies in the sentiment that the flogee is the powerless victim of the furious rage of a beautiful woman.' And short-stories which betray sadism combined with pathetic fantasy: 'The last cut left poor Reginald's bare bottom covered with blood. He rose from the block crying and sobbing like a child. It was not every day that a boy got so severe a flogging, and it made him so tame and gentle that he was quite kind to me all that day and helped me to pick out the broken bits of birch that were sticking in my flesh.' (From: *A Boy's First Flogging at Birchminster*.)

[206]

Swinburne's relations with women were not destined to be mutually satisfying. His brief liaison with the remarkable Adah Isaacs Mencken (see illustration 162), an imposing equestrienne and writer, who was said to have inspired the poem *Dolorida* (which Swinburne denied), was remembered by Julian Field as: 'a wild bet of Rossetti's'. Swinburne's part was relatively passive: 'He told me all about Mencken calling on him and telling him bluntly she had come to *sleep* with him',[22] and she is said to have reported back to Rossetti that she could not make the poet understand that 'biting is no good'.

The avoidance of conventional relations with adult women testifies to a powerful alienation from the mysteries and restraints imposed on and by the Victorian female. John Ruskin and Lewis Carroll seem to have felt aversion to the attitudes which surrounded sexual maturity and knowledge. Carroll (see illustration 163) ruthlessly dismissed his many girlfriends when they reached puberty: 'About nine out of ten of my child friendships get shipwrecked at the critical point where the stream and the river meet.'[23] Even his favourite Alice (Liddell): 'Alice seems changed a good deal and hardly for the better—probably going through the usual awkward stage of transition.'[24] Ruskin's life was ravaged by his love for young girls; one of his biographers, Joan Evans, notes: 'so soon as they began to be women they belonged to another world than his, into which his emotions could not follow them,'[25] and his marriage was brought to an unhappy end by his unfortunate attempt to rationalise away sexual relations with a wife he considered unsuitable for motherhood.

Part of the prevalent affection for children seems to have grown from an aesthetic preference for the childlike form over the deformities and restrictions which most Victorian women imposed upon themselves, and many artists used children as

162　*Algernon Charles Swinburne and Adah Isaacs Mencken*, photograph, 1868

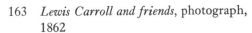

163　*Lewis Carroll and friends*, photograph, 1862

models. Frank Miles, who shared a house with Oscar Wilde before the latter's marriage, maintained a thirteen-year-old child model and shared her with other academicians until the police intervened. A less innocent interest was also widely shared and served by the massive trade in child prostitution, so spectacularly revealed by the activities of the journalist W. T. Stead.[26] The records of three London Hospitals for three years reveal two thousand seven hundred cases of venereal disease in girls between the ages of eight and eleven.

Even those with more conventional tastes may have found the company of their wives uninteresting, especially if the ladies were content with William Acton's demarcation of their role: 'Love of home, children and domestic duties are the only passions they feel',[27] and his assurance (with the apparent assumption that most Victorian men would have had sexual experience outside marriage) that there would be no danger of a wife demanding the sexual excitement that a courtesan might insist on. The narrow specifications of Victorian marriage with its strange combination of romance and chastity led in some cases to the idea of marriage as a justifiable but nevertheless degrading experience for the almost supernatural female. This attitude introduced a spiritual tension into the relationship which was intended to safeguard against disruption by disobedience or adultery. The Prince's description of his mother in Tennyson's poem *The Princess* suggests the exact opposite of Swinburne's Earth Mother, but both are roles imposed on a creature whose humanity was denied:

> *No angel but a dearer being, all dipt*
> *In angel instincts, breathing Paradise,*
> *Interpreter between the gods and men,*
> *Who look'd all native to her place, and yet*
> *On tiptoe seem'd to touch upon a sphere*
> *Too gross to tread, and all male minds perforce*
> *Sway'd to her form their orbits as they moved,*
> *And girdled her with music. . . .*

Richard Burton, who went on his extensive travels with a magnificently un-prejudiced mind and became an expert on sexuality in many societies, railed at the 'immodest modesty' of his age. He found the 'mysteries of the East' refreshing after the ritual complexities of male–female relationships in England, and he wondered at the 'mental prostitution' of so-called civilised women, who were 'unable to relieve the brain through the body'[28]—women who, through the agency of romantic novels and titillating and trivial journalism were: 'living in the rustle of (imaginary) copulation.'[29] In the Terminal Essay of Burton's magnum opus—the translation of the *Arabian Nights*—he proposed sex education for women (a subject hitherto ignored in contemporary treatises) as a move towards improving the health of society. It is ironic and indicative of the strength of conventional morality and the dictates of religious conventions that Burton's own remarkable wife and companion, Isobel, destroyed his diaries and the important manuscript of his translation of

The Perfumed Garden after his death. For that act and for the elaborate Catholic rites she arranged for his funeral, she earned a great deal of criticism, notably from Swinburne, who concluded his elegy: 'The corpse be theirs to mock; the soul is free,'[30] and from Ernest Dowson, one of the nineties poets, who castigated her devotion: 'To her one God—sterile Propriety.'[31]

At a time when sexual feelings which did not adopt narrow and conventional modes of expression were taboo, artists who developed a vocabulary and a set of attitudes centred around the appreciation of the beautiful came under suspicion. In England the path to a more explicit treatment of sexual themes lay through the struggle to relieve art of its moral responsibilities, and this was achieved by Aestheticism, combined with a new openness to the ideas of the Continental avant-garde. The 'life of the imagination' which Ruskin had tried to foster was taken up by later writers with less of his awe of nature and more of his respect for art. Words like 'precious' and 'intense' and 'amusing' which had been used by Keats, Ruskin, and Rossetti to focus sensitivity were adopted and used with less specific intentions in Aesthetic circles.

Walter Pater exerted a strong influence over most aspects of the 'Decadence',[32] although he, himself, led a discreet and withdrawn life. One biographer, A. C. Benson, noted his 'faded, sedentary air', and Henry James testified to his self-effacement: 'He is the mask without the face and there isn't in his total superfice a tiny point of vantage for the newspaper to flap his wings on.'[33] But there is little doubt that he was looked upon as a dangerous man in some quarters, with, Benson suggests, an inclination towards romantic homosexuality: 'his genius was for friendship rather than for love, and his circumstances and environment were favourable to celibacy; and thus he passed his life in a certain mystery, though the secret is told for those who can read it in his writings.'[34] But the subversive quality in Pater's work did not lie in this direction; ironically, by studying the works of writers who were standard academic fare at Oxford, he arrived at a position which negated the complex moral code of Victorian England. By studying Plato, Heraclitus, and Hegel, Pater seems to have come closer to a twentieth-century viewpoint on morality than any of his contemporaries. His modernity carried with it all the connotations of relative moral values. He rejected authority in favour of observation and experiment—an approach which Huxley had recommended for scientific research. He unerringly cultivated sensibility and subjectivity, emphasising the rarified atmosphere within: 'that thick wall of personality'. He was willing to accept the continuity of man with nature in a way that many contemporaries found contra-dictory to established religious and moral values. Pater's almost fearful sensitivity to beauty and the enervation attendant on overstimulation of the senses was evoked by him in both content and style and exaggerated by his followers into the mannerisms of Aestheticism and Decadence.

Lionel Johnson wrote of Pater's striving 'with cloistral jealousness of ardour',[35] and that apparent contortion of passion and aim became a model for his many followers. In *The Renaissance* Pater exhorted active appreciation: 'Great passions may give us this quickened sense of life, ecstasy and sorrow of love, the various forms of enthusiastic activity, disinterested or otherwise which comes naturally to many of us. Only be sure it is passion',[36] and this, taken in conjunction with the rejection of systems or theories, 'we have not identified with ourselves, or of what is *only* conventional', constitutes an inflammatory text which appears to condone personal gratification at the expense of authority. The Conclusion in which this doctrine appeared was withdrawn lest 'it might possibly mislead some of those young men into whose hands it might fall'.

Pater's attitude to the Greek ideal of beauty and the revaluation of male beauty in Greek statuary propagated by Winckelmann in the previous century, suggest some of the uneasiness which arose from the pervasive Grecian mood of Victorian education. Macaulay seems to have been one of the first to feel discomfort in his affection for Plato; he pointed out that the attitude to homosexuality had changed and that it was in modern times 'regarded as the most odious of all forms of immorality'.[37]

The new Hellenism was one of the areas of interest in which a more tolerant attitude to homosexual love becomes apparent, but some measure of acceptance is to be found in other connections. The contempt in which most women were held in intellectual circles fostered close comradeship between men which was reinforced by the great psychological barriers existing between the sexes. Medievalism, which permeated most areas of artistic and religious endeavour, offered the powerful precedent of chivalric codes—and stressed a high degree of homosexual intimacy, rust, and dependence —the Oxford Movement with its leaning towards Catholicism, suggested the cultivation of sensibility and a disposition to monastic celibacy and chaste friendships. G. M. Hopkins captures the strong element of comradeship in the face of religious experience in 'The Bugler's First Communion':

> *There! and your sweetest sendings, ah divine,*
> *By it, heavens, befall him! as a heart Christ's darling, dauntless;*
> *   Tongue true, vaunt- and tauntless;*
> *Breathing bloom of a chastity in mansex fine.*
>
> *Frowning and forfending angel warder*
> *Squander the hell-rook ranks sally to molest him;*
> *   March, kind comrade abreast him;*
> *Dress his days to a dextrous and starlight order.*

However, the most significant factor in the rise of homosexual literature towards the end of the century was the rise of Hellenism. Burton, who had the advantage of first-hand knowledge of sexual mores in the Near East, was in a position to compare the probable state of Ancient Greek morality with the nineteenth-century English interpretation, and he concluded: 'We are overapt to apply our nineteenth-century prejudices and prepossessions to the morality of the Ancient Greeks who would have specimen'd such squeamishness with Attic salt.'[38] Many who did not share the conventional tastes of society must have felt the teacher–pupil relationship to be a purer expression of love than the formalities of romantic love followed by marriage. Aleister Crowley expressed a characteristically forceful but not necessarily uncommon opinion: 'At school I was taught to admire Plato and Aristotle who recommend sodomy to youths. I am not so rebellious as to oppose their dictum; and, in truth, there seems no better way to avoid the contamination of woman and the morose pleasures of solitary vice.'[39]

The law, however, was quite firmly opposed to homosexual conduct between men. (Many Victorians believed with Queen Victoria that a female equivalent was 'unthinkable', although isolation from men and enforced idleness in the middle and upper classes resulted in many romantic attachments.) In 1885, the Criminal Law Amendment Act legislated against: 'acts of gross indecency' between male persons; the vagueness of its terms brought about the appropriate nickname: The Black-mailers' Charter.

The notorious application of the 1885 Act to the case of Oscar Wilde points up the revenge of society against an indiscreet flaunting of convention. Wilde (see illustration 164) was only one of a number of literary figures, including John Addington Symonds, Oscar Browning, and Edward Fitzgerald who shared similar tastes but managed their affairs with discretion. It is sometimes suggested that the years following Wilde's trial of 1895 saw a revolution in morality, a purge of Aestheticism and a move towards 'healthiness' in literature, represented by authors like Henley and Kipling. Kipling's poem 'The Mary Gloster' suggests a contempt for the 'unnatural' practices which were felt to lie behind Aesthetic attitudes:

164   *Oscar Wilde and*
      Lord Alfred Douglas,
      photograph, *c.* 1895

For you muddled with books and pictures an' china an' etchins and fans.
And your room at college was beastly—more like a whore's than a man's.

But the poetry of admiration if not of eroticism continued unabated. Edward Cracroft Lefroy's eulogies of footballers and cricketers betray a sentimental appreciation of male beauty closely tied to the rituals of public-school life, and represent a genre which continued well beyond the turn of the century:

> *If I could paint you, friend, as you stand there*
> *Guard of the goal, defensive, open eyed,*
> *Watching the tortured bladder slide and glide*
> *Under the twinkling feet; arms bare, head bare,*
> *The breeze a-tremble through crow-tufts of hair;*
> *Red-brown in face, and ruddier having spied*
> *A wily foeman breaking from the side,*
> *Aware of him—of all else unaware:*
> *If I could limn you as you leap and fling*
> *Your weight against his passage, like a wall;*
> *Clutch him and collar him and rudely cling*
> *For one brief moment till he falls—you fall;*
> *My sketch would have what Art would never give,*
> *Sinew and breath and body; it would live.*[40]

Wilde's *The Picture of Dorian Gray*, combined with the impact of his extravagantly 'camp' Aesthetic pose is evidence of a willingness to carry forward the attacks on two fronts initiated by his hero Baudelaire against the Bourgeoisie and by the Ruskin–Morris faction, which Wilde also subscribed to, against the Philistines. Not surprisingly, the book met with a great deal of criticism. The *Daily News* commented: 'It is a tale spawned from the leprous literature of the French Decadents —a poisonous book, the atmosphere of which is heavy with mephitic odours of moral and spiritual putrefaction.'[41] The romantic friendship between Lord Henry Wooton and the beautiful youth which is central to the story, was raised at the trial; the prosecution quoted:

Sir Edward Carson: ' "I grew afraid that the world would know of my idolatry." Why should you grow afraid that the world should know of it?'
Oscar Wilde: 'Because there are people in the world who cannot understand the intense devotion, affection and admiration that an artist can feel for a wonderful and beautiful personality. These are the conditions under which we live. I regret them.'[42]

The prosecution did not look far beyond *Dorian Gray*, some maxims and letters for courtroom evidence, but there is ample evidence elsewhere in Wilde's work of a sensitive and romantic appreciation of male beauty. 'Wasted Days', first published in 1877, was rewritten as 'Lily Girl' for the poems of 1881: it features:

> *A fair slim boy, not made for this world's pain,*
> *With hair of gold, thick-clustering around his ears,*
> *And longing eyes, half veiled by foolish tears*
> *Like bluest water seen through mists of rain:*
> *Pale cheeks whereon no love hath left its stain.*

A more extreme expression of that 'certain tendency', was Wilde's apparent involvement in *Teleny*; this book, published in a limited edition in 1893, was subtitled *The Reverse of the Medal—A physiological romance of today*. The result of a literary collaboration, the story achieved a fair literary standard combined with unusual frankness. Leonard Smithers published the prospectus in which he claimed, with some justification, that it was 'undoubtedly the most powerful and cleverly written erotic romance which has appeared in the English language during recent years'.[43] Interesting, as evidence of the increasing interest in the psychology of 'deviant' behaviour, is his mention in the same prospectus of the research of John Addington Symonds and Havelock Ellis. Wilde was to carry a recognition of the prevalence of homosexual feeling further with his essay *The Portrait of Mr W. H.* in which he explored the probable inspiration of Shakespeare's sonnets. By opening up that possibility he added the authority of England's greatest author (although he was approached with some timidity even by relatively open-minded writers like George Eliot and Charlotte Brontë) to the biblical precedent of David and Jonathan and the prevailing Greek Classics, which seemed to support a widened scope of homosexual affection, in spite of Jowett's attempts to explain away Plato.[44]

Shortly before Wilde's trial, Edward Carpenter, a friend and correspondent of the American poet Walt Whitman, and a sharer with him of the ideal of 'comradeship', lectured at Manchester on 'Homogenic Love'. Partaking of the rational mood of investigation which belongs to the nineties, this was one of the first attempts to raise the matter in public and to suggest positive elements in homosexual relationships. J. A. Symonds published his study on the same subject in 1891, in a limited edition under the title *A Problem in Modern Ethics*, and later continued his research and collaborated with Havelock Ellis to produce a collection of case-histories.

Carpenter mingled elements of socialist Utopian aims with quasi-mysticism. He proposed recognition of an 'intermediate sex'[45] and the acceptance of the theories of an Austrian writer, K. H. Ulrichs, who had suggested the term 'Urnings' (from *Uranos*, denoting beings of a higher order) to recognise the existence of the presence of female souls in male bodies and vice versa. Such people were seen as possible 'interpreters' between the sexes. Carpenter's theories suggest the urgency which had been expressed in various ways throughout the nineteenth century of freeing sexual roles of their polarity; and the realisation that the necessity of political and sexual change were linked. In exhorting women to free themselves from sexual domination he quotes Ferdinand Bebel: 'Women have as little hope from men as

[213]

workmen from the middle classes.' Like Wilde, Carpenter straddles the two main traditions of artistic non-conformity in Victorian England; his simple rural socialism belongs to the Arts and Crafts Movement, with which he had points of contact, but his writings on the associations of sexuality with mysticism (sex and star-worship: 'Between these two poles the human mind has swayed since the eldest time'[46]) links him closely with the preoccupations of *fin-de-siècle* Decadence.

The theme of mystical sexuality was taken up most consistently by remarkable figures like Count Stenbock, who dabbled in 'homosexual vampirism' and by Aleister Crowley, who experimented with a form of alchemy for which he used sexual fluids. His discoveries, he claimed, were paralleled by a European organisation known as Ordo Templi Orientis (one of many secret societies which flourished at the turn of the century), who were involved in reviving practices of the Knights Templars, whose activities traditionally included homosexuality linked with Satanism.

Crowley was an unusual combination of poet, explorer, and magician. His violent and sustained revolt against established religion may be seen as a reaction against the cruelly repressive atmosphere of his childhood, where he suffered the strictures of an extreme Plymouth Brethren upbringing. His poetry was rooted in the Decadence of the nineties when he associated with Beardsley and Yeats (a contemporary member of 'The Order of the Golden Dawn'). In 1898 he published a book of poems called *White Stains*[47] (limited to a hundred copies). Authorship was attributed, by way of vengeance, to a fanatically religious uncle—George Archibald Bishop—who was described as 'A Neuropath of the Second Empire'. The Introduction consists of a brief biography of that imaginary Decadent, which includes a significant tribute to Swinburne: 'Swinburne stands on his solitary pedestal above the vulgar crowds of priapistic plagiarists.' The poems, which are probably the most outspoken and perversely erotic products of the nineteenth century, owe a great deal to Swinburne in style, although they are specific where Swinburne is diffusive. Crowley intended the sequence to be read as a chronological record, showing a progressive dissipation and a resultant: 'increase of selfishness in pleasure' and 'diminution of sensibility to physical charms'. His avowed motive was one of sexual enquiry, an attempt to challenge Krafft-Ebing's contention that sexual aberration was the result of mental disease. In *White Stains* he hoped to evoke a number of progressive deviations and to show an intuitive understanding of each: 'I therefore invented a poet who went wrong, who began with normal and innocent enthusiasms, and gradually developed various vices. He ends by being stricken with disease and madness, culminating in murder.' In his poems he describes his downfall, always explaining the psychology of each act. Crowley undoubtedly enters into the spirit of the enterprise, but the didactic, scientific element which he claims is his starting point does not come over clearly in what reads as a versified collection of unlikely case-histories.

Rondels describes active homosexual love, and a variation of the theme is taken up in *A Ballad of Passive Pederasty*; *A Ballad of Burdens* mingles blasphemy with

venereal disease; *The Blood Lotus* describes 'doubtful liaisons with the grave';
Sleeping in Carthage violates several of the most rigid taboos of the Victorian age
and our own by taking for its theme the practice of cunnilingus with a menstruating
woman.[48]

> *The month of thirst is ended. From the lips*
> *That hide their blushes in the golden wood*
> *A fervent fountain amorously slips,*
> *The dainty rivers of thy luscious blood;*
> *Red streams of sweet nepenthe that eclipse*
> *The milder nectar that the Gods hold good—*
> *How my dry throat, held hard between thy hips,*
> *Shall drain the moon-wrought flow of womanhood!*
> *Divinest token of sterility,*
> *Strange barren fountain blushing from the womb,*
> *Like to an echo of Augustan gloom*
> *When all men drank this wine: it maddens me*
> *With yearnings after new divinity,*
> *Prize of thy draught, somewhere beyond the tomb.*

With Dog and Dame deals with tribadism and bestiality, *La Juive* portrays vicarious
sexual involvement in Christ's crucifixion, and *Necrophilia*, probably the climax of
Crowley's potential to shock, is a detailed description of buggery with a hanged
man (although it hardly explains the psychology of the act):

> *To gnaw thy hollow cheeks and pull*
> *Thy lustful tongue from out its sheath*
> *To wallow in the bowels of death,*
> *And rip thy belly and fill full*
>
> *My hands with all putridities;*
> *To chew thy dainty testicles;*
> *To revel with the worms in Hell's*
> *Delight in such obscenities.*
> *To probe thy belly, and to drink*
> *The godless fluids and the pool*
> *Of rank putrescence from the stool*
> *Thy hanged corpse gave, whose luscious stink*
>
> *Excites these songs sublime. The rod*
> *Gains new desire: dive, howl, cling, suck,*
> *Rave, shriek and chew; excite the fuck,*
> *Hold me, I come! I'm dead! My God!*

Quality aside, these poems testify to the lengths that reaction against repression was prepared to go.

The Wilde trial, although it did not pack every boat-train to France with evacuating homosexuals, did make it more difficult for the attitudes cultivated by Aestheticism to be tolerated. The Continent had always afforded refuge for moral rebels, and Venice was an especially congenial resort. J. A. Symonds had lived there and accomplished a liaison with a gondolier, and 'Baron Corvo', who was later to settle in Venice, spent a great deal of time in Italy in the 1890s, taking photographs of Italian youths which enjoyed popularity in English art magazines. Stories about Toto, an Italian peasant boy, appeared in *The Yellow Book* after the drive to purge that publication of the Decadent influences of Wilde and Beardsley.[49]

Frederick Rolfe, who went under the name of Baron Corvo, and was described by W. H. Auden as: 'a homosexual paranoid', led in Venice 'a life which he could neither have dared nor afforded to lead in England'.[50] The religious impulses which dominated his complicated life, seem to have arisen partly from a contempt for women and a corresponding attraction to young men, in a way which was probably not uncommon; in the words of his biographer, A. J. A. Symons, 'The attractiveness of Catholic priesthood to one so circumstanced can easily be understood. Set among those who had voluntarily embraced celibacy, his abnormality became, not a possible vice, but a sign of vocation.'[51] (Conversion to Catholicism often suggests ulterior motives in the artistic circles of the nineteenth century; the 'Aesthetic conversion' which went with an intense appreciation of ceremonial rites was complemented by the tendency which Holbrook Jackson noted: 'to experience the piquancy of being good after a debauch'.[52])

Corvo's distaste for women did not prevent him from employing female prostitutes, but, generally speaking, his antipathy to femininity seems to belong to the category of an aesthetic disregard for the ambience of Victorian womanhood; Nicholas Crabbe (Corvo's persona in his final novel *The Desire and Pursuit of the Whole*) objects to: 'vapid bunchiness and vacuous inconsequent patchworkiness',[53] and it is possible to sympathise in retrospect. The Aesthetic Movement had worked against these very tendencies in women's dress from 1870 onwards towards the realisation of a compound style based on the 'medieval' quality evident in Pre-Raphaelite painting and the loosely draped style influenced simultaneously by the new Hellenism and the vogue for Japonoiserie. The tendencies of taste moved in reasonable accord with the demands of female emancipation and the warnings of the medical profession against tight lacing. The use of corsets produced the exaggerated hips and thighs and the high, full, and agitated bosom which were favoured by conventional pornography, but were at once irrational, unhygienic and unaesthetic. Richard Burton, whose view of the female form was conditioned by un-English considerations of utility, complained, 'Our modern painters and sculptors, whose study of the nude is usually most perfunctory, have often scandalised me by the lank and greyhound-like fining off of the frame, which thus becomes rather simian than human.'[54] But artists and designers involved in the Aesthetic Movement, like

G. F. Watts and E. W. Godwin, seemed to favour the adolescent form unaccented by artificial means, and were both members of the Anti-Tight-Lacing League. Constance Wilde (wife of Oscar) edited *The Rational Dress Gazette*, and John Collier, a pupil of the Neo-classical artist Poynter, asserted the claims of the new Hellenism on the female form: 'A Greek woman never supposed she had a waist.' Pater, himself, protested against the over-ripe curves which were a feature of conventional fashion and design and approved a restrained and subtle line; he also pioneered the appreciation of youthful form: 'where the transition from curve to curve is so elusive, that Winckelmann compares it to a quiet sea'.[55] The nineties' avant-garde tended to favour the restrained quality of English tailoring; Beardsley is said to have dressed 'like an insurance man', and there is a tendency in his drawings to accommodate the 'New Woman' to this dandified reticence.

Corvo's *Desire and Pursuit of the Whole* provides an interesting example of a taste for the sexually ambiguous, a quality which is present at all levels in the *fin-de-siècle* from the Romantic–Symbolist myth of the hermaphrodite to the music hall impersonator. Max Beerbohm noted, 'that amalgamation of the sexes which is one of the chief planks in the decadent platform'.[56] The heroine Zilda, thrown on the mercy of Crabbe by a storm which also kills her relatives, had been treated as a boy from birth by her gondolier father and her boyish qualities are easy to equate with the fashion aesthetics of the 1920s or the 1960s and far removed from the Victorian woman: 'That slim, strong, brave-breasted athlete aloft there in a white guernsey and blue trousers. . . . He noted how splendidly vivid her sweet flesh was . . . how serene and simple and brave was her poise, how utterly artless was her expression.'

From these few examples it seems possible to suggest that sexual themes in the literature of Victorian England were largely explored by those who stood outside society or were driven to adopt a radical attitude by antipathy to the restricted fulfilment offered by connubial love. Inevitably, those most at odds with morality and the formidable machinery which was dedicated to upholding it were those whose tastes or appetites were expressed as rejections of the rigidly categorised inducements offered by the sexual status quo. Therefore, the most convincing erotic literature is concerned with a measure of 'deviancy'. The conflict in artistic terms only came to a head in the last decades of the century, when attitudes in art and literature emphasised the importance of the life of the artist. The necessary freedom of art to express all aspects of life, and the expression of artistic ideas through a life-style became the same cause: Wilde's defence of his sexual feelings was also a vindication of his rights as an artist.

Chapter 6

Twentieth-century Erotic Art

a: Compulsive Eroticism in Twentieth-century Art

Auguste Rodin is usually thought of as a nineteenth-century artist, the creator of essentially literary sculptures, whose effect, when concerned with physical love, is more often sentimental than truly erotic. His sweetly sexy marbles, for example *The Kiss* (1886; Tate Gallery, London) or *The Eternal Idol* (1889; Rodin Museum, Paris) seem to lack that compulsive urgency which distinguishes true eroticism; they are in fact the culmination of the nineteenth century's desire for respectful idealisation of the human figure, a desire which tended to stifle the compulsive nature of the Michelangelesque tradition in figurative art. But Rodin's later work shows an ambiguity and a restlessness which breathe new life into this tradition. His distorted and unfinished nude figures, often pushed into seemingly impossible positions, show how aware he had become in the early years of the twentieth century of the potential of the human figure as a means of expression.

Rodin's sensual nature made him a fervent womaniser, and he had a succession of mistresses, many of whom, like Camille Claudel, were first his models: it was his custom to kiss and fondle them in order to experience the bodies he intended to portray. Gustave Coquiot commented: 'He tells them, "Don't hurry to get undressed", and he gazes with greedy and sensuous pleasure.'[1] Edmond de Goncourt has described an occasion when Rodin was visiting Claude Monet: the sculptor looked at Monet's four daughters so directly and excitedly at dinner that they felt obliged to leave the table.[2] Rodin tended to conceive of woman as a violent and demanding creature, and the eroticism in much of his work is tinged with a sense of damnation characteristic of Baudelaire, whose *Fleurs du Mal* he had illustrated in a very free manner in the 1880s. Baudelaire's fascination for lesbianism is also reflected in various of Rodin's drawings and sculptures. It was especially in his drawings that Rodin gave free rein to his erotic feelings: in 1902 he executed twenty extremely frank lithographs for Octave Mirbeau's *Le Jardin des Supplices*, and at this period he produced drawings of both heterosexual and homosexual couples in intercourse, as well as many very explicit nudes, an example being *Reclining Female Nude* (c. 1905; Courtauld Institute, London), a pencil drawing in which the emphasis

[218]

is on the vulva. Arthur Symons wrote in 1906: 'In these astonishing drawings from the nude . . . every movement of her body, violently agitated by the remembrance, or the expectation, or the act of desire, is seen at an expressive moment. She turns upon herself in a hundred attitudes, turning always upon the central pivot of the sex.'[3]

Arthur Symons was a great and discerning admirer of Rodin's work and dedicated his book on William Blake to the sculptor with the words: 'his work is the marriage of heaven and hell.' Rodin described his marble of 1888, *The All-Devouring Female*, in these words: 'the woman dominates and forcibly exhausts the man whom she has leapt upon as if a prey, and he does not resist.'[4] His fascination with the sensual possibilities of the female's often violent desire for possession of the male culminated in *Christ and the Magdalene* (1894; Rodin Museum, Paris; see illustration 165), in which he depicted the nude figure of Mary Magdalene pressed against the nude Christ crucified on the cross in a clearly sexual embrace. The combination of Christian iconography and a situation involving physical love of a most extreme nature has produced here one of the most startling and provocative of all erotic works of art.

In spite of, or perhaps because of, his continual womanising, Rodin was at times suspected of homosexual inclinations, and this was especially true of his relationship with Nijinsky. Rodin was present at the first night of the controversial ballet *L'Après-midi d'un faune* in 1912 when the eroticism of Nijinsky's dancing caused a sensation, and the sculptor became a close friend and supporter of the dancer. In his diary,[5] Nijinsky has recorded how he posed in the nude for many hours while Rodin took

165   Auguste Rodin, *Christ and the Magdalene*, 1894

photographs and made sketches for a sculpture inspired by Michelangelo's *David*. But the work never materialised, owing perhaps to the jealousy of Diaghilev, who on one occasion discovered the sculptor and the dancer sprawled across a bed after a long modelling session and drew his own conclusions.[6] But Rodin did produce an extraordinary nude study of Nijinsky in plaster (1912; Rodin Museum, Paris) which certainly has much of the compulsive power of Michelangelo.

Besides Baudelaire, Rodin's most important literary source was Dante, and these two figures lie behind his most important project, *The Gates of Hell* (Rodin Museum, Paris) which occupied much of his time between 1880 and 1917. These gates with their mass of individually sculpted figures are Rodin's vision of the terrors of physical passion, a vision so aptly described by Symons as 'the marriage of heaven and hell'. Included are Paolo and Francesca, Orpheus and Eurydice, and Christ and Mary Magdalene; Eve is depicted along with figures representing lust and avarice; nudes writhe in the throes of love, as much in pain as in ecstasy. In the words of Rilke, 'it is still the eternal conflict of the sexes, but woman is no longer the forced or willing animal. Like man, she is awake and filled with longing, it is as though the two made common cause to find their souls.'[7]

The darker side of sensuality which fascinated Rodin was a preoccupation of many Middle European artists at the close of the nineteenth century and the beginning of the twentieth, especially the Austrian artists Klimt and Schiele. Like his contemporaries Moreau and Beardsley, Klimt was haunted by the image of the *femme fatale*, women like Salome and Judith. Klimt's painting of *Judith* (1901; Gallery of the Nineteenth and Twentieth Centuries, Vienna) shows a dark-haired woman with heavy-lidded eyes and half-open mouth clasping the severed head of her victim Holofernes in her long, wiry fingers as she cradles it against her half-naked torso; she wears rich golden jewellery, and one breast is laid bare while the other is thinly veiled by her heavily embroidered, transparent draperies. Similar figures from the past which obsessed Klimt included Leda and Danae; his *Myth of Danae* (*c*. 1905; private collection, Graz; see illustration 90) is perhaps the most erotic of all representations of this sexual incident which, as we have seen, had fascinated many artists before him. Klimt's *Danae* is a nude with long red hair, her body curled in a foetal position, her eyes closed and lips parted. One hand grips her breast while the other is held between her legs, guiding Jupiter in his manifestation as a shower of gold coins streaming out of the sky.

The history of art has few images of woman in a state of sexual excitement to rival Klimt's *Danae*, and he himself treated such a subject frequently. An example is *The Water Snakes* (1904–7; private collection, Vienna), which shows four nude girls with long flowing hair dappled with sparkling stars, their faces and bodies breathing a startling sensuality. One of these figures was inspired by Franz von Stuck's drawing of the *Allegory of Sin*. Stuck's painting of the same title (*c*. 1900; Pinakothek, Munich), is a typical example of kitsch eroticism, showing a bare-breasted girl with a python wrapped around her shoulders. But a more accurate comparison can be made between Klimt's erotic women and Edvard Munch's *Nude*

Madonna, a coloured lithograph of about 1895 with a printed frame depicting human sperms, in which the Madonna has similar sensually aroused facial features. Munch's work however tends more in the direction of emotionally charged images of sexual frustration, such as *Ashes* (1894; National Gallery, Oslo) and *The Beloved as Vampire* (lithograph).

Like so many revolutionary artists, Klimt was continually in trouble with authorities who did not approve of his attempts to advance the barriers of acceptability. His *Water Snakes* was attacked because no attempt had been made to disguise the pubic hair. In his drawings of nudes, Klimt usually draws attention to the pubic hair, as does Rodin, and indeed in some of them, the sexual area is the focal point of the whole drawing. Amongst his most vehemently condemned drawings were his illustrations to Lucian, published in Leipzig in 1907.[8] These show women, singly or in pairs, caught in their most private moments: one is of a nude lying on her bed masturbating (see illustration 166).

The most heavily condemned of all Klimt's works were his ceiling-decorations for Vienna University. These were commissioned in 1894 but rejected by the University when they were exhibited at the Vienna Sezession in 1900 and 1901, and destroyed by the Germans in 1945. The three huge oil paintings depicted *Philosophy*, *Medicine*, and *Jurisprudence*, and Klimt expressed these concepts by means of a procession of starkly nude figures symbolising varieties of human love and despair. In *Medicine*, the powerful figure of Hygeia, with a snake curled round her body, holds out the cup of healing, while behind her, nude figures are shown in various activities expressing love, ecstasy, procreation, motherhood, illness, and death. Although objections were made to the explicitness of the sexual activities that Klimt depicted, it was perhaps the overall mood of despair—so symptomatic of the period—that made these works especially unacceptable.

Vienna at the turn of the century was a lively artistic centre, but amongst its writers and musicians were some—like Hoffmansthal, Schnitzler, Mahler, Berg,

166   Gustav Klimt, *Woman Masturbating*, 1907

and Schoenberg—whose works showed an awareness that the society they lived in was suffering from a cultural instability that would soon end in its political dissolution. These men were explorers, and the area of exploration that caused the greatest uproar was the function of the sexual instinct: this was, after all, the period that saw the first writings of Freud[9] and Weininger.[10] The artist whose work best showed the inner emotional stresses of his time was Klimt's follower, Egon Schiele.

Schiele's drawings and paintings concentrate on the nude both male and female, but they have none of Klimt's sensual excitement; instead, they mirror the hardship of life for the young artist who gained little recognition and much opprobrium before his tragic death in 1918 at the age of twenty-eight. Schiele had a naïve love of life and of his fellow men, as his friend Otto Benesch recalled, but even when he produced a celebratory work such as the watercolour entitled *The Lovers* (1911; Fischer Fine Art, London; see illustration 167), he portrayed rather emaciated and

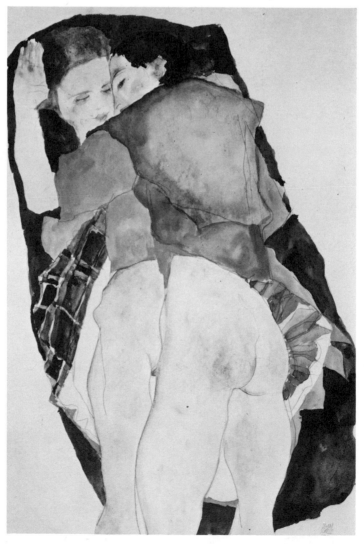

167   Egon Schiele, *Lovers*, 1911

awkward figures so that the resulting picture was full of a tension that belied mere sexual pleasure. The same is true of *Friendship* (1913; Galerie St Etienne, New York) in which a nude man nervously clutches at the breasts of a nude girl lying beside him.

Schiele saw close physical and emotional contact as one hopeful answer to the unhappiness of life, and so many of his works are on that theme. But such a subject could hardly have been expected to be welcome to the bourgeois connoisseurs of his day. Schiele was continually under attack for the explicitness of his work, culminating in a horrific sentence of twenty-four days imprisonment in 1912 for exhibiting 'pornographic' pictures.[11] In court he had to watch while the judge symbolically burnt one of his drawings. Yet he drew his figures in strange, ungainly postures that expressed at most an anguished and lonely eroticism of a strictly personal nature that contained no pornographic intentions at all. Whether depicting young girls (the subject which caused the biggest outcry), mature women, men, or his own body, he concentrates on the essential sexuality of the figure, taking great care to show the genital organs. It is this insistence that gives a burning eroticism to many of his works, for example, *Reclining Girl in a Blue Dress* (1910; private collection, London; see illustration 168) in which the girl's dress is pulled up to reveal the vivid red lips of her vulva, indicating a desire that perhaps will never be fulfilled. This same feeling characterises a rare *Self-Portrait* by Schiele (1910; private collection, London; see illustration 169), which shows the artist naked from

168 Egon Schiele, *Reclining Girl in a Blue Dress*, 1910

169 Egon Schiele, *Nude Self-Portrait*, 1910

the waist and with an erection. The staring eyes and slumped pose of the figure, with the bony hands grasping the penis, are movingly expressive of a desperation that leads the artist to a solitary attempt at sexual gratification as a temporary relief from unhappiness.

Another artist whose eroticism mirrored the times he lived in was George Grosz. Fighting reluctantly with the German army in the First World War, he was discharged with brain fever, redrafted, sentenced to death for desertion, reprieved, and incarcerated in a lunatic asylum. His contempt for mankind in general, but for the bourgeoisie of the short-lived Weimar Republic in particular, comes through in the acidly satirical drawings he produced between 1917 and 1924, which were published as *Ecce Homo* (1923)[12] and *Der Spiesser Spiegel* (1924).[13] With a ferociously masterful grasp of form and outline, Grosz laid bare the obscene decadence of post-war Germany in drawings which unmasked the private life of the ruling classes and thus exposed their moral hypocrisy. The two publications together constitute a merciless document of eroticism at its most nearly obscene, reducing the participants to their common animal nature and marking all their sexual activities as ugly and degrading. All pretensions of morality are stripped away in these visions of jaded or perverse sexuality: a lecherous uncle ogles his undressed niece; a sex murderer scrubs his hands after committing a particularly revolting crime; a foot-fetishist seeks his desperate satisfaction; an old man dreams of his past debauches; prostitutes parade their naked charms in the streets and cafés, or cater to the perverse tastes of bloated capitalists.

The political tone of Grosz's erotic drawings is all-important: they represented not an attempt at sophisticated titillation but a deliberate use of eroticism as a weapon against the oppressors of the proletariat, a technique that has been widely used since. This was recognised by the authorities, for Grosz was often fined for offences including 'corrupting the sense of shame and virtue innate to the German people', and many of the plates for *Ecce Homo* were confiscated. But none of the published drawings was as explicit or as damning as a series of very bold water-colours of sexual activities (see illustration 170) which brilliantly captured the complete and mindless degradation of the bourgeoisie during the Weimar Republic.

Grosz's deliberate use of erotic imagery to shock is characteristic also of the work of his colleague Max Beckmann. By 1932 when he fled from the Nazis to America, Grosz's work had lost the biting urgency of *Ecce Homo*, but on the other hand, the years of the rise of the Nazi party saw Beckmann produce his most powerful work. He fled to Holland in 1937 after being branded a 'degenerate' artist at the famous Munich exhibition of that year, having expressed his revulsion at the political climate in Germany in works such as the powerful triptych *The Departure* of 1932–33 (Museum of Modern Art, New York). Characteristically, this work is not so much a direct comment on contemporary events as an allegory with definite contemporary relevance. In the centre panel, a figure wearing a crown is seen leaving in a boat with his wife and child and a strange hooded figure. In the left panel, a man wields an axe in front of two figures tied to columns, one of which is nude and has had his hands chopped off. In the foreground a bound woman wearing only a corset is being tortured. And in the right panel, a partly unclothed couple are shown tied together, the man being upside down, while a drummer passes in the foreground and a masked man holding a giant fish stands behind them. However obscure this allegory might appear today, its relevance as a peculiarly erotic indictment of National Socialism was not lost on Beckmann's contemporaries.

The eroticism of Grosz and Beckmann is merely part of a purposeful display—more important in the first case than in the second, but nevertheless for both not much more than a channel for the expression of ideas unrelated to the basic philosophy of eroticism. We may read a certain amount into each artist's choice of subject-matter, but it would be imprudent to suggest that their erotic works tell us a great deal about themselves. With many twentieth-century artists, as with certain examples from earlier periods, the erotic works produced are valuable clues to the personality of the artist himself. In this connection one must mention the fellow-countryman of Grosz and Beckmann and fellow-sufferer at the hands of the Nazis, Hans Bellmer, whose 'degenerate' drawings and constructions on the theme of *The Doll* (see Appendix III a) are almost painfully revealing about the personal interests and sexual obsessions of their author.

Owing to the essentially personal nature of eroticism, many artists try to disguise the erotic meaning of their work or repudiate it altogether. It was possible in the nineteenth century for a figure such as Lewis Carroll to be unaware of the true motivation behind his photographs of little girls, but such naïvety would be highly suspect today. And yet the artist Balthus insists that in his many paintings of nude

170   George Grosz, *Couple Undressing,*
      1920s

or provocatively posed little girls, his only concern is with questions of composition and execution. The obvious degree of involvement with the subject-matter makes nonsense of this apologia, and in fact one of his earliest projects, a series of illustrations to Emily Brontë's *Wuthering Heights* drawn in 1933, was treated almost as autobiography. The drawings concerned only the first part of the book and related to the wooing by Heathcliff of the adolescent Cathy. Balthus portrayed himself as Heathcliff, and in the only painting connected with the book, *Cathy Dressing* (1933; private collection, New York), he sits tensely beside the nude girl as her hair is combed. The voyeur was to become a favourite subject with Balthus, and although later versions showed only the girl, the degree of voyeurism remained strong. Variations on this theme include many nude girls merely lying on their beds or sitting in chairs, perfect examples of the 'key-hole' art of Degas, and certainly showing as much concern with the technique of picture-making. *Getting Up* (1955; private collection, Paris) is a titillating female version of Caravaggio's highly provocative male nude known as *Love the Conqueror* (1598–99; Staatliche Museum, Berlin). And Balthus's girls are often accompanied by cats, potent sexual symbols in themselves. Examples include *Nude with Cat* (*c.* 1954; National Gallery of Victoria, Melbourne); *Girl and Cat* (1937; private collection, Chicago) and *The Dream* (1938; private collection, California). The two latter paintings depict pubescent girls sitting on chairs in an identical pose which reveals their upper thighs and tiny knickers under their dresses. Occasionally the situation is explicitly sexual, as in *The Guitar Lesson* (1934; private collection, Boston; see illustration 171), a beautifully composed and executed painting which shows a woman seated

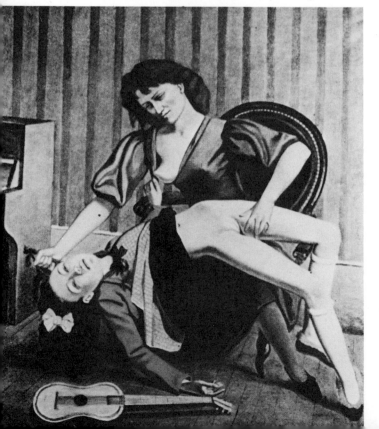

171 Balthus, *The Guitar Lesson*, 1934

on a chair with a half-nude girl lying across her lap. The woman holds the girl by the hair and fondles her clitoris while the girl tugs at the woman's dress, revealing a breast. But explicit sexual activity such as this is rare in Balthus's work.

In most of these erotic paintings there is a brooding, obsessive quality and a feeling of suppressed violence which Artaud early recognised as characteristic of Balthus's work.[14] These attributes are seen at their best in an enormous and extraordinary painting entitled *The Room* (1949–52; private collection, Switzerland). A nude girl is sprawled on a couch in the middle of the room, head back, one arm dangling towards the floor and legs apart. An evil-looking cat watches from a table as a menacing dwarf grips the curtains of a large window whose light illuminates the recumbent nude. It is an unforgettable picture which seems to puzzle, excite, and shock all at the same time. Is the dwarf closing the curtains on an incubus visitation of the sort enjoyed by Fuseli? Or is she, on the contrary, opening them to let in a radiant light filled with the sexual potency of Jupiter's visit to Danae? The brooding undertone of violence and the obsessively sexual atmosphere of the picture make it one of the most compulsive works of erotic art of this century.

This compulsive eroticism of Balthus has much in common with the works of this century's most avid explorers of sexuality, the Surrealists, who are discussed in detail in section b of the present chapter. The Surrealists were aware of the revolutionary nature of unfettered erotic expression, and they often insisted on excess, echoing the ideas and intentions of one of their heroes, de Sade. Thus, Surrealist erotic art has a compulsive intensity which cannot but have a deep effect on the viewer, communicating often on a direct subconscious level. For the Surrealists acted upon Freud's discovery that sexuality lay at the root of all creativity. But Surrealist art is a world away from pornographic exploitation of sexual impulses, and in fact the group disapproved of pornography. Their works show, in place of a concentration on genital organs, a transformation of the whole body into an erotic arena for exciting experiences. Magritte's *Rape* (1934; George Melly Collection, London; see illustration 198), Dali's *Young Virgin Autosodomized by her own Chastity* (1954; Alemany Collection, New York; see illustration 199), and the engravings and drawings of Bellmer (see illustration 250) may be cited as examples of this characteristic.

The Surrealists also valued very highly the world of dreams which they explored endlessly. The sexual content of dreams formed the basis of many Surrealist works, especially those of Paul Delvaux, whose silent dreamscapes are characterised by a haunting eroticism. *Venus Asleep* (1944; Tate Gallery, London; see illustration 172) shows the nude goddess reclining on an elaborate couch in a Classical courtyard, with nude women in some distress to the right and in the background, while to the left stands a clothed and impassive woman, or perhaps a tailor's dummy, confronting a skeleton. There is a note of disquiet therefore in this atmosphere of incipient eroticism which Delvaux has described: 'I tried in this picture for contrast and mystery . . . the psychology of that moment was very exceptional, full of drama and anguish. I wanted to express this anguish in the picture, contrasted with the calm

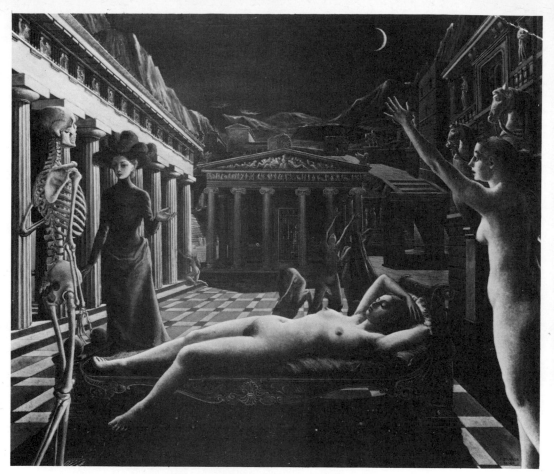

172 Paul Delvaux, *Venus Asleep*, 1944

of Venus.'[15] There is an element here of 'Eros Noir', by which writers such as Breton and Bataille characterised that dark, exciting, and taboo-laden atmosphere which was an essential aspect of eroticism to the Surrealists, and which gives so many of their art-works their compulsive force.

English artists this century seem to have been, on the whole, less concerned with eroticism than their Continental counterparts, a major exception being Allen Jones. But certain artists known in a different context have shown a very definite interest in erotic imagery in their more private work. Examples are the two religious artists Eric Gill and Stanley Spencer. Gill is best known for his carvings in Westminster and Guildford Cathedrals, but one of his earliest works was a stone carving of two lovers made in 1910 for Roger Fry, who wrote of it: 'It ought to be put up in a public place. It can't be until we are much more civilized in the real sense.'[16] Gill was a Roman Catholic convert, but many of his works (*e.g.* illustrations to *Song of Songs*, 1925) earned him the reproof of the Catholic Church. In 1926 he began to practise life drawing, and from then on he produced hundreds of life studies in which he drew especial attention to the sexual organs, which he called 'precious ornaments', 'the roses and the lilies', etc.[17] The less daring were published in albums,[18] and they tend to show a lack of real weight and volume, probably due to Gill's poor early training.

In London there are two collections of Gill's more private drawings and prints: that of his widow, given to the Victoria and Albert Museum,[19] and that of his brother Cecil, given to the British Museum.[20] Many show that he had some sort of phallic fixation: about seventy sheets show penises often highly finished and neatly coloured, some being depicted in both flaccid and erect state, with measurements carefully noted. There are also about ten drawings of vaginas and about thirty-five which show couples in intercourse (see illustration 173). Gill considered

173   Eric Gill, *Copulating Couple, c.* 1930s

that there should be no conflict between Catholicism and sexual honesty, and his annotations on certain drawings seem to show the artist trying to reassure himself of this. By a couple engaged in cunnilingus he has written: 'Man is matter and spirit, both real and both good.' On the back of a drawing of a man masturbating, he has made copious notes about man representing God's ideas of truth, beauty, etc. This religious concern perhaps explains in part the feeling of coldness about many of these drawings, obvious especially in those executed in his primitive style, such as a series of four showing males with erections or couples in intercourse (see illustration 174), with the hand of God in the top left corner giving the sign of divine blessing.

The vital importance of sex has, of course, been recognised by many clear-sighted people from the early Hindus and Taoists to the more recent philosophers

174 Eric Gill, *Copulating Couple with the Hand of God, c.* 1930s

Reich and Marcuse. Gill's contemporary, Stanley Spencer, wrote in 1936 of the horror of war: 'The only way to end the ghastly experience would be if everyone suddenly decided to indulge in every degree and form of sexual love, carnal love, bestiality, anything you like to call it. These are the joyful inheritances of mankind.'[21] But Spencer went further than this, for even more than Gill he saw a definite connection between sex and religion: 'In all my sex experience I notice the same degree of emotion as in religious experience.'[22] 'A man raises a woman's dress with the same passionate admiration and awe for the woman as the priest raises the Host at the altar.'[23] Sacred and profane love were therefore identical, and indulgence of sexual appetites brought one closer to God; thus every form of love was acceptable. This equation of spiritual and sexual ecstasy was not mere philosophy to Spencer: it was the starting point for all his important works, which were, in his opinion, meaningless without this knowledge: 'I am convinced that the physical urge in me is the very substance and core of the spiritual essence I am seeking.'[24] The intensity of Spencer's desire to communicate a deeply personal experience recalls Van Gogh, and both were concerned with the spirituality of nature in its totality. In a painting entitled *Sunflower and Dog Worship* (1937; W. A. Evill Collection, London), Spencer portrays himself with his first wife Hilda: they are passionately embracing sunflowers, experiencing, as Spencer explained, union with God, with nature, and with each other. The parallel with Van Gogh's ecstatic hymns of sunflower-worship is plain, whether Spencer was consciously aware of this or not. But in his sexual involvement Spencer goes beyond Van Gogh, and indeed in this painting he also depicts himself embracing a dog, while other dogs sniff each other and urinate.

[230]

In this way he demonstrates that all of nature is united through sex.

This painting is crucial for any understanding of Spencer's ideas, but events and attitudes have made such an understanding difficult. At the end of his life he wrote: 'Love is the generating force of my art. There are of course all sorts of odd kinds of love, emotional, sexual, and a sort of generalized benignity towards all things. They all of them contribute to my art. . . . I don't always like symbols, but because of the law must have recourse to them.'[25] His religious paintings abound with sexual symbols which are of great importance, and which his copious notes and correspondence help to clarify. In his official biography,[26] Maurice Collis touched on this subject but explained that Spencer's executors had forbidden him to include quotations or comments which would have been more explanatory. Not until Louise Collis was permitted to publish her account, which included the reminiscences of Spencer's second wife Patricia in 1972,[27] did an explanation of the artist's very personal use of sexual symbolism become possible. It then became clear that Spencer was all his life a sexual adolescent suffering from long periods of impotence, largely the result of a repressive childhood and a lack of sexual experience until he met his first wife (when he was already into his thirties). He was also a sado-masochist: many of his works show him as a small man at the mercy of large, powerful women, especially the *Beatitudes* series of 1937, and a pair of drawings squared up on canvas (1944; Astor Collection, London) which show him in a sexually excited state with each of his two wives. This desire to be dominated by women is a characteristic that shows clearly in his writings and in Patricia's memoirs, but at the same time it is noticeable that certain of his biblical paintings betray a sadistic tendency.

Spencer was also a fetishist who was sexually excited by women's clothes and shoes, and also by dirty smells. His painting entitled *The Dustman or The Lovers* (1934; Newcastle upon Tyne Art Gallery), which was rejected by the Royal Academy and led to Spencer's resignation, shows, in Spencer's words, 'the glorifying and magnifying of a dustman. His wife carries him in her arms and experiences the bliss of union which his corduroy trousers quicken.'[28] Spencer and other excited people can be seen with rubbish from the dustbins. And in *Love on the Moor* (1949–54; Fitzwilliam Museum, Cambridge), Hilda appears as a statue of Venus surrounded by an adoring crowd of people opening boxes of new clothes, which they excitedly try on or hold against each other, activities which lead many of them to make love. Patricia Spencer has described occasions when her husband would make her try on hundreds of dresses and pairs of shoes while he grew more and more excited. Many drawings from the early 40s in the Astor Collection refer to this fetish: God and a tailor hold up trousers for mutual admiration; a couple try on shoes; Stanley fondles Patricia's clothes as she dances in her underwear and God watches approvingly; Stanley buys Patricia new shoes and hats while God fondles her legs and feet.

In many of these works the presence of God, or of some reference to religion, is crucial, though all depictions of sexual activities were, of course, religious images to Spencer. One of his greatest ambitions—never realised, however—was to build a Temple of Love in which sex and religion would be one, and most of his sexual paintings and drawings were produced with this project in mind. This was the idea behind the eight *Beatitudes of Love* of 1937, of which he wrote: 'Each of the pictures shows the twined and unified soul of two persons.'[29] It was here that his equation of sacred and profane love was most carefully developed, where the religious nature of sexuality was most extensively explored. All show couples in a sexual connotation, although none shows the sex act, for Spencer had no wish to shock people to that extent. In *Worship* (W. A. Evill Collection, London), a tiny Stanley on the ground gazes excitedly at Patricia wearing a new dress; in *Seeing* (private collection, England; see illustration 175), Stanley gets undressed as a large, nude version of Hilda removes her clothes and at the same time appears in a crucifixion pose. Objections have been made more to the ugliness than to the sexuality of these pictures, but conventional ideas of beauty were meaningless to Spencer.

The Temple of Love was to have included altars dedicated to the women in Spencer's life, and the importance of these women was that they provided the fuel for his fantasies. His sex-life with them was never satisfactory: he was quite taken aback when both his wives expressed repulsion for his idea of living in a *ménage à trois* after he had divorced Hilda and married Patricia. In fact, he seems to have been happier acting out his fantasies in his sexual-religious paintings and in his interminable, and mostly unposted, love-letters to Hilda, which he continued to write throughout his marriage to Patricia and indeed even after Hilda's death. Making love by post or by painting brought him immense satisfaction, and two paintings in particular seem to show this. *Self-Portrait with Patricia* (1937; Fitzwilliam Museum, Cambridge) shows them both in the nude, he head and shoulders

175 Stanley Spencer, *Seeing*, from *Beatitides of Love*, 1937

only as he kneels by a bed, she lying full length on the bed, with breasts and pubic region visible. In *The Leg-of-Mutton Nude* (1937; Peyton Skipwith Collection, London; see illustration 176) the couple appear nude once more, Patricia lying on her back on the floor with her legs apart and Stanley crouching beside her in a fully frontal position. Spencer's handling of paint is often very unattractive, but in both these examples the drawing and modelling of the forms is excellent. A lot of care has gone into these works, and they were obviously important to the artist. They are not impersonal offerings of sexuality to the viewer as a straightforward nude might be; rather they express, through the artist's inclusion of himself, some sort of private wish-fulfilment concerning the relationship they celebrate.

We have discussed how certain major twentieth-century artists have used eroticism as a preferred means of self-expression, in some cases didactic and in others cathartic. At the same time there have been other minor figures who have specialised in erotic imagery in terms of illustration, either to their own texts or to those of others. The Belgian artist Louis Malteste wrote many novels of a sado-masochistic nature in the 1920s and '30s, and these he illustrated with drawings expressing an obsessive

176   Stanley Spencer, *Leg-of-Mutton Nude* (*Self-Portrait with Patricia*), 1937

fascination with flagellant scenes. These usually showed large-buttocked women submitting to the good-natured violence of their companions (see illustration 177), and were executed in a precise and skilful, if uninspired, manner. On the other hand, the large etchings by the Australian illustrator Norman Lindsay show a highly stylised grotesque eroticism in crowded scenes of latter-day *femmes fatales*. And the drawings by the Frenchman Pierre Klossowski, brother of Balthus, especially those to his novel *Roberte Ce Soir*,[30] express through their seeming clumsiness a fantasised violence that is full of a strange and haunting eroticism. The French artist Jules Pascin produced many highly assured drawings of nude women, often masturbating or in lesbian activities,[31] as well as a series of prints relating to the private fantasies of young girls which include lesbianism and relations with pet animals, and yet are completely without elements of salaciousness or crudity. The same can be said of a series of drawings entitled *Tableaux Vivants*[32] by the Hungarian Nicolaus Vadasz, which very explicitly illustrate the sexual experiences of boys and young men, somewhat in the manner and tone of the earlier prints by Vadasz's compatriot Zichy. A third Hungarian specialist in erotic genre scenes was Marcel Vertès, whose drawings and etchings for works by Carco, Apollinaire, and Colette and for his own series such as *Les Jeux du Demi-Jour* (*Twilight Games*) and *La Journée de Madame* (*Madame's Day*) treat subjects such as prostitution and illicit love with poetic humour in an unlaboured and economic style which recalls similar depictions by Toulouse-Lautrec and Degas.[33] More esoteric are the etchings entitled *Erbsünde* (*Original Sin*) by the German Walter Klemm, which show with

177   Louis Malteste,
Flagellation scene,
c. 1930

a perverse charm Eve's sexual relations with various animals in the Garden of Eden.[34]

The above artists are illustrators, and their works betray little of the compulsive urgency which characterises the most powerful works of eroticism. However, their work has both charm and honesty, attributes lacking in the works of certain other artists relevant to the present discussion, which may be labelled 'kitsch'. Nicholas Egon's paintings and drawings of the female nude are meticulous without being photographic, and titillating without being offensive. They express a completely bogus eroticism whose main appeal is purely decorative. But the artist does show self-awareness, a quality notably lacking in 'Britain's Modern Michelangelo', Anthony Brandt, whose highly finished nudes rejoice in such titles as *Crossed Legs*, *Amor Expectant*, and *Ecstasy*, and yet who insists his work is not 'erotic' but 'figurative in the great European tradition'. All his work is provocatively titillating and glossily superficial, as near to exploitation and as far from celebration of the nude as is possible.

The paintings and drawings of the young French artist Raymond Bertrand pose a different problem. The high finish and the superficiality of his nudes certainly ally him to the world of kitsch in spite of the heavy-handed fantasy which can seem at first glance to relate to Surrealist ideas. But a few of his drawings have an outrageous effrontery which can touch on deeper chords: they seem to express the violent sexual pleasure that could perhaps celebrate the obscene nuptials of de Sade or Hieronymus Bosch. And yet the shallowness is always there in the execution. It is as if the artist occasionally succeeds in spite of himself. Two sumptious volumes have recently been devoted to his work,[35] and their texts have been models of pretentious double-talk by so-called art critics. But the artist has been refreshingly honest in a recent interview: he is *not* trying to explore the nature of eroticism, he is *not* delving into the sexual subconscious, he is just painting what he likes to paint.[36]

On the borderlines of kitsch are certain 'underground' artists: the American Betty Dodson with her meticulously drawn female nudes and copulating couples, and also Tom of Finland (see illustration 178) and Spartacus with their no less

178 Tom of Finland,
Sauna-Bar, c. 1966

179 John Willie, *Girl
in Bondage, c.* 1947

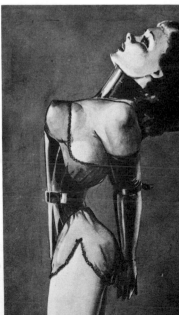

meticulously drawn male nudes and homosexual scenes. These last have a strong minority appeal which attracts avid collectors, as did the very different illustrations of the English artist John Willie (see illustration 179) in the 1940s and '50s. There are also highly talented underground comic illustrators such as Robert Crumb (see illustration 180), S. Clay Wilson, and Gilbert Shelton, with their deliberately

180   Robert Crumb, *Eggs Ackley among the Vulture Demonesses*, page from American comic strip, 1969

provocative and politically directed use of sexual imagery. We have already seen how earlier artists such as Grosz and Beckmann made use of the power of sexual pictures to shock. But one way to defuse this power is through humour, through the release mechanism which humour provides, and certainly the comic illustrators fall short of the powerful level reached by Grosz and Beckmann; instead, they recall the early sex-jokes of Salvador Dali (see illustration 181). Some artists have concentrated on sexual humour: in Germany, Michael Fingesten with his witty *Psycho-analytische Glossen* ('Psychoanalytic Caricatures') of 1915;[37] and more recently, in France, Siné with his cruel but outrageously funny *Picture Book*;[38] in Holland, the whimsical sex-cartoons of Willem;[39] and in America, Tomi Ungerer with his ingenious sex-machines.[40]

Another aspect of eroticism in twentieth-century art is provided by photography. Art-photography of an erotic nature, as opposed to photographic titillation or pornographic exploitation, seems to be a comparatively recent innovation. Francis Giacobetti produces glossy, gimmicky images of conventionally beautiful girls with little or no clothing (in a doorway in the middle of the desert; plucking a chicken; draped across a vintage car), to express his philosophy that 'females are a strange lot'. But he does not call his photographs erotic, for eroticism is 'an intellectual whim'.[41] Giacobetti believes in glamour, and so does Sam Haskins, but for Haskins glamour has to be subordinate: his photographs use a great deal of superimposition to create personal fantasies; they are 'quite simple: me, thinking in images'.[42] The images range from birds' eggs in a nest of pubic hair to a girl's face on an apple, but the result is often as gimmicky as a Giacobetti. Kishin Shinoyama's nudes form

181   Salvador Dali, *Alphabet drawing*, 1934

strange shapes in surrealistic landscapes or else pose in groups that seem to conjure up a truly erotic atmosphere in an indefinable way.[43] They seem to represent a convincing personal fantasy world, and the same is true of the very different images by David Hamilton, images of fifteen- and sixteen-year-old girls in natural settings, who express a seemingly quite unconscious sexual attraction in their flimsy night-dresses or neat underwear (see illustration 182).[44] The dreamily erotic atmosphere of his photographs recall a master like Lewis Carroll, and have had great influence on younger photographers like Peter Widdison (see illustration 183) with his visions of the bedroom world of young girls. All these photographers take care not to offend public taste, which perhaps provides them with a helpful guideline, but nevertheless inhibits them sadly in terms of sexual expression. They fear, with reason, that depiction of explicit sexual activity would be branded as pornography, yet they are the very people whose work could show up the terrible deficiencies of pornography and also allow photographers to give free rein to their sexual fantasies. This seems to be the aim of a recent German publication called *Softgirls*[45] (see illustrations 184 and 185), which includes explicit sexual photographs in beautifully controlled colours, showing single figures, couples, or groups in highly imaginative settings. The overall effect is of a powerful eroticism which does not at all aim at mere sexual arousal, but which can be enjoyed and appreciated in terms of poetry, imagination, and creativity.

The fascination of girls in childhood and adolescence has appealed to many English artists besides Carroll and Hamilton. Graham Ovenden has devoted his

182   David Hamilton, *Girl in Mirror*, 1970

183   Peter Widdison, *Two Girls*, 1972

184 *Lesbian Couple*, photograph from
Softgirls, Germany, *c*. 1969

185 *Couple*, photograph from *Softgirls*,
Germany, 1969

life to collecting Carroll photographs and to painting, drawing, and photographing young girls. His own works have a meticulous attention to detail which gives them an unusual directness of communication (see illustration 186). His little girls are certainly very sexual, but they are not painted as titillations for old men; they express a romantic nostalgia for the mystery of childhood, although they carefully avoid any hint of sentimentality. Basically, they express Ovenden's conviction that sexuality is an essential ingredient in childhood, a still unpopular belief and the cause of much bigoted criticism of his work. He is disarmingly honest about his feelings: 'I think that little girls are very romantic creatures . . . one paints the thing that moves one most in life . . . of course I fall in love with them. . . . I would be an absolute hypocrite if I said my work was lacking in any sexual feeling. It's paramountly obvious that they are very sexual things to me. . . . I have to admit to myself that I'm involved with something that can never be consummated. . . . It's a very painful experience.'[46]

The work of Barry Burman also revolves around young girls, and he too uses a meticulous technique. But the personal fantasy is different, and the similarity with Ovenden's pictures is a superficial one. Burman's work contains a real and barely hidden violence which threatens to erupt at any moment. His girls wear black leather gloves and hold severed heads or dainty dolls; sometimes they lie on black leather sofas or play with animals or poisonous snakes. For him, art is not an

[239]

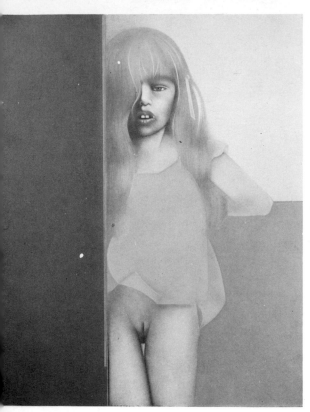

186   Graham Ovenden, *Belinda*, 1971   187   Barry Burman, *Judith*, 1969

intellectual process but intuitive, magical; thus he gives concrete form to private fantasies and fears which revolve around the idea of woman as a predatory creature. His work is a form of exorcism which relates to dualities—attraction and repulsion, the co-existence of innocence and corruption (or knowledge of forbidden things) in young girls for instance. These recognised dualities provide the tension which lies behind all Burman's images, especially his recent works relating to Henry James's *Turn of the Screw* and the story of Judith and Holofernes. His *Judith* (see illustration 187) is a young girl whose clothing is pulled up to reveal her vulva; with her long black leather gloves she grips the severed head of Holofernes as she gazes at it intently. The image owes something to Beardsley, but the drama simmering under the surface is the artist's own, and it recalls the obsessions of Michel Leiris: 'the insolent image of Judith as she must have appeared, emerging from Holofernes' tent (in which the treacherous creature had sought protection), her sharp nails dyed by murder like those of a woman lacquering hers red in the fashion of the twentieth century, her clothes rumpled, covered with sweat and dust and hastily pulled back on—in the greatest disorder—revealing here and there her flesh still sticky with ejaculations and blood. Like Holofernes with his head cut off, I imagine myself sprawling at the feet of this idol.'[47] Burman's disturbing and painful images breathe the atmosphere of compulsive eroticism.

[240]

Other specialists in erotic imagery have recently appeared in England, but their work has tended to lack the force of Ovenden and Burman and to relate more closely to the world of kitsch. Michael Mycock produces carefully air-brushed glossy pictures of girls with giant strawberries or rose-trees in poses derived from, and on the same cultural level as, girlie magazines.[48] John Holmes reflects a similar brand of watered-down Surrealism in what he describes as 'paintings to bring a lump to your trousers',[49] intricate images in wax crayon of female anatomy with strange appendages (*e.g.* a naked torso surmounted by a hand in a V-sign, whose two up-turned fingers are erect phalluses). More artistically valid are the images produced by artists who come under the general heading of Pop Art, whose source material has tended to come from the sexual hinterland of contemporary culture: fetish magazines, advertisements, and comic strips. David Hockney (see Appendix III c) has not concentrated on erotic subjects, but his *Cavafy* etchings and his painting entitled *The Room, Tarzana* (1967; McEwen Collection, London; see illustration 252), though primarily concerned with purely artistic problems, certainly express a fascination with homosexual love. More directly related to the sexual imagery of Pop Art are the paintings and sculptures of Allen Jones (see Appendix III b) which concentrate on the fascination of the female form in leather or rubber with stockings and high heels. Like the best erotic art, these beautifully executed products show a deep concern with the cerebral activity of image-making rather than merely the expression of a personal fantasy—although of course it is the deeply personal commitment which gives them their startling power to excite, astonish, or even horrify. But a painting such as *Woman with 2 Spheres (Float)* (1972; Marlborough Gallery, London; see illustration 251), rather than seeking merely to titillate him, invites the viewer to probe both his own and the artist's sexual imagination.

In America, a related fantasy world to that of Allen Jones is found in the paintings of Richard Lindner, images of colossal women in tight corsets and high-heeled shoes, full of a menacing sexuality that perhaps relates to the artist's early years as a Jew in Nazi Germany. Lindner's paintings have an indefinable fascination which partly results from the ambiguity of images made from both abstract and figurative elements. Women reign supreme: in *Woman* (1970; private collection, England; see illustration 188) the central figure with exaggerated sexual organs and encased in a tight-laced corset dominates the man in front of her, who in fact is no more than a face; like the pet dog in the foreground, he only exists in relation to the woman. Women have always fascinated and frightened Lindner: 'Women are more imaginative than men, they have secrets they don't even realize they have. . . . Every woman is a prostitute in the costumes of today. . . . Nature gives woman weapons very early—and secrets. . . . In my paintings, it is the woman who is the brighter and the stronger of the two—and she is also the sad one.'[50] Women also dominate the works of Tom Wesselman, whose neatly painted *Great American Nudes* (see illustration 189) unveil their sexual mysteries in matter-of-fact bedroom scenes. Wesselman's cool detachment is in marked contrast to the involvement of Lindner; Pop Art humour permeates his work, and is especially clear in *Bedroom*

[241]

188   Richard Lindner, *Woman*, 1970

189   Tom Wesselmann,
       Nude, 1966

Painting No. 20 (1969; Sidney Janis Gallery, New York), an image of an enormous brightly-coloured penis.

Many other American Pop artists have concentrated on the 'forbidden subject' of the penis, examples being Rauschenberg (*Carnal Clock*), Johns (*Penis Rubbing*), Brigid Polk (*Cock Book*), Oldenburg (*Capric Monument*), and Warhol (screenprints from *Blue Movie*). When in 1966 Jim Dine exhibited his *London Series* of pretty watercolour penises (see illustration 190), an effort to divorce the object from its usual pornographic context, the London gallery-owner was fined for committing a nuisance. Such battles between artistic freedom and entrenched prejudice have been fought and lost many times over. Van Dongen's *Madame Edmonde Guy* (Paris, collection of the artist), a fully frontal nude, caused a scandal in the twenties because it was a named portrait; Brancusi's *Princess X* (Philadelphia Museum of Art; see illustration 5), was refused space in an exhibition of modern art in Paris in 1916 owing to its clear phallic symbolism; and the nude

190   Jim Dine, *London Series No. 1*, 1966

studies and Classical scenes such as Leda and *The Rape of the Sabines* by D. H. Lawrence were confiscated by the police from his exhibition at the Warren Gallery in London in 1929—(these rather ugly pictures are nevertheless an interesting part of the art of this crusader for sexual honesty.)[51] Of course there have been victories as well: the vindication of Lawrence's *Lady Chatterley's Lover* in the British Law Courts in 1960[52]; the return of Warhol's film *Flesh* after it had been seized by the British police in 1969; and the dismissal of charges brought against the London Arts Gallery in 1970 for exhibiting John Lennon's artistically weak, but far from pornographic, lithographs (see illustration 191).

191   John Lennon, *John and Yoko*, 1970

Varying brands of sexual imagery abound in contemporary American art, from Nancy Grossman's leather sado-masochist sculptures and Edward Kienholz's terrifying reconstructions of illegal abortions and Negroes being castrated by the light of car headlights to Robert Graham's amazing miniature wax models of copulating couples, and the life-size but rather insensitive fibreglass and resin nude girls by John de Andrea, not to mention the delicately observed nudes drawn and painted by Norman Lundin (see illustration 192) and the notorious pastel by Lucas Samaras entitled *Lady Being Fucked by a Blue Dog*, which was removed by the police from the exhibition of contemporary erotica at the Van Bovencamp Galleries in New York in 1965.

A comparatively new phenomenon in America is erotic art created by women. The tradition of erotic art-works produced solely by men for men is being challenged by a politically orientated group of feminist artists who look to the example of

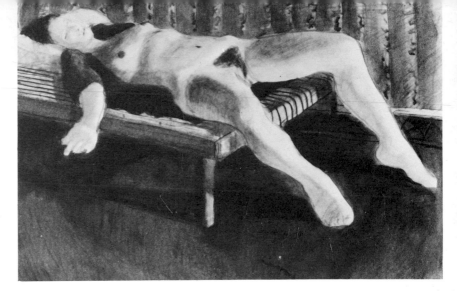

192   Norman Lundin,
       Nude, 1969

Georgia O'Keefe for their inspiration. Critics looked askance at O'Keefe's sexual symbols in the twenties simply because they were painted by a woman. There is a strong note of militancy in the sexual images produced by contemporary women artists in America: female genital forms by Judy Chicago and Hannah Wilke are seen as propaganda for sexual equality rather than simply as opportunities for erotic stimulation. These 'vaginal icons', as Barbara Rose has christened them,[53] follow the tradition of good erotic art in seeking to illuminate rather than merely to titillate. The strong psychological force behind such works is seen especially well in *Femme Couteau*, a marble sculpture by Louise Bourgeois of a woman's body turning into a phallic knife to express both the destructive and seductive aspects of women.

Wherever one looks in the Western world, it seems that artists are feeling increasingly free to give expression to their sexual fantasies, for which we can be grateful to the growing atmosphere of personal freedom engendered by the so-called permissive society. Of course, Scandanavia has been a pioneer: the erotic sculptures of Gustav Vigeland have been on public exhibition in Oslo since 1916, and Drs Phyllis and Eberhard Kronhausen were able to open the first international exhibition of erotic art in Lund, Sweden, and Aarhus, Denmark, in 1968 (see illustration 193).[54]

193   *Phyllis and Eberhard
       Kronhausen at the Lund
       Museum of Art,
       Sweden, with its
       director, Folke Edwards,
       and Picasso's Rape*
       (1963)

Contemporary erotic art in Denmark includes the obsessive drawings of copulating couples by Ernst Hansen and the Surrealistic collages and construction of Wilhelm Freddie; Sweden has the rather lightweight collages of Max Walter Svanberg and cartoon-drawings of Ulf Rahmberg. In Belgium, Roland Delcol paints startlingly photographic nudes in domestic scenes as 'aphrodisiac objets d'art', while in France, Mario Tauzin produces his delicately drawn yet explicit etchings of lesbians and copulating couples; and Leonor Fini and Felix Labisse continue their highly individual series of strangely erotic images redolent with Surrealist mystery (see illustration 202). Many Dutch artists use sexual themes: Karel Appel has painted startling scenes of animals copulating with women; Cornelis Doolaard paints his strange fantasy world of nude women, animals, and Freudian metaphors, usually with his own portrait included; and Melle produces meticulously executed paintings of stories like *Noah* and *Alice in Wonderland* (see illustration 194), which are full of fascinatingly inventive details loaded with sexual implication.

Contemporary erotic art in Germany tends to accentuate the implicit violence of sex; this is especially true in the graphic works of Horst Janssen and Paul Wunderlich. The latter, in particular, has produced various series of prints (*Qui s'explique*, 1959; *Leda and the Swan*, 1962; *Klein Anatomie*, 1963) which involve the violation of one being by another. These disturbing (and much confiscated) images seem to relate to a guilt-complex about the Nazi era. In Austria a group of artists practise Body Art: Günter Brus paints on the surface of the nude body, while Vito Acconci performs with his own body, posing in the nude with his penis hidden between his

194   Melle, *Alice in Wonderland*, 1966

legs so as to transform himself into a female, or masturbating under a wooden ramp while fantasising about the people walking above him (*Seedbed*, April 1972, Sonnabend Gallery, New York). The connections between these activities and erotic art seem tenuous in the extreme, but a recent critic wrote of Acconci's 'fusion of the Minimalist position in sculpture with a refreshed comprehension of the erotic implications in Duchamp's late sexual works, especially the *Wedge of Chastity* (1951)'.[55] More central to the discussion are the intricate, almost Dürer-like etchings of the Viennese artist Ernst Fuchs, which conjure up a rather nightmarish world of demonic sexual energy. Even the traditionally Roman Catholic countries show a concern with eroticism in art: the Galeria Vandrès of Madrid held an exhibition of Erotic Art in Spain in 1972, while in Italy, Marino Marini has for some years been producing sculptures under the title *Horse and Rider*, in which the horse's neck and head become a clear phallic metaphor. An interesting variant is *The Angel of the Citadel* (1949; Peggy Guggenheim Collection, Venice; see illustration 195), in which the ecstatic horseman is shown with an erect penis. The owner requested the artist to cast the penis separately, so that it could be 'screwed in and out at leisure'.[56]

It has been the purpose of this discussion to demonstrate the enormous range and variety of erotic art of this century. At the present moment it seems likely that posterity will adjudge Henry Moore and Pablo Picasso the two giants of early twentieth-century art. Eroticism is an important element in the work of each artist. Moore's tactile and sensuous natural forms relating to the human body have a clear erotic connotation, and certain writers have seen evidence in them of sexual symbolism in a psychological sense. In the interview which forms Appendix III d of this book,

195　Marino Marini, *The Angel of the Citadel*, 1949

Moore makes it clear that whether or not such interpretations are valid, sculpture
for him has always been an intuitive process. With Picasso, on the other hand,
eroticism was a conscious obsession throughout his long career. Asked shortly
before his death about the difference between art and eroticism, he replied with
great seriousness: 'But there *is* no difference',[57] a remark which says much about
his own work. His work concentrated on the female form consistently, from his
early Barcelona sketches to his last engravings and paintings, and his concern was
with the whole range of erotic feelings from love to hate. Sexual subjects appear
intermittently during his Blue Period and especially in the Neo-classical works
such as a series of drawings from 1920 of a centaur abducting a woman. By the
mid-'20s, the multiple aspects of sexual experience became an obsession, owing
largely to his hostility towards his wife Olga, and his infatuation with Marie-Thérèse
Walter in the early '30s reinforced this interest. Two recent commentators have
underlined the importance of Picasso's love-life to the sexual character of his work;[58]
one, Robert Rosenblum, wrote of the work of the late '20s and early '30s: 'At times,
sexual impulses, particularly those of women, are seen as menacing, brutal and
destructive; . . . elsewhere, eroticism is celebrated as a lyrical, tender experience
saturated with the magic of love and the miracle of procreation.'[59] During the late
'40s Picasso produced a number of paintings and drawings of a copulating couple,
and also a series of the artist painting, and making love to, his nude model. This
subject was continued in engravings of 1963–65, where the artist made love to his
model as often as he painted her. The personal concern of Picasso to capture the

196   Pablo Picasso, *Raphael and La Fornarina*, 1968

glories of erotic excitement is reflected in works which contain no hint of shame or guilt and which reflect the artist's deep attachment to Jacqueline Roque. By this time Picasso was in his eighties; his engravings of 1968 on the theme of Ingres's *Raphael and La Fornarina* developed the same theme and constituted one of the most moving of all his projects.[60] The artist who is depicted painting and—more importantly—making love to his model is now Raphael; Picasso himself appears in many of the prints as an old man watching the young couple with an expression that mixes excitement with wistfulness (see illustration 196). There is no false modesty: the details of intercourse are clearly represented in a firm and powerful technique that belies the artist's age. In many respects the nearest parallel to Picasso is the sensual Titian who painted until his death at the age of eighty-nine. These prints have candour, humour and also pathos. They give touching expression to the fantasies of an elderly painter looking back to the excitements of his youth. There is no prurience here and no desire to shock: the natural, guilt-free pleasures of the sex act are illustrated in a manner that ennobles rather than degrades. They are a true celebration of love.

---

b: Eros and Surrealism

by

ROBERT STUART SHORT[1]

About a century ago, Rimbaud declared that love had to be reinvented. Since its beginnings in the early 1920s, surrealism has accepted the challenge and, if it has not met it in full, it is still arguable that the surrealist conception of eroticism as at once a means of expression, a revolutionary weapon, a moral touchstone, a source of revelation, and a principle of ultimate harmony in the world is the only one appropriate and sufficient to the present human predicament.

Surrealism is unique among contemporary revolutionary movements in putting itself unreservedly at the service of Eros. Introducing the 1959 International Surrealist Exhibition, André Breton remarked that, in the last analysis, that which identified the works on show as surrealist, over and above the immense diversity of appearance, style, and techniques employed, was their eroticism. The surrealist aesthetic which made 'convulsiveness' a defining condition of beauty was infused with the values of erotic disruption. The image most frequently quoted as typifying the surrealist idea of beauty, Lautréamont's phrase from *Les Chants de Maldoror*— 'beautiful as the chance meeting on a dissection table of a sewing-machine and an umbrella'[2]—was a transparent metaphor for heterosexual copulation. In a rather different context, Breton claimed that the majority of the quarrels and schisms in the history of the surrealist group was caused by disagreements about the significance of love and not over divergences of political allegiance or personal incompatibility as had hitherto been inferred.

From their earliest experiments in automatic writing in 1919, the surrealists were aware of the intimate relationship between the verbal flow which this exercise uncorked within the subconscious and the awakening of erotic desires. Their consequent redefinition of art as an exploration of the hidden recesses of the psyche and the restimulation of the imagination, as distinct from the production of cultural commodities, led them to associate ever more closely the libidinous and the creative functions. Freud had shown that the source of creative drives, especially artistic drives, lay in sexuality. He had identified desire as the essence of man. The surrealists liked to describe art as 'the accommodation of secret desires'. André Breton once referred to the poetic image as 'the marvellous precipitate of desire', suggesting by the chemical metaphor the natural necessity of the process. Love and art speak the same language. Similarly, the response which each provokes is of the same quality. In *L'Amour Fou*, Breton insisted that there was only a difference in degree between the emotion provoked by poetry and erotic pleasure: sensuality and sensibility were one.

Welling up from the dark zones of the mind, both love and the imagination cast an enchanting new light, 'une lumière noire', on exterior reality and on human potential in this life. As related expressions of the pleasure principle, they challenge the restrictions, prejudices, and prohibitions imposed on men's freedom by submission to the reality principle. They vindicate for the adult the rights of the child and the free will of the game of chance, against stifling social pressures which impose routine, respectability, and the rhythms of the machine. If the Marxian revolution meant the reappropriation of labour by mankind whose labour was their defining feature, the surrealist revolution envisaged the complementing of this by the emancipation of desire. The surrealists reject Freud's pessimistic conclusion that repression is the price we have to pay for civilisation. Even if they may doubt the emergence of humanity into a new Eden of innocence and harmony, they set about the progressive destruction of the massed forces of surplus-repression, relying on the revivifying of a whole armoury of 'lost powers' within men to lift existence clear of its present 'derisory conditions' towards ever more exalted levels of possibility.

The *Abridged Dictionary of Surrealism* defines eroticism as a 'sumptuous ceremony in a tunnel'. In which case, the first act of the rite is certainly one of sacrilege and tumult. The surrealists fully approved Georges Bataille's observation in *Eroticism*: 'The passage from the normal state to that of erotic desire supposes within us a relative dissolution of the constituted being . . . the term "dissolution" recalling the familiar expression "dissolute" applied to erotic activity. For what is at stake in eroticism is always a dissolution of constituted forms.'[3] It is the dynamic behind the most intransigent expressions of human subjectivity: revolt, hysteria, perversion, and crime. Like dreams and automatism, love (or eroticism, for the surrealists did not distinguish between them) was an engine for sapping the structures of rational thought and of the world of appearances. Unleashed eroticism demands excess, blasphemy, subversion, even the blood-letting of the sadistic act. As such, it is an act of violence closely akin to a revolutionary act, with the special advantage that its negative movement of demystification also carries a promise of more generous alternatives.

The prevailing industrial ethic identifies the normal and the good with the useful. It stigmatises as unhealthy anything that is pleasurable for its own sake. Therefore surrealism has taken up the banner of de Sade who obeyed no injunctions other than those of desire. Surrealism has 'levelled at the brood of "basic duties" the long-range weapon of sexual cynicism' and has acclaimed the virtues of perversion in order to affront the utilitarian dogmas of profit and productivity. The Church as chief propagator of guilt about original sin and of obsessions with death has been a favourite target of blasphemous erotic provocation. Dali designed a habit for the 'new order of nuns' slashed at the front with a great opening in the shape of the cross, nicely contradicting the purposes of the usual enveloping vestments. In an orgy of combative black humour, Clovis Trouille painted a whole series of lecherous festivals for pantied priests and rampant nuns, exploiting all the clichés of commercial sex mixed up with the panoply of organised religion. In *Mes Funérailles* (see illustration 197), the fleshy buttocks of the officiants affirm the triumph of desire over death itself. Elaborating on the surrealist belief that love is the principle of evil

197   Clovis Trouille,
My Funeral, 1940

in bourgeois demonology, in his film *L'Age d'Or*, Luis Buñuel identified the figure of Christ with that of Sade's libertine Duke of Blangy emerging from the Chateau of Selliny after one hundred and twenty days of sodomy.

Time and again in surrealist art, everyday objects are diverted from their customary and respectable purposes and reallocated to louche and ambivalent symbolic roles. Hans Bellmer, for example, converts the dolls of innocent girlhood into all-purpose puppet-Lolitas (see illustration 249) which can be dismembered and reassembled according to the whims of perversity. Magritte's *Rape* (1934; George Melly Collection, London; see illustration 198), a portrait where breasts and pubis stand in for eyes and mouth, is as much a rape of the spectator's preconceptions as it is of the female face.

Having acclaimed as surrealist from the early date of 1924 'all discoveries changing the nature and purpose of a phenomenon', the movement has always been sympathetically predisposed towards sexual perversion. 'Eros noir' not only violates taboos and trespasses in forbidden domains, it also prospects in a country where desire is without limits and freedom intoxicating. Perversion rejects the concentration of erotic interest on the genital areas alone, convenient as the latter may be for a work ethic since it leaves the rest of the body available as an instrument of labour. Much surrealist art is about the multiplication of erotic possibilities, the sexualisation of the whole body, of the external world, and even, in some of Matta's works, presenting the universe in an endless cosmic copulation. Surrealism searches everywhere for fresh temptations, new stimuli, and satisfaction. Dali, in *The Young Virgin Autosodomised by her own Chastity* (1954; Alemany Collection, New York; see

198 René Magritte, *Rape*, 1934

199 Salvador Dali, *Young Virgin Autosodomised by her own Chastity*, 1954

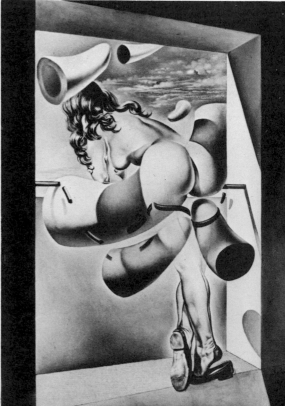

illustration 199), for instance, proposes his 'spectral woman': 'Thanks to dismantling or to deformation of the female anatomy, woman can satisfy her profound exhibitionism by detaching various sections of her anatomy and passing them round for people to admire.' In the paintings of Brauner, Svanberg, and Schröder-Sonnenstern, we find creatures with multiple eyes and orifices, tongues darting from breasts, heads sprouting on knees, comestible hair. The differences between the sexes lose their determinacy. In the photomontage *Sur le Pavois* (see illustration 200), the shaken spectator is confronted, amidst a rugger-scrum of heaving female limbs, with the black-hosed legs and spread buttocks of the artist himself—Pierre Molinier. As for Hans Bellmer, he carries the invention of anatomical analogies to the point of converting the whole body into an erogenous zone (see illustration 250), one great 'foyer of desire' as Xavière Gauthier has put it. 'The act of love is no longer a simple self-satisfaction, nor an act of possession, but rather an orgy of fantasies, of projections, substitutions, . . . of hallucinations.'

But now we have moved on from discussion of eroticism as a 'perturbation', an arm of revolt, to eroticism as a goal, as a paramount value in itself. Of all the areas of human experience in which the surrealists have prospected for a richer human consciousness—dreams, automatism, madness, objective chance, black humour—love offers the most intimate, most immediate, most verifiable, and most universally experienced revelations concerning man's unrealised possibilities. Jacques Brunius, for one, said that it was in the act of love that he first understood the meaning of 'the supreme point', that level of experience at which, Breton claimed, our fragmented and discontinuous view of things finally yields to an affectively experienced grasp of reality as a coherent totality. Again according to Breton, in *Arcane 17*, love is the event which comes closest to assuaging man's thirst for the absolute. The lover

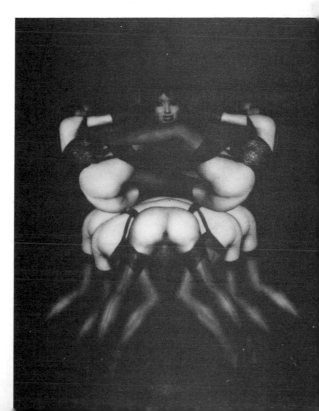

200   Pierre Molinier, *Sur le Pavois*,
photo-montage, *c.* 1950s

ceases to be aware of the rigid dualities of subject and object, of mental representation and physical perception. In love, desire and reality fuse. The imagined and the felt become one. Furthermore this exaltation surrealises not only the loved object but also the rest of the world. As Benjamin Péret put it: 'Everything I think lives and renews itself in the image of the loved one.' And in the *Ode to Charles Fourier*, Breton insisted that it was only after loving a specific human being that one could come to love humanity. Far from being in conflict with revolution, love was a spur to join the social struggle, especially as one came up against the obstacles thrown up by society in the path of love. Love, for the surrealist, is not an escape into a private paradise, nor, except in the direst circumstances, can it be seen as a compensation for general misery; rather it is a commitment, the cradle of altruism, the starting-point for a morality based on desire.

A necessary corollary of the expectations which the surrealists invested in love, without equal since Romanticism, has been their ecstatic celebration of man's partner in sexual alchemy, woman. To quote Breton: 'In Surrealism, woman will have been loved and honoured as the great promise, a promise that subsists even after it has been kept.' As the beloved who is herself an equal, active participant, woman acts as the medium between the lover and the 'other', the bridge between subject and object. Woman, as lover and mother, is the being who can transform the act of love into one of creation. The intermediary role of woman is personified in the legendary figure of Mélusine, evoked by Breton in *Arcane 17*, a siren who is equally at home in the elements of earth, air, and water, on intimate terms with the cosmic, animal, and vegetable forces which animate nature. The metaphorical role of woman in this sense is suggested in those paintings by Delvaux in which women, instead of legs, have trunks with roots plunging into the ground, in the telluric women of Masson's landscapes (see illustration 201), in the feminising of the metropolis by Aragon in *Paris Peasant*. By developing new 'myths' of womanhood, such as the child-woman and the 'femme sorcière', the surrealists have sought substitutes

201 André Masson,
*Metamorphosis of
Gradiva*, 1939

for the virgin–courtesan dichotomy of Christian tradition. The surrealist myths, by contrast, vindicate the independence and self-will of women and insist on the reciprocal nature of love. They have urged that salvation for the world will lie in the substitution of the female qualities of intuition and spontaneity for the presently prevailing masculine qualities of reason, calculation, and competition, which have served humanity so poorly.

The surrealist ideal love, the only love which they believe capable of operating the alchemical transmutation which will being harmony to the flesh and the spirit, is what they call 'elective love': a reciprocal attraction in which the couple incarnates the platonic but secularised allegory of the androgyne. In 'l'amour fou' or 'sublime love', according to Péret: 'the nature of the beloved object is suddenly recognised by the subject as a direct response to a desire which was only waiting the appearance of its object to become imperious.' Elective love is the outcome of a benign destiny which proves to be the working out of our own subconscious desires. Thus Breton could truthfully say to Elise: 'You know that when I saw you for the first time, I recognized you without hesitation.' Despite the experience of endless disappointments and repeated breakdowns of apparently 'elective' unions, the surrealists have kept faith with their ideal. They continue to insist that readiness to put all at risk, even for a lifetime, is the necessary *quid pro quo* for love's total gift.

It will now be apparent that surrealist eroticism derives its unique character from the tension involved in holding in suspense, at one extreme, the forbidden (the perverse and the taboo) and at the other extreme, the impossible (the perfect communion of the ideal couple). It struggles with dogged resolution to transcend the dichotomy between the consuming hunger of 'black eros' on the one hand and the purity of platonic love on the other.

In the same programme note in which Breton identified eroticism as the common factor in surrealist art, he also affirmed that the surrealist conception of eroticism outlawed anything in the order of the 'dirty joke', which, he said, committed the inexpiable crime of profaning the greatest mystery of human life. It is in fact striking that a movement which has gravitated around the carnal temptation for fifty years should have produced so little pornography. Surrealist beauty has generally been not only 'convulsive-fixed' and 'magic-circumstantial', but also 'erotic-veiled'. No doubt the surrealists have the same objections to pornographic representations of sexuality as they do to any other form of naturalism which slavishly copies the surface of reality without transposing it through the imagination and the subconscious. Just as surrealist revolutionary writing refuses to spell out the political slogans of the day, so eroticism in surrealist poetry and painting is latent rather than manifest.

If surrealism exalts eroticism in the language of religion—grace, profanation, interdict—it is because it claims back for human love all that has so long been alienated from it in adoration of the divine. Having achieved this reappropriation, surrealism denies that love requires much further demystification. It is already the most accessible model of all emancipations. Despite the explicitness of the surrealist

[255]

treatment of eroticism—their 'Enquiry into Sexuality', published in *La Révolution Surréaliste* in 1928–29 was unheard of at that date for its frankness—the surrealists prefer that, at the last, the subject should preserve its 'infracassable noyau de nuit'. Surrealism's attitude to the 'permissive society' is thus a highly unfashionable one. According to Robert Benayoun in his *Erotique du Surréalisme*,[4] the so-called 'sexual revolution' is leading to a sickening vulgarisation of eroticism. In promiscuity the depreciation of the act which links birth and death so that it becomes a casual diversion will lead speedily to boredom. Sex education reduces to a biological rictus what can only be properly comprehended in terms of the endlessly ramifying movements of psychic desire. No matter how blatant the hyperboles of commercialised sex, nor how athletic and ingenious the physical variations devised, this supreme recourse will become banal and demoralising if it is cut off from the more profound resources of the spirit.

Surrealism insists on the necessity for discrimination in the struggle for sexual emancipation. The destruction of prejudice, repressive censorship and their corollary, furtive lubricity, is one thing. But the reduction of sexuality to the instant gratification of primal libidinous instincts is another. In so far as eroticism is uniquely the proclivity of mankind as self-conscious beings, carnal love must not be divorced from spiritual love. Mental stimuli interact with and renew physical impulses. Far from abandoning himself once and for all to an orgy of primary sensation, the surrealist looks to his imagination to sensitise, poeticise, and amplify the instinctual drives, to discover enhancing equivalents, fetishes, and dream symbols. Far from being a repression, such sublimation is an enrichment of desire. No other terrain is more propitious than that of eroticism for the imagination to enlarge the area in which consciousness may continually surpass itself.

If surrealism has failed to 'reinvent love', it has enormously extended the frontiers and the scope of the expectations of the erotic consciousness. But while joyfully unleashing the disruptive energies of the libido, it has at the same time sought to survey this scene of ecstasy and abandon with lucidity, with what Dali very aptly called the 'paranoiac-critical' eye. Thus most surrealist erotic art appeals first of all not to the senses, as does that of the Impressionists or Expressionists, for instance, but to the mind. If the creations of Labisse (see illustration 202), Toyen, and Ernst (see illustration 203) are evidence enough, its preferred subject is not the flesh itself but the fantasm and the succubus. Its mythic space is that of the dream, nocturnal, and fetishistic. Set in endless vistas in a disconcerting perspective, the most turbulent dreams acquire a hieratic fixity—men stand like zombies—thanks to the serenity of the descriptive apparatus that the artist employs.

Not least among the merits of surrealism has been its stubborn confrontation of the contradictions which its rash enterprise has again and again brought into the open. Just as it struggles towards an accommodation between control and abandon in the artistic evocation of the erotic, so in its efforts to outline an ethic of desire it cuts a difficult path between sexual malthusianism on one side and permissiveness on the other. While protagonists of a sexual future of Edenic innocence and prophets

[256]

202   Felix Labisse, *The Strange Leda*, 1950

203   Max Ernst, Collage from *A Week of Happiness*, 1934

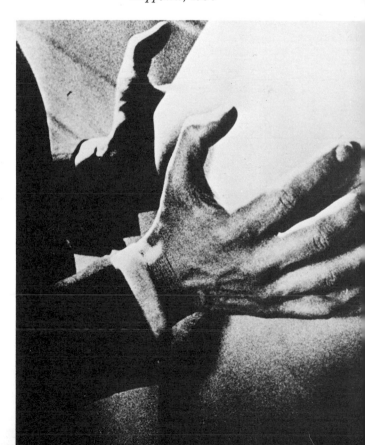

204   Luis Buñuel and Salvador Dali, *Un Chien Andalou* (*An Andalusian Dog*), 1928

of an erotic civilisation unshadowed by original sin have not been lacking in the movement—Breton himself has located his ideal in the Fourierist 'phalanstery'—surrealism has been too honest to deny that the exalted conception of a 'sacred' love does not require a concomitant sense of taboo and interdiction. If, as Breton admitted in his last years, and with due acknowledgment to Georges Bataille, the idea of the erotic is ultimately inseparable from the idea of transgression, then man is doomed to wage the moral war within his own heart into the most distant future, though hopefully at a level more worthy of his possibilities than he can reach today. The difficulty of this dilemma is admirably conveyed in a scene from Buñuel's film *Un Chien Andalou* (see illustration 204). The appearance of Simone Mareuil's breasts successively clothed and unclothed as Pierre Batcheff fondles them indicates simultaneously his desire for them to be naked and the fact that he feels them *beneath* the blouse. The clothing, says Xavière Gauthier, is both an obstacle and an aliment to his desire: 'His expression of mingled lasciviousness, wickedness and anguish indicate the complexity of this movement of desire.'[5]

In the last analysis, despite some stunning evocations of ultimate reconciliation in Breton's *L'Amour Fou* and the poetry of Paul Eluard, for example, surrealism is more absorbed in the quest for love than in the hoped for destination. Surrealism is a constantly ascending curve of desire. And desire, like liberty in surrealist eyes, can never reach a stable state; it is insatiable. To the surrealist, desire which defines man is also the force which perpetually drives him to break out of his specific condition. Surrealist eroticism is thus the motor and the matter of a project which will never be finally accomplished, the 'noyau de la comète' as it proceeds on its endless trajectory. 'A ce prix est l'amour.'

Chapter 7

The Erotic Novel—A Critical View

by

ALLAN RODWAY[1]

Among the dark gods of the psyche, Eros is a power so commanding that few novels could be classed as wholly unerotic. The present title, however, refers to something more specific: that class of novel whose sole or main purport is to arouse erotic feelings, and which stands to the wider class of novels about love, life, and society in much the same relationship as farce stands to comedy. Farce is laughter for its own sake—and why not? But that very fact renders it a lesser kind than comedy, wherein laughter subserves some point or purpose beyond itself. Eroticism for its own sake—and why not?[2]—is similarly limited; so the 'erotic novel' must also be accounted a minor kind. In literature as in life, though, it takes all kinds to make a world, and there is a case for preserving as many species as possible for pleasure as well as profit, for holiday as well as workaday use.

These terms sometimes spill over from literary to social contexts, and sometimes overlap with each other, or even change places (as, during the last war, pornography was put to workaday use by both sides for propaganda purposes). Not unnaturally, then, questions of social desirability are often confused with those of literary merit. Essentially, however, they are different questions; and this article concerns itself only with the erotic novel as a literary form, a minor kind within which it ought to be possible to sort out better from worse, more interesting from less, taking *l'homme moyen sensuel* as a rough starting-point for standards of judgement.

Such an approach must lead to some drastic revisions of current views. Selby's *Last Exit to Brooklyn*, for instance, can hardly be held to have been justly banned for a supposedly depraving and corrupting eroticism. It does not purport to be, and is not in fact, an erotic novel at all, in the sense defined. Certainly it presents a good deal of depraved and corrupt sexuality, but in such a way that no normal reader could possibly be more aroused than depressed by it. The sexuality, far from being erotic, is part and parcel of an off-putting grisly realism—open, if to any charge, only to that of a tendency to spread alarm and despondency. Sade's works,

[259]

too, seem properly classifiable on literary grounds as *anti*-erotic novels, though for the opposite reason. Their *un*realism is so extreme as to negate the erotic purport attributed to them, in this case rightly. So lacking are they in plot, plausibility—possibility even—in psychological insight, characterisation, variation, wit, humour, and so on; so demonstrably demolishable is the philosophy, so obsessive and exaggerated the performance, so puppet-like (and so happily, therefore, indestructible and unsuffering) the victims, that the final effect for the *literary* reader is one of queasy tedium, relieved only by a sense of exceptional, if mechanical, ingenuity, and by the appreciation of a few clever anti-theological quibbles. For the *sociological* reader Sade may be of much more interest. Were it felt that those not already lost would be led astray—unlikely, in view of the unconvincing nature of the fiction, even as fantasy—then it could be argued that these works were socially undesirable. On the other hand, it could be argued that working contrary to their own intent, they became socially desirable as Awful Warnings, cold textbooks whose mechanical permutations and extensions at last clarified and made classifiable a human characteristic long, and dangerously, underestimated. Neither case alters the fact that, again, they are not erotic novels as defined, though they try to be (as *Last Exit* does not).

Many novels that are erotic, however, draw upon Sade and subsequent psychiatric studies of the phenomenon of sado-masochism—sometimes to their benefit by enabling an intuitive perception to become fully conscious, as in Réage's *L'Histoire d'O* (*The Story of O*), sometimes to their detriment, by encouraging the admixture of good psychology with bad metaphysics, as in Bataille's *L'Histoire de l'Oeil* (*The Story of the Eye*), a characteristic shared by the Surrealist movement, in relation to which this book is of special interest. In general, and for obvious reasons, the more successful novels are those in which sado-masochism is only one ingredient—not too extreme—amongst others.

Yet to be as fully successful as the limitations of the kind allow, the erotic novelist must do more than ring the changes. For these limitations themselves make success more difficult to achieve, in some ways, than do the larger requirements of the major genres. A special talent is needed, which few seem to possess. Fantastic elaborations must always spring from basic buried realities, obsessions be preserved from boredom by some relationship with normality, and, even more importantly in this field than others, the writing must have integrity, must create a self-consistent world with which the narrator seems genuinely engaged. The whorish pretence of merely commercial productions, their calculated aping of authentically felt fact or fantasy, gives results in inverse proportion to their erotic potential.

Granted all this, which is true to some extent for all kinds of literature, there remains to be overcome a difficulty special to the genre. Like the sense of smell, our sexual sense tires rapidly. To counter this process by enlisting the aid of imagination, uninhibited introspection, and controlled invention, may indeed be one of the main justifications—if justification is needed—for the preservation of this particular literary species. Unfortunately, mind and body seem much alike in this area: arousal being relatively easy (especially through the opposite means of detailed fact and inventive fantasy), prolongation relatively hard, and re-arousal positively difficult—eventually becoming impossible no matter what the stimulation. In short, this is an area in which the law of diminishing returns applies with particular force. Even novelty rapidly loses its effect, for the most plausible and powerful ploys naturally get used up first, so that later invention carries a compound handicap. Moreover, however ingenious the variations, the method itself grows hackneyed, unless the novelties can be developed as part of an acceptable plot—a feat so far accomplished only by Gore Vidal's *Myra Breckinridge*, and approximated by Vladimir Nabokov's *Lolita*.

All this accounts for a paradox peculiar to the erotic novel: the more completely it fulfils its nature the less it achieves its end. Concentrated erotica turns out to be less erotic than the more diluted. Thus hard-core pornography, which clearly tries to be nothing but physically erotic, palls much more quickly than works such as Cleland's *Fanny Hill*, Pauline Réage's *Story of O*, Beardsley's *Under the Hill*, Southern and Hoffenburg's *Candy*, Lawrence's *Lady Chatterley's Lover*, Miller's *Tropics*, Roth's *Portnoy's Complaint*, and some others, which all in their different ways infuse some other element. In other words, erotic novels tend to be more successful *as such* in so far as they near the border of other genres rather than lying at the centre of their own.

Hard-core works do have an immediate effect on the novice reader, by appealing to that *nostalgie de la boue* which the necessary suppressions of civilisation accentuate; and shoddy production, poor style, and under-the-counter selling may well be part of the appeal, as Browning saw:

> *Or, my scrofulous French novel*
> *On grey paper with blunt type!*
> *Simply glance at it, you grovel*
> *Hand and foot in Belial's gripe.*[3]

But the law of diminishing returns there operates so drastically that it is tempting to replace it by the notion of overkill. For instance, one of its principal techniques is to call a spade a spade or preferably—and very frequently—a bloody shovel. Yet the characteristic sequence of 'sloppy snatches', clutches of 'cunts', or grosses of 'gashes'—to take one sort of example—are less effective than the mock-modest euphemisms of *Candy*: 'sweetening damp', 'pulsing jellybox', 'little sugar-scoop', 'precious little lamb-pit', and so on. Not only do these describe where the former merely name, but they also convey something of Candy's youth and sweetness, tone in with her own vocabulary, and moreover suggest smiling appreciation of adolescent sexuality (not excluding its innocent self-regard and self-deception); whereas the apparently more honest terms—at any rate in their customary context of uncouth dominance—suggest an underlying contempt and distaste, which further militates against the already precarious stimulation of reiterated taboo-words. At times, this suggestion becomes almost starkly explicit, as for example in Van Heller's *The Gang Way*:

> 'Sweetheart,' Dom said, 'you got a lovely lil' cunt.' He smirked at Sammy. 'She fucks like a bitch. Real nice pussy.'[4]

> He frigged her hard for a couple of seconds. 'Hi, baby,' he said. He wiped the finger on one of her tits. 'I'll see yuh around.'[5]

The differences in this small matter of vocabulary typify a general difference. What lifts *Candy* out of the ruck of unreadable, certainly unre-readable, rubbish is the variegated tints given to its eroticism by association with other elements. There is the parallel with Voltaire's *Candide*, in which another goodhearted innocent stumbles, ever-credulous, into the pitfalls of a philosophy designed by cynics to keep suckers sweet. There is the more specific satire on hypocrisy and self-deception in left-wing do-goodery; the humorous overturning of medical pedestals; the cutting-down to size of fashionable psychiatry. Above all, *Candy* has at least an elementary plot to sustain interest between sexual peaks, whereas most erotic novels are primitively episodic, and in trying to be all peaks become dull plateaus. In the culminating final scene the leitmotif of father-fixation is neatly joined with satire on mysticism.

Since *Candy* relies on cumulative effects, like all books that are wholes, not heaps, a good deal is lost by brief quotation; however, the climax of its amusing satire on the contemporary *guru* cult may go some way towards illustrating the fact that eroticism diluted increases in potency, becoming more re-readable in proportion as it is less simple-bodied:

> 'No, resume the basic yoga position', said Grindle, 'and I will continue with the instruction.'
> Candy lay back again with a sigh, closed-eyed, hands joined behind her head, and Grindle resumed his fondling of her sweet-dripping little fur-pie.
> 'Does the tingling sensation you referred to before continue, or increase?' he asked, after a moment or so.
> '. . . I'm afraid so,' said the girl sadly, panting a little.
> 'And do you experience feelings of creamy warmth and a great yielding sensation?' demanded Grindle.
> 'Yes,' Candy sighed, thinking he was surely psychic.

> 'Never mind your crass and absurdly cheap philistine materialist associations with it,' said Grindle crossly, as he adjusted her legs again and ranged himself just above her. 'Put those from your mind—concentrate on your *Exercise Number Four*, for always remember that we must bring *all* our mystical knowledge to converge on the issue at hand—even as does the tiger his strength, cunning and speed.'

[262]

'Now I am inserting the member,' he explained, as he parted the tender quavering lips of the pink honeypot and allowed his stout member to be drawn into the seething thermal pudding of the darling girl.

'Oh my goodness,' said Candy, squirming her lithe and supple body slightly, though remaining obediently closed-eyed and with her hands clasped tightly behind her head.

'Now I shall remove the member,' said Grindle, ' . . . not all the way but just so, there, and in again. You see? And again so, I will repeat this several times—while you do your *Exercise Number Four*.'

'Gosh,' said Candy, swallowing nervously, '. . . I don't think I can concentrate on it now.'

'Oh, yes,' said Grindle, encouraging her hips with his hands, setting them into the motion of the Cosmic Rhythm Exercise she had practised earlier in the rectent. And when she had satisfactorily achieved the motion, Grindle said: 'Now this, you see, approximates the so-called "sexual act".'

'I *know* it,' said Candy fretfully, greatly disturbed by the thought.

'I shall presently demonstrate still another mastery of glandular functions,' claimed great Grindle, 'that of the so-called *orgasm* or *ejaculation*.'

'Oh please,' said the adorable girl, actually alarmed, 'not . . . not inside me . . .I . . .I . . .'

'Don't be absurd,' said Grindle breathing heavily, 'naturally in willing the chemistry of the semen, I would eliminate the impregnating agent, spermatozoa, as a constituent—for it would be of no use to our purpose here you see.'

'Now then,' he continued after a moment, 'tell me if this does not almost exactly resemble the philistine "orgasm"?'

'Oh gosh,' murmured the darling closed-eyed girl, biting her lips as the burning member began to throb and spurt inside her, in a hot, ravaging flood of her precious little honey-cloister whose bleating pink-sugar walls cloyed and writhed as though alive with a thousand tiny insatiable tongues, '. . . *and how*!'[6]

Romantic love has been much criticised, and no doubt rightly, yet it seems to be a truth of experience that without it, or something serving a similar purpose, sexual life is diminished. Acts then are not enriched by meanings, nor absences pleasurably bridged by remembrance and anticipation. Much hard-core pornography appears to express brute reactions against this fact; buried rage at past rejections, at the inability of the body to live up to the aspirations of the mind, or more generally, rage at the paradox that wasting time and emotional capital on the extra-sexual should be a requirement of heightened sexuality. Literature, however, is not life, and the more subtle erotic novelist may avoid crude reaction and yet enrich his eroticism by evoking some ambience other than that of romantic love. Indeed he has to, for he must provide sublimation for the reaction mentioned and also allow play to fantasies incompatible with love, or for that matter with real life.

Aubrey Beardsley, in *Under the Hill*, adopts the artificial manner of rococo-pastoral for this purpose. That Dresden-china style turns the most outré eroticism into an aesthetic experience. A contradiction in terms, since the aesthetic requires distance, the erotic participation? Not quite, for polite manner may be held in tension with rude matter, especially if blended with a soupçon of humour. An aesthetic eroticism is improbable but, like sweet-sour sauce, it does exist:

> Now as Sparion and his friends began to grow tired and exhausted with the new debauch, they no longer cared to take the initiative, but, relaxing every muscle, abandoned themselves to passive joys, yielding utterly to the ardent embraces of the intoxicated satyrs, who waxed fast and furious, and seemed as if they would never come to the end of their strength. Full of the new tricks they had learnt that morning, they played them passionately and roughly, making havoc of the cultured flesh, and tearing the splendid frocks and dresses into ribands. Duchesses and Maréchales, Marquises and Princesses, Dukes and Marshals, Marquesses and Princes, were ravished and stretched and rumpled and crushed beneath the interminable vigour and hairy breasts of the inflamed woodlanders. They bit at the white thighs and nozzled wildly in the crevices. They sat astride the women's chests and consummated frantically with their bosoms; they caught their prey by the hips and held it over their heads irrumating with prodigious gusto. It was the triumph of the valley.[7]

> Poor Adolphe! How happy he was, touching the Queen's breasts with his quick tongue-tip. I have no doubt that the keener scent of animals must make women much more attractive to them than to men; for the gorgeous odour that but faintly fills our nostrils must be revealed to the brute creation in divine fullness.
>
> Anyhow, Adolphe sniffed as never a man did round the skirts of Venus. After the first interchange of affectionate delicacies was over, the unicorn lay down upon his side, and, closing his eyes, beat his stomach wildly with the mark of manhood.
>
> Venus caught that stunning member in her hands and laid her cheek along it; but few touches were wanted to consummate the creature's pleasure. The Queen bared her left arm to the elbow, and with the soft underneath of it made amazing movements upon the tightly-strung instrument. When the melody began to flow, the unicorn offered up an astonishing vocal accomplishment. Tannhäuser was amused to learn that the etiquette of Venusburg compelled everybody to await the outburst of those venereal sounds before they could sit down to déjeuner.
>
> Adolphe had been quite profuse that morning. Venus knelt where it had fallen, and lapped her little apéritif.[8]

Beardsley reinforces the aesthetic ambience, also, by frequent references to works of art and elaborate descriptions of dress and decoration—at times almost passing out of the area of 'the erotic novel' altogether (at the opposite side from Selby).

Fanny Hill, one of the most successful of erotic novels, remains well clear of the grey band that, rather than a sharp line, separates one literary genre from others, though it, too, avoids an unduly blatant, and therefore swiftly tiring, assault on the erotic taste-buds by recourse to the realm of art. Here, the case is not one of mock-euphemism, for this is not erotic comedy, nor is it a case of ironic tensions, but rather a matter of art-metaphor, seriously used to add an extra dimension to the merely sexual—and of course to exclude those accompaniments, like bad breath, that in real life tend to mar the desiderated ideal eroticism even of romantic lovers. The following characteristic descriptive passages, for instance, clearly use the critical register of eighteenth-century appreciations of landscape painting, landscape itself, and *objets d'art*:

. . . such a length, such a breadth of animated ivory! perfectly well-turn'd and fashioned, the proud stiffness of which distended its skin, whose smooth polish and velvet softness might vie with that of the most delicate of our sex, and whose exquisite whiteness was not a little set off by a sprout of black curling hair round the root, through the jetty sprigs of which the fair skin shew'd, as light aether through the branch-work of distant trees overtopping the summit of a hill; then the broad and blueish-casted incarnate of the head, and the blue serpentines of its veins, altogether compos'd the most striking assemblage of figures and colours in nature.[9]

Then lay exposed, or, to speak more properly, displayed, the greatest parade in nature of female charms . . . But what infinitely enrich'd and adorn'd them was the sweet intersection formed, where they met at the bottom of the smoothest, roundest, whitest belly, by that central furrow which nature had sunk there, between the relieve of two pouting ridges, and which, in this girl, was in perfect symmetry with the rest of her frame. No! nothing in nature could be of a beautifuller cut; then, the dark umbrage of the downy spring-moss that over-arched it, bestowed, on the luxury of the landscape, a touching warmth, a tender finishing beyond the expression of words or even the paint of thought.[10]

Her posteriors, plump, smooth, and prominent, form'd luxuriant tracts of animated snow, that splendidly filled the eye, till it was commanded down the parting of separation of those exquisitely white cliffs, by their narrow vale, and was there stopt, and attracted by the embowered bottom-cavity, that terminated this delightful vista and stood moderately gaping from the influence of her bended posture, so that the agreeable interior of the sides of the orifice came into view, and with respect to the white that dazzled round it, gave somewhat the idea of a pink slash in the glossiest white satin.[11]

Such passages do not alone account for the success of *Fanny Hill* as an erotic novel (any more than those using military or chemical metaphor, for active sexuality, wholly do so). But they all go to form a medium in which eroticism is supported and sustained by other interests, other feelings, and in which invented incident can be agreeably suspended. Moreover, they provide such a norm that stylistic bravura at moments of sexual crisis will seem not unnatural, but perfectly appropriate. And such bravura, it might be remarked, is the literary equivalent of that sophisticated play and variation by which human sexuality in life may transcend the lesser satisfactions of simple animality.

The Story of O differently transcends the limitations of sex in the raw: by relating O's masochism—though without ever using psychoanalytic jargon—to religion, with its similar openness to suffering, submission, and self-abandonment in the name of love:

Actually, the object of these procedures . . . [is] a good deal less to make you suffer pain, scream or shed tears than, by means of this pain, to enforce upon you the idea that you are subject to this constraint and to teach you that you utterly belong to something which is apart from and outside yourself.[12]

Thus he would possess her as a god possesses his creatures whereupon he lays hands guised as some monster or bird, as some invisible spirit or as very ecstacy. . . . The more he subjected her to, the more important to him she would become. The fact that he gave her to others was proof thereof; proof in his eyes, it ought to be proof in hers, that she belonged to him. He gave her so as to have her immediately back, and recovered her enriched a hundredfold in his eyes, as is an ordinary object that has served some divine purpose and thereby become infused with sanctity.[13]

Daily and, as it were, ritualistically soiled by saliva and sperm, by sweat mingled with her own sweat, she sensed herself to be literally the vessel of impurity, the gutter whereof Scripture makes mention. And yet in all, those parts of her body which were the most continually offended, having become more sensitive, seemed to her to have become, at the same time, more lovely, and as though ennobled.[14]

She considered herself fortunate, was happy to find that she was important enough to him to enable him to find pleasure in outraging her, as believers thank God for having humbled them.[15]

The sealed chateau of sadists clearly owes much to Sade, but the pains are mostly not so extreme as to make the production of masochistic pleasure improbable, and the physical paradox is not essayistically discussed in terms of an invalid philosophy, but is interfused with a psychology, made plausible in the characterisation of O, and validated by the phenomenon of religion, whose spiritual masochism finds sublimated expression in theological paradoxes almost identical with those felt by her. In this way, the well-written evocations of physical detail and sensation expand into psychological nuance, and O's progressively painful personal ecstasies acquire reverberations of wider significance.

Georges Bataille's *Story of the Eye* culminates in multiple sexual pollutions of priest, chalice, and Host, picking up the fertility rituals they derive from, but perverting them, presumably more to the benefit of Catholic readers than others. On the face of it, therefore, it is *The Story of O* in reverse: prostitution as sacrilegious rather than religious. Bataille's potty preface to the short-story in the same volume— pretentiously mingling Existentialism and Surrealism—indicates that it is supposed to be much the same thing: the achievement of holiness through anguish and the annihilation of personality in extreme sexual experience (much of it, though in a different way from O's, of a sado-masochistic kind). One of the less confused passages gives the *theory*:

> Pleasure would be a puny affair were it not to involve this leap, this staggering overshooting of the mark which common sense fixes—a leap that is not confined alone to sexual ecstasy, one that is known also to the mystics of various religions, one that, above all, Christian mystics experienced in the same way. The act whereby being—existence—is bestowed upon us is an *unbearable* surpassing of being, an act no less unbearable than that of dying.[16]

In *practice*—as the concluding psychoanalytic explanation of the preceding fantasies tends to confirm—the book's real achievement is not metaphysical but psychosomatic. Discounting the 'theology' and the rather special 'anguish' of this particular case-history (for not every child is lucky enough to possess a mad, blind, syphilitic, paralysed father and mother who, going mad in her turn, commits suicide), what emerges, in a form more blurred than it need have been, is an imaginative recapturing of the infantile eroticism of mess-making, through regressive sexual fantasy:

> At this point Simone developed a perfect craze for breaking eggs by squeezing them in her ass. She would place herself head down upon the seat of an armchair, her back pressed tightly against the back of the chair, her legs flexed towards me, and I would frig myself so as to squirt fuck in her face. Then I'd put the egg over her hole; she took pleasure in working it within that deep crack. At the moment my fuck sprang, her buttocks crushed the egg, she was convulsed, and I, burrowing my face in her ass, would soak myself in that abundance of impurity.[17]

What makes it inferior to the *Story of O* is that the theology and the psychology do not come over as illuminating extensions of the primal sexuality the book is really expressing—though infantile mess-making does seem to involve not only anguish but also feelings of sacrilege and omnipotence. They come over as rationalisations, as if the writer's muddled theory had diverted him from facing fully the real nature of his subject.

Henry Miller also misses a trick, so to speak, by separating his metaphysics from his physics. Practically all his erotic novels indeed could be very simply improved by scissoring out their windy balloons of rhetoric—which suggests a certain integrity in the untainted remainder. Yet much of the sexuality approximates to that in hard-core pornography, being basically that of a society in which men are emotionally too removed from women by convention and idealism; so that all three are contemptuously reacted against, and beautification is replaced by uglification. What saves Miller's work, by pointing up the healthy element in his particular reaction, are the good humour and resilience shown, the fearlessness with which the idealistic gaff is blown, and the social picture that accompanies the sexual episodes (and partly accounts for their tone). By these lights, the much-praised *Tropic of Cancer* ought to be considered inferior to the *Tropic of Capricorn*, where Miller is on home ground. For its hilarious savaging of the contemporary American scene his cornucopian rhetoric happens to be perfectly appropriate. There, people naturally grabbed for what they could get, before it was gone, in sex as in everything else:

I even accomplished the miracle of stopping the crazy turnover, something that nobody had dared to hope for. Instead of supporting my efforts they undermined me. According to the logic of the higher-ups the turnover had ceased because the wages were too high. So they cut the wages. It was like kicking the bottom out of a bucket. The whole edifice tumbled, collapsed on my hands. And just as though nothing had happened they insisted that the gaps be plugged up immediately. To soften the blow they intimated that I might even increase the percentage of Jews, I might take on a cripple now and then, if he were capable, I might do this or that, all of which they had informed me previously was against the code. I was so furious that I took on anything and everything; I would have taken on broncos and gorillas if I could have imbued them with the modicum of intelligence which was necessary to deliver messages. A few days previously there had been only five or six vacancies at closing time. Now there were three hundred, four hundred, five hundred—they were running out like sand. It was marvellous. I sat there and without asking a question I took them on in carload lots—niggers, Jews, paralytics, cripples, ex-convicts, whores, maniacs, perverts, idiots, any fucking bastard who could stand on two legs and hold a telegram in his hand.

The best thing about the new day was the introduction of female messengers. It changed the whole atmosphere of the joint. For Hymie especially it was a godsend . . . Despite the added work, he had a permanent erection. He came to work with a smile and he smiled all day long. He was in heaven. At the end of the day I always had a list of five or six who were worth trying out. The game was to keep them on a string, to promise them a job but to get a free fuck first. Usually it was only necessary to throw a feed into them in order to bring them back to the office at night and lay them out on a zinc-covered table in the dressing room.[18]

She must have had four or five orgasms like that, in the air, before I put her feet down on the ground. I took it out without spilling a drop and made her lie down in the vestibule. Her hat had rolled off into a corner and her bag had spilled open and a few coins had tumbled out. I note this because just before I gave it to her good and proper I made a mental note to pocket a few coins for my car fare home. Anyway it was only a few hours since I had said to Maxie in the bath house that I would like to take a look at his sister's quim, and here it was now smack up against me sopping wet and throwing out one squirt after another . . . But somebody had to pay for making me walk around in the rain grubbing a dime.[19]

Nabokov's *Lolita*, of course, is altogether more elegant in texture and structure; its erotic humour is more suave, its picture of the American scene and mentality more ironically sardonic, as befits an outsider's inside view. Kaleidoscopic, its shifts of place, pace, and personality provide variety within larger unities of plot and mood. If it is an erotic novel, then it is the best we have: a minor masterpiece. But *is* it? Or is it really a study of the psychology of unrequited consuming passion, the oldest of love-stories, here given one striking new twist?

At any rate, it is a debatable case—as is *Portnoy's Complaint*, of which it is arguable that the erotic, though bulking larger than any other element, is subordinated in importance to the comic psychological portraits of Portnoy himself and of his overwhelming Jewish mother. That the 'complaint' seems to refer at once to Portnoy's confession to his psychiatrist, to his sexual failing, and to his mother, indicates how intelligently witty the book is; hence the eroticism is often *dissolved* into a more inclusive comedy rather than *extended* by the sexualising of other areas of experience.

Nobody could accuse Lawrence of excessively witty intelligence; nevertheless, if *Lady Chatterley's Lover* fails (as the erotic novel it purports only ambiguously to be), it does so because it tries so hard to be intelligent. A process always vitiated in Lawrence by his belief in thinking with the solar plexus—one consequence of which legless footballing is that he is always much better on diagnosis than cure (one *feels* pains, but must *know* treatments). Witness the following conclusions of the inter-linked didactic themes of *Lady Chatterley's Lover*:

> They ought to learn to be naked and handsome, and to sing in a mass and dance the old group dances, and carve the stools they sit on, and embroider their own emblems. Then they wouldn't need money. And that's the only way to solve the industrial problem; train the people to be able to live and live in handsomeness, without needing to spend. . . . They should be alive and frisky, and acknowledge the great god Pan.[20]

> They were both silent. Then he roused himself and said: 'Yes, I do believe in something. I believe in being warm-hearted in love, in fucking with a warm heart. I believe if men could fuck with warm hearts, and the women take it warm-heartedly, everything would come all right.[21]

The feelings are fine, but even Marcuse could hardly take these recipes for the ills of our overcrowded world as anything but wishful thinking. In fine, the published version of this work—rather more than the first version—is too didactic for an erotic novel, too naïvely sensualist for a novel of ideas. Nothing of this length by Lawrence, of course, could lack all merit, and many passages do memorably convey the ugliness of the industrial environment and the beauty of sexual love at its best. But since they rise not from a background of matching eroticism, but from a didactic one, even they are haunted by the spectre of overwriting, and others undoubtedly fall victim to it. Had Lawrence been less of a puritan he might have written a major erotic novel, but *Lady Chatterley's Lover* tried to be something more and ended as something less.

Like Pauline Réage and Henry Miller, Lawrence usually insists so strongly on the traditional polarisation of sexual roles that his work sometimes gives the impression of compensating for a secret doubt. Indeed, many erotic works have the effect of seeming to reinforce a weakened sense of sexual identity through fantasy-experience. Gore Vidal's *Myra Breckinridge*, on the contrary, exploits modern uncertainties of identity and sexual role to make a novel at once genuinely comic and erotic, and, what is even rarer in this genre, brilliantly plotted. It may not be a great novel, but it is certainly a superlatively clever one.

The great erotic novel, in fact, has not yet been written. Quite possibly it never can be, for the relationship of novels in this mode to those in major modes is comparable to that between cookery and painting or music. Through the eye and the ear, as compared with the stomach, sensation is far more readily extensible into other, specially human areas, and thereafter is more retainable and revivable.

No one, however, would despise cookery for that reason. Indeed here, as in sex itself, surely, *vive la différence*! And, granted room for different kinds, we may be grateful that there exist a few chefs as well as too many cooks. With sauciness, selectivity, variety, cunning progression, aesthetic appearance, and ceremonial serving, these benefactors can transmute mere appetite into minor art. Though many cloy the appetites they feed, some, like Cleopatra, make hungry where most they satisfy. For this art, Auden's is a better recipe than Browning's:

> *Be subtle, various, ornamental, clever,*
> *And do not listen to the critics ever*
> *Whose crude provincial gullets crave in books*
> *Plain cooking made still plainer by plain cooks.*[22]

Chapter 8

Eroticism in Films

The cinema has been the most influential medium during the last thirty years, and in any discussion of eroticism it demands and deserves careful study. Eroticism in the cinema was suspect right from the very start, vexing self-appointed censors then as much as it worries the official censors today. Then as now, films were expected to pay lip-service to a code of ethics derived from Victorian morality. Then as now, righteous wrath was brought to bear on those who put freedom above prurience. In 1896, a couple were shown stealing a quick kiss in a film called *The Kiss*. One critic, Herbert S. Stone, described this event as 'absolutely disgusting', adding: 'All delicacy or remnant of charm seems gone from Miss Irwin, and the performance comes near being indecent in its emphasized vulgarity. Such things call for police interference.'[1] A film of *Fatima's Belly Dance* as performed at the Chicago World's Fair of 1893 was censored when shown in 1906, by having bars stencilled over the offending portions of the dancer's undulating torso.[2]

The erotic power of the early cinema was strong, but it did not depend on explicitly sexual behaviour. Owing to the stringent rules of censorship, nudity and sexual relations were shown extremely rarely, one exception being Gustave Machaty's *Extase* (1933), in which Hedy Lamarr went for a swim in the nude and then ran through the woods looking for her clothes (see illustration 205). The erotic appeal of the cinema was the erotic appeal of its stars. The creation of the star system provided audiences with agents for their own fantasies. Women identified with the sex goddesses of the screen; men fantasised about them. The stars were always identified with the parts they played; they acquired an extra dimension, becoming part-human and part-divine.[3] The characteristic appeal of each star was, however, quite different, and the trends in types of heroine provide an insight into the emotional climate of each period.

Previous to the First World War, studios did not name performers in their films in case it encouraged them to ask for more money. But by 1914 they had realised the drawing power of a personality, and the first true star of the cinema was created —Theodosia Goodman, a tailor's daughter from Cincinnati, renamed Theda Bara by William Fox, a far-sighted, independent producer. She was provided with a prefabricated screen-personality of a sex siren; her name was claimed to have been coined as an anagram of 'death Arab', and she was announced as the child of a sheikh and an Egyptian princess, who had been weaned on serpents' blood. At her personal appearances she would wear Arabian clothes, pretend not to speak English, and receive her admirers in an atmosphere reeking of incense and the

205   Hedy Lamarr in *Ecstasy*, 1933

perfume of lilies and roses. Her first film, *A Fool There Was*, was released in January 1915 and was an instant sensation. She played a vampire-like female pursuing her victims energetically and triumphing over them as they grovelled at her feet. With her dark eyes flashing a look of baleful eroticism, she was the epitome of sex appeal, and in 1917 was a great success in *Cleopatra* (see illustration 206). In no time she was christened 'The Vamp', and the star system was born.

A complete contrast to Theda Bara was Mary Pickford, America's sweetheart with the beautiful curls, playing the sexual innocent in weepies such as *Daddy Long Legs* (1919). Mary Pickford was discovered by D. W. Griffith and cast immediately as a sweet and sentimental girl in *Pippa Passes* (1909), a film based on the romantic verse-drama by Robert Browning. She was never to escape such type-casting, and became the victim of her screen personality, for her public would not allow her to be anything else, even when she was in her thirties. The sad result was that her acting-life was shortened by the persistence of the Pickford myth.

The third goddess of the silent screen was Clara Bow, the sexy flapper known to the world as the 'It Girl'. Elinor Glyn, Hollywood's authority on how film stars should make love, wrote a story about *It*, a strange magnetism which certain people

[272]

206   Theda Bara in *Cleopatra*, 1917

possessed. She chose Clara Bow to star in the film version of 1927, and *It* soon came to mean sex appeal. Clara Bow was a red-head, and red hair was thought to be very sexy in the '20s, just as black hair personified the vamp of the previous period and the platinum blonde was to be the sex-symbol of the '30s.

The first of the platinum-blonde screen goddesses, and the first sex star of the talkies, was Mae West, the good-time girl, the man-eater who refused to take herself too seriously (see illustration 207). 'Sex rampant and unrepentant, yet

207   Mae West in
She Done Him Wrong,
1933

redeemingly self-satirizing, is what Mae West represents; a sex goddess who mocks the very qualities she dangles before the public.'[4] She had the ability to load almost any action or remark with double meaning. She was continuously in trouble for the vivid sexuality of her every performance, from her early vaudeville days to her first appearance in the theatre, in her own play entitled *Sex* (1926). For this, she was indicted on a morals charge, fined and sent to jail for ten days, and she has been a controversial figure ever since. Yet she herself was far from debauched, and in her films she was much too busy enjoying sex to want to corrupt anyone. 'Because I portray sex with humour and good nature instead of as something shameful, I think my portrayals are accepted in the spirit in which I play them. I have excited and stimulated, but I have never demoralized.'[5]

Her most famous creation was the emancipated Bowery bawd, Diamond Lil, in *She Done Him Wrong* (1933), with the catch-phrase 'Come up and see me some time'. Her catch-phrases are part of cinema legend, as the one from *I'm No Angel* (1933): 'When I'm good I'm very good, but when I'm bad I'm better.' Mae West's acting career was sadly cut short in the '30s by a vicious purity campaign on the part of the Roman Catholic League of Decency, who were at that time trying to clean up films. She was too easy a target, and although she tried to present a reformed personality in *Klondike Annie* (1936), the result was not Mae West. She was completely self-made and completely brilliant in her great years, and her return in *Myra Breckinridge* (1970) was welcome, if only for reasons of nostalgia.

A very different sex goddess was Marlene Dietrich. Brought up in a Prussian officer's household, Dietrich learnt from an early age that any display of emotion or temperament was bad manners. In Josef von Sternberg's *The Blue Angel* (1930), she used this lesson to brilliant effect in the erotic atmosphere she created as a remote, mysterious *femme fatale*, with a deep, sensual, and attention-demanding voice. In almost all her films directed by Sternberg she played a woman who attracted men at the cost of suffering to them and sometimes to herself, a lonely yet fascinating woman, a figure that had immense appeal for cinema audiences in the '30s. But the purity campaign of the Roman Catholic League of Decency killed this Dietrich. In later films like *Destry Rides Again* (1939), she shed her mystery and her dignity and became very American, the epitome of brazen glamour, but a disappointment after the Dietrich of the early years.

The most mysterious of the sex goddesses of the screen was Greta Garbo, who had built up a fanatical following when she gave up her career in 1941 at the age of thirty-six. Garbo had a depressive personality, the result of a childhood conditioned by poverty, illness, and tragedy. The tense, withdrawn child became an enigmatic and mysterious actress who shunned the limelight. The catch-phrase 'I want to be alone' is said to be apocryphal, but it typifies her personality. Her very remoteness inspired curiosity and then immortality. She seemed to provide people with their need for something mysterious and inaccessible in life. To this extent Garbo was perhaps the greatest sex goddess the cinema has known. She was the embodiment of all that her admirers wanted her to be, for her remoteness ensured there would be no disillusionment. Her appeal was intensely erotic: her movements were animal-like, and in her love scenes, the feminine spirituality of her beauty was perfectly contrasted with the intensity of her sexual attack. Somehow she was able to excite her audiences with the seeming banality of the tragic heroines she played, such as *Camille* (1937) ('I knew I was too happy') and *Queen Christina* (1933) ('How wonderful to be happy for no reason'). Garbo was a great actress; she projected a new and sophisticated sexuality at a period when the public were tiring of the flapper girl and her philosophy of free love.

The film world has produced many other actresses with star quality, who fulfilled, for a while, their audiences' fantasies. Earlier examples included Pola Negri, the mysterious romantic, and Lilian Gish, the innocent virgin. In the '30s there was Jean Harlow, the original platinum blonde (see illustration 208), who pioneered the shift of erotic interest from the legs to the breasts, and whose blatant display of her body contained elements of strip-tease (*Platinum Blonde*, 1932). Harlow was very aware of her sexual attractiveness and used her body in a way that was later to be paralleled by Bardot, although the tragedy of her short career finds its reflection in that of Monroe. Later stars included Betty Grable with the voluptuous curves; Jane Russell with the startling bust; Katherine Hepburn, the woman of the world; Bette Davis and Joan Crawford, the passionate heroines of romantic melodramas; the cool and languorous Grace Kelly; the gamin simplicity of Audrey Hepburn; the poutingly provocative Brigitte Bardot; the Latin excitements of Sophia Loren and Gina Lollobrigida; the neurotic and fiery Elizabeth Taylor; the clinically pure Julie Andrews; Doris Day, the girl-next-door; the pneumatic Jayne Mansfield,

208   Jean Harlow in *Riff Raff*, 1935

Raquel Welch, and Ursula Andress; and, above all, the tragic innocent, Marilyn Monroe (see illustration 209).

An adoring public often confuses a star's public performances with his private life, and the greatest idols in fact have little chance of the luxury of a private life at all. They belong to their public, and their fans become emotionally infatuated with them. The resulting pressures can be too much to bear, and both Marilyn Monroe and James Dean can be seen as martyrs of the star system. It is especially easy to see Marilyn Monroe as the innocent victim of the world of Hollywood, progressing from the sweet blonde girl to the model for nude calendars and pin-ups, and on to the blonde bombshell exploited and manipulated by forces she could not understand or control, until she reached the unenviable position of belonging totally to a seemingly sex-starved world of cinema fans. The progress from happy unknown to desperately unhappy sex goddess was easy to follow in her very public private life and through her films from *Gentlemen Prefer Blondes* (1953) to *The Misfits* (1961); and the tragedy was made the more poignant by her combination of enormous physical attraction with wide-eyed innocence. She had the rare ability of exciting at one and the same time both the sexual appetite and the protective instinct. And in this way she differed from that other sex kitten Brigitte Bardot, for where Bardot offered herself completely and happily as an object of man's erotic desires, Monroe held something back, giving her films a touch of melancholy and making her supreme beauty and sexuality seem vulnerable rather than crudely available.

If Marilyn Monroe characterised eroticism at its best in the American cinema of

209   Marilyn Monroe

the '50s, Brigitte Bardot's variety was typical of the European films of the period, whose sexual sophistication began to permeate America in spite of the scissors of the Hays office. French films in particular reflected and boldly affirmed a philosophy of gratification of the senses. The one that introduced Bardot to Great Britain and America was *And God . . . Created Woman* (1956), directed by her husband, Roger Vadim, in which she played a bride who teased her brother-in-law into ripping off her clothes and raping her. In spite of extensive censoring on both sides of the Atlantic, the nudity and sexual antics that remained were unprecedented, and made Bardot, with her frankly animal sexuality and her wilful amorality and instant availability, an international star.

Bardot was only one of the French sex idols of the period. Martine Carol in *Caroline Chérie* (1950) was responsible for introducing extensive nudity and sexual antics into the French cinema, but few of her films were ever given certificates in Great Britain or America. Simone Signoret starred in *La Ronde* (1950), directed by Max Ophuls, a witty and cleverly made film about Viennese morals and manners at the turn of the century, concentrating on the inconstancy of lovers, rather than on the profligacy of the era. But scenes such as that where Signoret as a prostitute services a soldier standing upright in a dark alley were too much for the New York Board of Censors, who declared that it dealt with 'promiscuity, adultery, forni-fication and seduction', and hence constituted 'a clear and present danger to the good people of New York State'. The decision was reversed two years later by the U.S. Supreme Court, which tactfully pointed out that the film had already been shown in sixteen states without any appreciable effect on public morals.

One of the brightest stars of the French cinema in the '50s, and one whose reputation has grown ever since, was Jeanne Moreau, a far less obvious sex-symbol than Bardot, but one whose acting abilities are greater. Moreau was the star of Louis Malle's frankly erotic film *The Lovers* (1959), one of the most important of the *nouvelle vague* group of French films. The film told the simple story of a bored wife casually meeting a young man, falling in love with him and leaving home and husband to run off with him. The love scene on a bed and then in a bath-tub was beautifully photographed and the love-play was very explicit—including a graphic depiction of cunnilingus. The film obtained notoriety on various accounts. In England, it was heavily cut and the poster depicting Rodin's famous sculpture of *The Kiss* was banned by many local authorities. In the United States, many states refused it a licence, and it gave rise to a historic Supreme Court decision when an appeal against its total ban in Ohio was allowed, the Court declaring for the first time that 'national, not purely local, contemporary community standards' were to be used in determining whether or not a 'work of expression' was to be judged obscene.[6]

Jeanne Moreau also starred in Roger Vadim's *Les Liaisons Dangereuses* (1959), and François Truffaut's *Jules et Jim* (1961), continuing to project an image of an experi-enced sensualist determined to enjoy the sexual freedom traditionally reserved for men. The New York Censors decided not to cut *Les Liaisons Dangereuses*, but

[277]

instead to darken the lighting during the erotic scenes of the film. The director was delighted, as the result in his opinion was to give these scenes a sexier effect. The lighting was especially well handled in the scenes of nude love-making in *Hiroshima Mon Amour*, the film directed by Alain Resnais in 1959. The film showed a French actress having a brief affair with a Japanese architect in Hiroshima and included flashbacks to her relationship with a German soldier in Nevers during the occupation of France. The nudity was discreetly presented and the censors did not cut the film.

The climate of opinion in favour of eroticism in the cinema in Great Britain and America was greatly affected by these and other European imports in the '50s. From Italy came Fellini's *Nights of Cabiria* (1958), a warm-hearted film about a prostitute played by Giulietta Masina, and *Love in the City* (1954), partly directed by Antonioni, a Neo-Realist film based on newspaper reports of tragedies relating to sex. The sexual charms of Gina Lollobrigida were amply demonstrated in *Times Gone By* (1952), which also starred Vittorio de Sica as a lawyer defending La Lollo on a murder charge by revealing her physical attributes to the court and asking how anyone could want to remove such delights from the world. Sophia Loren was seen naked to the waist in two films, *It was He, Yes, Yes* (1951) and *Two Nights with Cleopatra* (1953). And by 1960, Antonioni's *L'Avventura* and Fellini's *La Dolce Vita* had become international successes that were to have great influence as representatives of a distinct style of film-making, often mysterious, often sexually provocative and always fascinating.

The '50s brought Swedish films to the attention of American and British audiences, largely due to the work of the great director Ingmar Bergman. Sweden had long accepted mixed nude-bathing in public, and so nudity played a natural part in Swedish films. Bergman's productions never take liberties for the sake of it. He features sex, extensive nudity, rape, adultery, incest, and various types of homosexuality, but for philosophic and moralistic purposes, giving concrete form with great artistry to legend and stories that have some mysterious contemporary relevance. *Summer with Monika* (1952) depicts the tragic consequences of thoughtless passion; *Sawdust and Tinsel*, also known as *The Naked Light* (1953), shows a clown, driven crazy with grief at the death of his promiscuous wife, carrying her nude body through a crowd of soldiers who have enjoyed her favours; *The Virgin Spring* (1960) includes a rape scene unprecedented for its realism, which becomes the central symbol in a brooding parable of tragedy and vengeance in the medieval world. *The Virgin Spring* bears comparison with the masterpiece of the new school of Japanese film-makers, Akira Kurosawa's *Rashomon* (1951). This brilliant film includes four re-enactments of the brutal rape by an outlaw of a beautiful woman in the presence of her husband and seen by a passing woodcutter. Each person tells the tale from his own self-protective point of view, and the beautifully directed yet terrifying film becomes a poetic riddle of the nature of truth and reality versus illusion.

Germany lagged far behind Sweden, France, Italy, and Japan as far as international film markets were concerned in the '50s. Her major sex star was Marion Michael, a lithe seventeen-year-old who was chosen out of 11,800 applicants for the title role in

Liane of the Jungle (1956). The film told of the love between the photographer of a scientific expedition and a female Tarzan discovered in the jungle, and a great deal of film-footage was devoted to scenes of Liane swinging through the trees with practically nothing on. Marion Michael displayed her charms in many other films, but the only German production to win a wide international audience at this period was *Rosemarie* (1958), an exposé of real-life corruption in high places that included some very candid sex scenes.

Overt eroticism was unknown in American films of the '50s, and American stars had to go abroad to show more of themselves to their public. Jayne Mansfield made the thriller *Too Hot to Handle* (1960) in England, and in one scene she wore a transparent evening gown that would not have been permitted in America. It was, in fact, British films that finally broke the taboos surrounding sex and nudity in the American market, where the influence of the Catholic League of Decency was slow to die. It was in the late-'50s that the *Carry On* films began, with their multitude of double meanings, but the period also saw many serious British films that treated sexual topics openly and portrayed extra-marital sex and homosexual relations in an honest and unprurient manner. These included *Look Back in Anger* (1958), *Espresso Bongo* (1959), *Saturday Night and Sunday Morning* (1960), *A Taste of Honey* (1961), and *A Kind of Loving* (1962). Christopher Isherwood's *I am a Camera* (1955) starred Julie Harris as an amoral girl who moves in with a struggling young writer and pays hie bills with money received from her American sugar-daddy. The film included a frank discussion about abortion, and lines such as 'What shall we do first, have a drink or go to bed?' In England it was chosen for the Royal Command Performance, but in America it was at first totally banned.

In America the most influential of the new school of English films was *Room at the Top* (1959), based on the novel by John Braine. Laurence Harvey played an ambitious young man who seduces his boss's daughter, has an affair with an older woman who loves and understands him, then marries the daughter to secure promotion, leaving the other woman to commit suicide. Harvey's love scenes with Simone Signoret as the woman who understands him were unprecedented in the English cinema for their frankness. He played a new type of hero, immoral and yet in the end rewarded, although the implication of unhappiness to come was made plain. A great success in England, the film was refused the Code Seal in America. Nevertheless it was shown there, received good reviews, and was booked for the big circuits. *Room at the Top* demonstrated the absurdity of censorship and showed that an honest view of society could also be honest entertainment.

During the '60s, American and British films became more adult, more realistic, more progressive—or as some would have it, more regressive. Sex and violence were accepted as important facets of the contemporary world, and were given their due prominence in the cinema, after the years of make-believe. Rear shots of nudity became commonplace: early examples of female or male variety occurred in such films as Carl Forman's *The Victors* (1963); *Darling* (1965) with Julie Christie; Joseph Strick's *Ulysses* (1967); *Zorba The Greek* (1965) with Anthony Quinn; and

[279]

The Family Way (1966) with the 'matured' Hayley Mills. Partial frontal nudity had appeared fleetingly in *Espresso Bongo* and reached its most blatant in Sidney Lumet's controversial *The Pawnbroker* (1965). Complete nudity appeared of necessity in John Houston's *The Bible . . . In the Beginning* (1966), with biblical authority, but the censors' guns were spiked, for Adam was created from the dust with one leg artistically crooked, and Eve was provided with an abundance of hair that adequately concealed her breasts. Whenever the couple were shown full-length on the screen, deftly positioned bushes or tree branches shielded their pubic regions, just as in depictions of Adam and Eve by Dürer and Cranach. Other discreet moments of nudity were Julie Newmar's underwater bathing scene with Gregory Peck in *Mackenna's Gold* (1968); a glimpse of Ursula Andress in *The Southern Star* (1968); and the marriage-night bedroom scene in Zeffirelli's beautiful film of *Romeo and Juliet* (1970; see illustration 210).

The nudity in *Romeo and Juliet* was so delicately staged and so absolutely consistent with the atmosphere of naturalness that characterised the whole film that no one could possibly have objected to it. And yet in a period when nudity was being considered by many filmgoers an end in itself, the poster for *Romeo and Juliet* depicting the young lovers in the nude scene may well have led some people to expect a quite different type of film. For it was in the '60s that film-makers became aware of the commercial possibilities of the voyeur film, or 'skin-flick', the film whose appeal and box-office success depended entirely on its degree of sexual titillation. In America and Great Britain, many 'clubs' or 'stag-houses' opened to show these uncensored films, and such places did not need to worry about details like certificates. The films they showed were more or less halfway between the real blue movie and the distributed feature film. The first of these 'skin-flicks' was made in 1959 by an unknown director by the name of Russ Meyer; it was called *The Immoral Mr Teas*.

210   Franco Zeffirelli,
Romeo and Juliet, 19

Russ Meyer, later to be known as the King of the Nudies, had been a war cameraman and then a glamour photographer. Finding Hollywood a closed shop in the '50s, he and a friend put up a thousand dollars each and made *The Immoral Mr Teas*, with the help of some army colleagues, in precisely four days. The total cost of the film was twenty-four thousand dollars. It is estimated to have made over one million dollars. The story concerns Mr Teas, a Hollywood messenger-boy whose contact with beautiful women in the course of his job causes him to have hallucinations in which they appear to him naked. He is a moral young man and tries unsuccessfully to escape from these visions. The film contains a great deal of nudity but no sexual activities and no pubic hair. It was judged not obscene in various test cases, and became phenomenally successful. By 1963, Meyer reckoned that there were about a hundred and fifty imitations of the film going the rounds, at least seven of which were made by him. A typical example was *Pardon My Brush*, which showed two housepainters who discovered that their paintbrush made walls transparent. The films were purely voyeuristic; they catered to the salacious interest of male audiences, but this interest did not last. They contained little scope for imaginative variation, and the genre was overtaken by the cinema industry itself.

In an effort to keep up the interest in such programmes, nudist films were imported to America from England, where they were enjoying some popularity. These films, with titles such as *Nudist Paradise* (1958) or *Take Off Your Clothes and Live* (1962), were ostensibly healthy, outdoor propaganda for nudism, and usually concerned bored secretaries who were persuaded to visit nudist camps for their holidays and found health and happiness when they did so. Sometimes they found their bosses there too, and after initial embarrassment ended up marrying them. Scenes of usually rather unattractive girls romping about in the nude, playing volleyball or coyly approaching the swimming pool with towels clutched strategically did little for nudism, yet these supremely immemorable films had the excitement of the forbidden, and the makers must have been aware of this. In America, where a 1958 Supreme Court decision held that nudity *per se* was not obscene, directors dropped all pretence of documentary and featured well-endowed starlets. As the need for more novelty was felt, fully fledged stars were given roles, and so Jayne Mansfield appeared in *Promises, Promises* (1963) and Mamie van Doren was featured in *Three Nuts in Search of a Bolt* (1964). Violent stories were sometimes used: Tony Orlando's *Lust and the Flesh* (1965) included rape, murder, graphic lesbianism, and a great deal of intercourse, but the film was narrated in a highly moral tone.

As more and more people jumped on the bandwagon of the 'skin-flick', demand exceeded supply, and so the European variety was imported into America and England. These had titles like *Sextroverts* (1969) ('Lust like theirs had only one end'); *Love me, baby, love me* (1969) ('The only cool moment in a hot and seductive love story is the shower scene'); *My Swedish Meatball* (1969) ('He lives and loves free from all morals'); *Inga, I have lust* (1968) ('Starring Marie Liljedahl, the Swedish sex bomb'). Most came from Denmark, Sweden, or Germany, countries which were at the same time producing a spate of 'sex education' films. These were more or less serious attempts to remove misconceptions about love-making and so enable people to enjoy a more satisfactory sex-life. The original intention was admirable, and the films were able to depict sexual activities with a frankness not permitted in feature films. However, the young audiences most in need of such films were not able to see them owing to certificate restrictions or club rules, and instead they played to the raincoat trade. Thus *The Anatomy of Love* (1969) was shown with a sex shocker called *Wild, Willing and Sexy* (1969), and *Techniques of Physical Love* (1968) went round with *The Sex Seekers* (1969). The best of these films was *The Language of Love* (1969), an intelligent discussion led by the Danish sexologists Stan and Inga Hegeler, and illustrated with films of couples having sexual intercourse, in which the basic techniques were very clearly and frankly demonstrated. Yet this was refused a certificate by the British Board of Film Censors. It was shown in London, where the Greater London Council gave it an X certificate, and also in one or two enlightened towns such as Brighton, which gave it an AA rating and thus allowed anyone over fourteen to see it.

Russ Meyer certainly had some influence on the acceptability of sexual freedom in the 'legitimate' cinema, but he found it difficult to keep one step in front. In 1969, he and his colleagues formed 'The Adult Film Producers' Association' in Los Angeles, to advise all 'skin-flick' makers on how far they should go in order to keep out of the courts, and they made great efforts to demonstrate the morality of their films. Meyer's *Vixen* (1969) has been called the best of the voyeur films; it features Erica Gavin as a nymphomaniac who grabs every man she meets and some girls too. Meyer has been at pains to point out that the aim of the film is to combat racial bigotry and communism.[7] In an interview in the late '60s, he explained why he thought his films were more successfully erotic than so-called 'art' films: 'At *The Killing of Sister George* people sat through 80 minutes of boredom to see one very erotic scene at the end. In my films they don't have to wait.' But he went on: 'I have never shown genitalia in any of my films. Once you have to show that to get people into the theatre, how many people are going to do it with taste? I have always been against censorship in any form, but I have also maintained that you should leave something up to the imagination.'[8]

Meyer realised in 1970 that he was in danger of appearing positively old-fashioned, and so full-frontal nudity appeared in both his films of that year, *Beyond the Valley of the Dolls* and *Cherry, Harry and Raquel. Beyond the Valley of the Dolls* (ironically made at the invitation of Twentieth Century Fox) tells of the adventures of an all-girl rock group in Hollywood and includes nymphomaniacs, transvestites, lesbians, homosexuals, male prostitutes, and drug addicts (see illustration 211). The climax of the film is an orgy at which absolutely anything goes, including a transvestite indulging in the pleasures of ritual murder. The entertainment value of the film comes from the hilarious effects of these deadly serious activities rather than from any degree of eroticism, and the usual moralising conclusion produces the biggest laugh of all. One hopes the whole film really *is* a send-up.

The commercial success of the voyeur or sexploitation films was an important factor in the cinema's desperate bid for survival in the face of television's threat in the '60s. The exciting adventure stories produced in Hollywood in the '50s became sex adventures: the film of Harold Robbins's *The Adventurers* (1970) was an attractive young man's odyssey in search of girls, and included a laughable depiction of sexual intercourse, with the camera zooming in and out in time with the panting couple, and interspersed with sudden cuts to intimate parts of nude sculptures. Candice Bergen said of her part in the activities: 'I may not be a great actress, but I've become the greatest at screen orgasms—ten seconds heavy breathing, roll your head from side to side, simulate a slight asthma attack and die a little.'[9]

In an earlier Harold Robbins-inspired film, *The Carpetbaggers* (1964), the same role was filled by Carroll Baker, who said of one scene where she reveals her all for a group of artists: 'I'm not a show-off by nature, but this scene was so important to the picture that I felt I had to do it.'[10] The same actress felt the same need in *Sweet Body of Deborah* (1967), when she took a shower with Jean Sorel in the first few minutes of the film. One critic was heard to say of this performance: 'Miss Baker takes off all her clothes whenever she has to scratch her elbow.'

Myra Breckinridge is another successful novel that has been made into a film. Gore Vidal's book was a clever and amusing parody of Hollywood, with its references to the stars of the past and its quotations from the 'sacred' writings of Parker Tyler. It was also a parody of the pornographic novel and depended very largely on the first-person narrative. Desperate to recoup their considerable losses, Twentieth Century Fox turned out the film *Myra Breckinridge* in 1970, the same year as their production of *Beyond the Valley of the Dolls*, but the film fell a long way short of the success enjoyed by the book, in spite of the acting talents of Raquel Welch, Mae West, and John Huston. The novel got away with being outrageous in a way which

211   Russ Meyer,
      *Beyond the Valley of the
      Dolls*, 1970

was impossible for the film: the written word was explicit enough to fire the sexual imagination, while the film seemed to show everything, and yet of necessity had to tone it down. The orgy and the attempted seduction of the female student seemed rather polite, and the crucial scene when Myra anally rapes with her dildo the handsome young stud on the examination table lost most of the erotic power of Vidal's description, especially when Myra's orgasm was represented by a quick cut to a shot of a dam bursting. The main fault of the film was that it was not daring enough, in spite of the free use of sexual terms in the dialogue. Either Mike Sarne was the wrong director or 1970 was too early. It was at times good entertainment, but like Ernest Lehman's film of Roth's *Portnoy's Complaint* (1972), it did not do justice to the erotic possibilities of the novel. And Raquel Welch was outshone by Mae West playing Letitia Van Allen, the talent agent with a giant bed in place of an office desk. When informed by a prospective young actor that he is six foot seven inches tall, she coolly drawls: 'Forget about the six foot, let's talk about the seven inches.'

One fault that *Myra Breckinridge* managed to avoid was boredom, the characteristic of most voyeur films. The simulated sex act is not in itself an erotic experience for most audiences. A successful erotic film will stimulate the imagination as well as the emotions; it will inspire a sort of empathy; it will engage the viewer intellectually through a subtle form of artistic presentation. The 'skin-flick' maker aims at a short-lasting physical thrill, which has little to do with real eroticism. The artist in the film medium tries to push the limits of sensory experience, and so freedom of sexual expression on film is one of his primary concerns. Directors like Fellini, Antonioni, Pasolini, Bergman, Polanski, Kurosawa, Godard, Truffaut, Makaveyev, Nichols, Schlesinger, Russell are serious artists concerned among other matters with providing new insights into man's basic sexual drives.

Any revolution turns up the good with the bad, and the sexual revolution in the cinema is no exception. Films trading on the new freedom, but with no real erotic content, exploiting rather than celebrating sex, have proliferated recently, and they are the price one must be prepared to pay for the great advance in the cinema. They include Aram Avakian's *End of the Road* (1970), written by Terry Southern, the author of the rather charming *Candy* (1968; see illustration 212). Avakian's film concerns a mentally deranged teacher's affair with the wife of a professor with a sexual leaning towards guns. Copulation, masturbation, and bestiality scenes are enlivened by a horrifying abortion, during which the patient drowns in her own vomit-filled oxygen mask. The film is not saved by its half-hearted attempt at some sort of social commentary.

Quiet Days in Clichy (1970), a soulless Danish film based on Henry Miller's autobiographical book, completely misses the vitality and joy of Miller's attempts to make the most of an unpromising world. Instead, the film is a hymn to blatant sexism, concentrating on pick-ups and bed-scenes enlivened by an orgy in a bath-tub which ends abruptly when the hero urinates. With underground film-makers, the new freedom often results in boredom, though a different variety of boredom

12 Christian Marquand,
    Candy, 1968, with
    Ewa Aulin

from that of the usual voyeur film. In Steve Dwoskin's *Moment* (1970), a girl's face
is observed for ten minutes as she smokes a cigarette while masturbating. Carolee
Schneeman's *Fuses* (1965) is a long glimpse of two people making love in a variety
of ways, but little can be seen owing to the fact that the surface of the film is overlaid
with collages, paint and scratch-marks.

It is, however, the real artists of the film medium who have used the new freedom
to create imaginative and enlightening erotic experiences, and one of these is Mike
Nichols. His film *Carnal Knowledge* (1971) traces the lives of two male under-
graduates through to middle age, and examines their continuing sexual problems.
The screenplay is beautifully written by Jules Feiffer, and it hints at the underlying
and subconscious homosexual bond that links the two men as they try to gain some
form of satisfaction from their relationships with the opposite sex. One revelation
of the film is the acting of their two lovers, Ann-Margret and Candice Bergen,
actresses previously considered no more than pin-up material. The sexual theme of
the film is treated in a very intelligent way: nudity is used sparingly, and not at all
in a prurient manner, and the two scenes of sexual intercourse are moving rather
than merely titillating, both because of their contexts and because of the use of the
soundtrack rather than the visuals in each case.

An intellectual approach to eroticism seems to have been characteristic recently
of certain Italian directors. Pasolini's complex films with sexual themes, *e.g.*
Theorem (1968) and *Pigsty* (1969), have been described by him as 'allegories that
plainly have to be interpreted and understood . . . I would like my work to be
comprehensible to the whole world, but the whole world must raise its standards,
not have the work lowered . . . I am committed to advancing and improving Society.'[11]

213   Pier Pasolini,
      Decameron, 1971

His film based on Boccaccio's *Decameron* (1971; see illustration 213), includes graphic depictions of many of the bawdiest tales, such as the one about a feigned deaf-mute who obtains a job as gardener in a convent and then proceeds to seduce all the nuns (needing to use no persuasion), stopping short only at the Mother Superior, for by then he is completely exhausted. Complete nudity of both sexes and bouts of copulation occur throughout, portrayed with beautifully unsophisticated wit in superb locations in and around Naples.

Fellini has also been concerned with sexual themes, from *La Dolce Vita* (1960) to *Juliet of the Spirits* (1965), and he too has recently filmed a classic of erotic literature, the *Satyricon* of Petronius (1970; see illustration 214). The story is set in Nero's Rome, and portrays all the peculiarities of sexual life that such a period

214   Federico Fellini,
      Satyricon, 1970

would find entertaining. Fellini's two heroes wander around in search of pleasure and excitement, never getting too involved and never passing moral judgement, but far from being a string of voyeuristic sequences, the film is a visually stunning and hauntingly rich exploration of dream-like realms of sexual fantasy. Image after image is conjured up: an enormous warren-like brothel with every desire catered for; a silent orgy with hundreds of naked men and women holding lighted candles in a large pool. Like Pasolini, Fellini sees parallels between the world of his film and his own world, although his attitude is rather different: 'Rome in its decline was quite similar to our world today. There was the same fury for enjoying life, the same violence, the same lack of moral principles and ideologies and the same self-complacency.'[12]

The theme of homosexuality, long a taboo subject for film-makers, has recently become quite common in the cinema. Robert Aldrich's *The Killing of Sister George* (1969) dealt quite openly with the relationship between Beryl Reid, a fading television actress, and her young friend Susannah York (see illustration 215). The actress's terror of the loneliness which will follow when her lover inevitably leaves her is very sympathetically portrayed, as in the play by Frank Marcus on which the film was based. But the love scene between Susannah York and Coral Browne, who plays a television executive with attractions that Miss Reid does not possess, was not in the original play and seems to have been included simply for its sensationalism, for the kissing, nipple-sucking, and breast-manipulation are certainly without precedent in a lesbian scene in the commercial cinema. Its inclusion tends to mar an otherwise sensitive film. John Schlesinger's *Sunday, Bloody Sunday* (1970) treats homosexuality in a more mature way: not as an extraordinary phenomenon but as a human fact of life. The middle-aged Jewish doctor (beautifully acted by Peter Finch) and his young artist lover behave absolutely naturally—talking, holding hands, kissing, making love. It may come as a shock to see two

215 Robert Aldrich,
The Killing of Sister George, 1969, with Beryl Reid and Susannah York

men making love together, but the love scene in *Sunday, Bloody Sunday* has a naturalness and a lack of prurience that distinguishes it from the scene in *Sister George*. The story of *Sunday, Bloody Sunday* (see illustration 216) revolves around the fact that the doctor has to share the young artist with a woman whose marriage has broken down (very sensitively played by Glenda Jackson). Both love him deeply, both know they can only have a part of him, and both know they will eventually lose him. In fact, the film is about sexual love, not about sex, an important distinction; and it is about the fact of love in a difficult situation, not a dramatisation of the forces that go to make such a situation. John Schlesinger said: 'It's the most difficult film I've ever made, in that it's all understatement. We weren't trying to make a film about the two aspects of sexuality. The film is about the different emotional stages that people go through and about the business of coping with life. . . . Right from the start, the idea was not to make a great dramatic film about the subject but to delicately expose the moments of pressure.'[13]

Glenda Jackson's low-key acting in *Sunday, Bloody Sunday* surprised many of her fans, who thought of her as Ken Russell's leading lady. Russell has now established himself as England's most controversial, and some would say finest, film director of recent years, and his films tend to be characterised by larger-than-life, convention-flouting outrageousness, as *The Music Lovers* and *The Devils*. In a recent interview, he showed how different was his attitude from that of Schlesinger: 'There seems to be a general distrust of freely expressed emotion these days—a feeling that there's a virtue in understatement. I don't believe that.'[14]

Understatement is certainly not the keynote of Russell's style, but his early film *Women in Love* (1969) did not go to the extremes of his next two. The film was a very faithful adaptation of the novel by D. H. Lawrence, and Russell shares Lawrence's passion for honesty and outspokenness. The novelist's belief that sexual love is a basic necessity which allies man to nature and is only denied to his great

216 John Schlesinger,
Sunday, Bloody Sunday
1970, with
Glenda Jackson and
Murray Head

detriment was beautifully conveyed in images of people in the wilds of the country-side, making love and running naked; also in the scene where Glenda Jackson, as Gudrun, the 'emancipated' school teacher, strips off her clothes and offers herself to Oliver Reed to comfort him on the death of his father. But the scene that caused the most comment was where Oliver Reed and Alan Bates (playing his childhood friend) strip naked and wrestle with each other in the firelight (see illustration 217). The incident was faithful to the novel, and told a lot about the intimate yet un-expressed relationship of the two men; Russell insisted that the actors should be naked and he persuaded them to perform the very difficult scene with a bottle and a half of vodka. In fact there was no prurience about this or any other nude scene in the film, and Russell's feelings about nudity are summed up in his remark, 'the full nude has a dignity that half a body does not have'.[15]

Glenda Jackson also starred in Russell's *The Music Lovers* (1970), a none-too-reverent film about the composer Tchaikovsky, and there was certainly no under-statement here. Russell described how he set up this project: 'I went to United Artists. They asked me what the plot was, and I said it was about this homosexual who married a nymphomaniac, and they said, "Great, go ahead".'[16] The finished product was advertised by a quotation from the *People*: 'These scenes of raving and hysterical sex are certainly the most daring you have ever seen.' Miss Jackson played the composer's nymphomaniac wife who ended up as a savage mad-woman, and in one scene in a railway sleeping-compartment, she lay naked on the floor, writhing ecstatically in a vain attempt to awaken some sexual interest in her husband. The excesses of the film were too much for many critics, but Russell was un-repentant: 'Of course *The Music Lovers* was excessive, crude, flamboyant, that was what fascinated me about the subject, the excessive romanticism. I was intrigued by the contrast between this destroyer, this monster, and the accepted picture of the unhappy, homosexual lovely man, that most people have.'[17]

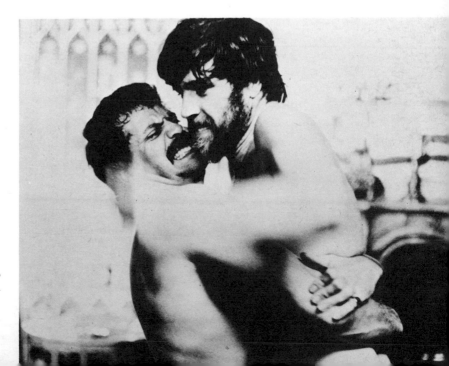

217 Ken Russell,
Women in Love, 1969,
with Oliver Reed and
Alan Bates

The cult of Ken Russell really depends on an act of faith, a willingness to believe in the master's integrity whatever he does. Miss Jackson—certainly one of Britain's most intelligent actresses—is a great admirer of Russell; in a recent communication to the author she described him as 'enormously talented and fascinating to work with', and went on to point out that he does not pander to the audience as far as the sex in his films is concerned: 'I don't think any performance of mine has been erotic in the sense of attempting to stimulate the audience. The character however probably was attempting to stimulate the other character or characters in a particular scene or scenes. As eroticism to work surely has to be intensely personal and most films tend to be intensely generalised, I doubt eroticism exists in films, let alone is important.'[18]

Eroticism is, of course, a personal experience, but that does not mean it cannot exist in the generalised world of the cinema. A film is an externalised utterance of the concept of a group of people, but it is also a concept in the mind of the individual viewer.

Ken Russell's film *The Devils* (1971) got away with more nudity than any of his previous films, but the erotic effect of hundreds of hysterical naked nuns cavorting in a forest, or a hump-backed Mother Superior's body being subjected to hideous and undignified tortures was such as to appeal to only a minority audience. The role of the Mother Superior erotically obsessed by a priest in seventeenth-century France was first offered to Glenda Jackson, but she appears to have had doubts and so Vanessa Redgrave appeared in the film. Miss Jackson's doubts were echoed by almost every critic: words used to describe the film ranged from 'camp' and 'prurient' to 'repulsive' and 'vicious'. Scenes of nude nuns masturbating themselves with altar candles and the Mother Superior eagerly licking the stigmata of her lover whom she is imagining as a crucified Jesus shocked many hardened critics, and the censor removed one glimpse of a pectoral cross being used as a dildo. But the real question posed by such scenes was were they artistically and historically justified or were they merely self-indulgence on the director's part? The act of faith required to believe in Russell's integrity became difficult at such moments and yet it could well be argued that the result was superb in terms of excitement, spectacle, and visual presentation. Oliver Reed gave a fine and restrained performance as Father Grandier, the priest whose carnal hold over the minds of the Ursuline nuns is exploited by Cardinal Richelieu to bring about his politically expedient execution. Russell clearly saw that Grandier's celebration of sexual passion as a way to God made him a relevant figure to our own day, but the political implications of the film were somewhat blurred by the sheer spectacle. Alexander Walker wrote: 'Almost every serious question raised by the historical situation is thrown away by Russell in order to flaunt a taste for visual sensation that makes scene after scene look like the masturbatory fantasies of a Catholic boyhood.'[19]

The relationship between the new politics and the new sexual morality has been reflected recently in the cinema. One of the most notorious of recent films has been *I am Curious* (*Yellow*) (see illustration 218), made by the Swedish director Vilgot

218 Vilgot Sjoman,
     I am Curious (*Yellow*),
     1967

Sjoman in 1967 but not released abroad until 1969. It is a film within a film, and
sets out to analyse the international youth revolution and its opposition to political
oppression and materialistic social values. The director's girlfriend is given the role
of inquiring reporter in the film being made, and then proceeds to fall in love with
her leading man just as she is meant to in the film. The reporter indulges in all sorts
of sexual experimentation as part of her revolt against authority, and at the same
time the actress frequently makes love to her leading man as their relationship
deepens. The scenes of sexual intercourse are very graphically shown and the
degree of nudity was unprecedented at that time. The effect is not particularly
erotic—the love-making is straightforward, and the couple have clearly not been
chosen for their anatomical attractions. At times, the effect is more comical than
erotic, as when they copulate in the middle of a stream, in the branches of an oak
tree (a position lacking in the *Kama Sutra*), and on the balustrade of the Swedish
Royal Palace (to the obvious discomfiture of the soldier on duty). In one scene,
the girl kisses and plays with the man's penis; later, in a dream, she kills and then
castrates him. The film was the subject of a celebrated court-case in New York in
1968, which the distributors of the film eventually won, at which glowing testimony
as to its artistic and social value was given by Norman Mailer ('One of the most
important pictures I have ever seen in my life . . . I think it is a profoundly moral
movie'[20]), and Parker Tyler ('Demonstrably a serious work of art'[21]). This court-case
and the battle with the British censor (it was eventually passed after 10 per cent had
been chopped out) gave the film an unfortunate notoriety, for although it is at times
boring, it is not sensation-seeking or prurient.

[291]

One of the most highly praised films of 1971 was *W.R.—Mysteries of the Organism*, made by the Yugoslavian director Dusan Makavejev, already famous for his *Switchboard Operator* (1967). The initials W.R. are those of Wilhelm Reich, whose philosophy of free sexuality being the key to socialism (and therefore happiness) lies at the root of the film. One section is made up of documentary clips and narrative about Reich, and includes interviews with his family and disciples and a hilarious transvestite named Jackie Curtis; there is also a sequence in which a girl makes a plaster cast of a man's erect penis. Intercut with this section is a story about a Yugoslavian girl and her frigid Russian boyfriend. The girl harangues her friends about the relation between orgasm and revolution and conversely between sexual repression and fascism. When she finally persuades her boyfriend to make love to her, he is overcome with guilt and kills her. Thus the second theme is a fictional expression of the philosophy founded in the first theme, and the conclusion to the story recalls that Reich was hounded to death and his works were burnt. The intricacy with which the themes are intercut is astonishing and the resulting film is a beautiful work of art, enlightening and moving, a perfect example of the intelligent use of the new freedom of sexual expression.

Underground film-makers have been claiming such freedom for themselves for some years now, and one of the most accomplished of this group is Kenneth Anger. His *Scorpio Rising* (1963) is a brilliant study of a group of neo-Nazi homosexual motorcyclists, and *Inauguration of the Pleasure Dome* (1954) is an exotically costumed masquerade inspired by the neo-paganism of Aleister Crowley. His early film *Fireworks* (1947) was one of the first outstanding products of the American underground, and represented an attempt to make the audience empathise with the feelings of a teenage homosexual. The boy is shown in bed with an erection visible under the sheets; he then dreams he meets some sailors in a bar, who lead him on and then beat him, cut him about, and pour a trickle of symbolic cream over his face. But he is not demanding sympathy; the beating has an orgasmic effect on him, and we see him dressed as a sailor, with a giant artificial penis protruding from his trousers. He sets a match to it and it erupts into shooting stars.

Among the more recent examples from the American underground are Ed Emshwiller's *Relativity* (1963), which attempts to relate man to the universe by exploring the beauty of a female body and contrasting it with the deformity and decay of the world she inhabits; and Tom O'Horgan's *Futz* (1970; see illustration 219) which gives graphic depictions of bestial fantasies. A more bizarre film is Sandy Daley's *Robert Having His Nipple Pierced* (1971; see illustration 220), in which Robert undergoes this painful operation in the arms of his boyfriend, while his unseen girlfriend gives a hilarious commentary which includes an uninhibited account of Robert's homosexual adventures and her own sexual hang-ups. If the images become too harrowing, the sound-track can be enjoyed with the eyes closed.

The best-known American underground film-maker is Andy Warhol. Films such as *Flesh* (1968; see illustration 221) and *Trash* (1970; see illustration 254), which are discussed in Appendix IV, are now becoming overground, and they are in any

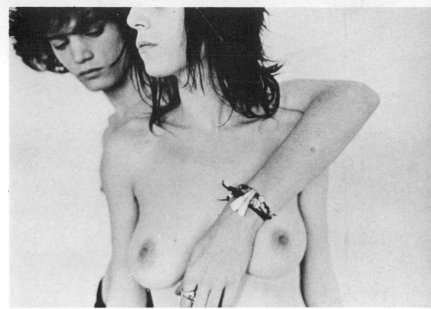

220 Sandy Daley, *Robert Having his Nipple Pierced*, 1971

219 Tom O'Horgan, *Futz*, 1970

case the work of his assistant, Paul Morrissey. Warhol's earlier films, such as *Chelsea Girls* (1966), were realist to the extreme, with cameras in a fixed position recording what happened in front of them, and when people were involved, sex was usually the main subject. With *Lonesome Cowboys* (1968) (see illustration 222), Warhol advanced to the stage of using props and locations and presenting a narrative—in this case, a group of cowboys who ride into a ghost town and meet a ranch owner (Viva) and her 'nanny' (Taylor Mead). The film includes scenes of Viva being raped by some

221 Andy Warhol and Paul Morrissey, *Flesh*, 1968, with Joe Dallesandro

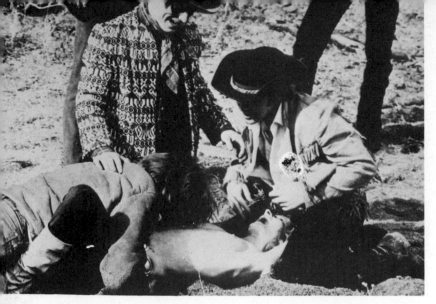

222 Andy Warhol and
Paul Morrissey,
Lonesome Cowboys,
1968, with
Joe Dallesandro and
Viva

of the cowboys, while Mead tries to seduce Joe Dallesandro. The sex is honest and straightforward, not especially erotic, but certainly far from pornographic. This parody of a Western hints strongly at the bisexuality that lies dormant in almost all straight Westerns, but the serious element is counter-balanced by the fact that the film is extraordinarily funny.

Compared with America, England's underground film-makers have made little impression so far, but two of them deserve mention: Robert Stuart Short, whose films (for example, *The Voluptuous Martyrdoms of the Magnificent Masturbators*) tend towards Surrealistic amalgams of sex and death in the spirit of Georges Bataille; and Tony Rayns who visualises sexual fantasies, as in *Hellbound*, a meditation on maleness and masturbation.

It is questionable whether the underground has yet produced a masterpiece. If it has, then it is surely none of the recent American films, but a silent black and white film made in 1953 by the French author Jean Genet, *Chant d'Amour* (or *Song of Love*) (see illustration 223). The film is based on Genet's own experiences and

223 Jean Genet, *Chant d'Amour* (*Song of Love*), 1953

concerns homosexuality in a prison, where a brutal warder spies on the men in solitary confinement. The camera dwells with heart-rending detail on two men's efforts to contact each other through the wall that divides their cells. One pulls a straw from his mattress, pushes it through a hole and puffs smoke through it. The other inhales the smoke with an expression of complete ecstasy. As the film opens, one swings a flower from his barred window, always just missing the outstretched hand of his friend in the neighbouring cell. The film closes with a shot of the second man catching the flower triumphantly. There is little sexual activity: the men masturbate in their cells, or roll on the ground together during a remembered country walk. But the greatness of the film lies in its ability to create a poignant and moving atmosphere in which the two men, and their warder, act out their fantasies about each other. Genet succeeds in stimulating the viewer intellectually as well as emotionally through a combination of his sexual preoccupations and his visual artistry. The result is a fine example of eroticism in the cinema.

Few films have been as successful in creating an erotic effect as *Chant d'Amour*, which reinforces the truism that explicitness of sexual activity is not necessarily a guarantee of erotic excitement. In 1973, Bertolucci's *Last Tango in Paris* (see illustration 224) became the centre of controversy when passed by the British Board of Film Censors, for it was reported to be more daring than any film previously accepted for public showing in this country. Further, Pauline Kael described it as 'the most powerfully erotic movie ever made'.[22] The film starred Marlon Brando as a middle-aged American in Paris whose wife had recently committed suicide. A casual meeting with a girl (Maria Schneider) who like Brando is inspecting an empty apartment leads to a very physical relationship which, decrees Brando, must remain on a totally anonymous level. There follow many scenes of copulation, some tender and some brutal: at one point, Brando uses butter to facilitate forced buggery, a scene Mr Murphy felt constrained to cut by ten seconds. Since the protagonists rarely undress before performing, there is little nudity; in any case, the sight of a sensual but decaying Brando desperately copulating with the beautiful Miss Schneider as he swears crudely and orders her to shove two fingers up his arse loses

224   Bernardo Bertoluzzi,
       Last Tango in Paris,
       1973, with
       Marlon Brando and
       Maria Schneider

in erotic power what it gains in vivid realism. It would be wrong to criticise the film as sexploitation, for it is a very skilfully constructed study of a relationship which develops tragically when Brando tries to break his own rule of anonymity on realising that he has fallen in love. The film thus tends to underline the connections between love and death which have so often been the preoccupation of artists.

An interesting aspect of *Last Tango in Paris* is its pioneering attempt to introduce the verbal and visual explicitness of the underground cinema into the overground, without merely achieving titillation for its own sake, as is the case with the notorious American film by Gerard Damiano, *Deep Throat* (1973). A girl finds that her clitoris is situated at the back of her throat; this unlikely discovery is the excuse for scenes of explicit oral sex. The film is badly directed and Linda Lovelace cannot act. The sex scenes are poorly handled and the film is a total disappointment, falling between the two stools of masturbatory pornography and erotic excitement.

Eroticism in the contemporary cinema seems to be moving in two directions. On the one hand, Just Jaeckin's French film *Emmanuelle* (1974) is a beautifully photographed and meticulously directed account of a young woman's voyage into sexual discovery during a visit to Bangkok. Typically French is the rather heavy-handed sexual philosophising with which the story ends, and although the film gains much from its intelligent use of explicit sexual scenes (too explicit for the British Censor), the end result is glossily superficial. In contrast, the Mitchell Brothers in America have produced two fantasy sex-films, *Resurrection of Eve* and *Behind the Green Door* (both 1973), which explore the possibilities of sexual excitement without the artful direction and self-conscious philosophising of *Emmanuelle*. In *Behind the Green Door*, a girl is kidnapped and persuaded to take part in a superior form of live sex-show at an exclusive club. The result is an astonishingly powerful kaleidoscope of stimulating visual images which puts any blue film to shame. The same can be said of Wakefield Poole's American film *Bijou* (1973), which depicts the sexual experiences—both real and imaginary—of a young man who finds in the street an entry ticket to a strange palace of erotic delights. The film is an intelligent, creative, and visually stunning amalgam of absolutely explicit sexual encounters, both heterosexual and homosexual; the viewer is presented with the erotic experience of simultaneous aesthetic, emotional, and physical excitement.

Continental film-makers seem to suggest that sex is a serious business, whereas the new American sex-film prefers to concentrate on the sheer joy and excitement of sex; viewers in Britain, however, are prevented by the Censor from judging for themselves either variety in the original form. It remains to be seen which direction the erotic film will take, but the likelihood is a combination of the two. But one thing is certain: the serious film-maker has recognised that eroticism is a vital area in which the cinema can progress as an art form; he has at last claimed the right to stimulate his audience sexually as well as to make them laugh and cry.

Chapter 9

Eroticism in the Performing Arts

by

DAVID F. CHESHIRE[1]

Introduction

It would seem that it is confusing enough trying to arrive at a universally accepted definition of 'eroticism' when it is considered merely as a philosophical concept, or as an aesthetic concept in relation to verbal, static visual (*i.e.* 'fine art', photographic), or moving visual (*i.e.* film) representations of erotic subjects. When live people of all sexes are performing variously before, or with, live people of all sexes, in the same room or area, then the problem of discovering whether an erotic art emerges becomes virtually unsolvable, especially if a large world, and time, view is adopted.

All that is attempted here, therefore, is a survey of *some* of the theatrical performances that have at various times and in various places been considered 'erotic' in the most general meaning of that term. No attempt is made to decide whether these performances were, or are, 'pornographic' or 'obscene'.

Dance

Dancing is one of the basic human arts. In African villages and Classical Greek cities, dance celebrated, and derived its movements from, 'birth, copulation and death', seen from both the religious and secular angles.

Much African 'primitive' dancing is obviously erotic, and Les Ballets Africains de Keita Fodeba's 1957 tour of the major British variety theatres made an important contribution to the increasing permissiveness of the theatre at that time, largely by shattering the 'static nude only' rule. But they demonstrated, also, how much more vital dance could be if theatrical and social conventions currently prevailing were ignored. Fodeba's treatment of African dance was undoubtedly inspired by Katherine Dunham's theatrical arrangements of Haitian dance in the 1940s, which similarly caused violent reactions, as many of the items featured 'the common element in obscenity and pornography and in the erotic as well . . . the portrayal or disclosure of a tabooed and forbidden reality.'[2] For example, in *L'Ag'Ya* Miss

Dunham appeared to be dancing erotically under the effect of a Voodoo love-potion, and the most controversial item in her repertoire—*Rites of Passage*—recreated as graphically as possible in the theatre a young male's initiation ritual.

The ritual dances presented by Fodeba and Dunham were erotic in intention, and people of other cultures understood them to be so. But when Asian dances are presented outside their true venues, or before non-native audiences at home, there is the chance that such audiences will misinterpret what they see, since:

'the whole question of eroticism in Asia is a complex one. . . . Hindu culture has to the Western eye immense areas of unmitigated and abandoned sexuality—in its mass of *mithuna* temple carvings . . . in its dances where *devadasi*, who can even be prostitutes, perform as an integral part of religious worship. . . . But certain elements of the dance outside India imply a potential 'immorality', and the Westerner is apt to be deceived by first impressions. . . . Asians delight in artistic interchange—boys dancing as girls, women as men, immature girls flirting like prostitutes. . . . If you suggest to an Asian that women playing women and men playing men would be better, he is amazed. Obviously, you have missed the point and are trying to thrust eroticism where it is not.[3]

Unfortunately, much Asian dancing (and indeed 'primitive' dancing in general) has been degraded by contact with Western ideas, or by commercial considerations. This is true even of the most potentially erotic of European dances—those of the Spanish gypsy, commonly known as *flamenco*. Originally a private dance, it was first presented in public in cafés in the nineteenth century, and theatres in the twentieth. It is still capable of rousing the passions of both gypsy and 'foreign' audiences, even though (or possibly because) 'in modern times the [*flamenco*] dance tends towards bi-sexuality, as do many of its interpreters. . . .'[4] whereas originally there was a clear distinction: 'The male dancer emphasized the footwork, a symbol of strength and virility, and the female dancer . . . the "dance of the arms", symbol of feminity and passions.'[5]

Obviously dancing can be an auto-erotic activity. One of the few descriptions of this aspect concerns *flamenco*:

It would be hardly ten o'clock. Until two in the morning Caroline Otero would dance and sing—for her own enjoyment, she cared little for ours. From a handsome forty she became a lovely seventeen. The bathwrap tossed aside, she danced in her petticoat . . . the only garment essential to Spanish dancing. Soaked with sweat, her fine lawn chemise clung to her loins; her moist skin gave off a delicate scent, a dusky scent, predominantly of sandalwood, that was more subtle than herself. There was nothing base in her violent and wholly selfish pleasure. It was born of a true passion for rhythm and music.[6]

To non-gypsies, the dance is the main attraction, whereas the gypsy considers the singing (usually of songs dealing with erotic themes) and the guitar-playing as more important. The latter can be erotic, especially where the Spanish guitar is concerned, for it assumed its modern shape only after Antonio Torres, in the mid-nineteenth century, had 'revised the curves . . . narrowing and shortening the bottom part of the feminine form, and widening and prolonging the breast part.'[7]

Spanish dancing has many affinities with Oriental and especially Egyptian dancing. But as the paintings of Egyptian dancers gave little documentary idea of how they moved, any recreation of the most famous 'Egyptian' dance of all may be correct. It would, however, be difficult for a real dancer to be quite as erotic as J.-K. Huysmans's description of Gustave Moreau's painting of *Salome dancing before Herod* (compare illustration 133: *The Apparition*):

> with a withdrawn, solemn, almost august expression on her face, she begins her lascivious dance which is to rouse the aged Herod's dormant senses; her breasts rise and fall, the nipples hardening at the touch of her whirling necklaces; the strings of diamonds glitter against her moist flesh. . . .[8]

But many dancers have attempted the feat: for example, Maud Allen, who was a more reliable 'Isadora Duncan' of the pre-1914 music-hall stage. Even actresses in presentations of Oscar Wilde's play *Salome* (banned not because of the dance, but because it called for the representation of biblical characters on stage) have attempted to recreate the scene. None could have been more successful than Ludmilla Tcherina, wearing only a transparent body-stocking in the 1970 French-television adaptation filmed in Gaudi's Guell Park, Barcelona.

Wilde's play is less frequently performed than Richard Strauss's opera based upon it, even though the key aria calls for Salome to pour out an ecstatic necrophiliac invocation to John's decapitated head, before sinking her face into the gory remains. At the Royal Opera House, Covent Garden, in 1910 the censor decreed that the plate should be empty. But it was very full for the 1970 production there, in which the lithely beautiful Grace Bumbry managed to fuse the erotic and vocal aspects of the part better than most, in both that aria, and the dance of the seven veils. Mary Garden (one of the first American singers of the part) was emphatic that her dance should not be staged in 'hoochie-koochie' style, insisting that the 'spiritual' side should be emphasised. At the same time, Isadora Duncan was concentrating on the 'spiritual' aspects of Ancient Greek dance. Not for her the Bacchanalian orgy, or Dionysian rite:

> Other festivals of a more or less erotic character were the Dionysia . . . and the Lenea, the feast of the wine-presses. This festival was marked by a great banquet, heavily subsidised by the state, and a dance through the city in fancy dress . . . accompanied by wanton practical jokes of every kind, although primarily erotic. Dances were performed by beautiful boys; in the evening people lay in the streets on couches, drinking heavily.[9]

[299]

In spite of reports of such scenes, early Christian leaders had accepted dancing in Church ceremonies, and St Basil the Great (344–407) had praised and described the angels dancing in Heaven. But even he was forced to admit that some women were taking advantage of appearances in church to 'shamelessly attract the attention of everyman. With unkempt hair, clothed in bodices and hopping about, they dance with lustful eyes and loud laughter; as if seized by a kind of frenzy they excite the lust of youths.'[10] The anti-dance faction took this sermon as their guide, and after a persistent campaign, managed to force the Church to declare, in 1298, that dancing was a grievous sin. Allegedly 'religious' dance manifested itself again soon afterwards, particularly during the Black Death, when auto-erotic dance manias swept through Europe. Some, like the Italian 'Tarantellism' epidemic, caused the dancers to collapse completely after going into ecstatic trances. Occasionally, dancers died from their exertions.

Four hundred years later, a British music-hall singer and dancer, Lottie Collins, devised a Tarantellic dance to accompany the English, slightly deodorised, version of an American bordello 'bump-and-grind' song: *Tar-ra-ra-boom-de-ay!* Her frenetic whirling around the world's stages with red skirts and hair flying in all directions obsessed everybody from 1892–96. Many young people (*e.g.* Holbrook Jackson) saw her as a symbol of youth kicking the stuffiness out of Victorian Britain, one of the first examples of an erotic performance being welcomed for political reasons in modern times. Lottie Collins's dance had obvious connections with the can-can, which was at the height of its popularity during the 1890s. Some of the erotic appeal of both dances lay in the possibility that 'forbidden' areas of female anatomy might be glimpsed—either partially, or occasionally completely, unclothed. This possibility exists in many similar 'folk' dances: the fact that a photograph revealed that she was pantless during a cabaret performance led to the virtual end of Carmen Miranda's Hollywood career as a Brazilian dancer during the 1940s.

Some observers, however, thought that Lottie Collins added a further dimension to her performance: often her intense concentration took her into a dervish-like trance, so that she seemed, like Loie Fuller, not to be taking part in a variety show, but in a religious rite. Recent events in some churches have given the impression that some clergy are intent on making it appear that they are not taking part in a religious rite, but in a variety show, while many more are trying to return the dance to the service of the Church, with one American theologian insisting that this will make people feel first and think later, with the result that there will be a complete 'eroticization of the liturgy'.[11]

Whether Isadora Duncan would have approved of this is doubtful—but there can be no doubt that she is one of those who have been responsible for creating the atmosphere where such a statement is possible. For it is an example of 'America fighting the battle against Americanism . . . and Isadora led the way into the fight . . . with her naked and strong body and her bold character, vivid as an Amazon'.[12] Isadora was a great believer in genuine nudity on stage, not the fake nudity usually offered until recently. When she appeared in *Tannhäuser* at Bayreuth in 1905, the transparent tunic, showing every part of my dancing body . . . created some stir amidst the pink-covered legs of the ballet. . . . Many times I declaimed myself hoarse on the subject of just how vulgar and indecent these salmon-coloured tights were and how beautiful and innocent the naked human body was when inspired by beautiful thoughts.[13]

'Beautiful thoughts' is nicely vague, and undoubtedly many found her perform-ances erotic, as although she appeared completely naked on stage rarely (preserving such displays for private parties where stimulating refreshments and sympathetic companions had created a wholly congenial atmosphere), she sometimes 'accidentally' allowed her coverings to slip off—as she did on the famous occasion in Boston. Her costumes (as close inspection in the archives of the Library of the Performing Arts in New York confirms) were, however, truly transparent, and as she invariably shunned underwear, it would have been impossible for her not to show every part of her body—probably to even greater effect than if she had danced nude. However, it is recorded that on at least one occasion she did reveal herself fully. Tchaikovsky's grand-niece recalled, 'Isadora dancing the *Pathétique* on the stage of the Bolshoi Theatre, Moscow . . . wearing a purple mantle, which on the final chord she allowed to fall to the ground, revealing her naked, middle-aged body. Everybody rose to their feet: there was silence, then applause.'[14]

Poses Plastiques, Nude-shows, Striptease

Nudity in a ballet may have started with Picabia's *Relâche* (1924), in which appeared a naked man (Marcel Duchamp) and woman posing as Lucas Cranach's *Adam and Eve*. But that was more in the manner of music-hall *poses plastiques*, as the figures were motionless, and only illuminated intermittently. This type of performance had long been popular as a private *divertissement*. One of the most famous of the pioneer public poseurs whose efforts have been recorded was Emma Hart.

She first attracted attention in 1780 when she demonstrated various pieces of 'scientific' apparatus (including a mud bath) in one of the leading 'quack' shows of the day: Dr Graham's Temple of Hymen in the Adelphi, London, to what advertise-ments called 'Les Amateurs des délices exquises de Venus'. Here she gained fame posing lightly draped as the goddess Hebe Vestina. George Romney found her a congenial friend and model, and his many paintings of her made her reputation in London Society. She was also portrayed by Reynolds, Fuseli, Lawrence, Nollekens, and Angelica Kauffmann. Soon she became the mistress, and later the wife, of the art-loving British Ambassador to Naples, Sir William Hamilton, who, in the words of Goethe:

. . . had made for her a Greek costume, which becomes her extremely. Dressed in this, and letting her hair loose, and taking a couple of shawls, she exhibits every possible variety of posture, expression and look, so that at the last the spectator fancies it is a dream. One beholds here in perfection, in movement, in

ravishing variety, all that the greatest of artists have rejoiced to be able to produce.
. . . The old knight holds the light for her, and enters into the exhibition with
his whole soul. He thinks he can discern in her a resemblance to . . . the *Apollo
Belvedere* itself. . . .[15]

Thereafter, 'posing' suitably clothed in *tableaux vivants* became a popular pastime
in upper-class drawing-rooms, and simultaneously, with less regard for decorum,
in the better-class London brothels. Special venues were organised:

These places of voluptuousness are situated in the neighbourhood of Waterloo
Place, and Waterloo Road, and are almost entirely frequented by such of the
frail sisterhood as are of French nationality . . . about 'The witching hour of
night' commence what may really be termed the orgies of the Cyprian goddess.
Girls of every state, from complete nudity to the half-dressed, go through the
most voluptuous exhibitions—and perform the most spirit-stirring dances.[16]

Poses Plastiques were staged in public during the 1830s, and thereafter they were
ubiquitous, though frequently controversial, acts in European music halls for over
a century. Initially the participants—both male and female—wore all-enveloping
tights made to simulate the marble surfaces of the sculptures they were representing.
It was this 'artistic' content that enabled them to escape the attentions of many who
would have censored the display of so much apparent nakedness under less elevating
circumstances (see illustration 225).
One of the other 'Paphian Revel' venues was 'THE WINDMILL SALOON . . .

225 The Sellons in *Poses Plastiques* (*The Winning Post*), London *c.* 1905

situated in Windmill Street, Piccadilly . . . [part of an old waxwork show, but now] the dead dodge is done by living creatures in what is called *tableaux vivants*, for the ladies *go* entirely naked, and the gentlemen dress without clothes; nor is this *all* that is, for there is a . . . nocturnal meeting, wines, music, song and dance.'[17]

A later Windmill Theatre provided London with its most famous selection of erotic entertainment from 1932 to 1966 (see illustration 226). All their sketches and tableaux had to be passed by the Lord Chamberlain, for it was a public theatre and thus under his jurisdiction. The Windmill's last manager, Sheila van Damm, remarked, after she had given up the theatre and it had been converted into a cinema:

> The screening of 'nudies' at the Windmill and other West-End cinemas, without a cascade of white-hot letters scorching the doormat of the Lord Chamberlain's Office, shows how drastically public reaction to nudity has changed in recent years. . . . But [in] 1932, the year Father decided to put nudes on the Windmill stage . . . even if a carefree mood of strip, strip, hooray prevailed in Surrey's new sun-bathing society, it was definitely an exception. . . . Much to everyone's surprise, the Lord Chamberlain agreed to Father's proposal. . . . Father . . . emphasised that the presentation would be artistic, while the Lord Chamberlain insisted that the nudes remain completely immobile, and the lighting subdued. . . .[18]

The appeal of the Windmill was essentially to the innocent out-of-town visitor, for nothing untoward occurred on stage, although fan-dancers did drop their fans 'accidentally' at frequent intervals. By the mid-'50s, however, the Windmill's proud ex-Second World War motto—'We never closed'—seemed in danger, as

226 *Revudeville*, Windmill Theatre, London, 1930s

anomalies in the London licensing of entertainment laws meant that while the Windmill had to be licensed as a theatre, and its sketches, therefore, submitted to the Lord Chamberlain, the strip-clubs mushrooming in Soho did not come under his jurisdiction. The Windmill found that its discreetly illuminated static nudes were no longer enough, and its audience gradually declined.

Simultaneously, dying British variety theatres were being kept barely alive by an infusion of sub-Windmill nude (or as they were known colloquially 'Tit and Bum') shows. Often it seemed that more effort went into the choice of title (*e.g. My Bare Lady, She Strips to Conquer, Yes We Have No Pyjamas*) than into the staging of the actual shows, which usually played to a dozen or so patrons in thousand-seater theatres. Although all played on the 'Frenchness' of the entertainment offered, with Montmartre backcloths for can-can dancing, and occasionally an attempt at that most stunning piece of sadistic eroticism—The Apache Dance—English girlie-shows at all levels rarely indulged in the spectacular costumes and scenery which had been the trademark of the big Parisian theatres specialising in 'Les Girls'.

Virtually nude showgirls in wildly imaginative postures had been the staple fare in Parisian music halls throughout their history. Initially they were static, but movement gradually increased (see illustration 227). Occasionally men posed in the near-nude (*e.g.* Feral Benga and Frédéric Rey at the Folies Bergère in 1931 and 1950 respectively). But by the '60s the static, not-bare-bosomed nude was made to seem passé by the increasingly erotic displays at the more intimate night-clubs, *e.g.* The Crazy Horse Saloon in Paris. Reports of visits to nude shows usually remark on the apparently subdued audiences.

227 *Folies-Bergère*, Paris, late 1940s

It could be that such audiences are too erotically involved to make a normal response visible to the uninformed observer. Kenneth Tynan maintained that 'the best sexual experiences that I've had in theatre were all a very long time ago in . . . the old Howard Theatre in Boston . . . which was on a much higher level than the average burlesque house. But even in the burlesque theatres that were supposed to arouse you to a great pitch of sexual delight, the ushers would be walking up and down the aisles with torches to see if people were masturbating—you see, the double standard.'[19] Raymond Durgnat has suggested, however, that 'The shows are soothing rather than aphrodisiac. You know they'll strip, so there's no tease. The routines are grindingly similar, and their succession is numbing. The men seem solaced rather than stirred, by contemplating, coveting and/or worshipping the various totems of female nudity.'[20]

During the late-'60s, strippers all over the world gradually became so indiscreet that to some connoisseurs the erotic effect was dissipated completely. For as the name implies, 'tease' and 'strip' should be represented equally. Thus the most renowned stripper in the world disapproved wholeheartedly of the nudity prevalent in the theatre just before she died. Gypsy Rose Lee 'had little censor trouble for her act was more tease than strip. Her gimmick was a ball gown, long white gloves, a lady-like demeanour—and a sense of humour. "I never try to stir up the animal in 'em. . . . Did you ever hold a piece of candy or a toy in front of a baby—just out of his reach? Notice how he laughs? That's your strip audience." '[21]

Miss Lee was, of course, a 'straight' stripper. She just took her clothes off slowly. Others, to liven up their acts, do interesting things with feather boas, real boas, whips, or pillars supporting the roof. Some have their clothes whipped off (often literally) by male partners, by female partners, by baby elephants, or even by dolphins—underwater. In fact, whatever your fancy, it can be catered for. In 1970, in spite of defence pleas that laughter was the main aim, a Soho strip-club owner was jailed for thirty months, and fined a thousand pounds, for showing in a 'lewd and obscene stage show' rituals depicting sexual themes including 'sadism, bestiality, homosexuality and necrophilia'.

This type of act has long been available to interested parties, but has received little publicity in the public prints until recently. A sign of the times, however, was the appearance in the January 1972 issue of *Men Only*, complete with glorious technicolour photographs, of a lesbian act at The Crazy Horse Saloon, Paris, where the manager had given the two artistes concerned complete freedom to do whatever they liked.

A long way from this were the most internationally famous girl shows: the Ziegfeld Follies, staged by Florenz Ziegfeld in New York between 1907 and 1931, and from which Hollywood drew not only some of its stars (*e.g.* Billie Dove, Ruby Keeler, Mae Murray), but also ideas for the staging of early sound musicals— Busby Berkeley's numbers are but technically expanded versions of the type of chorus numbers so beloved of Ziegfeld's audiences. For although great vaudevillians appeared (*e.g.* Fanny Brice, W. C. Fields, Will Rogers), it was the Ziegfeld Girls who drew the crowds—especially the Ben Ali Haggin numbers which incorporated fantastic costumes and discreet nudity. Marjorie Farnsworth comments that Ziegfeld 'was the leading entrepreneur of sensual desire, desire in chiffon and lace . . . and the bailiff of glorification of the American girl . . . in a fabulous era which seemed to those who lived in it the utmost of sophistication, and which seems to us now both Byzantine and naïve'.[22]

Live Sex Shows

Couples, or groups of persons, of various sexes involving themselves in live sex-acts have always been available for the *cognoscenti* all over the world in waterfront dives, nightclubs, brothels, and (by special arrangement) in private homes, while acts in which single performers (usually female—with champagne bottles) masturbate have been openly available in Munich nightclubs for many years. However, the existence of such shows was not publicised widely (in the United Kingdom) until Lord Longford visited Copenhagen, and 'walked out of two sex shows after only a few minutes. I saw enough for science and more than enough for enjoyment . . . what repelled me most was that some sort of audience participation seemed to be expected.'[23]

With news of such displays, if not such displays themselves, readily available, it is little wonder that the leading entrepreneur of striptease in the United Kingdom (Paul Raymond), in spite of strong possibilities of prosecution for misleading advertising, dubbed his Revuebar 'the world centre of erotic entertainment' in 1971, and maintained that he was presenting 'a sensual revue' (see illustration 228). It is perhaps significant that in 1973 exactly the same show was presented to the general public without any 'club' restrictions, Mr Raymond having successfully applied for a theatrical licence.

228 *Raymond Revuebar strip-tease,* London, 1973

Theatre

Female Impersonation
All this is a long way from 'the belly dance to the St Louis Blues' for which, in her
own play *Sex*, Mae West was successfully prosecuted in New York in 1927, and sent
to prison for 'corrupting youth'. Mae West claimed to have invented sex plays. She
did not, but she was one of the first comediennes to treat her erotic appeal as a joke.
She did extend the range of sexual subjects permissible in theatre, as in her play *The
Drag* (1928) about the 'gay boys' sad lot', which contained a drag-ball scene not
repeated until John Osborne introduced one into *A Patriot for Me* (1965). Mae
West's behaviour on stage and screen (her innuendoes were the final decisive factors
in the campaign for the introduction of censorship into Hollywood—in spite of her
claims that her words and actions were intended to promote laughter not lust) was
such that as long ago as 1934 she was described by George Davis in *Vanity Fair* as
'the greatest female impersonator of all time'.

Female impersonation is one aspect of potentially erotic theatre that raises more
problems than most. Obviously, to those so inclined the sight of men dressed and
made-up to look as much like women as possible can be powerfully erotic, others
will consider it a sad spectacle, while still others will find it hilariously funny. To
achieve their disguise some female impersonators have surgical operations to bring
out or emphasise their female qualities. This would seem to destroy the theatrical
impact of the act, although such treatment might be justified on psychological
grounds. But some 'drag' stars (*e.g.* Danny La Rue) really work in the tradition of
the hermaphroditic fools. Thus, after his initial glamorously deceptive appearance,
Danny La Rue rarely uses any but his own voice, continually draws attention to his
false breasts and makes frequent reference to the uncomfortableness and difficulty
of hiding masculine appendages inside tight-fitting dresses. Most of his audience
is female, whereas the audiences of the majority of 'drag' shows are male—both
homosexually and heterosexually orientated.

In a uniquely serious anthropological study of popular entertainment, it is
suggested that:

men are excited by transvestites who (with the help of padding and rouge)
display big, shaking breasts, voluptuous bodies, dancing, shimmying buttocks,
nice voices and beautiful faces. . . . Finally the sheer strangeness of the transvestite
(who like the Greek satyr, combines bodily elements not ordinarily combined)
shocks and fascinates: people exclaim 'God Damm' . . . 'Fuck!' when transvestites
step out on the stage. (Since shock is expressed by exclaiming 'Fuck!' shock and
sex are related.) . . . Probably the transvestite's relationship to the kampung
[low-life area] male's family life enhances the transvestite's attractiveness. To a
man living with a tough . . . household boss, the gentle transvestite must look good.
Also the transvestite because she (*sic*) can spawn no child does not bid to become a
household boss . . . [and] he evokes fantasies of *sexual* escape from adult responsi-

[307]

bilities. He is mixed up with forbidden fantasies of returning to adolescence, returning to childhood, eroticism without procreation. . . .[24]

Fools

Non-drag buffoons, fools, and clowns have always been associated with erotic behaviour—usually in a highly exaggerated fashion, for example, the gross artificial phalluses of the Greek and Roman mimes or Harpo Marx's motor-horn. The British contemporary comedian Ken Dodd also indulges in this type of humour, to a certain extent on television, but fully only in the theatre. At intervals throughout his hectic act he produces 'tickling-sticks' which gradually increase in size from small feather duster size, with which he tickles himself, to a massive one with which he can tickle a woman some twenty or thirty feet from the stage. Like the majority of comedians, he makes great play with *doubles-entendres* and with the conversion of an apparently innocent word or motion into something 'ruder' by the quick insertion of a catch-phrase: 'Well they can't touch me for it', 'As the actress said to the bishop', etc.

The Italian *Commedia dell'Arte* character Harlequin originally wore an artificial phallus, later changed to a large sword-like bat which he carries. Mr Punch is forever belabouring the other characters with a truncheon, but as he is considered now a minor theatrical figure, of interest only to children, this aspect of his character was generally overlooked until Harrison Birtwistle wrote an opera *Punch and Judy* (1968), in which he most strikingly and successfully brought out the sado-erotic aspects of the main character. It need not be emphasised, therefore, that 'the fool's bauble is, like the king's sceptre, phallic'[25] (see illustration 229). Indeed, the

229 *The Fool and Sexual Desire,* anonymous sixteenth-century German woodcut

derivation of the word 'fool' has been traced back to the Latin word 'follis' meaning 'bellows, windbag, but probably here in the specific sense of *scrotum*; *cf.* It. *coglione* . . . (a fool) . . . lit. testicle; also L. *gerro*, fool, from a Sicilian name for pudendum'.[26]

Comedians have dealt with erotic themes at times when more 'serious' or 'artistic' treatments have been disallowed. A recent authority has written:

> Jokes about excretion and sex usually play upon restrictions, but it is equally possible for such jokes to play upon cultural permissiveness toward these processes. Thus the night-club comedian Lenny Bruce, famous for his 'sick' humour, was arrested for violation of a New York State law which forbids any 'obscene, indecent, immoral, or impure' public performance. The judges who handed down the decision against Bruce remarked that his language 'clearly debased sex and insulted it'. This is very far from the view that the explicit dwelling upon sex is itself bad. What was bad to the judges was rather the comedian's attack upon its dignity and nobility by means of gutter words for incest, sodomy, and excrement.[27]

Like Bruce, the British comedian Max Miller was always in trouble with various authorities for his allegedly lewd and immoral act, although he was not harried quite as much by such large authorities as the American. If his act is analysed, however, it will be found that the 'lewdness' is not directly referred to. He relied on another time-honoured fool's device, and played up to his audience's pre-conceived notion of what was being referred to, or going to be referred to, at the end of the sentence. For example, watching the microphone disappear into the stage: 'Did you see that, Ivor? Must be the cold weather . . .'; A little song 'Last Night I was In the Mood— Tonight I Must Get Some Sleep'; 'I want it to flow all the time . . .'; (tuning his guitar) 'Ooh that's nice Maxie, Ooh I like that Maxie . . .'; 'You can put your bit to mine' (in context that can *only* refer to money); 'Go on make something of that— you filthy lot!' He ended his act invariably with one of his own sentimental songs (*Be Sincere, My Old Mum*) sung without any innuendoes at all. George Orwell placed him in the tradition of Donald McGill's seaside postcards.

Variety

Virtually any type of performance can be presented (or thought of) as erotic— contortionists (both male and female) who can twist and turn themselves into a wide range of intriguing shapes and positions; gleaming-with-sweat-and-grease, half-naked wrestlers who, with partners of the same sex, seemingly thrash each other senseless, often by adopting a intriguing variety of 'holds'; and, of course, acrobats. J.-K. Huysmans described their erotic appeal in *Against Nature*:

> Heading the procession of mistresses . . . [was] an American girl with a supple figure, sinewy legs, muscles of steel, and arms of iron. . . . The more he admired her suppleness and strength, the more he thought he saw an artificial change of sex operating in her; her mincing movements and feminine affections became less

obtrusive . . . she seemed to have . . . become an integral, unmistakable man . . . he got to the point of imagining that he for his part was turning female; and at this point he was seized with a definite desire to possess the women. . . . But when at last his wishes were granted, he suffered immediate and immeasurable disappointment. . . . Miss Urania was a mistress like any other, offering no justification for the cerebral curiosity she had aroused.[29]

There are even more esoteric possibilities; as after this fiasco Des Esseintes, the hero of Huysmans's novel became fascinated with a ventriloquist but:

. . . it was not so much the woman as the artiste that appealed to him. . . . As he lay holding the woman in his arms, a husky, drunken voice would roar from behind the door . . . he would temporarily hurl himself upon the ventroloquist, whose voice went blustering on outside the door. He derived extraordinary pleasure from this panic-ridden hurry of a man running a risk, interrupted and hustled in his fornication.[29]

'Legitimate' Theatre before 1968

As can be seen, the non-legitimate theatre has often had a much freer attitude to erotic themes and performances than the legitimate theatre, upon which, however, virtually all the controversies of the late '60s concentrated. Isadora Duncan explained this:

People have an entirely false conception of the importance of words in comparison with other modes of expression, just as potent as words. An entire audience of so called respectable people, who would leave the theatre if anyone appeared to blaspheme or to use indecent words, will sit through a performance in which someone makes indecent movements which, if translated into words, would make the audience rush from the theatre. A seemingly modest girl would not think of addressing a young man in lines or spoken phrases which were indecent and yet the same girl will arise and dance these phrases with him in such dances as the Charleston and Black Bottom, while a negro orchestra is playing *Shake that thing*.[30]

Erotic plots have been present in written plays from Greek times onwards. Greek tragedy dealt with many combinations of human sexual relationships more frankly than even many modern plays, and the pantomime artistes and comic writers dealt with them in an even more explicit and (to modern spectators) outrageous manner. But under the influence of the Christian Church performances of these plays gradually ceased. The Church's own plays presented erotic situations when the biblical stories upon which they were based required, *e.g.* the wardrobe list for a Cornish Mystery play reveals: Adam and Eve 'an aparlet in whyte lether' with 'fig leaves redy to cover their members'; The Wakefield Second Nativity Play contained some really broad folk-humour. In fact, the humour gradually became so bold that the plays were banned from performance inside churches or under Church authority.

Secular entertainment continued the tradition; and a miniature in the Berlin State Museum shows Minerva, Juno, and Venus completely naked in a *tableau vivant* of *The Judgement of Paris* presented in the triumphal entry of Juana de Castile into Brussels in 1497.

Around 1539 actresses reappeared on Continental stages, and there is a Renaissance Florentine stage direction which reads: 'Now goes the King to Rome and you meanwhile make four women, naked, or clothed in flesh coloured cloth, rise waist-high from the sea, with tresses to the wind, and let them sing as sweetly as may be.'[31]

But, as J. Huizinga points out in *The Waning of the Middle Ages*, Medieval and early Renaissance drama 'treated love matters only exceptionally; sacred subjects were its substance. There was, however, another form of representation, namely, noble sports, tourneys and jousts. Sportive struggles always and everywhere contain a strong dramatic element and a strong erotic element. In the medieval tournaments these two elements had so much got the upper hand, that its character of a contest of force and courage had been almost obliterated by its romantic purport. With its bizarre accoutrements and pompous staging, its poetical illusion and pathos, it filled the place of drama in a later age.'[32]

This tournament aspect is evident throughout Elizabethan and Jacobean drama, which similarly mingled pageantry, violent death, and splendid costumes in 'games' often motivated by love, but with the added dimension of verse to express it. The result was a genuine popular entertainment, enjoyable on various levels.

The majority of these plays held the stage even after the introduction of the censor led to the banning of new plays on similar themes, Shelley's *The Cenci* being one of the few 'classic' plays banned by the Lord Chamberlain. Often these older plays work on a more sophisticated erotic level than many recent ones. Even in 1969 John Webster's *The White Devil* (*c.* 1608), in a striking National Theatre production at the Old Vic, seemed very 'modern' in its treatment of perverted sensuality, especially at the climax: 'Flamineo, Vittoria, and her Moorish servant are strapped to the wall and slowly, protractedly, disembowelled. It is an erotic consummation for the killed as well as the killers: an orgasmic union that leaves three exhausted and three dead.'[33]

1969 also saw a production of William Wycherley's *The Country Wife* (*c.* 1672) at Chichester, where 'modern outspokenness about sex . . . [seemed] mealy-mouthed lisping beside the merrily scabrous Restoration *Country Wife* . . . seen for the first time since theatre censorship was lifted. This play (written before censorship was thought of) surprises—so much sharper its eye, so much harder its bite—than any more recent reports on the war between the sexes. . . .'[34]

Wycherley's play was one of those that triggered off the major Puritan pamphlet on the theatre: Jeremy Collier's *Short View of the Immorality and Profaneness of the English Stage* (1698). The Puritans had driven the theatre underground during the Interregnum, and it is frequently forgotten by those who defend greater freedom in the arts to portray more explicitly sexual behaviour that among those that oppose them are many to whom the whole idea of dressing up and pretending to be other than 'real' is an immoral and profane act in itself, no matter what situations are concerned.

So many plays deal with erotic themes either explicitly or implicitly that it would be impossible to detail even a fraction here. In fact the very construction of the play itself has been likened to the sexual act—a wide variety of plot-constructions leading in every case to a similar variety of climaxes. One has only to think of the presentation of Shakespeare's plays in five 'acts' each consisting of scenes of varying lengths, with a false climax at the end of act three, a frequently diffuse fourth act, and a fifth act with sometimes a satisfactory climax and sometimes a contrived climax involving the introduction of material not previously used. Then there are the tightly constructed 'well-made' plays, especially popular in Edwardian England and France, and Brecht's rambling 'epic' plays (behind which were his theories on the subject formulated in the Weimar Berlin of George Grosz). Brecht's plays consist of a lot of short, frequently unconnected scenes, which either peter away, or reach an artificial climax. There are, too, the playwrights who specialise in one-act plays only, sometimes for only one player, among them, Samuel Beckett. The possibilities are infinite. Even the different types of play have erotic connotations according to American dramatist Robert Anderson: 'Comedy is like petting: it's fun and no one gets hurt. A serious play is more like intercourse: if you don't have an orgasm, you end up frustrated.'[35]

It was possibly because of the difficulty of deciding whether the most innocent-seeming theatrical event was potentially erotic or not that the American Commission on Obscenity and Pornography in 1969 omitted theatre from their investigations, even though in their Preface they referred to the more blatant pieces of erotic theatre:

> The Commission did not investigate directly the phenomenon of 'live' sex shows, such as simulated or actual sexual activity on the stage, or before an audience. These activities are governed most often by local laws regulating actual sexual conduct, such as prohibitions upon indecent exposure, disorderly conduct, fornication, or sodomy. The terms of such prohibitions vary widely from locality to locality and the reasons for them may diverge substantially from the concerns underlying obscenity prohibitions. The Commission, therefore, did not deem recommendations in these various areas of sexual conduct to be within its primary assignment.[36]

Because of this, and because it makes more exciting copy, most of the recent controversy on erotic theatre has concentrated on the question of nudity. Often nudity has been introduced as a director's idea, as in *The Knot Garden*, where it was not called for in the original text, and where its presence would not have been missed. However, in the production of an adaptation of *Lady Chatterley's Lover* at the Arts Theatre Club in 1961, the fact that the lovers were obviously not naked in bed did rather detract from the realism of the eroticism at the première. Subsequently they *appeared* to be completely unclothed beneath the sheets in which, however, they were so well entwined that they revealed far less of themselves than two actresses did in the Royal Shakespeare Company's production of Jean Anouilh's *Becket* at the Aldwych in the same year.

In the 1960–61 season five plays were running in London's West End which all signposted the way to greater permissiveness: *The World of Suzie Wong* (an American musical), *Irma La Douce* (a French musical), *The Hostage* (Brendan Behan's play), and two English musicals: *The Crooked Mile* and *Fings Ain't Wot They Used T'be*. All were set in, or around, brothels. All were passed by the Lord Chamberlain—in script form. But into the performance of *Fings*, at least, crept incidents which caused one of his subordinates to visit the show after it had opened and request the management to delete certain unauthorised pieces of business, *e.g.*: 'Indecent business of Rosie putting her hand up Red Hot's bottom. . . . The interior decorator is not to be played as a homosexual and his remark . . . "Excuse me, dear, red plush, that's camp that is" is to be omitted, as is the remark "I've strained meself." The builder's labourer is not to carry the plank of wood in the erotic place and at the erotic angle that he does, and the Lord Chamberlain wishes to be informed of the manner in which the plank is in future to be carried. . . . Tosher, when examining Red Hot's bag, is not to put his hand on Rosie's bottom with finger aligned as he does at the moment. . . . Tosher is not to push Rose backwards against a table when dancing in such a manner that her legs appear through his open legs in a manner indicative of copulation.'

The House of Commons's Report recommending the abolition of the Lord Chamberlain's power of censorship (which the then Lord Chamberlain fully agreed was a complete anomaly) was published in June 1967. But intent on exercising his authority until the end, he refused permission for the proposed transfer of Jean Claude Van Itallie's *America Hurrah* from the Royal Court Theatre Club to a public theatre in the West End. This was in spite of the fact that the section to which he objected—*Motel* (1963)—was a trenchant satire on permissive sex without love: 'Two giant dolls, rubbing their papier-maché nakedness against each other in an obscene parody of loveless sex, go beserk in an hotel room, vandalising the fittings, scrawling filthy words and drawings on the walls. . . .'[37] But as Harold Hobson pointed out in the *Sunday Times*, many who objected to it failed to realise that 'it is an exaggerated example of that exaggerated Puritanism, the *saeva indignatio* of Swift which it is easy to mistake for pornography.'[38]

The Lord Chamberlain's powers of theatrical censorship were legally terminated in September 1968; subsequent events in the theatre are discussed in Chapter 10.

Happenings

Many of the erotic theatrical performances of the last five years owe something to that ubiquitous artistic manifestation of the '60s: the happening. Happenings are direct descendants of dada and surrealist events, and so 'the symbolical or oblique treatment of sexual material, a frequent Surrealist concern, is central to many Happenings.'[39]

In March 1961, Michael Kirby included a partly naked, crouching figure of a girl in *A Spring Happening* at the Reuben Gallery, New York, while in September, 1963, Alan Kaprow staged the first British happening at the Edinburgh Festival International Drama Conference. In this, a nude female model was whisked across the organ loft on a trolley. A court-case ensued, but the model was acquitted, one of the arguments being that she represented the Soul of the Festival, and that artists have always used nude women to represent the soul. Such a brief glimpse of a naked female figure was not considered to be quite as erotic as the sight of Carroll Baker wriggling along the tops of the seats in the auditorium immediately after Miss Kesselar's appearance. Ken Dewey recalled that 'she looked very beautiful in her long gold pants, stretched across three or four rows.'[40]

In 1964, Carole Schneeman added another erotic possibility in her *Meat Joy*. In this, 'several people moved about with dead chickens' heads in their mouths and the rest of the chicken hanging down. The sight was heightened by the sexual implication of voluptuous, scantily clad girls playing provocatively with the decaying carcasses . . . prehistoric sensuality was the hall-mark.'[41]

By 1972 Miss Schneeman had developed the idea even further in her scenario for *Genital Play Erotica Meat Room*:

A large, curving space filled entirely with wonderfully fashioned, over life-size pricks, balls, nipples, clitorises, labia majoria, labia minoria, cunts and ass holes. They will be life-like in variations of detail, color, aroma and moisture; constructed from flesh-like material, they completely cover floors, walls, ceiling. They are electrically charged and when handled properly they will undergo life-like transformations and as they are touched they communicate to the toucher, flood the toucher with the most extreme sensations they could normally feel. The genitals-meat are disposed so that it is possible to climb on them, swing on them, ride, run and jump among them—all the time receiving an ecstatic electrical current. . . . In your own time your own way with another no one can predict how this room will effect them how will they effect this room (let insights follow delight).[42]

The elder statesmen of surrealism and dada were, however, unimpressed: 'The happening, offspring of *Hellzapoppin!*, seems to me to run one of the gravest risks; that of sexual promiscuity.'[43] wrote André Breton in 1964, and three years later, Marcel Duchamp was quoted as saying: 'I went to another Happening. . . . Nothing happened, just some woman or other naked on a heap of coal. . . . The tattiest thing one could imagine. . . .'[44]

Ballet

Early ballet dancers would not have exuded much more erotic appeal on the stage than they would have in ordinary everyday clothes, except when they donned a particularly striking 'symbolic' costume. For then, as now only occasionally, dancers were used primarily as symbolic rather than real figures. Camargo, however, altered things slightly by shortening her skirts. This innovation led eventually to the short classical dress with which many still associate ballet entirely—the tutu: 'derived from the French child's word *tutu* (i.e. *cul-cul*), 'bottom', and by extension the slang term used to describe the very short petticoat sewn together between the legs, made and un-made at each performance, and worn by danseuses to conceal that part of their anatomy. Today it designates the short classical ballet skirt. . . . Camargo in 1730 introduced the entrechat . . . shortening the skirt to above the instep and wearing knickers, a wise precaution when performing steps of elevation as shown by the unfortunate experience of Mlle. Mariette (in 1727) who, catching her dress on a piece of scenery, was obliged to pose in the nude for a full minute. . . .'[45]

Thereafter, the propriety of dancers' dresses became a perennial topic. For although bosoms were virtually on open-display, legs were not revealed off-stage to the extent they were in ballets until after 1918. They were, therefore, the principal objects of erotic contemplation. The introduction of fleshlings by Maillot at the Paris Opera after the French Revolution resulted in the hypocrisy Isadora Duncan detested. Whether the Pope's subsequent decree that fleshlings in the theatres under his jurisdiction must be blue, so that they were not suggestive of flesh, was more or less hypocritical must be a matter for debate.

In late-nineteenth-century London, the Empire and Alhambra Theatres were the homes of English ballet. Both employed massive companies, whose dress and allegedly 'low' off-stage behaviour came in for adverse comment. Even more adverse comment fell upon the management for allowing prostitutes to ply for hire in their promenades and foyers. A campaign was launched in 1894 to get rid of this social menace from the Empire and those other theatres where prostitutes were allowed to trade untroubled by the managements. During the campaign Mrs Ormision Chant criticised the erotic movements in certain ballets, and in true Women's Lib manner suggested that the dancers were being forced to prostitute themselves to appease the greed of the monopolists and capitalists who were making vast (eighty per cent) profits by exploiting the barely draped female form. She suggested that things would be very different if men were forced to display themselves in similar fashion. But since 1894 the number of male dancers has increased enormously, and there has been a steady flow of adverse comment on erotic aspects of male dancers' costumes, particularly from provincial audiences. Their prejudices when faced with a dancer (or actor in costume part) wearing tights has been neatly summarised by John Osborne in *The Entertainer*:

> I was in a show with a couple of male dancers once. And wherever we went, on the Monday night some woman would complain about their tights bulging. Wherever we went. Every Monday night. I'm sure it was the same woman each time. I used to call her the Camp Follower.

Remarkably enough even in January 1971, in New York of all places, Rudolf Nureyev was adversely criticised for wearing 'practically transparent tights' in the

Australian Ballet Company's *Don Quixote*.

Fokine's *Scheherezade*, created for Diaghilev's Ballets-Russes in 1910, to selections from Rimsky-Korsakov's symphonic poem of the same name, brought imaginatively staged eroticism into the open, although it had been implicit in many of the great classical ballets, *e.g. The Sleeping Beauty* (1890). Benois's strident designs, the overwhelming violence of the brilliantly choreographed orgy scene, and above all Nijinsky's dancing as the Negro Slave enamoured of the Shah's favourite wife, created a furore whenever it was staged.

An even bigger furore occurred in 1912 when Nijinsky choreographed another ballet to an already composed score by Claude Debussy: *L'Après-midi d'un Faune*. In this, 'Nijinsky took the subject—the creative act—for sex itself; the shock lay in that "the unmentioned object" had been heretofore unmentionable. Convention canonized copulation; masturbation was heresy. Mallarmé [in the eclogue to which Debussy's music was the 'Prelude'] wished to depict, not the object, but the effect it produced. In obscure verse this was safe; in danced action obscene. Nijinsky was no simple narcissist. He was an artist and a naïve philosopher with ultimate aspirations towards sainthood. In three ballets he paralleled Freud's chart of man's developing psyche: in *Faune*, adolescent self-discovery and gratification; in *Jeux*, homosexual discovery of another self or selves; in *Le Sacre du Printemps*, fertility and renewal of the race.'[46] The subject, therefore, was basically 'a recognition through auto-eroticism of adolescent sex'.[47] The production was in the 'Greek' style; the 'story' was simple: a faun tries to play with some passing nymphs, they are frightened, one drops a scarf, the faun is left alone again. But 'the Faun's final act, thrusting his body onto the nymph's scarf, caused a scandal, which the press whipped up into a *cause celèbre*. The sculptor Rodin defended Nijinsky; the Russian embassy was horrified; Diaghilev delighted'[48] (see illustration 230).

Prince Peter Lieven later recalled:

230 Vaslav Nijinsky in
L'Après-Midi d'Un
Faune, Paris, 1912

There are several versions of the origin of this phallic movement. Prince Argoutinsky has told me that one of the . . . [glass grapes on Nijinsky's costume] broke . . . and when Nijinsky lay down on the veil, he could not immediately find a position in which the broken glass didn't hurt . . . and only later, when it was seen what an invaluable advertisement was provided by the . . . controversy aroused, it became a definite feature . . . Grigorieff, however [said] the scene was rehearsed deliberately . . .. In 1916 after the first performance . . . in New York, Diaghileff tried to revive a similar sensation. Notices appeared of rumoured police ban . . . but the uproar created in Paris . . . could not be equalled.[49]

Fokine was criticised sharply for ignoring Rimsky-Korsakov's own 'programme' when he choreographed *Scheherezade*, and in *L'Après-midi* Nijinsky departed to a certain extent from Debussy's intention, but when *Le Sacre du Printemps* was premiered in 1913, Nijinsky's choreography was purely a visualisation of the erotic programme already present in Stravinsky's commissioned score. The result was 'an absolutely pure work, harsh, bitter . . . brutal . . . frank, limpid, coarse . . . sociological'[50] about 'the rebirth of life after winter sleep, also a metaphor of deep changes in adolescent sexuality'.[51] It climaxed with a sacrificial dance, and the self-immolation of a virgin, whose 'rigid corpse, raised high to the rising sun, is run off stage. In group dances, terrified women [were] thrown as if by centrifugal force, out of the turning, swarming crowd, lashed by the orchestra's whips, snapped up by the instrumental cyclone. . . .'[52]

In 1960 Maurice Béjart revived *Le Sacre* but abandoned the original scenario, and instead used the savage religious elements of the score as the basis for a mass spectacle with sex as the overt driving force, and for the climax, the virgin copulated instead of dying. Recent revivals of this interpretation have become even more erotic as the dancers have been able to discard the fleshlings they wore initially.

The American dancers Ted Shawn and Ruth St Denis included *poses plastiques* in their early repertoire, and Shawn himself—always a staunch advocate of nudity in ballet—danced nude (except for a minuscule fig-leaf) in *Death of Adonis* in the mid-'20s. However, their most famous student, Martha Graham, was the next major choreographer after Nijinsky to deal more or less explicitly with erotic topics. But there was one vital difference: 'Her females have characters in depth, but the male . . . is demoted to object status, just a means to satisfy female lust'.[53]

Ardent Song (1954) contains some of Graham's most striking erotic moments:

Aphrodite lurches about the stage. It is a lurid, sickening, erotic, drunken and unclean movement. As she gathers up the serpent, holding a head in each hand, so the music quickens and the serpent heads begin to convulse. The body of Aphrodite seems shaken by their violence, the climax of the ejection of the serpent's poison coincides with her own orgasm. The stage is filled with light— it is moon-high—exposing this obscene ritual. . . . The sense of thralldom to lust, of the dark night of depravity, the terrible, relentless and inexorable impetus of

[317]

passion, have rarely been so sickeningly and superbly portrayed in the theatre.[54]

Roland Petit has choreographed one ballet with a highly erotic theme: *Le Jeune Homme et La Mort* (1946) and another: *Carmen* (1949), with one of the most memorably erotic scenes in ballet. In *Le Jeune Homme*, written by Jean Cocteau, and performed to Bach's *Passacaglia in C*, a young poet in the depths of despair is visited and tempted by a female figure of death. In *Carmen* the theme is also man bewitched by woman. In a bedroom scene, a valiant attempt is made to match classical dancing with realistic love-making in a realistic setting with generally most convincing results, especially when the leading parts were danced by Petit himself and Renée Jeanmaire. But, as in *Le Jeune Homme*, the most erotic scene involves the love/death syndrome. In the final scene the bullfight within and the exchanges between Carmen and Don José outside are convincingly paralleled. And, after she has provoked her lover into stabbing her with his knife: 'Clasping Don José, Carmen gives a final spasmodic twitch of her legs in the most realistic death scene in all ballet.'[55]

Jerome Robbins's *The Cage* (1951) and Kenneth Macmillan's *The Invitation* (1960) were essentially in this 'French' tradition of erotic melodrama. The Peter Darrell–David Rudkin ballet *Sun into Darkness* (1966) dealt with similar erotic themes, and even went further in its study of violence in a small Cornish village by incorporating incidents involving flagellation, onanism, sodomy, and copulation. Unfortunately, inadequate choreography and unconvincing staging mitigated its effect.

America provided the *Jeune Homme* of the '60s: Robert Joffrey's *Astarte* (1967). It was the first multi-media work to be presented by a major ballet company, and also the first to successfully use a 'rock' score (by the Crome Syrcus). A young man walks onto the stage from the audience, strips off his clothes, and experiences his first trip (to complete sexual satisfaction) with Astarte—the Phoenician goddess of love. This was a serious work seriously performed. The Joffrey Ballet Company's repertoire also includes Gerald Arpino's *Valentine*, a wittily devised satire on heterosexual love-making—staged as if it was a boxing bout. To give added piquancy Jacob Druckman's music is scored for a solo contrabass. Its player is also on stage and, like the contestants, ends flat on his back, completely exhausted, but in his case he has been overwhelmed by his instrument's powerful performance.

Most ballets deal with male–female relationships (although of course spectators may interpret what is seen according to their own predilections). But in Glen Tetley's *Freefall* (1967) there are 'duets of a ferociously sexual nature not only for men with women, but man with man and woman with woman: the work digs into human nature for some underlying needs or desires.'[56]

Much recent erotic dance has featured complete nudity. Whether this adds or detracts from the erotic effect is a matter of personal taste. There is not, however, as much as publicists would make it appear. The most extensive use of nudity (seven minutes) occurs in Tetley's *Mutations* (1970; see illustrations 231 and 236) created for the Nederlands Dans Theater. Their visit to Sadler's Wells caused Richard Buckle to reflect: 'To those of us who have never seen a naked body before, the

231 Glen Tetley,
Mutations (Nederlands
Dans Theater),
London, 1970

difference between men and women is at once apparent. Women's pubic hair grows
in a more implacable way. Apart from this there is one feature which men have and
women are without, in sculpture and painting it can be stylised, but in ballet apparently not. This is a pity for, after all, a dancer's training stylises his body and
renders it godlike; so if nothing can be done about that feature I think naked male
dancers should wear artificial ones of ideal proportion.'[54]

Opera

Opera rarely deals with purely abstract themes, and as in the 'legitimate' theatre,
nearly every opera contains some erotic content. Only a minute number of examples
can be cited here.

Plots are usually mechanised by 'straightforward' sexual desire: Bizet's *Carmen*
(1875); unusual sexual urges: Berg's *Lulu* (1937); desire on a more sophisticated
level: Cavalli's *La Calisto* (1651); a subtle combination of all the foregoing: Mozart's
The Marriage of Figaro (1786). Increasing stage-permissiveness has forced many
singers to reveal more of themselves than was usual before, *e.g.* Valerie Masterson as
Eurydice in the current Sadler's Wells production of Offenbach's *Orpheus in the
Underworld* (1861), takes a bubble-bath in true Bardot manner; at the height of the
abnormal-sex-on-stage craze (1965) Peter Hall produced the orgy in Schoenberg's
Moses and Aaron (1957) at the Royal Opera House, Covent Garden, with painstaking
attention to detail: striptease dancers from Soho appeared as the Four Virgins.

To many people, however, the true erotic content of opera lies not in the visual
aspect but in the music. And of all opera composers Wagner was the one most

[319]

dedicated to the idea of representing Love on stage; in his own words, he sought: 'release from the present, for absorbtion into an element of endless love, a love denied to earth and reachable through the gates of death alone. . . . How absurd, then, must those critics seem to me, who, drawing all their wit from modern wantonness, insist on reading into my *Tannhäuser* a specifically Christian and impotently pietistic drift!'[58]

Tannhäuser (1845) revolves around the hero who, after a year's absence in the court of Venus, returns to earth and takes part in a singing competition on the theme of Love. His passionate song in praise of non-selfless Love horrifies the listeners, and he is forced to seek the Pope's absolution. His plea is rejected, and he dies so that he may return to Venus (see illustration 232). Immediately, the Pope's staff, borne by passing Pilgrims, sprouts leaves 'in token that God (if not the Pope) has forgiven Tannhäuser'.

But it is in Act II of *Tristan and Isolde* (1865) that Wagner's most erotic music is to be found:

The Love Motive rises with ever increasing passion until Isolde's emotional exaltation finds expression in the Motive of Ecstasy. The music seethes with passion as the lovers greet one another, the Love Motive and the Motive of Ecstasy vying in the excitement of this rapturous meeting. Then begins the exchange of phrases in which the lovers pour forth their love for one another . . . [in] the duet: '*Oh, sink upon us, Night of Love*', and there is nothing in the realms of music or poetry to compare in suggestiveness with these caressing, pulsating phrases.[59]

232 Richard Wagner, *Tannhäuser* (Covent Garden), London, 1955

The opera throughout is on the same consistently, all-enveloping passionate level and, as the Earl of Harewood has written, 'all who have made a study of opera, and do not regard it merely as a form of amusement, are agreed that the score of *Tristan and Isolde* is the greatest setting of a love-story for the lyric stage. It is a tale of tragic passion, culminating in death, unfolded in the surge and palpitation of immortal music.'[60]

It is obvious, therefore, why many opera-lovers think that such incidents as the introduction by Peter Hall of the first nude principal soprano—in *The Knot Garden* at the Royal Opera House in 1970—are merely publicity gimmicks, usually not necessary to the overall conception of the production, which in the latter was a gallant attempt by Michael Tippett to deal with more complicated erotic themes than Wagner experienced in as convincing manner as possible on the modern opera stage.

Popular Music

At the Berkeley Experimental Arts Foundation Open Theater in California, Ben Jacopetti has for some years been trying, through happenings such as *Revelations* (1966), to create erotic experiences for his audiences: 'There are times when every-thing works up there: the bodies, the objects, the music, the voices, the sounds, the breathing, the lights, the colors; these are the times when the complexity and intensity of the sensual experience are literally breathtaking.'[61]

Such a result is aimed at by all theatrical performers, especially those in the field of popular music. Unfortunately, publicists for each new popular singer have frequently during the last hundred years built up their artiste by disparaging the achievements and performances of his predecessors. Thus much of the revolutionary novelty claimed for the erotic content of the songs, and on-stage and off-stage behaviour, of many of the 'progressive' singers of the late-'60s ignored the fact that virtually everything they were doing had been done before. For example, R. Meltzer devotes several paragraphs of *The Aesthetics of Rock* to the substitution of rude or erotic words for the written words in rock songs, without a single reference to the fact that this has been a popular pastime since the first non-rude or non-erotic song was written, and was especially popular in Regency and Victorian glee clubs and sporting rooms.

The 'realistic' erotic content of 'blues' (and folk-song in general) has been contrasted frequently with the 'sentimental' erotic content of 'commercial' popular song. But the songs that deal with erotic subjects most blatantly are those sung in servicemen's bars and Rugby Football Club baths and bars. It has been observed, however, that whereas 'recognised traditional song is mostly concerned with the social aspects of sexual activity—pregnancy and cuckoldry. . . . Rugby songs are technical. Beyond that they deal not with people, but with grotesques; the subjects are ten-foot genitals, monstrous pubic hairs, astonishing feats of endurance, ladies insatiable even with mechanical aids.'[63]

Certain pop songs have, however, been very explicit in their verbal imagery, such as Max Romeo's 'Wet Dream' (1968) with its refrain: 'Lie down gal, let me push it up, push it up.' In spite of the record company's insistence that the situation involved a hotel-room drama in which the man was telling the woman to lie down while he pushed up the window since someone was shooting into the room at them, the record was banned from the air waves by the BBC and many similar corporations. Other recently banned records include 'Jump up and down and wave your knickers in the air' by St Cecilia and 'My Ding-a-Ling' by Chuck Berry in England and the ambivalent and fascinating 'Lola' by the Kinks, in Australia. The most exciting but least-known pop record of this variety is 'Stickball' by Rod McKuen. This incredible record describes in explicit detail a male fantasy of unusual copulatory techniques building up to an orgasmic climax; it appeared in America in a very small, clandestine edition in 1973. The following year, the album of the sexual musical, *Let My People Come*, by Earl Wilson Junior, was issued commercially in America with very good explicit songs such as 'Come in my mouth', 'Dirty words', and 'The cunnilingus champion of company C'. The record was not available in London when the show opened there later in 1974. But, as with all the theatrical arts, in all types of music it is definitely a case of 'whatever turns you on' being potentially erotic. 'Rhythm 'n' Blues' music is often straight sex, as with songs like 'Work with me Annie' and 'Baby Let Me Bang your Box'. In 'jazz' and 'Rock 'n' Roll' the very words for the music-form should be enough to warn the unwary that the erotic content is bound to be high.

Jazz started as the background music in New Orleans brothels, and eroticism is rarely absent—even from such apparently cerebral music as that provided by the Modern Jazz Quartet. It was the supremely elegant Duke Ellington (still exuding charm and sex appeal until the end) who wrote a suite based on the idea that 'A drum is a woman'. But his own drummers tended to be (like the composer himself) essentially gentle, although they attempted occasionally to provide those timpanistic pyrotechnics frequently demanded by jazz audiences. If Ellington's comparison was correct, it is that supremely accomplished big band drummer—Buddy Rich—who, with his ferocious displays of seemingly perpetual rhythmic dexterity, comes closest of all jazzmen to a symbolic representation of one of Bataille's definitions of eroticism: 'What does physical eroticism signify if not a violation of the very being of its practitioner?—a violation bordering on death, bordering on murder?'[63]

The phallic possibilities of the trumpet (Louis Armstrong was rarely seen without his 'horn' in his hand) and saxophone need no emphasising, while Charlie Mingus manages to produce tremendously erotic sounds from his swaying double-bass—especially in 'Tijuana Moods', where he provides a stirring blend of flamenco, limbo, and American striptease music.

Many find the eroticism of jazz and dance music too blatantly obvious (*e.g.* Isadora Duncan) and turn (like Miss Duncan) to 'classical' music for inspiration or solace, as it can provide a full range of sounds—from brightly mechanical Bach to the all-enveloping shroud of Mahler. The work of the most blatantly 'erotic' composer has, however, not been well received by music-lovers and critics, although his 'ordinary' piano pieces are performed frequently. For the Russian composer Alexander Scriabin exceeded even Wagner (and came close to the ideas of many modern artists) in his Theosophically-inspired versions of a New Art which would combine music (both instrumental and vocal) with synchronised colour-effects, dancing, and sexual activity in an erotic Mystery performed in the elaborately decorated, perfumed temple he planned to build in India. The diversity of musical erotic experience is apparent when it is learned that 'A cultured Chinese gentleman . . . once remarked that he found the pulsating rhythms of the US Marine Band uncomfortably stimulating.'[64]

Even the very act of putting a record on the player can give an erotic thrill. For the record-player has 'affinities to Marcel Duchamp's sex machine metaphor . . . one can then penetrate the aptly supplied (vaginal) center hole with an erect steel spindle projecting from the revolving turntable. Once the spindle has fully penetrated, the record is in contact with the turntable and they both move with the same precise rhythm. While in such intimate contact, in a perfectly consistent repetitive circle (Aristotle's symbol for perfect motion), the sex machine now produces aural manifestations of the game in which it is indulging. . . .'[65]

These 'aural manifestations' have multiplied with the development of recording and reproduction techniques. In post-LP days it is easier to use recorded music as a prelude or accompaniment to erotic play—for obvious reasons. Domestic tape-recorders, and a wider range of commercially-released 'documentary' records have meant that sounds to thrill even Des Esseintes are available (*e.g.* the stereo storms from the soundtrack of *La Dolce Vita*). Tape-recorders can be used also to compose 'music', and a recent piece by Japanese avant-garde composer Takematsu consists of 'a 72-minute tape montage condensed into 4 minutes 9 seconds consisting of one man and one woman repeating the word "Ai" in different ways composed on tape by manipulating the recorder.' This is, however, only a 'serious' use of the deep-breathing device employed by Jane Birkin and Serge Gainsbourg on their notorious bedroom record, 'Je t'aime—moi non plus' (1969) which itself was derived from Stan Freberg's hit record of the early-'50s, 'John and Marsha', and perhaps also the palpitating and orgasmic 'Erotica' by Rita (1969).

In spite of recent reports, pre-1956 songs and performers were not all unerotic, although it was Elvis Presley who brought explicit eroticism to white audiences with his pelvic movements adapted from the Negro dance of the '20s—the Snake Hips, and from coloured singers like Bo Diddley, and even white singers like Johnnie Ray, whose performances of 'Oh What a Night it Was' caused a sensation in the early-'50s. Modern pop singers owe most to black dances and black performers, who themselves owe much to African dancers, who gain their stimulating effect by exploding outwards from the hips, whereas in European social dance the body is usually held stiffly erect. This was the stance adopted by the leading white singers of the '30s and '40s (*e.g.* Bing Crosby and Frank Sinatra), who were nevertheless able to stir the passions of their fans by their voices alone—although in Sinatra's case the baby-boss image undoubtedly helped.

[323]

233   Elvis Presley

Presley was definitely the boss figure (see illustration 233). It has been suggested by George Melly that his importance lay in the fact that:

> he was the first male white singer to propose that fucking was a desirable activity in itself and that, given sufficient sex appeal, it was possible for a man to lay girls without any of the traditional gestures or promises. It's true that his immediate predecessor Johnnie Ray had offered in fairly open terms a musical equivalent to the sex act. 'Oh What A Night It Was' is remarkably specific for its period, but Ray was always a vulnerable figure, suggesting the seduced rather than the seducer. Presley, on the contrary, came on as though confident in his ability to attract women without appealing in any way to their protective instinct. He was the master of the sexual simile, treating his guitar as both phallus and girl, punctuating his lyrics with the animal grunts and groans of the male approaching orgasm. He made it quite clear that he felt he was doing any woman he accepted a favour. He dressed to emphasize both his masculinity and basic narcissism, and rumour had it that into his skin-tight jeans was sewn a lead bar in order to suggest a weapon of heroic proportions.[66]

It may be significant to record that Mick Jagger was reputed to give himself a similar 'well-endowed' effect by padding his trousers with a pocket handkerchief.

Presley's gyrations on his first TV show caused an uproar, and subsequently he

[324]

was photographed only from the chest up. That brought a similar number of complaints, and so he was put into evening dress and photographed full-length, but told to stand still. All to no avail; audiences, and his music, demanded he move. In his 1969 NBC-TV Special he showed that even standing still he could make disturbingly erotic gestures—by wiggling his very supple little finger. Presley wriggled, fell to the floor, but he did not hurl himself wildly about the stage as many of his contemporaries and descendants did. There have been many singers in this 'crying', 'orgasmic' vein, but little written evidence of their acts. That of Al Braggs—whose act contains most of the elements of this style of musical eroticism —has been described in some detail:

> Braggs usually concludes his part of the show by pulling out all the vocal and choreographic stops with a cry routine in the general manner of James Brown or Little Richard. Normally this is a direct orgasmic appeal to the fairer sex but, as Braggs does it, pleading plays a secondary part to gymnastics. He screams; he groans; he crawls rhythmically across the stage on his stomach dragging the microphone behind him; he leaps over, under, and around the microphone cord; he lies on his back and kicks his feet in the air; he does some syncopated push-ups; he falls halfway over the edge of the stage and grabs the nearest hands . . . he does the limbo; he bumps and grinds; and gradually manoeuvres himself off stage with a flying split or two, still twitching and shouting.[67]

The dress of non-Progressive Pop singers has certain standardised features: 'Cry singers invariably appear in José Greco outfits, removing coat, tie, and some-times the shirt, as their stunts become more strenuous.'[68] Tom Jones is a typical performer in this style:

> The leading male sex icon . . . [has] improved over his previous Vegas appear-ance . . . [when] jokes about his tight trousers with extra dimensional frontal effect . . . captured more interest than his songalog. . . . Virility rites are accentuated with Jones' very fluid moves, stimulating the audience noticeably. There was more restraint shown from his devotees on opening nights. Perhaps it was the large amount of children present that kept the sacrifical offerings to mere napkins, rather than the collection of lingerie, room keys and strange feminine flotsam that have been cast upon stage during other noteworthy sessions.[69]

Shirley Bassey is a typical female equivalent of Tom Jones. In 1957:

> Hobbled in a bright silver sheath she leans towards her master, the microphone; totters between numbers in tiny circles, wide-eyed and beaming beneath close-cut, silver-streaked hair, slim boyish arms outstretched as though to keep her balance. . . . Her throat pulses, her fingers curve and clutch in predatory slashes . . . and when in case we should fail to grasp what is really meant by songs about

'burning my candle at both ends', or 'Fire Down Below', she strokes her thighs
. . . a vestigial indifference . . . blurs the professional attack.[70]

Twelve years later her act had changed more than somewhat, and at least one critic
maintained (with a nice piece of aesthetic discrimination it would be difficult to
support) that by 1970 she was:

> a show business personality rather than a singer, presenting a totally vulgar act
> that strays rather near the border of tastelessness . . . she prowled around . . .
> throwing out 'bloodies' like a fishwife and making some rather dubious innuendoes
> (was there any need for her to talk of her 'jock-strap—I mean—G-string'). . . .
> Yet . . . the sheer outrageousness of her between-song conversation was refresh-
> ingly novel.[71]

Such demeanour on stage is far removed from that of Marlene Dietrich, who has
for forty years epitomised sophisticated show-business eroticism. In fact, she
rarely appeared on stage from 1928–42, but since then she has refined a stage-act
originally devised to entertain the troops into one of the most striking ever given
in the theatre. Her deliberate, husky delivery, her pale, mysteriously aloof appearance, the androgynous enigma of her costumes—she regularly wears male dress
both on- and off-stage—are incomparable. It has been suggested that her performance combines 'maximum eroticism with minimum physical exposure',[72] but she
did pioneer the see-through dress in 1953. In her version of 'Johnny' Dietrich also
emphasises the potential symbolism of the microphone by caressing it gently on
its stand as the verses rise to exciting climaxes. J. W. Lambert called the microphone
Shirley Bassey's 'master' in the passage quoted above, but since 1957 the increasingly
smooth, cylindrical shape of this reproductive aid has made the symbolism even
more explicit. Dietrich's use of it is, however, considerably more subtle than the
rather blatant symbolic fellatio participated in (either wittingly or unwittingly) by
many other popular singers, both male and female.

Bassey and Dietrich epitomise flamboyant, well-groomed glamour. But there are
female singers (*e.g.* Edith Piaf and Judy Garland) who have at times been anything
but well-groomed on stage, and yet have had their own erotic effect. Like all actors
and actresses, part of their aim was to make their audiences love them, usually only
figuratively speaking, but Piaf (see illustration 234) was at her compulsive best if
she knew that a new lover was in the stalls or wings. The power such singers have
over their audiences is exemplified by the following description of the finale to a
Judy Garland concert at The Palace, New York, in 1968:

> At 11.43 she began to let them touch her. They had been after her flesh a long
> while, but it is only now, after she is done and it is ended, that she allowed them
> contact. Just the barest graze. Her fingertips to theirs as she moved, as always,
> jerkily, parallel to the footlights. . . . And if she expected her flesh to quiet them,
> she was only wrong, the din, already painful, somehow went up a notch . . . a

234   Edith Piaf

young boy . . . is staring up at her wringing his hands. He cannot and will not stop . . . even though his constant wringing pressure has forced his skin to burst and bleed.[73]

There have been female 'Rock' stars (*e.g.* Janis Joplin whose act was very similar to Garland's), but undoubtedly this area of singing is dominated by males, albeit males often with what has been considered in recent years female characteristics— long hair and brightly coloured clothes: 'Suddenly it was Mick [Jagger]. In a white, bow-buttoned billowing frock over tight white pants, a gold-studded leather collar. . . .'[74]

There are many others in the anarchic-erotic manner of Jagger, such as Jimi Hendrix: 'an outrageous ham showman . . . he camped it up like mad . . . [but] carried real conviction. He was mesmeric. He was ferocious and sexy.'[75] 'That Hendryk [sic] is masturbating, as his fingers pump madly up and down the phallic shaft of his guitar, is clear.'[76]

If that *is* clear, it must be wondered what The Who are up to when they smash their guitars during their act—allegedly as a protest against the false values of a materialistic society; or Frank Zappa, whose erotic hold over his girlfriend caused a man to hurl the singer into the orchestra pit at the Rainbow Theatre, London, in 1971, breaking his leg; or Elton John, who sometimes sports a codpiece which gives a flash (of light) when he strikes a particular chord on his guitar; or Jim Morrison, 'self-styled "King of Orgasmic Rock" . . . [who was charged with] lewd and lascivious behaviour in public by exposing his private parts and by simulating

[327]

masturbation and oral copulation' in Miami in 1969.[77] His 'lewd' behaviour has been emulated by spectators. For example, in 1972: 'At one Osibisa gig recently . . . a guy started to strip off, leaped on to the stage for a frenzied nude bop, . . . started a craze and five other fellows followed suit, careering undraped among the rest of the audience in abandoned ecstasy.'[78]

Such basic erotic behaviour results, in Jeff Nuttal's opinion, from:

> . . . the fact that the music is dangerous. It precipitates not mere copulation, but wholesale orgy, not seduction but rape, not mere vigour but cruelty. It is a music of pain. . . . The artifacts are of almost unprecedented obscenity. The semi-quavers gobble down to the bridge of the guitar like the drooling mouth of a nymphomaniac in transports of passion shrieking towards fellatio. . . . The top strings wail and plead and threaten. The bass guitars snort and grunt in bestial spasms. . . . The amplifiers are abused to the point when they become actually painful and while their eardrums strain and split, the audience explode their brainmatter with chemicals . . . behind the figures and the rituals and the broken young minds [looms] a spectre of unearthly grace and freedom, a figure whose unsurpassed beauty warms the horrified mind and promises a magic and a life from deep in the gut that will transcend the essentially trivial evils of a trivial society.[79]

Chapter 10

The Theatre of Celebration

In this book we have already seen that the way to end the pathetic dependence on tawdry pornography which so many people feel today is not by suppressing it but by eliminating the 'exacting, selfish and ruthless morality', as Freud calls it, which drives people to such desperate searches for satisfaction. What is needed is not tough repression but free expression, and this is as true in daily life as it is in the realm of the arts. In early 1967, Richard Schechner wrote: 'An expressive society would have need for neither pornography nor oppressive controls. Replacing them would be celebratory sexual art and expression: the phallic dances of the Greeks, the promiscuity of Elizabethan England. . . . We are beginning to understand the difference between masturbatory and celebratory sex.'[1] Schechner saw the theatre as being the most suppressed of art forms, but he detected hopeful signs that censorship was on the wane. Eight years later his hopes have been realised in many parts of the Western world, and we have begun to experience what might be termed the theatre of celebration, wherein theatrical events openly celebrate the joys and disappointments of erotic sexuality, without relying purely on masturbatory fantasies.

The theatre offers a unique experience. Reading is a solitary activity; book reviewers are sent one copy of a book, while film and theatre reviewers receive two tickets. Going to the cinema or theatre is assumed to be an experience which we share with people who are emotionally close to us. The vibrating energies generated by a film or a play bring a high level of involvement. Film is a more abstract, fictionalised art than theatre, for in a play the actors are seen to be real people, and the urge to participate in events with them can become a very real one, as recent playwrights have recognised. This is one reason why there have for so long been strong strictures against open sexuality on the stage. Richard Schechner wrote: 'Overt and graphic sexuality would destroy the aesthetic fabric of any (traditional) performance. . . . And it is only within the framework of celebration that sexuality can be both graphic and aesthetic.'[2]

The archetypal theatre of celebration is the tribal dance (*cf.* Chapter 2 a) in which there is total participation often of an orgiastic nature, which is considered to be of immense value to the community. Such total participation is suspect today, but many artists are trying, through happenings, to obliterate distinctions between art and life and to involve audiences in events. Participation is a new code-word for students, black people, and workers, and the theatre has a part to play in the revolution of our time. The *Marat/Sade* (1965) is one of the most important plays in this connection; in it, Peter Weiss tries to ensure the audience's involvement in what is happening on stage by making them part of the play. Richard Schechner quotes the Marquis de Sade as describing in the play: 'the revolution of the flesh which will make all your other revolutions seem like prison mutinies', and he adds, 'this atavistic, cohesive and participatory revolution is the new expression'.[3]

Only with the removal of the absurd restraints relating to sexual explicitness could the theatre truly celebrate—through both the actors and the audience—that complete freedom of expression which Schechner described. In both England and America this has only been achieved very recently, and after long and arduous campaigns. In England, until 1968, theatrical censorship lay in the hands of the Lord Chamberlain, the Keeper of the Queen's Household. This incredible anachronism had its roots in the eighteenth century. In 1736, Henry Fielding and his friends staged various plays in London which attacked the current evils of gambling, bribery and corruption in high places, lampooning in particular Robert Walpole, the Prime Minister, who was known to be especially culpable.[4] As a result, Walpole introduced an act into Parliament which would empower the Lord Chamberlain to prohibit certain plays, and although vigorously attacked by Lord Chesterfield, the Licensing Act became law in 1737. This law, modified in 1843 as the Theatre Regulations Act, remained in force for two hundred and thirty years, in spite of a near-successful attempt to abolish it in 1949.

Censorship of the theatre had existed since Elizabethan times, but only as far as attacks on royalty or the Church and insults to foreign powers were concerned. Public propriety and moral standards were in no way the concern of the censors in Tudor and Stuart reigns. Only in the late-eighteenth century did prudery begin to make itself felt, and this changed to bigotry in 1824 when George Coleman became Chief Censor under the Lord Chamberlain, the Duke of Montrose. Coleman had been an author, and indeed one of his plays had earlier been banned for indecency. He now set out to purify the English stage, and censored all swear-words and religious allusions, as well as anything he considered obscene. In this direction he was helped by the notorious Thomas Bowdler, whose 'polite' family-edition of the works of Shakespeare first appeared in 1818. Later in the nineteenth century, plays by Ibsen, Tolstoy, Wilde, and Zola were banned in spite of remonstrations by George Bernard Shaw (whose *Mrs Warren's Profession* [1894] was also banned).

In our own century, theatrical censorship became slowly modernised, though by the 1960s, 'Christ' and 'Jesus' could still not be used as expletives, and lesbianism and homosexuality were still taboo subjects which could occasionally be mentioned if in a suitably serious context. In 1957, John Osborne had to make numerous cuts in *The Entertainer*, from Archie Rice's remark, on holding up a brassière, 'Now what about this: "Lift up Your Hearts" ' to 'the vicar's got the clappers', which was altered to 'the vicar's dropped a clanger'.[5] Another author who suffered from such pettiness was Peter Nichols. When he directed a new production of his first play *A Day in the Death of Joe Egg* in 1971, he recalled how the play had been examined by the censor in the '60s: 'Michael Blakemore and I had one of those ludicrous interviews with him at St James's Palace. . . . "This speech here," he said, "where the character cries 'Down Rover!' Is this accompanied by an obscene gesture of any kind?" and he vaguely motioned towards his flies. I explained that it wasn't and that it was simply an imitation of the breathing pattern of a mother during natural childbirth. "Oh well," he said, "in my job you can't be too careful." '[6] Until 1968, any theatrical text had to be submitted for the Lord Chamberlain's approval with a fee of two guineas before it could be performed, and he could ban a play absolutely or for as long as he thought fit, or 'as long as necessary for the preservation of good manners, decorum or the public peace so to do'.[7] There was no appeal against the verdict of this gentleman, who breathed the niceties of court etiquette, but had little or no knowledge of the theatre. The Lord Chamberlain's power of censorship ceased at last on 26 September, 1968. The ending of stage censorship was greeted with joy by most people in the British theatrical world, and with great apprehension by guardians of public morality. These latter people considered that theatres would become over-run by obscene plays and that family entertainment would be doomed. Such fears can now be seen to have been un-justified, for only a minority of the plays produced in London since 1968 have included scenes which would have been unacceptable before the demise of the censor, and the new freedom has been used on the whole in an intelligent and responsible manner. As always happens, the great British public has voted with its feet. The theme of homosexuality and lesbianism has been successfully treated in such plays as *Fortune and Men's Eyes* (1968), *Spitting Image* (1968), *Boys in the Band* (1969) and *The Killing of Sister George* (1969). Rolf Hochhuth's *Soldiers* (1969) was able to show a great statesman of the recent past (Sir Winston Churchill) in an unfavourable light. And Edward Bond's *Saved*, in which bored and frustrated teenage boys stone a baby to death, was hailed as a great play by the serious press in 1969 after being prosecuted when produced privately at the Royal Court Theatre in 1965.

The aspect of the new theatrical freedom which has caused most concern and gained most headlines has been sex and nudity. The ending of censorship was celebrated by the London opening of the superb American musical *Hair* in November, 1968, and its nude scene and free language had a violent impact; by the early seventies, the audiences for *Hair* were largely made up of Women's Institute coach-parties and middle-aged suburban couples. *Hair* was soon followed by *Narcolepsy*, a Japanese mime play (1969), in which the main character, a young man, was naked throughout almost the entire performance. *The Stage* called the play 'pornographic', although very little sexual activity took place. Nudity was also an important feature of the Living Theatre's *Paradise Now* (1969), Ken Tynan's *Oh! Calcutta!* (1970), Tom Eyen's *The Dirtiest Show in Town* (1971), and Andy Warhol's *Pork* (1971). Helen of Troy appeared in the nude in Marlowe's *Dr Faustus* at the Royal Shakespeare Theatre in Stratford-upon-Avon in 1968; another Marlowe play to benefit from the new freedom was *Edward II*, for in the Prospect Theatre's

[331]

beautiful production in 1969 the homosexual king passionately kissed his lover on stage (see illustration 235). One of the most startling plays in the London theatre since censorship ended has been Michael Mclure's *The Beard* (1968), a brilliant dialogue between Jean Harlow and Billy the Kid after their deaths. In the final scene, Billy performs cunnilingus on the former sex idol.

Most of the above-mentioned plays came to London from America, where there has never been organised censorship of the theatre. But Vigilance Societies tend to be especially active in America, and so police prosecution of plays on the grounds of 'public indecency' is not uncommon. *The Beard* was prey to such charges in certain states, as was *Oh! Calcutta!*, but the most controversial case arose in New York over *Che*. This play involved extensive nudity and simulated sex acts (press reports suggested that some of the sex acts were real), the whole adding up to a plea for the freedom for which Che Guevara died. The cast was arrested and another cast immediately took its place. The play folded when the director ran out of actors, yet it was innovatory in its attempt to use sexual metaphor to express a political idea.[8]

The American situation is similar to that in France, where nudity has been a part of theatrical life for a long time. The first completely nude female to appear on the legitimate stage in Paris was probably an actress in Marlowe's *Dr Faustus* in 1891,[9] but more recently there have been numerous occasions, one of the more famous being the extensive nudity in Arrabal's *Le Grand Cérémonial* (1968). In 1971, an eight-hour double bill, *Prologue* and *Deaf Man's Glance*, based on a true story of a young black boy who went deaf after seeing his mother murder his two brothers with an axe, was presented in Paris by Robert Wilson. The marathon starred the boy himself, and was a 'happening' of the Allan Kaprow variety involving numerous naked people. The director reportedly said that the purpose was to let the participants

235 Christopher Marlowe,
Edward II, London,
1969, with
Ian McKellen and
James Laurenson

learn to understand their bodies and relieve their inner tensions, but audiences may have found the eight hours less therapeutic.[10]

Theatrical celebration of sexuality is of course easily open to abuse, and the whole question of stage nudity has brought its own problems. When jobs are scarce, many actors and actresses can be persuaded to act in a manner repugnant to them. Equity, the Actor's Union, has formulated a set of rules to try to curb abuses of this sort, and these seem to have met with some success in both Britain and America.[11] But Equity is not against stage nudity. Most of those who are make their stand on moral grounds, although to be disgusted by nudity is really a form of self-disgust. Some actors object on more reasonable grounds; Dorothy Tutin has said: 'I'm totally against stage nudity, not out of any prudishness; but because an actor is there to pretend. And without clothes you are simply yourself. Nudity is an end product, while the theatre is a place for transformation.'[12] In an article in *The Times*, Lord Kennet suggested that nudity on stage could be—but rarely is—justifiable, and objected to plays whose popularity was to an extent the result of their inclusion of nude scenes.[13] This carefully veiled and misplaced puritanism led him to write: 'We ought now to remember that good art is good morals', a tendentious and extremely debatable statement.

One incidence of nudity to which Lord Kennet objected was *Mutations* (see illustration 236), a nude ballet by Glen Tetley performed by the Nederlands Dans Theater in London in 1970. Alexander Bland wrote of the performance: 'Nudity is used in this ballet as a stimulating but serious ingredient which completely justifies itself artistically. . . . I find the spectacle of beautiful naked bodies exciting. Their introduction in this ballet induced a glow of added interest which it was painfully easy to analyse.'[14] Coming from a distinguished critic, the first remark commands

236   Glen Tetley, *Mutations* (Nederlands Dans Theater), London, 1970

our respect; the rest of the quotation should also command our respect for its honesty. Four young men and one girl danced throughout the ballet in full spotlight, without the slightest feeling of shame, and their five beautiful naked bodies were indeed exciting to watch, adding as they did a new (to our generation at least) experience in dancing. This was indeed the theatre of celebration and nudity was an essential part of it.

We are now able to accept nudity simply as a theatrical device and can now question whether a play involving nudity makes good theatre, rather than whether a play should involve nudity at all. Nudity no longer has to justify itself. The brief nude scenes in such plays as Ronald Millar's *Abelard and Heloise* (1970), about one of the greatest love tragedies, or Edward Whitehead's *The Foursome* (1970), about four very ordinary young people's day on the beach, are not absolutely crucial to the plays, but contribute to fine pieces of theatre. In *Sweet Eros* (1971), Terrence McNally puts a naked girl on the stage and subjects her (and the audience) to a fifty-minute monologue from her captor. The play is to be criticised as bad theatre rather than as exploitation of nudity. The same can be said of *Maybe That's Your Problem* (1971), a musical about premature ejaculation that turns out to be a witless and hypocritical attack on society's morbid preoccupation with sex. The new maturity can be seen in Harold Hobson's critique of Francis Warner's *Lying Figures* (1971): 'In this play, Katharine Schofield and Nova Llewellyn appear either partially or wholly nude. They seem to me to be as exquisite as the paintings of Van Dongen or the *Venus of Urbino*. It is morally risky to condemn them. The spectator who sees nothing but nakedness in *Lying Figures* may honestly feel that he is upholding high moral principles, but in fact he is merely revealing himself as the victim of a disagreeable psychological obsession.'[15] The revolution that is implicit in this review by a leading establishment critic, acceptance of the naked body in the theatre, is a major achievement of the avant-garde.

The revolution began with the 'tribal love-rock musical', *Hair*, which opened in an off-Broadway theatre in 1967 under the direction of Tom O'Horgan, one of the original Café La Mama troupe. It was written by two young actors, James Rado and Gerome Ragni, and owed a great deal to the general life-style and attitudes of the Hippy Movement. The direction was influenced by happenings and the La Mama open-stage idea, and nudity and drug-taking were both featured. The main reason for its runaway success was the brilliant score by Galt Macdermot, which included such songs as 'Aquarius', 'Good-morning Starshine', 'I got Life', and 'Let the Sunshine in', which soon became standards. But apart from the memorable songs, the show's importance lay in the way it presented a new life-style in realistic theatrical terms. The use of nudity, acid trips and explicit discussion of sexual matters was simply an extension of that life-style, and replaced the artificiality of almost all previous theatrical entertainment. Since the life-style was new and—to many people—shocking, the show gained a scandalous reputation that was out of all proportion to its real importance. Now that we can place it in its historical perspective, it can be seen as basically an excellent entertainment involving music,

237   James Rado and Gerome Ragni, *Hair*, London, 1968

humour, pathos, and insight, but at the same time an enormously influential exercise in the theatre of celebration.

The strength of *Hair* (see illustration 237) was that it had something important to say through the medium which it created for itself. Its authors wrote in the programme notes: 'Our spiritual beings are stultified by the unnatural and inhuman way of life. *Hair* is holy; the curls belong to God.' Their intention was to show people where modern life was taking them, and to demonstrate the hippy philosophy of love, happiness, and freedom, as expressed in the song 'Aquarius':

> *Harmony and understanding,*
> *Sympathy and trust abounding;*
> *No more falsehoods or derisions;*
> *Golden living dreams of visions*[16]

The mystical religion of love lay behind everything in the show, and that religion included the freedom to take drugs and remove clothes, just as much as to make love. The part played by sex in the show was in proportion to other aspects of the desired utopia, and sex was treated much more honestly than in most 'legitimate' stage productions. The famous nude scene, in which the cast emerged from under an enormous sheet and stood completely naked in the half-light, singing and holding hands, was a symbolic demonstration of the young generation's freedom from the

[335]

impurities of the life led by their parents. The embarrassment felt by many spectators arose from their own uptight and prurient attitudes. It was to them that the last song was addressed: 'Let the Sunshine in'.

After *Hair*, one of the most controversial shows has been *Oh! Calcutta!*, although the two have nothing in common apart from their sexual explicitness. *Oh! Calcutta!* (see illustrations 238 and 239) was a sophisticated evening of erotic entertainment with the accent on sophistication. Its curious title was a play on the French 'Oh! Quel cul t'as!' ('Oh! What an arse you have') referring to the naked woman on the poster painted by Clovis Trouille, but recalling Duchamp's *LHOOQ* ('*Elle a chaud au cul*'). Kenneth Tynan, who masterminded the show, explained that 'it occurred to me that there was no place for a civilized man to take a civilized woman to spend an evening of civilized erotic stimulation. At one end there's burlesque, at the other an expensive night club, but no place in between. We're trying to fill that gap with this show.'[17] He brought together the talents of such people as Joe Orton, Samuel Beckett, John Lennon, Jacques Levy, and Allen Jones to create an entertainment that included singing, dancing, and very explicit sexual comedy. One sketch concerned the history of women's underwear, another demonstrated the techniques and surprises of suburban wife-swapping. John Lennon's contribution, *Four in Hand*, featured four men masturbating in front of screens on which their fantasies appeared. Three screens showed pin-ups while the fourth was blank until the *William Tell Overture* came booming in and the Lone Ranger appeared, producing groans of satisfaction from one of the men but outbursts of anger from the others. This scene was retained when the show moved from New York to London in 1970, but others were removed, including an orgy involving elderly babysitters ('Let me chew on your garter belt, Ella. It's the only thing that makes me horny. . . .' 'I don't think you're gonna get hard, Ralph. Better go get the cane'). This was replaced in London by Joe Orton's glimpse of life in a stately home where the main problem facing the family of landed gentry was how to satisfy Auntie's need for a man after years of making do with wooden spoons, rolled copies of *The Times*, and other assorted objects, some of which had remained *in situ*.

Critical reaction to *Oh! Calcutta!* was mixed in both countries, ranging from those who dismissed it as a boring evening out for smug middle-class voyeurs to those who hailed it as a theatrical breakthrough, or as Jack Kroll wrote in *Newsweek*: 'a beautifully textured, witty, sweet and impudent theatrical poetry of the body and of our ingrown attitude toward it'.[18] Predictably, guardians of morality broke into hysteria: in London, the Dowager Lady Birdwood made an unsuccessful application to a magistrate to have the theatre closed, and David Holbrook wrote in *The Times*: 'God knows what will follow on stage if *Oh! Calcutta!* can get away with criminal acts of corruption and depravity. . . . Such a crime against human dignity and value. . . . I no longer wish to belong to a society which causes me so much pain by allowing the dear humanity I cherish to be openly and savagely abused.'[19] These people failed to realise that *Oh! Calcutta!* presented them with none of the ideological danger implicit in *Hair*; all Kenneth Tynan wanted to do, as he said in an interview

238　Kenneth Tynan and others,
　　Oh! Calcutta!, New York, 1970

239　Kenneth Tynan and others,
　　Oh! Calcutta!, New York, 1970

in *Theatre Quarterly*, was to 'remove sexual embarrassment and shame'.[20] Far from being a revolutionary tool of destruction, *Oh! Calcutta!* was in fact a rather reactionary piece of voyeuristic entertainment that questioned nothing, but merely confirmed received ideas and opinions, albeit in an often very amusing manner.

In the same interview, Kenneth Tynan also said he wanted to titillate the audience: 'To titillate well, to give the fullest, most delicate sensual pleasure, is given to very few people. . . . Salvador Dali in one of his autobiographies describes two people who know each other so well that eventually they can enter opposite corners of a large hall dressed from head to foot in all-enfolding robes with simply eye-slits, and by looking at each other can provoke orgasm: that would be the ideal erotic show, I suppose. . . . If that were the climax of a play in the course of which you got to know these two people intimately—physically and mentally—you would share the orgasm.'[21] Although the art of titillation is a perfectly justifiable one, the theatre of titillation in the long run is less satisfying and less enriching than the theatre of celebration. At one point *Oh! Calcutta!* achieved the celebration of physical love in theatrical terms: *One on One*, a lyrical and tender *pas de deux* danced by Margo Sappington and George Welbes in the nude to a funky country-blues song. This was in a world of its own, standing out from the hard-bitten sophistication of the rest of the show.[22]

Titillation tended to be the keynote of another production that started in New York and later opened in London, *The Dirtiest Show in Town* (see illustrations 240 and 241), in which almost the entire cast spent the second half of the show completely naked on stage in full lighting, performing various types of simulated intercourse in the most explicit manner ever seen on the London stage. Outside the Duchess Theatre were large photographs of the cast in the nude and emblazoned across the building were the words: *The Dirtiest Show in Town:* 'It's true. It is.' (*The Sun*). Small wonder that the audiences were largely composed of the raincoat brigade. In the programme, the author, Tom Eyen, described the show as 'a documentary of the destructive effects of air, water and mind pollution in New York City', and throughout the proceedings, the cast intoned the refrain: 'There's just so much loneliness a person can bear.' The play began, in fact, as an experimental underground programme at the Café La Mama in New York; Tom Eyen later explained: 'The original conception was sexuality not pollution. I wanted to take the masculine-feminine syndrome and destroy it, which I think we are doing right now. . . . The whole show started with no nudity.'[23] Between the original conception and the London production, something had changed drastically, and the English press comments reflected this: 'It is as clear-cut an example as I have seen of the commercial filtering process: what began in the cafés and church theatres of New York's East Village has been packaged and sterilized for the expense account public who want a daring night out';[24] 'To me, it looked a transparent excuse for nudity.'[25]

Although *The Dirtiest Show in Town* included a certain amount of insight into the pollution problem (of the world and of the mind) and the homosexual way of life, and had the occasional daring joke (*e.g.* 'Last night I was gang-fucked by the whole baseball team.' 'Aren't you ashamed and humiliated?' 'Yes, it was the opposing

240   Tom Eyen, *Dirtiest
Show in Town*, London,
1971

team'), the whole production as seen in London was directed at the voyeur; most
of the press were highly critical, and took little serious notice of the original intention
behind the play. One critic challenged the cast to keep their clothes on and keep
the show running.[26] The challenge was not accepted and the play was all set for a
highly successful run. But the audiences of titillation seekers depressed the cast,
who saw more in the play than sex. In a conversation with the author, one of the

241   Tom Eyen, *Dirtiest Show in Town*,
London, 1971

242 Tom Eyen, *Dirtiest
Show in Town*,
London, 1971, with
Philip Sayer

English cast, Philip Sayer (see illustration 242), said: 'The audiences are terrible—
they don't understand what it's all about. They come for the skin, and resent having
to sit through one hour of "boredom" first. This is the fault of the London production,
not of the play. It's being sold as sex, which it isn't. But all the promoters are
interested in is the easiest way to make money. The commercial theatre is death to
an ideas play like this. The situation was very different in New York where it was a
great artistic success.' What did he feel about the nudity in the show, and about sex
in the theatre in general? 'I don't personally think the nudity in *Dirtiest Show* is
especially erotic or aesthetically beautiful, but in the context of the play it is certainly

243 Andy Warhol and Anthony Ingrassia, *Pork*, London, 1971

valid. It's not our fault that in the London production the nudity is no more than titillation, and that it attracts the wrong audiences; these people are not interested in the acting or in ideas. So there is no feed back for the actors. Sex is beautiful, and it's an important part of life, so it has to be an important part of the theatre. But the theatre isn't the place for mere stimulation. Fucking is beautiful on the cinema screen as a visual image, but on stage it would not be beautiful, even if it were possible (which I doubt), and would merely attract the wrong sort of audience. Anyway, the trend is reversing now—it's avant-garde to wear clothes on the stage!'

Finally, what were his reactions to appearing in the nude on the stage? 'The first time for me was the audition for *Dirtiest Show*. I was terrified—it was very difficult. And it was worse in the actual play. It's not just acting one's part—there are terrible hang-ups involved—you feel so *vulnerable* in the nude in front of 400 people. It's difficult not to imagine that everyone in the audience is critically judging your "size". But I was never worried about getting an erection—you are too tense—too aware of the audience. Although one evening someone sucking my toe in the "orgy" turned me on for a moment! But in retrospect I'm glad I dared to appear in the nude. I'm certainly less uptight about my body now—I really feel nudity is natural and beautiful.'[27]

One play that went further than any other seen in London as far as the refinements of sex were concerned was Andy Warhol's *Pork* (see illustration 243). This lasted just four weeks in August 1971, and featured masturbation, fornication (both hetero- and homo-sexual) and defecation—all simulated, of course. A prostitute was seen doucheing in preparation for her next customer; there was a detailed discussion of abortions; and a transvestite described the fascination of different varieties of excrement. There was a certain amount of light-hearted nudity, including two young boys with pastel-tinted pubic hair and a girl who enjoyed making her breasts revolve in different directions. It all seemed rather too strong for London. *The Times* was abusive, the *Daily Telegraph* was repulsed by the whole thing, and the *News of the World* described it as 'a new low in permissiveness . . . the most amazing scenes of nudity and immorality ever performed on stage . . . it made *Hair, Oh! Calcutta!* and *The Dirtiest Show in Town* look like a vicarage tea party.'[28] In tones of smug hypocrisy, *Penthouse* said: 'With its unique blend of excremental obsession and blatant nudity, it transmogrifies the wholesome, exciting process of sexual stimulation into a degrading version of amateur night at the sewage works drama society.'[29] On frequent nights, the play was interrupted by outbursts from outraged citizens, though one might with reason have asked them why they were there in the first place, since the advertisements read: 'Warning: this play has explicit sexual content and "offensive" language. If you are likely to be disturbed, please do not attend.' But at the same time favourable reviews appeared in the *Guardian* and *New Society*, whose critics were able to perceive that more lay behind the play than sexual innuendo and the desire to exploit people's sexual susceptibility. The keys to the play were humour and observation, and there were marvellous performances from Geri Miller (of

Trash) as the exuberant, breast-twirling prostitute with a heart of gold, and Wayne County as the bitchy transvestite with a taste for shit amongst other little eccentricities.

The most obvious positive asset of *Pork* was that a lot of it was incredibly funny, but the real skill behind it lay in the fact that it made its group of weirdies so believable. The play was edited by the director, Anthony Ingrassia, from two hundred hours of the original by Andy Warhol, whose intention was simply to make a play out of the lives of the people around him in New York whom he personally found interesting. The programme quoted him as saying: 'I still care for people but it would be so much easier not to care . . . it's too hard to care . . . I don't want to get too involved in other people's lives', and the central character in the play, a flaxen-haired movie-maker called B. Marlow clearly representing Warhol himself, coolly observed the strange people around him without appearing to be involved with any of them. This character held the play together, acting as the vital catalyst that made the hang-ups of a group of New York weirdies into an entertainment. But Warhol is no crusader; in his play he was not trying to expose hidden truths or strike a blow against puritan morality, but simply to observe with cool curiosity and dry humour, and to communicate his observations to the audience. They, in turn, were free to see parallels in the play with real life as they knew it or to treat the whole evening's events as fantasy to be appreciated or rejected out of hand.

Sex plays a large part in the activities of *Pork*, presumably because sex plays a large part in the lives of the people depicted, just as it plays a large part in the lives of just about everyone who is *not* depicted. The question that presents itself is whether the sexual realism of the play is justified by its context or whether it is merely exploitation; whether in fact it is erotic theatre or pornographic display. The author put this to the director, Anthony Ingrassia: '*Pork* is definitely erotic, that is it connects you physically, makes your mouth go dry, makes you quiver. It does this by word and gesture as well as by visuals. It is not pornographic, for pornography is merely visual, unamusing, in the long run boring, in fact just a demonstration of sex. Eroticism connects sexually and concerns the human condition. People don't have many erotic experiences in everyday life, and the theatre can and should give them some through plays like *Pork*. Nudity has its natural place in erotic theatre, and if it offends you, that's your hang-up, not the author's or the director's. People perform sexual acts of a wide variety in their private lives, but if those same acts are performed on the stage, there's an outcry. It's absurd to think that people need protecting from sex.'[30] Does he foresee the advent of real sex on the theatrical stage? 'If you can kiss on stage why shouldn't you fuck? It will be difficult, but it will happen. But it must be relevant, it must illuminate a relationship, otherwise it will merely cater to the tired businessman in search of a thrill, and that's not what people like me are here for: that would be a sad day for the theatre, a real sell-out, and some people seem to be moving in that direction in search of a means to make the theatre more popular. The answer is not censorship but the education of society. People must develop as people not as animals. What I object to is the wrong use of nudity. I saw *Othello* at the Mermaid Theatre recently, with a nude Desdemona. Why shouldn't she be nude in her own bedroom? But the actress was ugly and her body tan showed the clear outlines of her bikini. She should have stayed clothed, or else they should have given Ann-Margaret the part. And then your film censor refuses to pass Warhol's *Trash*, saying he doesn't mind the nudity but he can't allow the drugs, when in fact the film can only turn people off drugs. A bit of sense is needed.'

Finally, why was *Pork* not a success in London? 'England is not a sexual country. Anything sexual upsets English people. You're still wondering why there should be any need for nudity in the theatre. You don't try to come to terms with your sexual motivations. *Pork* is about the connection between food and sex, drink and sex, talk and sex, fantasy and sex; nobody noticed. Everyone was so hung-up on the fact that it was about sex at all that they ignored the fact that it was a serious artistic play. It was a mistake to publicize it as a sex show, and the press comments did immense harm, especially the *News of the World* article by a journalist who was nice and friendly to everyone and then made us all out to be sex-fiends. In fact, *Pork* is a good slice of erotic theatre.'

Better written than *Pork* and a more serious piece of theatre, Peter Shaffer's *Equus*, presented by the National Theatre Company at the London Old Vic in 1974, also tackled a sexual taboo: bestiality. The seventeen-year-old hero has been sent to an asylum for having blinded six horses. The play slowly uncovers his motivations: he has been able to find real sexual fulfilment only when riding horses while naked, and when a girl tries to seduce him in the stable, he finds he is impotent: hence his horrible revenge on his beloved horses. The importance of the play lies in the dilemma recognised by the boy's psychiatrist: society insists he should seek to replace the boy's totally fulfilling if unconventional sexual fixation with the prosaic and short-lasting thrill of a normal marital relationship. The nudity of the seduction scene and the very explicit orgasm on horseback are fine examples of the intelligent use of the theatre's new freedom.

An attempt has been made in the present chapter to differentiate between the theatre of celebration and the theatre of exploitation: clearly *Equus* belongs to the former category, and the same can be said of a very different production, *Let My People Come*. This sexual revue which opened in New York early in 1974 and in London later in the year featured songs and sketches by Earl Wilson Junior on topics such as homosexuality, lesbianism, fellatio, and cunnilingus. It included extensive nudity and explicit language, together with a lot of humour and some very good songs. The music was in fact better than that in *Oh! Calcutta!*, and the whole tone of the show was more joyous and less sophisticated than its forerunner. While hardly great theatre, it was certainly good adult entertainment. In their totally different ways, both *Equus* and *Let My People Come* are concerned with celebration.

It has been the purpose of this argument to show, through discussions of certain plays and conversations with people concerned, that the removal of censorship

[343]

of the theatre has facilitated the open and exciting celebration of sex in a way that does not depend on exploitation: a process described as 'the revolution of the flesh'. This exhilarating liberation of the stage is part of a general movement towards an exploration of sexual motivations and a new maturity in the understanding of the difference between pornography and eroticism, between masturbatory and celebratory sex.

Appendix I

Aretino, Giulio, Marcantonio and The Sonnets

Pietro Aretino was one of the most notorious of all Italian writers of the sixteenth century, and his reputation has lasted well. As a recent commentator has put it: 'like some Italian Falstaff, he lied, cheated, drank and whored his way through 64 years of his country's history'.[1] In the world of erotic literature, Aretino was undisputed master of his time. As an exile in Venice, he wrote lives of the saints and penitential psalms at the same time as highly obscene dialogues, reflecting the variety of life in a city whose prostitutes were only rivalled by those of mid-Victorian London. He enjoyed fame throughout Europe, and amongst his benefactors were King Henry VIII of England, King Francis I of France, and Pope Julius III. He was most famous for his *Ragionamenti* (or *Discussions*), which were published in Venice between 1534 and 1536 and recorded a dialogue between Nanna (a prostitute) and Antonia about the future of Nanna's daughter, Pippa. The prostitute describes the sexual behaviour of nuns, married women, and courtesans, in language which is honest and obscene, as one would expect from Aretino. Nanna says at one point, 'I shall say *fucking* and not *indulging the passions* . . . for no other reason than because people speak so in my place.'[2] The book is distinguishable from straightforward pornography by the author's witty observations of contemporary life and the sharp satire which must have related to real people of his day. Antonia's cynical advice at the end of the dialogue is: 'thou shouldst make a whore of thy Pippa, since the nun betrays her vows and the married woman violates the sacrament of matrimony; the whore at least dishonours neither Monastery nor Husband: she does as the soldier, who is paid to ravage all.'[3]

Aretino's life reflected the variety of his writings, and he is characteristically represented in Titian's portrait which shows him as a redoubtable figure in doublet and cloak, with a tall forehead and black, penetrating eyes, set against a full beard and a shock of dark hair. Pope Julius III made him a knight of St Peter and first magistrate of Arezzo, and he narrowly missed being made a cardinal. And yet scandal was never far away. In 1525 he was almost killed in a street brawl by an assassin who objected to an Aretino sonnet that poked fun at his mistress. Rumour put it about that he used his literary earnings to ensure for himself a plentiful supply of boys as well as women. It is known that he had at least one illegitimate child. The unproven account of his death in October 1556 suggests an attack of apoplexy caused by a fit of laughter at an obscene joke about his own sister.

The fame of Pietro Aretino was especially well established in England. In 1802, a fictitious book entitled *The Amours of Peter Aretin* earned its author James Aitkin a six-months' jail sentence as a result of a prosecution brought by the Society for the Suppression of Vice. In 1827, George Cannon published *The Accomplished Whore* as being by Aretino, although the original Italian text had no connection with him. As early as 1658, an English adaptation of the *Ragionamenti* had been published as *The Crafty Whore, or The Misery and Iniquity of Bawdy Houses laid open*, but the most enterprising piracy of Aretino was an attempt by the students of All Souls College, Oxford, in 1674 to print their own secret edition of his *Postures* or *Sonnets* by using the University press at night. Unhappily, the enterprise was thwarted by an unexpected visit from the Dean. Ben Jonson mentions the *Postures* in his play *The Alchemist*, and the Earl of Rochester's notorious *Farce of Sodom* (*c.* 1680) is set in an 'Antichamber hung round with Aretino's *Postures*'. Further proof of the fame of this book in England is found in an anonymous anti-feminist satire of 1722, *Whipping Tom; or a Rod for a Proud Lady*, whose author complained of the vogue among women for snuff-boxes 'painted with more obscene and lascivious Pieces than can be shewn in Aretino's *Postures*'.

The *Sonnets* or *Postures* of Aretino is one of the most widely discussed and yet least known of all works of erotic art. Everyone has heard of it, yet no complete copy is known to exist. The original title was *Sonetti lussuriosi di Pietro Aretino*, and it was probably first published in Venice in 1527. It consisted of sixteen (later commentators suggested twenty) engravings of copulating couples by Marcantonio Raimondi, each accompanied by a sexually explicit poem in the form of a sonnet by Aretino. Marcantonio had published his series of engravings in Rome in 1523, basing them on drawings by Raphael's greatest pupil, Giulio Romano. Aretino wrote later that Giulio drew 'sixteen erotic postures showing the various manners, attitudes and postures in which lewd men have intercourse with lewd women'[4] on a wall in the Vatican because Pope Clement VII was unpunctual with payments. The room is now the Sala di Costantino, and it must be assumed if Aretino is correct, that Giulio later covered the drawings with his frescoes relating to the Emperor Constantine. It is, however, more likely that Giulio had merely drawn a set of Love Stories of the Gods, which have long since disappeared. Such sets of mythological erotica were common in sixteenth-century Italy. Meanwhile, Marcantonio had seen Giulio's drawings and had decided to engrave them. He is known to have had a great interest in erotic subjects, as any major Print Room can demonstrate. A comparatively recent discovery of an etching by Marcantonio, now in the Stockholm Print Room, shows a nude woman standing in a landscape enjoying herself with an early type of dildo.[5] The prints after Giulio were published in 1523 in Rome, and caused an immediate scandal.[6] Cardinal Giberti had Marcantonio thrown into prison and made strong attempts to destroy the plates and all copies of the prints. Giulio meanwhile fled to Mantua to work for Federico Gonzaga II, and in the Palazzo del Te he later created two of the most famous of all erotic paintings, the frescoes showing *Jupiter as a sea serpent revealing himself to Olympia* (see illustration 79) and *Parsiphae concealing herself in the statue of a cow made by Daedalus, in order to receive the love of the bull.*[7]

[346]

Pietro Aretino was in Rome in the early 1520s, and he much admired Marcantonio's engravings of the *Postures*. In the letter quoted above, which was written later in Venice, he claimed he had been responsible for arranging Marcantonio's release from prison, although this was untrue. He went on to say: 'When I saw the prints I was touched by the same inspiration which moved Giulio Romano to draw them.' He therefore decided to improvise sonnets to illustrate each of the sixteen (or twenty) prints, as a gesture against the hypocrisy that had caused Marcantonio's imprisonment. 'I disassociate myself from the bad judgement and piggish custom which forbids the eyes to see what gives them most pleasure. What harm is there to see a man on top of a woman? Must animals have more freedom than we?' So Aretino published his sonnets, printed beneath the designs of Marcantonio after Giulio, although it is not known whether he was able to obtain original plates which had escaped Cardinal Giberti or merely had copies made, or even perhaps commissioned a further set of prints from Marcantonio, since no copy of either the edition of 1523 or the original Aretino volume is now known.

Aretino's sonnets caused a storm of controversy when they were published in about 1527, and this is clearly reflected in the factually inaccurate account by the artist and historian Giorgio Vasari written in 1550: 'Giulio Romano next employed Marcantonio to engrave twenty plates of figures, the character of which was highly offensive; and what was worse still, Messer Pietro Aretino wrote a most indecent sonnet for each, insomuch that I do not know which was the most revolting, the spectacle presented to the eye by the designs of Giulio or the affront offered to the ear by the words of the Aretine.'[8] Since Vasari's day, little effort seems to have been made to ascertain the truth about the *Postures*, although a spirited defence of them was published by Lodovice Dolce in 1557.[9] In his standard work on Marcantonio published in Paris in 1887, Delaborde dated the engravings 1524 and discussed at length whether there were originally sixteen or twenty; he added: 'It is lucky for Marcantonio that these witnesses to his immorality no longer exist.' The most recent authority on Giulio Romano, Frederick Hartt, mentions *The Twenty Poses*: 'the tale of the pornographic engravings is universally known, at least in Vasari's pious version. . . . The twenty sonnets of Aretino were engraved by Marcantonio.' He goes on to refer to their 'special emphasis on abnormal and spectacular attitudes, on acute physical strain, and on frustration',[10] which suggests he had little or no first-hand knowledge of the prints.

The sonnets were soon published in other editions and other languages, often with spurious poems added and with new illustrations; at the same time, many campaigns were mounted, especially under the Inquisition, to destroy copies of the work. In his *Essai de Bibliographie Aretinesque* (1909), Guillaume Apollinaire listed editions originating in Venice, 1556; Paris, 1757; Venice, 1779; Rome, 1792; Leiden, 1864; Brussels, 1865; Paris, 1882; and Berlin, 1904; and by the last French edition there were no less than thirty poems.[11] Apollinaire was trying to separate fact from fiction, and in this he was following the pioneering examples of Christopher von Murr, who had published an article on Aretino's volume in 1785,[12] and L. J.

Hubaud, who had attempted a bibliography in 1857.[13] The first known translation into English appeared in the 1920s; the introduction made a fanciful attribution: 'So far as the knowledge of the compiler of this work goes, Oscar Wilde made the only English translation known, the one contained herein.'[14] The literary standard is far below that of Wilde, and although the translation appears to be reasonably accurate, it does not manage to reproduce the vulgarity of the brothel world which characterises Aretino's flavour of sensuality:

Sonnet Number Four

Place your leg, dearest, on my shoulder here,
And take my truncheon in your tender grasp,
And while I gently move it, let your clasp
Tighten and draw me to your bosom dear.

And should I stray from front to hinder side,
Call me a rogue and villain, will not you?
Because I know the difference 'twixt the two,
As stallions know how lusty mares to ride.

My hand shall keep the turgid dart in place,
Lest it might slip and somehow get away,
And I should see a frown on your fair face.

Backsided joys enchant but one, they say,
But surely this both you and me doth grace,
So let us spend and quickly, too, I pray.

And I'll be loth to leave a sport so gay,
Dear one, for such a valiant lance
Was ne'er possessed by any King of France.[15]

Another English translation appears in *Works of Aretino* by Samuel Putnam, published in Chicago in 1926. The author declares his position by pointing out that a literal translation is undesirable as it would be pornographic. His version is better poetry than the earlier translation, but completely misses the spirit of the original.[16]

In spite of the fact that no copies of the editions of 1523 or 1527 are known, we can still form a good idea of what inspired the famous volume of Aretino because we have some good clues. These include: a set of nine etched fragments in the British Museum;[17] one complete etching, also in the British Museum,[18] and an identical one in the Vienna Print Room; an early edition of the sonnets in the collection of Mr Walter Toscanini of New York; a set of twenty wash drawings in the British

Museum, and an almost identical set in the Bibliothèque Nationale, Paris.[19]

The nine fragments (see illustration 244) are almost certainly the remains of an original set of the Marcantonio prints, either from the 1523 edition or from Aretino's edition of *c*. 1527. The fragments are postage-stamp size, except for two slightly larger ones which are shaped like cameos. All show heads of various figures, with occasional glimpses of naked shoulders. They are all clearly the results of an attempt to make polite a set of indecent pictures; they are the sad proof of a prejudiced mind. In spite of this, they denote a powerful and creative hand which relates them stylistically to Marcantonio. How they came to be mutilated is a matter for conjecture. However, a clue is to be found in a letter written by the French collector Mariette to his agent in Italy in May 1756: 'I am very obliged to you for your researches relating to the "free" prints by Marcantonio. They must be exceedingly rare. I will have to be content with what I have received from you: fragments which I must regard as the only surviving examples. They are the more precious to me in that I can display them without blushing or making others blush, since they have been reduced to only the heads.'[20] The British Museum acquired its fragments from the collection of Sir

244 Marcantonio Raimondi (after Giulio Romano), fragments of *Postures*, 1523

Thomas Lawrence in 1830: in the catalogue of the sale, they are described as being from Mariette's collection. A letter written by Monsieur Joly, Keeper of the Paris Print Room, on 14 December, 1775, is of great interest in this connection; he is discussing the sale of Mariette's collection: 'You know of course that M. Mariette was the only person in the world who owned vestiges of those dirty subjects which caused so much trouble for the engraver, the painter and the poet.'[21]

There is, however, another story in a lithographed French manuscript (one copy in the British Museum, another in the Bibliothèque Nationale) written in the nineteenth century by someone who clearly had knowledge of the fragments. This quotes the catalogue of the Mariette sale in Paris in 1775: 'Item 38, suite of the Loves of the gods in twenty pieces, extraordinarily rare', and goes on to say that the French sculptor Gérard found eleven prints being used by his grocer as wrapping paper during the early nineteenth century, which he recognised as being Marcantonio's *Postures* presumably from the Mariette sale. They were eventually sold to an English Duke, and were burnt after his death. This author also wrote that the British Museum's fragments were obtained from a Mr Willett. The catalogue of the Mariette Sale also lists at Item 39: 'Ten other little pieces of the same sort also rare.' It is known that many prints by Marcantonio were bought at the Mariette sale by an English collector, Ralph Willett; nine fragments by the same artist appear in the

245   Marcantonio Raimondi (after Giulio Romano), plate from *Postures*, 1523

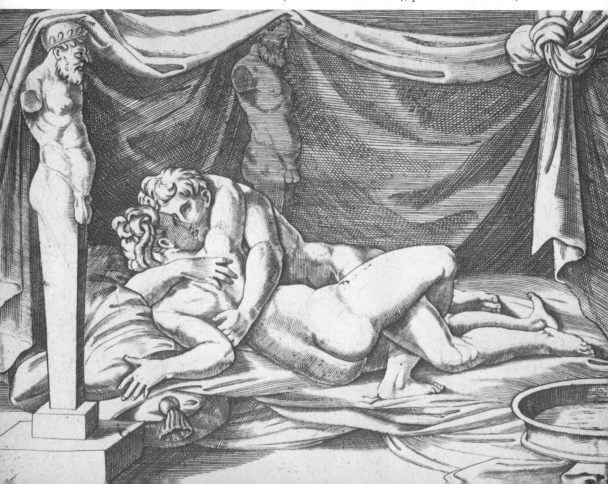

246 Friedrich von Waldeck (after Marcantonio Raimondi), Drawing No. 8 from
Postures, *c.* 1858

catalogue of the Willett sale in Paris in 1812. These presumably found their way to
the Lawrence collection and then to the British Museum.[22]

The two versions of the one surviving complete engraving show a nude couple
engaged in intercourse on a bed (see illustration 245). The scale is identical to that of
the fragments, and on stylistic grounds they would certainly seem to be by the same
artist. Their provenances are not known, but there are records of erotic prints very
like them in the Wellesley collection of Oxford which was sold at Sotheby's in 1858.
Adam Bartsch, the famous keeper of the Albertina Gallery in Vienna in the nineteenth
century, and author of the monumental *Peintre-Graveur* series of books, wrote of
'the loves of a god and a goddess engraved by Marcantonio after Giulio Romano.
These prints are so excessively rare that one would doubt their existence without
Vasari's positive account. We are unable to give any indication as to what the prints
depicted; of the twenty items in the suite, we have only seen one' (*i.e.* the print in the
Vienna Print Room).[23]

The early edition of the *Sonnets* is ascribed by its owner to the late-1520s, and is
illustrated with woodcuts. Fourteen poems and illustrations are present; two (or six)
of each appear to be missing.[24] The faces and poses of the figures in these prints
correspond to those in the set of nine fragments and one is identical to the two single
prints. This would appear to be a very early reprint of Aretino's original volume,
illustrated with very crude woodcuts executed after Marcantonio's prints.

The two sets of twenty drawings are in pen and ink with grey watercolour wash
(see illustration 246). They are almost certainly copies made by Baron Frédéric de

[351]

Waldeck (or Count Friedrich von Waldeck) in the nineteenth century. The British Museum acquired their set from Messrs Colnaghi of London in 1868 and no further provenance is known. The drawings are identical in scale to the fragments and the two complete prints, and these latter correspond to the drawing numbered *one*. Ten of the drawings are identical to the woodcut illustrations to the early edition; one of the other ten is only the same in respect of one area that corresponds to one of the fragments, the rest of the design being altered. This would suggest that their author knew ten of Marcantonio's original prints and also knew the fragments. The British Museum possesses a sheet of mounted photographs of wash drawings in the same style as their set of twenty, but which are copies of the fragments (see illustration 247). The nineteenth-century French manuscript in the Museum's collection, which is referred to above, makes it clear that its author knew of the fragments; it also goes on to describe how 'a picture lover' found a complete set of twenty prints by Marcantonio after Giulio in a convent in Mexico on 31 January, 1831.

All evidence points to Waldeck as being the author of both the twenty drawings and the manuscript. Baron Frédéric de Waldeck was born in Prague in 1766 and died in Paris at the age of one hundred and nine in 1875.[25] He appears to have been a born adventurer. After studying painting and drawing under Vien and Prudhon in

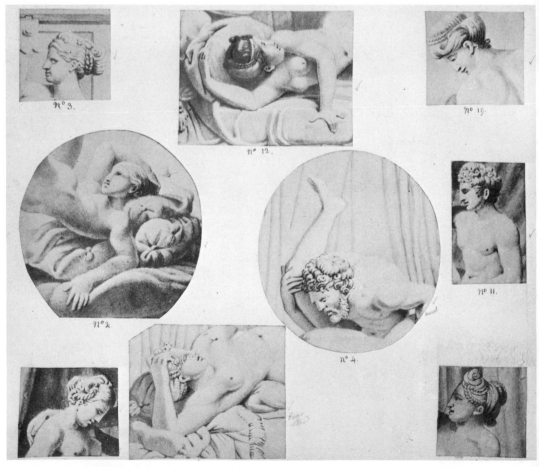

247   Friedrich von Waldeck (after Marcantonio Raimondi), fragments from
       Postures, c. 1858

248 Friedrich von Waldeck (after Marcantonio Raimondi), Drawing No. 4 from
Postures, c. 1858

Paris, he sailed round the world, being alternately soldier, camp-follower, and
pirate. In 1822 in London he was commissioned to execute lithographs for a book
on Mexico; he travelled there and spent the next twelve years as an engineer in a
silver mine. He claimed to have found a set of prints by Marcantonio Raimondi after
Giulio Romano in a convent in Mexico City, which he was allowed to copy. Back in
Paris in 1858, he produced a pamphlet about his discovery; it is reasonable to assume
that this is the lithographed manuscript of which the British Museum and the
Bibliothèque Nationale possess copies. Further, it is reasonable to assume also that
Waldeck was the author of the two sets of twenty drawings in the same collections,
which he executed partly as copies of originals he saw in Mexico, partly as copies
of the prints which the sculptor Gérard had found in Paris, and partly as imaginative
reconstructions based on the fragments which he saw at some time in Paris or London
and also copied. His manuscript ends by referring to 'the present suite of drawings
made from Raimondi's original compositions', which is destined for national
collections and is in a very small edition at a high price, in order to put it out of the
reach of the public and 'vicious idlers'.

All the evidence we have suggests that the original drawings by Giulio must have
been extraordinarily powerful, and indeed his nudes in the Vatican and at the

[353]

Palazzo del Te in Mantua would confirm the likelihood that this was so. His was a strong and highly personal style of drawing, and it must be counted a major loss that these erotic works were destroyed or otherwise lost. Marcantonio's talent was of a very high order too, for he was more than merely a copyist. His print of *The Judgement of Paris* after Raphael (see illustration 78) is one of the finest examples of high-Renaissance engraving. What remains of his interpretations of the Giulio originals makes it clear that these, too, are a sad loss. Louis Dunand in his interesting pamphlet on sixteenth-century Italian erotic engravings calls the prints 'true masterpieces',[26] and even Delaborde, who so strongly objected to the immorality of the prints, was forced to admit that they had a dignity and majesty which put them among Raimondi's finest works.[27]

The Waldeck drawings are a disappointment when we can imagine what the works by Giulio and Marcantonio must have been like. All the dynamic power is gone. The erotic scenes have been translated into an impersonal and rather anaemic Neo-classical style which owes too much to Prudhon and Vien. But they certainly have a documentary value, for they constitute an important part of the missing link in this complicated story. For instance, drawing number four (see illustration 248) shows that the two large oval fragments in the British Museum were originally part of the same print, and that the portion cut away from the lower half of one oval was the woman's hand grasping the man's erect penis. This drawing also demonstrates clearly that the original design was the inspiration for Aretino's Sonnet Number Four, quoted above, which begins:

> *Place your leg, dearest, on my shoulder here,*
> *And take my truncheon in your tender grasp.*

Some of the pieces of the puzzle are missing and others do not fit too well, but nevertheless the Aretino–Giulio–Marcantonio collaboration can still be seen to have produced one of the most powerful and intriguing works of Western erotic art, a work in the genre usually confined to the Oriental world.

Appendix II

The Restricted Collections of the British Museum and the Victoria and Albert Museum

Throughout the present work, reference has been made to works of art or literature which are kept in the Restricted Collections of the British Museum and the Victoria and Albert Museum. It will perhaps be instructive to enlarge upon these mysterious collections. The fact of the matter is that London possesses the finest all-round collection of erotica in the world, a fact that is to be explained by both historical and social factors.

Of course, restricted collections are not the prerogative of England's capital, even though Victorian prudery is responsible for ours remaining unseen by the general public. In Paris, both the Louvre and the Bibliothèque Nationale possess items which are not considered suitable for public exhibition, ranging from Greek pottery and European prints and drawings to a fine collection of explicitly sexual literature. The Vatican in Rome is said to have a private museum of sexual art and literature; little information is given on the subject, although it is certain that the Vatican Palace contains a bathroom decorated in an erotic manner by Raphael and his assistants (see Chapter 4 a). The National Museum at Naples has a 'secret cabinet' in which are kept sexual objects and paintings found at Pompeii and items from the collection of Sir William Hamilton, British Ambassador in the eighteenth century (see Chapter 2 b).[1] The Museo Nacional at Mexico City has a 'salon segreto' which contains sexual images from Pre-Columbian Mexico (see Chapter 2 a). In America, the Library of Congress in Washington has a large collection of sexual literature, and the Institute for Sex Research at Bloomington, Indiana, has for some years been gathering art objects of a sexual nature and literature relevant to a study of eroticism and pornography. Some of these collections are richer in one specialised area than London, but none can match the scope and quality of the erotic material in the London museums.

The Victoria and Albert Museum has one of the world's finest art libraries, and most items can be obtained without even applying for a ticket. Special application to the Keeper is necessary to consult certain books, among them an almost complete set of Eduard Fuchs's studies in erotic art, the very rare pioneering enterprise of the early years of this century: the library has twelve of the thirteen volumes (see Chapter 4 a).[2] But the rarest items in the library are probably manuscripts relating to the notorious John Wilmot, 2nd Earl of Rochester, courtier, soldier, playwright, poet, and rake. These are two volumes entitled *The Earle of Rochester's Verses, for which he was Banished*,[3] and they include many fine examples of bawdy Restoration poems such as 'A Description of Maidenhead' and 'One Writing Against His Prick'. One poem is dedicated to the licentious King Charles II:

> *In the Isle of Britain, long since famous grown*
> *For breeding the best Cunts in Christendome,*
> *There now do's live, ah! let him long survive,*
> *The easiest King, and best bred Man alive. . . .*
> *Peace is his aim, his gentlenesse is such,*
> *And Love, he loves, for he loves Fucking much,*
> *Nor are his high desires above his strength;*
> *His Scepter and his Prick are of a length*
> *And she that plays with one, may play with tother*
> *And make him little wiser than his Brother. . . .*

Rochester's famous play *The Farce of Sodom* is also included, this being one of the very few manuscripts of it known (others are in the British Museum[4] and Hamburg Library). Rochester was frequently banished from court because of his bawdy lampoons, but always recalled by Charles who missed his wit and charm. *The Farce of Sodom* was acted before the King, and is one of the wittiest and best-written pieces of bawdy in the English language. It is in fact a satire on court life, and the characters include King Boloximian of Sodom, his Queen Cuntigratia, and their children Prince Prickett and Princess Swivia, as well as Pockenello, Pimp, Catamite and Favourite to ye King, Borastus, Buggermaster Generall, and Buggeranthus, Generall of the Army. The King believes that sexual pleasure is all that matters:

> *My laws shall act more pleasure than command,*
> *And with my Prick I'll govern all the Land. . . .*
> *Henceforth, Borastus, set the Nation free.*
> *Let conscience have its force of Liberty.*
> *I do proclaim that Buggery may be used*
> *O're all the land, so Cunt be not abus'd.*

His new-found delight in sodomy is catered for by Pockenello and Borastus, but his wife feels neglected and so finds solace with Buggeranthus, while their children spend their time in bed together. The play ends with the Queen having died of a surfeit of sex and dildoes, the Prince with syphilis, the Princess out of her mind, and the King—leaning on his faithful Pockenello—shouting defiance to any army of fiery demons:

> *Let Heavens descend, set the World on fire,*
> *We to some darker caverne will retyre,*
> *There, on thy Bugger'd Arse I will expire.*

The Indian Department at the Victoria and Albert Museum does not differentiate between erotic and non-erotic art, and so all items in their collection are freely available on application. These include a variety of drawings and sculptures of a sexual nature. One late-eighteenth-century scene of intercourse from Nepal (see Chapter 3 b) is on permanent exhibition,[5] and its popularity is attested by the heavily worn floor in front of it. Erotic prints from Japan are not, however, available. They are kept in the Restricted Collection of the Print Room. The museum owns well over a hundred *shunga*, including fine examples by Shuncho, Haronobu, and Kiyonaga, and a set of the famous *Uta-Makura* by Utamaro of 1788 (see Chapter 3 e).[6] The Print Room also has erotic works by such artists as Rowlandson, Fuseli, and Eric Gill, none of them appearing in the catalogue. There are fifty prints by Rowlandson (see Chapter 4 b) including all the best examples[7] making this at least the equal of any collection of Rowlandson erotica in the world. There is a very intriguing drawing by Fuseli (see Chapter 4 b) which holds an important place in his work,[8] together with similarly erotic drawings by his associates, Von Holst and Wainewright.[9] There are also eleven engravings by Eric Gill in a folder marked 'Gill engravings withdrawn from main collection—safe E'.[10] The Japanese prints and works by Rowlandson and Fuseli are kept in the same safe, E perhaps standing for erotic. The Gill engravings (see Chapter 6 a) show couples in intercourse, some with the hand of God giving the sign of blessing above them.

Rowlandson and Gill are also represented in the Restricted Collection of the Print Room at the British Museum. This houses one of the finest collections of erotic drawings and engravings in the world, although they are almost completely unknown to anyone other than museum staff, hidden away as they are in the Sheepshanks Cabinet. This is an enormous cupboard in the Assistant Keeper's office which contains, as well as the erotic works, such priceless objects as Dürer's woodblocks for the *Little Passion* series, etched plates by Turner and Sickert, and also Blake's woodblocks for *Thornton's Virgil* and copperplates for *The Book of Job*. With them are Rowlandson's eight etched copperplates for his notorious series entitled *Pretty Little Games for Ladies and Gentlemen* (discussed in Chapter 4 b). The prints themselves are there, together with many other erotic works by Rowlandson, including copies of Rubens, Titian, Boucher, and Francesco Albano.

There are also two albums of very detailed sexual drawings by Eric Gill labelled *Studies of Parts*. One, showing a clothed man mounting a nude girl, is on the back of an advertisement for a book on trains. An inscription explains that the artist observed the couple in Hyde Park on 14 May, 1925, at 10 p.m.: 'he looked like a student or journalist, she like a girl in business.' There are ten drawings of nude women with their legs apart and thirty of couples in intercourse, often with inscriptions of a religious nature (see Chapter 6 a). But the vast majority of these drawings are of penises or of nude males. There is a note from the artist (dated 23 October, 1940) suggesting that these drawings be given after his death to the Royal College of Surgeons: 'In my opinion anatomy books are not well illustrated in respect of the male organ,' but also a note from the College (dated November 1948) declining the offer 'as the drawings are not showing any pathological conditions'. In many of these depictions, the penis is shown both flaccid and erect, with carefully noted measurements: most show the artist himself, either glimpsed masturbating in a mirror, or having traced his penis on a table-top, or reclining on a bed, showing the body from the chest to the feet. They offer a fascinating view of the artist's most private world.

Some of the finest and most valuable of the items in the Sheepshanks Cabinet are Italian sixteenth-century engravings by or after Raphael, Giulio Romano, Carracci, Parmigianino, Jacopo di Barbari, Enea Vico, etc. (These are discussed in Chapter 4 a.) Many are the very rare first state of a print usually known only in later altered states. Especially interesting is the print by Marcantonio Raimondi after Giulio Romano of a couple in intercourse, which is one of the only remaining Aretino illustrations; this, and the fragments of others in the series and the set of nineteenth-century copies by Waldeck all preserved in the Sheepshanks Cabinet are discussed at length in Appendix I. Other rarities in this collection include the eighteenth-century French *Histoire Universelle* with its watercolour illustrations of erotic scenes from mythology, history, and the Bible (see illustration 99); a series of prints by Rops; Zichy's lithographs entitled *A Cycle of Love* (see illustration 129); and erotic prints by Beardsley and Von Bayros (all of these mentioned in Chapter 4); also the fifteen illustrations to Lucian's *Dialogues* by Gustav Klimt (see illustration 166 and Chapter 6 a).[11] These last were published in 1907, and, together with five other volumes of modern German prints, were sent to the British Museum by the Director of Public Prosecutions in March 1923. Among the most intriguing of all items in the collection are the erotic drawings by Turner which Ruskin failed to find and destroy. At least eight of Turner's sketchbooks contain drawings of a sexual nature; and one of my greatest finds was one large separate folded sheet which has two very explicit ink and chalk drawings on one side and one on the back. One drawing[12] (see illustration 114) is very carefully executed, with wash added for the highlights on the bodies of the nude man and the nude woman whose clitoris he is playing with (see Chapter 4 b).

The British Museum has many Oriental erotic books, albums, and prints. The finest Japanese *shunga* albums are kept locked away in the Department of Oriental Antiquities; until I asked to see them, they were uncatalogued and unexamined. The rich collection includes examples by the earlier artists, Kiyonobu and Harunobu, as well as Kuniyoshi and Hiroshige from the nineteenth century, and highlights include three albums by the great Utamaro, one being the *Poem of the Pillow*, and Hokusai's famous *The dream of the fisherman's wife* (see illustration 65 and Chapter 3 e). The Department of Oriental Manuscripts keeps its erotic drawings, watercolours, and related books in a special restricted cupboard.[13] The Chinese and Japanese albums are not of the highest quality, and date mostly from the nineteenth century. Among the books are items from Ashbee's famous collection, including editions of the *Kama Sutra, Ananga Runga, Kama Shastra*, and *Perfumed Garden* (see Chapter 3), side by side with such recent studies on oriental erotic art as Van Gulik's *Sexual Life in Ancient China*[14] and *Erotic Colour Prints of the Ming Period*[15], *Erotologie de la Chine*, by Woo Chan Cheng[16] and Robert Surieu's *Sarv e Naz, an essay on love and the representation of erotic themes in Ancient Iran.*[17]

The *Annual Returns of the British Museum* for 1865–66 mention on page 14 the receipt of 'a collection of antiquities illustrating what the donor has termed *Primitive Worship*'. The donor was George Witt, F.R.S., and his collection has proved something of an embarrassment ever since. The *Annual Returns* for the following year state on page 26 that a room has been provided in the basement for the Witt Collection of 432 specimens plus 431 items already in the Museum 'illustrating superstitions connected with the evil eye and nature worship'. This basement room contained a large collection of erotic objects from all over the world, coming from the Payne Knight, Townley, Hamilton and Morel bequests as well as the Witt items, but of course it was not easily accessible. One visitor was Henry Spencer Ashbee, the erotic bibliographer, whose collection of books was later to cause an even greater embarrassment. Ashbee wrote in 1877: 'The objects left to the nation by Knight and Witt now form one collection, which to the shame of the British Museum authorities, is consigned to a dark room in the basement, difficult of access, and where the interesting specimens it comprises can be inspected only under the greatest disadvantages.'[18] If Ashbee were alive today he would have more reason to complain, for by 1912 the basement museum of erotica was no more and from that date its items have been dispersed to locked cupboards in various of the Museum's other departments.

Any conception of what the visitor to that museum of erotica would have seen is difficult to form since many of its items have mysteriously disappeared. The items themselves do not appear in the published Museum catalogues, and those that remain are practically unknown even to the Museum staff. The residue of the collection is in a large cupboard in the Department of Medieval and Later Antiquities, together with a leather-bound manuscript catalogue dating from the 1870s, with some later additions. My efforts to locate items mentioned in the original catalogue were made with the fullest co-operation of the staff of the various departments concerned, and it was certainly not their fault that my searches were not always successful. The catalogue is a most carefully prepared document, complete with tiny drawings of certain of the items, and the occasional fascinating footnote. Under numbers W432–4, three bronze phallic objects, the compiler has written that these came to the Museum with a note dated 7 July 1902 in a female hand which said: 'If these Phallae (which are genuine) can find no place in the Museum, the sender hopes that if there is anyone in the Bronze Department who would care to have them, he will keep them for his own private collection, should they be worthy. One word of acknowledgement in either the *Daily Telegraph* or *Daily Mail* to Ariadne would gratify the sender greatly.'

Many of the items listed in the catalogue are now in the Museum Secretum of the Greek and Roman Department (see Chapter 2 b). These include Greek vases and amphora decorated with erotic scenes; one, which has recently been restored, depicts a seilenos balancing a bowl on the end of his erect penis (see illustration 33), whereas previously, thanks to Victorian prudery, the bowl seemed to float in mid-air, as photographs show. With the pottery are a large number of small phallic amulets of various types from the ruins of Pompeii, ithyphallic figurines of Priapus or Hermes, lamps shaped like phalluses, and also fragments of phalluses removed from statues as an alternative to fixing a fig-leaf. It is interesting to note that the catalogue also mentions a 'gilt penis, part of a Mummy of the Ptolemaic period'. Apart from Greece, Rome and Egypt, other countries and cultures represented in the catalogue include Peru (erotic drinking-vessels), Australia (erotic carvings), Easter Island (wooden figure), Yucatan (gold bas-relief) and Africa (erotic lamps): all these items are now kept in the Ethnographical Department.

There are many curiosities among the items kept in the Department of Medieval and Later Antiquities, including an iron chastity belt, whose genuineness is open to question; a German medieval bottle in the form of a phallus; an Egyptian pottery figure of a dwarf with a giant phallus which passes round his neck; two diplomas awarded by the Beggars Benison Society, an eighteenth-century rake's club; various watches and snuff-boxes with erotic decorations; and two contraceptive sheaths made from animal membrane and dating from the late-eighteenth century, which could have been owned by Casanova himself. In terms of aesthetic value the outstanding object is a hitherto unrecorded terracotta sculpture of a satyr having intercourse with a goat,[19] a copy of a famous Roman sculpture, made by the English sculptor Joseph Nollekens in the 1760s (see illustration 42 and Chapter 2 b). All these are entered in the manuscript catalogue; among other entries which seem to have disappeared are a Roman lamp with a depiction of a crocodile having intercourse with a woman; a Chinese fan, which showed flowers when opened conventionally, and two figures making love when opened the opposite way; an elaborate Hindu shrine with a brass lingam surrounded by four figures and two elephants; plaited horsehair 'used by Patagonian women to excite the men putting it into their vagina'; and perhaps the most serious loss, a mediaeval full-length stone Shelah-na-Gig fertility figure from Ireland, which is reproduced in the second edition of Payne-Knight's *Discourse on the Worship of Priapus* (see Chapter 4 a).[20]

The Restricted Collection at the British Museum that is best known to the public is that held by the library, thanks mainly to Peter Fryer and his book entitled *Private Case—Public Scandal: Secrets of the British Museum Revealed*.[21] While researching for a book on birth-control, Mr Fryer applied in the library for Iwan Bloch's *Sexual Life in England Past and Present* (1938), but had to submit to an oral examination about his motives for wanting to consult the book before he was finally allowed to see it. Upon further enquiry, Mr Fryer discovered that the library possessed a large collection of books which, although they were listed in the general catalogue (like Bloch's) were only available to serious researchers. These were known as 'cupboard books'. Irritation became real concern when Mr Fryer made a further discovery: upon suggesting that the library acquire *The Slang of Venery* (Chicago, 1916), he was informed that a copy was already in the collection, but was in the category of books that were not listed in the general catalogue. These were known as 'private case books'. Mr Fryer was informed that on no account could he see the catalogue of these items; he could, however, inquire as to whether a certain book was in this category, and if it was, he could make a special application to see it. It might, however, be in a third category, 'suppressed books' or 'S.S.', in which case it could on no account be seen.

Mr Fryer's book on the library's secrets was published in 1966; since then about half of the private case books have been listed in the general catalogue and the rest will eventually be listed as well. It is still impossible to consult S.S. books, mainly books that have figured in libel actions, but private case books may be obtained by those with a long-period reader's ticket who have submitted in advance a letter from a professor or publisher certifying the seriousness and respectability of their intentions. It is still impossible to see the private case catalogue; it seems that the policy of the library is not merely to discourage 'frivolous' enquirers, but to make it as difficult as possible for anyone to consult those books which are considered 'problematical', that is, for the most part, books of a sexual nature.[22] And yet the British Museum Library has the finest collection of erotica in the world, far surpassing the Vatican, the Library of Congress, the Bodleian in Oxford, the Kinsey Institute at Bloomington, Indiana, and even the famous Enfer of the Bibliothèque Nationale in Paris. And all these libraries include their erotica in their main catalogues.

In the course of my research for this book, I applied for and obtained permission to see any book in the cupboard and private case collections. The only difficulty was to know what items to apply for, since my request to consult the private case catalogue met with a predictable refusal. Peter Fryer's book was valuable in giving titles of certain items, but he did not give their Museum pressmarks. However, an item in the private case entitled *Registrum Librorum Eroticorum* by 'Rolf S. Reade' (Alfred Rose, a London bookseller) gave pressmarks and titles for many of the books in the private case in the year of its publication, 1936.[23] I also made friends with a counter assistant, who kindly made time among her other duties to check whether items that interested me were in the private case catalogue, and also give me hints as to what other items that might interest me were listed. As a result of all my detective work I was actually able to sit at the special table under the eyes of the vigilant officials in the North Library and thumb my way through books denied to lesser mortals.

The impression of joining a select group is not only the result of the workings of the library's regulations. Connoisseurs of erotica have always tended to be 'top people', owing especially to the cost and the general difficulty in obtaining material. Famous collectors have included Francis I and Louis XV of France, the Duc d'Orléans, George IV, Lord Houghton, and more recently, the 27th Earl of Crawford and the 2nd Marquess of Milford Haven, not to mention a recently deceased member of the Royal Family. The private case includes books from more than one of these collections, and also material from Dr Simon Ward that came to light during the Profumo scandal. But the core of the collection is the bequest of Henry Spencer Ashbee, a rich businessman, who left 15,229 volumes of erotica and editions of *Don Quixote* to the Museum in 1900, the stipulation being that the

Cervantes items could not be taken without the more esoteric material.

Ashbee was the author of the famous erotic bibliographies published in the 1870s and '80s under the pseudonym, Pisanus Fraxi, and the author's annotated copies are in the private case, together with such other essential documents as Forberg's *Manual of Classical Erotology* (1887), the four volumes of the *Bilder-Lexicon* edited by Schidrowitz (Vienna and Leipzig, 1928–31), the numerous volumes of *Geschichte der erotischen Kunst* by Eduard Fuchs (Munich, 1912–26), and *Love's Picture Book* by Brusendorff and Henningsen (Copenhagen, 1959–62). Among other items are *My Life and Loves* by Frank Harris (1922); Casanova's *Autobiography* (1894) and Harris's *List of Covent Garden Ladies: or man of pleasure's Kalendar* for 1788–90 and 1793. Also included are the complete works of the Marquis de Sade and Restif de la Bretonne's *Anti-Justine* (1798); Andrea de Nerciat's *Le Diable au Corps* (1803); and Michel Millot's *L'Escole des Filles* (1655), the book which Pepys read 'for information' and then hastily burnt. Books in the private case which are discussed in Chapter 5 b of the present work include *Teleny or the Reverse of the Medal*, attributed to Oscar Wilde (1893); Walter's *My Secret Life* (c. 1890); *The Whippingham Papers*, to which Swinburne contributed (1888); and Aleister Crowley's *White Stains* (1898).[24] Among books recently transferred from the private case to the cupboard is *Fanny Hill: Memoirs of a Woman of Pleasure* by John Cleland (1749), perhaps the greatest classic of English erotica (see Chapter 7). It is, perhaps, not surprising that another book in the cupboard is Peter Fryer's *Private Case—Public Scandal*, although it would have been an inspired stroke of irony to have placed it in the private case. Among other items in the private case discussed elsewhere in the present work are Hancarville's three illustrated volumes on the sexual exploits of figures from Roman history and mythology (see Chapter 2 b); Aretino's *Sonnets* (Appendix I); and a collection of eighty catalogues and prospectuses relating to pornographic and erotic material mounted in an album presented by George Mountbatten, 2nd Marquess of Milford Haven (see Chapter 5 a).

The Museum Library cupboard includes many works by famous authors which are listed there owing to the frankness of their sexual imagery. Examples include John Donne's 'A Defense of Women for their Inconstancy' (c. 1600) and certain of his poems including 'Batter My Heart' and 'To His Mistress, Going to Bed'; and a volume of the poems of Robert Herrick entitled *Hesperides* (1648), which includes 'Upon the Nipples of Julia's Breast' and 'To Anthea'. In the private case is the notorious *Essay on Woman* by John Wilkes, MP, which was printed privately in 1763 for Sir Francis Dashwood's fraternity of Medmenham Abbey with its shrine dedicated to St Francis covered with indecent frescoes where orgies of the Hell-Fire Club took place. It was pirated and circulated by Wilkes's enemies in Parliament, where the philistine rake Lord Sandwich described it as 'a most scandalous, obscene and impious libel'. Many of Wilkes's opponents had recognised themselves as caricatured in the poem, and Wilkes was imprisoned for a year, but nevertheless he later became Lord Mayor of London. The poem is dedicated to Miss Fanny Murray, the famous courtesan, and opens:

Awake, my Fanny, leave all meaner things;
This morn shall prove what rapture swiving brings!
Let us (since life can little more supply
Then just a few good fucks and then we die)
Expatiate free o'er that loved scene of man,
A mighty maze, for mighty pricks to scan; . . .
Observe how Nature works, and if it rise
Too quick and rapid, check it ere it flies;
Spend when we must, but keep it while we can:
Thus godlike will be deem'd the ways of man.

The *Essay on Woman* is signed: Pego Borewell, Esq, and is in fact a very clever line-by-line parody of Alexander Pope's *Essay on Man*, complete with learned footnotes. The poem ends:

Heaven from all creatures hides the Book of Fate
All but the page prescribed, the present state . . .
Oh! blindness to the future, kindly given,
That each may enjoy what fucks are marked by Heaven,
Who sees with equal eye, as God of all,
The man just mounting, and the virgin's fall.
Prick, cunt, and bollocks in convulsions hurled,
And now a hymen burst, and now a world.
Hope humbly for clean girls; nor vainly soar;
But fuck the cunt at hand, and God adore.
What future fucks he gives not thee to know,
But gives that cunt to be thy blessing now.[25]

A volume of short works by Jonathan Swift, *Dean Swift's Medley*, has recently been transferred to the cupboard. These all reveal their author's definitely lavatorial sense of humour. One item is entitled: 'A scheme humbly offered, for making Religion and the Clergy useful, with the author's observations on the Cause and Cure of the Piles: and some useful Directions about wiping the Posteriors'; another, 'The County Squire and his Man John', is an extended joke about a man defecating after eating too much apple pie; a third, 'Strephon and Chloe', tells of Strephon's strenuous efforts not to fart in bed on his wedding night:

And love such nicety requires,
One blast will put out all his fires.[26]

A notorious item in the cupboard is *The Merry Muses of Caledonia* by Robert Burns. This is a collection of bawdy songs noted down in a lost Burns manuscript, and it is now clear that a number are by Burns himself. Wordsworth was one of many people who refused to believe this possible, though Byron showed more understanding when he wrote: 'The mixture or rather contrast of tenderness, delicacy, obscenity and coarseness in the same mind is wonderful.'[27] The songs are frank and humorous, treating subjects like outsize penises and non-stop ejaculations in a healthy, unprurient manner. Some, like the famous 'Ball o' Kirriemuir', are barrack-room material but others have a robust charm of their own, such as 'Nine Inch Will Please a Lady', which is almost certainly by Burns himself:

'Come rede me, dame, come tell me, dame,
My dame come tell me truly,
What length o' graith, when weel ca'd hame,
Will sair a woman duly?'
The carlin clew her wanton tail,
Her wanton tail sae ready—
'I learn'd a sang in Annandale,
Nine inch will please a Lady.

But for a koontrie cunt like mine,
In sooth, we're nae sae gentle;
We'll tak twa thumb-bread to the nine,
And that's a sonsy pintle:
O leeze me on, my Charlie lad,
I'll ne're forget my Charlie!
Tway roarin handfu's and a daud,
He nidge't it in fu' rarely.

But weary fa' the laithron doup,
And may it ne'er be thrivin!
It's no the length that makes me loup,
But its the double drivin.
Come nidge me, Tam, come nudge me, Tam,
Come nidge me o'er the nyvel!
Come lowse and lug your battering ram,
And thrash him at my gyvel!'[28]

Very different are the charming and delicately erotic poems by Paul Verlaine, recently transferred from the private case to the cupboard: *Hombres* (1891)[29] and *Femmes* (1890).[30] Verlaine was able to be explicit without being in anyway offensive, whether writing about homosexual love (in the first volume, one poem being written in conjunction with Arthur Rimbaud) or heterosexual love (in the second). Works of literature like these belong to the world, not just to rich connoisseurs or erudite researchers. Like the wealth of drawings, prints, and other art objects in the various departments of both the Victoria and Albert Museum and the British Museum, they represent experiences of the mind and body which should be, and hopefully soon will be, available to everyone.

Appendix III

Eroticism in Twentieth-century Art: Interviews with Contemporary Artists

a: Hans Bellmer[1]

'I want to reveal scandalously the interior that will always remain hidden and sensed behind the successive layers of the human structure and its last unknowns.' In these words from his book *L'Anatomie de l'Image*,[2] Hans Bellmer has explained the extraordinary power of his work to horrify, to excite, to illuminate, and to intrigue. The artist is now seventy and confined to his bed as the result of a stroke,* but the firm hand-shake and the bright, piercing eyes are still those of the man whose provocative manipulations and distortions of female anatomy in his photographs of dolls and in his sculptures such as *La Mitrailleuse en Etat de Grâce*[3] not only scandalised the art-loving bourgeoisie of the thirties, but also incurred the wrath of the Nazi Party. I was fortunate enough to meet this great contemporary erotic artist while visiting Paris to see his retrospective exhibition in January 1972. Bellmer has lived in a tiny apartment in one of the less well-known areas of Paris, under the watchful eye of his devoted housekeeper, since his beloved companion, the artist and writer Unica Zurn, committed suicide in 1970.

Bellmer has known many tragedies in his life, one of the greatest being the death of his wife Margarete in Berlin in 1937. It was during his wife's long illness that he began to give expression to his sexual dreams and desires by constructing the articulated figure of a young girl, inspired to an extent by a performance of *The Tales of Hoffmann* and also by his wholly innocent infatuation for his fifteen-year-old cousin Ursula, who was living nearby. His doll was made up of a collection of plaster parts that could be assembled in various different ways, and he photographed his creations in order to have a record of the doll's different manifestations. Sometimes he arranged two pairs of legs around the central core of a stomach; at other times, the doll wore a petticoat and was provided with a face and long hair but no limbs (see illustration 249); then again she would appear as a tangle of anatomical parts festooned with lace and artificial flowers.

These photographs expressed a powerful and disturbing eroticism·in a painfully

* Hans Bellmer died in Paris on 24 February 1975.

[366]

249 Hans Bellmer, *Doll*,
photograph, *c.* 1934

honest manner, and when Bellmer sent examples to André Breton in Paris, the Surrealists were very excited by such irrational images of erotic dreams. Some were reproduced in *Minotaure* Number 6 (December 1934) and others illustrated a special article by Bellmer in *Cahiers d'Art* (1936). Two years later, Paul Eluard published a collection of prose-poems inspired by the photographs, entitled *Les Jeux de la Poupée.*[4] After the death of his wife, and when under danger of arrest by the Nazis as a 'degenerate' artist, Bellmer fled to Paris to join the Surrealists in 1938. During the war he was interned (along with Max Ernst), but afterwards he began a long series of drawings and etchings which further developed the violent eroticism of his dolls. Inspired by the works of Baudelaire, de Sade, and Georges Bataille, he produced sets of illustrations which are works of art in their own right: these are often ambiguous superimposed images conjuring up visions of far-from-innocent little girls taking part in advanced sexual exercises, or strange anatomical inventions made up of sexual apertures and throbbing organs. These exciting, honest, and totally un-prurient creations are always executed in a marvellously refined and elegant technique, culminating in the large and highly complex two-colour etchings entitled *Petit Traité de la Morale* (1968; see illustration 250), which illustrate the sexual dreams of young girls and at the same time the sexual fantasies of their author. These ten prints constitute one of the finest expressions of eroticism in twentieth-century art, and they show the uniqueness of Bellmer's erotic art in that they are *non-naturalistic*, graphic transcriptions of mental images relating to erotic desire.

Bellmer's large retrospective exhibition held at the National Centre for Contemporary Art in Paris was a beautifully arranged survey of work over four decades. To many people it provided a revelation of the enormous talent of this single-minded and courageous artist, whose work is still little known and appreciated outside France and Germany. A powerful level of sustained eroticism characterised the whole exhibition, which included over one hundred drawings, about twenty paintings, a selection of doll photographs, ten sets of engravings, and six sculptures and constructions. The centre of attraction was a completely black room hung with enlarged doll photographs. In the middle were two sculptures inspired by the doll, and at the far end, dramatically lit by two spotlights, was a bed covered with black velvet on which lay all that remains today of Bellmer's seminal doll. This consisted of two pairs of legs, wearing white socks and school-girls' shoes, joined to a nude torso, behind which was the top half of another torso with a head and black velvet neckband and one single arm caressing the four-legged figure. It is impossible to convey in words the powerful and moving effect of this room dedicated to Bellmer's doll.

I began my interview by asking Bellmer whether he had been able to visit the exhibition. 'Yes, they kindly took me there to have a look. I thought it was beautifully arranged, especially the doll room. It was a deep experience for me. I have kept those parts of the doll all this time—the rest I had to leave behind when I fled from Germany in the thirties. I feel very honoured that such an exhibition should be arranged by the Ministry of Cultural Affairs.' I remarked that it was a pity London was not willing or able to give him such an exhibition. 'Yes, English people do not seem ready for my work yet. My exhibition of de Slade illustrations was closed by your police in 1966 and although there have been small shows since then[5] I have had no

250   Hans Bellmer, *Petit Traité de la Morale*, etching, 1968

major exhibition in London. My work is too erotic—and too *openly* erotic—for Puritan England, I am afraid. Your country is still in the nineteenth century—I hope your book will help to change that. Germany is very different, and so is France, where there is now a very free and easy atmosphere for artists. After all, my exhibition is arranged by an official ministry in an official building. But I think one day soon my work will be more appreciated in your country.'

I asked Bellmer his feelings about being known exclusively as an erotic artist. 'All my work is erotic—it always has been. The idea of eroticism is an essential part of life, so it's right that artists like me should devote themselves to exploring that idea. Eroticism has always been of the greatest importance to me.' I suggested that some people might find his idea of eroticism very far from their own—what was his concept of the erotic? 'I agree with Georges Bataille that eroticism relates to a knowledge of evil and the inevitability of death, it is not simply an expression of joyful passion.' Bellmer pointed to the powerful erotic images in Bataille's novel *L'Histoire de l'Oeil*,[6] which he himself had tried to conjure up in his illustrations to the book. I asked him if the writings of de Sade had meant as much to him as those of Bataille. 'I admire de Sade very much, especially his idea that violence towards the loved one can tell us more about the anatomy of desire than the simple act of love, but I find I can't read very much of his work. I prefer the poems of Baudelaire, the stories of Lewis Carroll, and *Là-Bas* by Huysmans. But the most important book of all to me has been Lautréamont's *Les Chants de Maldoror*[7]—that made a very deep impression on me.' I pointed out that, nevertheless, some of his most powerful graphic work had been inspired by de Sade—for example, ten prints entitled *A Sade* (1961) and ten prints entitled *Petit Traité de la Morale* (1968). He admitted that this was so, but said that some of the plates of *Petit Traité de la Morale* (see illustration 250) were extensions of ideas he had expressed in the love-letters published in his *Anatomie de l'Image* in 1957:

> As for me, I wonder if I will wear the skin-tight trousers made from your seamless legs and adorned on the inside with spurious excrement? And do you think that, presuming I do not first faint away, I shall button on to my chest the heavy and trembling under-garment of your breasts? As soon as I am ready under the pleated skirt made of your fingers . . . you will breathe into me your sweet fragrance and feverish excitement so that my sexual organ will appear from inside yours.[8]

I suggested that the disturbing nature of these quite recent prints could be traced back to the doll photos of the 1930s, which a critic had described as 'menacing variations on the theme of desire'.[9] Bellmer became quite emotional when recalling the tragic years of persecution during which his wife died, and then his escape from Nazi Berlin to the Surrealists in Paris. 'Yes, my dolls were the beginning. Obviously there was a convulsive flavour to them because they reflected my anxiety and un-happiness. To an extent they represented an attempt to reject the horrors of adult life as it was in favour of a return to the wonder of childhood, but the eroticism was all-important, they became an erotic liberation for me. Eroticism has to be personal, of course, so I find difficulty in discussing it.' Bellmer's difficulty is easy to appreciate, but nevertheless he reminded me of what he wrote in his first album of doll photographs published in Karlsruhe in 1934:

> What transpired by the staircase or the crack in the door when the little girls were playing doctors up in the loft, what oozed from those juicy enemas (dare I say the sour juice of raspberries?)—all of this could easily take on the appearance of seduction, could even excite desire. . . . Would it not be in the doll's very reality that the imagination would find the joy, the ecstasy and the fear that it sought? Would it not be the final triumph over the adolescent girls with wide eyes which turn away if, beneath the conscious stare that plunders their charms, aggressive fingers were to attack their plastic forms and slowly construct, limb by limb, all that sense and brain had appropriated?[10]

I suggested to Bellmer that the construction of the dolls and the photographing of them had not only served a cathartic purpose, but had also represented a conscious attempt at communication. 'To a certain extent you are right. I wanted to help people lose their complexes, to come to terms with their instincts as I was trying to do. I suppose I wanted people to really experience their bodies—I think this is only possible through sex. The photographs blended the real and the imaginary, but they had to be provocative to be effective.' I presumed that they provoked a hostile reaction because of the mutilation and reorganisation to which he subjected the dolls. 'Yes, and this was deliberate, because I was aware of what I called the physical unconscious, the body's underlying awareness of itself. I tried to rearrange the sexual elements of a girl's body like a sort of plastic anagram. I remember describing it thus: the body is like a sentence that invites us to rearrange it, so that its real meaning becomes clear through a series of endless anagrams.[11] I wanted to reveal what is usually kept hidden—it was no game—I tried to open people's eyes to new realities: this is as true of the doll photographs as it is of *Petit Traité de la Morale*. The anagram is the key to all my work. This allies me to the Surrealists and I am glad to be considered part of that movement, although I have less concern than some Surrealists with the subconscious, because my works are always carefully thought out and controlled. If my work is found to scandalise, that is because for me the world is scandalous.'

---

b: Allen Jones[1]

PETER WEBB: Your image has remained reasonably constant, hasn't it—the '40s woman with high-heeled shoes and black stockings—can you now point to what it was that led to the choice of image?

ALLEN JONES: I wanted to paint a picture free from the ideas about picture-making that had become almost a dogma whilst I was living in New York in 1964. I wanted to paint a pictorial affront. Whereas before the subject was enmeshed in painterly gestures I now wanted to insinuate it upon the viewer. The choice of a leg for my image meant that I had to consider shoes; to consider a shoe is to consider a style and I did not want to date my pictures in that way. I wanted the epitome of a shoe just as I wanted the epitome of a leg. The high-heel black shoe became an inevitable choice. From Freud to Fredericks it is the archetypal shoe. In retrospect I can see how the fetishistic content must have been important, and I can recognise the Freudian implications of the high heels.

P.W.: You seem to avoid mentioning your mental involvement in the subject-matter, the erotic idea of the leg, the high-heeled shoes, the close-fitting shiny black stockings. You didn't, after all, just like it as a nice image surely?

A.J.: The image satisfied myself and the requirements of the picture. I liked the idea of a saucy image and I can see now that the eroticism had a latent attraction for me from the start. I am, of course, aware of the fetish element in my work but I think this is suggested as much by my treatment of the painted surface, detail and repetition of a theme, as by any particular obsession of mine. Repetition has another function, it depersonalises the image. I do not want the figures to represent an individual. I want the image to be a sign for woman not a portrait of her.

P.W.: In your two books[2] you have collected a lot of '40s and '50s fetishistic material in the form of photographs and drawings, so this clearly has a great attraction for you.

A.J.: Yes, I discovered an incredible amount of literature existed on this sort of stocking theme, which used to be very easily obtainable. I had collected a cross-section of the styles of drawing that appeared in fetish magazines, mail order catalogues, decals, movie posters, pin-ups, etc. They represented a refreshing directness in dealing with the figure, a vitality that was foreign to the subject when handled by the Fine Art media. In New York there was an incredible sublimation of sexual interest into drawing; there wasn't any photographic hard pornography around, as there was in Europe. I got very turned on to the books, for the artists were communicating and obtaining some kind of tactile response. The drawings had much more vitality than any of the work I saw in Art Schools while I was teaching. The difference between the drawings done commercially in the little stocking books and the drawings done in the life class was remarkable and this interested me a lot, so over the years I have collected drawings of the figure made outside the Fine Art area. They all have a potency, whether they are done in lunatic asylums or for stocking magazines, and the mail-order catalogues are an absolute fund of drawings and visual information of this kind. The creativity is staggering. And because they are out of period, they become like Japanese pillow prints or Indian erotic miniatures; because these things are removed from one's own society, a lot of the erotic charge tends to be removed, and then one can see the art in the drawing; and it's the same with Bronzino's *Venus, Cupid, Folly and Time* in the National Gallery (see illustration 85). We don't look at it with the same eyes as the people for whom it was painted—it was a private commission, for them alone, not to be viewed in public.

P.W.: In your second book, *Allen Jones Projects*, you included some boot and lash drawings, such as *Miss Marchant's Diary of Discipline* and *Suzanne's Punishment School*, which have a very specific variety of erotic appeal.

A.J.: That was the specific area being dealt with in a sketch I was supposed to do for *Oh! Calcutta!* called *Homage to St Dominics*, which was about punishment in a girls' school. As I have never spanked the arse of anybody, I tried to gather as much visual material on the subject as possible. These pictures in the book are all that remains of my sketch, as the resident designer took it over in the end.

P.W.: But your project for the history of knickers entitled *The Empress's New Clothes* was used in *Oh! Calcutta!* wasn't it?

A.J.: Yes, I was very happy about that. Now that I come to think of it, the set that I designed consisted of a tall column flanked at its base by two discs!

P.W.: In your paintings, is the erotic content the most important element to you?

A.J.: Yes, the content must be the most important element in a picture, but it does not necessarily occupy most of my thinking time. When an idea has been conceived, I still have to paint the picture. After the formal considerations have been solved, the 'making' process evaporates into the totality of the picture. People contemplating the picture always ask 'why?', and painters always ask 'how?'.

P.W.: So it would be wrong to describe your work as the painful process of making an erotic and private anxiety into a visual statement?

A.J.: I don't give it much thought; that would be for a psychiatrist to work out. I think it is possible to talk about a lot of painting in psychological terms, and an artist who deals closely with a figure is always fair game for the pundits. I certainly used to do a lot of automatic drawing under the influence of Surrealism, but I'm not looking for visual equivalents of erotic hang-ups.

P.W.: You told me the other day that your recent painting of a *Woman with two Spheres (Float)* has been a problem of geometry and colour relationships mainly (see illustration 251).

A.J.: Well, the picture consists of two discs or spheres with a woman floating above them. It does obviously have a phallic connotation but that realisation no longer surprises me. The actual problem was to manipulate these two circles with the acute accent above them until the picture jelled.

P.W.: So if someone sees Freudian implications in the painting, you would agree, but insist that they were purely subconscious during the working out of the picture so far as you were concerned?

A.J.: Yes.

P.W.: I believe some 'Women's Lib' supporters have objected to your seeming exploitation of the female as a sexual object, especially in your sculptures?[3]

251   Allen Jones, *Float*, 1972

A.J.: Yes, but I think that the cause of female emancipation is trivialised when someone gets uptight about a piece of sculpture, whilst enormous problems of inequality still exist amongst live human beings. Suppose my sculptures did underline a human condition; when Goya painted a blood bath, it did not follow that he condoned it.

P.W.: Can we discuss the differences between an artist who is very deeply involved in his erotic subject-matter, to an almost painful degree: Hans Bellmer, and you, who as you have said have refined the fetish and fantasy world of your subject-matter to the extent that you are more concerned with visual and painterly and colour problems now?

A.J.: I have some Bellmer prints, and I admire him very much. When confronted with a Bellmer, I find myself reflecting on the man more than the picture. Perhaps this is a clue as to why he stands outside the mainstream of painting. Artists usually sublimate or intellectualise their obsessions, egos, etc., into abstract visual problems, and so it becomes the picture that is worthy of contemplation, not the artist. I don't want to exist outside current artistic preoccupations. I feel that if the only thing of interest is the curiosity value of what kind of private life

[373]

I must lead or what kind of private problems I might have, then I'm not interested in speaking about it.

P.W.: But you are quite aware of the fact that there must be a lot of yourself in your work.

A.J.: Of course. But the reason I never discuss my own obsessions in this context is that I do not want to *limit* the interpretation of the picture.

P.W.: And what is your reaction to those people who are turned on by what they see as the expression of a fetish in your work?

A.J.: That's okay with me. If they look at my work and are turned on by it, that's a hell of a good reason for wanting to buy it.

P.W.: And what of those people who say they ought to be turned on but aren't because it doesn't seem sufficiently erotic, it seems too beautiful and superficial?

A.J.: That's okay too. If my work elicits a strong reaction, then I can ask no more —after all, people bare themselves, their understanding and their prejudices when making their value judgements.

P.W.: What is your feeling about being treated in this present context as an important example of eroticism in modern art?

A.J.: A nice feeling, but it passes quickly.

P.W.: Would you agree that, as in the case of Bellmer, we can come to terms with art by knowing the experiences that produced it?

A.J.: Biography is always interesting, especially to art historians, but I do not think that looking at a painting should be prefaced with such information. I knew nothing of Bellmer's life, yet still I responded to certain of his works. I think one brings one's own experience to a picture; it is like a mirror, it reflects those things we expect to see and sometimes, something new in the background is added to our perception. I think Bruce Nauman said 'the true artist helps the world by revealing mystic truths'.[4]

P.W.: What do you think about Balthus?

A.J.: It is a matter of temperament, I suppose, but I never really connect with Balthus. He uses an atmospheric kind of modelling that represents a different kind of illusionism; I like clearly delineated forms that establish a strong pattern on the surface, even if these surfaces are highly modelled, as with Ingres. The reason why the work of Balthus doesn't turn me on is that it seems to be a picture of a situation, it never seems to go beyond that. But I do appreciate the stillness of his pictures. Whatever activity seems to occur within a picture, I think all great painting has this quality of stillness.

P.W.: And what about Wesselmann and Lindner?

A.J.: Well, they are good examples, they keep right there on the surface. Their erotic pictures mean much more to me, therefore, than those of Balthus. Wesselmann paints a nude so that you know it isn't a nude, but you get the feeling of the nudeness being nude. He's created something *real* without creating the illusion of something being there which isn't there.

P.W.: Could you put into words what you really think eroticism is?

[374]

A.J.: As a motor reaction, it seems to me to be something that might cause the chest to tighten or the pulse to quicken. Eroticism is something that demands an emotional response and generally speaking I think erotic art can only have this direct connection to someone living within the social or cultural background that produced it. Of course one can appreciate the style, art, etc., of another age as with Indian sculpture, but I think this is reduced to an objective cerebral appreciation. One can never identify with the emotional charge that the work had for its immediate audience. But basically, eroticism is an absolutely universal subject which relates you to every other human being.

P.W.: And you think eroticism is an important theme in the arts today?

A.J.: Yes, it has to be.

---

c: David Hockney[1]

PETER WEBB: Although your work as a whole does not really come under the heading of erotic art, it seems to me that some of your projects show a definite interest in eroticism. Are you conscious of this?

DAVID HOCKNEY: I think eroticism is interesting as a subject, but it should come naturally. I have never deliberately accentuated the eroticism in my work—humour plays a more dominant part than eroticism for me, though, of course, the two can be related. I think even the *Cavafy* etchings weren't really erotic because the poems aren't erotic, they're matter-of-fact poems about certain situations about love, they are rather old fashioned even.

P.W.: But the idea of boys making love to each other must be erotic in some way.

D.H.: Well, of course it's erotic—it's just like a man making love to a woman. But the poems try to make it matter-of-fact—so many incidents are included—and so there is less of the erotic about it. You see I think the erotic is about the particular, I don't think it can really be just about the general, and those poems weren't about the particular, so are not in that sense erotic, and in the same way my etchings weren't.

P.W.: What about your painting *The Room, Tarzana* (see illustration 252)?

D.H.: That has more elements of the erotic, because it is about a particular incident and a particular person. The way the buttocks are painted, and emphasised, is of course a deliberate erotic element.

P.W.: Did you have the Boucher painting of *Mlle O'Murphy* (see illustration 95) in mind?

D.H.: Not in mind, no, but of course I knew it and it no doubt was subconsciously

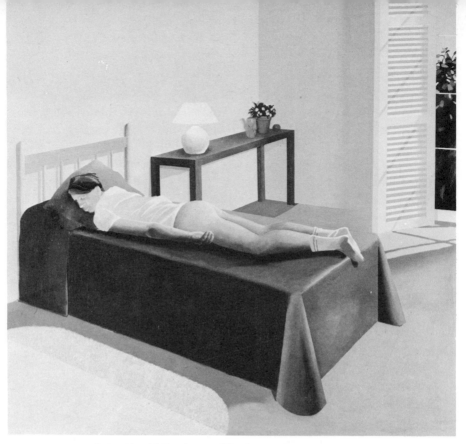

252   David Hockney, *The Room, Tarzana*, 1967

in my mind. In fact, the picture started in an unerotic way, from an ad in the *San Francisco Examiner* for Macy's Department Store, which showed a bedroom, and I wanted to add a figure. The painting therefore became an erotic picture. But it's difficult to isolate eroticism in my work; after all, I am a figurative painter and I think almost any figurative artist is bound to have elements of eroticism in his work because the nude body is erotic, and certainly my nude drawings are erotic and are meant to be. Kenneth Clark points out in his book *The Nude* that there are bound to be elements of eroticism in any nude picture and I think he's absolutely right there. But it has not been a dominating interest in my work as it has in the work of Bellmer, or Allen Jones, who has been obsessed with a certain kind of eroticism for a long time.

P.W.: You told me that eroticism plays an important part in your private life, why is that not carried over very much into your work?

D.H.: One's life and one's work are not always all that closely related. An artist controls his work; if he doesn't, he's not an artist. Art is not a therapy for me as it is for some people. I'm not an expressionist who works very emotionally; I know what my picture will be like before I start.

P.W.: But your subject-matter does seem to be closely related to your personal interests—you paint a nude boy in a bedroom rather than a bikini-clad blonde on the beach at Cannes.

D.H.: Yes, that's true. At the Royal College of Art, one was supposed to draw from the nude, but I hated doing that because the models were fat women who did nothing for me at all, and I could never accept that idea of Cézanne's that everything is an apple. In the end, I got my own models, and I got boys because I think they are much more attractive and so I enjoy drawing them more than fat women. An artist should always start with his own conception of beauty; this has always been the case. Renoir obviously loved plump girls and painted them all his life; thin girls didn't do anything for him. Michelangelo liked muscular young men, and they dominate his art because they are his ideal of beauty. Beauty is here a better word than eroticism, although eroticism comes into it. But I think you would find it difficult to find any figurative artist who did not do something explicitly erotic at some time—he can't help it.

P.W.: I agree, but the pictures are usually hidden from the public eye, aren't they? That's why people don't realise how much erotic art exists and always has existed.

D.H.: Yes, certainly. But I expect there to be a normal amount of eroticism in all figurative art, so when I think of erotic artists, I am thinking of people who have specialised and taken a stronger interest in that subject than normal. I have done some very explicit erotic drawings as presents for my friends, but they were not part of my main work.

P.W.: Would you consider Bellmer and Balthus to be among the most interesting of erotic artists?

D.H.: Yes, I admire Bellmer, although he is not one of my favourite artists. Balthus I admire even more, even though his eroticism doesn't really appeal to me— young adolescent girls do nothing for me. But for me his work is very fine art— I admire his skill and his enthusiasm. Bellmer is also a fine artist in a formal way, but he has had very little influence on my work, whereas Balthus has influenced me. He is one of the very few modern painters who uses conventional means, and as I am a very conventional painter, I naturally feel close to him.

P.W.: What art do *you* find erotic, what turns you on?

D.H.: I very much like the drawings in the American male magazines by Tom of Finland (see illustration 178) and Spartacus; they're not great art but they're very good, the artists know exactly what they are trying to do and they do it very well. They draw beautiful muscular men in leather or in the nude.

P.W.: Can you define what eroticism means to you?

D.H.: Something that excites me physically.

P.W.: But that could as well be a pornographic photo.

D.H.: Not necessarily. Most pornography bores me. Whenever I see pornographic films they bore me, and the reason is because they are not made by artists. A movie is an art form, and in art if you want to heighten something you've got to contrast it with something, otherwise everything is bland. The films you see on 42nd Street in New York are like that now. I suppose pornographic films will improve. They have, in fact, already improved, because until last year erections weren't allowed in the New York cinemas, so you had incredible films with naked people doing anything to each other as long as they didn't get an erection!

[377]

These will become period pieces—people will think, why weren't they excited? Didn't they enjoy it? Now the films are much more natural, so perhaps artists will get involved. I'm sure I could make a much more erotic pornographic film, in fact I keep meaning to do so. I suppose pornography must satisfy some people, perhaps the dirty old men—they're dying out now aren't they, but some are left —perhaps they have a rather low standard of visual sense. I'm not criticising them—if it gives them a thrill, then that's pretty good.

P.W.: What films do you find erotic?

D.H.: I like Warhol's films. *Trash* (see illustration 254) is a great film, better than *Flesh*. His films are very accurate portrayals of a certain variety of life in New York. *Trash* is a very honest piece of art. The sexual explicitness is part of the appeal, of course, but Warhol doesn't overdo that aspect. Like Bogdanovich's *The Last Picture Show*, which has a few nude scenes because life is like that, but which is not specially concerned about trying to be an erotic film, it's just showing that people are always interested in sex. I don't just like Warhol's films because they are sexually explicit. The nudity is valid for artistic reasons—Warhol is an extremely talented artist. His films are far more artistic than sexploitation movies.

P.W.: The erotic is obviously much more interesting and important to you than the pornographic.

D.H.: Yes—the erotic is so much more inventive than the pornographic because it's produced by artists.

P.W.: Would you like to be more concerned with eroticism in your own work? Would you like to feel you were turning people on all over the world?

D.H.: Well, I like to feel I'm doing that anyway! But people don't really need art to turn them on to sexual pleasure, do they?

d: Henry Moore[1]

PETER WEBB: What role does eroticism play in your work?

HENRY MOORE: As I do my work I am not conscious of erotic elements in it, and I have never set out to create an erotic work of art. My work is mainly intuitive. But of course it is true that almost any sculptured form can be seen as erotic and can arouse erotic associations in the mind of the viewer; in nature many simple things, the petals and stamen of a flower, can become erotic forms to some eyes. I have no objection to people interpreting my forms and sculptures erotically, relating my figures to erotic imagery in their own thinking. Part of the excitement of sculpture is the associations it can arouse, quite independent of the original

253 Henry Moore, *Composition*, 1933

aims and ideas of the sculptor. But I do not have any desire to rationalise the
eroticism in my work, to think out consciously what Freudian or Jungian symbols
may lie behind what I create. That I leave for others to do. I started to read Erich
Neumann's book on my work, *The Archetypal World of Henry Moore*,[2] in which
he suggests a Jungian interpretation, but I stopped halfway through the first
chapter, because I did not want to know about these things, whether they were
true or not. I did not want such aspects of my work to become henceforth self-
conscious. I feel they should remain subconscious and the work should remain
intuitive. Perhaps the associations it can arouse are all the stronger for that very
reason. Anyhow, for me, making my sculpture is an intuitive process without any
conscious intention to create erotic images (see illustration 253).

Appendix IV

Censorship in the Cinema

The Oxford English Dictionary defines *censor* as 'official examining plays, books, news, correspondence, etc., to suppress what is immoral or seditious or inopportune; person assuming the right of judging others'. As far as the cinema is concerned, immorality has been the prime target of the censor (closely followed by violence); but with fast-changing concepts of personal morality, the job of censoring films has become increasingly difficult. And the film censor is especially aware of the vulnerability of anyone who assumes the right of judging others. As the world grows more aware of the true meaning of personal freedom as guaranteed in a democratic society, the authoritarian nature of censorship becomes abhorrent to an ever increasing number of people. Far from fulfilling a protective role, censorship is seen as reflecting a society's lack of confidence in itself. Neville March Hunnings puts the position into perspective in *Film Censors and the Law*: 'Censorship has an extremely complicated network of causes: psychological—many people have a compulsive need to prevent others from uttering thoughts or images which are disturbing or distasteful to them; political—governments and governing bodies have an interest in preserving stability and in preventing utterances which might upset their own policies; paternal—parents have an interest in ensuring that their children are exposed only to influences which will cause them to develop along desirable lines; social—administrators and citizens have an interest in the preservation of a healthy society and in the prevention of criminal and deviant conduct. Against these causes, the tendency of which is opposed to change and which incline towards preservation of the *status quo*, is the philosophic concept of freedom, based on metaphysical uncertainty and hence on humility and the willing sufference or even encouragement of experiment and change in a continual search for improvement in all spheres, especially social, political and moral.'[1]

Cinema audiences in many countries are denied the basic freedom to choose what they wish to see, for the film is almost universally dependent on administrative sanction rather than, as with the other arts, judicial control. Judicial prosecution after publication or exhibition is the accepted regulator for writers, artists, playwrights, etc., but film-makers have to submit to administrative censorship before presentation to the public. This seems to result from fear of the cinema's extraordinary power of suggestion, coupled with its wide popularity, its intimacy as a medium, and its ability to bridge social, racial, and age barriers. These factors seem to strike terror into the hearts of guardians of morality in particular, who have tended to see every cinema as a potential sink of iniquity. During the trial of *La*

Ronde in America in 1952, a prosecution lawyer asked in horror: 'But do you realize that this picture will be seen by a large group of people in a *darkened* theatre?'

Censorship has always been a matter of controversy in countries where personal freedoms are guaranteed by a constitution or bill of rights. Apologists declare that even if a constitution protects freedom of expression, a system of censorship is in the public interest to maintain standards of morality. Such systems are left in the hands of administrative agencies who are usually immune from judicial control, for little or no attempt is made to reconcile the needs of both public interests and the constitution.

Film censorship seems to have developed universally out of a failure to recognise the cinema's potential. 'Living pictures' were initially regarded as merely one amusement among many to be found in showmen's booths or the music halls, and so control was exercised as a matter of course. Once a system of control was in operation, it tended to be maintained, even when the cinema outgrew its fairground origins and became a serious art form. In Denmark, where film censorship has now been abolished, a law was passed in 1922 which gave Parliament the power to regulate and control the cinema. In France and England, the political climate did not allow for such legislation, but a system of censorship control was instituted which worked through the local authorities in each country, for they had the power to regulate minor entertainment. The cinema was in the category of 'spectacles de curiosité' in France and 'public dancing, music or other public entertainment of the like kind' in England, and the division of public entertainment into 'dramatic' and 'minor' categories prevented the cinema from being considered on a level with the theatre. Even when the new entertainment had clearly outgrown its original classification, no attempt was made in France or England to rethink the established system of censorship, although in England the film industry organised its own advisory board—the British Board of Film Censors—to protect itself against the vagaries of local authorities.

In America the attitude towards the cinema was the same; in a famous case in 1915, it was referred to as 'a business pure and simple',[2] and therefore it did not enjoy the protection of the First Amendment to the American Constitution ('Congress shall make no law . . . abridging the freedom of speech'), which is considered as prohibiting censorship. Ironically, only Soviet Russia saw the potential of the cinema, which Lenin called, at the founding of the Soviet Film Industry in 1919, 'the most important of all the arts'. Whereas America did not consider the cinema a serious enough medium for communicating ideas, Russia quickly recognised the capabilities of the film and set about exploring them for political ends. The Communist Party, therefore, exercised a strong power of censorship over the Russian film industry which is still much in evidence. As Krushchev said in his famous speech of 8 March, 1963: 'Art belongs to the sphere of ideology. On questions of creative art the General Committee of the Party will demand of everyone that he abides unswervingly by the Party line.'[3] In America film censorship later came to be controlled by a similarly totalitarian group of the Roman Catholic Legion of Decency, although their motives were dissimilar. The development of film censorship in the United States is incredibly complicated, partly because of the Constitution which theoretically guarantees freedom of expression, and partly because of the division of power between central government and the individual states. The film industry set up its own organisation to regulate itself in 1922, under the leadership of Will H. Hays, ex-Postmaster-General of the Federal Government, after an abortive attempt had been made to enforce censorship nationally through the National Board of Censorship. The self-regulating body was known officially as the Motion Picture Producers and Distributors of America, Incorporated, but because of its leader's powerful personality it soon became known as the Hays Office. Its aims included 'establishing and maintaining the highest possible moral and artistic standards in motion picture production'.[4] For this purpose, a list of guidelines for film-makers was issued, and this became known as the 'don'ts and be carefuls'. Hollywood was already established as the centre of American film production; by the end of the '20s, the rules of the Hays Office were accepted and enforced among Hollywood producers.

During the early-'30s, there was a great scare about the effects of films on children. In 1933, the Catholic Church formed the Legion of Decency to fight for an improvement in the moral standards of films, and members of the Church pledged themselves to boycott films listed by the Legion as offensive. The Legion's activities were supported by the Protestant and Jewish communities, and so clearly the Hays Office had to take its decisions into account. The result was the formation of a Production Code Administration under Joseph I. Breen, second-in-command to Hays, and this group produced the famous Breen Code, which was to hamstring the American cinema for over thirty years. Among the stipulations of the Code were: 'If two people are shown on a bed, they must have at least one foot on the floor,' and 'No inside thigh of a female may be shown between the garter and the knickers.' Double beds were forbidden in bedroom scenes, words like 'adultery', 'virgin', and 'damn' were forbidden and 'God' or 'Lord' could only be mentioned in church. Hollywood allowed itself to be tied down to this ridiculous Code rather than face the possibility of Federal censorship, and so the world its films depicted was a totally unreal one.

This obsession with an appearance of moral uprightness was characteristic of the cinema in America up until the late '50s. Films that had received a 'C' (condemned) rating from the League of Decency, or an 'X' rating from the Hays Office were thought unlikely to attract paying customers, but during the '50s, a series of foreign films was shown with great success in the United States. These had not been submitted to the MPPDA, and so were automatically given an 'X' rating, and according to the rules they should therefore not have achieved any success. In fact, many foreign films were prosecuted as being obscene, and test cases such as *The Miracle*, *M*, and *La Ronde* were won by the film-distributors. These films were franker and more sensational than their American counterparts, and clearly there was an audience for them; the hallowed Breen Code gradually lost all credibility with the public. The judgement in the case of Roberto Rossellini's film *The Miracle* in

1952 made it clear that the cinema's freedom of expression was guaranteed by the First Amendment and therefore censorship was unconstitutional.

The old-style censorship was clearly doomed. The League of Decency was still giving 'C' ratings to such classic films as *Jules et Jim, Knife in the Water, L'Avventura,* and *Saturday Night and Sunday Morning* in 1964, but by 1966 it had done some rethinking and was handing out awards to *Darling* and *Juliet of the Spirits.* And in the same year, the Breen Code was rewritten in such a way that practically everything was left to the discretion of the producer and the director. Today there is no actual censorship of films in America, though a system of codes is still provided, the main purpose being the protection of children. Sometimes the Code seal is refused, although this appears to do little harm to the films. Much the same system operates in Denmark, Sweden, Belgium, and Uruguay, and other countries including West Germany and Holland are fast moving in the same direction. But America's move into the realms of intelligence did not please everyone. Ronald Reagan said recently: 'What writing does it take simply to have two people undress and get into bed? Call me a square if you want to, but I think the business has degenerated.'[5]

In France, regulation of films is in the hands of the Commission de Contrôle, a government body created in 1916 when it was entirely made up of police officers. Since that date, representatives of the film industry have been added, but the majority of its members are still civil servants. It is no surprise, therefore, to find that French film censorship has concerned itself much more with political questions than with the moral issues of sex and violence. Thus Renoir's *La Grande Illusion* was banned in 1939 for making a German officer too sympathetic, and Chris Marker's *Cuba Si* was denied a certificate until 1963 because it was considered to amount to a defence of the Castro regime. Stanley Kubrick's much admired *Paths of Glory* has never been publicly shown in France because the First World War event on which it is based is considered to show France in a bad light. Local authorities have retained their power to ban locally films approved by the official censors, but they cannot overrule a government ban on a film. As in America, the Catholic Church takes an active interest in films in France, and unofficially wields great influence in moral terms. Buñuel's masterpiece *L'Age d'Or* has never been given a certificate because of Catholic pressure. But morally questionable films are not as carefully scrutinised as those considered politically dangerous. It is known that Losey's *The Servant* was passed with no cuts at all because only two members of the Commission were present at its screening, and both slept throughout the film.[6] In Italy, Spain, Portugal, Norway, and New Zealand, a form of government censorship of films similar to that in France is in operation, and in the first three countries, the Catholic Church plays a strong part in the process of censorship. In Canada, each province has its own board of film censors, although Ontario has generally set the pattern for others to follow. In Ontario, the Board of Censors has the power to cut films or ban them completely, and also to classify them as adult entertainment only. No film which has not been approved by the Board may be shown in the province, although an appeal against a ban may be made to the provincial Minister of Travel and Publicity.

Although Australia has, like Canada, a Federal structure, film censorship is not primarily in the hands of the states, for they do not appear to have taken any interest in exercising such powers. With their more or less passive support, film censorship is operated by the Commonwealth Government through the Customs. The very few locally produced films are subject to the Commonwealth Film censorship, but imported films have to apply for a registration from the Customs, and this is only provided on the authorisation of the Film Censor. Registration is likely to be refused for films containing 'objectionable characteristics' as laid down in the Report of the Council for Public Education of 1922. These include: 'Indecent, suggestive or insufficient dress; embraces over-stepping the limits of affection or which would be contrary to propriety in ordinary life; nude figures; positions of the actors which are suggestive of sexual passion or desire; scenes which might be morally harmful to the young especially of both sexes.' Appeals may be made to an Appeal Censor. The states have their own facilities for film censorship, but the Commonwealth Censor's decisions and classifications are almost universally approved, with the result that film censorship in Australia is less liberal than almost anywhere in the world outside the Soviet bloc.

One country where censorship of films is even more reactionary than Australia is India. The disastrous effects of the Victorian puritanism of the days of the Raj are still in evidence in a country that once bore witness to the most completely integrated sexuality in the world. The Central Board of Film Censors categorises films as totally unacceptable, or suitable for unrestricted public exhibition, or suitable only for audiences over eighteen. Cuts in films are very frequently made, and for a wide variety of reasons, although the reasons are usually related to sex in some way. The directive governing Board-policy sets out three general principles:

1. No picture shall be certified for public exhibition which will lower the moral standards of those who see it. Hence the sympathy of the audience shall not be thrown on the side of crime, wrong-doing, evil or sin.

2. Standards of life, having regard to the standards of the country and the people to which the story relates, shall not be so portrayed as to deprave the morality of the audience.

3. The prevailing laws shall not be so ridiculed as to create sympathy for violation of such laws.[7]

The directive also gives details as to what is permitted in the representation of vice, crime, immorality, relations between the sexes, exhibition of the human body, etc. Two of the main concerns are correct coverage of the breasts and restrictions against licentious kissing and petting. Kissing is forbidden in Indian films and yet tolerated in foreign ones; a recent Commission on Film Censorship recommended that kissing and nudity should both be allowed if necessary for aesthetic reasons. The Board's decisions are valid throughout India, and open to appeal, but the certificates it grants may be, and sometimes are, withdrawn by the Central Government (for example, *Road to Bali*, 1953; *Dial M for Murder*, 1955; *Baby Doll*, 1958; *Nine Hours to Rama*, 1963).

If a country has to censor films at all, it is certainly more consonant with freedom of speech that the censorship should not be controlled by the Government. In Great Britain, every film shown publicly has to be passed first of all by the British Board of Film Censors. This is an independent body which was set up in 1912 by the Film Industry as a buffer against hostile criticism from the public and also against the vagaries of local authorities, who had been given the power in the 1909 Cinematograph (Fire Precautions) Act to interfere with publicly shown films.

Concern about fires in theatres was at its peak during the late-nineteenth century. Drury Lane and Covent Garden theatres were both burned down during the century and lives were lost. Disastrous fires had also destroyed theatres in St Petersburg, Quebec, New York, Vienna, Liverpool, and Exeter. Many laws were passed which enforced fire-protection measures, the first being in 1878, and after the tragic fire at the film show in the Paris Charity Bazaar in 1897, premises showing films in England were subject to strict rules. The Cinematograph Act of 1909 was the result of public pressure, and gave local councils the power 'to make better provision for securing safety at Cinematograph and other Exhibitions'. The Act was never intended to apply to anything other than safety matters, but right from the start, the powers it gave were interpreted very widely indeed by local authorities. In 1910, the London County Council announced that film shows would not be permitted on Sundays, and other local authorities followed this example, in spite of objections that this had nothing to do with the question of safety.

From this position it was only a short step to controlling the content of films that cinemas were allowed to exhibit. In 1910, Blackburn County Council insisted that owners of premises licensed for the showing of films should not exhibit any pictures of an objectionable character, and this attitude began to be found throughout the country. The film industry realised that the 1909 Act was being turned into a stick with which local Councils could beat it mercilessly, and in 1912 the Cinematograph Exhibitors Association was formed to review the situation. Self-censorship was seen to be the only solution; as the trade journal *Bioscope* expressed in an editorial: 'It must at once be admitted that it would be far better for the trade to censor its own productions than to see all films at the mercy of an arbitrary authority.'[8] The result was the setting up in 1912 of the British Board of Film Censors, 'a purely independent and impartial body, whose duty it will be to induce confidence in the minds of the licensing authorities, and of those who have in their charge the moral welfare of the community generally.'[9]

From the start, the Board's main concern was, therefore, to preserve a standard of morality in films so that local authorities would honour its recommendations, for it was invested with no legal powers at all. It was many years, in fact, before all local Councils agreed to take note of the Board's Certificates, and even today its recommendations are occasionally overruled by certain Watch Committees. For a long period of time, therefore, the Board saw its role as that of keeping the cinema inoffensive and uncorrupting, and took a strong conservative line. Although it had only two specific rules—no nudity and no portrayal of Christ—in practice it was very difficult to please. Cecil Hepworth, who managed to obtain permission to show the American dancer Loie Fuller's erotic film of *The Serpentine Dance* after changing its title to *Salome Dancing before Herod* in the early 1900s, would have had more difficulty ten years later.[10] Nevertheless, the Board's decisions were often attacked or ignored. A film called *Five Nights* was given an adult's certificate in 1915, but banned in Preston, Birmingham, St Helens, and Leicester on the grounds of immorality.

Successive Presidents of the Board ignored the importance of the principle of freedom of expression, concerned only that no film should offend a reasonable number of reasonably-minded people. In the report of a Cinema Commission of Inquiry in 1917, the then President of the Board, T. P. O'Connor, mentioned the forty-three rules of the Board, among which were a wide variety of taboos including: excessively passionate love scenes; bathing scenes passing the limits of propriety; incidents having a tendency to disparage our Allies; scenes holding up the King's uniform in contempt or ridicule; subjects dealing with India, in which British officers are seen in an odious light; scenes suggestive of immorality; indelicate sexual situations; men and women in bed together; illicit sexual relationships; cruelty to young infants and excessive cruelty and torture to adults, especially women; gruesome murders and strangulation scenes; realistic horrors of warfare; scenes depicting the effect of veneral diseases, inherited or acquired; materialisation of the conventional figure of Christ.[11]

Over the years priorities have altered, and the political overtones of some of these rules would be quite unacceptable to the Board today. Religion is no longer a touchy subject, and many films have been passed which included depictions of Christ. The two problem-areas that remain are sex and violence. Under the Secretaryship of John Trevelyan (1958–71), the Board reflected a more liberal attitude towards sex, and most of the sexual taboos in T. P. O'Connor's list became commonplace in films passed by the Board in the 1960s. This relaxation of restraint had great importance for the British film-maker in his efforts to perfect the art of the cinema. But both John Trevelyan and his successor, Stephen Murphy, are on record as having said that they consider violence the biggest problem that faces the Board. Violence made quite a small showing in T. P. O'Connor's list, but the obsession with intense realism among film-makers recently has led to a marked increase in films that depict the extremes of violence. This in turn has led the Board to concern itself especially with the protection of children, the one aspect of censorship that most liberals would welcome.

The Board was, of course, created by the film industry, but it has maintained a strict independence from interference by any part of the industry. Nevertheless, it has tended to reflect the attitudes of the distributing and exhibiting sides of the industry, where marketability counts for more than integrity. Artistic and aesthetic concerns have not played a great part in the Board's work, except for the briefly tolerated Secretaryship of John Nicholls in 1957 to 1958, but because it represents protection from a more official type of censorship film-makers have worked hand in hand with the Board. When John Trevelyan in 1971 praised film-makers for so successfully disguising the cuts he had to make in their films, Kenneth Tynan, the critic and ardent opponent of censorship, likened this to praising a eunuch for his mastery of self-castration. Not all film-makers are co-operative: Joseph Strick once described John Trevelyan as 'your friendly neighbourhood film mortician'.[12] And Derek Hill of the New Cinema Club, which shows films without certificates, once said 'film censorship is a sort of protection racket run by the film industry for the film industry'.[13]

It must surely seem incredible that a civilised society in the 1970s should still feel it necessary to deny a basic freedom to its adult citizens under the guise of protecting them from what they are unable to recognise for themselves as dangerous. Censorship is paternalistic, and implies that there are those who know best in a society and who can therefore help the dim and silent majority who crave their protection. As Federico Fellini put it: 'I think that censorship is a horrible thing. . . . It is as if you said that we are all babies and therefore need to be held in arms. Now if we are all babies, then the censors are babies too, and what confidence can we have in them?'[14]

The defenders of censorship feel so assured of the inherent wrongness of anyone being stimulated to sexual behaviour by a film (or play or book or painting) and of the wrongness of anyone being deeply shocked or discomforted by any of these media, that they feel morally justified in making sure that such results are prevented or at least made extremely difficult. To appear civilised, such people make allowances for what they call 'artistic integrity', meaning that they are prepared to make exceptions in cases where they themselves feel that the material is justified as being sufficiently artistic. Of course, this makes them artistic dictators as well as moral guardians, and in any case assures the denial of personal freedom of choice to the vast majority. Freedom should mean that a man can make a good or bad film, work well or badly, paint a good or bad picture, on any theme he chooses; it should also mean that no one is compelled to pay attention to any film, book or picture. Society is a collective force that can corrupt as well as bless. The creative arts must reflect all aspects of society freely and fearlessly, and we do society no service at all when we attempt to limit that freedom.

Apologists for film censorship always stress the need to protect that minority of people whose minds might be unbalanced by what they see, but the reports of both President Nixon's Inquiry on Pornography in America and the Arts Council's Committee on Obscenity in England made it clear that expert opinion disagrees with the censors on this point. Much has been written about the effect of sexually explicit films on the people concerned with making them, but this is usually to confuse fantasy with reality. The author recently asked Glenda Jackson (the *Marat/ Sade*, *Women in Love*, *The Music Lovers*, etc.) how she felt about appearing in the nude, and about censorious attacks on her nude appearances: 'Nudity, if necessary (and not all nudity is), is no more or less a part of the actor's responsibility than learning his lines. Puritanical outbursts against myself or anyone else for that matter are worrying only for the "outburster", surely? There is no justification, except regarding children, for censorship in the cinema.'[15] And Janet Lynn, star of the X film *Cool it, Carol*, said: 'I'm just an actress playing a part. My friends and family who have seen the film realise I'm just doing a job of work. It's not really me there on the screen. I wouldn't stand there and strip off—not in a million years. I'm just playing a character who does that sort of thing. . . . Acting is a tough profession. . . . All I want is to keep working and do my job well.'[16] The only valid excuse for censorship is the protection of children—although some people would argue that children reared in the right environment do not need such protection to be imposed by law—and many countries are now in the process of following Denmark's example in abolishing censorship of the cinema altogether and merely retaining age restrictions.

Stephen Murphy has pointed out that responsibility for film censorship in Great Britain rests ultimately with local authorities, although the British Board of Film Censors has an enormous amount of influence through its granting or withholding of certificates. The trend is towards protection of children even here, for in 1970 the Board announced changes in age restrictions. The minimum age for admission to X films was raised from sixteen to eighteen, so that films in this category could be more 'candid'. A new category, AA, was introduced allowing admission to anyone over fourteen. An A certificate no longer required that a child be accompanied by an adult, but implied that the film contained material that some parents might consider unsuitable for their children. A film with a U certificate was, as before, recommended for all ages. Any of the six hundred local authorities has the power to overrule the Board and give its own certificate to a film it wishes to have shown, but in practice it is very rare for the Board's decisions to be altered in this way, for most local authorities tend to be very conservative in this respect. An exception was *Fanny Hill*, refused a certificate by the Board but given an X by eighteen authorities, an A by forty-four, and a U by four. But often the effect is the reverse, and films passed by the Board are banned in various parts of the country. And it is of interest to note who it is that can exercise such control. In Stockport, for instance, films are vetted by the Markets and Trading Standard Committee; in Southend, the Public Protection Committee; in Manchester, the Licensing and Fire Brigade Committee; in Bradford, such powers are exercised by the Standards and Cemeteries Executive Group.[17]

Under John Trevelyan's Secretaryship, the Board's decisions certainly became more liberal. The progress that was made can be gauged by the astonishment we now feel that there was ever any fuss at all over such films as *Room at the Top* of 1959, *Saturday Night and Sunday Morning* of 1960 and *A Taste of Honey* of 1961. These films brought about a revolution: from then on, the British cinema was allowed to show that unmarried people sleep together, and to admit that homosexuals actually exist and are quite ordinary people. The Censor's decisions during the next decade brought onto cinema screens almost every area of life that had been previously forbidden. *A Kind of Loving* (1962) showed Alan Bates going into a chemist's shop and buying a condom; *Rachel, Rachel* (1967) included a woman being told by her lover to 'fix herself up'. *The Pawnbroker* (1965) caused a storm when a woman bared her breasts to the camera, although we had earlier been allowed glimpses of breasts in *Espresso Bongo* (1959) and various of Ingmar Bergman's films, such as *Summer with Monika* (1952).

The cavortings of nude couples were featured in the French *Hiroshima Mon Amour* (1959) and *Une Femme Mariée* (1964), the Japanese *Woman of the Dunes* (1967), and the Czech *A Blonde in Love* (1965); but the censor made sure that we caught no glimpses at all of the various protagonists' sexual areas. The first view of female pubic hair was a split second in Antonioni's *Blow-Up* of 1966, soon followed by a more leisurely opportunity in Lindsay Anderson's *If* in 1968, and the prolonged view of Glenda Jackson in the nude trying to seduce Richard Chamberlain in Ken Russell's *The Music Lovers* (1970). Although there was an absurd fuss about naked men appearing on the screen in the French documentary on New Guinea, *The Sky Above, the Mud Below* in the early-'60s, the first actor's penis to be seen on the screen was that of Terence Stamp in Pasolini's *Theorem* (1968), and few people even noticed it. Alan Bates was much more obviously nude in the back-to-nature sequence of Ken Russell's *Women in Love* (1969), a film which also showed him wrestling naked with Oliver Reed (see illustration 217). By 1970, Joe Dallesandro was seen in close-up in Warhol's *Flesh* with an erection.

Female masturbation was featured in *The Silence* (1962), *The Fox* (1967) and *I, a Woman* (1967); and Polanski's *Repulsion* (1965) contained a very vivid orgasm, although it was only heard off-screen. The same director showed rape in *Rosemary's Baby* in 1968, although the censor curtailed the sequence, but Kurosawa's *Rashomon* (1951) and Bergman's *Virgin Spring* (1960) had included rape scenes many years earlier. It was only a matter of time before the actual details of sexual intercourse were shown on the British screen. The film which the censor allowed to create such a precedent was the so-called 'educational' film *The Language of Love*, made by the Danish sexologists Inge and Stan Hegeler in 1969.

Previous to the '60s, certain words were taboo in the British cinema. Frank Sinatra astonished audiences by using the word 'penis' in *The Detective* in 1968 and then going on to refer to 'semen-stains' on a sheet. The word 'bugger' was first used in 1966 in *Who's Afraid of Virginia Woolf* (by Elizabeth Taylor), and 'fuck' was heard for the first time in Joseph Strick's *Ulysses* (1967). The first mention of the word 'lesbian' was in Sidney Lumet's *The Group* (1966), and the first film to show a lesbian kiss was Strick's version of Genet's *The Balcony* (1962) with Shelley Winters and Lee Grant, soon followed by Chabrol's *Les Biches* (1967) and the more explicit *The Killing of Sister George* (1968). The first film to mention the word 'homosexual' was *Victim* (1961), which was banned in America for that reason. Homosexuality had been hinted at in earlier films such as Charles Vidor's *Gilda* (1946) and Howard Hughes's *The Outlaw* (1940), but Rod Steiger was the bestower of the first homosexual kiss in 1968 in *The Sergeant*. This was soon followed by *Staircase* (1968), *The Boys in the Band* (1970), and *Fortune and Men's Eyes* (1968), which treated homosexuality in a very open manner. But it was not until John Schlesinger's *Sunday, Bloody Sunday* (1971) that two men were shown making love together.

The very process of cataloguing these hard-won innovations points to the sadness and stupidity of censoring films for adults, an activity that can only result in films drawing audiences who are more attracted by broken taboos than by real artistic merit. Of course, the censor has often had to change his mind about harsh decisions. In 1968, he insisted on fifteen seconds being cut out of *Hugs and Kisses*, a Swedish film that was very well reviewed by the critics. The offending section showed a naked girl looking at herself in a full-length mirror. Many local authorities passed the film without any cut. When it was pointed out that *If* had been given a certificate without any cuts being demanded the Censor agreed to restore the offending fifteen seconds. Since then, the Board's decisions against Axel's *Danish Blue* (1968) and Warhol's *Flesh* and *Trash* (1968 and 1970) have been reversed.

The spectacle of the Censor growing ever more liberal in order to reflect the movement of public opinion and to appear less out of touch with contemporary ideas is a sad one. Stephen Murphy has gained wide respect for his liberalising efforts; Jimmy Vaughan, distributor of Warhol's films in the United Kingdom, has described him as 'an honest man in a thoroughly dishonest profession'.[18] But the job is incredibly difficult, and in early 1972 Mr Murphy was viciously attacked in the Press by certain local authorities for his liberality, and called upon to resign. The truth is that he is fighting a losing battle, and he knows it, in spite of his protestations that he performs a necessary function. Torn between liberal and conservative pressures, he finds himself able to satisfy no one. Thus in February 1973, he passed Bertolucci's *Last Tango in Paris*, only to have his decision challenged by the Greater London Council.

Of all the criticisms aimed at the Board, one of the most damning is its seeming lack of consistency. We are told we need to be protected from violence, drug-taking, and gratuitous sex because these are anti-social. So chunks are cut out of *Performance* (1970), and *Trash* is at first refused a certificate. Meanwhile, a film like *Vanishing Point* (1971) passes through unscathed. This film seems dedicated to the idea of the joys of dangerous driving, consisting as it does of one long and pointless car chase. It is characterised by glamorised violence and the romanticisation of drug-taking. It was released in the same week as *Puppet on a Chain* (August 1971), which features interminable killings (especially of beautiful girls) and much unconvincing moralising about drugs. These two films were soon followed by *Straw Dogs* (1971), which features seven horrific murders, a double rape, and a lynching, besides nympho-maniacs, voyeurs, and a slaughterer of pets. The Board passed the film because they considered it was based on the theme of anti-violence, but the critics were less happy. Scenes of a man being garrotted, another being battered to death, and a third having his foot shot off disgusted practically all the critics of the serious papers: 'The violence is presented as entirely laudable and justified in its own terms;'[19] 'Sex and

violence are consistently equated in this film. The gun and the cock are inter-
changeable'.[20] 'For the first time in my life I felt concern for the future of the
cinema'.[21] The critics were not saying that such a film should not be shown. They
were with justification asking why *Straw Dogs* should get the certificate which *Trash*
had not at that time been allowed.

Warhol's *Trash* (see illustration 254) was rejected by the Board at the same time
that the three above-mentioned films were passed, yet the critics of *The Times*, the
Guardian, the *Sunday Times* and the *Observer* all enthused over it. Stephen Murphy
has said that he felt unable to pass *Trash* because it might help create a drug problem
in Great Britain. The film is about a heroin addict who is unable to have sex because
of his addiction. Far from encouraging drugs, the film takes a highly moral line in its
own terms, as it shows graphically the physical dangers and unhappiness of addiction.
Scenes of Joe Dallesandro as the addict being hopelessly provoked into gaining an
erection by various astonishing girls are more likely to turn people off drugs than any
righteous moralising. The film is easier to follow than most of Warhol's films, as it
makes more concessions to main-stream film-making, and like *Flesh*, it is largely the
work of Warhol's assistant, Paul Morrissey. Its observation of life on the fringes of
society is funny and accurate, and its treatment of the mechanics of sex is honest and
explicit, yet in no way does it cater to the pornographic interest.

Another victim of the Censor was *Performance* (1970), in which James Fox plays a
gangster on the run, who by chance finds his way into the house of an ex-pop singer
(Mick Jagger), who has lost the element of violence that made him a superstar. A
psychological cat-and-mouse game develops, in which the personalities of Jagger
and Fox merge in a kaleidoscope of sex and drugs. Although John Trevelyan liked

254 Andy Warhol and
Paul Morrissey, *Trash*,
1970, with
Joe Dallesandro and
Holly Woodlawn

the film, he made extensive cuts. A Samson-like ceremony of shaving the head of a chauffeur as a warning to his employer was foreshortened in case people tried it out for themselves. The scene where James Fox is beaten up was partly cut, and the flashbacks to him fucking and whipping a girl during the beating—to show that his whole world is violence and he knows no other world—were cut out. This all helped to mute the effect of his meeting Jagger and rejecting violence for a world where getting high and having sex are more important. The opposing personalities of Fox and Jagger merge into one as the film's allegory develops, and this is shown especially in a scene where Jagger, his girlfriend, and Fox have a nude threesome on a great big bed (see illustration 255). Most of this scene was cut by the Censor

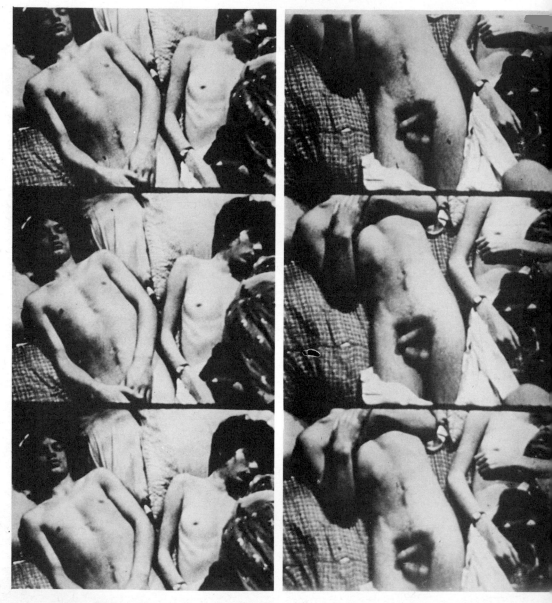

255 Nicholas Roeg, *Performance*, 1970, with Mick Jagger and Anita Pallenberg

including the vital moment when Jagger and Fox embrace passionately. The mutilation of *Performance* is a perfect example of the short-sightedness and destructiveness of film censorship.

While *Trash* and *Performance* suffer at the hands of the Censor, a film like *Doctors' Wives* passes unscathed. The critics could only deride it: 'Real life operations in full colour share the screen with assorted doctors and their wives in an orgy of fornication, blackmail, drugs, attempted suicide, hysteria, and discreet nudity';[22] 'the film is replete with more vulgar language, tasteless decor and badly photographed actresses than I've seen in years';[23] 'the hoot of the week . . . Dialogue sample: Bitchy wife: "It took a good funeral to make her sober." Reformed alcoholic: "No it didn't, honey, it took a good lay with my ex-husband." '[24] And two other films which were quite happily given certificates were *Percy* (1970) and *The Statue* (1970), the former about the first penis-transplant and its new owner's efforts to see where it had been before, and the latter about a man who finds that his wife has sculpted him in the nude but given him someone else's penis, leading him off on a hunt for his faithless wife's model, armed with a photograph of the relevant area of the statue. Both films are careful to avoid showing any penises, or even mentioning the word, and they depend entirely on the snigger and sly-wink approach to sex. And yet honestly sexual films are unacceptable to the British Board of Film Censors.

Violence appears to cause the Censor the most trouble nowadays, but it has, of course, been a part of films from the earliest times. *The Perils of Pauline* (1913) was a silent comedy in which a girl was tied onto a railway line and left to her fate. *The Cat and the Canary* (1939) was an early psychological thriller which included a scene where a girl is attacked in a cellar by a maniac with a knife. Famous moments of violence in the cinema include the scene in *Un Chien Andalou* (1928) by Luis Buñuel and Salvador Dali where a woman's eye is sliced open by a razor, and the Odessa steps sequence in Eisenstein's *Battleship Potemkin* (1925), with the close-up of the screaming governess's blood-spattered face and smashed spectacles. In the '60s the Censor objected to the explicit violence of the Italian film *Bitter Rice* (1948) with its young man strung up on a meat-hook, and *Hari Kiri* (1962), the Japanese film which depicted a very realistic scene of a man ceremonially disembowelling himself. The heroes of films like *Bonnie and Clyde* (1967) and *Pigsty* (1969) were shown suffering brutal deaths which were clearly just desserts, but very different were the factually correct and almost unbearably realistic hangings of the Clutter family murderers in the film of Truman Capote's *In Cold Blood* (1967), with its implicit message that capital punishment is wrong.

A killing such as that of Janet Leigh in Hitchcock's *Psycho* (1960) had great shock value at a time when the extremes of violence were the quick and clean shootings of Clint Eastwood's cowboy films *A Fistful of Dollars* and *For a Few Dollars More* (1964, 1965). But this was all changed by the end of the '60s and the early '70s when films like *The Wild Bunch* (1968) and *Soldier Blue* (1970) were able to show a great deal of very explicit and brutal killing.

The controversy over violence in the cinema ranged around two viewpoints: either explicitly violent films would encourage violence in society, or they would benefit that society by releasing its tensions. Stephen Murphy took up an ambivalent position, passing *Straw Dogs* and *A Clockwork Orange* (1972) but rejecting eight other films on the grounds of violence in his first six months in office. His yardstick of public acceptability begged the question, for how was anyone to judge what was publicly acceptable? Expert opinion on the effects of violence in the media is divided.[25] Dr Robert Shields wrote recently: 'Just because somebody is shocked doesn't necessarily mean their values will be changed.'[26] Professor James Halloran of Leicester University has said: 'Violence in films may be a marginal contributory factor to violence in society, but it's not the major factor. And ought we not to be asking first and foremost what *are* the major factors causing violence and frustration? Censorious people tend to use the media as scape-goats.'[27]

Meanwhile, numerous horror films were quietly being made on both sides of the Atlantic with hardly a murmur of protest, even though they often tended to portray extremely explicit violence. Hammer films, the very successful British horror-film company, even began to produce films like *When Dinosaurs Ruled the Earth* (1969) containing the unbeatable combination of sex and violence used earlier in *King Kong* (1933), *Hounds of Zaroff* (1932), and *The Tingler* (1959). Adrienne Corri, who in *A Clockwork Orange* is stripped and raped to the tune of 'Singing in the Rain', pointed to the different standards employed: 'I have just done a Hammer horror and its brimming over with lots of sex and blood. Yet nobody will object, because the violence is treated as a joke. It's like a strip cartoon. But the moment you get near to reality in a film, people get upset. Kubrick treats violence seriously and causes an uproar. Hammer treats it as a joke and no one's concerned. Where's the logic?'[28]

Obviously, people are able to enjoy violence for fun, as in Tom and Jerry cartoons or Hammer films, just as they can enjoy sex for fun in the *Carry On* films. But violence and sex in real terms hit people very hard. If they cannot laugh they tend to be frightened, and fear lies at the root of censorship. As far as the cinema is concerned, the urge to protect people from something whose danger they cannot see for themselves is still riding high in certain countries, notably Great Britain. But it is riding for a fall.

The general trend throughout the world seems to be towards the abolition of censorship for adults and concentration on classification for the protection of children, and this should be welcomed by every civilised being. Censorship is paternalistic, an affirmation of the censor's own superiority, and it is also basically anti-democratic. A matter of personal taste becomes a matter of law, but law and art make unsatisfactory bed-fellows, and legal sanctions are a great hindrance to the urgent necessity of the arts to experiment. Yet experimentation is essential if the cinema is to progress as an art form, and eroticism is one of the most important areas in which such progress can be made. The film is rightly expected to move people, but not much further than laughter or tears. Only when it is universally accepted that the film-maker has an equal right to excite his audience sexually will the cinema be able to achieve total maturity as an art form.

Appendix V

Pornography: A Brief Survey

Pornography is available in the form of magazines, films, and photographs. The range of magazines on offer to the fantasy-collector is enormous, and is better described by Gillian Freeman's term 'undergrowth of literature' than by using the narrow term 'pornography'. The most obvious, and most easily obtainable, are the pin-up magazines, which sell the titillation of the desirably unattainable by means of photographs of provocatively posed pneumatic lovelies. At the cheaper end of the range are the English mini-magazines with monosyllabic titles such as *Spick*, *Span*, *Wink*, *Kink*, and *Spank*, harmless little bundles of fun for randy servicemen and football fans. *Spick* says proudly on its title page: 'We believe man should be left in no doubt that woman has the superior shape,' and proceeds to show buxom women in their underwear who could turn on only the very unsophisticated. The articles extol the qualities of each model (*e.g.* ' "By gad," said Chad, "she's rather adorable, ain't she?" ' starts the piece on 'swinging Goldilocks Amery, a London dolly who has an infallible way of dealing with wolves'). America has its equivalents, for example, *Scamp*, 'the sparkling companion for men', which intersperses its photographs with articles on such subjects as 'Are men losing the Battle of the Sexes?'

In the middle of this range are the more glossy magazines with regular feature articles. American examples tend to have male-ego-boosting titles like *Man to Man* (with its nude of the month and articles such as 'when sexy art was public and proper'), *Stag* ('What you should know about women who are nymphomaniacs, promiscuous, lesbians') and *Male* ('The truth about organ size, male and female' and a monthly feature on 'You and Women'), though there is nothing to match the level of the forerunner *Esquire* with its high class pin-ups drawn by Petty (in the '30s) and Vargas (in the '40s). In England the tone is gentler: there is *King* and *Knave* as well as *Titbits* (with covergirl and a lively letters page) and *Fiesta* (with serious articles on subjects like 'Revolution in the Theatre' and 'Tribute to Henry Miller'). There was also the short-lived *Sex International News* which described itself as 'the specialist newspaper for the sex scene', but which was just a collection of chatty articles about sexual happenings, interspersed with pin-ups and frontal nudes both male and female, in the style of the German tabloids, *Sexy* and *Die Nachrichten* and the American *San Francisco Ball*.

At the top of the pin-up magazine range, as far as price is concerned at any rate, are the expensively produced glossies aimed at the affluent market, such as Paul Raymond's publications so often confiscated by the police, *Men Only* (see illustration 256) and *Club International*, but there is nothing now to match the fantasy world of

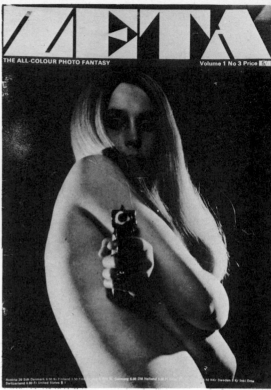

256   *Men Only*, London,
      1972

257   *Zeta*, London, 1967

the beautifully produced but sadly defunct *Zeta* (see illustration 257). The leaders
in this range are *Playboy* (America) and *Penthouse* (England), which give the same
service (though probably more effectively), but add a veneer of culture, vying with
each other to attract the big names as contributors (*Playboy* has recently offered its
readers the pearls of Ken Tynan, Terry Southern, Timothy Leary, John Cassavetes,
Woody Allen, Robert Morley, Tomi Ungerer, Joan Baez, John Wyndham, Len
Deighton; *Penthouse* has come up with Julian Huxley, Wolf Mankowitz, Colin
Wilson, Alan Sillitoe, Alex Trocchi, Germaine Greer, Shepherd Mead, David
Benedictus, Alex Comfort). You must expect to pay more for the intellectual features
sandwiched between the more down-to-earth delights of the beautiful models, but
you also get a remarkably high standard of photography for your money. Interest
centres on the famous centre-spread features—*Penthouse* Pet of the Month (see
illustration 258), and *Playboy* Playmate of the Month, gorgeous, amply-endowed
females who always seem, according to the accompanying articles, to combine healthy
outdoor activities with the occasional intellectual interest, and who presumably do
not realise that they are being exploited as sexual objects. And the editors seem at
pains to keep up with the magazines' pseudo-serious image: for example, Heidi,
Playboy Playmate of the Month, is shown almost nude, sitting on a cane-bottomed
chair. The caption runs: 'Van Gogh saw the art in a chair. His was yellow and
cloggish and square. Ours is round and slicker, being whicker. But we cheated. We

sat the art on it. Heidi's the name.' The special appeal of these tantalising visions of femininity used to be that they kept their pubic hair well hidden at all costs, symbolising the fantasy of the unattainable. Alas, things have changed in our permissive age, and now almost anything goes, even in *Playboy* and *Penthouse*! And the same is true of their continental counterparts, *Lui* (France), *Er* (Germany), and *Playmen* (Italy), which recently caused a sensation with its frontal nude photographs of Jacqueline Kennedy Onassis, taken secretly and in questionable circumstances.

Apart from the advertisements on the Underground, these pin-ups are the staple diet of titillation for the average man. But it is not difficult to find further and perfectly legal excitement if nude girls are the required commodity, for certain photographers make their living this way: photographs of nude women with shaved pubic hair like Rosanna of Guernsey (see illustration 259) are easily obtainable. The nude photographs and films of Harrison Marks all show full frontals, but either with the pubic hair shaved or else with evidence of deft brushwork on the negative. These clinical and supremely unerotic productions have made Mr Marks a fortune, but their *kitsch* level of taste is at least preferable to the pre-war nudist magazine 'art studies' by Roye such as *Tomorrow's Crucifixion* (1938), an air-brushed nude woman wearing a gas-mask and nailed to a cross.[1] One of Roye's nude studies was reproduced in the *Daily Mirror* in 1938, the first occasion on which a British national daily newspaper published a nude photograph;[2] another such breakthrough was the publication in the Oxford student magazine *Oxymoron* in 1967 of *Sun Worship* (see illustration 260), Jean Straker's female nude study, with pubic hair left in. This was the first time such a photograph had been published in a British paper, and in retrospect the outcry that greeted this event seems absurd. It was fitting that Jean

258 *Pet of the Month*, from *Penthouse*, London, 1971

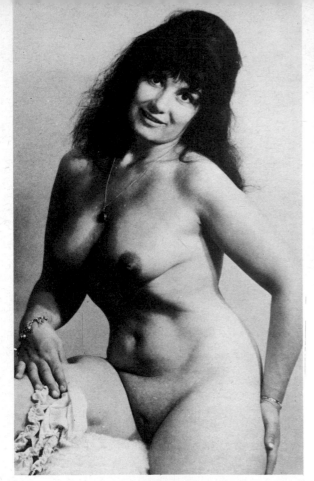

260   Jean Straker, *Sun Worship*, 1967

259   *Rosanna of Guernsey*, 1967

Straker should be the photographer to accomplish this, for he has campaigned tirelessly and through much harassment from the law for complete freedom for the artist.[3]

For honest, straightforward full-frontal nudes of both sexes, one has only to turn to the publications of the various nudist associations (or naturists as they prefer to be called). Of these, the most common are *Sun and Health* and *Sun Seeker* (see illustration 261) in Great Britain, and *Nudism Today* and *Nude Living* in America. The law likes to believe that since nudism is a healthy activity, nudist magazines will only be read by healthy people, and so takes no exception to these magazines. But the circulation they enjoy bears absolutely no relation to the small numbers of nudists in the world. The articles in these magazines range from 'Is Milk a Protection against Cancer?' to 'Nudism and Sex in Marriage', and the most obvious difference between them and the pin-ups is the total lack of any attempt at titillation in the photographs; in fact it is difficult to see how anyone can find these pictures erotic (see illustration 262). The editors cannot be unaware of the fact that most of their customers are in no way interested in the serious subject of nudism, though I have seen no evidence of deliberate attempts to pander to such readers. However, the success of such publications is now on the wane, now that pin-up magazines are able to be so much more daring.

Until very recently, the student of sex in all its forms had little or no alternative

[398]

262　*Nude Camper* from *Sun Seeker*, London, 1967

261　*Sun Seeker*, London, 1967

to the above materials if he wished to stay the right side of the law. But now we are experiencing in Great Britain a new phenomenon—the sex magazine. The pioneer in this field was *Forum*, 'The Journal of Human Relations', the longest-running and still the most serious, which takes a very academic approach to sex and uses no photographs. While its integrity and honesty are beyond question, it does tend to make sex sound rather boring. *Forum* is a small-format magazine, and has many imitators, including *Fact* (The Intimate Journal'), *In Depth* (whose article on 'The Orgasm' starts: 'The fuses become heated, bells ring out, you mutter "I love you" then explode, thrusting, panting, your body loses control of itself, you fall exhausted to the sheet, ecstatic!'), *Search* ('For Adam and Eve Together') and *Open* ('For the Open Mind'), none of which matches up to the original.

Forum has no appeal to the visually prurient interest, but this is provided by the glossy sex magazines, whose serious content tends to be proportionately diminished. *Man and Woman* was a weekly which built up in ninety-eight parts to become *The Marshall Cavendish Encyclopaedia of Adult Relationships*, and was designed to cause the least possible offence. The result fell between the two stools of polite family reading and serious sexual exploration. *Curious* is a full-colour glossy subtitled 'The Sex-Education Magazine for Men and Women'. The occasional scholarly and informative article tends to be lost among the photographs, which often outdo *Playboy* for erotic effect and have featured full-frontal nudes, both male and female.

[399]

It is certainly very alive, even after a heavy fine under the Obscene Publications Act. *New Direction* ('The Magazine of the Sexual Revolution') seems to try to go further than any other in the daring quality of its photographs while sanctimoniously declaring that it is 'carefully edited to avoid any element of titillation since this is not (our) purpose'. One of the most recent of these is *Probe*, a semi-serious, glossily illustrated sex-counselling magazine, but the best is *Scorpio* ('Explorations in Sexuality'), which is exactly what it says it is, with well-researched articles on everything from abortion and censorship to aphrodisiacs, as well as inquiries into pornography and sexual aids. Its historical articles are good as well, and the illustrations are of a high quality (see illustration 263); in fact, *Scorpio* makes a fair attempt at providing the great lack in British journalism, a magazine of eroticism. France has *Plexus*, a serious monthly publication which includes features on people connected with the world of eroticism from Dali to the Kronhausens, and from Sade to Bataille, interspersed with examples of erotic art and photography. America had its counterpart, *Eros*, until its editor Ralph Ginzburg was jailed after an absurd obscenity trial in 1963.[4] In its four issues, *Eros* published the brothel prints of Degas, little-known erotic writings by Mark Twain, D. H. Lawrence, Robert Burns, and Ovid, and features on Marilyn Monroe, Frank Harris, Victorian pin-ups, and Indian temple sculptures. In 1971 a magazine called *The Image* appeared in England which featured the work of contemporary artists and photographers like Richard Hamilton, Graham Ovenden, Peter Till, and Bruce Lacey: the accent was on eroticism, but the quality of the art-work diminished in successive issues, and the magazine failed to reach the level of *Plexus* or *Eros*.

Side by side with the sex magazines have appeared fully illustrated manuals of

263   *Fetish photograph* from *Scorpio*, London, 1971

sex technique. Among English examples are *Making Love* ('For Married Couples Only'), which is described by its publishers, Pellen Personal Products Ltd, of London, as 'showing a young nude couple, husband and beautiful wife, making love in imaginative positions, with the added beauty of coloured bodies and settings', and *Variations on a Sexual Theme*, which has to do without coloured bodies and settings but contains photographs and descriptions of forty ways to have intercourse, plus rather pedestrian essays on the plumbing mechanism. It is all very far removed from the excitements of the *Kama Sutra*.

The publishers of these and other such books have had trouble with the law in England, even though they are at pains to make sure that no one can catch sight of a sexual organ, or even a pubic hair. Full lip-service is paid to modesty and morality: the models' faces are always turned away from the camera, and the girl's wedding ring is prominently displayed. Such books may well help couples to a fuller sex-life; the prurient interest of the illustrations is negligible. Similar books in America, Denmark, and Sweden leave nothing to the imagination and cater for all interests with an enviable honesty and openness: a good example is the American publication *The Joy of Sex* by Dr Alex Comfort.[5] In England, sex manuals are sold mainly in sex boutiques or sex supermarkets, another recent and highly controversial innovation, though already common in Holland, America, Germany, Sweden, Denmark, and Norway, where they provide a very necessary service.

Gillian Freeman estimates that ninety per cent of the pornography imported into England is sado-masochistic (see illustration 264). This is probably an exaggeration, but certainly violence plays a large part in hard-core pornography. Of course, sex and violence have always gone hand in hand for the sexually sophisticated, and the

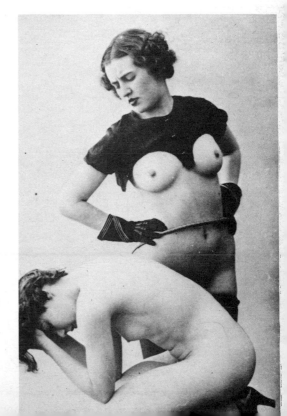

264   *Flagellation photograph*, Germany?,
c. 1935

very act of sex has violent undertones. Psychologists have noted that perfectly normal people often react sexually to news, or even experiences of brutality or tragedy. Mary McCarthy described recently on television how she tends to respond sexually to cruelty on the screen. From the widespread wearing of long leather boots to the steady demand for the services of the 'governesses' who advertise their 'discipline' on notice-boards in Soho and 42nd Street, the smell of violence hovers around the citadel of sex.

In her book, Gillian Freeman equates the enormous demand for sado-masochist literature in Great Britain with our tradition of ritualistic punishment by caning (in schools) and flogging (in the services; in prisons). 'Schools, prisons and colonial territories were, and are, places where fantasy has been allowed to leak unpleasantly into real life, under the guise of discipline.'[6] Although there is a germ of truth here, this is dangerous ground, and ignores the fact that America, Germany, and Japan all consume an enormous amount of sado-masochist literature; and that both de Sade and the authoress of *Histoire d'O* were French. The English have no corner on sado-maschism; the connection between sex and violence is a part of the human psyche. As Peter Fryer has pointed out: 'Today we can look more honestly into the human heart, for we know there are tendencies towards, and

265   Robert Crumb, *Eggs Ackley among
the Vulture Demonesses*, page from
American comic strip, 1969

fantasies of, both cruelty and submission in "normal" people.[7] Or as Jung said on a famous occasion, 'Give me a normal man and I will cure him'.

Whether through corporal punishment or not, children certainly come into contact with violence very early on. Their reading material caters for their need for fantasy, and violence plays a part in most children's books. In comics this is especially true. Whilst not usually pornographic, these often contain features of adult fetishism. Batman wears tight shorts, satin cape, high boots, long leather gloves, and a rubber hood and mask. Robin is masked and booted, and their relationship is overtly homosexual. Then there is Rubber Man, Plastic Man, and Captain America (who wears a tight rubber hood), not to mention Wonder Woman, with her steel bracelets and gold-plated bra, and her high-heeled boots 'made of special Amazon material'. Cruelty and discipline stalk the pages of *Wham*, *Smash*, *Eagle*, and *Dandy*. Violence and fetishism lurk between the pages of the 'unapproved' new-style American comics such as *Zap* and *Mr Natural*, with their brilliant art-work by Robert Crumb and S. Clay Wilson. Robert Crumb's 'Vulture Demonesses' (see illustration 265) with their exotic outfits and long leather boots, would turn on many a fetishist; this comic strip achieved world fame as the model used by Vivian Berger for his *Oz Schoolkids Issue* Rupert Bear cartoon (see illustration 266).

266 *Rupert finds Gipsy Granny*, page from
Oz Schoolkids Issue, London, 1971

Dr Frederic Wertham sees a great danger in such material: 'The short circuit which connects violence with sex is a primitive pattern slumbering in all people.'[8] He argues that violent comics are psychologically harmful to children, but his case is certainly not proven. Gillian Freeman is nearer the mark: 'I feel that if sexual fetishes are developed in the very young, the masks, capes, boots, manacles, and violence in children's comics are perhaps just as likely to exorcise a child's fantasy needs as they are to feed a grown-up's.'[9]

Soft pornography often reflects this primeval interest in violence (see illustration 267). *Penthouse* once conducted a lively forum on the subject of disciplining girls: 'To my mind the normal school cane is far too heavy, thick and rigid. My husband on one of his business trips to Singapore brought me a more suitable type. It is three foot long, quarter of an inch thin, light and very pliable with a curved handle'; and *Playboy* recently included a photo-fantasy entitled 'Brides of Fu Manchu'.

There is, however, a whole world of specialised pornography devoted to 'fladge'. At one end are the light-weight magazines consisting of carefully posed photographs telling a 'story', such as *Domestic Problem* ('Angelique was Sonya's own personal maid, but quite often she just didn't act like a proper servant girl should. . . . Finally Sonya could no longer tolerate Angelique's incorrigible behaviour. She took the wilful young maid in hand and with the aid of an ominous-looking snakeskin whip made her point quite clear and firm.' Both Angelique and Sonya are shown clothed in tight-fitting black latex); or *Macabre Punishment* (a girl is depicted in chains in a dungeon; various tortures are applied; the ketchup is used liberally). Then there are the specialist periodicals: *e.g. Slave Mistress, Justice Monthly, Rubber News,*

267   *Bondage photograph*, England, *c.* 1932

268   John Willie, *Bondage drawing*, *c.* 1947

Sunday Spankers, Teenage Discipline, Leather Boys, Spankers' Monthly (typical extract: 'Little did they realize that I, Duchess of Pain, was hungry for the whip and to be whipped. Little did they realize that when I took a man into my castle he wielded the whip on me. I had the same whip turned on him by me. This is my Pleasure'). *Justice Monthly*, like many others, runs a personal-advertisements service ('Thirty year old Anglo-Saxon male, docile, with pleasant manners and good education, would like to meet aggressive female of any age interested in the subject of discipline'). *Leather Boys* and *Rubber News* are two of many publications directed at the fetishist, though *Rubber News* went out of business in June 1967 when the Editor was fined one thousand pounds for corrupting the innocent. This was a pity, because it was a serious and intelligent publication which had a large following: 'By far the majority of rubber-lovers are just ordinary folk, living Godly and sober lives, but having this unusual interest in something added. But if you look at it coldly, it is for certain that a liking for rubber is by no means as odd as a passion for fox-hunting.' The magazine did a survey of its readers' initiations into their fetish: 'My own introduction to rubber was at a very early age—about four years old, I think, when I gradually realized that a rubber hot-water bottle meant more to me than just a bed warmer'; 'I can now remember that my first appreciation of rubber was when I was issued with a rubber cape-cum-groundsheet in the school OTC.' And the service it offered was much appreciated: 'It is a relief to find so many other people who are "rubber-slaves". One normally feels so alone and rather guilty.' The most well-known fetishistic magazine is *Bizarre* (America, 1946–59), a now-defunct product which combined high-class photography and art-work by

269 John Willie, drawing from *Sweet Gwendoline and the Missing Princess*, *c.* 1948

270 *Bondage photograph*, America?, *c.* 1948

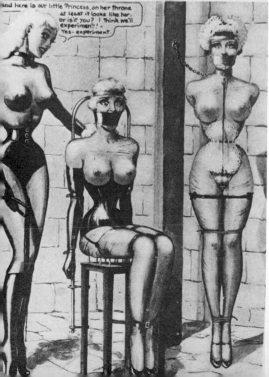

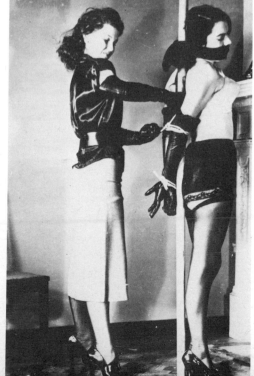

271   *Bizarre Illustrated*,
Pennsylvania, 1968

the famous English illustrator John Willie (see illustrations 268, 269, and 270) with
good articles, and is now a collector's item, as is its forerunner, *London Life* (late-
'20s–mid-'40s). They have had many imitators, among them *Bizarre Capers*,
Bizarre Fun, and *Bizarre Illustrated* (see illustration 271). These productions meet
a real need: 'The fetishist has displaced his desire from an area in which it can be
fulfilled to an area in which it cannot. It has been moved from a sensation to an
idea.'[10] (See illustration 272.)

272   *Fetish photograph*, suit
by Atomage of
London, *c.* 1970

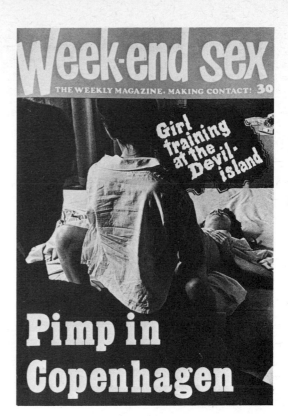

273   *Weekend Sex*, Copenhagen, 1972

In its most extreme form, fetishism involves subjects which must be repugnant to even the most liberal-minded. An advertiser in *Weekend Sex* (a Danish magazine, see illustration 273) writes: 'Slave wants mistress or couple or others. Would you like to make me really filthy with urine, etc.? I would like to be your toilet and lick your anus for your great pleasure. Discretion wanted and given. All letters will be answered.' Magazines cater even for him: *e.g. Grotesque*, a Danish product aimed apparently at the German market, which consists of photographs of leather-clad men in chains, some covered with excrement, others being made to eat it. Although possibly faked, these photographs must turn some people on.

Many magazines, including *Grotesque*, show a special liking for Nazi uniforms, and this seems especially true of certain American productions, *e.g. Man, Man's Story, Men Today, Dominate* (typical feature: 'Hideous secrets of the Nazi Torture Cult'). Gillian Freeman mentions a story in *Man* called 'Soft Flesh for the Nazi Fanged Doom' headlined: 'Fashionable or not, pleasant or not, the bloody account of the darkest era of history must be told and retold.' She comments: 'And heaven knows, it is told and retold and retold and retold, week after week after week.'[11] This market is also catered for by paperback books with titles like *Orgies of Torture and Brutality* ('Sadistic rituals . . . savage fertility rites') and *Gerda, the Bestial Wardress of Belsen* ('Dip his balls in boiling fat . . .'). De Sade and Sacher-Masoch are left far behind.

There are many paperback books of this sort aimed at the fetishist and the sado-masochist. My favourite title is *Rubber Family Robinson* ('The life of an offbeat

[407]

family—this is a fun book, nothing more. It does not seek to probe anyone's psyche.') There is a series called *Betty Page in Bondage* in which the lady endures being trussed up, gagged, hoisted on pulleys, and many other such delights. Then one can savour *Pussies in Boots* ('nearly 200 pages packed with photos of gorgeous girls in boots'). On the dedication page is the quotation: ' "Kick me" said the masochist. "No" said the sadist.' Other titles are *Holiday in Fetterland, Sadistic Cults and Abnormalities, The Lure of Leather, Buttocks and Breasts, Domestic Discipline, The Mini-skirt and Beyond, a Voyeur's View*. An interesting example is *Erotic Variations* by John Barry, which purports to be a series of interviews with sexual deviants, followed by the author's enlightened comments. 'The purpose of this book is to establish a guide line so that the citizen will be equipped with a proper background in the field of deviation. . . . I dedicate this book to the thinkers of America. Our one and only hope for survival.' A typical case: 'As a male I am very fond of wearing a rubber girdle. This I wear at home and sometimes to work if the desire is very strong. I've tried to get my wife to be a convert to a rubber girdle and panties, but so far no luck. For casual wear about the house I wear mesh stockings and a rubber girdle along with a bathing cap.' The enlightened comment: 'There are a host of fetish items. They all add up to one fact that they are but an erotic symbol which is used as a substitute for regular sexual relations.'[12] Such pseudo-scientific publications are the stock-in-trade of Soho and 42nd Street.

Magazines and paperbacks are not, of course, the only type of pornography available. Sets of photographs are more easily obtainable now than in the days when one had to haggle with the dirty-postcard sellers of Paris or Port Said, and of much higher quality. And recently there has been an enormous demand for pornographic films. Porn shops sell them, and they are obtainable by post from Denmark and Sweden in all varieties. One is advertised as *The Swingers:* 'Two young girls are dancing around in a room. Suddenly they discover a beautiful penis sticking out from an open cupboard.' Another, *Phantom Fucker*, caters for more exotic tastes: 'Three girls are sitting on a sofa, when two masked men force their way in. The girls are made to undress. The men beat them and force them to suck one man and have intercourse with him. They are then made to lick up his sperm and drink a glass of his urine. A film which really shows sexual sadism.'

One very common theme in pornography is lesbianism, which appeals to men as well as women, unlike male homosexuality, which women usually find revolting. It has been suggested that a large number of men enjoy watching lesbian activities because of a latent fear of the psychological demands of a heterosexual relationship. Certainly, it would appear that almost all lesbian photo-pornography is bought by men. They can choose between scenes of torrid love-making in *Lesbian Climax* or *Black Lesbian* (from Sweden) and the more violent happenings of *Chok* (from Denmark); and many fetishist magazines depict lesbian activities. There are, however, some lesbian magazines aimed specifically at lesbians, including *Ladder* and *Lesbian* (America) and *Arena Three* and *Sappho* (England). All are serious publications with no interest at all for the prurient. Instead, they feature articles on law reform, censorship, etc., and reviews of books and films of interest to their readers.

Pornography is aimed almost exclusively at men, for it is generally assumed that women are romantic creatures who are not sexually aroused by photographs but prefer to use their imagination: 'Whereas a man can be sexually aroused by a nude pin-up, women are more attracted by a man's personality which only shows in his manner and movements. Women need something more tangible than flat pictures to be aroused.'[13] From my own observations of my students I am convinced that this broad generalisation is nonsense. Many women react more quickly—and more critically—to sexual images than men, and if the images appeal to them, they are often more deeply aroused. But women have been conditioned to accept that obvious sexual excitement is unseemly, and the Victorian rule that they should not expect pleasure from sex is still unfortunately alive in some sections of the community. For instance, sex-instruction diagrams for both boys and girls very rarely include the clitoris; and the public suspiciousness of sexual pleasure is reflected in the fact that certain American states still make it illegal for married couples to practise fellatio or cunnilingus, and in England anal intercourse in marriage is also against the law. But attitudes are of course changing: *Cosmopolitan* is one American women's magazine that has featured male pin-ups. For its birth in Great Britain in 1972, it promised its new readers a male pin-up who would 'reveal all', but the photograph disappointed many because the model was shown coyly bending one leg to hide his penis.[14] Curiously, his navel had been retouched, although a glimpse of pubic hair remained. In retaliation, *Oz* magazine then published a fully frontal nude photograph of the same model.[15] In America, 1973, and in England, 1974, saw the arrival of two pin-up magazines aimed specifically at women: *Playgirl* and *Viva*; both contained discreet male frontal nudes, but the papers were from the same stables as *Playboy* and *Penthouse* respectively, and shared the same rather unliberated sexual philosophy. Nevertheless they were a step in the right direction. In January, 1973, a man's magazine in England, *Knave*, 'a new concept in eroticism', began to feature articles for women readers which included photographs of male frontal nudes. And at the same time at least four calendars featuring the same sort of photographs went on sale in Britain and America, and a half-length nude poster of Olympic swimmer Mark Spitz sold by the thousand. Male nudity has also begun to appear in British advertising, although many women have objected to the 'effeminacy' of the models; in Europe, however, such advertisements have been common for some time.

Male homosexual magazines appeal only to homosexuals, but if sales are a good yardstick, then homosexuals form a sizeable proportion of the population. Unlike lesbianism, male homosexuality is frowned upon by the law in almost every country. Only since 1967 have male homosexual relationships been legal in Great Britain, and the age of consent is still twenty-one, whereas for heterosexuals it is sixteen. In America it is the same in those states where homosexuality is legal, but in Denmark and Sweden, the age of consent for homosexuals is eighteen and will shortly be changed to fifteen, as for heterosexuals.

Strictures against homosexuality apply also to magazines which cater for homosexuals. Of course many of these are hard-core pornography, for example *Tabasco* (from Germany), *Pagan Male* and *Homo Triangle* (from Denmark), and *Hot Rod* and *Hard Up* (from America): the Americans appear to be more imaginative. These show photographs of homosexuals in action, sometimes with a tenuous story-line. There are also some for sado-masochists: *Kick* (from Germany) and *Gay Wheels*, subtitled 'Teasy Rider, for Leather or Worse' (from America). These show men in leather uniform and out of it, and also feature motor-bikes: the modern counter-parts of the cowboy and his horse.

There are also homosexual publications of a more serious type. These include *Amigo* (from Denmark), *Eos* (from Sweden), *Mattachine Review* and *Tangent* (from America). They include articles and photographs of special interest to their readers, book reviews, cinema and theatre surveys, and personal advertisement columns. *Tangent* is the best produced, and sets out to attack widespread generalisations and misunderstandings about the 'gay' life. They are, of course, illegal in Great Britain, and the personal contact service they offer was provided for a while in this country by *International Times* and *Time Out*, members of the so-called underground press. However, *International Times* had to stop doing so as the result of a prosecution in 1970, which showed the degree of prejudice against homosexuality still prevalent, and *Time Out* followed suit.

In April 1969, a new magazine appeared on the bookstalls in England: *Jeremy*, subtitled 'The Magazine for Modern Young Men'. This was a brave if shortlived attempt to provide homosexuals with a legal and easily obtainable magazine in this country. The editors promised all the features of any other lively magazine, and the first issue offered its readers advice on the latest styles in underwear and cosmetics, cooking hints, a guide to restaurants and clubs that welcomed homosexuals, film and theatre reviews and a special horoscope ('Aquarius: Should those around you criticize you for not holding yourself erect, remember that the feeling's mutual. Don't thrust yourself indiscriminately at your associates, you will only rub them up the wrong way'). It was all a bit coy, but it sold. Unfortunately, the printers and distributors were unhappy about the magazine, and after efforts were made by the editors to give it a less restricted appeal in order to get round these difficulties, it sadly folded up. Prejudice had won another victory. A pale imitation of *Jeremy* appeared in Britain in 1972, *Jeffrey*: 'We shall be wanting to satisfy the keen football fan amongst our readers as well as the domesticated gay guy who may want to try a new recipe or knitting pattern.' *Jeffrey* supplies information and features of interest to homosexuals, but has none of the sparkle of its predecessor. Far more worthwhile are the more politically orientated British publications, *Gay News* and *Lunch*: the former uses a newspaper format and tries to supply the services of a newspaper, while the latter is a heavily political broadsheet. And there is also *Come Together*, the official paper of the Gay Liberation Movement. These are the equivalents of *Spare Rib* and *Shrew*, the Women's Liberation papers, and as with the lesbian magazines

Arena Three and *Sappho*, the prurient appeal is absent. Nevertheless, they have to be constantly wary since the police keep an eye on them. But at their best these publications achieve the high level of informed comment and liberated entertainment of their American counterparts such as *Gay Sunshine* (San Francisco), *Advocate* (Los Angeles), and *Gay Scene* (New York).

A quite different phenomenon are the legal British and American homosexual magazines which pretend to be physique magazines for body-builders. There are hundreds of these, on both sides of the Atlantic, with titles such as *Physique Pictorial*, *Male Classics*, *Tomorrow's Man* ('filled with photos of up and coming physique stars'), *Body Beautiful*, *Male Models* ('Honi Soit Qui Mal y Pense'), *Physique Artistry*, *Big* ('Big's point of view should serve to inspire the development toward perfection of mind, body and health'). They contain endless photographs of young men in very brief posing pouches, or nude but carefully positioned, with details of their vital statistics and addresses for obtaining 'further studies' of them. Very rarely do they even mention body-building (*Man's World* is the exception here), yet in theory they exist solely to further their readers' interest in physique development. *Junior* describes itself as 'The Boy's Guide to Physical Fitness', but has features such as 'Up-stairs and down with Bucky Brown' (a pretty youth posing coyly on the stairs in his birthday suit) and only two pages that have even a remote connection with physical fitness. With lack of subtlety, it proclaims across its front cover: 'The Strength of America lies in its Youth'. One of the distinctions of these magazines, however, is their use of male nude drawings by Quaintance, Spartacus, and especially by the highly talented Tom of Finland (see illustration 178).

In America, these magazines now get away with full-frontal nudity, genitals and all (though not in a state of arousal), but this is too dangerous for Great Britain. I have seen a copy of the uncensored American *Male Models* in Soho for two pounds, and then found the same issue on open sale in a bookshop for thirty pence, with all the genitals carefully blacked out for the English market (see illustrations 274 and 275). People must be employed full time to touch up photographs of male nudes! The advent of full-frontal nudity brought problems in America, as we learn from *Physique Pictorial*'s article on 'The Big Basket Fraud': 'When the physique magazines could show models only in posing straps, we described the then prevalent practice of stuffing the straps with dildos, sausages and other such nonsense. But now that the full-nude era is upon us, a far more sophisticated technique of "cheating" is being practiced. Many of the "outrageously sized" appendages displayed in the books making their primary appeal to the "tumescophiles" have been photographically added on. We have no intention of joining the frantic contest to see who can display the largest pudenda. In the words of a certain cigarette advertisement, "It's not how long you make it, but how you make it long." We feel that some people are trying to push too much too fast.' Laudable sentiments, especially when you print nearby a photograph of 'Randy Anderson' (with decidedly enlarged penis) 'who wants to be an airline pilot'. It is to be regretted that the laws of two of the most civilised countries in the world make the dishonesty of these magazines a necessity.

[411]

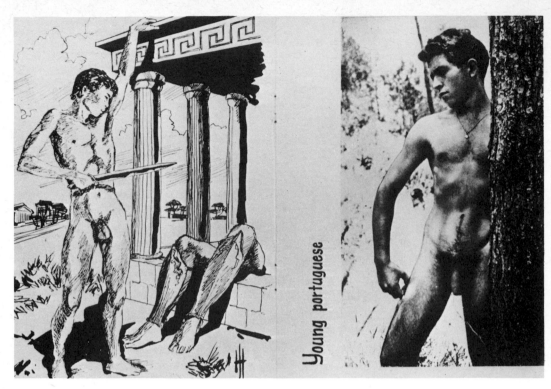

274   Page from *Male Models* number 4, American edition, 1963

275   Censored page from *Male Models* number 4, English edition, 1963

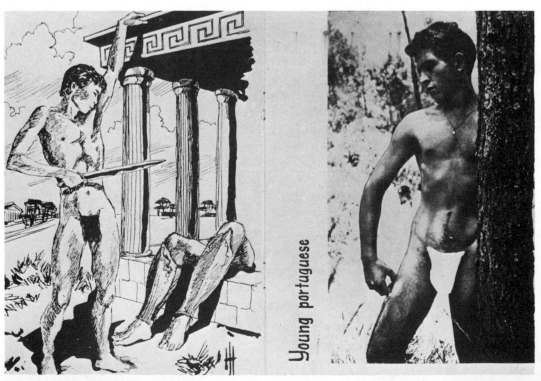

One of the biggest shocks I experienced during my research on pornography was my first view of *Animal Bizarre*. This is a Danish magazine which shows very explicit full colour photographs of people having sexual relationships with animals. Both males and females are depicted, and the animals include dogs, pigs, and donkeys. There is apparently a big market for such magazines, especially in Denmark and Germany, and others available include *Donkey Sex* and *Animal Orgy*. One famous model for these is Bodil, a Danish girl who describes how she really loves her animals and does not just make-believe for the photographer. She also appears in a beautifully made film (*A Summer's Day*) which I saw in a Copenhagen cinema, in which she advises people not to try to make love to a stallion as it will probably kill them. In fact, this pornography provides a strong and needed fantasy for certain types of people, and I am assured that they very rarely have any desire to make the fantasy a reality.

The most widespread pornography depicts straightforward heterosexual intercourse, and since there are only a limited number of possible permutations and camera-angles, this tends to become incredibly boring (see illustration 4). *Colour Climax* (from Denmark) and *Loving Sweden* have an enormous circulation for their monthly issues, and must provide a continual headache for those who think up the 'plots'. Like *Kis* and *Colour Sperma* (from Denmark) and *Private* (from Sweden), they use very high-quality colour photography (and no text) to tell a little 'story'. A typical example starts with a young couple watching television. Bored with the programme, they begin heavy petting, and then undress each other. Finally they move to the bedroom and start running through the *Kama Sutra* range. The couples in these publications are always clothed at the beginning, start undressing by page 4, and are more or less nude by page 7. Visible male orgasm is almost invariably shown at the end.

These publications tend to appeal to perfectly normal people who find the need for visual stimulation in their sex lives, not necessarily on their own but more usually with their partners. The idea that pornography is only bought by dirty old men to masturbate over is incorrect. But of course many lonely people do buy pornography. These tend to be people whose sexual needs cannot be met in reality, either because of shyness or more often as a result of repression in childhood or lack of understanding shown to them by their fellow adults. Hostility from the law and from society makes such people search for a compensating fantasy world in pornography, especially the less straightforward varieties described above. Such people do not constitute a danger; on the contrary, they deserve every sympathy. Their fantasies are not, however, likely to be catered for by the sexpapers *Suck* (Amsterdam, English language) and *Screw* (New York), which are nevertheless treated by the law as pornography and unobtainable in Great Britain. They are not concerned merely to titillate sexual appetites; they are politically and philosophically orientated in the direction of complete freedom for the individual, looking forward, perhaps over-optimistically, to a freer and happier society.

Soft-core pornography is legal in Great Britain, but the real hard-core material is not (the difference between the two being, I suppose, that between a soft and a hard organ). It is illegal to have it in your possession for gain (*i.e.* to sell it), and also to cause it to be sent through the post or to bring it into the country. Presumably the law is concerned to protect her Majesty's Postal and Customs Officers from the deadly product. But it is not illegal merely to possess hard-core porn. After all, an Englishman's home is still his castle.

All evidence points to the fact that the Obscene Publications Act is unworkable and undesirable. A recent *Observer* inquiry into the financial background to pornography in Great Britain summed up: 'Prohibition does not work. It merely puts up prices, drives the business underground and provides a potential source of corruption for those charged with enforcing the laws against it. A free and legal market, through the mail and from shops with no window displays, would probably result in a market glut, falling prices, and satiated customers.'[15]

In 1967 Denmark became the first country to abolish restrictions on pornography. It was a calculated and carefully considered decision, and a parliamentary committee on censorship spent nearly two years looking at evidence and opinion from all quarters before recommending it. From the start, this was a political decision by a democratic government committed to the ideal of individual freedom, but it was also considered an experiment—one that could always be stopped. This has not been found necessary. In fact, in the eyes of the Danes, the experiment has been a success. Sweden and West Germany have now repealed their legislation on pornography and Holland is expected to follow suit in the near future.

There was a certain amount of anxiety at the outset in Denmark about possible effects of the experiment. Fears were expressed that pornography would affect children and give them a callous attitude to sex, and that it would lead to promiscuity and stimulate sex crimes. These fears appear to have been allayed during the seven years that the experiment has been in operation. A leading Copenhagen psychologist has said: 'We opened the forbidden door at the end of the corridor and we did not find it half as alarming as some expected. There is a distinct change of mood once the unnatural fear has gone out of it.'[17] As far as public opinion is concerned, a government poll taken in 1970 revealed that fifty-seven per cent of Danes approve of full liberation; eighteen per cent are undecided; and twenty-five per cent have reservations—mainly about shop-window displays rather than about the basic principles involved.

Denmark is ideally suited for this type of experiment, with its small, highly educated, affluent society. It does not possess—or claim to have—a monopoly on the availability of pornographic material, for Sweden, West Germany, Holland, and the United States all have as many outlets of one sort or another, and Great Britain is not far behind. What distinguishes Denmark is the essential fact that it was the first country which gave its citizens the freedom to choose or reject pornography as part of its social policy. The law states that anyone over the age of sixteen can choose to see, read or buy any photograph, magazine, film, or play that he wishes. The experiment has been in operation long enough to offer significant lessons to more hesitant countries.

On a visit to Copenhagen in the summer of 1971, I found the lack of interest shown in pornography by young people very obvious. There was a large number of clearly marked porn shops, some on main streets, but it was rare to find young people in them. The proprietor of one of these shops told me that the vast majority of his clients were middle-aged men. Most young people I spoke to considered pornography an irrelevance to them, merely a commodity which people could easily obtain if they needed it. I did not see children giggling at the pornographic magazines and photographs displayed in shop windows.

This open and quite unavoidable display of sexual material in the streets of Copenhagen is the one obvious factor in the Danish experiment which can be attacked. Guarantees of freedom presumably extend to those who do not wish to be confronted by window displays of a sexual nature when they are doing their daily shopping. Surely they are missing out here? I put this question to Dr Birge Wilcke, a leading police lawyer with special responsibility for pornography. He told me that this was a big problem. 'We had hoped that the porn shops would confine themselves to one area of Copenhagen, but they have spread onto the major shopping streets. We have a law that no scenes of intercourse of any kind may be shown in a shop window —although straightforward nudes are permitted—and this we try to uphold. We take action if we receive a complaint. There was a successful prosecution only two weeks ago. The Director of Public Prosecutions himself went to see the offending window display before taking steps against the shop concerned.'

I asked Dr Wilcke to clarify the laws protecting young people in Denmark. He explained that it was illegal for anyone below the age of sixteen to buy pornography, and for anyone below the age of eighteen to take part in homosexual activities. The latter age restriction would soon be lowered to fifteen to bring it in line with the law relating to heterosexual activities. It was illegal to commit rape or incest, and also to force anyone to take part in pornographic photography.

The effect of liberalisation on young people was one of the main discussion points at the beginning of the Danish experiment, and it certainly appears that the result has triumphantly exonerated the liberals. There is good reason for countries such as Great Britain and the United States to take note of this fact, for this same topic is still put forward as a strong reason against liberalisation in these countries.

The other main worry expressed at the time of Denmark's abolition of restrictions on pornography was the effect this might have on the rate of sex crimes. The government committee in 1967 went no further than saying that the crime rate would not go up with a change of the laws. They have been proved right. On paper, the sex-crime figures appear to show a dramatic drop of sixty-three per cent between 1959 and 1969. Dr Wilcke was cautious about claiming too much credit for this, but did say that since sexual gratification was easier to obtain now—whether from prostitutes or from pornography—it was to be expected that the rate for minor sex crimes (*e.g.* voyeurism, exhibitionism, etc.) would drop.

An important study of this question was made by Dr Berl Kutschinsky of the University of Copenhagen's Institute of Criminal Science for the American Commission on Pornography in 1970. Although President Nixon rejected the Commission's recommendations, there is no doubt that the evidence collected was scholarly and significant. Dr Kutschinsky reported that the rate of serious crimes such as rape had remained constant, as the experts had expected, although it is of interest to note in passing that such crimes are very rare in Denmark. The big decrease was in such offences as indecent exposure, voyeurism, and indecent assault on women and children, and this could be directly attributed to the increased availability of pornography, through its substitution of a sexual fantasy which could relieve frustrations. The report emphasised that its conclusions were tentative, but more recently Dr Kutschinsky has made it clear that he has no doubt at all that there is a direct relationship between censorship and sexual crimes. To those who believe that pornography becomes an addiction, like a dangerous drug, leading to perversion, he says that on the contrary, once people's initial curiosity has been satisfied, most people lose interest in pornography. 'I call it the banana boat effect. When bananas first appeared in Copenhagen after the war, everyone ate themselves sick.'[18]

My experience in Copenhagen certainly confirms what Dr Kutschinsky says about people losing interest. Most Danish people appear to be completely bored by the whole subject, and rather embarrassed that the world outside associates them with pornography rather than with bacon or ceramics. They would clearly be happier if tourists sought out historic castles and picturesque farmhouses rather than clinical porn-shops, but at the same time they are realistic enough to see the value of this unusual tourist market to their balance of payments.

In 1967 there was a rush to buy pornography, and sales rose steadily until the boom year of 1969, when they reached the staggering figure of thirty million pounds. But already boredom had set in, and most of that figure came from exports and sales to tourists. The present sales-figure is nearer twelve million pounds a year, and something approaching ninety per cent of that is from export sales. All porn-shop owners I spoke to were agreed that the market was very dull in Denmark now, and that except for the usual raincoat brigade they depended on tourists for their livelihood. So much for the idea that pornography is dangerously addictive.

The most refreshing fact of life in Denmark to me is the absence of prejudice, that bugbear that still haunts England and manages successfully to slow or stop our attempts to move in Denmark's direction. Some Danes may dislike pornography, but they do not presume to impose their opinion on others. While I was in Copenhagen, another investigation was taking place there too, though with better financial backing and more publicity. This was Lord Longford and his Commission of Inquiry into Pornography (see illustration 276). Lord Longford is in his late-'60s and his co-investigators in Denmark were in their '20s. Not surprisingly, there was some conflict of opinion between them about the effects of liberalisation. The younger members tended to be little harmed by what they saw, and to believe the experts who told them of the success of the experiment. One was quoted as saying:

PORNOGRAPHY
Lord Longford v Peter Webb
a debate illustrated with slides
**Main College Room B Wednesday December 15th
at 2pm**

276 *Lord Longford,* poster of debate with Peter Webb, Hornsey College of Art,
London, 1971

'I found Dr Kutschinsky's theory convincing. It is a formidable argument for
liberalizing the censorship laws'.[19] Lord Longford, however, was singularly un-
convinced, and the Press had a field day reporting his expressions of shock and
disgust as he dutifully travelled from porn-shop to sex-show to film-show and back
to porn-shop, all in the interests of research and for the greater good of England:
'We must grit our teeth and see for ourselves. We shall come out unscathed.'[20]

When Lord Longford's report on pornography was published in September,
1972,[21] it was exactly what all the preliminary publicity had led one to expect: an
unintellectual and unscientific document demanding harsher legislation against
'the evils of pornography' (which included cinema, theatre, and broadcasting as
well as magazines and photographs). Opinions from worthy local church-groups

[417]

were quoted as authoritative, while the American Commission and the Arts Council Report were brushed aside. In fact, the Longford Commission pointed out the value of common sense as opposed to expert opinion, the usual stance of prejudiced groups, and its report gave the appearance of being an official document rather than a private investigation. Its new definition of pornography as 'that which outrages contemporary standards of decency', together with its demand for the abolition of the legal defence of 'public good', were mere sops to conservatism. Fortunately, the Government refused its request for immediate action.

The live sex-shows that so horrified Lord Longford were provided originally as an attempt to recapture the attention of Danes who were bored by porn-shops and pornographic magazines. Their owners fixed their hopes on the perfect mixture of the outrageous and the slightly furtive, and at first the good citizens of Denmark paid their seven pounds or so. When I visited one, the audience was entirely made up of tourists, and the whole show was conducted in English for their benefit (though Italians, Frenchmen, Germans, and Japanese were present too). I was accompanied to the 'club' (a euphemism to extract a membership fee as well as an admission fee) by a 'sex guide', one of many girls who distribute leaflets in the streets and 'sell' the sex-shows to the tourists. My guide—a delightful girl named Vibeke who worked as a nurse in the daytime—became disarmingly honest when I told her of my professional interest in Copenhagen: 'The show is very far from erotic. You will probably hate it. Notice how the same girls keep appearing, but with a change of wig so you will think there are more of them. See that one—she is three months pregnant but needs the money. If you think the show is boring, imagine how boring it is for the girls. You won't see any Danes here—they either couldn't care less or just laugh.' I found the show a sad travesty of sexual excitement on the whole, but the final act—'real intercourse'—was really quite stimulating and seemed far removed from the endless striptease and simulated lesbian encounters. The couple were both young and beautiful, and actually seemed to be enjoying themselves once the problem of obtaining an erection was overcome. My guide told me they were in love and living together, which no doubt helped. 'It's not as nice as this at most of the clubs,' she told me.

Before I left Copenhagen I asked Dr Wilcke if he was happy about the way the experiment had developed. 'I am not proud of the sex clubs and it is sad that they attract people from all over the world, though I can't deny it is good for the tourist trade. But people should be free to see and to buy what they like. The liberalisation of the laws relating to sex has certainly meant that the police can get on with more important tasks. Of course, we hope that in the long run sex illnesses and sex crimes will virtually disappear, and all our efforts will be justified. But one thing is clear —what we have here in Denmark is true democracy.'

My reaction to Copenhagen was one of admiration mixed with sadness. Admiration that the God-fearing, home-proud Danes had had the courage to put democracy into effect with their experiment in liberalisation, and sadness that they had paid the penalty for being first by becoming a mecca for sex-hungry foreign tourists, with sex blaring from shops, cinemas, and clubs all over Copenhagen. I am sure that sex will be put into its proper perspective there as soon as other countries learn to cater for their own citizens' sexual needs.

Notes

INTRODUCTION

1. Anthony Storr, *Sexual Deviation*, Harmondsworth, Penguin, 1964, pp. 9–10, 14.
2. Marshall McLuhan, *The Mechanical Bride: Folklore of Industrial Man*, London, Routledge & Kegan Paul, 1951, p. 22.
3. *The Times*, 26 April, 1971.
4. Wilhelm Reich, *Die Funktion des Orgasmus*, Leipzig, Vienna, Zurich, 1927; English translation, *Function of the Orgasm*, New York, Farrar, Straus & Giroux, 1942 and 1961.
5. Herbert Marcuse, *Eros and Civilization*, New York, Beacon Press, 1955; London, Sphere Books, 1969.
6. Norman Brown, *Life Against Death*, Middletown, Connecticut, Wesleyan University Press, 1959; London, Routledge & Kegan Paul, 1959.
7. Geza Roheim, *The Origin and Function of Culture*, New York, Doubleday, 1943 and 1971.
8. The *Guardian*, 27 September, 1971.
9. *The Idler*, 20 January, 1761.
10. Breasts had appeared, although covered with soap-suds, in a Breeze soap advertisement in 1960, and many papers insisted on blocking out the nipples. The Enkasheer advertisement showed completely naked breasts. The designer was quoted as saying: 'We are not trying to say to readers—if you wear stockings with Enkasheer, you'll get laid. And we didn't put in nipples just to get attention. It was a matter of identification—we wanted to try to put the reader in the position where she's actually enjoying the sensation of putting on her stockings.' (Quoted in Jeremy Bugler, 'The Sex Sell', in *New Society*, 15 May, 1969.)
11. In *The Naked Ape* (London, Cape, 1967), Desmond Morris describes an E-type Jaguar as a 'penis on wheels', and points to the connotations in this context of words like 'parking', 'power', and 'performance'. In the late '60s, advertisements for Chrysler cars in American papers featured the faces of beautiful girls, with captions such as 'Don, I might . . . if you drove a Chrysler' and 'Perhaps we could, Paul . . . if you owned a Chrysler'. The designer stated: 'The ads are not meant to be sexy.' (Quoted in 'Is Yours as Good as Grant's?' by Geoffrey Wagner, in *The Spectator*, 3 October, 1970.)
12. The designer of the advertisement was quoted as saying: 'We had a choice of places to show it being applied . . . We wanted to underline that Fabergé is unusual and a bit adventurous, so we didn't want the most conventional place . . . The phallic symbolism was accidental, in that the pack came first. We didn't deliberately say—we must get a phallic symbol. But when it evolved, we didn't mind.' (Quoted in Jeremy Bugler, *op. cit.*)

CHAPTER 1: ART AND PORNOGRAPHY

1. Morris L. Ernst and William Seagle, *To the Pure*, London and New York, 1929.
2. Quoted from Charles Rembar, *The End of Obscenity*, New York, Random House, 1968, p. 24. Rembar was the lawyer who successfully defended *Lady Chatterley's Lover*, *Tropic of Cancer*, and *Fanny Hill* before the United States Supreme Court.

[421]

3. This famous definition is traced by G. Legman in *Rationale of the Dirty Joke* (London, Panther, 1972), to the eighteenth-century Maréchale de Luxembourg, who said of an erotic work by Count Benseval: 'It can be read with only one hand.'

4. Quoted from Sir Alan Herbert.

5. Georges Bataille, *Eroticism*, London, Calder, 1966.

6. D. H. Lawrence, *Pornography and Obscenity*, Paris, This Quarter, 1929, reprinted in *A Propos of Lady Chatterley and Other Essays*, Harmondsworth, Penguin, 1967, p. 67.

7. Steven Marcus, *The Other Victorians*, London, Corgi, 1969, pp. 283–84.

8. Morse Peckham, *Art and Pornography*, New York and London, Harper & Row, 1971, p. 36.

9. *Ibid.*, p. 42.

10. *Ibid.*, p. 47. Dr Peckham is at pains to point out that this is only a 'procedural definition'.

11. Drs Phyllis and Eberhard Kronhausen, *Erotic Art*, London, W. H. Allen, and New York, Grove Press, 1971.

12. Cf. *Report from the Danish Forensic Medicine Council to the Danish Penal Code Council*, Copenhagen, 1966; *Report of the Arts Council of Great Britain on the Obscene Publications Act*, London, 1969; *Report of the American Presidential Commission on Obscenity and Pornography*, Washington, D.C., 1970. See also Appendix V of the present work.

CHAPTER 2: SEXUAL THEMES IN ANCIENT AND PRIMITIVE ART

a: *Ancient and Primitive Cultures* (by John H. Field)

1. John H. Field is Principal Lecturer in the History of Art at Middlesex Polytechnic. He was invited to contribute this chapter because of his interest in archaeology and anthropology. The material gathered proved to be so fascinating and abundant that he now intends to write on the subject at greater length.

2. See Peter J. Ucko and Andrée Rosenfeld, *Paleolithic Cave Art*, London, Weidenfeld & Nicolson, 1967, an excellent critical summary of interpretations of the meanings of Paleolithic art.

3. André Leroi-Gourhan, *The Art of Prehistoric Man in Western Europe*, London, Thames & Hudson, 1968 (Paris, 1965), p. 513: chart xxxii, p. 514: charts xxxiii–xxxvii.

4. Annette Laming-Emperaire in *La Signification de l'Art rupestre paleolithique*, Paris, Picard, 1962, suggested that horses symbolised the female and bison the male principle, the opposite of Leroi-Gourhan's theory. According to the latter, even a bull bison stands for the female principle.

5. Leroi-Gourhan, *op. cit.*, pp. 173–74.

6. *Ibid.*, p. 142: fig. 63; pp. 144–47; pp. 300, 404: figs. 254–55. Also well illustrated in Siegfried Giedion, *The Eternal Present, Vol. I: The Beginnings of Art*, London, Oxford University Press, 1962, p. 183: fig. 112; p. 184: fig. 113; p. 186: fig. 116; p. 189: fig. 120.

7. Ucko and Rosenfeld, *op. cit.*, p. 111: fig. 65. Photographic illustration in Nancy K. Sandars, *Prehistoric Art in Europe*, Harmondsworth, Penguin, 1968, plate 33.

8. Ucko and Rosenfeld, *op. cit.*, p. 210: fig. 90; p. 211: fig. 91. Giedion, *op. cit.*, pp. 478–83. G. Charrière, *La Signification des représentations érotiques dans les arts sauvages et préhistoriques*, Paris, G. P. Maisonneuve et Larose, 1970, p. 44: fig. 21 illustrates the related horse.

9. Giedion, *op. cit.*, p. 196: fig. 129; pp. 214–16.

10. *Ibid.*, p. 210: fig. 145. Ucko and Rosenfeld, *op. cit.*, p. 61: fig. 33.

11. P. Mouton and René Joffroy, 'Précisions nouvelles sur les stations magdaleniennes de Farincourt (Haute Marne)' in *Revue archéologique de l'Est et du Centre Est*, Vol. 7, Dijon, 1956, pp. 193–223. Also illustrated in Charrière, *op. cit.*, p. 119: fig. 41.

12. Giedion, *op. cit.*, p. 197: fig. 130. Other phallic staffs are illustrated in Leroi-Gourhan, *op. cit.*, pp. 396–97: figs. 178–95; p. 402: figs. 227–28; p. 500: chart xi and discussed pp. 59–63. See also Charrière, *op. cit.*, p. 25: fig. 10 (m–y) and p. 198; and Frank Bourdier, *Préhistoire de France*, Paris, Flammarion, 1967: p. 281: fig. 106. Bourdier suggests (p. 282) that these phallic staffs might have been used for ritual defloration.

13. Giedion, *op. cit.*, p. 201: fig. 134. The line drawing is inaccurate. Leroi-Gourhan, *op. cit.*, p. 401: fig. 216.

14. Giedion, *op. cit.*, p. 174: fig. 107; p. 194: fig. 125; p. 210: fig. 146; pp. 238–39: fig. 167; pp. 469–77: figs. 314–21. The enigmatic 'double' figure was interpreted by its discoverer Dr Lalanne as a representation of either copulation or childbirth. Giedion interprets it along with other ambiguous figures as possibly a primal hermaphrodite. Leroi-Gourhan interpreted it as an unfinished 'Venus'. See Ucko and Rosenfeld, *op. cit.*, pp. 183–84 and p. 92: figs. 58 and 59.

15. G. H. Luquet in *The Art and Religion of Fossil Man*, London, 1930, pp. 109–10, rejected the fertility-magic interpretation of the paleolithic 'Venus' figurines, which he felt portray 'not the generative, but the voluptuous character of women . . . the thought of the artist was associated much less to the idea of the eventual prosperity of the social group than to the memory or the imagination of his own sensual satisfactions . . .' See also P. Ucko and A. Rosenfeld, *op. cit.*, p. 230. A statuette from Ostrava Petrkovice, Czechoslovakia, dated *c.* 25,000 B.C., is exceptional in its slender proportions comparable with those of the modern erotic idol Raquel Welch, who, though she is a multipara, is not generally thought of as a 'mother-figure'.

16. F. Hancar, 'Zum Problem der Venusstatuetten in eurasiatischen Jungpaläolithikum' in *Prähistorische Zeitschrift*, (Berlin), Vol. 30, 1939, pp. 144–50 and Vol. 31, 1940, pp. 85–156.

17. René Neuville, 'Statuette érotique du desert de Judée' in *L'Anthropologie*, (Paris), Vol. 43, 1933, pp. 558–60, fig. 1. This sculpture, now in the British Museum, is also illustrated in James Mellaart, *Earliest Civilisations of the Near East*, London, Thames & Hudson, 1965, p. 30: fig. 11.

18. The Swiss jurist Johann J. Bachofen in *Das Mutterrecht*, Basel, 1861, alleged that many ancient cultures had been 'matriarchal' (rule by the mother). Karl Marx and Friedrich Engels enthusiastically adopted the theory of 'primitive matriarchy' as a pre-capitalist stage of social evolution. (See F. Engels, *The Origin of the Family, Private Property and the State*, Zurich, 1884.) Under Stalin it became the official Party line for Marxist archaeologists and pre-historians that Matriarchal Neolithic farmers had lived in peaceful classless communism until the coming of aggressive patriarchal warrior-pastoralists, who brought war, private wealth, the class system and social injustice. (See M. W. Thompson's 'Translator's Foreword' to A. L. Mongait, *Archaeology in the U.S.S.R.*, Moscow, 1955; Harmondsworth, Penguin, 1961, pp. 29–30, 121.) Many writers including Robert Briffault, *The Mothers* (3 vols.), London, Allen & Unwin, 1927; Robert Graves, *The White Goddess*, London, Faber & Faber, 1948, and *The Greek Myths* (2 vols.), Harmondsworth, Penguin, 1955; Erich Neumann, *The Great Mother: An Analysis of the Archetype*, New Jersey, Princeton University Press, 1955, have popularised the matriarchal hypothesis and it has passed into Women's Lib 'herstory', *e.g.* Elizabeth G. Davis, *The First Sex*, London, Dent, 1973. However, see Simone de Beauvoir's existentialist critique of 'primitive matriarchy' in *The Second Sex: A Study of Modern Women*, Paris, 1949; London, Jonathan Cape, 1953, pp. 79 ff., 92 ff., especially p. 96: '. . . in truth that Golden Age of Women is only a myth . . . Society has always been male; political power has always been in the hands of men . . .' Although prehistoric matriarchy is probably a myth, women's economic and technological contributions to cultural progress have been unfairly neglected. Such major Neolithic innovations as weaving, pottery-making, and possibly even agriculture, may have been women's inventions. Nevertheless, the high social status of women suggested by Neolithic imagery was probably due to man's religious venera-tion of the 'female mysteries' of sexuality.

19. J. Mellaart, *op. cit.*, pp. 92 and 95: fig. 73, and J. Mellaart, *Çatal Hüyük: A Neolithic Town in Anatolia*, London, Thames & Hudson, 1967, pp. 18 ff. and plates 67, 68, IX, fig. 52.

20. J. Mellaart, *Earliest Civilisations . . .*, p. 108: fig. 94 and J. Mellaart, 'Excavations at Hacilar: 4th Preliminary Report' in *Anatolian Studies: Journal of the British School at Ankara*, (Ankara), Vol. 11, 1961, pp. 56, 59: fig. 21.

21. Stuart Piggott, *The Neolithic Cultures of the British Isles*, London, Cambridge University Press, 1954, pp. 42, 46, 61, 86–88 including plate 48, fig. 14; see Preface to 2nd unrevised edition 1970. All Neolithic dates have been drastically revised in recent years, extending the British Neolithic back to the fourth millennium B.C. Objects of various

sizes, shapes, and materials from several Neolithic and Bronze Age sites in Britain have been tentatively interpreted as images of the phallus, often without great plausibility. The unambiguous chalk phallus illustrating this chapter was excavated by H. St George Gray at Maumbury Rings, Dorchester, Dorset in 1912, and is displayed in the Dorchester Museum. See Harold St George Gray, 'Interim Report on the Excavations at Maumbury Rings, Dorchester' in *Proceedings of the Dorset Natural History and Antiquarian Field Club*, (Dorchester), Vol. 34, 1913, pp. 81–106 (re phallic artifact no. 309, p. 103) and his 'Fifth Interim Report on the Excavations at Maumbury Rings, Dorchester', *ibid.*, Vol. 35, pp. 88–118 (re two more phallic fragments, artefacts nos. 378 and 409, pp. 95, 112, 116).

22. R. Rainbird Clarke, *Grime's Graves, Norfolk*, London, H. M. Stationery Office, 1963, pp. 21, 22, 29, 31. The discovery of the first phallus is described in Canon William Greenwell, 'On the Opening of Grime's Graves in Norfolk', *Journal of the Ethnological Society of London*, London, new series, Vol. 2, 1870, pp. 419–39 (re chalk carving of glans penis see pp. 430–31). A. L. Armstrong's discovery of the chalk phallus associated with an obese 'goddess' statuette in his 1939 excavation of Pit 15 remains unpublished except at second hand. The present author was not permitted to examine the two chalk phalluses from Grime's Graves which are in the Prehistoric and Romano-British section of the British Museum.

23. Like many deities, Atum was bisexual. His masturbating hand became the female consort of his phallus and was deified as the Hand Goddess, Iusas. In some versions Atum created Shu and Tefnut by 'spitting', in others he ejaculated into his hand, transferred the semen into his mouth and then spat it forth. See R. T. Rundle Clark, *Myth and Symbol in Ancient Egypt*, London, Thames & Hudson, 1959, pp. 41 ff., and Jack Lindsay, *Men and Gods on the Roman Nile*, London, Frederick Muller, 1968, pp. 293–94.

24. 'Bnbn' = 'pyramidion' and also 'to become erect' with reference to outflowings, including seminal emission. See Henri Frankfort, *Kingship and the Gods: A study of Ancient Near Eastern Religion as the Integration of Society and Nature*, Illinois, University of Chicago Press, 1948, pp. 153, 380–81 (Fns 26 and 27).

25. E. A. Wallis Budge, *The Book of the Dead: An English Translation*, London, Routledge & Kegan Paul, 1969, p. 98. Boris de Rachewiltz, *Black Eros: The Sexual Customs of Africa from Prehistoric Times to the Present Day*, (Milan, 1963), London, Allen & Unwin, 1964, p. 31, suggests that this passage relates to circumcision. His Chapter 2: 'Sacred and Profane Love in Ancient Egypt' is a useful and well-illustrated introduction to the subject with an extensive bibliography.

26. *Ibid.*, p. 40. B. de Rachewiltz quotes P. Buzon, *La Médecine et les Religions*, Paris, 1904, stating that women accused of lesbianism were made to submit to the sexual attentions of a buck, who by his ardour or disdain indicated whether the woman was innocent or guilty.

27. R. C. Faulkner, 'The Bremner-Rhind Papyrus (I)', *The Journal of Egyptian Archaeology*, (London), Vol. 22: part 2, Dec. 1936, p. 125.

28. G. D. Hornblower, 'Phallic Offerings to Hat-hor' in *Man*, London, Vol. 26, May 1926, pp. 80–83, plate E.

29. W. M. Flinders Petrie, *Coptos*, London, 1896. One statue is illustrated in B. de Rachewiltz, *op. cit.*, p. 42. The statues are well illustrated and discussed by S. Giedion, *The Eternal Present*, Vol. 1: *The Beginnings of Art*, London, Oxford University Press, 1962, pp. 204–6: figs. 137–40 and Vol. II: *The Beginnings of Architecture*, 1964, pp. 82–89: figs. 40–44.

30. 'Latuca sativa longifolia', a succulent with thick, milky-white sap, identified with semen. In Egypt it is still considered an aphrodisiac promoting fertility.

31. H. Frankfort, *op. cit.*, pp. 168–69, 175–80, 188–90, 390 (fns. 23–29).

32. Eberhard Otto, *Egyptian Art and the Cults of Osiris and Amon*, Munich, 1966; London, Thames & Hudson, 1968, pp. 58–64, including Plutarch's second century A.D. account of the Osiris myth.

33. H. Te Velde, *Seth, God of Confusion: A Study of his Role in Egyptian Mythology and Religion*, Leiden, E. J. Brill, 1967, pp. 28 ff. Although a sexually perverted villain in the Osiris myths, Seth had a more positive role among the Asians and Egyptians of the Nile Delta where he seems to have been worshipped as a 'strong god' of power and fertility, comparable with Min.

34. E. Otto, *op. cit.*, plates 16–20 and accompanying notes. p. 69.

35. Joseph Kaster, *The Literature and Mythology of Ancient Egypt*, London, Allen Lane, 1968, pp. 237–56.

36. *Ibid.*, pp. 249–51, 256.

37. J. Lindsay, *op. cit.*, pp. 351–56, 369. R. Clark, *op. cit.*, p. 144.

38. W. M. Flinders Petrie, *Amulets, illustrated by the Egyptian Collection in University College, London*, London, Constable, 1914, p. 145, plate 27 (no. 145 z).

39. James E. Quibell, *Excavations at Saqqara 1905–1906* (2 vols.), Cairo, Service des Antiquités de l'Egypte, 1907. B. de Rachewiltz, *op. cit.*, p. 40, cites Vivant Denon's report of a mummy of a Theban lady found to have a mummified phallus of a large animal, probably a bull, placed between her thighs. A lotus was often placed above a mummy's vulva as the appropriate symbol of the female genitals and of rebirth.

40. *Ibid.*, pp. 34, 37.

41. E. W. Budge, *op. cit.*, pp. 176, 182.

42. *Ibid.*, p. 557.

43. Rundle Clark, *op. cit.*, p. 161: fig. 23; p. 169.

44. *Ibid.*, pp. 125–28. J. Lindsay, *op. cit.*, pp. 48–56. H. Frankfort, *op. cit.*, pp. 190 ff. Erwin R. Goodenough, *Jewish Symbols in the Greco-Roman Period*, Vol. 5: *Fish, Bread and Wine*, New York, Pantheon Books, 1956, pp. 141 ff., 163 ff., an excellent discussion of Egyptian sexual symbolism with full references.

45. J. Lindsay, *Leisure and Pleasure in Roman Egypt*, London, Frederick Muller, 1965, p. 24. Giuseppe Lo Duca, *Histoire de l'Erotisme*, Paris, La Jeune Parque, 1969, p. 132. E. Goodenough, *op. cit.*, pp. 179–81.

46. J. Quibell, *op. cit.*, pp. 12–14, 28–29, frontispiece and plates 26, 29, 31.

47. B. de Rachewiltz, *op. cit.*, pp. 44–45. Albert Moll, *Handbuch der Sexual Wissenschaften*, Leipzig, F. C. W. Vogel, 1912, pp. 573–75, fig. 317 a–z.

48. Flinders Petrie, *Amulets . . .*, pp. 11–12, 27, 37, plates 1, 14, 27, 30, 49.

49. J. Kaster, *op. cit.*, pp. 313–16. Giuseppe Lo Duca, *A History of Eroticism*, Paris, 1961; London, Rodney Books, 1966, pp. 30–33. Adolf Erman, *The Literature of the Ancient Egyptians*, London, Methuen, 1927, reprinted in paperback as *The Ancient Egyptians: A Sourcebook of their Writings*, New York, Harper Torchbooks, 1966, pp. xxxvi–xxxvii, 243–51. The following quotations were revised and adapted from these translations.

50. B. de Rachewiltz, *op. cit.*, pp. 49–50. Kurt Lange, Max Hirmer *et al.*, *Egypt: Architecture, Sculpture, Painting in 3,000 Years*, London, Phaidon, 4th edition, 1968, p. 431. A drawing of the Divine Copulation relief is illustrated in E. Goodenough, *op. cit.* (Vol. 5), fig. 156.

51. B. de Rachewiltz, *op. cit.*, p. 50. G. Lo Duca, *Histoire de l'érotisme*, p. 125, top right, apparently illustrates this unique scene but does not give the source of the illustration.

52. B. de Rachewiltz, *op. cit.*, pp. 60, 63, 64.

53. A copy of the erotic drawings of the Turin papyrus is illustrated in Otto J. Brendel, 'The Scope and Temperament of Erotic Art in the Greco-Roman World' in Theodore Bowie and Cornelia Christianson eds., *Studies in Erotic Art*, New York, Basic Books, 1970, pp. 49–51, 65–66: fn. 69, plate 30.

54. Samuel N. Kramer, 'Mythology of Sumer and Akkad' in S. N. Kramer ed., *Mythologies of the Ancient World*, Garden City, N.Y., Doubleday Anchor, 1961, p. 97. Shocked by this brutal rape, the other gods exiled Enlil.

55. S. N. Kramer, 'Enki and Ninhursag: A Paradise Myth' in James B. Pritchard ed., *Ancient Near Eastern Texts Relating to the Old Testament*, New Jersey, Princeton University Press, 3rd edition, 1969, pp. 37–41. G. S. Kirk, *Myth: Its Meaning and Function in Ancient and Other Cultures*, London, Cambridge University Press, 1970, pp. 90–98 attempts to interpret these myths according to Claude Levi-Strauss's structuralist theories.

56. S. N. Kramer, 'Sumerian Sacred Marriage Texts' in J. Pritchard ed., *op. cit.*, p. 643 S. N. Kramer, *The Sacred Marriage Rite: Aspects of Faith, Myth, and Ritual in Ancient Sumer*, Bloomington, Indiana, Indiana University Press, 1969, p. 59.

57. The Sumerian Earth Mother was known by various titles such as Ninmah or Ninhursag. Inanna-Ishtar was her 'daughter', but as wife and mother was identified with her. She was also Mistress of Beasts, wild and tame. In addition to being Goddess of Sexuality and

Fertility, Inanna-Ishtar was the ferocious War-Goddess. Her aspect as Death Goddess is suggested in the myth of her Descent into the Underworld and her vengeful pursuit of her lover Dumuzi-Tammuz, whom she had dragged down into the Land of the Dead. There are parallels in the myth of the fatal love of her 'elder sister' Erishkigal, Queen of the Underworld, for Nergal.

58. Thorkild Jacobsen, *Toward the Image of Tammuz and Other Essays on Mesopotamian History and Culture*, Cambridge, Mass., Harvard University Press, 1970, pp. 73–101. Re Dumuzi and the 'Sacred Marriage' see also Elisabeth Douglas Van Buren, 'The Sacred Marriage in Early Times in Mesopotamia' in *Orientalia*, (Rome), new series: Vol. 13, 1944, pp. 1–72. See S. N. Kramer's critical comments on Jacobsen and Van Buren in *The Sacred Marriage . . .*, p. 159.

59. *Ibid.*, p. 92.

60. *Ibid.*, p. 94.

61. T. Jacobsen, *op. cit.*, p. 95.

62. S. N. Kramer, *op. cit.*, p. 104.

63. Herodotus, *The Histories*, Harmondsworth, Penguin Classics, rev. ed. 1972, Book One: pp. 121–22. Herodotus's report is not specifically confirmed by surviving native texts and some scholars have thought that he misinterpreted the well-documented activities of professional 'Sacred Prostitutes'. But the distinctions between such customs as the ritual offering of their virginity by virtuous women and the practice of prostitution, sacred or profane, were well known within the Classical world. On Mesopotamian prostitution see H. W. F. Saggs, *The Greatness that was Babylon: A Survey of the Ancient Civilisation of the Tigris-Euphrates Valley*, London, Sidgwick & Jackson, 1962, pp. 185 ff., 191 ff., 348–51, 360 ff., 381 ff. (This book is the best easily available and up-to-date account of Mesopotamian sexual mores in English.) See also Erich Ebeling, 'Liebeszauber im alten Orient' in *Mitteilungen der Altorientalischen Gesellschaft*, (Leipzig), Vol. 1, No. 1, 1925, pp. 1–56.

64. Ephraim A. Speiser, 'The Epic of Gilgamesh' in J. B. Pritchard ed. *Ancient Near Eastern Texts . . .* pp. 73–74. ff.

65. Her ill-fated lovers had included Dumuzi-Tammuz and a herdsman whom she transformed into a wolf, a gardener whom she metamorphosed into a mole, a bird, a lion, and a stallion. The animal lovers whom she 'broke' probably refers to her role as 'Mistress of Beasts'. Hindu erotic art shows the archetypal 'Sacred Prostitute', or love goddess, copulating with many animal species. See Philip Rawson, *Erotic Art of the East: The Sexual Theme in Oriental Painting and Sculpture*, New York, Prometheus Press, 1968, p. 182, plate XIII, fig. 121.

66. Adding injury to insult the heroes killed the Bull of Heaven sent to punish them at Inanna-Ishtar's request. Enkidu contemptuously tossed the dead bull's 'right thigh' in the goddess's face. Some commentators have interpreted this 'thigh' as a euphemism for the phallus as in the Bible.

67. Thorkil Vanggaard, *Phallos: A Symbol and its History in the Male World*, London, Jonathan Cape, 1972, pp. 117–18.

68. Max E. L. Mallowan, *Early Mesopotamia and Iran*, London, Thames & Hudson, 1965, vase from Tell Agrab, *c.* 3100 B.C. p. 24: fig. 10.

69. André Parrot, *Sumer*, London, Thames & Hudson, 1960, p. 45: plate 60 (d). Ishara, 'Mistress of Life', was an aspect of the Great Goddess associated with the marriage bed.

70. Georges Contenau, *La Déesse nue Babylonienne: étude d'iconographie comparée*, Paris, Paul Geuthner, 1914. Marie-Therèse Barrelet, 'À propos d'une Plaquette trouvée à Mari' in *Syria: Revue d'art oriental et d'archéologie*, (Paris), Vol. 29, 1952, pp. 285–93 and *idem*, 'Les Déesses armées et ailées' in *Syria*, (Paris), Vol. 32, 1955, pp. 222–60.

71. Nude woman alone on bed. Charlotte Ziegler, *Die Terrakotten von Warka (Ausgraben der Deutschen Forschungsgemeinschaft in Uruk-Warka*, Vol. VI), Berlin, Gebrüder Mann, 1962, plate 32: figs. 416 a and b. Couple in sexual embrace on bed: Bruno Meissner, *Die Babylonische Kleinplastiken*, Leipzig, Hinrichs, 1934, p. 23: fig. 13; Pierre Amiet, *Elam*, Auvers-sur-Oise, Archée, 1966, p. 328; Roman Ghirshman, 'Suse: Campagne de Fouilles 1962–1963, Rapport préliminaire' in *Arts Asiatiques*, (Paris), Vol. 10, 1964, pp. 3–20, p. 13: fig. 7;

Marie-Thérèse Barrelet, *Figurines et Reliefs en Terre Cuite de la Mesopotamie Antique*, Paris, Paul Geuthner, 1968, pp. 292, 319, plate 59: fig. 628; plate 71: figs. 743, 744.

72. E. Ebeling, *Tod und Leben nach den Vorstellungen der Babylonier*, Berlin-Leipzig, 1931, pp. 49, 51.

73. Walter Andrae, 'Die jüngeren Ischtar-Tempel in Assur', in *Wissenschaftlichen Veröffentlichungen der Deutschen Orient Gesellschaft*, (Berlin), No. 58, 1935, pp. 90–93 and plate 36.

74. *Ibid.*, pp. 103–4, plates 45, 46.

75. L. Legrain, *Archaic Seal Impressions* (*Ur Excavations vol. III*), Oxford University Press, Trustees of British Museum and University of Pennsylvania Museum, Philadelphia, 1936, plates 18 (nos. 365 68), 19 (no. 370), 20 (no. 385). See also nude woman in genital display, or birth, position with heraldic scorpions: plate 14 (nos. 268–70). Ephraim A. Speiser, *Excavations at Tepe Gawra vol. I*, Philadelphia, University of Pennsylvania Press, 1935, pp. 124–25, plates 55 (b), 58 (nos. 40, 41). See also pp. 49, 99, 165 and plates 27 (a), 46 (b), 74 (no. 204). Arthur J. Tobler, *Excavations at Tepe Gawra vol. II*, 1950, p. 183 ff., plates 89 (c), 163 (nos. 86–88). Ruth Opificius, *Das altbabylonische Terrakottarelief*, Berlin, Walter de Gruyter, 1961, pp. 166–68, plate 20 (no. 612). Marie-Thérèse Barrelet, *Figurines et Reliefs en Terre Cuite . . .*, pp. 292, 319, plates 50 (no. 527), 56 (no. 591), 59 (no. 628), 63 (no. 675), 71 (no. 744).

76. Re late survival of this theme into the Achaemenid Persian period see Louis Delaporte, *Musée du Louvre: Catalogue des Cylindres, Cachets et Pierres gravées de Style oriental vol. I*, Paris, Hachette, 1920, p. 79, plate 52 (no. 21 and compare no. 20). Hans H. Von der Osten, 'The Ancient Seals from the Near East in the Metropolitan Museum: Old and Middle Persian Seals' in *The Art Bulletin*, (Chicago and New York), Vol. 13, No. 1, 1931, pp. 221–41, p. 232 and figs. D and 14b.

77. Charlotte Ziegler, *op. cit.*, p. 55 (plate 10: fig. 168) described a plaque from Uruk-Warka showing a couple copulating as 'two bearded' figures, but possibly misinterpreted the bending figure.

78. Re anal copulation in ancient Mesopotamia see H. Saggs, *op. cit.*, p. 185, 'A text refers to the high priestess permitting intercourse *per anum*', and Briggs Buchanan, 'A Snake Goddess and her Companions: A Problem in the Iconography of the early Second Millennium B.C.' in *Iraq*, (London), Vol. 33, 1971, pp. 1–18 re 'Sacred Prostitutes': p. 4: 'The intercourse is commonly anal, a sure method of birth control.' Ibn Washya in his 'Book concerning Nabean Agriculture' described a magical ritual for grafting fruit-trees 'contrary to nature' in which 'the branch to be grafted must be held in the hands of a very beautiful maiden, while a man is having shameful and unnatural sexual intercourse with her; during coitus the girl grafts the branch on to the tree.' (See Mircea Eliade, *The Forge and the Crucible*, London, Rider, 1962, p. 35). Re preference for anal copulation in the Islamic East, despite the prohibition of the *Koran*, see Allen Edwardes and R. E. L. Masters, *The Cradle of Erotica: A Study of Afro-Asian Sexual Expression and an Analysis of Erotic Freedom in Social Relationships*, New York, Julian Press, 1963, pp. 195–226.

79. Henri Frankfort, 'Gods and Myths on Sargonid Seals' in *Iraq*, (London), Vol. 1, 1934, pp. 2–29, re a cylinder seal from Tell Asmar (32/934): p. 8 and plate 1 (b); *idem*, *Cylinder Seals: A Documentary Essay on the Art and Religion of the Ancient Near East*, London, Macmillan, 1939, p. 75; *idem*, *Stratified Cylinder Seals from the Diyala Region* (Oriental Institute Publication 72) University of Chicago, 1955, p. 38 and plates 34 (no. 340), 53 (no. 559). Briggs Buchanan, *Catalogue of Ancient Near Eastern Seals in the Ashmolean Museum*, Vol. 1 (*Cylinder Seals*), Oxford, Clarendon Press, 1966, pp. 5–7, 24, 38, 49 and plates 20 (no. 254), 72 (no. 796).

80. E. Goodenough, *op. cit.*, pp. 123 ff.

81. B. Buchanan, *op. cit.*, p. 49 suggests that plate 20 (no. 254) and Frankfort (*Diyala*) plate 34 (no. 340) illustrate 'both normal and, presumably, anal intercourse', the latter re standing couples beside bed.

82. Léon Heuzey, *Découvertes en Chaldée par Ernest de Sarzec* (2 vols.), Paris, Ernest Laroux, 1884–1912; Vol. 1: pp. 319, 320, plate 30 bis:21. L. Delaporte, *op. cit.*, p. 8 and plate 4

(no. 6-T.88). Neither of these early photographic illustrations of the seal impression show the phallus of the reclining figure. Gerard Zwang in *Le Sexe de la Femme*, Paris, La Jeune Parque, 1967, p. 387 gives an enlarged photographic illustration of this scene which clearly shows the phallus entering the woman's vagina, but this phallus may be a retouched 'restoration'. On the same page Zwang shows drawings after the seal from Paul Toscanne, 'Les fonctionnaires Bata, Lupa et Naru' in *Revue d'Assyriologie* (Paris), Vol. 7, 1909, p. 61, illustrated without the phallus, and a similar drawing from *Bilder Lexikon der Erotik* (4 vols.), Vienna and Leipzig, Verlag für Kulturforschung, 1928–1930, which includes the allegedly 'bowdlerised' phallus. However, the latter illustration is later than, and apparently based on, P. Toscanne's article. The present author, not having had the opportunity to examine the original seal in the Louvre, cannot say who has been guilty of phallic falsification in this case.

83. G. Zwang, *op. cit.*, gave his illustration the title 'Murder of adulterers'. Joseph Campbell, *The Masks of God*, Vol. 2: *Oriental Mythology*, London, Secker & Warburg, 1962, p. 42 interpreted the scene as a ritual human sacrifice of the couple who had performed the 'Sacred Marriage' fertility ritual. See H. Saggs, *op. cit.*, pp. 361 ff. for a discussion of the controversial theories about the 'Royal Tombs' of Ur which inspired Campbell's interpretation.

84. L. Heuzey, *op. cit.*, pp. 319, 320 suggested, as an alternative to a mere representation of 'bad morals', the depiction of a demonic succubus. George Contenau, *La Magie chez les Assyriens et les Babyloniens*, Paris, Payot, 1947, pp. 94–95 also suggested that the scene depicts the 'ardat lili' succubus. The Hellenistic Greek relief is discussed and illustrated in J. Brendel, *op. cit.*, pp. 14–15 and plate 4.

85. André Parrot, *Nineveh and Babylon*, London, Thames & Hudson, 1961, p. 287: fig. 358 and p. 258: fig. 330. *Idem, Sumer*, p. 300: fig. 367. See M.-T. Barrelet's two articles cited in note 70 for a detailed discussion of this type of figure. G. Contenau, *op. cit.*, pp. 94–96 discusses the female demons 'ardat lili' and 'lamashtu'. He quotes a spell, 'He on whom the "ardat-lili" has cast her eye; the man whom the "ardat-lili" has stretched out on the ground . . .'. The Lamashtu demon was the prostitute daughter of Anu, who attacked pregnant woman, causing abortions, and stole new-born babies.

86. Re Lilith see also Robert Graves and Raphael Patai, *Hebrew Myths: The Book of Genesis*, London, Cassell, 1964, pp. 12, 65–69, 98. On p. 69 Graves commented that Greek witches, too, preferred the superior posture. His reference to 'early Sumerian representations' would include, in addition to the Akkadian seal in the Louvre, a damaged painting of a similar couple (the phallus unambiguous) on a vase from Tepe Ali Abad, Musiyan, Iran. See J. E. Gautier and G. Lampre, 'Fouilles de Moussian' in *Délégation en Perse: Memoires*, (Paris), Vol. 8, 1905, pp. 59–148, pp. 135 and 136: fig. 266. Donald E. McCown and Richard C. Haines, *Nippur vol. 1: Temple of Enlil, Scribal Quarter and Soundings*, Chicago, University of Chicago Press, 1967, illustrated more terracotta plaques of erotic themes. Plate 137.6 seems to show a woman in an upright position 'impaling' her vagina on a phallus and may relate to the theme discussed here. Two other images, plates 127.6 and 134.8, show the legs of a frontal nude woman flanked by heraldic phalluses with testicles. One of these (plate 134.8) may show a feathered wing-tip of the 'ardat-lili' type.

87. John Gray, *The Canaanites*, London, Thames & Hudson, 1964, p. 136. Theodor H. Gaster, *Thespis: Ritual, Myth and Drama in the Ancient Near East*, Garden City, N.Y., Doubleday Anchor, revised edition, 1961, pp. 406–35.

88. Louis Hughes Vincent, *Études bibliques: Canaan d'après l'exploration récente*, Paris, Librairie Victor Lecoffre & J. Gabalda, 1907, pp. 168–69: fig. 115, a Canaanite-Phoenician terracotta, then in the collection of Baron Ustinov, Jaffa.

89. Cyrus Gordon, *Ugarit and Minoan Crete: The Bearing of their Texts on the Origins of Western Culture*, New York, Norton, 1966, p. 90. H. L. Ginsberg, 'Ugaritic Myths, Epics and Legends' in J. B. Pritchard ed., *Ancient Near Eastern Texts . . .*, p. 142. E. Lipinski, 'Les Conceptions et couches merveilleuses de "Anath" ', in *Syria*, (Paris), Vol. 42, Paris, 1965, pp. 45–73, pp. 56, 61, 63, 68.

90. J. Gray, *op. cit.*, plates 19, 29, 30, 38. James B. Pritchard, *Palestinian Figurines in Relation to certain Goddesses known through Literature*, New Haven, Conn., American Oriental Society, 1943 is a careful, but inconclusive, attempt to identify the subjects of these icons. Marie-Thérèse Barrelet, 'Deux Déesses Syro-Pheniciennes sur un Bronze du Louvre' in

Syria, (Paris), Vol. 35, 1958, pp. 27–44 made a similar iconographic examination of the Syrian material.

91. The older interpretations of allegedly phallic artifacts were conveniently listed in William Robertson Smith, *Lectures on the Religion of the Semites*, London, A. & C. Black, 3rd edition with additional notes by Stanley A. Cook, 1927. To W. R. Smith's Appendix, 'The supposed Phallic Significance of Sacred Posts and Pillars' (pp. 456–57 in the original edition), S. A. Cook added a note 'Phallic Symbols', pp. 687–88, giving many references up to the 1920s. However, these articles deserve critical scepticism. Robert A. Stewart Mac-Alister, *The Excavation of Gezer 1902–1905 & 1907–1909* (3 vols.), London, John Murray, 1912, Vol. 2, p. 446: 'A large number of phalli of soft limestone were found, especially in the High Place enclosure, where they came to light in basketfuls.' But the illustrations plate 223 (nos. 15–18) are not very convincing.

92. *Ibid.*, Vol. 2, pp. 385–89. L. H. Vincent, *op. cit.*, pp. 112 ff., 127 ff., 142 ff. Phallic interpretation of 'massaboth' standing stones is now out of fashion. See J. Gray, *op. cit.*, pp. 66–68, 75–76.

93. *Genesis* 24:2 and 9 is interpreted to mean that the oath was sworn while touching the patriarchs' genitals. *Genesis* 9:22–25; *Deuteronomy* 25:11; *Job* 18:17.

94. C. Gordon, *op. cit.*, p. 23. Theophile J. Meek, *Hebrew Origins*, New York, Harper Torchbooks (revised edition 1950), 1960, pp. 134–36, 141–45, 160–70, 224. E. O. James, *Myth and Ritual in the Ancient Near East*, London, Thames & Hudson, 1958, pp. 60–68, 125–28. *Idem, The Cult of the Mother Goddess*, London, Thames & Hudson, 1959, pp. 78–84.

95. *II Kings* 23: 4–7.

96. S. Kramer, *The Sacred Marriage* . . ., pp. 85–106. *Hosea* 2.

97. *Jeremiah* 44: 15–19.

98. C. Gordon, *op. cit.*, p. 31.

99. Raphael Patai, *Man and Temple in Ancient Jewish Myth and Ritual*, London, Thomas Nelson & Sons, 1947, pp. 89, 92–93. Theodor Reik, *Pagan Rites in Judaism*, New York, Farrar, Straus & Giroux, Noonday, 1964, pp. 66–79. A psychoanalyst's essay on the re-emergence of the mother goddess in Judaism, based on his childhood memories.

100. Herbert A. Strong, translator, introduction and notes by John Garstang, *The Syrian Goddess, being a Translation of Lucian's 'De Dea Syria' with a Life of Lucian*, London, Constable, 1913.

101. Theodor H. Gaster, ed., *The New Golden Bough: A New Abridgment of the Classic Work by Sir James George Frazer*, Garden City, N.Y., Doubleday Anchor Books, 1961, pp. 164–70, 210–17. Wolf W. F. Baudissin, *Adonis und Esmun: Eine Untersuchung zur Geschichte des Glaubens an Auferstehungsgötter und an Heilgötter*, Leipzig, J. C. Hinrichs, 1911. Roland de Vaux, 'The Cults of Adonis and Osiris' in *The Bible and the Ancient Near East*, Paris, 1967. London, Darton, Longman & Todd, 1971, pp. 210–37.

102. T. Gaster, ed., *op. cit.*, p. 178.

103. Re caves as 'wombs' see M. Eliade, *op. cit.*, pp. 21, 41. Gertrude R. Levy, *The Gate of Horn: A Study of the Religious Conceptions of the Stone Age, and their Influence upon European Thought*, London, Faber & Faber, 1948, pp. 214 ff. Re Çatal Hüyük aniconic stalagmite-stalactite idols see: J. Mellaart, *Çatal Hüyük* . . ., pp. 178 ff., 184.

104. Re double-axe as symbol of Neareastern weather god see Arthur B. Cook, 'The Cretan Axe-Cult outside Crete' in *Transactions of the 3rd International Congress for the History of Religions*, (Oxford), Vol. 2, 1908, pp. 184 ff. Charles Picard, *Les Religions préhelleniques (Crète et Mycenes)*, Paris, Presses Universitaires, 1948, pp. 99, 190, 200–201. Re double-axe as symbol of the Cretan goddess, perhaps used to sacrifice bulls see: Agnes C. Vaughan, *The House of the Double Axe: The Palace of Knossos*, Garden City, N.Y., Doubleday, 1959, pp. 168–75. Richard W. Hutchinson, *Prehistoric Crete*, Harmondsworth, Penguin, 1962, pp. 224–25. Jacquetta Hawkes, *Dawn of the Gods*, London, Chatto & Windus, 1968, p. 131, concurred but also saw the 'phallic' shaft thrust through the hole of the double 'female triangle' as an 'effective piece of sexual imagery', following the 'lingam-yoni' analogy first proposed by David C. Hogarth, 'Aegean Religion', in James Hastings, ed., *Encyclopedia of Religion and Ethics*, Vol. 1, Edinburgh, T. & T. Clark, 1908–, pp. 143–44. Robert S. McCully, 'A Psycholo-

gist looks at Prehistoric Art' in *Art International*, (Zurich), Vol. 16, No. 9, Nov. 1972, pp. 63–66, 99 (p. 64 conjectured that the double-axe was used by the Cretan goddess to castrate her young paramour as in a myth concerning Kybele, the Phrygian mother goddess and the unfortunate Attis).

105. Early Bronze Age Cycladic figurines represent nude women with strongly defined pubic triangle. Nudity also occurs in a 'folk-art' clay group of dancers from Kamilari dated *c.* 1500 B.C. A gold repoussé emblem from Mycenae of the sixteenth century B.C. portrays a nude woman, probably a goddess, with three birds. See illustrations in J. Hawkes, *op. cit.*, pp. 47, 126, 228. Another nude figure occurs on a signet-ring, apparently representing a funerary scene. See G. Levy, *op. cit.*, p. 221 and plate 29 (c). On fragments of a Middle Minoan I pot from Mallia a crude incised figure may represent the Great Goddess in a pose of fully frontal genital display. See Pierre Demargne, 'Deux Représentations de la Déesse minoënne dans la Necropole de Mallia (Crète)' in *Mélanges Gustave Glotz* (2 vols.), Paris, Presses Universitaires de France, 1932, Vol. I, pp. 305–14.

106. Martin P. Nilsson, *The Minoan-Mycenean Religion and its Survival in Greek Religion* (2 vols.), 2nd revised edition, 1950, reprinted New York, Biblo & Tannen, 1972, pp. 119, 496, 303, 593. Although he discussed fully the phallic elements in later Greek religion, he emphatically and repeatedly denied that there is any trace of phallic imagery in Minoan culture. However, Stephanos Xanthoudides, *The vaulted Tombs of Mesara: An Account of some early Cemeteries of southern Crete*, London, Hodder & Stoughton (University of Liverpool Press), 1924, tentatively identified as phallic symbols a number of clay objects discovered near the tombs at Koumasa. John D. S. Pendlebury, *The Archaeology of Crete: An Introduction*, London, Methuen, 1939, pp. 117 ff., rejected Xanthoudides's interpretation. Recently Keith Branigan, *The Tombs of Mesara: A Study of Funerary Architecture and Ritual in Southern Crete, 2800–1700 B.C.*, London, Duckworth, 1970, accepted Xanthoudides's phallic identification and conjectured about their possible ritual significance. Heinrich Schliemann had identified as phalluses various artifacts excavated at Troy. See Wilhelm Dörpfeld *et al.*, *Troja und Ilion: Ergebnisse der Ausgrabungen in den vorhistorischen und historischen Schlichten von Ilion 1870–1894,* (2 vols.), Athens, Beck & Barth, 1902, p. 384 and plate facing p. 368. Herbert Schmidt, *Heinrich Schliemann's Sammlung trojanischer Altertümer*, Berlin, Staatliche Museum, 1902, pp. 282–83. However, Carl Blegen in his later reassessment of Troy refrained from phallic interpretations and classified such objects as pestles, which does not necessarily disprove Schliemann's theory since mortar-and-pestle have significance as symbols of copulation in various parts of the world. For recent references to this controversial subject see Nicholas G. Hammond, *History of Macedonia*, Vol. 1: *Historical Geography and Prehistory*, Oxford, Clarendon Press, 1972, pp. 231, 244, 247, 267. Hammond asserts that allegedly phallic artifacts found at Malik (*Π*) and Servia (*Π*) can be associated with the Greek-speaking Indoeuropeans from the late Neolithic to the early Bronze Age *c.* 2600 B.C.

107. J. Hawkes, *op. cit.*, pp. 131–32, 153.

108. For a recent discussion of the problems of Indo-European origins see Stuart Piggott, *Ancient Europe from the Beginnings of Agriculture to Classical Antiquity: A Survey*, Edinburgh, Edinburgh University Press, 1965, pp. 77 ff.

109. Emmanuel Anati, *Camonica Valley: A Depiction of Village Life in the Alps from Neolithic Times to the Birth of Christ as Reflected by Thousands of Newly-Found Rock Carvings*, London, Jonathan Cape, 1964, p. 164.

110. Peter Gelling and Hilda E. Davidson, *The Chariot of the Sun and other Rites and Symbols of the Northern Bronze Age*, London, Dent, 1969, re 'Sacred Marriage': pp. 48 (fig. 22e), 49, 57 (fig. 25d), 58–59, 66–78, 161–63. Ithyphallic man plowing with bulls: p. 74 (fig. 35d), 79.

111. T. Vanggaard, *op. cit.*

112. Arthur T. Hatto, 'Stonehenge and Midsummer: A New Interpretation' in *Man*, (London), July 1953, article 151, pp. 101–6. R. J. Atkinson, *Stonehenge*, London, Hamish Hamilton, 1956; Harmondsworth, Penguin, 1960, pp. 174–75, mentions that different-shaped megaliths at Avebury Circle have been interpreted as 'male' and 'female'.

113. P. V. Glob, *The Bog People: Iron-Age Man Preserved* (London, Faber & Faber, 1969), London, Granada-Paladin, 1971, p. 116.

114. N. Sandars, *op. cit.*, pp. 214–15, plate 218. Walter Torbrügge, *Prehistoric European Art*, Baden-Baden, 1968; New York, Harry N. Abrams, n.d., pp. 147–48.

115. *Tacitus on Britain and Germany*, Harmondsworth, Penguin, 1948, pp. 133–34. P. Glob, *op. cit.*, pp. 117 ff.

116. *Ibid.*, pp. 126–28 and unnumbered plates.

117. Marie-Louise Sjoestedt, *Gods and Heroes of the Celts*, Paris, 1940; London, Methuen, 1949, pp. 3, 7. Alwyn and Brinley Rees, *Celtic Heritage: Ancient Tradition in Ireland and Wales*, London, Thames & Hudson, 1961, pp. 29, 146, 155, 165, 246. Proinsias MacCana, *Celtic Mythology*, London, Paul Hamlyn, 1970, pp. 58, 117. Estyn Evans, *Prehistoric and Early Christian Ireland: A Guide*, London, Batsford, 1966, pp. 175–76.

118. Giraldus Cambrensis, *Topographia Hibernica* (A.D. 1185), quoted by M.-L. Sjoestedt, *op. cit.*, pp. xvii–xviii, comparing this Irish rite with one from the extreme opposite end of the Indoeuropean spread, the Aryan Hindu rite of 'asvamedha', a horse sacrifice in which the king's principal wife simulates copulation with the sacrificial stallion to promote fertility. See J. Campbell, *op. cit.*, pp. 193–97. P. Rawson, *op. cit.*, p. 182, figs. 69, 121, plate XII. Men copulate with equine quadrupeds in Prehistoric rock engravings: E. Anati, *op. cit.*, p. 128, P. Gelling and H. Davidson, *op. cit.*, p. 66 (fig. 30e).

119. M.-L. Sjoestedt, *op. cit.*, pp. 38–42.

120. *Ibid.*, p. 35.

121. *Ibid.*, p. 36.

122. *Ibid.*, pp. 65–66, re connection of 'battle ardour' and 'rut' see p. 58 and 62: 'From his skull rises a stream of black blood as high as the mast of a ship.' A psychoanalyst would describe this as the tumescent phallus 'displaced upward'.

123. *Ibid.*, p. 66, referring to Pliny, *Natural History*, Book 22: 2.

124. A. and B. Rees, *op. cit.*, p. 292.

125. W. Torbrügge, *op. cit.*, p. 190.

126. *Ibid.*, p. 194.

127. Paul Jacobsthal, *Early Celtic Art*, (2 vols.), Oxford, Clarendon Press, 1944, Vol. 1: pp. 193–94; Vol. 2: plate 157: fig. 308. J. V. S. Megaw, *Art of the European Iron Age: A Study of the Elusive Image*, Bath, Adams & Dart, 1970, p. 86, plate 101. In a Norse tale the 'trickster' Loki amuses the gods by tying his genitals to a she-goat's beard.

128. J. Megaw, *op. cit.*, p. 78, plate 78. Anne Ross, *Pagan Celtic Britain: Studies in Iconography and Tradition*, London, Routledge & Kegan Paul, 1967, pp. 62–63, plates 26a, 83b.

129. P. Jacobsthal, *op. cit.*, Vol. 2: pp. 8–9, plate 218b. Donna C. Kurtz and John Boardman, *Greek Burial Customs*, London, Thames & Hudson, 1971, pp. 179, 241–44, are sceptical about the phallic interpretation of Greek gravestones but provide a useful bibliography of the subject.

130. P. Jacobsthal, *op. cit.*, Vol. 1: p. 166, Vol. 2: plate 11: fig. 12 and plate 218b.

131. O. Hermelin, 'Stenkloten på Ättehögarne' in *Svenska Fornminnesföreningens Tidskrift*, (Stockholm), Vol. 2, 1873–1874, pp. 165–205, p. 173. Haakon Shetelig, *Scandinavian Archaeology*, (Oxford), 1937, pp. 247–48, 413.

132. G. Charrière, *op. cit.*, pp. 172–75. Bénard le Pontois, *Le Finistère préhistorique* (Publications de l'Institut Internationale d'Anthropologie no. 3), Paris, Émile Nourry, 1929, pp. 258–72. P. R. Giot, J. L. Helgouach, J. Briard, *Brittany*, London, Thames & Hudson, 1960, pp. 179 ff.

133. J. Megaw, *op. cit.*, p. 97, plate 129, 'The carefully preshaped stone, phallic in outline to those who would see it that way . . .'. E. Evans, *op. cit.*, pp. 124–25, 'The Turoe stone must be considered phallic in form . . .'.

134. Stuart Piggott, 'The Hercules Myth: Beginnings and Ends' in *Antiquity*, (London), Vol. 12, No. 47, 1938, pp. 323–31. A. Ross, *op. cit.*, pp. 381–82. H. S. L. Dewar, *The Giant of Cerne Abbas* (West Country Folklore, pamphlet no. 1), St Peter Port, Guernsey, Toucan Press, 1968.

135. Brian Branston, *Gods of the North*, London, Thames & Hudson, 1955, pp. 118, 134, 158–59, derives the name 'Frigg' and Frey's alias 'Fricco' from the Indoeuropean root 'prij' = love, from which the modern sexual vulgarisms 'frig' and 'prick' allegedly derive.

136. Re Freyja see Hilda R. Ellis Davidson, *Gods and Myths of Northern Europe*, Har-

mondsworth, Penguin, 1964, pp. 114–24. Re love-songs (illegal) see Eric Oxenstierna, *The Norsemen*, Stuttgart, 1959; London, Studio Vista, 1966, p. 205.

137. H. Shetelig, *op. cit.*, p. 415.

138. T. Vanggaard, *op. cit.*, pp. 76–86, 118–22.

139. E. Oxenstierna, *op. cit.*, p. 206. In the last century peasants still called the bridal bed 'hammer-bed' and a customary prank was to hide a large hammer in the bed. The first wedding toast was drunk to Thor. German peasants believed that for a newly-wedded wife to carry something heavy in the first thunderstorm after her wedding brought good luck. Like the Neareastern storm-god's axe, Thor's thunder hammer was a fecundating phallic symbol.

140. Adam of Bremen, 'Gesta Hammaburgensis Ecclesiae Pontificium' (*c.* A.D. 1070) quoted by Johannes Brøndsted, *The Vikings: An Illustrated History of the Vikings, their Voyages, Battles, Customs, and Decorative Arts*, Harmondsworth, Penguin, 1960, p. 265. Re archaeology of the site see Hilda R. Ellis Davidson, *Pagan Scandinavia*, London, Thames & Hudson, 1967, pp. 141–44. Mårten Stenberger, *Sweden*, London, Thames & Hudson, 1962, pp. 153–55.

141. Hilda R. Ellis Davidson, *Scandinavian Mythology*, London, Paul Hamlyn, 1969, p. 55.

142. H. Davidson, *Gods and Myths . . .*, pp. 96–97.

143. *Ibid.*, pp. 93–94. P. Glob, *op. cit.*, pp. 130–32. From *Flateyjarbók*, a fourteenth-century M.S. of the 'Saga of King Olaf Tryggvason'.

144. J. Brøndsted, *op. cit.*, p. 267. P. Gelling and H. Davidson, *op. cit.*, p. 169. From poem '*Volsapáttr*' in *Flateyjarbók*.

145. Leo Frobenius, *Ekade Ektab: Die Felsbilder Fezzans*, Leipzig, Otto Harrassowitz, 1937, pp. 42–55, plates 50, 60–62. Fabrizio Mori, *Tadrart Acacus: Arte rupestre e Culture del Sahara preistorico*, Turin, Giulio Einaudi, 1965, pp. 68–73, figs. 34, 37, 38, 41–43. B. de Rachewiltz, *op. cit.*, pp. 14–25. G. Charrière, *op. cit.*, pp. 12–15, 30, 34, 38, 164.

146. Byron de Prorock, *In Quest of Lost Worlds*, London, Frederick Muller, 1935, pp. 255–59. *Idem, Dead Men do tell Tales*, London, George Harrap, 1943, pp. 108–14.

147. William B. Seabrook, *Jungle Ways*, London, George Harrap, 1931, pp. 274–79, quoting the Hogoun of Aru.

148. Geoffrey Parrinder, *African Mythology*, London, Paul Hamlyn, 1967, pp. 23–24, 61–63. Lucy Mair, *Witchcraft*, London, Weidenfeld & Nicolson, 1969, pp. 95–96, 98–99.

149. G. Parrinder, *op. cit.*, pp. 45–48, 68–69, 76. B. de Rachewiltz, *op. cit.*, p. 83.

150. G. Parrinder, *op. cit.*, pp. 61–63, 99–103.

151. Bruno Bettelheim, *Symbolic Wounds: Puberty Rites and the Envious Male*, London, Thames & Hudson, 1955, pp. 234–38.

152. Père Azaïs and R. Chambard, *Cinq Années de recherches archéologiques en Ethiopie, Province de Harar et Ethiopie meridionale*, (2 vols.), Paris, Paul Geuthner, 1930–1932, Text vol.: pp. 217, 223 ff. Plates vol.: plates 69–78, 95.

153. Christopher R. Hallpike, *The Konso of Ethiopia: A Study of the Values of a Cushitic People*, Oxford, Clarendon Press, 1972, pp. 19, 30, 101, 113, 134, 147–54, 186, 251, 254, 264, 266, 280, 287–89, 292. Adolf E. Jensen, *Im Lande des Gada: Wanderungen zwischen Volkstrümmern Südabessiniens*, Stuttgart, Strecker & Schröder, 1936; pp. 207, 281, 329, 333, 361, 389, 434–35, 448 ff., 481, 563, plates 28, 29, 33.

154. Geoffrey Gorer, *Africa Dances: A Book about West African Negroes*, Harmondsworth, Penguin, 1945, pp. 124, 137.

155. B. de Rachewiltz, *op. cit.*, p. 84.

156. Maya Deren, *Divine Horsemen: The Voodoo Gods of Haiti*, London, Thames & Hudson, 1953, re Papa Legba pp. 96–102. Deren wrote that the Dahomean Legba was the sun, the fire of life, primal procreative energy and his cosmic phallus was the vertical world-axis linking the visible, mortal world with the invisible immortal world. Re Ghede see pp. 34–38, 102–14.

157. B. de Rachewiltz, *op. cit.*, pp. 94, 106.

158. *Ibid.*, pp. 74–75.

159. Herbert M. Cole, 'Mbari is Life' in *African Art/Arts d'Afrique*, (Los Angeles), Vol. 2, No. 3, Spring 1969, pp. 8–17, 87, illustration p. 13. (Two more articles by Cole appeared in Vol. 2, No. 4, Summer 1969, pp. 42–51, 79 and Vol. 3, No. 1, Autumn 1969,

pp. 34–41, 88.) See also Ulli Beier, *African Mud Sculpture*, Cambridge, Cambridge University Press, 1963.

160. P. Amaury Talbot, *Some Nigerian Fertility Cults*, London, Frank Cass, 1927, pp. 10–33.

161. H. Cole, *op. cit.*, pp. 13–14.

162. Ronald M. Berndt, *Djanggawul: An Aboriginal Religious Cult of North-Eastern Arnhem Land*, London, Routledge & Kegan Paul, 1952.

163. William L. Warner, *A Black Civilization: A Social Study of an Australian Tribe*, New York, Harpers, 1937, pp. 244–334. Ronald M. Berndt, *Kunapipi*, Melbourne, F. W. Cheshire, 1951. Geza Roheim, *The Eternal Ones of the Dream*, New York, International Universities Press, 1945, pp. 171–73. Karel Kupka, *Dawn of Art: Painting and Sculpture of Australian Aborigines*, Sydney, Angus & Robertson, 1965, pp. 112–20, 144 (colour plate of bark painting of the myth of the Wawilak sisters).

164. R. Bettelheim, *op. cit.*, p. 195.

165. L. R. Hiatt, 'Secret Pseudo-Procreation Rites among the Australian Aborigines' in L. R. Hiatt and C. Jayawardena, ed., *Anthropology in Oceania: Essays presented to Ian Hogbin*, Sydney, Angus & Robertson, 1971, pp. 77–88, p. 88: fn. 18.

166. G. Roheim, *op. cit.*, pp. 85–86.

167. *Ibid.*, pp. 84 ff., 100–101.

168. Richard A. Gould, *Yiwara: Foragers of the Australian Desert*, New York, Charles Scribner's Sons, 1969, p. 148. G. Roheim, *op. cit.*, pp. 42–45.

169. I. M. Crawford, *The Art of the Wandjina: Aboriginal Cave Paintings in Kimberley, Western Australia*, London, Oxford University Press, 1968, pp. 94–95 (fig. 84).

170. Roslyn Poignant, *Oceanic Mythology*, London, Paul Hamlyn, 1967, p. 135. K. Kupka, *op. cit.*, p. 57.

171. G. Roheim, *op. cit.*, pp. 175, 257.

172. *Ibid.*, pp. 81–84.

173. *Ibid.*, p. 264.

174. A. P. Elkin, Catherine and Ronald M. Berndt, *Art in Arnhem Land*, Melbourne, F. W. Cheshire, 1950, pp. 80–81, 84–91, plates 8, 9, 18, 22. R. Poignant, *op. cit.*, p. 137.

175. G. Roheim, *op. cit.*, pp. 94–95.

176. Paul Wirz, 'La Signification du serpent et de l'oiseau sur le Territoire du Sepik (Nouvelle Guinée)' in *Bulletin des Musées royaux d'Art et d'Histoire*, (Brussels), 4th series, 1955, pp. 63–76. Referred to in Douglas Fraser, 'The Heraldic Woman: A Study in Diffusion' in Douglas Fraser, ed., *The Many Faces of Primitive Art: A Critical Anthology*, Englewood Cliffs, N.J., Prentice Hall, 1966, pp. 36–99, an interesting survey of the motif of a woman exhibiting her vulva and flanked by heraldic animals, with a useful bibliography.

177. Carl A. Schmitz, *Oceanic Art: Myth, Man, and Image in the South Seas*, New York, Harry N. Abrams, 1972, pl. 77.

178. For a parallel in another area see Robert Heine-Geldern, 'Some Tribal Art Styles of Southeast Asia' in D. Fraser, ed., *op. cit.*, pp. 165–71. The Naga tribe of Assam erect phallic monoliths in connection with severed enemy heads to secure fertility. Gregory Bateson, *Naven: A Survey of the Problems Suggested by a Composite Picture of the Culture of a New Guinea Tribe Drawn from Three Points of View*, Cambridge, 1936; Stanford, California, Stanford University Press, 2nd edition, 1958, pp. 138–41.

179. *Ibid.*, p. 163, plates 25, 27, 28. Heinz Kelm, *Kunst vom Sepik* (3 vols.), Berlin, Museum für Volkerkunde, 1968, Vol. 3: sculpture no. 89. C. Schmitz, *op. cit.*, plate 25.

180. G. Bateson, *op. cit. Idem*, 'Music in New Guinea' in *The Eagle*, (St. John's College, Cambridge University), Vol. 48, No. 214, Dec. 1934, pp. 158–70

181. Anthony Forge, 'Art and Environment in the Sepik' in *Proceedings of the Royal Anthropological Institute of Great Britain and Ireland, 1965*, (London), 1966, pp. 23–31, pp. 26–28, 31: footnote 5. (Reprinted in Carol F. Jopling, ed., *Art and Aesthetics in Primitive Societies: A Critical Anthology*, New York, E. P. Dutton, 1971, pp. 290–314.) My thanks to B. A. L. Cranstone of the British Museum, Dept. of Ethnography, for bringing this article to my attention.

182. *Ibid.*, p. 29.

183. Douglas Newton, *Art Styles of the Papuan Gulf*, New York, Museum of Primitive Art, 1961, p. 10. Gunnar Landtman, *The Kiwai-Papuans of British New Guinea*, London, Macmillan, 1927, pp. 351–52, 355, 359–60.

184. G. Roheim, *op. cit.*, pp. 127–29. Paul Wirz, *Die Marind-Anim von Holländisch-Süd-Neu-Guinea*, (2 vols.), Hamburg, L. Friedrichsen, 1922–1925, Vol. 1, Part 1: p. 35, Part 2: pp. 13, 22, 47 fn 4, 154 fn 4; Vol. 2, Part 3: pp. 1–5, 8, 16–17, 19, 23, 28, 30, 35–36, 38, 43, 89–90, 93, 98, 114, 147.

185. Margaret Mead, *The Mountain Arapesh*, (3 vols.), Garden City, N.Y., Natural History Press, 1970, Vol. 3 (*Arts and Supernaturalism*), pp. 401–11.

186. A. Forge, *op. cit.*, p. 28. See also Ian Hogbin, *The Island of Menstruating Men: Religion in Wogeo, New Guinea*, Scranton, Penn., Chandler, 1970, pp. 86–99.

187. A. Forge, *op. cit.*, p. 30.

188. G. Bateson, *Naven* . . ., p. 149. I have changed Bateson's 'copulate with' to 'fuck' because the latter expresses the aggressive tone more accurately.

189. *Ibid.*, pp. 12, 20–21. In the Naven ceremony a man praising his nephews impersonates the maternal role, dressed in dirty, ragged female garments and speaking falsetto. He satirises female sexual passivity by 'presenting' his buttocks to his nephews with an orange-coloured fruit protruding from his anus to simulate a woman's 'anal clitoris'. In debates men ferociously threaten to rape other men. In their manhood initiation ordeal, boys are bullied and called 'wives', and are made to handle the penises of the initiators. See also Margaret Mead, *Male and Female: A Study of the Sexes in a Changing World*, New York, William Morrow, 1969; Harmondsworth, Penguin, 1962, p. 105.

190. Andrew and Marilyn Strathern, *Self-Decoration in Mount Hagen*, London, Duckworth, 1971.

191. R. F. Fortune, *Sorcerers of Dobu: The Social Anthropology of the Dobu Islanders of the Western Pacific*, (1932) New York, E. P. Dutton, 1963, pp. 295–97.

192. Edmund R. Leach, 'A Trobriand Medusa?' in *Man*, (London), Vol. 54, article 158, July 1954, pp. 103–5. See also controversial comments in *Man*, Nos. 65, 90, 160, 1958 and 3, 66, 67, 1959. This article was reprinted in C. Jopling, ed., *op. cit.*, pp. 45–54.

193. Bronislaw Malinowski, *The Sexual Life of Savages in North-Western Melanesia: An Ethnographic Account of Courtship, Marriage and Family Life among the Natives of the Trobriand Islands, British New Guinea*, London, George Routledge & Sons, 1929, pp. 232 33.

194. *Ergebnisse der Südsee Expedition 1908–1910: II (Ethnographie), B (Mikronesien)*: Augustin Krämer, *Palau* (5 vols.) Vol. 1, 1917 and Vol. 2, 1919, Vol. 3, 1926, Hamburg, L. Friedrichsen. Vols. 4 and 5, 1929, Hamburg, Friedrichsen & De Gruyter. Re unmarried men's hous ('bai') and custom of cohabitation of unmarried young people see Vol. 3: 229 ff., 274 ff., 332–32 and Vol. 4: pp. 2 ff. Re sculpture and painted reliefs of 'bai' houses see Vol. 1: plate 1, Vol. 2: pp. 245, 277–79, 332, Vol. 5: pp. 2 ff. and plates 1, 4, 8, 15 and double-page plates at back of volume. Re grossly ithyphallic wooden statue of a spirit see Vol. 3: p. 340 and plate 18 (also in C. Schmitz, *op. cit.*, plate 279, see also 'Dilukai' figure, plate 280). See also Jan S. Kubary (ed. by J. D. E. Schmeltz), *Ethnographische Beiträge zur Kenntnis des Karolinen Archipels*, (3 parts), Leiden, P. W. M. Trap, 1892–1895; Part 3, 'Die Palausche Baukunst' (1895), plates 31–33, 35–37, 40: figs. 17 and 20, 43: fig. 3.

195. A. Krämer, *op. cit.*, vol. 3: pp. 245, 277–79. Re Polynesian parallel of a maiden fertilised by the sun's rays while she sat with her thighs parted see *idem*, *Die Samoa Inseln*, (2 vols.), Stuttgart, 1902, vol. 1: pp. 403–404. These references are summarised in D. Fraser, *op. cit.*, pp. 60–62.

196. A. Krämer, *op. cit.* (*Palau*), Vol. 4: p. 8 and Vol. 5: double plate 1d.

197. Re tattooing of 'mons veneris' see *ibid.*, Vol. 3: p. 35: fig. 19, 36. Re lengthening of clitoris and labia see Paul Tabori, *Dress and Undress: The Sexology of Fashion*, London, New English Library, 1969, p. 199, referring to Otto Finsch, 'Ueber die Bewohner von Ponapé (östl Karolinen), nach eigenen Beobachtungen und Erkundigungen' in *Zeitschrift für Ethnologie: Organ der Berliner Gesellschaft für Anthropologie, Ethnologie und Urgeschichte*, (Berlin), Vol. 12, 1880, pp. 301–32 (pp. 304, 311–12, 316) and re Sonsol, J. Kubary, *op. cit.*, Part 1, pp. 88–90.

198. A. Krämer, *op. cit.*, Vol. 4, p. 168 and Vol. 5, double-plate 20 e.

199. *Ibid.*, Vol. 4, p. 125 and Vol. 5, double-plate 14 a.

200. Edwin G. Burrows, *Flower in my Ear: Arts and Ethos of Ifaluk Atoll*, Seattle, University of Washington Press, 1963, pp. 71–74.

201. *Ibid.*, p. 229.

202. *Ibid.*, p. 230.

203. *Ibid.*, p. 243.

204. *Ibid.*, p. 256.

205. Antony Alpers, *Legends of the South Seas: The World of the Polynesians seen through their Myths and Legends*, London, John Murray, 1970, p. 372.

206. *Ibid.*, pp. 73–75 and notes, p. 371.

207. J. Frank Stimson, *Songs and Tales of the Sea Kings: Interpretations of the Oral Literature of Polynesia*, Salem, Mass., Peabody Museum, 1957, p. 19.

208. Peter Buck (Te Rangi Hiroa), *The Coming of the Maori*, Wellington, Whitcombe & Tombs, 1949, p. 510.

209. Edward Dodd, *Polynesian Art: The Ring of Fire*, (New York, 1967) London, Robert Hale, 1969, p. 292. Terrance Barrow, *Maori Wood Sculpture of New Zealand*, Wellington, N.Z., A. H. & A. W. Reed, 1969, pp. 18, 19, 112 (fig. 149).

210. P. Buck, *op. cit.*, p. 510.

211. A. Alpers, *op. cit.*, p. 109 and notes p. 374. For penis with bent tip see E. Dodd, *op. cit.*, pp. 291, 293.

212. Donald S. Marshall, *Island of Passion: Ra'ivavae*, London, George Allen & Unwin, 1962, p. 293. Terrance Barrow, *Art and Life in Polynesia*, London, Pall Mall, 1972, p. 117 (fig. 192) and E. Dodd, *op. cit.*, p. 135.

213. Antony Alpers, *Maori Myths and Tribal Legends*, London, John Murray, 1964, pp. 28 ff.

214. Ralph Linton, 'Marquesan Culture' in Abraham Kardiner, ed., *The Individual and His Society*, New York, Columbia University Press, 1934, p. 178. Re women taboo during canoe-building see Raymond Firth, *We the Tikopia: A Sociological Study of Kinship in Primitive Polynesia*, London, G. Allen & Unwin, 1936, p. 470 (Chapter 14, 'Sociology of Sex', was omitted from the 2nd edition, 1957).

215. T. Barrow, *Maori Wood Sculpture . . .*, pp. 13–14, 19.

216. Terrance Barrow, 'Maori Decorative Art: An Outline' in *The Journal of the Polynesian Society*, (Dunedin, N.Z.), Vol. 65, No. 4, Dec. 1956, pp. 305–31, 325. Paul S. Wingert, *Primitive Art: Its Traditions and Styles*, Cleveland and New York, World Publishing-Meridian Books, 1965, p. 325 (fig. 108).

217. E. Dodd, *op. cit.*, p. 250. T. Barrow, *Maori Wood Sculpture . . .*, pp. 78 (fig. 98), 116 (fig. 154), 117 (fig. 155), 123 (fig. 162), 143 (fig. 199), 145 (fig. 205), 147 (figs. 208–10).

218. E. Dodd, *op. cit.*, p. 249. T. Barrow, *Art and Life . . .*, p. 112 (figs. 183–85). This idol was brought home as a trophy to the London Missionary Society. The missionary William Ellis, *Polynesian Researches during a Residence of nearly Six Years in the South Sea Islands* (2 vols.), New York and London, 1829, frontispiece to Vol. 2 illustrates the statue wearing a chaste loincloth. The divine creative copulations of this deity opened the 'Arioi' cult performances.

219. T. Barrow, 'Maori Decorative Art . . ., p. 323, *idem, Maori Wood Sculpture . . .*, pp. 18, 76, 116.

220. E. Dodd, *op. cit.*, pp. 255–59. T. Barrow, *Art and Life . . .*, pp. 55, 124–25 (figs. 209–10). R. Poignant, *op. cit.*, pp. 55–56. These staff-gods are thought by some scholars to represent either Tangaroa, or his son Oro, deity of the 'Arioi' cult.

221. Elsdon Best, *The Maori* (2 vols.), Wellington, N.Z., H. H. Tombs, 1924, pp. 556–57

222. *Ibid.*, Vol. 1, p. 43 (illustration). E. Dodd, *op. cit.*, pp. 80, 117. J. F. Stimson, *op. cit.*, p. 218: 'Our Supreme Goddess . . . who was said to be the Bailer, having inset as its handle the Divine Clitoris, called Fledgling-within-its-nest . . .'.

223. E. Dodd, *op. cit.*, pp. 151–52.

224. J. L. Young, 'Remarks on Phallic Stones from Rapanui' in *Occasional Papers of the Berenice Pauahi Bishop Museum of Polynesian Ethnology and Natural History*, (Honolulu), Vol. 2, No. 25, 1904, pp. 171–72. Alfred Métraux, 'Ethnology of Easter Island' in *Berenice P.*

Bishop Museum Bulletin, (Honolulu), No. 160, 1940, pp. 3–432, pp. 105–6, 264. D. Marshall, *op. cit.*, pp. 19, 198–99, 249–51, 266–67, 273, 276–77.

225. Margaret Mead, *Coming of Age in Samoa: A Study of Adolescence and Sex in Primitive Societies*, (1928), Harmondsworth, Penguin, 1943, pp. 112, 117, 217.

226. Augustin Krämer, 'Der Phallusberg von Molokai (Hawaii-Inseln)' in *Globus: Illustrierte Zeitschrift für Länder- und Völkerkunde*, Vol. 73, Braunschweig, 1898, pp. 8–10.

227. August Eichorn, 'Alt-hawaiisch Kultobjekte und Kultgeräte' in *Ehrenreich Baessler-Archiv: Beiträge zur Völkerkunde*, (Leipzig and Berlin), Vol. 13, 1929, pp. 1–30, pp. 17 (figs. 26 and 27), 18.

228. D. Marshall, *op. cit.*, p. 200.

229. J. F. Stimson, *op. cit.*, p. 218.

230. Katherine Scoresby Routledge, 'Survey of the Village and Carved Rocks of Orongo, Easter Island, by the Mana Expedition' in *Journal of the Royal Anthropological Institute of Great Britain and Ireland*, (London), Vol. 50, 1920, pp. 425–51. A. Métraux, *op. cit.*, pp. 105–106, 264, 309–41. Thor Heyerdahl, Edwin N. Ferdon, Jr *et al.*, *Archaeology of Easter Island: Reports of the Norwegian Archeological Expedition to Easter Island and the East Pacific* (2 vols.), Stockholm, Forum Publishing House, Vol. 1: 1961, Vol. 2: 1965. Vol. 1: pp. 131, 157, 244, 334, 359, 452–56, 471, 512 ff.

231. Albert Wilhelm Geisler, *Die Oster-Insel: Eine Stätte prähistorischer Kultur in der Südsee*, (Berlin), 1883, p. 35. Knut Hjalmar Stolpe, 'Über die Tätowirung der Oster-Insulaner', article No. 6 in *Festschrift fur A(dolf) B(ernhard) Meyer: Abhandlungen und Berichte des königlichen Zoologischen und Anthropologisch-Ethnographischen Museums zu Dresden*, Dresden, 1899, pp. 1–13, pp. 6, 10–11. A. Métraux, *op. cit.*, pp. 109, 243, 248.

232. *Ibid.*, pp. 264, 266, 298. T. Heyerdahl *et al.*, *op. cit.*, Vol. 1: pp. 240, 244, 359, 452–53, 471.

233. Carlo Gay, *Chalcacingo*, Graz, Akademische Druck-und Verlagsanstalt, 1971, pp. 33–34 (fig. 9). Similar vulva symbols were painted on the cave-walls of 'shelter D' at Chalcacingo. See pp. 19 (fig. 1), 29. A similar stalactite penis was discovered in a cave on an island in the Tesechoacan River in northern Oaxaca. See Auguste Genin, 'Notes d'Archeologie mexicaine' in *Journal de la Société des Américanistes de Paris*, (Paris), Vol. 3, No. 1, 1900, pp. 1–42, (pp. 38–39).

234. Robert Ravicz and A. Kimball Romsey, 'The Mixtecs' in *Handbook of Middle American Indians*, Vol. 7, Austin, University of Texas Press, 1969, pp. 367–99, (p. 394).

235. C. Gay, *op. cit.*, pp. 39 (fig. 9a: relief 2), 45 (fig. 17), 46. Miguel Covarrubius, *Indian Art of Mexico and Central America*, New York, Alfred A. Knopf, 1957, p. 64 (fig. 24) illustrates another drawing of this relief which differs in several details. The serpent-faced figures may be carrying instruments of thunder and lightning like the 'lelem' lightning machetes of the Mayan 'Chac' rain deities, and the sticks used by the Mexican Tlalocs to break the water-jars of the rain.

236. Re 'Mam' see Guy Stresser-Péan, 'Montagnes calcaires et sources vauclusiennes dans la religion des Indiens Huastèques de la Région de Tampico' in *Revue de l'Histoire des Religions*, (Paris), Vol. 141, No. 1, Jan.–March, 1952, pp. 84–90. *Idem*, 'Ixtab, Maximon et Judas: Croyances sur la Pendaison chez les Mayas du Yucatan, du Guatemala et de la Huasteca' in *Actas del XXXIII Congresso Internacional de Americanistas, 1958*, San José, Costa Rica, 1959, Vol. 2: pp. 456–64. Erwin P. Dieseldorff, *Kunst und Religion der Mayavolker in alten und heutigen Mittelamerika*, (3 vols.), Berlin and Hamburg, 1926–1933. Vol. 1 reprinted from *Zeitschrift für Ethnologie*, Vol. 57, Berlin, 1925, pp. 1–45, 53 (plates), includes many illustrations identified as *Mam*. Ferdinand Anders, *Pantheon der Maya*, Graz, Akademische Druck-und Verlagsanstalt, 1963, pp. 301–2, 330–34. John Eric S. Thompson, *Maya History and Religion*, Norman, Okla., University of Oklahoma Press, 1970, pp. 118, 173, 275, 286, 336, 352. The Huastecs and Mayas are related cultures, both pre-Mexican and probably deriving from the ancient Olmecs.

237. *Ibid.*, p. 253 and plates 9–10. Edward H. Thompson discovered subterranean rain-water cisterns at the Mayan site of Xkichmook, Yucatan. On the walls of one was a stucco relief of a phallus and testicles; another had images of a frog, turtle, and snake, all associated

with rain, and an ithyphallic monkey, associated with sexuality. See E. H. Thompson, 'Ruins of Xkichmook, Yucatan' in *Publications of the Field Columbian Museum:* Anthropological Series, Vol. 2, No. 3 (publication 28), Chicago, July 1898, pp. 207–29 (p. 225 and fig. 28 facing p. 224).

238. *Dresden Codex*, folios 17a, 21c. See F. Anders *op. cit.*, p. 301.

239. The most beautiful and elaborate statuette of this theme is in the National Gallery, Washington, D.C. (Bliss collection). See George Kubler, *The Art and Architecture of Ancient America: The Mexican, Maya and Andean Peoples*, Harmondsworth, Penguin, 1962, plate 81. Coarser specimens are illustrated in: Irmgard G. Kimball, *Maya Terrakotten*, Tübingen, E. Wasmuth, 1960, plates 26, 28, 38. Ferdinand Anton, *Art of the Maya*, London, Thames & Hudson, 1970, plate 203. Hasso von Winning, *Pre-Columbian Art of Mexico and Central America*, London, Thames & Hudson, 1969, p. 441. Catalogue of loan exhibition: *Maya Sculpture and Pottery from Mexico: The Manuel Barbachano Ponce Collection*, London, Ethnography Department of the British Museum, 1971, No. 87.

240. *Ibid.*, Nos. 1, 96. Re Ix Chel see J. Eric Thompson, 'The Moon Goddess in Middle America, with Notes on related Deities' in *Contributions to American Anthropology and History* (Carnegie Institute, Washington, D.C., publication 509), Vol. 5, No. 29, Washington, D.C., June 30, 1939, pp. 127–73.

241. The 'Plumeria', or 'Frangipani' was associated with sexual desire and used in love-magic. Intoxicated by its smell a ruler of Chichen Itza lustfully coveted his guest's bride and thus caused the downfall of his city.

242. See Salvador Toscano, 'Arte Precolombino del Occidente de Mexico' in *Cuadernos Americanos*, (Mexico City), Vol. 27, No. 3, May–June, 1946, pp. 223–26 and 22 unnumbered plates (15th plate 'Colima Personaje'). Phyllis and Eberhard Kronhausen, *Erotic Arts* (2 vols.), New York, Grove Press, Vol. 1: 1968, Vol. 2: 1970; London, W. H. Allen, Vol. 1: 1971, F. Anton, *op. cit.*, fig. 70, fragment of a painted dish from Uaxactún. Nude females are rare in Pre-Columbian art, but see Jaina terracotta figurine in I. Kimball, *op. cit.*, plate 27.

243. Phyllis and Eberhard Kronhausen, *op. cit.*, Vol. 1: plate 230, Vol. 2: plates 234, 235, 239. Ferdinand Anton, *Ancient Mexican Art*, (Leipzig, 1965; London, Thames & Hudson, 1969, p. 282 and plate 145. Dieter Eisleb, *Westmexikanische Keramik der Museum für Volkerkunde*, Berlin, Museum für Völkerkunde, 1971, p. 26 and plate 8. C. Gay, *op. cit.*, p. 66 suggested a link between Olmecoid Chalcacingo and Colima-Michoacan. José Corona Nuñez, 'Relaciones arqueologicas entre las Huastecas y Regiones al Poniente' in *Huastecos, Totonacos y sus Vecinos* (special volume of: *Revista Mexicana de Estudios Antropologicos*, [Mexico City]), Vol. 13, 1952–53, pp. 479–83, discusses probable contacts between the two main areas of phallic imagery, the east coast: Huasteca and the west coast: Colima-Michoacan. Some contacts between the Peruvian coastal cultures (see below) and the latter area are also likely.

244. Anonymous, 'Relatione fatta per un Gentil'huomo del Signor Fernando Cortese' in Giovanni Battista Ramusio, ed., *Delle Navigationi . . .*, 1606, Vol. 3, p. 257. This account probably dates from *c.* 1519 and may relate to the city of Cila.

245. A. Genin, *op. cit.*, pp. 32–38. Jules Claine, 'Découverte de documents du culte phallique au Mexique' in *Société d'Anthropologie de Paris*, (Paris), Series 4, Vol. 4, Dec., 1892, pp. 222–23. Nicolas León, 'El Culto al Falo en el Mexico Precolumbiano' in *Anales del Museo Nacional, Mexico época 2*, Mexico City, Vol. 1, 1903, pp. 278–80 (illustrations pp. 279 and 280). One of the three stone phalluses from Yahualica, measuring respectively 1 m 57, 1 m 62, 1 m 55 in length, was sent to the Museo Nacional, Mexico City, where it was a feature of the restricted 'Salon Segreto' where numerous examples of Pre-Columbian sexual imagery were displayed to the 'chosen few'. See Ramón Mena, *Catalogo del Salon Secreto (Culto al Falo)*, Mexico City, Museo Nacional de Arqueologia, Historia y Etnografia, 2nd edition, 1926. Many of the items illustrated are of questionable erotic significance. Guy Stresser-Pean, 'Première Campagne de Fouilles à Tamtok près de Tamuin, Huasteca' in *International Congress of Americanists, 1962*, Mexico City, 1964, Part 1: pp. 387–94 re a stone slab carved with a schematised symbol of a vulva.

246. Selenite statuette in National Gallery, Washington, D.C. (former Bliss collection). The goddesses of fertility and sexuality overlapped. Xochiquetzal was also said to be the

mother of Cinteotl. Women who died in childbirth were associated with witch-demonesses and were honoured like dead warriors for their bloody self-sacrifice.

247. Cottie A. Burland, *The Gods of Mexico*, London, Eyre & Spottiswoode, 1967, pp. 122–24, 162.

248. Francisco Guerra, *The Pre-Columbian Mind: A Study into the aberrant Nature of Sexual Drives, Drugs affecting Behaviour, and the Attitude towards Life and Death, with a Survey of Psychotherapy in Pre-Columbian America*, London-New Tork, Seminar Press, 1971, pp. 112–13, 275, 278.

249. *Codex Laud (MS Laud Misc. 678)* *Bodleian Library, Oxford*, (Codices Selecti, Phototypice Impressi, Vol. II), Graz Akademische Druck-und Verlagsanstalt, 1966; and London, Phaidon, 1968, a colour facsimile with an Introduction by Cottie A. Burland.

250. Colour facsimile with notes by E. T. Hamy: *Codex Borbonicus: Manuscrit mexicain de la Bibliothèque du Palais Bourbon (Livre divinatoire et rituel figuré)*, Paris, 1899, pp. 20–30. Francisco del Paso y Troncoso, *Discripción Historia y Exposición del Códice Pitórico de los Antiguos Náuas que se conserva en la Biblioteca de la Cámera de Diputados de París (antiguo Palais Bourbon)*, Florence, Salvador Landi, 1898, pp. 133–60. Georg Eduard Seler, *Codex Borgia: Eine altmexikanische Bilderschrift der Bibliothek Congregatio de Propaganda Fide*, Berlin, privately printed for the Duke de Loubat, 1903, pp. 158–59 and fig. 344. *Idem*, 'Die holzschnitze Pauke von Malinalco und das Zeichen *atl-tlachinolli*' in *Mitteilelungen der Anthropologische Gesellschaft in Wien*, Vol. 34 (3rd Series: Vol. 4), Vienna, 1904, pp. 222–74 (pp. 229: fig. 17b, 232). Konrad Theodor Preuss, 'Phallische Fruchtbarkeits-Dämonen als Träger des altmexicanischen Dramas: Ein Beitrag zur Urgeschichte des mimischen Weltdramas' in *Archiv für Anthropologie*, Vol. 29 (n. s. Vol. 1), Braunschweig, 1904, pp. 129–88 (p. 130: fig. 1, pp. 135 ff.). *Idem*, 'Der Unterbau des Dramas' in *Vorträge der Bibliothek Warburg 1927–28*, Leipzig and Berlin, 1930, pp. 1–88 (pp. 67 ff. and plate 41: fig. 60). Carlos R. Margain Aranjo, 'La Fiesta Azteca de la Cosecha Ochpanistli' in *Anales del Instituto Nacional de Antropologia e Historia, Mexico (1939–40)*, Mexico City, Vol. 1, 1945, pp. 157–74.

251. C. Burland, *op. cit.*, pp. 93, 148–64. The source for the statement p. 93 re Quetzalcoatl: 'his loincloth is a special shape with a rounded end, because he was reputed to have a magnificent penis which was hidden by this special cloth', unfortunately is not given by Burland. Such a loincloth is represented on a body-stamp of Quetzalcoatl-Ehecatl from Tezcoco, illustrated by F. Anton, *Ancient Mexican Art*, p. 68. Together with other rounded wind-forms associated with Ehecatl this motif probably derived from the Gulf Coast. The Huastecs were notorious for *not* hiding their genitals with loincloths. Clay figurines of the god from Tezcoco have a knobbed cylindrical head-dress which could be interpreted as phallic and similar forms appear at Mayapan, Yucatan as 'column-altars'. Bernardino Sahagun, *Universal History of New Spain: The Florentine Codex* (translated by Arthur J. Anderson and Charles E. Dibble), Santa Fe, New Mexico, University of Utah Press, 1952, Book 3: p. 31 the exiled Quetzalcoatl 'set up a huge rock'. Eduard Seler translated 'vejtepol tetl' as 'phallus rock'. Re Quetzalcoatl's Huastec origin see Joaquin Meade, *La Huasteca: Epoca Antigua*, Mexico City, 1942, pp. 107–14. Doris Stone, 'An Interpretation of Ulna Polychrome Ware' in *38ste Internationalen Amerikanisten Kongress: Stuttgart-Munich, 1968*, Munich, 1970, Vol. 2, pp. 67–76; p. 70: 'Quetzalcoatl was a god of rain and subsequently fertility . . . It may be that the copulating pairs represent the idea of the Mexican rain god, Quiatect. . . . Certainly the Feathered Serpent could easily merge with the crocodile, Cipactli, who besides being a symbol of fertility and the earth was accompanied by a copulating pair . . .' Re 'copulating' pairs motif see F. Anton, *Art of the Maya*, fig. 53.

252. B. Sahagun, *op. cit.*, Book 3, Chapters 4 and 5, pp. 15–18. Primo Feliciano Velasquez, trans., 'Codice Chimalpopoca: Anales de Cuahtitlan y Leyenda de los Soles' in *Universidad Nacional Autonoma de Mexico*, Mexico City, Instituto de Historia, 1945, pp. 7–8, 13. Fernando de Alva Ixtlilxochitl, *Obras Historicas* (ed. by Chavero), Mexico City, 1891–92. F. Guerra, *op. cit.*, pp. 100–102, 159–60. C. Burland, *Gods of Mexico . . .*, pp. 155–62.

253. John Eric S. Thompson, 'Dating of certain Inscriptions of non-Maya Origin' in *Carnegie Institute of Washington, Division of Historical Research: Theoretical Approaches to Problems* No. 1, Washington, D.C., July, 1941, pp. 49–54, 59–64. *Idem, The Rise and Fall of Maya Civilization*, Norman, Okla., University of Oklahoma Press, 1954, pp. 93, 97, 133–34.

Idem, Maya History and Religion, pp. 20, 45–46, 319. Alfred M. Tozzer, 'Chichen Itza and its Cenote of Sacrifice: A Comparative Study of contemporaneous Maya and Toltec' in *Memoirs of the Peabody Museum of Archaeology and Ethnology*, Vols. 11 and 12 (plates), Cambridge, Mass., Harvard University Press, 1957, p. 111.

254. *Ibid.*, pp. 34, 44, 111.

255. Re 'House of the Turtles' phallic rainwater sprouts see Ignacio Marquina, *Estudio Architectonico Comparativo de los Monumentos Arqueologicos de Mexico*, Mexico City, 1928, plate preceding p. 65. *Idem, Arquitectura Prehispanica*, Mexico City, 1950, p. 789. This detail has been discreetly omitted from the restored ruins. Re 'Temple of the Phalluses', Uxmal, see Alberto Ruz Lhuillier, *Uxmal: Official Guide of the Instituto Nacional de Antropologia y Historia*, Mexico City, 1956, p. 45.

256. G. Kubler, *op. cit.*, pp. 191–200 and plate 101. Karl Ruppert, 'The Mercado Chichen Itza, Yucatan' in *Carnegie Institute, Washington: Contributions*, Vol. 8, No. 43, Washington, D.C., 1943, figs. 19 and 20. J. E. Thompson, *Maya History and Religion*, p. 20.

257. *Ibid.*, pp. 20, 46. *Idem, Rise and Fall . . .*, p. 134. F. Guerra, *op. cit.*, pp. 172–73.

258. E. Wyllys Andrews, 'A Group of Related Sculptures from Yucatan' in *Contributions to American Anthropology and History*, No. 26, *Carnegie* Institution, Washington, publication 509, Washington, D.C., 1939, pp. 71–79. *Idem*, 'The Archaeology of Southwestern Campeche' in *Contributions . . .*, Nos. 40–43, Carnegie Inst. Publ. 546, 1943, pp. 82–86. Re hanging and its erotic significance and a link with the god 'Mam' see G. Stresser-Péan, *Ixtab, Maximon et Judas . . .*, pp. 459–60. Román Piña Chan, 'Informe preliminar sobre Mul-Chic, Yucatan' in *Anales del Instituto Nacional de Antropologia e Historia*, Vol. 15, No. 44, Mexico City, 1962–63, pp. 98–118 (p. 111 and plate 12) illustrates a mural from structure A which shows a captive hanged from a tree, perhaps grasping his erect penis. The Mexican *Codex Vaticanus No. 3773 (Codex Vaticanus B): An Old Mexican Pictorial Manuscript in the Vatican Library*, elucidated by Dr Eduard Seler, Berlin, privately printed for the Duke de Loubat, 1902, London, 1903 (printed by T. & A. Constable, Edinburgh) shows images from various codices of a naked penitent adulterer strangling with a rope and/or the blood-red serpent of sexuality around his neck, pp. 18–19, 29: fig. 73, 35, 36: figs. 106 and 107, 41–42.

259. Diego de Landa, 'Relacion de las Cosas de Yucatan' (translated and annotated by Alfred M. Tozzer) in *Peabody Museum Papers*, Vol. 18, Cambridge, Mass., 1941, pp. 116–18.

260. I. Marquina, *Arquitectura Prehispanica . . .*, p. 867, (fig. 440), 868 (fig. 441), 869. The illustrations are a reconstruction by Miguel Angel Fernàndez of the ceiling of the ruined north temple of the ceremonial ball-court. Compare with text by Diego Garcia de Palacio, *Collection of rare and original Documents and Relations concerning the Discovery and Conquest of America, chiefly from Spanish Archives*, Vol. 1: '*Carta dirijda al Rey de Espana . . .*' (*1576*), translated by Ephraim G. Squier, New York, 1860, pp. 65, 67.

261. Thomas W. F. Gann, 'The Maya Indians of Southern Yucatan and Northern British Honduras' in *Smithsonian Institute: Bureau of American Ethnology Bulletin 64*, Washington, D.C., 1918, pp. 60–67.

262. D. de Landa, *op. cit.*, p. 113: note 522. G. de Palacio, *op. cit.*, pp. 75, 87.

263. F. Guerra, *op. cit.*, p. 155, quoting Antonio de Herrera y Tordesillas, *Historia general de los hechos de los Castellanos en las Islas y Tierra Firme del Mar Oceano* (1601–15), Vol. 4, p. 242 re Nuño de Guzman's expedition of 1531.

264. F. Guerra, *op. cit.*, p. 56, quoting Gonzalo Fernàndez de Oviedo y Valdes, *Historia general de las Indias* (1535), folios 48–50. The jewel had been acquired at Santa Marta on the north coast of Columbia by Pedrarias Davilus's expedition of 1514 and was destroyed at Darien by Oviedo y Valdes.

265. Victor W. von Hagen, *The Desert Kingdoms of Peru*, London, Weidenfeld & Nicolson, 1965, was one of the first non-specialist books in English to illustrate Peruvian erotic art and gives a good general account of the whole culture area. Elizabeth P. Benson, *The Mochica: A Culture of Peru*, London, Thames & Hudson, 1972 includes an interesting discussion of the wide range of Mochica iconography including erotic subjects. Rafael Larco Hoyle, *Checan: Essay on Erotic Elements in Peruvian Art*, Geneva, Nagel, 1965 is a magnificent collection of plates, mostly in colour, with an interesting, although quirky, text. Paul H. Gebhard, 'Sexual Motifs in Prehistoric Peruvian Ceramics' in T. Bowie and C. Christianson, eds., *op. cit.*,

pp. 109–44 is an interesting and well-illustrated statistical analysis of Peruvian erotica by Alfred Kinsey's collaborator and the present Director of the Institute for Sex Research of Indiana University. F. Guerra, *op. cit.*, pp. 255–59, includes a somewhat different statistical analysis in his study of Pre-Columbian *mores*. P. and E. Kronhausen, *op. cit.*, illustrate more Peruvian specimens. Morse Peckham, *Art and Pornography: An Experiment in Explanation*, New York, Basic Books, 1969 in the paperback edition, New York and London, Harpers & Row–Icon, 1971, illustrates two more pots, pp. 22–23.

266. R. Larco Hoyle, *op. cit.*, p. 129.

267. *Ibid.*, p. 103 (see also p. 130, bottom). P. Gebhard, *op. cit.*, plate 49.

268. *Ibid.*, plate 51. R. Larco Hoyle, *op. cit.*, p. 128.

269. P. Gebhard, *op. cit.*, p. 118.

270. *Ibid.*, plate 67. R. Larco Hoyle, *op. cit.*, pp. 108–9, 113, 140. E. Benson, *op. cit.*, pp. 134–35, 144.

271. M. Peckham, *op. cit.*, paperback edition only.

272. R. Larco Hoyle, *op. cit.*, pp. 23, 24. P. Gebhard, *op. cit.*, plate 64.

273. *Ibid.*, plate 54. R. Larco Hoyle, *op. cit.*, p. 132. E. Benson, *op. cit.*, p. 143 (figs. 6–16).

274. *Ibid.*, pp. 142–46.

275. Statisticians disagree: R. Larco Hoyle, *op. cit.*, p. 110 states less than 5% vaginal and more than 95% anal intercourse. P. Gebhard, *op. cit.*, p. 257 states re Mochica erotic ceramics, a minimum of 21% anal copulation. F. Guerra, *op. cit.*, p. 257, heterosexual anal sodomy 31%. As to the motivation for heterosexual anal intercourse E. Benson, *op. cit.*, p. 148, vaguely supposes a ritual significance; F. Guerra, *op. cit.*, p. 258, suggests that priests who guarded the 'Virgins of the Sun' may have avoided dire punishment by resorting to anal intercourse leaving them technically 'intact'. But many of the women depicted in this sexual act are apparently ordinary wives and mothers. P. Gebhard, *op. cit.*, p. 126 suggests that contraception may have been the motive.

276. F. Guerra, *op. cit.*, p. 257 asserts that 3% of depictions of anal sodomy are homosexual and identifies as males at least two fellators. R. Larco Hoyle, *op. cit.*, p. 112 found no certain specimens of homosexuality.

277. V. von Hagen, *op. cit.*, pp. 54–55. R. Larco Hoyle, *op. cit.*, p. 122. F. Guerra, *op. cit.*, pp. 57, 114, 227, 241.

278. *Ibid.*, pp. 257–58. R. Larco Hoyle, *op. cit.*, pp. 76, 82–83, 93, 101, 105, 126–27.

279. *Ibid.*, pp. 21, 80, 84, 118, 121. Larco Hoyle suggested (pp. 108, 123–27) that the skeletal figures lacking lips and cheeks were exemplary figures of the horrible consequences of insatiable lust punished by gruesome tortures. This view was rejected by P. Gebhard, F. Guerra and E. Benson. E. Benson, *op. cit.*, pp. 151–54 notes the erotic element in human sacrifice as signified by naked prisoners with prominent genitals and a rope around their necks. The 'rope' is sometimes a snake nibbling the victim's penis (see footnote 262 above).

280. The 'Kokopelli' is a large dipterous insect, a sort of locust or an Assassin or Robber Fly. See Jesse W. Fewkes, 'Hopi Katchinas drawn by Native Artists' in *Smithsonian Institution: Bureau of American Ethnology: 21st Annual Report for 1899–1900*, Washington, D.C., Government Printing Office, 1903, pp. 13–126 (p. 86 and plate 25). Florence Hawley, 'Kokopelli of the Prehistoric Southwestern Pueblo Pantheon' in *American Anthropologist*, new series: Vol. 39, Menasha, Wisconsin, 1937, pp. 644–46. Elsie C. Parsons, 'The Humpbacked Flute Player of the Southwest' in *American Anthropologist*, Vol. 40, 1938, pp. 337–38. Mischa Titiev, 'The Story of Kokopele' in *American Anthropology*, new series: Vol. 41, 1939, pp. 91–98. Watson Smith, 'Kiva Mural Decorations at Awatovi and Kawaika—A, with a Survey of other Wall Paintings in the Pueblo Southwest. (Report of the Awatovi Expedition no. 5)' in *Papers of the Peabody Museum of American Archaeology and Ethnology, Harvard University*, Vol. 37, Cambridge, Mass., 1952. Harold S. Colton, *Hopi Kachina Dolls, with a Key to their Identification*, Albuquerque, N.M., University of New Mexico, revised edition 1959, pp. 35–36. Frederick J. Dockstader, 'The Kachina and the White Man: A Study of the Influences of White Cultures on the Hopi Kachina Cult' in *Cranbrook Institute of Science Bulletin 25*, Bloomfield Hills, Mich., May, 1954, pp. 1–186. Frank Waters, *Book of the Hopi*, New York, Viking Press, 1963, and Ballantine, 1969, pp. 44–47, 50–52, 73. Re petroglyphs of ithyphallic Kokopelli see J. W. Fewkes, 'Cliff Ruins in Fewkes Cañon, Mesa Verde'

in (*Col. William H.*) *Holmes Anniversary Volume*, Washington, D.C., 1916, pp. 96–117 (pp. 107: fig. 2, 108). Earl Morris, 'The Aztec Ruin' in *Anthropological Papers of the American Museum of Natural History*, Vol. 26, Part 1, New York, 1919, p. 92 and fig. 66a. Alfred V. Kidder and Samuel J. Guernsey, 'Archaeological Explorations in Northeastern Arizona' in *Smithsonian Institution: Bureau of American Ethnology Bulletin 65*, Washington, D.C., 1919, pp. 1–228 (pp. 195: fig. 96, 196). Forrest Kirkland and W. W. Newcombe, Jr, *The Rock Art of Texas Indians*, Austin, University of Texas Press, 1967, pp. 179 (plate 127), 187 (plate 137), 196 (plate 147), 200.

281. M. Titiev, *op. cit.*, pp. 91–93.

282. W. Smith, *op. cit.*, pp. 59, 60: fig. 7 f., 221: fig. 17 r, s, t, 296, 299–302 and fig. 53 and notes on facing page. F. Dockstader, *op. cit.*, pp. 48 (fig. 126), 50–53. Awatobi pueblo was a focus of Christian missionary activity. Leaders of traditional religion resorted to the drastic and atypical expedient of massacring their irredeemably corrupted tribesmen for the good of the Hopi nation in 1700. The site was abandoned but a few men and women were spared to transplant certain erotic fertility rites to other Hopi puebloes. See F. Waters, *op. cit.*, pp. 315–29.

283. Jesse W. Fewkes, 'Archaeological Expedition to Arizona 1895' in *Bureau of American Ethnology: 17th Annual Report for 1895–96*, Part 2, Washington, D.C., 1898, pp. 519–742 (p. 633 and plate 129c). Sikyatki was abandoned before 1540. Another ithyphallic figure on a bowl from the same site is in the Florence Hollenback collection and is illustrated, captioned Kokopelli, and dated A.D. 850, in Alice Marriott and Carol K. Rachlin, *American Indian Mythology*, New York, T. Crowell, 1968, and New American Library-Mentor, 1972.

284. F. Waters, *op. cit.*, p. 291. See also A. Kidder and S. Guernsey, *op. cit.*, plate 90 f. Note elongated clitoris and labia.

285. This bowl was excavated from a grave by Thomas V. Keam and was purchased by the Königliche Museum für Volkerkunde, Berlin (Catalogue no. IV B.3252). It disappeared in the Second World War but had been illustrated in K. Preuss, 'Phallische Fruchtbarkeits-Dämonen . . .', pp. 127–28, 131 (fig. 2) and *idem*, 'Der Unterbau des Dramas . . .', plate 30: fig. 43.

286. Ritual hair-washing is a part of the purification of initiates, a ceremony associated with this dance. F. Waters, *op. cit.*, pp. 175–79.

287. The Mamzrau woman's society and its 'brother' societies, the Wucim and Tataukyam men's societies, derived their erotic rituals from Awatobi. Jesse W. Fewkes, 'The New Fire Ceremony of Walpi' in *American Anthropologist*, new series: Vol. 2, No. 1, 1900, pp. 80–138 (pp. 123–31 and plate 3). Due to the prudery of that time Fewkes felt unable to illustrate the Awatobi bowl and the erotic details of the dance. A. Stephen, *op. cit.*, pp. 929, 936, 948, 971, 978, 979 (fig. 487, vulva symbol carried by dancers). J. Fewkes and A. Stephen, *Mamzrauti . . .* p. 235. Note vulva and maize symbol illustrated p. 220 (plate II: fig. 5). The Mamzrau society is now extinct, but their function is performed by the Maraw society. See F. Waters, *op. cit.*, pp. 186–87, 287–91.

288. Jesse W. Fewkes, 'Sun Worship of the Hopi Indians' in *Smithsonian Institute: Annual Report, 1918*, Washington, D.C., 1920, pp. 493–526 (pp. 503–7). Hamilton A. Tyler, *Pueblo Gods and Myths*, Norman, Okla., University of Oklahoma Press, 1964, pp. 194–208.

289. *Ibid.*, pp. 202–4. The Hopi Yaya society was notorious for its un-Hopi excesses. Originally concerned with a benign magical relationship with the powers of wild animals it degenerated into black magic acquiring the evil reputation of being ever ready to 'bugger a man or ravish a woman or maid'. See F. Waters, *op. cit.*, pp. 293–301 and A. Stephen, *op. cit.*, Vol. 2: pp. 1007–8, 1322.

290. *Ibid.*, Vol. 1: pp. 328–31. Other acts of obscene clowning: Vol. 1: pp. 175, 230–31, 365, 383, 385, 402–6, 489, 554; Vol. 2: p. 947.

291. Don Talayseva and Leo W. Simmons (ed.), *Sun Chief: The Autobiography of a Hopi Indian*, New Haven, Conn., Yale University Press, 1942, p. 190.

292. F. Dockstadter, *op. cit.*, pp. 128–30.

293. Re anthropological and psychoanalytic significance of 'tricksters' and obscene 'polymorphous-perverse' clowns, see Paul Radin, Carl Gustav Jung, Karl Kerenyi, *The Trickster: A Study in American Indian Mythology*, London, Routledge & Kegan Paul, 1956.

294. James O. Dorsey, 'A Study of Siouan Cults' in *Bureau of American Ethnology: 11th Annual Report for 1889–90*, Washington, D.C., 1894, pp. 351–553 (pp. 456–57: fig. 191 and plates 45 and 48). George A. Dorsey, 'The Cheyenne' (2 parts) in *Field Columbian Museum* (*publication no. 99*): *Anthropological Series*, Vol. 9, Nos. 1 (March) and 2 (May), Chicago, 1905, pp. 1–186 (pp. 97–98, 117). E. Adamson Hoebel, *The Cheyennes: Indians of the Great Plains*, New York, Holt, Rinehart, Winston, 1960, pp. 11–16. Re other Cheyenne sexual *mores*, see pp. 77–79, 90, 95–96. Black Elk and Joseph E. Brown (ed.), *The Sacred Pipe: Black Elk's Account of the Seven Rites of the Oglala Sioux*, (Norman, Okla., University of Oklahoma Press, 1953) Harmondsworth, Penguin, 1971, pp. 67–100. Black Elk (pp. 72 and 79) described the votive buffalo figure as 'chief of all the four-leggeds [*i.e.* animals]' and the ithyphallic man as the chief representative of all people. E. Hoebel (p. 14) wrote that the human figure represents enemy tribesmen to be killed like their other prey the buffalo. The entrance of the Cheyenne Sun Dance was open to the East to receive the sun's fertilising rays, a parallel with A. T. Hatto's interpretation of Stonehenge (see note 112 above). For an illustration of Oglala Sioux rawhide ithyphallic figures, see Norman Feder, *American Indian Art*, New York, Harry N. Abrams, plate 36.

295. E. Hoebel, *op. cit.*, pp. 15, 17.

296. Gene Weltfish, *The Lost Universe: The Way of Life of the Pawnee*, New York, Basic Books, 1965, and Ballantine-Walden, 1971, pp. 129–43.

297. George Catlin, *O-kee-pa: A Religious Ceremony and other Customs of the Mandans*, London, Trübner, 1867. Reprint: John C. Ewers, ed., New Haven, Conn., Yale University Press, 1967, including the optional supplementary 'Folium Reservatum' relating sexual details. Prince Maximilian von Wied-Neuwied, *Travels in the Interior of North America*, Coblenz, J. Hoelscher, 1839–41; London, Ackermann, 1843, pp. 343, 369, 373–77.

298. Similar black and white symbols are worn by the frightening Hopi Mastop Kachinas, who mime copulation with women-onlookers. See F. Waters, *op. cit.*, p. 190. George A. Dorsey and Henry R. Voth, 'Oraibi Soyal Ceremony' in *Field Columbian Museum Anthropological Series*, Vol. 3, No. 1, Chicago, 1901, pp. 1–59 (p. 45 and plates 23–25).

299. Karl F. P. Martius, *Das Naturell, die Krankheiten, das Arzttum und die Heilmittel der Urbewohner Brasiliens*, Munich, 1843, pp. 111–13, quoted in I. Bloch, *op. cit.*, pp. 107–8.

b: *The Classical World*

1. See *Winckelmann: Writings on Art*, edited by David Irwin, London, Phaidon and New York, Praeger, 1972.

2. Museums which still contain secret collections of Classical art include the British Museum, the Louvre, the Naples Museum, and the Vatican Museum in Rome.

3. Quoted in H. Montgomery Hyde, *A History of Pornography*, London, Four Square, 1966, p. 42.

4. Quoted in Jean Marcadé, *Eros Kalos, an Essay on Erotic Elements in Greek Art*, Geneva, Nagel, 1962, p. 101.

5. Reproductions of pottery with explicit sexual depictions are to be found in Jean Marcadé, *op. cit.*

6. Quoted in Jean Marcadé, *op. cit.*, p. 85.

7. Bells were considered to be effective in driving away evil spirits, and such a belief can be traced to Isis, the Egyptian deity who used a bell to drive away Typhon after he had mutilated the body of her husband Osiris. Egyptian and Jewish priests wore bells attached to their garments, and Hindu Buddhas were often furnished with bells which were sounded during the temple rites. The Christian Church took over the custom, which can be traced back to the rites of phallic worship. See Richard Payne Knight, *An Inquiry into the Symbolical Language of Ancient Art and Mythology*, London, 1818, pp. 145–46; and George Ryley Scott, *Phallic Worship*, London, Panther, 1970, p. 180.

8. Sir James Frazer, *The Golden Bough: A Study in Magic and Religion*, (1890), London, Macmillan, 1950, p. 349.

9. St Augustine, *The City of God*. Translation by John Healey (1610), quoted in E. Royston Pike, *Love in Ancient Rome*, London, Muller, 1965, p. 187.

10. Letter from Sir William Hamilton to Sir Joseph Banks, Naples, 1781, published as the Preface to Richard Payne Knight, *An Account of the Remains of the Worship of Priapus*, London, T. Spilsbury, 1786, p. 10. Plate I illustrates similar 'vows' from Sir William's collection which he presented to the British Museum.

11. John Mathias, *Pursuits of Literature*, London, 1808, p. 119.

12. James Gardner, *The Faiths of the World*, Edinburgh, 1858, Vol. 1, p. 809.

13. Jean Marcadé, *Roma Amor: An Essay on Erotic Elements in Etruscan and Roman Art*, Geneva, Nagel, 1965, p. 124.

14. Some of these paintings are still *in situ*, but many are now in the Restricted Collection of the Naples Museum. A large selection is illustrated in Jean Marcadé, *op. cit.*

15. No examples of Greek painting survive, but there are records of erotic pictures by such famous artists as Apelles, Xeuxis, and Philoxene; in the same way, many authors refer to erotic stories by a famous Greek courtesan, Elephantis, though none has survived.

16. Otto J. Brendel, 'The Scope and Temperament of Erotic Art in the Greco-Roman World', in *Studies in Erotic Art*, New York and London, Basic Books, 1970, pp. 3–69.

17. Jean Marcadé, *op. cit.*, pp. 100, 105.

18. *Cf.* Suetonius, *Lives of the Caesars*, section on the Emperor Tiberius, XLIV. See *The Twelve Caesars*, translated by Robert Graves, Harmondsworth, Penguin, 1957, p. 131.

19. For example, Epigram 3 by Martial: 'Why can no one prove they've fucked Thais? Everyone wants her—why does she seem so chaste? Because she likes sucking.' Epigram 105: 'Ganymede was honoured by Jupiter's attentions, yet when you surprise me in bed with a young boy, wife, you complain that your arse is just as good. Juno said that to Jupiter, yet he preferred Ganymede.'

20. For example, Juvenal's Sixth Satire against women: 'I prefer sleeping with Pusio to sleeping with a woman, for he is quiet all night, doesn't ask for gifts, and doesn't complain if you don't pay attention to him all the time.'

21. Pierre-François Hughes d'Hancarville, *Monumens de la Vie Privée des Douze Césars*, Rome, l'Imprimerie du Vatican, 1786 (actually Nancy, 1780); *Monumens du Culte Secret des Dames Romaines*, Rome, l'Imprimerie du Vatican, 1790 (actually Nancy, 1784); and *Veneres et Priapi*, Paris and London, *c.* 1785. British Museum Library Private Case numbers: 1: PC 15-d.f.8 and PC 31-b.13; 2: PC 13-f.f.9 and PC 18-b.10; 3: PC 31-f.6 and 7.

CHAPTER 3: EROTICISM IN ORIENTAL ART AND RELIGION

a: *Introduction*

1. Philip Rawson, *Erotic Art of the East*, New York, Prometheus Press, 1968; London, Weidenfeld & Nicolson, 1973, p. 29.

2. Alex Comfort, Introduction to Rawson's *Erotic Art of the East*, p. 22.

b: *India* (ed. by P. Webb from a lecture given by Philip Rawson)

1. Philip Rawson is Curator of the Gulbenkian Museum of Oriental Art at the University of Durham. He is author of *The Art of South East Asia*, London, Thames & Hudson, 1967 and *Erotic Art of the East*, New York, Prometheus Press, 1968, and London, Weidenfeld & Nicolson, 1973. The present essay is an edited and expanded version by Peter Webb of a lecture given in the Erotic Arts course at Hornsey College of Art by Philip Rawson in October, 1971.

2. Reproduced in Philip Rawson, *Erotic Art of the East*, plate 1.

3. In Sanskrit there is a play on words here: fall is *pat*, husband is *pati*, and wife is *patni*.

4. *Cf.* Mulk Raj Anand, *Kama Kala: Some Notes on the Philosophical Basis of Hindu Erotic Sculpture*, Geneva, Nagel, 1958, and Max-Pol Fouchet, *The Erotic Sculpture of India*, London, Allen & Unwin, 1959.

5. Reproduced in Rawson, *op. cit.*, plate xii.

6. *Kama Sutra of Vatsyayana*, translated by P. F. Arbuthnot and Sir Richard Burton, London and Benares, 1883; London, Panther Books, 1968, p. 65.

7. *Idem*, p. 62.

8. Both reproduced in Rawson, *op. cit.*, plates 112 and xiii respectively.

9. *Cf.* catalogue of *Tantra* exhibition, Hayward Gallery, London, 1971.

10. *Cf.* Giuseppe Tucci, *Rati-Lila, an Interpretation of the Tantric Imagery of the Temples of Nepal*, Geneva, Nagel, 1969.

c: *Islam*

1. David James, 'Islam', in Rawson's *Erotic Art of the East*, p. 220.

2. Quoted in Allen Edwardes, *The Jewel in the Lotus: A Historical Survey of the Sexual Culture of the East*, New York, Julian Press, 1959; London, Tandem Books, 1965. See p. 35.

3. *Ibid.*, p. 17.

4. *The Perfumed Garden of Sheikh Nefzawi*, translated by Sir Richard Burton, Cosmopolis, [London], 1886.

5. *The Kama Sutra of Vatsyayana*, translated by Sir Richard Burton, Cosmopolis, [London], 1883.

6. Alan Hull Watson, Introduction to *The Perfumed Garden of Sheikh Nefzawi*, London, Panther, 1964. See p. 29.

7. *Ibid.*, p. 129.

8. David James, *op. cit.*, p. 211.

9. *The Book of the One Thousand Nights and a Night*, translated by Sir Richard Burton, Benares [London], 1885, quoted in Edwardes, *op. cit.*, p. 19.

10. From a poem by the thirteenth-century Persian poet, Sa'adi, quoted in Robert Surieu, *Sarv e Naz, Essay on Love and the Representation of Erotic Themes in Ancient Iran*, Geneva, Paris, Munich, Nagel, 1967, p. 85.

11. From *Divan of Shams al-Din Tabrizi* by the thirteenth-century Persian poet, Jalal al-Din Rumi, quoted in Surieu, *op. cit.*, p. 109.

12. From the *Rubaiyat* by the twelfth-century Persian poet Omar Khayyam, translated by Edward Fitzgerald, London, Adam & Charles Black, 1909, p. 134.

13. Surieu, *op. cit.*, p. 92.

14. Now in the Bibliothèque Nationale, Paris; reproduced in Surieu, *op. cit.*, plates 138–41.

15. *Cf. Dalliance*, Safavid period, in the Victoria and Albert Museum, London, reproduced in Surieu, *op. cit.*, plate 117.

16. Now in the Edinburgh University Library; reproduced in Rawson, *Erotic Art of the East*, plate xvii.

d: *China*

1. *Cf. The Book of Changes*, translated by James Legge, New York, Dover Books, 1963, p. 1.

2. From *The Art of Love* by Master Tung-Hsuan, quoted in Professor Etiemble, *Yun Yu, An Essay on Eroticism and Love in Ancient China*, Geneva, Paris, New York, Nagel, 1970. See p. 34.

3. *Cf.* Rawson, *op. cit.*, plate 154.

4. From a treatise on love-making by Master Jung-Cheng, quoted in Etiemble, *op. cit.*, p. 41.

5. Reproduced in Rawson, *op. cit.*, plate 162.

6. Eighteenth-century poem by Fei-Su-Huang, quoted in *Anthologie de la Poésie Chinoise*, Paris, Gallimard, 1969. (Author's translation.)

7. *Cf.* R. H. van Gulik, *Sexual Life in Ancient China*, London, 1961.

8. Reproduced in Etiemble, *op. cit.*, plates 37–40.

9. Reproduced in Etiemble, *op. cit.*, plates 60–71.

10. Reproduced in Etiemble, *op. cit.*, plates 102–8.

e: *Japan*

1. Reproduced in Philip Rawson, *Erotic Art of the East*, see plate 209. This album contains the earliest-known *shunga*.

2. Shimabara is the subject of a large six-panel lacquered screen from the Ukiyo-e School of the late seventeenth century, entitled *The Reserved Quarter at Kyoto*. The screen is now in the Boston Museum of Fine Arts in America, and is reproduced on pp. 5 and 36–37 of Charles Grosbois, *Shunga, an Essay on Erotic Elements in Japanese Art*, Geneva, Paris, Munich, Nagel, 1966. Yoshiwara is the subject of an album by Kiyonaga dating from the early 1780s, entitled *Yoshiwara Scenes*. The album is reproduced in Rawson, *op. cit.*, plate 244.

3. Reproduced in Rawson, *op. cit.*, plate xxx (a).

4. Quoted in Grosbois, *op. cit.*, p. 111.

5. Quoted in Grosbois, *op. cit.*, p. 121.

6. Reproduced in Grosbois, *op. cit.*, p. 92.

7. Reproduced in Rawson, *op. cit.*, plate xxiii.

8. Quoted in Grosbois, *op. cit.*, p. 147.

9. Reproduced in Rawson, *op. cit.*, plate xxx (c).

CHAPTER 4: EROTICISM IN WESTERN ART

a: *Middle Ages to 1700*

1. Eduard Fuchs, *Geschichte der Erotischen Kunst*, Munich, Albert Langen, 1912–26, Vol. I, p. 1 (author's translation).

2. S. Alexander, *Beauty and other forms of Value*, London, Macmillan, 1933, p. 127.

3. Kenneth Clark, *The Nude*, New York and London, John Murray, 1956, p. 6.

4. *Cf.* Georges Bataille, *Eroticism*, Paris, Editions de Minuit, 1957; London, Calder & Boyers, 1966.

5. *Cf.* Lo Duca, *Erotique de l'Art*, Paris, La Jeune Parque, 1966.

6. Quoted in Jean-Louis Vaudoyer, *The Female Nude in European Painting*, London, Longmans Green, 1957, p. 6.

7. The extent to which priests were encouraged to pry into people's private sexual habits is made clear in Leo Taxil, *Les Livres Secrets des Confesseurs*, Paris, Librairie Anti-Cléricale, 1883 (a copy is in the British Museum Library, Restricted Collection number CUP 403 P6) and also *The Confessional Unmasked*, Dublin, 1836, and London, Protestant Evangelical Union, 1860 (discussed in Pisanus Fraxi (Henry Spencer Ashbee), *Centuria Librorum Absconditorum*, London, privately published, 1879, a copy of which is in the same Restricted Collection, number PC 14 de 4). These books quote two eighteenth-century theologians: Petrus Duns from Flanders and Alphonsus di Liguori from Italy, who wrote books explaining the sort of sexual practices which priests must unmask among their congregations, and the type of questions they must ask in order to find out whether a confessor's sex-life was permissible or sinful. Both theologians made generous allowances for the sexual prurience of the priests concerned in these activities.

8. Reproduced in Sir Frank Stanton, *The Bayeux Tapestry, a Comprehensive Survey*, London, Phaidon, 1957, plate 15.

9. In the 1865 edition of Payne Knight's *Discourse on the Worship of Priapus*, London, [John Hotten], an essay attributed to Thomas Wright entitled 'The Worship of the Generative Powers during the Middle Ages of Western Europe' states: 'They represented a female exposing herself to view in the most unequivocal manner ... People have given them the name of Shelah-na-Gig, which, we are told, means in Irish Julian the Giddy, and is simply a term for an immodest woman; but it is well understood that they were intended as protecting charms against the fascination of the evil eye' (p. 132). Reproductions of seven Irish examples are given ('all yet known'). An article entitled 'Figures known as Hags of the Castle, Sheelas or Sheela na Gigs' in Vol. 24 (March, 1894) of the *Journal of the Royal Society of Antiquaries of Ireland* (pp. 77–79) lists thirty-two known Irish examples as well as others at Dunraven Castle; Binstead churchyard, Isle of Wight; Church Stretton, Shropshire; and the Church of St Radegonde at Poitiers in France. The writer states that the name was invented by a peasant when interviewed by an early nineteenth-century researcher, and has been retained. Vivian Mercier, in *The Irish Comic Tradition*, London, Oxford University Press, 1962, concludes

that these figures symbolise a goddess of creation and destruction of the sort in which Celtic mythology abounds, but they are almost certainly linked also to protection, fertility, and regeneration. See also Douglas Fraser, 'The Heraldic Woman: a study in diffusion' in *The Many Faces of Primitive Art, a critical anthology*, New Jersey, Prentice-Hall, 1966, pp. 44–45; and T. Clifton Longworth, *The Worship of Love*, London, Torchstream Books, 1954, where ten Shelah-na-Gigs are illustrated.

10. Jean-Louis Vaudoyer, *op. cit.*, p. 7.

11. For a discussion of the problems relating to the missing Leonardo and the copies, see Frank Arnau, *3,000 Years of Deception in Art and Antiques*, London, Jonathan Cape, 1961, pp. 68–69; for the destroyed Michelangelo version, see Maurice Roy: 'La Léda de Michelange et celle du Rosso', in *Gazette des Beaux Arts*, (Paris), February, 1923.

12. From G. Bottari, *Raccolta di Lettere sulle Pittura*, Milan, 1822–25, quoted in Giuseppe Lo Duca, *Histoire de l'Erotisme*, Paris, La Jeune Parque, 1969, p. 412. Author's translation.

13. Walter Pater, *The Renaissance*, London, Fontana Books, 1964, p. 123.

14. Sigmund Freud, *Leonardo da Vinci, a Psychosexual Study of an Infantile Reminiscence*, London, Routledge & Kegan Paul, 1932.

15. Leo Steinberg, 'The Metaphors of Love and Birth in Michelangelo's Pietàs', in *Studies in Erotic Art*, New York and London, Basic Books, 1970, pp. 231–85.

16. One of the most famous of his mistresses was the subject of his painting *La Fornarina* (Cracow Gallery, Poland; *c.* 1514), a baker's daughter, Margherita di Francesco Luti from Sienna. It is recorded that Agostino Chigi could only get Raphael to complete the decorations to his villa near Rome by forcibly abducting Margherita and keeping her imprisoned there, although this is probably apocryphal. Picasso's erotic engravings of 1968 relate to the amatory exploits of this couple. It has also been suggested that the subject of his painting *La Donna Velata* (Pitti Palace, Florence; 1513) was one of his mistresses. He was engaged to marry Maria Bibbiena; according to Vasari, he died from a fever caught from a 'secret visit' to his fiancée.

17. These prints are described, and some reproduced, in Louis Dunand, *Le Lascivie du Graveur Augustin Carrache*, Lyon, Bulletin des Musées Lyonnais, Vol. 6, No. 1, 1957. A volume of engravings by Coiny after the originals was published in 1798, *L'Aretin d'Augustin Carrache, ou Recueil de Postures Erotiques, d'après les Gravures à l'eau forte par cet Artiste célèbre*. A la Nouvelle Cythère [Paris, P. Didot, 1798].

18. E. Rodocanachi, *Histoire de Rome, Le Pontificat de Leon X, 1513–1521*, Paris, 1931.

19. Patrick O'Donovan, 'Secret Vatican', with photographs by Dante Vacchi, London, *Observer Magazine*, 27 February, 1972. Reference to the bathroom was made in *I Palazzo Vaticani* (Rome, Capelli, 1967, pp. 109–13) by the Director General of the Vatican Museums, Redig de Campos. The author's recent request to Dr de Campos for further information and for permission to visit the room met with no success.

20. A retouched copy is in the Louis Dunand collection, France, and is reproduced in Louis Dunand, *Les Amours des Dieux*, Lyon, Albums du Crocodile, 1964, plate 4.

21. British Museum Department of Prints and Drawings, Restricted Collection, No. BXV-48-4.

22. See Otto Kurz, 'Four forgotten paintings by Agostino Carracci', London, *Journal of the Warburg and Courtauld Institutes*, Vol. xiv, Nos. 3–4, 1951.

23. Adam Bartsch, *Le Peintre-Graveur*, Vienna, 1813, Vol. xviii, Nos. 123–35.

24. B.M. no. BXVIII-109-134 (Restricted Collection).

25. B.M. no. BXVIII-102-114 (Restricted Collection).

26. B.M. no. BXVIII-109-132 (Restricted Collection).

27. B.M. no. BXVIII-110-136 (Restricted Collection).

28. These three prints are reproduced in Louis Dunand, *Le Lascivie du Graveur Augustin Carrache, op. cit.* This is a very interesting and useful article.

29. B.M. no. BXV-294-27 (Restricted Collection).

30. B.M. no. 1851-3-8-1053 (Restricted Collection).

31. Giorgio Vasari, *Lives of the Artists*, translated by Mrs Jonathan Foster, London, 1851, Vol. 3, p. 370.

32. B.M. no. BXIII-247-6 (Restricted Collection).

33. B.M. no. BXV-463-4 (Restricted Collection).

34. One of these, *The Rape of Helen*, of the 1540s, is now in the Bowes Museum, Barnard Castle, County Durham.

35. Andrew Martindale, *Man and the Renaissance*, London, Paul Hamlyn, 1966, pp. 101–2.

36. Erwin Panofsky, *Studies in Iconology*, New York and London, Harper & Row, 1962, pp. 87–90.

37. The eroticism inherent in the stories of Judith and of Lucretia, who killed herself out of shame after being raped by Tarquin, is beautifully evoked by Michel Leiris in his autobiographical study, *L'Age d'Homme* (Paris, Gallimard, 1939), translated as *Manhood* (New York, Grossman, 1963 and London, Jonathan Cape, 1968); see also Chapter 6a of the present work.

38. Georges Bataille, *Les Larmes d'Eros*, Paris, Pauvert, 1964. Bataille says that the violence of the spasmodic joy of orgasm is at the same time the heart of death: 'je saisis, dans le désordre de mes rires et de mes sanglots, dans l'excès des transports qui me brisent, la similitude de l'horreur et d'une volupté qui m'excède, de la douleur finale et d'une insupportable joie!' (p. 8). ('In the confusion of laughing and sobbing, in the excesses of passion which completely shatter me, I glimpse the similarity between horror and an overpowering voluptuousness, between the final pain and an unbearable joy!' Author's translation.)

39. Another erotic version is *Madonna with a Long Neck* of c. 1535 (Pitti Palace, Florence), which was once known as *Venus and Cupid*. One of the attendants behind the Madonna is clearly recognisable as the courtesan Antea who was Parmigianino's mistress: *cf*. his *Portrait of Antea* in the Naples Museum.

40. The theme of Mary Magdalene's love for Christ can be traced from the ninth-century writer Rabanus Maurus, via medieval Passion Plays, to Savonarola's *Tractato dello Amore di Jesu Christo*, Florence, 1492. See Helen M. Garth, *St Mary Magdalene in Mediaeval Literature*, Baltimore, Md., 1950, Chapter 4; also Steinberg, *op. cit.*, pp. 247–48, 277–80.

41. Forty erotic drawings by Titian were reportedly discovered in Fontainebleau in about 1960, and Georges Bataille is said to have seen them. Titian has inspired varied poetic reactions, from the notorious limerick:

> *When Titian was mixing rose madder,*
> *His model posed nude up a ladder.*
> *Her position to Titian suggesting coition,*
> *He nipped up the ladder and 'ad 'er.*

to the poem *Musée Secret* by Theophile Gautier:

> *Aussi j'aime tes courtisanes,*
> *Amant du vrai, grand Titien,*
> *Roi des tons chauds et diaphanes,*
> *Soleil du ciel vénitien.*
> *Sous une courtine pourprée*
> *Elles étalent bravement,*
> *Dans sa pâleur mate et dorée*
> *Un corps vivace où rien ne ment.*

> *'I love your courtesans, great Titian,*
> *Lover of truth, King of warm and diaphanous colours,*
> *Sun in the Venetian sky.*
> *In the shadow of purple draperies,*
> *They display their immortal bodies of pale gold,*
> *Which tell no lies.'*—Author's translation.

42. Mlle Lange was a famous actress in the Directoire period, and was once imprisoned for the sexual explicitness of her acting. She became a fashionable courtesan and later married a rich banker; see Florent Fels, *L'Art et L'Amour*, Paris, Arc-en-Ciel, 1953, Vol. 2, p. 46. Girodet's painting is an allegorical representation of the actress's life, and Cupid who helps her to gather the gold coins is in fact her daughter, who was an important source of income for

her; see G. Levitine, 'Girodet's New Danae: the iconography of a scandal', in *The Minneapolis Institute of Arts Bulletin*, No. 58, 1969, pp. 69–77.

43. One of the King's famous exploits was the seduction of a girl in a cottage just outside Fontainebleau. The site was renamed *Cour du Roi*, a play on words meaning both courtyard and courtship of the King.

44. Examples by all three are in the Vienna Albertina Collection: *Man Playing with a Kitchen Maid* (Teniers), *Erotic Scene in a Hostelry* (Ostade), and *Man Masturbating, Watched by a Woman* (Steen).

45. Bernini has depicted a young angel standing over Saint Theresa, holding an arrow which points at the Saint's lower anatomy. This refers to Saint Theresa's mystic vision of the 1550s: she recounted a visit from an angel bearing a long golden spear with a fiery tip, who 'plunged it into my deepest inward. When he drew it out, I thought my entrails would have been torn out too, and when he left me I glowed in the hot fire of love for God. The pain was so strong, and the sweetness thereof was so passing great that no one could wish ever to lose it.' (Autobiography published posthumously in 1587, quoted in Wayland Young, *Eros Denied*, London, Corgi, 1968, p. 274.)

46. The Marchese Giustiniani found it expedient to keep his painting of *Love the Conqueror* (1598–99) by Caravaggio behind a special curtain. The work, which shows a provocatively nude youth, is now in the Staatliche Museum, Berlin.

47. André Malraux, *Saturne, Essai sur Goya*, Paris, Gallimard, 1950. Translated as *Saturne, An Essay on Goya*, London, Phaidon, 1957, p. 66.

48. *Ibid.*, p. 67.

49. The Spanish word *maja* means courtesan; however, an unsubstantiated legend grew up after Goya's death that the model for the nude and clothed versions of the picture was the notorious Duchess of Alba, with whom the artist is known to have had an affair. This was celebrated in the limerick:

> *Said the Duchess of Alba to Goya,*
> *'Remember that I'm your employer.'*
> *So he painted her twice,*
> *Once clothed to look nice,*
> *And once in the nude to annoy her.*

50. Reproduced in G. Lo Duca, *op. cit.*, p. 425.

b: *Eighteenth and Nineteenth Centuries*

1. Edmond and Jules de Goncourt, *L'Art au Dix-Huitième Siècle*, Paris, 1856; English edition, *French 18th Century Painters*, London, Phaidon, 1948 (translated by Robin Ironside), p. 55.

2. *Idem*, p. 8.

3. Reproduced in Cary von Karwath, *Die Erotik in der Kunst*, Vienna and Leipzig, C. W. Stern, 1908. A close friend of Watteau, the Comte de Caylus, reported that the artist destroyed some of his indecent works a few days before his death in 1721. A recent commentator (Donald Posner, *Watteau's Lady at her Toilet*, London, Allen Lane, 1973) has pointed out that three of Watteau's works, *The Morning Toilet* (*c.* 1715; Paris, Private Collection), *The Remedy* (*c.* 1714–15; Paris, Private Collection), and *The Lady at her Toilet* (*c.* 1716–17; London, Wallace Collection), mark the beginnings of the erotic genre scene, later to become so popular in France; also that the small dog in the latter picture recalls that such pets were sometimes used for lascivious purposes in eighteenth-century France (*cf.* Fragonard's *The Ring Biscuit, c.* 1770, reproduced in Posner, *op. cit.*, p. 83).

4. The album is kept in the Restricted Collection of the Department of Prints and Drawings at the British Museum. The style appears to be School of Boucher or Fragonard; in his *Centuria Librorum Absconditorum* (London, privately published, 1879), Henry Spencer Ashbee attributed the drawings to Charles Antoine Coypel (p. 403).

5. Goncourt, *op. cit.*, p. 65.

6. *Mes Loisirs*. Petit Recueil pour exciter la ferveur des fidèles, aux Matines de Cythère, par un Amateur de l'office. Paris, 1764.

NOTES

7. Roger Portalis, *Les Dessinateurs d'Illustrations au 18 siècle*, Paris, 1877, p. 524. Ashbee, *op. cit.*, describes the book on p. 400.

8. *Histoire de Dom B. Portier des Chartreux, écrite par lui-même*, A Rome, chez Philotanus, n.d. A copy is in the private case of the British Museum Library, no. PC.23b.10.

9. *Dictionnaire des Oeuvres Erotiques, Domaine Français*, Paris, Mercure de France, 1971.

10. Eduard Fuchs, *Die Grossen Meister der Erotik*, Munich, Albert Langen, 1928; Cary von Karwath, *op. cit.*

11. Michael Kitson, *The Age of Baroque*, London, Paul Hamlyn, 1966, p. 130.

12. Quoted in Nancy Mitford, *Madame de Pompadour*, London, Hamish Hamilton, 1954 (p. 165), a book which gives much useful background information to this period.

13. Kenneth Clark, *op. cit.*, p. 140.

14. Quoted in Jacques Thuillier, *Fragonard*, Geneva, Skira, 1967, p. 27.

15. Reproduced in Eduard Fuchs, *Illustrierte Sittengeschichte, Die Galante Zeit*, Munich, Albert Langen, 1910, p. 129.

16. 'Cease, beautiful young things, from defending yourselves against this kind invention. To extinguish the fire that sparkles in your eyes would take a quite different sort of water-jet.' (Author's translation.)

17. Quoted in Goncourt, *op. cit.*, pp. 84–85.

18. Quoted in Eliza Pollard, *Boucher and Greuze*, London, Methuen, 1904, p. 44.

19. Quoted in Gershon Legman, *Rationale of the Dirty Joke*, London, Panther, 1972.

20. Lawrence Gowing, *William Hogarth*, Catalogue of exhibition at the Tate Gallery, London, 1971, p. 28.

21. Reproduced in Gowing, *op. cit.*, p. 30, in the engraved version.

22. John Milton, *Paradise Lost*, Part II, ll. 648 ff.

23. *Cf. The Public Advertiser*, 6 January, 1792, three weeks before the date of Gillray's print: 'The Duchess of York's birthday shoes will distance all competition as much by their value as by their size. They will be covered with ornaments of diamonds.' Quoted in Draper Hill, *Fashionable Contrasts: Caricatures by James Gillray*, London, Phaidon, 1966, p. 164.

24. *Pretty Little Games for Young Ladies and Gentlemen. With Pictures of Good Old English Sports and Pastimes*, by T. Rowlandson. A few copies only printed for the Artist's Friends. London, J. C. Hotten, (c. 1872). A fictitious date of 1845 appeared on the title page. A copy is in the British Museum (Restricted Collection). The titles of the prints are: *Rural Felicity or Love in a Chaise; The Hairy Prospect or The Devil in a Fright; The Country Squire New Mounted; The Larking Cull; The Sanctified Sinner; New Feats of Horsemanship; The Wanton Frolic; The Toss-Off; The Curious Wanton; The Willing Fair or Any Way to Please.*

25. Henry Spencer Ashbee lists one hundred and seven prints and eight drawings in his *Centuria Librorum Absconditorum*. He calls these erotic works 'generally charming and talented productions' (pp. 393–94).

26. Bernard Falk, *Thomas Rowlandson: His Life and Art*, London, Hutchinson, and New York, Beechhurst Press, 1952, p. 11.

27. Joseph Grigo, *Thomas Rowlandson*, London, Chatto & Windus, 1880, pp. 217 and 219. The print is illustrated on p. 218.

28. Quoted in Kurt von Meier, *The Forbidden Erotica of Thomas Rowlandson*, Los Angeles, Hogarth Guild, 1970, pp. 14–15.

29. Quoted in Grigo, *op. cit.*, p. 18.

30. Gert Schiff, *The Amorous Illustrations of Thomas Rowlandson*, New York, Cythera Press, 1969, pp. xxxii–xxxiii.

31. The Empress Catherine II of Russia was notorious for her insatiable sexual appetite. She had a total of two husbands and thirteen favourites during her sixty-seven years, and was said to have been in the habit of choosing a bed-partner when reviewing her Guards. She was also believed to have a collection of erotic art. The Palace of Gatchina near St Petersburg (now Leningrad) was built as a gift for one of her favourites between 1765 and 1770, and decorated with erotic furnishings and frescoes. These were lost in a fire in 1944. A recent book, *The Passions and Lechery of Catherine The Great* by Bernard Gip (Geneva, Nagel; and London, Skilton; 1971) published photographs purporting to be of the original furnishings and frescoes. The two items of furniture, a round table supported on giant phalluses and a

large chair with decorations including modelled male and female sexual organs and copulating nudes, appear to be in the Art Nouveau style, and the frescoes, showing well-developed satyrs copulating with excited nymphs, would seem to be late-nineteenth-century works of little artistic merit.

32. *Acts*, Chapter 17, Verse 18.

33. John Knowles, *The Life and Writings of Henry Fuseli*, London, 1831, p. 55.

34. Allan Cunningham, *Lives of the Painters—Fuseli*, London, 1829, quoted in Eudo C. Mason, *The Mind of Henry Fuseli*, London, Routledge & Kegan Paul, 1951, p. 142.

35. Allan Cunningham, *ibid.*, recounts Fuseli's testy reply to an inquiry as to his age: 'How should I know? I was born in February or March, it was some cursed cold month, as you may guess from my diminutive stature and crabbed disposition.' Quoted in Nicolas Powell, *The Drawings of Henry Fuseli*, London, Faber & Faber, 1951, p. 11.

36. Frederick Antal, *Fuseli Studies*, London, Routledge & Kegan Paul, 1956, p. 117. Antal's otherwise brilliant book is rather weak on analysis of Fuseli's erotic works, while a more recent work (Peter Tomory, *Life and Art of Henry Fuseli*, London, Thames & Hudson, 1972) completely fails in this respect.

37. A drawing and an oil painting by Fuseli of *The Incubus* (1781) are in the Kunsthaus in Zurich. Incubi (who visited females) and succubi (who visited males) were the subject of an ecclesiastical controversy for many centuries, St Augustine and St Thomas Aquinas being amongst the believers in their existence. In the fifteenth century, William the Good wrote: 'That there exist such beings as are commonly called incubi and succubi, and that they indulge in their burning lusts, and that children, it is freely acknowledged, can be born from them, is attested by the unimpeachable and unshakeable witness of many men and women who have been filled with foul imaginings by them, and endured their lecherous assaults and lewdness.' Many of the victims were nuns, and their accounts often remark upon the similarity of appearance of their incubus to that of their confessor! See Bernhardt J. Hurwood, 'Devil in the Flesh', *Penthouse* magazine, (London), Vol. 5, No. 4, 1970, p. 63; and George Ryley Scott, *Phallic Worship*, London, Panther, 1970, pp. 107–9. See also, Nicolas Powell, *Fuseli's The Night-mare*, London, Allen Lane, 1972.

38. *The Toilet*, reproduced in Mason, *op. cit.*, opposite p. 161.

39. Sacheverell Sitwell, *Splendours and Miseries*, London, Faber & Faber, 1943, p. 224.

40. Both are reproduced in Mervyn Levy, *The Artist and The Nude*, London, Barrie & Rockliffe, 1965, as plate 74. Of the latter, Levy writes: 'It is a study of breathtaking eroticism with the ecstasy already mounting to a crescendo of bliss as the man swings back the woman's head for the stab of his kiss.' (P. 25.)

41. *The Autobiography and Journals of Benjamin Robert Haydon*, London, 1853; London, Macdonald, 1950, p. 412.

42. Allan Cunningham, quoted in Mason, *op. cit.*, p. 215.

43. Sitwell, *op. cit.*, p. 224. Mr Sitwell states that forty abscondita by Fuseli turned up at a London dealer's in 1938–39, and more appeared at a country house sale in Oxfordshire.

44. Ruthven Todd, *Tracks in the Snow*, London, Grey Walls Press, 1946. See p. 82 and plates 24 and 25. These drawings are briefly mentioned in Antal, *op. cit.*, p. 126. The drawings were formerly in the collection of the Countess of Guildford, who bought as many of Fuseli's drawings as she could find after his death. They were later in Sir Hugh Walpole's collection, and are now in the Victoria and Albert Museum, London (Restricted Collection, nos. E106-109, 1952). There are also fifteen Fuseli drawings catalogued as 'obscene' in the collection of the Horne Foundation, Florence, nos. 6062–76.

45. Paul Ganz, *Hans Heinrich Fusseli's Zeichnungen*, Bern, Oltera, 1947. Translated as *The Drawings of Henry Fuseli*, London, Max Parrish, 1949. A more recent commentator, David Antin, is equally mistaken: 'Fuseli treats all erotic situations as scenes of stupid lust. The point of view of his erotic work is that of the satirist or voyeur . . . in this cold fascination with the erotic-ridiculous.' See David Antin, 'Fuseli, Blake, Palmer', in *The Grand Eccentrics*, New York, Collier Books, and London, Collier-Macmillan, 1971, p. 117.

46. Mason, *op. cit.*, pp. 142–43.

47. William Michael Rossetti, who helped Ruskin sort through the massive number of drawings left by Turner, wrote that Ruskin came across 'several which from the nature of

their subjects it seemed undesirable to preserve'. These 'were burned by him on the authority of the Trustees of the National Gallery'. *Cf.* W. M. Rossetti, *Rossetti Papers*, London, 1903, p. 383. A more sensational and far less credible account appears in Frank Harris, *My Life and Loves*, London, 1923, Vol. 2, p. 263.

48. Walter Thornbury, *The Life of J. M. W. Turner*, London, Chatto & Windus, 1862.

49. In his interesting study of Turner (a psychological rather than critical biography), Bernard Falk comes to the conclusion, from an examination of Turner's letters and the one notebook with erotic drawings that he has seen, that the artist was certainly no whole-hearted bohemian, and that he valued respectability even if he did not always conform to it. Falk considers Turner merely had a dread of entering into a legal state of matrimony, and likens the relationship in later life with Sophia Booth to that between Rembrandt and Hendrickje Stoffels. *Cf.* Bernard Falk, *Turner the Painter: His Hidden Life*, London, Hutchinson, 1938. A glimpse of the private world of another English artist is provided by a recently discovered wood-engraving by Thomas Bewick of a boy being beaten on the naked buttocks (published by Liverpool Polytechnic in 1972 in a limited edition), which refers to many similar childhood experiences recalled in Bewick's memoirs.

50. Tate Gallery nos. T.B. 5493 and T.B. 5517.

51. *Cf.* Adrian Stokes, *Painting and the Inner World*, London, Tavistock Publications, 1963. The chapter on 'The Art of Turner' gives a psycho-analytical view of his work, see especially pp. 61–65 and 72–76.

52. *Swiss Figures Sketch Book*, 1802. B.M. no. T.B. LXXVIII (S.25), p. 1; reproduced in Jack Lindsay, *J. M. W. Turner, a Critical Biography*, New York, New York Graphic Society; and London, Cory, Adams & Mackay, 1966, fig. 11.

53. A. J. Finberg, *Complete Inventory of the Drawings of the Turner Bequest*, London, His Majesty's Stationery Office, 1909.

54. *Lowther Sketch Book*, 1809–10, B.M. no. T.B. CXIII (S.39), pp. 5, 6a, 9, 40a, 43a, 44a, 45a (reproduced in Jack Lindsay, *op. cit.*, fig. 10), and 46a (reproduced in Graham Reynolds, *Turner*, London, Thames & Hudson, 1969, fig. 39).

55. *Woodcock Shooting Sketch Book*, 1810–12, B.M. no. T.B. CXXIX (S.42), p. 116a.

56. *Petworth Sketch Book*, 1830, B.M. no. T.B. CCXLIV (M), pp. 69 and 70.

57. *Colour Studies Sketch Books*, 1834, B.M. nos. T.B. CCXCI (b) and (c) (S.100 and S.103).

58. *Academy Auditing Sketch Book*, 1824, B.M. no. CCX (a) (S.38), pp. 19, 22, 23, 28, and 32–34.

59. *Indecent Subject*, B.M. no. T.B. CCCLXVa (Restricted Collection).

60. *Cf.* Georges Grappe, *Henry Monnier*, Vol. I of *Meisterwerke der Erotischen Kunst Frankreichs*, Leipzig, 1909.

61. For examples of the work of these illustrators, see the scholarly catalogue of *Libertine Literature* relating to a sale held at the Parke-Bernet Galleries, New York, 27 April, 1971. The catalogue was compiled by Jeff Rund. See also *The Satirical Drawings of Martin van Maele*, New York, Cythera Press, 1970.

62. Mario Praz, 'Canova: Ice and Eros', in *Academic Art*, New York and London, Collier-Macmillan, 1971, p. 167.

63. *Cf.* Robert Baldick, *Dinner at Magny's*, Harmondsworth, Penguin, 1973, p. 145.

64. One is reproduced on p. 77 of Giusseppe Lo Duca, *Histoire de l'Eroticisme*, Paris, La Jeune Parque, 1969. The Victoria and Albert Museum in London has a small oil sketch of a reclining nude which is a study for the highly erotic *Sleeper of Naples* by Ingres, which disappeared in 1815.

65. *Cf.* Louis Dunand, 'A propos de dessins dits "secrets" légués par J.-D. Ingres au Musée de Montauban et copiant des estampes du 16ème siècle', *Bulletin des Amis du Musée Ingres de Montauban*, (Montauban), No. 23, July, 1968.

66. Charles Baudelaire, *Fusées*, in *Oeuvres Complètes*, Paris, Bibliothèque de la Pléiade, 1958, p. 1191. (Author's translation.)

67. This painting was reproduced in Gerald Zwang, *La Sexe de la Femme*, Paris, La Jeune Parque, 1967, opposite p. 18, with the provenance: 'Museum of Fine Arts, Budapest, formerly collection of Professor Hatvany'. However, in a communication to the author dated 4 Feb-

ruary, 1972, the Director of the Museum of Fine Arts at Budapest (Dr Klara Garas) wrote, 'Courbet's painting has never been in our museum; it was in a private collection in Budapest and disappeared during the war.' During a visit to Budapest in October, 1972, the author learned that the painting had been stolen by the Germans during the war and had then been appropriated by the Russians. Professor Hatvany had bought it back and later taken it to Switzerland. Wayland Young in *Eros Denied*, London, Corgi, 1968, p. 96, mentions a rumour that the painting was sold in America in 1958.

68. Maxime du Camp, *Les Convulsions de Paris*, Paris, c. 1867, Vol. II, pp. 263–64.

69. See Jacques Lethève, *Impressionistes et Symbolistes devant la Presse*, Paris, Colin, 1959.

70. A few contemporaries made efforts to point out the hypocrisy behind the admiration of academic nude paintings, for instance Louis Morin, in *La Revue des Quat' Saisons*, No. 1, Jan.–April, 1900: 'The mother takes her daughter to the salon, stops her in front of the nymphs and bathers of the charming Jules Lefebvre and the juicy Bouguereau. Suppose these nymphs and bathers were to climb down from their frames and walk around the gallery, displaying their pink and white charms, just imagine the headlong flight of these ladies and their cries of horror! If the picture is charming, why is the reality so despicable?' (Author's translation; quoted in Patrick Waldberg, *Eros Modern Style*, Paris, Pauvert, 1964, p. 99.)

71. Maupassant, *La Maison Tellier*, Paris, Vollard, 1935. Lucian, *Mimes des Courtisans*, Paris, Vollard, 1935 and Paris, Cercle des Editions Privées (in French and English), 1973. The monotypes are discussed and illustrated in Jean Adhémar and Françoise Nora, *Degas, Gravures et Monotypes*, Paris, Arts et Métiers Graphiques, 1973.

72. 'When one touches on such subjects, the result is often pornographic, though always imbued with a desperate sadness. It took someone of the calibre of Degas to give *The Madame's Birthday Party* both an atmosphere of happiness and the grandeur of an Egyptian bas-relief.' (Author's translation.)

73. Quoted in Douglas Cooper, *Toulouse-Lautrec*, London, Thames & Hudson, 1955.

74.   *You, whom my soul has tracked to lairs infernal,*
      Poor sisterhood, I pity and adore,
      For your despairing griefs, your thirst eternal,
      And love that floods your hearts for evermore!

(*Femmes Damnées*, translated by Roy Campbell, in Charles Baudelaire, *The Flowers of Evil*, London, Routledge & Kegan Paul, 1955.) Baudelaire was found guilty of an offence against public morality and six poems from his *Fleurs du Mal* were banned in 1857.

75. The paintings are reproduced in J.-B. de la Faille, *The Works of Vincent Van Gogh*, London, Weidenfeld & Nicolson, 1970, on pp. 158 and 159.

76. See *The Complete Letters of Vincent Van Gogh*, London, Thames & Hudson, and Greenwich, Conn., New York Graphic Society, 1959, Vol. 3, pp. 474–525, especially letters B9, B16, B19 and B19a.

77. See *Peter Fendi, 40 Erotic Aquarelles*, Los Angeles, Hogarth Guild, 1970.

78. See *The Erotic Drawings of Mihály Zichy*, New York, Grove Press, 1969.

79. See *The Amorous Drawings of the Marquis von Bayros*, North Hollywood, Brandon House, 1968.

c: *Decadent Art* (by Simon Wilson)

1. Simon Wilson is a writer and lecturer living in London; he has contributed an introductory essay to Robert Melville's *Erotic Arts of the West*, London, Weidenfeld & Nicolson, and New York, Putnam, 1973 and is author of *The Surrealists*, London, Tate Gallery Publications, 1974, and *Pop*, London, Thames & Hudson, 1974.

2. *Cf.* Sigmund Freud, *Civilisation and its Discontents*, and *Civilised Sexual Morality and Modern Nervousness*, 1908, Standard Edition, London, 1962; Wilhelm Reich, *The Function of the Orgasm* and *The Sexual Revolution*, New York, 1969 (4th revised edition); Herbert Marcuse, *Eros and Civilisation*, Boston, 1966.

3. *E.g.*, Alex Comfort, *The Anxiety Makers*, London, Nelson, 1967; Wayland Young, *Eros Denied*, London, Weidenfeld & Nicolson, 1965; Stephen Marcus, *The Other Victorians*, London, Basic Books, 1964.

4. Herbert Marcuse, *Zur Kritik des Hedonismus*, cited by Robinson in *The Sexual Radicals*, London, Paladin, 1972.

5. Georges Bataille, *Eroticism*, London, Calder, 1966, p. 11; see also Georges Bataille, *Les Larmes D'Eros*, Paris, Pauvert, 1961.

6. John Cage, *Silence*, Middletown, Conn., Wesleyan University Press, 1961. Quoted in *John Cage*, edited by Richard Castelanetz, London, Allen Lane, 1971, p. 134.

7. Salvador Dali, address delivered at MOMA 1934. Cited by Julian Levy in *Surrealism*, New York, Black Sun Press, 1936, p. 7.

8. *Cf.* Sigmund Freud, *Beyond the Pleasure Principle*, 1922, translated by J. Strachey, London, Hogarth Press, 1971, p. 32.

9. D. G. Rossetti, letter of 26 March, 1871 (author's italics), published in Virginia Surtees, *Rossetti*, London, Oxford University Press, 1971, pp. 93–94.

10. J. K. Huysmans, *Against Nature*, translated by Robert Baldick, Harmondsworth, Penguin, 1959, pp. 64–66.

11. *Ibid.*, pp. 67–68.

12. *The Goncourt Journal*, 6 March, 1868.

13. Jules Barbey D'Aurevilly, *Les Diaboliques*, Paris, Dantu, 1873; quoted from *Oeuvres Complètes*, Paris, Alphonse Lemerre, n.d., p. 3. (Author's translation.)

14. Aubrey Beardsley, letter to Smithers, 26 March, 1896, quoted in *The Letters of Aubrey Beardsley*, edited by Henry Maas and others, London, Cassell, 1970, p. 120.

CHAPTER 5: SEXUAL ATTITUDES IN VICTORIAN ART AND LITERATURE

a: *Erotic Themes in Victorian Art and Photography*

1. Steven Marcus, *The Other Victorians*, Bloomington, Ind., Indiana Institute for Sex Research, 1966; London, Corgi, 1969.

2. Alex Comfort, *The Anxiety Makers*, London, Nelson, 1967.

3. Peter Fryer, *The Birth Controllers*, London, Secker & Warburg, 1965. Introduction to *Prostitution* by William Acton, London, MacGibbon & Kee, 1968.

4. Ronald Pearsall, *The Worm in the Bud: The World of Victorian Sexuality*, Harmondsworth, Penguin, 1971.

5. Reproduced in William Gaunt, '19th Century Nudes', in *The Saturday Book*, No. 28, London, Hutchinson, 1968, p. 242.

6. Milton Rugoff, *Prudery and Passion*, London, Rupert Hart-Davis, 1972.

7. *Cf.* Lloyd Goodrich, Introduction to catalogue of *Thomas Eakins Exhibition*, New York, Whitney Museum of American Art, 1970.

8. Alessandro di Marco was the model for Walter Crane's *Birth of Venus* (Tate Gallery, London), for Crane's wife did not like him to use female models. Leighton was not taken in; when he saw Crane's rather muscular Venus, he said 'Why, that's Alessandro!' (Quoted by William Gaunt, *op. cit.*, p. 246.)

9. Reproduced in Gaunt, *op. cit.*, p. 252.

10. Reproduced in Ernest Rhys, *Frederic Lord Leighton*, London, Bell, 1900, opposite p. 34.

11. A. Lys Baldry, *Leighton*, London, Jack, and New York, Stokes, n.d., p. 61.

12. Quoted in Helen Zimmern, 'L. Alma-Tadema, his Life and Work', *Art Journal Annual*, London, 1886, p. 28.

13. Jean Lorrain, *Pall Mall Magazine*, London, April 25, 1898. For the full account, see Patrick Waldburg, *Eros Modern Style*, Paris, Pauvert, 1964, pp. 97, 99, 101.

14. *Cf.* Jiri Mucha and others, *Alphonse Mucha*, London, Academy Editions, 1971, in which are reproduced some drawings done from the photograph and also the finished poster.

15. Stuart Dodgson Collingwood, *Life and Letters of Lewis Carroll*, London, T. Fisher Unwin, 1898, p. 80.

16. Helmut Gernsheim, *Lewis Carroll, Photographer*, London, Max Parrish, 1949, and New York, Dover Publications, 1969, p. 21.

17. These photographs are discussed, and two are reproduced, in Graham Ovenden and

Robert Melville, *Victorian Children*, London, Academy Editions, and New York, St Martin's Press, 1972. Graham Ovenden writes: '[Carroll] created in his pictures of his little girl friends some of the most sensitive yet latently sexual images ever seen in art. . . . They are the product of human love and are innocent in the true sense.' Beautiful nude photographs of little girls by O. G. Rejlander and attributed to J. T. Withe are also reproduced.

18. Quoted in Gernsheim, *op. cit.*, p. 21.

19. *Cf.* Collingwood, *op. cit.*: 'But those who loved him would not wish to lift the veil from these dead sanctities, nor would any purpose be served by so doing,' p. 355.

20. *Cf.* Gernsheim, *op. cit.*, Preface to second edition, 1969, p. v, evidence of Wing Commander Caryl Hargreaves, son of Alice Liddell.

21. *The Exquisite*, British Museum Library no. PC 20 b 1–3.

22. This album contains eighty catalogues and prospectuses from the 1890s and early 1900s; British Museum Library no. PC 16 i 2.

23. *Teleny; or the Reverse of the Medal*, Introduction by H. Montgomery Hyde, London, Icon Books, 1966; unexpurgated edition, California, Collectors Publications, 1968.

24. Pisanus Fraxi (Henry Spencer Ashbee), *Index Librorum Prohibitorum*, London, privately printed, 1877; *Centuria Librorum Absconditorum*, London, privately printed, 1879; *Catena Librorum Tacendorum*, London, privately printed, 1885; British Museum Library no. PC 18 b 9.

25. *The Pearl, a journal of voluptuous reading*, New York, Grove Press, 1968.

26. Quoted in Ralph Ginsburg, *An Unhurried View of Erotica*, London, Secker & Warburg, 1959, p. 77.

27. Aubrey Beardsley, *The Story of Venus and Tannhäuser*, unexpurgated and illustrated edition, New York, Award Books, and London, Tandem, 1967.

28. Letter of *c.* 15 July, 1896, quoted in *The Letters of Aubrey Beardsley*, edited by Henry Maas and others, London, Cassell, 1970, p. 145.

29. Letter of 11 August, 1896, quoted in Maas, *op. cit.*, p. 150.

30. *Cf.* Eduard Fuchs, *Die Karikatur der europaischen Volker von 1848 bis zur Gegenwart*, Berlin, Hofmann, 1903. 'We must freely admit that we have seldom seen anything so repugnantly filthy. It is sheer indulgence in dirt,' p. 1. (Author's translation.)

31. Brian Reade, *Aubrey Beardsley*, New York, Viking Press, and London, Studio Vista, 1967.

32. Malcolm Easton, *Aubrey and the Dying Lady*, London, Secker & Warburg, 1972.

33. Brigid Brophy, *Black and White, a portrait of Aubrey Beardsley*, London, Jonathan Cape, 1968, p. 28.

34. *Idem.*, p. 11.

35. *Idem.*, p. 36.

b: *Erotic Themes in Victorian Literature* (by Barry Curtis)

1. Barry Curtis is Senior Lecturer in Art History at the Faculty of Art and Design of Middlesex Polytechnic (formerly Hornsey College of Art); he has made an extensive study of the Victorian period, and has also written articles on German Neo-classical Architecture. This essay is the revised text of a lecture given as part of the Erotic Arts course.

2. Quoted from *The Edinburgh Review* in Muriel Jaeger, *Before Victoria: Changing Standards and Behaviour 1787–1837*, London, Chatto & Windus, 1956, p. 121.

3. *Vide*: 'Incomprehensible? But some vices were then so unnatural that they did not exist. I doubt if Mrs Poulteney had ever heard of the word "lesbian"; and if she had, it would have commenced with a capital, and referred to an island in Greece; it was to her a fact as rock-fundamental as that the world was round or that the Bishop of Exeter was Dr Philpotts, that woman did not feel carnal pleasure. . . . No doubt here and there, in another milieu, in the most brutish of the urban poor, in the most emancipated of the aristocracy, a truly orgastic lesbianism existed then; but we may ascribe this very common Victorian phenomenon of women sleeping together far more to the desolating arrogance of contemporary man than to a more suspect motive. Besides, in such wells of loneliness is not any coming together closer to humanity than perversity?' John Fowles, *The French Lieutenant's Woman*, London, Jonathan Cape, 1969, pp. 154 and 156.

[454]

4. Harold Nicolson, *Tennyson*, London, Gray Arrow, 1960, p. 157.

5. Tennyson, quoted in Fawn Brodie, *The Devil Drives*, Harmondsworth, Penguin, 1971, p. 369.

6. Reference to Tennyson's poem 'Lockesly Hall':

> *I, the heir of all the ages, in the foremost files of time.*

7. Quoted in Steven Marcus, *The Other Victorians*, London, Corgi, 1969, p. 153.

8. Quoted in *Ibid.*, p. 16.

9. Quoted in John Milner, *Symbolists and Decadents*, London, Studio Vista, 1971, p. 20.

10. 'The Fleshly School of Poetry and Other Phenomena of the Day', London, *Contemporary Review*, October, 1873.

11. See G. H. Fleming, *That Ne'er Shall Meet Again*, London, Michael Joseph, 1971, p. 362.

12. Quoted in Graham Hough, *The Last Romantics*, London, Oxford University Press, 1961, p. 223.

13. Quoted in G. H. Fleming, *op. cit.*, p. 362.

14. Buchanan, *op. cit.*

15. G. H. Fleming, *op. cit.*, p. 167.

16. Buchanan, *op. cit.*

17. *Ibid.*

18. Sir Maurice Bowra, *The Romantic Imagination*, London, Oxford University Press, 1959, p. 207.

19. Quoted in Albert Mordell, *The Erotic Motive in Literature*, London, Collier Books, 1962, p. 61.

20. T. S. Eliot, 'Swinburne as a Poet', *Selected Essays*, London, Faber & Faber, 1963, p. 327.

21. Quoted in Rupert Croft-Cooke, *Feasting with Panthers*, London, W. H. Allen, 1967, p. 22.

22. Adah Isaacs Mencken, *A Fragment of Autobiography by X.Y.Z.*, 1917 (British Museum Private Case).

23. Quoted in Helmut Gernsheim, *Lewis Carroll: Photographer*, New York, Dover, 1969, p. 18.

24. Ronald Pearsall, *The Worm in the Bud*, London, Weidenfeld & Nicolson, 1969, p. 498.

25. Joan Evans, *John Ruskin*, London, Jonathan Cape, 1954.

26. Stead's evidence landed him in Holloway Prison, but was probably instrumental in raising the age of consent from thirteen to sixteen years in 1885.

27. Quoted in Marcus, *op. cit.*, p. 32.

28. Quoted in Brodie, *op. cit.*, p. 368.

29. Sir Richard Burton, *Love, War and Fancy: the social and sexual customs of the East*, edited by Kenneth Walker, London, William Kimber, 1964, Editor's Introduction, p. 12.

30. Quoted in Brodie, *op. cit.*, p. 414.

31. Ernest Dowson, 'Against My Lady Burton: On Her Burning the Last Writing of Her Dead Husband', written 1891; collected in *Poetry of the Nineties*, edited by R. K. R. Thornton, Harmondsworth, Penguin, 1970, p. 161. The bibliographic activities of Burton's friend Henry Spencer Ashbee were similarly disclaimed by his family (see Appendix II).

32. 'Decadence': An explanation of the meaning of this term is best provided by Arthur Symons, a nineties poet and critic and author of an article entitled 'The Decadent Movement in Literature' (which first appeared in *Harper's New Monthly Magazine*, November, 1893); he found in the most representative contemporary literature certain common qualities: 'all the qualities that mark the end of great periods, the qualities that we find in the Greek, the Latin decadence: an intense self-consciousness, a restless curiosity in research, an over subtilising refinement upon refinement, a spiritual and moral perversity.'

33. Quoted in Philippe Jullian, *Oscar Wilde*, London, Paladin, 1971, p. 44.

34. A. C. Benson, *Walter Pater*, London, Macmillan & Co., 1926, p. 188.

35. Lionel Johnson, 'Walter Pater', a poem quoted in full on p. 135 of Ferris Greenslet, *Walter Pater*, London, William Heinemann, 1904.

36. Conclusion of Walter Pater, *The Renaissance*, (1873), London, Macmillan & Co. (Pocket Edition), 1925, p. 252.

37. Quoted in Jaeger, *op. cit.*, p. 150.

38. Brian Reade, *Sexual Heretics* (*The Arabian Nights Terminal Essay*, Section D., Pederasty) by Sir Richard Burton, London, Routledge & Kegan Paul, 1970, p. 165.

39. Aleister Crowley, *The World's Tragedy*, quoted by Timothy d'Arch Smith, *Love in Earnest*, London, Routledge & Kegan Paul, 1970, p. 95.

40. Edward Cracroft Lefroy, 'A Football Player', collected in *Poets and Poetry of the XIX Century: Bridges to Kipling*, London, Routledge, 1906, p. 444.

41. Quoted in Hesketh Pearson, *The Life of Oscar Wilde*, Harmondsworth, Penguin, 1960, pp. 151–52.

42. Quoted in *ibid.*, p. 299.

43. *Teleny, or The Reverse of the Medal* (expurgated), quoted in the Introduction by Montgomery Hyde, London, Icon Books, 1966, p. 10.

44. See Pearsall, *op. cit.*

45. See Edward Carpenter, *Love's Coming of Age*, London, Allen & Unwin, 1948, p. 132.

46. *Ibid.*, p. 185.

47. Aleister Crowley, *White Stains*, London, [Leonard Smithers], 1898, (Edition of 100), recently reissued with Introduction by John Symonds, London, Duckworth, 1973, in an edition of 1000.

48. This 'perversion' has retained its effectiveness as a potent 'mind-fucking' weapon for present-day rebels against the moral order—celebrated by Hell's Angels with red wings insignia. The taboos against menstruation in modern societies have recently been clarified by writers concerned with Women's Liberation.

49. *The Yellow Book* had drawn criticism from its first appearance, largely because of its association with the French 'yellow novel'. The *Westminster Gazette* of 25 April, 1894 accused it of being 'semi-obscene, epicene and sham erotic'. Spurious connection with Oscar Wilde (the press reported that he was carrying 'a yellow book' [not *The Yellow Book*] when arrested) effected a firm editorial disassociation from Decadence and Beardsley, the art editor, was forced to leave. For information on the contents and reception of *The Yellow Book* see Katherine Lyon Mix, *A Study in Yellow*, Kansas, University of Kansas Press, and London, Constable, 1960.

50. F. R. Rolfe (Baron Corvo), *The Desire and Pursuit of the Whole*, Introduction by W. H. Auden, 3rd edition, 1961, p. v.

51. A. J. A. Symons, *The Quest for Corvo*, Harmondsworth, Penguin, 1966, p. 258.

52. Holbrook Jackson, *The Eighteen Nineties*, Harmondsworth, Penguin, 1950.

53. Rolfe, *Desire and Pursuit of the Whole*, *op. cit.*, p. 13. Rolfe draws a clear picture of the elements of dress which obstructed an aesthetic or sexual approach to the conventional Victorian–Edwardian female and suggests the attractiveness of uninitiated girls: 'You should have observed his [Nicholas Crabbe's] furious forbearance with the scraggy ladies of rectors, or with the tailor-made females who still hoped to allure a man with their motley mangy boas and hybrid hand bags and clinking beads and heterogeneous high heels and foolish fat stockings and hard waists (O Aphrodite Anadyomene) and tabby hats like crumpled wrecks of flea bitten birds' nests of felt plastered with the scratchings of rag bags and gigantic withered old cauliflowers. But sometimes he did admire a young girl at a distance, and only for her fresh wholesome youth, her lithe strength, her dainty adroitness. And then, an appalling prevision of what she would have to hide, or what she was likely to become, made him wipe her from the mirror of his mind.' (Pp. 13–14.)

54. Burton, *Love, War and Fancy*, *op. cit.*, p. 160.

55. Pater, 'Winckelmann', *The Renaissance*, *op. cit.*, p. 230.

56. Max Beerbohm, 'A Defence of Cosmetics', first published in *The Yellow Book*, April, 1894, London, John Lane: The Bodley Head.

NOTES

CHAPTER 6: TWENTIETH-CENTURY EROTIC ART

a: *Compulsive Eroticism in Twentieth-Century Art*

1. Quoted in Robert Descharnes and Jean-François Chabrun, *Auguste Rodin*, London, Macmillan, 1967, p. 232.
2. See *The Goncourt Journal*, Vol. V, 1889, incident reported to the Goncourts by Octave Mirbeau; English edition, *Pages from the Goncourt Journal*, edited by Robert Baldick, London, Oxford University Press, 1962, p. 350.
3. Arthur Symons, *Studies in the Seven Arts*, London, Archibald Constable, 1906, pp. 18–19.
4. Quoted in Denys Sutton, *Triumphant Satyr*, London, Country Life, 1966, p. 82.
5. *The Diary of Vaslav Nijinsky*, London, Jonathan Cape, 1963, pp. 121–22.
6. See the Memoirs of Jacques-Emil Blanche, quoted in Descharnes and Chabrun, *op. cit.*, p. 256.
7. Rainer Maria Rilke, *Auguste Rodin*, Berlin, J. Bard, 1903; London, Grey Walls Press, 1946, p. 30.
8. *Hetärengespräche des Lukian*, with fifteen etchings by Gustav Klimt, Leipzig, Zeitler Verlag, 1907.
9. Sigmund Freud, *A Case of Treatment by Hypnotism*, Vienna, 1892.
10. Otto Weininger, *Sex and Character*, Vienna, 1903.
11. See Alessandra Comini, *Schiele in Prison*, London, Thames & Hudson, 1974.
12. George Grosz, *Ecce Homo*, Berlin, Malik Verlag, 1923; Introduction by Henry Miller, London, Methuen, 1967.
13. George Grosz, *Der Spiesser-Spiegel*, Berlin, Malik Verlag, 1924; translated as *Image of the German Babbit*, Introduction by Walter Mehring, New York, Arno Press, 1968.
14. Antonin Artaud, 'Balthus at the Galerie Pierre', reprinted in catalogue of Balthus exhibition, Tate Gallery, London, 1968.
15. Quoted in Ronald Alley, *Tate Gallery Foreign Paintings and Sculptures*, London, 1959, p. 63.
16. Letter of 15 February, 1911, quoted in Robert Speaight, *Life of Eric Gill*, London, Methuen, 1966, p. 53.
17. *Autobiography of Eric Gill*, London, Jonathan Cape, 1940.
18. *First Nudes* (London, Spearman, 1926 and 1954); *25 Nudes* (London, Dent, 1938); *Drawings from Life* (London, Hague & Gill, 1940).
19. Victoria and Albert Museum, Safe E, nos. E 989–991; 1212–1215; 1376–1377; 1661–1662.
20. British Museum, Sheepshanks Cabinet, three albums.
21. Quoted in Maurice Collis, *Stanley Spencer, a Biography*, London, Harvill Press, 1962, p. 139.
22. Quoted in *ibid.*, p. 142.
23. Quoted in Louise Collis, *A Private View of Stanley Spencer*, London, Heinemann, 1972, p. 71.
24. Quoted in Maurice Collis, *op. cit.*, p. 142.
25. Quoted in *ibid.*, p. 223.
26. *Idem.*
27. Louis Collis, *op. cit.*
28. Quoted in Maurice Collis, *op. cit.*, p. 114.
29. Quoted in *ibid.*, p. 141.
30. Pierre Klossowski, *Roberte Ce Soir*, Paris, Editions de Minuit, 1953; New York, Grove Press, 1969.
31. *Pascin; 110 drawings*, Introduction by Alfred Werner, New York, Dover, 1972.
32. *Tableaux Vivants*, fifteen erotic tales with drawings by Nicolaus Vadasz, New York, Grove Press, 1969.
33. *Cf.* Maurice Glosser, *The Erotic Perceptions of Marcel Vertès*, Los Angeles, Avanti Art Editions, 1972.

34. *Cf.* 'Original Sin', in Poul Gerhard, *The Pillow Book or a History of Naughty Pictures*, London, Words and Pictures, 1972, pp. 122–25.

35. *Dessins Erotiques de Bertrand*, Paris, Eric Losfeld, 1969; *Dessins Erotiques de Bertrand, Numĕro II*, Paris, Eris Losfeld, and London, George Proffer, 1971.

36. 'Bertrand et les rigueurs de la passion', in *Zoom*, (Paris), No. 1, Jan., 1970, pp. 90–96.

37. *Cf.* 'Fingesten's Erotic Wit', in Gerhard, *op. cit.*, pp. 150–52.

38. *Cf. Siné Picture Book*, Amsterdam, Thomas Rap, n.d. (*c.* 1970).

39. *Cf.* Willem, *Forty Dirty Drawings*, Amsterdam, Thomas Rap, n.d. (*c.* 1969).

40. *Cf.* Tomi Ungerer, *Fornicon*, New York, Rhinoceros Press, 1969.

41. Quoted in *4 Masters of Erotic Photography*, Munich, Wilhelm Heyne, 1970, p. 50.

42. *Ibid.*, p. 6.

43. Examples of the work of Shinoyama, and also of Giacobetti, Haskins, and Hamilton, are to be found in the above-mentioned catalogue.

44. *Cf.* David Hamilton and Alain Robbe-Grillet, *Dreams of Young Girls*, London, Collins, 1971.

45. Bettina Von Heuenstein and Jan Lue Verrou, *Softgirls*, Germany, Zero Press, n.d. (*c.* 1969).

46. 'One paints the thing that moves one most: Chris Robbins talks to Graham Ovenden', London, *The Image*, No. 2, 1972, pp. 32–39.

47. Michel Leiris, *L'Age d'Homme*, Paris, Gallimard, 1946; translated as *Manhood*, London, Jonathan Cape, 1968, p. 132.

48. *Cf.* Eddie Wolfram, 'Look and See', in *Arts Review*, (London), 22 April, 1972, p. 238.

49. *Cf.* Eddie Wolfram, 'Other Realities', in *Art and Artists*, (London), July, 1972, pp. 24–27.

50. 'Interview with Lindner', in catalogue of Lindner exhibition, University of California, 1969, pp. 7 and 11.

51. *Cf. The Paintings of D. H. Lawrence*, edited by Mervyn Levy, London, Cory, Adams & Mackay, and New York, Viking Press, 1964.

52. *Cf.* C. H. Rolph, *The Trial of Lady Chatterley*, Harmondsworth, Penguin, 1961.

53. *Cf.* Barbara Rose, 'Vaginal Iconology', in *New York Magazine*, February 1974: 'At issue in vaginal iconology is an overt assault on the Freudian doctrine of penis envy, which posits that all little girls must feel that they are missing something.' See also Dorothy Seiberling, 'The Female View of Erotica', in the same issue.

54. *Cf.* Introduction to Drs Phyllis and Eberhard Kronhausen, *Erotic Art*, New York, Grove Press, 1968; London, W. H. Allen, 1971. The Kronhausens opened their International Museum of Erotic Art in San Francisco in 1973.

55. Robert Pincus-Witten, 'Vito Acconci and the conceptual performance', in *Artforum*, (New York,) April, 1972, p. 47.

56. Peggy Guggenheim, *Confessions of an Art Addict*, London, André Deutsch, 1960, p. 130.

57. Quoted in Roland Penrose, *Picasso: His Life and Work*, Harmondsworth, Pelican, 1971, p. 465.

58. Robert Rosenblum, 'Picasso and the Anatomy of Eroticism', in *Studies in Erotic Art*, New York and London, Basic Books, 1970; John Berger, *Success and Failure of Picasso*, Harmondsworth, Penguin, 1965.

59. Rosenblum, *op. cit.*, p. 338.

60. *Picasso: 347 Engravings*, Paris, Galerie Louise Leiris; and London, Institute of Contemporary Arts, 1968.

b: *Eros and Surrealism* (by Robert Stuart Short)

1. Robert Stuart Short is Senior Lecturer in the School of European Studies at the University of East Anglia; he is co-author with Robert Cardinal of *Surrealism: Permanent Revelation*, London, Studio Vista, 1970.

2. Le Comte de Lautréamont (Isidore Ducasse), *Les Chants de Maldoror*, translated by Alexis Lykiard, London, Allison & Busby, 1970, p. 177.

3. Georges Bataille, *Eroticism*, Paris, Editions de Minuit, 1957; London, John Calder, 1966, p. 17.

4. Robert Benayoun, *Erotique du Surréalisme*, Paris, J. J. Pauvert, 1965.

5. Xavière Gauthier, *Surrealisme et Sexualité*, Paris, Gallimard, 1971.

CHAPTER 7: THE EROTIC NOVEL: A CRITICAL VIEW (by Allan Rodway)

1. Dr Allan Rodway is Reader in English Literature at Nottingham University; his publications include *The Common Muse*, London, Chatto & Windus, 1957, *The Romantic Conflict*, London, Chatto & Windus, 1963, and *The Truths of Fiction*, London, Chatto & Windus, 1970. He has contributed to the *Pelican Guide to English Literature*, the *British Journal of Aesthetics*, *Comparative Literature Studies*, and *Twentieth Century*.

2. 'It is one of the effects, perhaps one of the functions of literature to arouse desire, and I can discover no ground for saying that sexual pleasure should not be among the objects of desire which literature presents to us, along with heroism, virtue, peace, death, food, wisdom, God &c.' (from Lionel Trilling's review of *Lolita* entitled 'The Last Lover', in *Encounter*, October, 1958, p. 10).

3. Robert Browning, 'Soliloquy of the Spanish Cloister', VIII, in *Poetical Works*, edited by Ian Jack, London, Oxford University Press, 1970.

4. Marcus Van Heller, *The Gang Way*, New York, Ophelia Press, 1970, p. 23.

5. *Ibid.*, p. 62.

6. Terry Southern and Mason Hoffenburg, *Candy*, Paris, Olympia Press, 1958; New York, Putnam, 1965, pp. 205–8.

7. Aubrey Beardsley, *Under the Hill*, London, John Lane, 1904; and Olympia Press, 1966, p. 45.

8. *Ibid.*, p. 60.

9. John Cleland, *Fanny Hill: Memoirs of a Woman of Pleasure*, London, G. Featon, 1749; Paris, Obelisk Press, 1950, p. 90.

10. *Ibid.*, pp. 139–40.

11. *Ibid.*, p. 143.

12. Pauline Réage, *Histoire d'O*, Paris, Pauvert, 1954; translated as *The Story of O*, Paris, Olympia Press, 1959, p. 21.

13. *Ibid.*, p. 36.

14. *Ibid.*, p. 48.

15. *Ibid.*, p. 86.

16. Georges Bataille, *L'Histoire de l'Oeil*, Paris, K-éditeur, 1944; translated as *Story of the Eye*, Hollywood, Brandon House, 1968, p. 114.

17. *Ibid.*, p. 21.

18. Henry Miller, *Tropic of Capricorn*, Paris, Olympia Press, 1939; London, Panther, 1966, pp. 26–27.

19. *Ibid.*, p. 193.

20. D. H. Lawrence, *Lady Chatterley's Lover*, Florence, Guiseppe Orioli, 1928; Harmondsworth, Penguin, 1960, p. 315.

21. *Ibid.*, p. 215.

22. W. H. Auden, 'The Truest Poetry is the most Feigning', in *The Shield of Achilles*, London, Faber & Faber, 1955, p. 44.

CHAPTER 8: EROTICISM IN FILMS

1. Quoted in Terry Ramsaye, *A Million and One Nights*, New York, Simon & Schuster; and London, Frank Cass, 1964, p. 259.

2. Reproduced in Michael Milner, *Sex on Celluloid*, New York, Macfadden-Bartell, 1964, p. 161.

3. *Cf.* Edgar Morin, *The Stars*, New York, Grove Press, and London, John Calder, 1960.

4. Alexander Walker, *Sex in the Movies*, Harmondsworth, Penguin, 1968, p. 64.

5. *Cf. Goodness had Nothing to do with it: The Autobiography of Mae West*, London, World Distributors, 1962, p. 212.

6. *Cf.* Arthur Knight and Hollis Alpert, 'The History of Sex in Cinema', *Playboy Magazine* (New York), Dec., 1966.

7. *Cf.* Knight and Alpert, 'Sex in Cinema 1969', *Playboy Magazine* (New York), November 1969.

8. *Time Magazine*, 13 June, 1969.

9. *Sunday Mirror*, 29 Aug., 1971.

10. Quoted in Milner, *op. cit.*, p. 44.

11. Quoted in Stacy Waddy, 'Contradiction without Concession', the *Guardian*, 2 July, 1971.

12. Quoted in Gillian Hanson, *Original Skin: Nudity and Sex in Cinema and Theatre*, London, Tom Stacy, 1970, p. 97.

13. Quoted in Michael Billington, 'John Schlesinger', *The Times*, 30 June, 1971.

14. Quoted in Lee Langley, 'The Right to be Outrageous', *Observer Magazine*, 18 Aug., 1971.

15. Quoted in Hanson, *op. cit.*, p. 175.

16. Quoted in Philip Oakes, 'The Rival Tchaikovskys', the *Sunday Times*, 9 Nov., 1969.

17. Quoted in Langley, *op. cit.*

18. Communication to Peter Webb from Glenda Jackson, London, 8 Oct., 1971.

19. *Evening Standard*, 22 July, 1971.

20. Quoted in programme notes, *Forbidden Film Festival*, New Cinema Club, London, July–Sept., 1971, p. 10.

21. Parker Tyler, *Sex, Psyche Etcetera in the Film*, New York, Horizon Press, 1969; Harmondsworth, Penguin, 1971, p. 59. *Cf.* Chapter Six, 'Pornography and Truthfulness: A Report on I am Curious'.

22. *New Statesman*, 17 March, 1973.

CHAPTER 9: EROTICISM IN THE PERFORMING ARTS (by David F. Cheshire)

1. David F. Cheshire is the Librarian, Faculty of Art and Design, Middlesex Polytechnic, London. He is the author of *Theatre: a reader's guide*, London, Bingley, 1967 and *Music Hall in Britain*, Newton Abbot, David & Charles, 1974. He has contributed articles to *Dancing Times*, *Gibraltar Chronicle*, *The Saturday Book*, *Theatre Quarterly*, etc.

2. Thomas Robischon, 'Chronicle of a rear-guard action', in *Arts and Society*, (Madison, Wisc., University of Wisconsin Press), Vol. 7, No. 1, 1970, p. 88.

3. Faubion Bowers, *Theatre in the East*, London, Nelson, 1956, p. 230.

4. D. E. Pohren, *The Art of the Flamenco*, Morón de la Frontera, Spain, Society of Spanish Studies, 1967, p. 63.

5. *Idem.*

6. Colette, *My Apprenticeships*, Harmondsworth, Penguin, 1967, p. 18.

7. D. E. Pohren, *op. cit.*, p. 284.

8. J. K. Huysmans, *Against Nature*, translated by Robert Baldick, Harmondsworth, Penguin, 1959, pp. 65–66.

9. Burgo Partridge, *A History of Orgies*, London, Spring Books, 1964, p. 20.

10. Quoted in Harvey Cox, *The Feast of Fools*, Cambridge, Mass., Harvard University Press, 1969, p. 50.

11. *Continuum*, Winter 1968, p. 734.

12. Max Eastman, 'Isadora Duncan is Dead', in Isadora Duncan, *The Art of the Dance*, edited by Sheldon Cheney, New York, Theatre Arts Books, 1969, p. 39.

13. Isadora Duncan, *My Life*, London, Gollancz, 1928, pp. 169–70.

14. Richard Buckle, *Sunday Times*, London, 26 Jan., 1969, p. 59.

15. J. W. von Goethe, *Travels in Italy*, London, Bell, 1892, p. 199. For further information about Lady Hamilton, see also J. T. Herbert Baily, *Emma, Lady Hamilton*, London, W. G. Menzies, 1905; Hugh Tours, *Life and letters of Emma Hamilton*, London, Gollancz, 1963; *Lady Hamilton*, catalogue of exhibition at Kenwood, London, 1972.

16. The Hon. F. L. G., *The Swell's Night Guide Through the Metropolis*, London, *c.* 1840, pp. 93–94.

17. Lord Chief Baron, *The Swell's Night Guide*, London, 1846.

18. Sheila van Damm, *We Never Closed*, London, Hale, 1967, pp. 62–63.

19. Kenneth Tynan, 'The Critic Comes Full Circle', in *Theatre Quarterly* (London), Vol. 1, No. 2, April–June, 1971, p. 38.

20. Raymond Durgnat, 'Strippers', in *International Times* (London), 28 Nov.–11 Dec., 1966, p. 11.

21. Mabel Elliott, *Daily Telegraph*, London, 28 April, 1970, p. 19.

22. Marjorie Farnsworth, *The Ziegfeld Follies*, London, Peter Davies, n.d. [1956], p. 11.

23. *Evening News*, London, 25 Aug., 1971, p. 1.

24. James L. Peacock, *Rites of Modernization*, Chicago, Chicago University Press, 1968, pp. 198–204.

25. William Willeford, *The Fool and His Sceptre*, London, Arnold, 1960, p. 170.

26. Ernest Weekley, *A Concise Etymological Dictionary of Modern English*, London, Secker & Warburg, 1952.

27. Willeford, *op. cit.*, pp. 126–27.

28. Huysmans, *op. cit.*, pp. 110–12.

29. *Ibid.*, p. 115.

30. 'Dancing in Relation to Religion and Love', in Cheney, *op. cit.*, p. 125.

31. Quoted in Rosamond Gilder, *Enter the Actress*, New York, Theatre Arts Books, 1931, p. 51.

32. J. Huizinga, *The Waning of the Middle Ages*, London, Arnold, 1924, pp. 68–69.

33. Frank Marcus, *Sunday Telegraph*, London, 16 Nov., 1969, p. 14.

34. John Barber, *Daily Telegraph*, London, 10 July, 1969, p. 21.

35. Quoted in William Goldman, *The Season*, New York, Bantam Books, 1970, p. 91.

36. *Report of the Commission on Obscenity and Pornography*, New York, Bantam Books, 1970, p. 5.

37. Alan Brien, *Sunday Telegraph*, London, 6 Aug., 1967, p. 10.

38. Harold Hobson, *Sunday Times*, London, 6 Aug., 1967, p. 21.

39. Michael Kirby, *Happenings*, New York, Dutton, 1965, p. 38.

40. Quoted in Richard Kostelanitz, *The Theatre of Mixed Means*, London, Pitman, 1970, p. 156.

41. Al Hansen, *A Primer of Happenings and Time/Space Art*, New York, Something Else Press, 1965, pp. 26 and 29.

42. Carole Schneeman, 'Parts of a Body House', in *Schmuck*, (London), March, 1972, p. 47.

43. André Breton in *Nouvel Observateur*, 10 Dec., 1964.

44. Marcel Duchamp in *New Writers IV*, London, Calder, 1967, p. 37.

45. G. B. L. Wilson, *Dictionary of the Ballet*, London, Cassell, 1961, pp. 296–97.

46. Lincoln Kirstein, *Movement and Metaphor*, London, Pitman, 1971, p. 199.

47. *Idem.*

48. *Idem.*

49. Prince Peter Lieven, *The Birth of the Ballets-Russes*, London, Allen & Unwin, 1965, pp. 176–77.

50. Jacques Rivière, quoted in Kirstein, *op. cit.*, p. 206.

51. *Ibid.*, p. 207.

52. Emile Vuillermoz, quoted in Kirstein, *op. cit.*, p. 207.

53. Nicholas Dromgoole, *Sunday Telegraph*, London, 16 April, 1967, p. 11.

54. James Roose-Evans, *Experimental Theatre*, London, Studio Vista, 1970, pp. 134–35.

55. Arnold L. Haskell, *Baron at the Ballet*, London, Collins, 1950, p. 210.

56. John Percival, *Modern Ballet*, London, Studio Vista, 1970, pp. 113–14.

57. *Sunday Times*, London, 8 Nov., 1970, p. 25.

58. Albert Goldman and Evert Springhorn, *Wagner on Music and Drama*, London, Gollancz, 1970, p. 258.

59. The Earl of Harewood (ed.), *Kobbe's Complete Opera Book*, London, Pitman, 8th edition, 1969, p. 199.

60. *Ibid.*, p. 190.

61. Ben Jacopetti, 'Revelations', in *Playboy* (New York), March, 1966, p. 154.

62. Tony McCarthy, 'Rugby folk' in *New Society*, London, 2 April, 1970, p. 550.

63. Georges Bataille, *Eroticism*, London, Calder, 1966, p. 17.

64. Ralph Ginzberg, *An Unhurried View of Erotica*, London, Secker & Warburg, 1959, p. 21.

65. R. Meltzer, *The Aesthetics of Rock*, New York, Something Else Press, 1970, p. 111.

66. George Melly, *Revolt into Style*, Harmondsworth, Penguin. 1970, pp. 36–37.

67. Charles Keil, *Urban Blues*, Chicago, Chicago University Press, 1966, p. 122.

68. *Ibid.*, p. 172.

69. 'Tom Jones at Caesar's Palace, Las Vegas' in *Variety*, 28 April, 1971, p. 65; see also Richard Dyer, 'The Meaning of Tom Jones' in *Working Papers in Cultural Studies*, University of Birmingham, Spring 1971, p. 58, which quotes Tom's reply to a woman who asked him whether he padded his crutch: 'There's nothing false about me but my nose.'

70. J. W. Lambert, *Sunday Times*, 28 July, 1957, p. 17.

71. Ray Connolly, *Evening Standard*, 14 April, 1970, p. 16.

72. Michael Billington, *The Times*, 23 April, 1970, p. 16.

73. William Goldman, *op. cit.*, p. 5.

74. Richard Neville, *Playpower*, London, Paladin, 1971, p. 91.

75. Nik Cohn, *AWopBopaLooBopLopBamBoom*, London, Paladin, 1970, p. 222.

76. Jeff Nuttall, 'Applications of Ecstasy' in Joseph Berke, *Counter Culture*, London, Peter Owen, and New York, Fire Books, 1969, p. 211.

77. Unidentified newspaper report, quoted in *Rolling Stone* (U.S.A.), 5 Aug., 1971, p. 32; see also Geoffrey Cannon, 'Doors of Perception' in the *Guardian*, 16 July, 1971.

78. *Record Mirror* (London), 12 February, 1972, p. 20.

79. Jeff Nuttall, *op. cit.*, pp. 210–11.

CHAPTER 10: THE THEATRE OF CELEBRATION

1. Richard Schechner, 'Pornography and the New Expression', *Atlantic Monthly*, Jan., 1967, p. 76.

2. *Ibid.*, p. 28.

3. *Idem.* It is of interest to note that the *Marat/Sade* was the first play in New York to feature male nudity; this was, however, not permitted in the London production.

4. His plays included *The Author's Farce* (moral: 'If you would ride in a coach, deserve to ride in a cart'), *Rape Upon Rape, or The Justice caught in His Own Trap* (moral: 'If you cannot pay for your transgressions like the rich, you must suffer for them like the poor'), and *The Historical Register for the Year 1736*, starring Walpole flimsily disguised as Quidam the fiddler, who makes people dance to his tunes by bribery. See Richard Findlater, *Banned, A Review of Theatrical Censorship in Britain*, London, MacGibbon & Kee, 1967, pp. 39–46, a very useful survey of this subject.

5. See Richard Findlater, *ibid.*, pp. 214–15.

6. Quoted in Michael Billington, 'Joe Egg's Dad', the *Guardian*, 2 Dec., 1971.

7. See Richard Findlater, *op. cit.*, p. 8.

8. For an account of police harassment of *Che*, see the *Daily Telegraph*, 31 March, 1969 and 1 April, 1969. The charges on which the cast were found guilty included consensual sodomy, public lewdness, and obscenity. *Time* magazine described the play as a kind of genital love-hate profile of American relations with revolutionary regimes.

9. *Cf.* Patrick Waldberg, *Eros Modern Style*, Paris, Pauvert, 1964, p. 93.

10. *Cf.* Richard Roud, 'Haute Culture', in the *Guardian*, 1 July, 1971.

11. *Cf.* Peter Gladstone Smith and Peter Birkett, 'Actors Seek Rules for Nude Scenes', in the *Sunday Telegraph*, 10 Jan., 1971; also *Plays and Players*, (London), July and Nov., 1969.

12. The *Sunday Times*, 7 May, 1972.

13. Lord Kennet, 'The Morality of Stage Nudity', in *The Times*, 26 June, 1971.

14. Alexander Bland, 'When Fig Leaves Fall', in the *Observer*, London, 8 Nov., 1970.

15. Harold Hobson, 'Beauties and the Beast', in the *Sunday Times*, London, 29 Aug., 1971.

16. The author would have liked to quote the whole of this verse, which expresses beautifully the yearning for 'the mind's true liberation' which lies at the heart of the original message of *Hair!*. Unfortunately, the publishers of the lyrics, United Artists Music of Monmouth Street, London, have demanded a fee of £50 to quote even one more line, and have threatened to sue if more is quoted without payment. Alas for the original message of *Hair!*

17. Kenneth Tynan, 'Oh! Calcutta!' in *The Village Voice*, (New York), July, 1969.

18. Jack Kroll, 'Oh! Calcutta!' in *Newsweek*, 7 July, 1969.

19. David Holbrook, 'Art or Corruption?' in *The Times*, London, 14 Oct., 1970.

20. Kenneth Tynan, 'The Critic Comes Full Circle', in *Theatre Quarterly* (London), Vol. I, No. 2, April–June, 1971, p. 38.

21. *Ibid.*, p. 38.

22. In an interview in *Playboy Magazine*, July, 1970, Margo Sappington said: 'Society is so funny—when we bump into people on the street, we say "I'm sorry" instead of "It's good". Everybody in the show is *glad* to touch each other, and it's not being naughty. Of course, it's harder for the men because there's the outward sign of being aroused. And men haven't been accepted naked on stage as women have, from belly dancers on up. Everyone wants to know how they keep from getting erections. Well, they *do* get them: yesterday there was a honey of a hard-on. But we don't feel like lovers. It becomes a warm, open, almost brother-sister thing, a *family* feeling' (p. 76).

23. 'Tom Eyen on Tom Eyen and the Dirtiest Show in Town', in *Time Out* (London), No. 64, 7–13 May, 1971, p. 37.

24. Irving Wardle in *The Times*, 12 May, 1971.

25. Felix Barker in the *Evening News*, 12 May, 1971.

26. *Idem.*

27. Conversation between Philip Sayer and Peter Webb, London, 13 Sept., 1971.

28. Weston Taylor, 'This Show's a Shocker', in *News of the World*, 11 July, 1971.

29. *Penthouse Magazine*, (London), Vol. 6, No. 8, Summer 1971, p. 58.

30. Conversation held in London, 17 Sept., 1971, between Peter Webb and Anthony Ingrassia, formerly actor with John Vaccaro's Playhouse of the Ridiculous in New York; author of *Sheila*, *The Adventures of Pussy Red* and *Identity, a Comedy of Errors* (both performed by his own company in New York, 1970); Editor and Director of *Pork*.

APPENDIX I: ARETINO, GIULIO, MARCANTONIO, AND THE SONNETS

1. Donald Thomas, 'Master of Renaissance Erotica', *Penthouse* (London), Vol. 5, No. 6, 1970, pp. 63–66.

2. Pietro Aretino, *Ragionamenti*, with Introduction by Peter Stafford, Libra Collection, London, 1970, p. 104.

3. *Ibid.*, p. 184.

4. Letter to Battista Zatti of Brescia, written from Venice in November or December, 1527. The full text is in a document in the possession of the British Museum.

5. The print is discussed in *Repertorium für Kunstwissenschaft*, Berlin, XXXI, 1908, by Paul Kristeller and described as 'not suitable for reproduction'. A photograph is in the Restricted Collection of the Department of Prints and Drawings at the British Museum. The Museum's Library has a French album of erotic prints 'after originals by Giulio Romano in Rome', B.M. no. PC 31 1 5.

6. For contemporary evidence, see Ariosto, *Suppositi*, Rome, 1526, a play in verse which mentions Raimondi's series of postures prints.

7. Sala di Psyche, Palazzo del Te, Mantua, 1520s. Other evidence of Giulio's erotic work includes a print depicting a nude woman trying to escape from the grasp of a nude man with an erection (Restricted Collection of the Department of Prints and Drawings at the British

Museum, no. BXV-48-4); and *Jupiter and Semele*, a print showing a very overt treatment of the legend, a retouched copy of which is in the Louis Dunand Collection, France (reproduced in Louis Dunand, *Les Amours des Dieux*, Lyon, Albums du Crocodile, 1964, fig. 4).

8. Giorgio Vasari, *Lives of the Artists*, translated by Mrs Jonathan Foster, London, 1851, Vol. 3, p. 504.

9. Lodovico Dolce, *Dialogo della pittura intitolato l'Aretino*, Venice, 1557; translated as *Aretin: A Dialogue on Painting*, London, 1770; quoted in Klein and Zerner, *Sources and Documents in the History of Art: Italian Art 1500–1600*, New Jersey, Prentice-Hall, 1966, see especially p. 62.

10. Frederick Hartt, *Giulio Romano*, New Haven, Conn., Yale University Press, 1958, pp. 280–81.

11. Guillaume Apollinaire, *Essai de Bibliographie Aretinesque* in *L'Oeuvre du Divin Arétin*, Paris, Bibliothèque des Curieux, 1909. See Vol. 2, pp. i–v.

12. Christopher von Murr, 'Notice sur les Estampes gravées par M.-A. Raimondi et accompagnées des Sonnets de l'Aretin', in *Journal zur Kunstgeschichte und zur Allgemeinen Litteratur*, Nurnberg, 1785, Vol. 4. Von Murr was a curator of the Museum of Baron Paul de Praun, a collection of erotic art in Nuremberg.

13. L. J. Hubaud, *Dissertation bibliographique sur un recueil de sonnets Italiens de Pierre Aretin*, Marseille, 1857.

14. *The Lascivious Sonnets of Pietro Aretino*, privately printed, London, n.d., p. 1.

15. The last verse is inaccurate. The last line in the original reads: 's'io ben credessi campar il Re di Francia!'; the meaning is thus 'I would never leave you even if I thought I could set free the King of France'. This refers to François I who was captured at the Battle of Pavia in Italy in 1525. Aretino had written a letter of condolence to the King in prison on 24 April, 1525. The text was later altered, since the allusion would be lost, to: 'se me lo comandasse il Re di Francia!', meaning 'even if the King of France commanded me [to leave you].' The English translator has either misunderstood the text, or used an even more corrupt version.

16. The author refers in passing to the earlier translation: 'There is also a very lewd rendering of the *Sonetti Lussuriosi* by an English poet, rumoured to be from the hand of Oscar Wilde, but which those who have read it assure me Oscar undoubtedly never saw.'

17. The Restricted Collection of the Department of Prints and Drawings, British Museum, no. BXIV-186-231a.

18. *Ibid.*, no. BXIV-186-231.

19. *Ibid.*, nos. 1868-3-28-376 to 395; Bibliothèque Nationale Print Room, Reserved Collection No. Ae 52.

20. Quoted in *Raccolta di Lettere sulle Pittura*, Vol. 4, Rome, 1764. Réprinted in *Les Sonnets luxurieux de l'Aretin*, Paris, Isadore Liseux, 1882, pp. 86–87. Author's translation. This edition has a very interesting introduction by Alcide Bonneau. Liseux was later fined for publishing a second edition of the sonnets in 1904. This edition was illustrated by 'ancient copies of the originals by Giulio Romano', which were in fact coy and clumsy pen and ink drawings of the late eighteenth century.

21. Quoted in Louis Dunand, *op. cit.*, p. 9. Author's translation. This interesting pamphlet includes a detailed discussion of much of the evidence relating to the Marcantonio prints.

22. Ralph Willett bought ten fragments at the Mariette sale, Paris, 1775; Sir Mark Sykes bought nine fragments at the Willett sale, Paris, 1812; Sir Thomas Lawrence bought nine fragments at the Sykes sale, Sotheby's, London, 1824; the British Museum bought nine fragments at the Lawrence sale, Christies, London, 1830.

23. Adam Bartsch, *Le Peintre Graveur*, Vienna, 1813, Vol. XIV, p. 180, No. 231.

24. Information from letters in the possession of the British Museum. The author has not seen the volume.

25. See *Grand Dictionnaire Universal du XIX siècle*, Paris, Larousse, 1876, Vol. XV, p. 1252.

26. Louis Dunand, *op. cit.*, p. 49.

27. Delaborde, *Marcantonio Raimondi*, Paris, 1887. More recently, they were described as mostly 'serious, noble, balanced, open' in *Eros Denied* (London, Corgi, 1968) by Wayland

Young, who discussed the whole project, and especially the poems, in some detail (Chapter 9 and Appendix 2).

APPENDIX II: RESTRICTED COLLECTIONS OF THE BRITISH MUSEUM
AND THE VICTORIA AND ALBERT MUSEUM

1. In August 1973 it was announced that the museum would soon put its secret collection on public display.

2. Victoria and Albert Museum Library nos. 66P 1–12.

3. V & A Library nos. 25F 37 and 38 (Dyce Manuscript 43). For further information about the Earl of Rochester, see Henry Blyth, *The High Tide of Pleasure*, London, Weidenfeld & Nicolson, 1970, Chapter 1.

4. British Museum Harleian Manuscript 7312.

5. No. S-15-1967, exhibited in Room 41.

6. Nos. E 94–104 (Utamaro); E 220–225; E 1205–1236. The museum staged an exhibition of Japanese prints entitled *The Floating World* in the autumn of 1973 which included erotic items by Utamaro, Haronobu, and Shuncho.

7. Nos. E 110–158.

8. No. E 108.

9. Nos. E 106–7; 109.

10. Nos. E 989–91; E 1212–15; E 1376–77; E 1661–62.

11. *Hetärengespräche des Lukian*, illustrated by Gustav Klimt, Leipzig, Julius Zeitler Verlag, 1907, No. 201 A9.

12. No. CCCLXVa.

13. No. OR 59 e.

14. Van Gulik, *Sexual Life in Ancient China*, Leiden, E. J. Brill, 1961.

15. Van Gulik, *Erotic Colour Prints of the Ming Period*, Tokyo, privately printed, 1951.

16. Woo Chan Cheng, *Erotologie de la Chine*, Paris, Pauvert, 1963.

17. Robert Surieu, *Sarv e Naz*, Geneva, Nagel, 1967.

18. Henry Spencer Ashbee ('Pisanus Fraxi'), *Index Librorum Prohibitorum*, London, privately printed, 1877, p. 8 (footnote). B.M. Library no. P.C. 18 b 9 (Restricted Collection).

19. No. M 550, $6\frac{1}{4}$ inches high, from the Townley Collection.

20. See Richard Payne Knight, *Discourse on the Worship of Priapus*, London, Chiswick Press, 1865, plate 30: fig. 3. B.M. Library no. CUP. 820 s 2 (Restricted Collection). The Shelah-na-Gig figure was found, after an extensive search, in December, 1972.

21. Peter Fryer, *Private Case—Public Scandal: Secrets of the British Museum Revealed*, London, Secker & Warburg, 1966. B.M. Library no CUP. 701 h 5 (Restricted Collection).

22. In November, 1973, however, the author was given the unique favour of access to the Private Case Catalogue. It consists of two large, thick leather-bound volumes, in which the gaps in the entries indicate recent transferral to the General Catalogue. Items still listed, however, include Apollinaire's *Le Verger des Amours*, Aubrey Beardsley's *Lysistrata*, Boccaccio's *Decamerone*, Robert Burns's *Merry Muses of Caledonia*, William Burroughs's *Naked Lunch*, John Cleland's *Fanny Hill*, the Marquis de Sade's *Juliette* and *La Nouvelle Justine*, the Earl of Rochester's *Sodom*, Lautréamont's *Maldoror*, Alfred de Musset's *Gamiani*, Pauline Réage's *Histoire d'O*, Aretino's *Sonnets* and *Ragionamenti*, Sacher-Masoch's *Venus in Furs*, Laurence Sterne's *Tristram Shandy* and *Sentimental Journey*, Paul Verlaine's *Hombres* and *Femmes*, Walter's *My Secret Life*, Oscar Wilde's (?) *Teleny*, Wilkes's *Essay on Woman*, and Burton's translations of *The Arabian Nights*, *The Kama Sutra*, and *The Perfumed Garden*. Other incredible listings include *Cythera's Hymnal or Flakes from the Foreskin* (1870) and *The Times* for January 23, 1882, 'remarkable for the account of an indecent interpolation in the speech of the Home Secretary, Sir W. V. Harcourt, at Burton-on-Trent, see fourth column of page seven, fifty-third line from the bottom'. The interpolation was actually the compositor's: 'The speaker then said he felt like a little fucking. I think that is very likely [laughter].'

23. Rolf S. Reade (Alfred Rose), *Registrum Librorum Eroticorum*, London, privately printed, 1936, B.M. Library no. CUP. 504 g 18 (Restricted Collection).

24. *Teleny, or the Reverse of the Medal* (1893), B.M. Library no. P.C. 31 f 37 (Restricted Collection): recent editions, London, Icon Books, 1966, with Introduction by H. Montgomery Hyde, and California, Collectors Publications, 1968 (unexpurgated edition); Walter's *My Secret Life* (*c.* 1890), B.M. Library no. P.C. 13 b 1 (Restricted Collection): recent editions, London, Poly Books, 1967 (excerpts), and New York, Grove Press, 1968 (complete); *The Whippingham Papers* (1888), B.M. Library no. P.C. 27 a 35 (Restricted Collection); *White Stains* (1898), B.M. Library no. P.C. 13 ff 7 (Restricted Collection): recent edition, London, Duckworth, 1973, with Introduction by John Symonds.

25. John Wilkes, *Essay on Woman and Other Pieces*, London, privately printed, 1871, pp. 13–15 (first quotation); pp. 19–20 (second quotation). B.M. Library no. P.C. 31 k 7 (Restricted Collection). There is also a spurious edition, Aberdeen, James Hay, 1788, B.M. Library no. P.C. 31 g 18 (Restricted Collection). For further details of Wilkes, Dashwood, and the Hell-Fire Club, see Burgo Partridge, *A History of Orgies*, London, Bestseller Library, 1962, pp. 134–48.

26. *Dean Swift's Medley*, Dublin and London, privately printed, 1749, p. 110. B.M. Library no. CUP. 804 a 6 (Restricted Collection).

27. Letter from Byron to Hodgson, dated 14 December, 1813, quoted in *The Merry Muses as Folklore* in Gershon Legman, *The Horn Book*, New York, University Books, 1964, p. 180.

28. Robert Burns, *The Merry Muses of Caledonia*, Kilmarnock, D. Brown, 1911, p. 55. B.M. Library no. CUP. 804 a 4 (Restricted Collection). See also the edition edited by James Barke and Sidney Goodsir Smith, London, W. H. Allen, 1965, pp. 58–59. B.M. Library no. CUP. 804 p 2 (Restricted Collection).

29. Paul Verlaine, *Hombres*, Paris, privately printed, 1891. B.M. Library no. CUP. 1001 c 1 (Restricted Collection).

30. Paul Verlaine, *Femmes*, Paris, privately printed, 1890. B.M. Library no. CUP. 1001 c 3 (Restricted Collection).

APPENDIX III: EROTICISM IN TWENTIETH-CENTURY ART:
INTERVIEWS WITH CONTEMPORARY ARTISTS

a: *Hans Bellmer*

1. Interview between Peter Webb and Hans Bellmer held in Paris on 15 January, 1972.

2. Hans Bellmer, *L'Anatomie de l'Image*, Paris, Le Terrain Vague, 1957.

3. *La Mitrailleuse en Etat de Grâce* is a construction dating from 1937 which depicts some sort of strange weapon to which a female head and breasts have been added. A literal translation would be *Machine-Gun in a State of Grace*, but this misses the pun, for the word for machine-gun is feminine in French and can also mean a female machine-gunner.

4. Hans Bellmer and Paul Eluard, *Les Jeux de la Poupée*, Paris, private edition, 1938 and Berggruen, 1949.

5. Robert Fraser Gallery, London, 1966 (closed by police; see Terry Southern, 'The Show that never was', in *Art and Artists*, London, Vol. I, No. 8, Nov., 1966, pp. 10–13); Robert Self Gallery, London, 1966; Editions Graphiques Gallery, London, 1972.

6. Georges Bataille, *L'Histoire de l'Oeil*, Paris, K-éditeur, 1944; English translation, *The Story of the Eye*, Hollywood, Brandon House, 1968.

7. Le Comte de Lautréamont (Isadore Ducasse), *Les Chants de Maldoror*, Brussels, Lacroix, Verboeckhoven, 1869; Paris, E. Wittman, 1874; English translation by Alexis Lykiard, London, Allison & Busby, 1970. This fascinating book with its weirdly erotic imagery was of enormous importance to the Surrealists.

8. *L'Anatomie de l'Image, op. cit.*, author's translation.

9. Sarane Alexandrian, *Surrealist Art*, London, Thames & Hudson, 1970, p. 118.

10. Hans Bellmer, *Die Puppe*, Karlsruhe, privately printed, 1934; French translation, *Naissance de la Poupée*, Paris, Cahiers GLM, No. 1, 1936, pp. 20–24; author's translation.

11. *Cf.* Hans Bellmer, *Notes au Sujet de la Jointure à Boule*, Paris, 1937, quoted in *Hans Bellmer*, Paris, CNAC Archives, 1971, p. 94.

b: *Allen Jones*

1. Interview between Allen Jones and Peter Webb, held in London, July, 1972.
2. *Allen Jones Figures*, Milan, Edizioni O, and Berlin, Galerie Mikro, 1969; *Allen Jones Projects*, London, Mathews, Miller & Dunbar, and Milan, Edizioni O, 1971.
3. See in particular Laura Mulvey, 'You don't know what is happening to you, Mr Jones', in *Spare Rib*, No. 8, Feb., 1973, pp. 13–16, which suggests that the work of Allen Jones is not about women at all but expresses his castration complex. The sculptures discussed include *Table*, *Hatstand*, and *Chair* (all of 1969) and *Green Table* and *Secretary* (of 1972).
4. Bruce Nauman's neon sculpture entitled *The true artist helps the world by revealing mystic Truths* of 1967 (subtitled *Window or Wall Sign*) is reproduced in an exhibition catalogue, Los Angeles County Museum, 1972, No. 25.

c: *David Hockney*

1. Interview between David Hockney and Peter Webb, held in London, June 1972.

d: *Henry Moore*

1. Statement made by Henry Moore to Peter Webb, Much Hadham, Hertfordshire, 1 December, 1971.
2. Erich Neumann, *The Archetypal World of Henry Moore*, New York, Pantheon Books, 1959.

APPENDIX IV: CENSORSHIP IN THE CINEMA

1. Neville March Hunnings, *Film Censors and the Law*, London, Allen & Unwin, 1967, p. 383.
2. *Mutual Film Corporation v. Industrial Commission of Ohio*, 1915. Quoted in Hunnings, *op. cit.*, p. 160.
3. Quoted in Nikita Khrushchev, *The Great Strength of Soviet Literature and Art*, London, Soviet Booklets, 1963, p. 31.
4. Resolution of 26 February, 1924, quoted in Hunnings, *op. cit.*, p. 155. See also R. Molcy, *The Hays Office*, New York, Bobbs-Merrill, 1945.
5. Quoted in Gillian Hanson, *Original Skin*, London, Tom Stacey, 1970, p. 56.
6. *Cf.* Peter Graham, 'Cinema in France', in *Censorship*, London, No. 2, Spring 1965, p. 16.
7. *Directive to Examining Committees of the Central Board of Film Censors regarding the principles to be observed in determining whether a film is or is not suitable for public exhibition*, Delhi, September 1954. Quoted in Hunnings, *op. cit.*, p. 237.
8. *Bioscope*, London, 8 February, 1912.
9. *Bioscope*, London, 21 November, 1912: letter from representatives of the Cinematograph Associations.
10. *Cf.* Cecil Hepworth, *Came the Dawn*, London, Phoenix House, 1951, pp. 33–34.
11. For the full list, see Hunnings, *op. cit.*, pp. 408–9.
12. Quoted in Hanson, *op. cit.*, p. 50.
13. Quoted in *Time Out* (London), No. 63, 30 April–6 May, 1971, p. 27.
14. Quoted in Michael Milner, *Sex on Celluloid*, New York, Macfadden-Bartell, 1964, p. 9.
15. Communication to Peter Webb from Glenda Jackson, London, 8 October, 1971.
16. Quoted in the *Daily Mirror*, 2 July, 1971.
17. *Cf. Today's Cinema* (London), September 1971; and *Cinema and TV Today* (London), 12 February, 1972.
18. Quoted in the *Guardian*, 14 March, 1972.
19. David Robinson, in the *Financial Times*, 26 November, 1971.
20. George Melly, in the *Observer*, 28 November, 1971.

21. Dilys Powell, in the *Sunday Times*, 28 November, 1971.

22. Tom Milne, in *The Times*, 2 July, 1971.

23. Alexander Walker, in the *Evening Standard*, 1 July, 1971.

24. Derek Malcolm, in the *Guardian*, 1 July, 1971.

25. *Cf. The Influence of the Cinema on Children and Adults*, UNESCO, 1961; *Television Violence and Delinquency*, U.S.A., 1972; *Independent Television Authority Code on Violence*, London, 1972.

26. Quoted in the *Observer*, 23 January, 1972: 'Ultra-Violence, the New Wave' by John Heilpern.

27. *Idem.*

28. *Idem.*

APPENDIX V: PORNOGRAPHY: A BRIEF SURVEY

1. Roye, *Nude Ego*, London, Hutchinson, 1955, reproduced opposite p. 79. Mr Roye states: 'I find that lack of breeding often expresses itself in a gracelessness of movement and a want of sympathy . . . an amazing proportion (of my models) have been daughters of clergymen' (p. 134).

2. 'The Glory that is perfect womanhood', in *Daily Mirror*, 14 Sept., 1938, p. 14. The first book to be published in England with photographs of male and female frontal nudes was probably Frances and Mason Merrill, *Among the Nudists*, London, Douglas, 1931, though very discreet nudity had appeared in Maurice Parmelee, *Nudity in Modern Life*, Introduction by Havelock Ellis, London, Douglas, 1929.

3. See *The Nudes of Jean Straker*, London, Charles Skilton, 1958. Mr Straker is the Founder of the Academy of Visual Arts and the Freedom of Vision Society, both of which have their headquarters at Ashurstwood in Sussex; the members are devoted to the ideal of complete freedom for the artist.

4. See Ralph Ginzburg, 'Eros on Trial', published as Vol. 2, Issue 3 of *Fact Magazine* (New York), May–June 1965.

5. Alex Comfort, *The Joy of Sex: A Gourmet's Guide to Lovemaking*, New York, Crown Publishers, 1972.

6. Gillian Freeman, *The Undergrowth of Literature*, London, Panther, 1969, p. 89.

7. Peter Fryer, *Private Case—Public Scandal*, London, Secker & Warburg, 1966, p. 123.

8. Fredric Wertham, *Seduction of the Innocent*, New York and Toronto, Rinehart, 1954, p. 179; London, Museum Press, 1955.

9. Freeman, *op. cit.*, p. 209.

10. Anthony Storr, *Sexual Deviation*, Harmondsworth, Penguin, 1964, p. 57. The author suggests that 'women have no need of fetishes because they do not have to achieve or sustain an erection' (p. 54).

11. Freeman, *op. cit.*, p. 101.

12. John Barry, *Erotic Variations*, Hollywood, Brandon House, 1967; London, K and G Publications, 1968, pp. 107 and 113.

13. A psychiatrist, quoted in Jill Evans, 'This Woman's World', *Daily Mirror*, 30 March, 1972. For a more sane view, see 'Lust Lib' by Gillian Freeman and 'What do we want from male pin-ups?' by Germaine Greer in *Nova* (London), Oct. 1973, pp. 46–47, 51–54.

14. *Cosmopolitan* (London), April 1972, pp. 76–77. The American edition's most famous male nude pin-up showed Burt Reynolds; however, he managed to conceal his penis with his arm.

15. *Oz* (London), No. 42, May–June 1972, p. 55.

16. *Observer*, 15 August, 1971.

17. *Observer*, 29 August, 1971.

18. *The Times*, 23 April, 1971.

19. *Sunday Times*, 29 August, 1971.

20. *Daily Mail*, 27 August, 1971.

21. *Pornography: The Longford Report*, London, Coronet Books, 1972.

Critical Bibliography

This is not a complete inventory of works consulted in the preparation of this book: details of most of these appear in the notes and references above. Instead, it is a critical bibliography of works relevant to the theme of eroticism in the arts. It is arranged under four headings, *General, Art, Literature,* and the *Performing Arts,* rather than simply in accordance with the order of subjects discussed in this book; thus it will have a wider use, for to the author's knowledge this is the first critical bibliography of the whole range of erotica to be published.

The *General* section includes recommended works which cover large areas of the field of this book, *e.g.* Taylor's *Sex in History,* Hyde's *History of Pornography,* Bloch's *Sexual Life in England,* and Young's *Eros Denied.* These are well-known books whose appeal is far wider than the scope of the present work. There are, however, few specialist books that can be wholeheartedly recommended, owing to the fact that we are still in the early stages of serious study of eroticism in the arts. The other three sections include a wide range of material relevant to their subjects, much of which is of limited value, but among the more important works are the Fuchs series, the Nagel series, Bowie and Christenson's *Studies in Erotic Art,* Rawson's *Erotic Art of the East,* Clark's *The Nude,* Bataille's *Eroticism,* and Durgnat's *Eros in the Cinema.* Others have appeared very recently, and too late to be of use in the writing of this book: these include Rawson's *Primitive Erotic Art,* Melville's *Erotic Art of the West,* Hess and Nochlin's *Woman as Sex Object* and Elsom's *Erotic Theatre.* The section headed *Art* covers prehistoric, primitive, oriental and western art; *Literature* includes the novel, poetry, and pornography; the *Performing Arts* covers theatre, cinema, ballet, opera, and music.

SECTION 1: GENERAL

Baynes, Ken, *Art and Society: Sex.* London, Lund Humphries, 1972. Interesting and amusing collection of illustrations showing society's preoccupation with sex.

Beauvoir, Simone de, *A History of Sex. The Second Sex.* London, Four Square, 1960; 1961. Translation from French (*Le Deuxième Sexe,* Paris, Gallimard, 1949); history of women's role in society; Marxist, Freudian and Existentialist interpretations.

Becker, Raymond de, *L'Erotisme d'en Face.* Paris, Pauvert, 1964. Translated as *The Other Face of Love,* London, Neville Spearman, 1967. Balanced discussion of homosexual love (male and female) in Ancient Egypt, Greece, Rome, Middle and Far East and the contemporary world; the French edition is very much better illustrated than the English one.

Bloch, Ivan, *Sexual Life in England.* London, Corgi Books, 1965. Translated from the German classic, *Das Geschlechtsleben in England,* Berlin, 1901–3; a mine of useful background information; short chapters on erotic art and literature are thin and inaccurate; bibliography. An adapted and illustrated edition was published in 1934 (New York, Panurge Press) and 1938 (London, Panurge Press).

Brantôme, Abbé de, *Lives of Gallant Ladies.* London, Panther, 1965. Translation of erotic anecdotes of sixteenth-century French raconteur; good background reading; interesting introduction by Martin Turnell.

Chesney, Kellow, *The Victorian Underworld*. Harmondsworth, Penguin, 1972. Contains useful chapter on prostitution; illustrated; references.

Cleugh, James, *Love Locked Out*. London, Anthony Blond, 1963. Interesting background information on sexuality and censorship in the Middle Ages in Western Europe; bibliography.

Comfort, Alex, *The Anxiety Makers*. London, Nelson, 1967. Very good survey of medical efforts to promote chastity and inhibit sexual behaviour, concentrating on the nineteenth century; illustrated.

Dulaure, Jacques Antoine, *Les Cultes Priapiques*. Paris, Losfeld, 1953. Originally published 1825, and still interesting; classic source work with Knight; discusses phallic cults, ancient, mediaeval, and modern, but especially classical; illustrated.

Epton, Nina, *Love and the English. Love and the French. Love and the Spanish*. Harmondsworth, Penguin, 1964. Interesting background information; all volumes are illustrated.

Flacelière, Robert, *Love in Ancient Greece*. London, Muller, 1962. (*L'Amour en Grèce*, Paris, Hachette, 1960.) Less scholarly than Licht, but full of useful information.

Fowles, John, *The French Lieutenant's Woman*. London, Jonathan Cape, 1969. Recent novel which gives excellent insight into effects of sexual repression in Victorian England.

Fryer, Peter, *The Birth Controllers*. London, Secker & Warburg, 1965. Well-researched survey of efforts towards scientific birth-control; bibliography.

Fryer, Peter, *The Man of Pleasure's Companion, an Anthology of Secret Victorian Vices*. London, New English Library, 1969. Nineteenth-century Victorian sexual habits; gives insight into Victorian morality and secret sex lives; bibliography.

Fryer, Peter, *Mrs. Grundy, Studies in Sexual Prudery*. London, Dobson, 1963. Well-researched and revealing study of prudery in language, literature, entertainment, fashion, etc.; full references and bibliography; illustrated.

Henriques, Fernando, *Love in Action: The Sociology of Sex*. London, Panther, 1964. Scholarly comparative survey of sexual behaviour in many societies; illustrated; extensive footnotes.

Henriques, Fernando, *Prostitution and Society*, Volume I, *The Pretence of Love* (primitive Classical, and oriental worlds); Volume II, *The Immoral Tradition* (the Western world); Volume III, *Modern Sexuality* (up to modern times). London, Panther, 1970. Scholarly and well-researched discussions of the importance of prostitution in various societies; illustrated; full references.

Hunt, Morton M., *The Natural History of Love*. London, New English Library, 1962. Interesting background information on concept of love in the West from Classical to modern times; useful though outdated bibliography.

Hurwood, Bernhardt T., 'Devil in the Flesh', *Penthouse* magazine, London, Volume 5, Number 4, 1970. Interesting short article about incubi, succubi, mediaeval-church attitudes to sex, etc.

Hyde, H. Montgomery, *A History of Pornography*. London, Four Square, and New York, Dell, 1966. Pioneering study of pornography in the widest sense of the word; full of useful information though occasionally inaccurate; concentrates on erotic literature of Western Europe, but mentions Classical and oriental; erotic art discussed briefly; useful bibliography.

Jennings, Hargrave, *Phallism celestial and terrestrial, heathen and Christian, its connexion with the Rosicrucians and the Gnostics and its foundation in Buddhism*. London, George Redway, 1884. Curious compendium of information with a strong slant towards mysticism; covers a very wide field of inquiry.

Jones, Ernest, *Life and Works of Sigmund Freud*. New York and London, Basic Books, 1953–57. Provides invaluable basic knowledge and information for the study of erotic art, but this should be used with discretion.

Kiefer, Otto, *Sexual Life in Ancient Rome*. London, Routledge & Kegan Paul, 1941. Scholarly work; strong on quotations; illustrated.

Knight, Richard Payne and Wright, Thomas, *Sexual Symbolism: A History of Phallic Worship*. New York, Julian Press, 1962. Introduction by Ashley Montagu; includes

Discourse on the Remains of the Worship of Priapus and *Worship of the Generative Powers during the Middle Ages of Western Europe*, originally published 1865, and still very useful; with original illustrations.

Laurent, Gisèle, *Les Sociétés Secrètes Erotiques*. Algiers, S.P.E., n.d. (*c*. 1962). Rather unintellectual account of sexual customs among secret societies; illustrated.

Lewinsohn, Richard, *A History of Sexual Customs*. London, Longmans Green, and New York, Harper Brothers, 1958 (*Eine Weltgeschichte der Sexualität*, Hamburg, Rowohlt Verlag, 1956). Scholarly account of Ancient and modern world; full references; well illustrated.

Licht, Hans, *Sexual Life in Ancient Greece*. London, Routledge & Kegan Paul, 1949. (*Sittengeschichte Griechenlands*, Stuttgart, Gunther Verlag, 1959.) Scholarly and well-annotated work; illustrated.

Macy, Christopher (ed.), *The Arts in a Permissive Society*. London, Pemberton Books, 1971. Conference of the Rationalist Press Association, 1970: Peter Faulkner on 'The Historical Perspective'; John Calder on 'The Novel'; Roger Manvell on 'Cinema and Television'; Daniel Salem on 'Is Social Theatre Possible?'. Four very useful and thought-provoking articles relating to the general topics of censorship and eroticism in the arts.

Pearl, Cyril, *The Girl with the Swansdown Seat*. London, Muller, and New York, Signet Books, 1958. Entertaining glance at Victorian sexual habits.

Pearsall, Ronald, *The Worm in the Bud: the World of Victorian Sexuality*. Harmondsworth, Penguin, 1971. Painstaking examination of prostitution, pornography, sex instruction, sexual perversions, etc. in Victorian England; full notes and references.

Pike, E. Royston, *Love in Ancient Rome*. London, Muller, 1965. Less scholarly than Kiefer, but useful; illustrated.

Rougemont, Denis de, *Passion and Society*. London, Faber & Faber, 1962. Pioneering study (translated from French, first published 1940); learned treatise on the conflict between passion and marriage, reflected especially in European mediaeval literature; full references; published as *L'Amour et l'Occident*, Paris, 1956, and *Love in the Western World*, New York, Pantheon Books, 1956.

Rugoff, Milton, *Prudery and Passion*. London, Hart-Davis, 1972. Interesting discussion of prudery in America in nineteenth century.

Salthus, Edgar, *Love Throughout the Ages*. London, Camden Publishing Company, n.d. (*c*. 1930). Rather superficial survey of history of love in the Western world.

Scott, George Ryley, *All that is Strange in Sex*. London, Luxor Press, and Lucknow, Madnuri Press, 1963. Curious little compendium of strange sexual practices; not very scholarly; illustrated.

Scott, George Ryley, *Phallic Worship*. London, Panther, 1970. Well-researched study of importance of phallic worship in primitive, Classical, oriental, and Western religions; illustrated; good glossary and bibliography.

Simons, G. L., *A History of Sex. Sex in the Modern World. Sex Tomorrow*. London, New English Library, 1969; 1970; 1971. Carefully researched, but short on insight and analysis.

Tabori, Paul, *Dress and Undress*. London, New English Library, 1969. Well-researched and amusing discussion of clothing and sexuality.

Taylor, Gordon Rattray, *The Angel-Makers*. London, Secker & Warburg, 1973. Study of changes in social behaviour in Europe, 1750–1850, especially sexual morality; written from a psychological viewpoint; long bibliography.

Taylor, Gordon Rattray, *Sex in History*. New York, Ballantine Books, 1962; London, Thames & Hudson, 1968. Classic study (first published 1953) from psychologist's rather than historian's point of view; very informative background material; only discusses Western Europe from the Middle Ages; long bibliography.

Thomas, Donald, 'Vice Society', *Censorship* Magazine, London, Volume 3, number 1, winter 1967. Informative article on Victorian anti-vice groups.

Vries, Leonard de, and **Fryer, Peter,** *Venus Unmasked, or an Inquiry into the Nature and Origin of the Passion of Love*. London, Barker, 1967. Anthology of events and writings relating to love in the eighteenth century; illustrated with contemporary engravings; bibliography.

Westropp, Hodder M. and **Wake, C. Staniland,** *Phallism in Ancient Worships.* New Delhi, Kumar Brothers, 1970. Reprint of papers written in 1870; includes some useful information but very dated; illustrated.

Young, Wayland, *Eros Denied.* New York, Grove Press, 1964; London, Corgi, 1968. Intelligent discussion of attitudes over the centuries to erotica of all kinds and from all societies; facts occasionally inaccurate; illustrated.

SECTION II: ART
A. Prehistoric and Primitive Art

Bettelheim, Bruno, *Symbolic Wounds: Puberty Rites and the Envious Male.* London, Thames & Hudson, 1955. Interesting psychoanalytical interpretation of the psychosexual significance of tribal customs; full references; bibliography.

Bloch, Ivan, *Strange Sexual Practices.* California, Brandon House, 1967, and England, K & G Publications, 1968. Learned survey of sexual customs in primitive, Classical, oriental, and Western societies; patronising tone throughout; translated from German late nineteenth century work; no illustrations or bibliography.

Brend, William A., *Sacrifice to Attis: A Study of Sex and Civilisation.* London, Heinemann, 1936. Fair text; illustrated.

Danielsson, Bengt, *Love in the South Seas.* London, Allen & Unwin, 1958. Well-written popular anthropology; illustrated.

Forge, Anthony, *Primitive Art and Society.* London and New York, Oxford University Press, 1973. Very scholarly collection of essays, many dealing with erotic aspects, including 'Style and Meaning in Sepik Art' (A. Forge) and 'The Spatial Presentation of Cosmic Order in Walbiri Iconography' (Nancy D. Munn); full references; well illustrated.

Goldberg, B. Z., *The Sacred Fire: The Story of Sex in Religion.* London, Jarrolds, 1931. Covers a very wide field; rather sensationalised text; poorly illustrated.

Goodland, Roger, *A Bibliography of Sex Rites and Customs.* London, George Routledge & Sons, 1931. Very useful bibliography of works before 1930.

Gordon, Pierre, *Sex and Religion.* New York, Social Sciences Publishers, 1949. Translated from *L'Initiation Sexuelle et L'Evolution Religieuse*; scholarly; footnotes; fairly good.

Hartland, Edwin Sidney, 'Phallism', article in *Encyclopedia of Religion and Ethics* (ed. by James Hastings), Edinburgh, Clark, 1917. Good summary, though now rather outdated.

Hoyle, Rafael Larco, *Checan: Essay on Erotic Elements in Peruvian Art.* Geneva, Paris, Munich, Nagel, 1965. Beautifully illustrated; maps and chronological tables; good introduction to subject.

Laurent, Emile and **Nagour, Paul,** *Magica Sexualis, mystic love books of black arts and secret sciences.* California, Brandon House, 1966. Interesting examination of sex rites related to witchcraft; illustrated; bibliography.

Longworth, T. Clifton, *The Devil a Monk Would Be: A Survey of Sex and Celibacy in Religion.* London, Joseph, n.d. (*c.* 1945). Intelligent discussion of the ancient and modern worlds; short bibliography.

Longworth, T. Clifton, *The Worship of Love, A Study of Nature Worship Throughout the World.* London, Torchstream Books, 1954. Useful illustrations and text on sex rites in British Isles, Europe, Africa, Egypt, Rome and Greece, India, China, Japan, Americas; also Christian sex rites.

Malinowski, Bronislaw, *Sex, Culture and Myth.* London, Hart-Davis, 1963. Collection of scholarly essays on the role of sex and religion, based on anthropological research, but related to the modern world.

Malinowski, Bronislaw, *The Sexual Life of Savages in North-Western Melanesia: An Ethnographic Account of Courtship, Marriage and Family Life among the Natives of the Trobriand Islands, British New Guinea.* London, Routledge, 1929; New York, Halcyon House, 1941. Very well researched, pioneering anthropology; illustrated.

Mantegazza, Paolo, *The Sexual Relations of Mankind.* North California, Brandon House,

1966. Pioneering, though now outdated, study of sexual customs in various cultures, written in a crusading spirit; first published 1885; many illustrations.

Marshall, Donald S. and **Suggs, Robert C.** (ed.), *Human Sexual Behaviour: Variations in the Ethnographic Spectrum*. New York and London, Basic Books, 1971. Collection of scholarly essays on sexual behaviour in various communities, mainly primitive; full references; good critical bibliography.

Mead, Margaret, *Male and Female: A Study of the Sexes in a Changing World*. Harmondsworth, Penguin Books, 1962; New York, Morrow, 1949. Classic study of the range of different cultural definitions of sex roles in various tribal cultures; bibliography.

Ploss, Herman Heinrich and **Bartels, Max and Paul,** *Femina Libido Sexualis*. New York, Tower Books, 1967. Female sexual behaviour in primitive cultures; classic German work translated from *Das Weib* (1897).

Rachewiltz, Boris de, *Black Eros: The sexual customs of Africa from prehistoric times to the present day*. London, Allen & Unwin, 1964 (*Eros Nero*, Longanesi, 1963). Very scholarly; well illustrated; full bibliography.

Rawson, Philip (ed.), *Primitive Erotic Art*. London, Weidenfeld & Nicolson, and New York, Prometheus Press, 1973. Includes 'Early History of Sexual Art' (Rawson), 'Celtic and Northern Art' (Anne Ross), 'North America' (Cottie Burland), 'Middle America' (Cottie Burland), 'Central Andean Region' (Harold Osborne), 'Africa South of Sahara' (Cottie Burland), 'Equatorial Islands of the Pacific Basin' (Tom Harrisson); scholarly and informative text on each of the main areas; very well illustrated; important book.

Sex Worship: (1) *Phallicism* (Lingams, Crosses); (2) *Ophiolatreia* (Serpent worship); (3) *Phallic Objects* (Monuments, Towers); (4) *Cultus Arborum* (Tree worship); (5) *Phallic Faiths* (Fishes, Flowers, Fire). London, A. Reader, 1890. Anonymous little books; quaint, rather simplistic; unillustrated.

Suggs, Robert C., *Marquesan Sexual Behaviour: An Anthropological Study of Polynesian Practices*. New York, Harcourt Bruce, and London, Constable, 1966. Best work on Polynesian sexual behaviour; bibliography; illustrated.

Vanggaerd, Thorkil, *Phallos: A Symbol and its History in the Male World*. London, Jonathan Cape, 1972. Danish psychoanalyst's interesting study of the significance of sexual dominance among men with special reference to Ancient Greece and Viking Scandinavia; illustrated.

Walker, Benjamin, *Sex and the Supernatural*. London, MacDonald Unit 75, 1970. Brief discussion of sexual beliefs in many civilisations; short on insight and analysis; illustrated; brief bibliography.

Wall, O. A., *Sex and Sex Worship*. St Louis, Missouri, Mosby ,1932. A curiously idiosyncratic and unreliable book; some interesting illustrations; phallic worship in Primitive, oriental, Classical and modern societies; bibliography (titles only).

SECTION II: ART
B. The Oriental World

Allgrove, George, *Love in the East*. London, Panther, 1963. Interesting account, concentrating on the present day; short on history and literature; misleading title as only concerned with Arab world.

Anand, Mulk Raj and **Kramrisch, S.,** *Hommage to Khajuraho*. Bombay, 1960. Well-illustrated survey of the erotic temples.

Anand, Mulk Raj, *Kama Kala: Some Notes on the Philosophical Basis of Hindu Erotic Sculpture*. Hamburg, Geneva, Paris, Nagel, 1963. Beautifully illustrated; good introduction to subject.

Beurdeley, Michel, *The Clouds and The Rain, The Art of Love in China*. Fribourg, Switzerland, Office du Livre, and London, Hammond, Hammond & Co., 1969. Especially good on *Taoism and Sexuality* and *The Erotic Novel in China*; useful bibliography; beautifully illustrated; well researched.

Brough, John (Introduction by), *Poems from the Sanskrit*. Harmondsworth, Penguin, 1968.

Indian poems, many on erotic themes, translated from Sanskrit; dating from *c.* fourth–tenth century A.D.; interesting Introduction.

Burton, Richard, *Love, War and Fancy: the Social and Sexual Customs of the East.* London, William Kimber, 1964. Complete text of Burton's important *Terminal Essay* to his translation of *The Arabian Nights* (1885–87), with introduction by Kenneth Walker.

Burton, Richard (trans.), *Ananga Ranga: The Hindu Art of Love.* New York, Medical Press, 1964. Classic Indian treatise on love; illustrated with photographs of Hindu erotic sculpture.

Burton, Richard (trans.), *The Book of the Thousand and One Nights.* London, Panther, 1964. Unexpurgated selection of the erotic tales; edited by P. H. Newby.

Burton, Richard (trans.), *The Kama Sutra of Vatsyayana.* London, Panther, 1968. The classic Indian treatise on physical love.

Burton, Richard (trans.), *The Perfumed Garden of Sheikh Nefzawi.* London, Panther, 1964. The classic text of Islamic sexual behaviour; interesting Introduction by Alan Hull Walton.

Chou, Eric, *The Dragon and the Phoenix: Love, Sex and the Chinese.* London, Corgi Books, 1973. Good account of sexual attitudes in China, past and present; bibliography.

Dehoi, Enver E., *L'Erotisme des Mille et Une Nuits.* Paris, Pauvert, 1961. Dictionary of eroticism in *1001 Nights*; well illustrated.

Densmore, Marianne, *Les Estampes Erotiques Japonaises.* Paris, Cercle du Livre Précieux, 1961. Interesting illustrations.

Edwards, Allen and **Masters, R. E. L.,** *The Cradle of Erotica.* London, Odyssey Press, 1970. Study of Afro-Asian sexual behaviour in the nineteenth and twentieth centuries; some interesting information; bibliography.

Edwards, Allen, *The Jewel in the Lotus: A Historical Survey of the Sexual Culture of the East.* London, Tandem Books, 1965. Not very scholarly; interesting information, though sensationalised; only concerned with Arabs and Indians; useful but very uncritical bibliography.

Ellis, Albert (Introduction by), *The Love Pagoda: The Amorous Adventures of Hsi Men and his Six Wives.* California, Brandon House, 1965. Erotic portions of *Chin Ping Mei*, second half of sixteenth century.

Etiemble, Professor, *Yun Yu: An Essay on Eroticism and Love in Ancient China.* Geneva, Paris, Munich, Nagel, 1970. Beautifully illustrated; many quotations from Chinese texts; good introduction to subject.

Fouchet, Max-Pol, *The Erotic Sculpture of India.* London, Allen & Unwin, 1959. (*L'Art Amoureux des Indes*, Lausanne, 1957.) Superior form of guidebook; nice illustrations.

Girchner, Lawrence E., *Erotic Aspects of Chinese Culture.* U.S., Private Edition, 1957. Not very reliable.

Grosbois, Charles, *Shunga, Images of Spring: Essay on Erotic Elements in Japanese Art.* Geneva, Paris, Munich, Nagel, 1966. Beautifully illustrated; good introduction to subject.

Gulik, R. H. van, *Erotic Colour Prints of the Ming Period.* Tokyo, Private Edition, 1951. Useful text; well illustrated.

Gulik, R. H. van, *Sexual Life in Ancient China: A Preliminary Survey of Chinese Sex and Society from circa 1500 B.C. to 1644 A.D.* Leiden, E. J. Brill, 1964. Very sound and informative.

Humana, Charles, *The Keeper of the Bed – a study of the Eunuch.* London, Arlington Books, 1973. Interesting study of castration with particular reference to the Islamic world; illustrated.

Humana, Charles and **Wu, Wang,** *The Ying-Yang: The Chinese Way of Love.* London, Tandem, 1971. Bibliography; interesting.

Ishihara, Akira and **Levy, Howard S.,** *The Tao of Sex: Chinese Introduction into the Bedroom Arts.* New York and London, Harper & Row, 1970. Good book; scholarly bibliography; illustrated with drawings.

Lal, Kanwar, *The Cult of Desire—Interpretation of Erotic Sculpture of India.* New York, University Books, and London, Luxor Press, 1967. Attempt to relate Indian sculpture to religion; well illustrated.

Lal, Kanwar, *The Religion of Love.* Delhi, Arts and Letters, 1971. Indian religion related to concepts of love; illustrated; references.

BIBLIOGRAPHY

Leeson, Francis, *Kama Shilpa: A Study of Indian Sculpture Depicting Love In Action.* Bombay, D. B. Taraporevala, 1965. Well illustrated; good survey of subject.

Legge, James (trans.), *I Ching.* New York, Dover Books, 1963. Good edition of classic Chinese text on sex and life.

Leigh, Edward, *The Erotic Traveller—Sir Richard Burton.* London, Ortolan Press, 1966. Fair introduction to Burton's life, with quotations from his writings on Oriental sexuality.

Lesoualch, Théo, *Erotique du Japon.* Paris, Pauvert, 1968. Not very scholarly, but interesting attempt to relate present-day Japan (religion, films, night-clubs) to sexual customs of the past; illustrated.

Levy, Howard S., *Chinese Footbinding: the history of a curious erotic custom.* London, Spearman, n.d. (c. 1972). Painstaking study of a little-known aspect of Chinese sexual life; illustrated.

Martin, Richard (trans.), *The Before Midnight Scholar (Ju Pu Tuan* of Li Yu). London, André Deutsch, 1965, and New York, Grove Press, 1963. Translation of seventeenth-century erotic Chinese novel.

Rawson, Philip, *Erotic Art of the East.* New York, Prometheus Press, 1968; London, Weidenfeld & Nicolson, 1973. Extremely scholarly essays on each of the major centres for erotic art: India—Rawson, Islam—David James, China—Rawson, Japan—Richard Lane; beautifully illustrated; important book; introduction by Alex Comfort.

Rawson, Philip, *The Art of Tantra.* London, Thames & Hudson, 1973. First complete survey of Tantric Art; extremely well illustrated; authoritative text on all aspects of Tantra; vastly expanded version of introduction to Hayward Exhibition catalogue.

Rawson, Philip (Introduction by), *Tantra.* London, Arts Council of Great Britain, 1971. Fascinating introduction to major exhibition at Hayward Gallery; five hundred and forty-eight exhibits are illustrated, many in colour.

Rawson, Philip and **Legeza, Laszlo,** *Tao.* London, Thames & Hudson, 1973. Relates Chinese erotic art to philosophy of people for whom it was created; excellent text; well illustrated.

Saikaku, Hara, *The Life of An Amorous Woman.* London, Transworld Publishers, 1964. Seventeenth-century Japanese erotic novel; introduction by Nana Morris.

Sheng, Wu Shan, *Erotologie de la Chine.* Paris, Pauvert, 1963. Fair text; well illustrated.

Surieu, Robert, *Sarv E Naz: An Essay on Love and the Representation of Erotic Themes in Ancient Iran.* Munich, Geneva, Paris, Nagel, 1967. Beautifully illustrated; long quotations from Islamic texts; good introduction to subject.

Thomas, P., *Kama Kalpa: Hindu Ritual of Love.* Bombay, Taraporevala, 1960. Mainly concerned with sexual life and religion in India in the past; well illustrated; good scholarly text.

Tucci, Guiseppe, *Rati-Lila: An Interpretation of the Tantric Imagery of the Temples of Nepal.* Munich, Paris, Geneva, Nagel, 1969. Beautifully illustrated; good introduction to subject.

Watts, Alan and **Elisfon, Eliot,** *The Temple of Konarak—Erotic Spirituality.* London, Thames & Hudson, 1971. Fair text; beautiful photographs.

Waley, Arthur (Introduction by), *The Mandarin and His Six Wives.* London, New English Library, 1962. Translation of the classic Chinese erotic novel of the sixteenth century, *Chin Ping Mei, The Golden Lotus*; expurgated.

Waley, Arthur (Introduction by), *The Pillow Book of Sei Shonagon.* London, Unwin Books, 1960. Translation of tenth-century Japanese diary.

Walker, Kenneth (Introduction by), *The Hindu Art of Love.* London, Kimber, 1963. Burton and Arbuthnot's translation of the *Ananga Ranga,* together with Jowett's translation of Plato's *Symposium.*

SECTION II: ART
C. The Western World

Aulnoyes, François des, *Histoire et philosophie de l'érotisme.* Paris, Pensée Moderne, 1958. Complicated and unhelpful text with strong psychological slant; illustrations include a few art works but are mainly very dated pin-ups.

Balthus: 'Balthus' by J. Leymarie, *Art International*. London and Paris, Feb. 1972. Good short article on eroticism in work of Balthus; illustrated.

Balthus: Exhibition catalogue, Tate Gallery, London, 1968. Introduction by John Russell underplays the eroticism; texts also by Camus, Artaud and Eluard; many illustrations.

Bataille, Georges, *Eroticism.* Paris, Editions de Minuit, 1957, and London, Calder & Boyars, 1966. Fascinating interpretation of eroticism in art and literature in highly personal manner; illustrated.

Bataille, Georges, *Les Larmes d'Eros.* Paris, Pauvert, 1964. Continues certain ideas from *Eroticism, e.g.* closeness of erotic excitement to violence and pain; important book; fascinating collection of illustrations.

Bayros: *The Amorous Drawings of the Marquis von Bayros.* California, Brandon House, and New York, Cythera Press, 1968. Very good selection of erotic work by Bayros.

Beardsley: *Aubrey and the Dying Lady* by Malcolm Easton. London, Secker and Warburg, 1972. Intriguing examination of Beardsley's relationship with his sister Mabel; some rather far-fetched ideas; full references; well illustrated.

Beardsley: *Black and White: A Portrait of Aubrey Beardsley* by B. Brophy. London, Jonathan Cape, 1968. Very good examination of the psychology behind Beardsley's eroticism; illustrated; bibliography.

Bell, Cyrus, 'Saucy Pictures You're Not Allowed To See', *Saturday Tit-bits*, London, 28.11.70. Sensationalised article on secret collections in museums; illustrated.

Bellmer, Hans: *L'Anatomie de l'Image.* Paris, Le Terrain Vague, 1957. Essential source material for the appreciation of Bellmer; illustrated.

Bellmer, Hans: *Hans Bellmer* by Sarane Alexandrian. Paris, Editions Filipacchi, 1971. Very good text; beautifully illustrated.

Bellmer, Hans: Paris, CNAC Archives, 1971. Souvenir of the important retrospective exhibition in Paris; texts by Hans Bellmer, Nora Mitrani, Paul Eluard and Bernard Noël; well illustrated.

Bellmer, Hans: *The Drawings of Hans Bellmer.* London, Academy Editions, 1972; New York, St Martin's Press, 1973. *Les Dessins de Hans Bellmer.* Paris, Denoël, 1966. *Die Zeichnungen von Hans Bellmer.* Berlin, Propyläen Verlag, 1969. Good introduction by Constantin Jelenski; ninety-seven drawings are reproduced.

Bellmer, Hans: *L'Oeuvre Gravé.* Paris, Denoël, 1969; with supplement of work to 1973. Interesting introduction by André Pieyre de Mandiargues; illustrates Bellmer's complete graphic work.

Benayoun, Robert, *Erotique du Surréalisme.* Paris, Pauvert, 1965. Brilliant discussion of the role of eroticism in Surrealist cinema, literature, and art; very well illustrated.

Berger, John, *Ways of Seeing.* Harmondsworth, Penguin Books and London, BBC Publications, 1972. Chapter Three contains an interesting, if at times simplistic argument that the female nude in European painting has almost always been designed as an image to flatter men or a particular man, so that the woman has been made an object; illustrated.

Bertrand: *Dessins Erotiques de Bertrand.* Paris, Losfeld, 1969. *Bertrand—Dessins Erotiques II.* Paris, Losfeld, 1971, and London, Proffer, 1971. Erotic Art bordering on Kitsch.

Bilbo, Jack, *Famous Nudes by Famous Artists.* London, Modern Art Gallery, 1946. Lightweight discussion of nudes from prehistoric and primitive to modern; odd selection of reproductions.

Bolen, Carl von, *Geschichte der Erotik.* Vienna, Verlag Willy Verkauf, 1951. Heavy Germanic account of eroticism in past and present in art and literature.

Boucher: 'Who was Boucher's best beloved?' by Jean Cailleux in *Burlington Magazine*, London, February 1966. Interesting short well-illustrated article postulating that Boucher depicted his wife in some of his erotic works.

Boucher: 'Four artists in search of the same nude girl' by Jean Cailleux in *Burlington Magazine*, London, April 1966. Interesting short well-illustrated article tracing the pose of a female nude in works by Rembrandt, Watteau, Lagrenée and especially Boucher.

Boullet, Jean, *La Belle et La Bête.* Paris, Le Terrain Vague, 1958. Confused and uninspired text touches on Jupiter's transformations and their appeal to artists; a few interesting illustrations, but too many are from horror movies.

BIBLIOGRAPHY

Bowie, Theodore and **Christenson, Cornelia V.** (ed.), *Studies in Erotic Art*. New York and London, Basic Books, 1970. Very scholarly and well-researched essays on 'The Scope and Temperament of Erotic Art in the Greco-Roman World' (Otto J. Brendel), 'Sexual Motifs in Prehistoric Peruvian Ceramics' (Paul H. Gebhard), 'Erotic Aspects of Japanese Art' (Theodore Bowie), 'The Metaphors of Love and Birth in Michelangelo's Pietàs' (Leo Steinberg), and 'Picasso and the Anatomy of Eroticism' (Robert Rosenblum); full references; well illustrated.

Brusendorff, Ove and **Henningsen, Poul**, *Love's Picture Book: Love, Lust and Pleasure*. Copenhagen, Thaning and Appels, and London, Polybooks, 1973. Enthusiastic but not very scholarly account of role of eroticism in various civilisations; copiously illustrated; four volumes.

Brusendorff, Ove and **Henningsen, Poul**, *A History of Eroticism*. Copenhagen, Thaning and Appels, 1963, and New York, Lyle Stuart, 1965–67. Mainly concerned with a survey of erotic art and literature, and sexual sociology, with some interesting quotations but little insight; numerous illustrations, rarely relating to text; six volumes.

Burland, Cottie, *Erotic Antiques or Love is an Antic Thing*. Scotland, Galashiels, Lyle Publications, 1974. Brief introduction to a collection of amusing illustrations.

Cabanne, Pierre, *La Psychologie de l'Art Erotique*. Paris, Edition Samogy, 1970. Fair text; well illustrated.

Campagne, Jean-Marc, *Clovis Trouille*. Paris, Pauvert, 1969. Good text; well illustrated.

Canova: *Academic Art* by T. B. Hess and J. Ashberry. New York, Collier Books, and London, Collier-Macmillan, 1971. Includes Mario Praz, 'Ice and Eros', an interesting short essay on the repressed eroticism of Canova's sculpture.

Carr, Francis, *European Erotic Art*. London, Luxor Press, 1972. Superficial amalgam of received opinions and indiscriminate quotations; little insight and minimal research; illustrated in monochrome on pink paper.

Carracci: *Les estampes composant 'Le Lascivie' du graveur Augustin Carrache*, by L. Dunand. Lyons, *Bulletin des Musées Lyonnais*, No. 1, sixth year, 1957. Scholarly article on Carracci's erotic prints; illustrated.

Carroll: *Life and Letters of Lewis Carroll* by S. D. Collingwood. London, Fisher Unwin, 1898. Standard work with chapter on 'child friends' which ignores any erotic interests; illustrated; bibliography.

Carroll: *Lewis Carroll – Photographer* by H. Gernsheim. New York, Dover Publications, 1969, and London, Constable, 1969. Includes many photographs of girls though not nude, but discusses the question of the nude ones; bibliography.

Cichy, Bodo (Introduction by), *The Nude in Art*. London, Batsford, 1959. Mainly a picture-book; numerous illustrations cover European and non-European painting, from early Egyptian to twentieth century; careful though rather superficial Introduction.

Clark, Kenneth, *The Nude*. Harmondsworth, Penguin Books, 1960. Classic history of the nude in art; polite and erudite; illustrated; extensive footnotes.

Comfort, Alex, *Darwin and the Naked Lady: Discursive Essays on Biology and Art*. London, Routledge & Kegan Paul, 1961. Discusses psychology behind certain erotic paintings, especially Surrealist; illustrated.

Dali: 'Salvador Dali on Eroticism', *Penthouse Magazine*, London, Vol. 2, No. 8, June–July 1967. Amusing short illustrated article.

Daniels, Jeffrey, 'A Man's World', *Art and Artists*, London, November 1972. Interesting article on Winckelmann and the effects of his homosexual ideas on the concept of Neo-classicism in the late eighteenth century; illustrated.

Degas: *Mimes des Courtisanes* (Lucian) with illustrations by Degas. Paris, Cercle des Editions Privées, 1973. Lucian's text translated into French and English; Preface discusses the monotype brothel scenes by Degas.

Degas: 'Degas et les Maisons Closes' by F. Nora, *L'Oeil* Magazine. Paris, October 1973. Interesting article on Degas and brothels; illustrated with his monotypes of prostitutes.

Delvaux: *Paul Delvaux* by P.-A. de Bock. Brussels, Laconti, 1967. Very good selection of illustrations.

Demoriane, Hélène, 'Les Pervertis', *Connaissance des Arts*, Paris, May 1973. Interesting article on Binet, illustrating many of his erotic illustrations for works by Restif de la Bretonne.

Dine: catalogue of exhibition at Robert Fraser Gallery, London, September–October 1966. Interesting introduction by Cyril Barrett; illustrations include three of the London penis drawings and two of the Dine-Paolozzi vulva collages, all of which were confiscated by the London police.

Dunand, Louis, *Les estampes dites découvertes et couvertes.* Paris, *Gazette des Beaux-Arts,* April 1967. Interesting article on the habit of censoring sixteenth-century and later prints by altering the plate (adding drapery to nudes, etc.); illustrated.

Dunand, Louis, *Louise Labé dans l'esprit de son époque.* Lyons, *Albums du Crocodile,* 1962. Interesting article on the sixteenth-century French writer and courtesan; illustrated.

Dunand, Louis, *Les rapports de l'amour et de l'argent dans les estampes des 16. et 17. siècles.* Lyons, *Bulletin des Musées Lyonnais,* 1969. Discussion of prints showing people offering money for sexual relations; illustrated.

Dunlop, Ian, *The Shock of the New.* London, Weidenfeld & Nicolson, 1972. Includes chapter on Manet's *Déjeuner sur L'herbe* and the Salon des Refusés, 1863.

Erotic Art '66, catalogue of exhibition at Sidney Janis Gallery, New York, October 1966. Thirty-three items are catalogued, and eighteen are illustrated, including Rosenquist, Segal, Wesselmann, Lindner, Rivers, Marisol, Dine, Kitaj, Jones, Warhol and Klein; quality of works is generally not high.

Erotic Art: 'Seized', *Art and Artists,* London, Vol. I, No. 8, November 1966. Includes articles on erotica, Terry Southern on Bellmer, review of Janis Gallery Erotic Art Exhibition, Christopher Finch on *Synthetic Pubism,* etc.

Erotic Art by Women: 'The Female View of Erotica' (Dorothy Seiberling) and 'Vaginal Iconology' (Barbara Rose). *New York Magazine,* February 1974. Valuable short articles written from the feminist viewpoint; illustrated with erotic works by contemporary women artists.

Erotica: *Bilder-Lexikon der Erotik.* I *Kulturgeschichte;* II *Literatur und Kunst;* III *Sexualwissenschaft;* IV *Ergänzungsband.* Vienna, Institut für Sexualforschung, 1928–31. Massive documentation of anything relating to erotica; illustrated; source work.

Erotica: *Die Erotik im 20. Jahrhundert: Die Welt Eros.* Basel, Verlag Kurt Desch, 1967. Includes translations from French: Patrick Waldberg, 'Eros Modern Style'; Anatol Jakovski, 'Eros du Dimanche'; Lo Duca, 'Technique de L'Erotisme', Jean Boullet, 'Symbolisme Sexuelle'; very interesting texts; well illustrated.

Erotica: *Lexique Succinct de l'Erotisme.* Paris, Losfeld, 1970. Small, not too serious, dictionary of personalities and concepts, from Surrealist viewpoint.

Erotica: *Sixty Erotic Engravings from Juliette.* New York. Grove Press, 1969. Etchings from 1797 edition; very explicit, amusing, not great works of art.

Etty: *Etty and the Nude* by W. Gaunt and F. G. Roe. Leigh-on-Sea, Sussex, F. Lewis Publishers, 1943. Straightforward biography with useful collection of illustrations of Etty's nude paintings and drawings.

Fels, Florent, *L'Art et L'Amour.* Paris, Editions Arc-en-ciel, 1953. Well-illustrated chronological discussion of the role of sex in French art; two volumes.

Fendi: *Peter Fendi: Forty Erotic Aquarelles.* Los Angeles, Hogarth Guild, 1970. Introduction by Karl Merker; all the paintings are reproduced in colour.

Forberg, Friedrich Carl, *The Manual of Exotica Sexualia.* California, Brandon House, 1965; originally published as *Manual of Classical Erotology* (*De Figuris Veneris*), London, 1887. Erotica in Classical art and literature; standard work; scholarly, though takes a very cold, unenthusiastic attitude.

Fragonard: 'The True Path of Fragonard's Progress of Love' by D. Posner, *Burlington Magazine.* London, August 1972. Scholarly article on cycle of paintings; illustrated.

Freud, Sigmund, *Leonardo da Vinci.* London, Kegan Paul, 1932. Contains the famous sexual interpretation of Leonardo's childhood reminiscence.

Fuchs, Eduard, I: *Die Karikatur der Europäischen Volker von 1848 bis zur Gegenwart,* Berlin, A. Hofmann & Co., 1903. II: *Das Erotische Element in der Karikatur,* A. Langen, Munich, 1904. III: *Die Frau in der Karikatur,* Albert Langen, Munich, 1907. IV: *Illustrierte*

BIBLIOGRAPHY

Sittengeschichte vom Mittelalter bis zur Gegenwart: Vol. 1. *Renaissance* (1909) and
Ergänzungsband (1928); Vol. 2. *Die Galante Zeit* (1910) and *Ergänzungsband* (1928); Vol. 3.
Das Bürgerliche Zeitalter (1911) and *Ergänzungsband* (1928); V: *Geschichte der Erotischen
Kunst,* Munich, A. Langen, 1912. VI: *Geschichte der Erotischen Kunst:* Vol. 1. *Das
Zeitgeschichtliche Problem* (1922); Vol 2. *Das Individuelle Problem* I (1923); Vol. 3. *Das
Individuelle Problem* II (1926); Vol. 4. *Erweiterung und Neuarbeitung des Werkes Das
Erotische Element in der Karikatur mit Einschluss der Ernsten Kunst* (1912). VII: *Die Grossen
Meister der Erotik, ein Beitrag zum Problem des Schöpferischen Malerei und Plastik*, Munich,
A. Langen, 1928. Pioneering works of great interest, though not very scholarly, and not
strong on insight; no bibliographies; very interesting collections of illustrations.

Fuseli: *Fuseli's The Night-Mare* by N. Powell. London, Allen Lane, 1972. Good discussion;
illustrated.

Fuseli: *Fuseli.* London, Tate Gallery, 1975. Very well illustrated catalogue of important
exhibition; Introduction by Gert Schiff ('Fuseli, Lucifer and the Medusa') makes interesting if at times far-fetched suggestions about the erotic basis of much of Fuseli's work.

Gaunt, William, '19th-Century Nudes', *Saturday Book No. 28*. London, Hutchinson, 1968.
Informative but short article; interesting illustrations.

Gauthier, Xavière, *Surréalisme et Sexualité*. Paris, Gallimard, 1971. Women's Liberation
critique of Surrealists' attitudes to sex; their attitudes to women found wanting; illustrated.

Gerdts, William H., *The Great American Nude: A History in Art*. London, Phaidon, and
New York, Praeger, 1974. Comprehensive survey of the nude in American art; full references; bibliography; very well illustrated.

Gerhard, Poul, *The Pillow Book, or A History of Naughty Pictures*. London, Words and
Pictures, 1972. Interesting collection of erotic illustrations, including lesser known artists,
Peter Fendi, Antoine Borel, Henri Lemott, Otto Schoff; poor text.

Gerhard, Poul, *Pornography or Art*. London, Words and Pictures, 1971. Interesting collection of illustrations of erotic art, especially lesser known artists—Zille, Vertès, Zichy;
text of little value.

Gip, Bernard, *The Passions and Lechery of Catherine the Great*. Geneva, Nagel, and London,
Skilton, 1971. Poor discussion of Catherine's erotic interests; photographs of her furniture
and art works are clearly fakes.

Grand-Carteret, John, *Die Erotik in der Französischen Karikatur*. Vienna and Leipzig,
C. W. Stern, 1909. Fair text; well illustrated.

Grand-Carteret, John, *Le Décolleté et le Retroussé: quatre siècles de Gauloiserie*, 1500–1870.
Paris, Bernard, n.d. (*c*. 1905). Interesting discussion of eroticism in women's clothing as
seen in French art, especially eighteenth and nineteenth centures; very well illustrated.

Grimley, Gordon (ed.), *Erotic Illustrations*. New York, Grove Press, 1973. Good selection
of drawings for erotic novels from eighteenth century to today.

Grosz, George, *Ecce Homo*. Berlin, Malik Verlag, 1923. Introduction by Henry Miller,
London, Methuen, 1967; New York, Grove Press, 1966. Free drawings of prostitutes, etc.;
good introduction.

Grosz, George, *Der Speisser-Spiegel*. Berlin, Malik Verlag, 1924; translated as *Image of the
German Babbit*, Introduction by Walter Mehring, New York, Arno Press, 1968. Free
drawings of sexual underworld, includes autobiographical article.

Haskell, Francis, 'Eroticism and the Visual Arts', *Censorship* magazine, London, Vol. 3,
No. 1, Winter 1967. Interesting and informative unillustrated short article about underlying
eroticism in Western painting, and people's ambivalent attitudes to it.

Haskins, Sam, *Five Girls*. London, Bodley Head, 1962. *Cowboy Kate and Other Stories*.
London, Bodley Head, 1965. *November Girl*. London, Bodley Head, 1967. Collections of
Haskins's erotic photographs.

Hamilton, David and **Robbe-Grillet, Alain,** *Dreams of Young Girls*. London, Collins,
1971. Good selection of Hamilton's photographs of nude young girls.

Hess, Thomas B. and **Nochlin, Linda** (ed.), *Woman as Sex Object: Studies in Erotic Art,
1730–1970*. New York, Art News Annual, No. 38, 1972 and London, Allen Lane, 1973.
Very interesting and well-researched essays on topics including the chauvinism behind
erotic art being created by males for males; the corset as erotic alchemy; the *femme-fatale*;

pin-ups; and eroticism in the works of Ingres, Fuseli, Courbet, Manet, Renoir, Klimt and Picasso; full references; well illustrated.

Hester, George M., *The Classic Nude*. New York, American Photographic Book Publishing Company, 1973. Portfolio of beautiful photographs of the nude—full frontals of both sexes. Artistic, imaginative lighting.

Howe, Eric, *How to Draw Pin-Ups*. London, Studio Books, 1963. Brief history of eroticism preceeds discussion of pin-ups; illustrated.

Ingres: *A propos des dessins dits secrets légués par J.-D. Ingres au Musée de Montauban* by L. Dunand. Montauban, Bulletin des Amis du Musée Ingres, No. 23, July 1968. Scholarly discussion of Ingres's fourteen drawings after sixteenth-century erotic prints; illustrated.

Ingres: 'Ingres – The Fierce Twilight' by R. Huyghe, *Réalités*, Paris, January 1972. Good discussion of eroticism in works of Ingres, especially late work, *Le Bain Turc*; well illustrated.

Jones, Allen, *Figures*. Milan, Edizioni O, and Berlin, Galerie Mikro, 1969. *Projects*. London, Matthews, Miller & Dunbar, and Milan, Edizioni O, 1971. *Waitress*. London, Matthews, Miller & Dunbar, 1972. Attractive collections of source material and works.

Kahmen, Volker, *Eroticism in Contemporary Art*. London, Studio Vista, 1972. Published as *Erotic Art Today*, New York, Graphic Society, 1972. Translated from *Erotik in der Kunst*, Tübingen, Wasmuth, 1971. Very uncritical reading of Freud has led the author to see sex in everything from a Cologne water-tower to a Mondrian abstract; tedious and often unintentionally hilarious; illustrated with very poor-quality works of art.

Karwath, Cary von, *Die Erotik in der Kunst*. Vienna and Leipzig, C. W. Stern, 1908. Scholarly attempt at pioneering study of erotic art; well illustrated.

Klimt: *Gustav Klimt* by F. Novotny and J. Dobai. Salzburg, Welz, and New York, Praeger, 1970. Discusses eroticism in Klimt's work; well illustrated.

Klimt: *Gustav Klimt: 100 Drawings* by A. Werner, New York, Dover Publications, 1972. Good short Introduction and many erotic drawings; illustrated.

Knight, Richard Payne, *An Inquiry into the Symbolical Language of Ancient Art and Mythology*. London, 1818. Pioneering study; still interesting and useful.

Kronhausen, Drs Phyllis and Eberhard, *Erotic Art, a survey of erotic fact and fancy in fine arts*. New York, Grove Press, 1968; London, W. H. Allen, 1971. *Erotic Art 2*. New York, Grove Press, 1970. Introduction is mainly guidebook material, for these are luxury catalogues for the exhibition of Erotic Art held in Sweden, Denmark and West Germany in 1968; very well illustrated.

Kronhausen, Drs Phyllis and Eberhard, *The International Museum of Erotic Art*. New York, Ballantine Books, 1973. Selection from the Kronhausen Collection on show in San Francisco; well illustrated.

Kyrou, Ado, *Un Honnête Homme*, with English translation by Alan Hull Walton as *An Honest Man*. Paris, Le Terrain Vague, and London, Rodney Books, 1964. Illustrations include many good examples of turn-of-the-century erotic postcards.

Lacey, Peter, *The History of the Nude in Photography*. London, Corgi, 1969. Mainly concerned with recent photographers of the female nude, with brief references to examples from the late nineteenth and early twentieth centuries; brief text; many illustrations.

Laver, James, *Homage to Venus*. London, Faber & Faber, 1948. Interesting collection of works illustrating the story of Venus; informative but brief introduction.

Lawrence: *The Paintings of D. H. Lawrence* M. Levy (ed.). London, Cory, Adams & MacKay, 1964. Includes sensible essay by Herbert Read; fully illustrated.

Lejard, André, *Le Nu dans la Peinture Française*. Paris, Editions du Chêne, 1947. Interesting collection of French paintings of the female nude; brief Introduction.

Levey, Michael, *The Nude*. London, Trustees of the National Gallery, 1972. Very readable and informative booklet about paintings of the nude in the collection of the National Gallery; illustrated.

Levy, Mervyn, *The Artist and the Nude*. London, Barrie & Rockcliffe, 1965. Anthology of drawings of nudes with very sensitive Introduction.

Levy, Mervyn, *The Moons of Paradise—Reflections on the Breast in Art*. London, Arthur Barker, 1962. Fascinating personal exploration of the sexuality of women (and in particular their breasts) as seen in art from the Classical and Oriental worlds to the twentieth century; especially good on Fuseli; illustrated.

Lindner: *Richard Lindner* by D. Ashton. New York, Abrams, n.d. (*c* 1968). Good text; very well illustrated.

Lippard, Lucy, 'New York Letter', *Art International*. Lugano, Switzerland, April, 1965. Good short article on eroticism and pornography; reference to Klimt, Schiele, Wesselman, Jones, Samaras; with review of Contemporary Erotica exhibition at Van Bovenkamp Gallery, New York.

Lo Duca, Guiseppe, *Erotique de l'Art*. Paris, La Jeune Parque, 1966. Thematic but unscholarly text; very well illustrated.

Lo Duca, Guiseppe, *Dictionnaire de Sexologie*. Paris, Pauvert, 1962. General topics related to sex; profusely illustrated.

Lo Duca, Guiseppe, *Histoire de l'Erotisme*. Paris, La Jeune Parque, 1969. Thematic but unscholarly text; very well illustrated with art works.

Lo Duca, Guiseppe, *A History of Eroticism*. London, Rodney Books, 1966. (*De Erotica I: Histoire de l'Erotisme*. Paris, Pauvert, 1960.) Very Freudian interpretation of eroticism in art and literature; interesting selection of illustrations.

Lucie-Smith, Edward, *Eroticism in Western Art*. London, Thames & Hudson, 1972. Uneven and unsatisfactory; lack of real intellectual argument or depth of research; discussion of symbolism often very fanciful; brief bibliography; well illustrated.

Maas, Jeremy, 'Victorian Nudes', *Saturday Book No. 31*. London, Hutchinson, 1971. Short article; interesting illustrations.

Man Through his Art—Love and Marriage. London, Educational Productions Ltd., 1968. Intelligent essays on artworks from all civilisations; concentration is not on eroticism; well illustrated.

Marcadé, Jean, *Eros Kalos: Essay on Erotic Elements in Greek Art*. Geneva, New York, Paris, Hamburg, Nagel, 1962. Beautifully illustrated; many quotations from Greek authors; good introduction to the subject.

Marcadé, Jean, *Roma Amor: Essay on Erotic Elements in Etruscan and Roman Art*. Geneva, Paris, Munich, Nagel, 1965. Beautifully illustrated; many quotations from Roman writers; good introduction to the subject.

Melly, George, 'Pornography and Erotica', *Art and Artists*. London, August 1970. Brief article pointing out triviality of pornography compared with eroticism of Jones, Picasso, Bellmer.

Melville, Robert, *Erotic Art of the West*, with a short history of Western Erotic Art by Simon Wilson. London, Weidenfeld & Nicolson, and New York, Prometheus Press, 1973. Fascinating yet unsatisfactory; historical introduction good but far too brief; chapters of book divided into subjects *e.g.* 'Act of Love', 'Object of Desire', 'Violence and Violation', 'Erotic Symbolism', etc., which makes for confusion in spite of the moments of real insight; very well illustrated.

Mentone, Frederick, H., *The Human Form in Art*. London, The Naturist, 1944. Chatty little book about great painters of the nude; illustrated.

Mitford, Nancy, *Madame de Pompadour*. London, Reprint Society, 1955. Interesting background information to French eighteenth-century art; illustrated; bibliography.

Moore: *The Archetypal World of Henry Moore* by E. Neumann. New York, Pantheon, 1959. Interesting psychological interpretation of eroticism in Moore's work; illustrated.

Mucha: Graham Ovenden: *Mucha Photographs*. London, Academy Editions and New York, St Martin's Press, 1974. Short introduction to good selection of Mucha's photographs, including some of his nudes.

Newton, Eric, *Masterpieces of Figure Painting*. London and New York, Studio Publications, 1936. Interesting essay on the treatment of the human body as 'a thing of intrinsic dignity and beauty'; few illustrations.

Norgaad, Erik, *With Love: The Erotic Postcard*. London, MacGibbon and Kee, 1969. Amusing collection of illustrations.

Ovenden, Graham, *Pre-Raphaelite Photography*. London, Academy Editions, and New York,

St Martin's Press, 1972. Interesting comparisons of images of women by Rossetti, Lewis Carroll, J. M. Cameron, Arthur Hughes, etc.

Ovenden, Graham and **Melville, Robert,** *Victorian Children.* London, Academy Editions and New York, St Martin's Press, 1972. Beautiful collection of photographs of girls, many of them nude, by Carroll and Rejlander, and from the collection of J. T. Withe.

Ovenden, Graham and **Mendes, Peter,** *Victorian Erotic Photography.* London, Academy Editions and New York, St Martin's Press, 1973. Beautiful selection of Victorian photographs of the female nude; short Introduction.

Peppiatt, Michael, 'Balthus, Klossowski, Bellmer: three approaches to the flesh', *Art International.* Paris and London, October 1973. Very good long article on three important contemporary erotic artists; well illustrated.

Peyrefitte, Roger, *Un Musée de l'Amour.* Paris, Editions du Rocher, 1972. Interesting account of the author's personal collection of erotica; illustrated.

Photography: *Vier Meister der Erotischen Fotografie.* Munich, Wilhelm Heyne, 1970. Documentation of exhibition in Munich and London. Articles on, and photographs by, Sam Haskins, David Hamilton, Francis Giacobetti, Kischin Shinoyama. English translation as *Four Masters of Erotic Photography*, 1970. Very well illustrated.

Picasso: *347 gravures.* Paris, Galerie Louise Leiris, 1968; London, I.C.A., 1968; and New York, Random House, Maecenas Press, 1970. Illustrations of Picasso's erotic engravings of 1968.

Piper, Reinhard, *Die Schöne Frau in der Kunst aller Zeiten.* Munich, Piper Verlag, 1923. Profusely illustrated; rather heavy text.

Reichardt, Jasia, 'Censorship, Obscenity and Context', *Studio International.* London, November 1966. Intelligent short article pointing to the danger of erotic art having to justify itself as being for the public good.

Rickards, Maurice, *Banned Posters.* London, Evelyn Adams & MacKay, 1969. Well-illustrated, short discussion.

Rodin: *Triumphant Satyr* by D. Sutton. London, Country Life, 1966. Interesting study of Rodin, especially erotic aspects of his work; well illustrated.

Romano: *Les compositions de Jules Romain 'Les Amours des Dieux' gravés par M.-A. Raimondi* by L. Dunand. Lyons, Albums du Crocodile, 1964. Scholarly article on the Aretino prints; illustrated.

Romi, *La Conquête du Nu.* Paris, Editions de Paris, 1957. Entertaining but unscholarly discussion of nudity in Western art; some interesting illustrations.

Romi, *Mythologie du Sein.* Paris, Pauvert, 1965. Interesting collection of illustrations of female breasts from earliest times to contemporary art, films, photography, and advertising; rather pedestrian text.

Rops: 'Towards an Art of the Shiver' by R. Melville, *Architectural Review.* London, November 1971. Interesting short article on the strange eroticism of Rops; illustrated.

Rops: *Felicien Rops.* London, Academy Editions and New York, St Martin's Press, 1972. Very brief Introduction by Victor Arwas; fair selection of plates, not including the most erotic.

Rops: *Pornocrates* by Charles Brison. London, Skilton, 1969. Disappointing; fails to illuminate eroticism in Rops's work; many prints illustrated, but not the most erotic.

Rops: *The Graphic Work of Felicien Rops.* New York, Land's End Press, 1968. Introduction by Lee Revens; includes important essay by Huysmans, 'Instrumentum Diaboli', on Rops and his place in erotic art; excellent selection of prints, including the most erotic.

Rowlandson: *The Amorous Illustrations of Thomas Rowlandson.* New York, Cythera Press, 1969. Interesting Introduction by Gert Schiff; good selection of illustrations.

Rowlandson: *The Forbidden Erotica of Thomas Rowlandson.* Los Angeles, Hogarth Guild, 1970. Poor Introduction by Kurt von Meier; good selection of illustrations.

Rund, Jeff, *Libertine Literature.* New York, catalogue of sale at Parke-Bernet Gallery, 27 April 1971. Many reproductions of French eighteenth- and nineteenth-century erotic illustrations; scholarly.

Schiele: *Schiele in Prison* by A. Comini. London, Thames and Hudson, 1974. Interesting but very brief discussion of Schiele's imprisonment for his 'obscene' drawings of little girls; only one of these is reproduced.

Segal, Muriel, *Dolly on the Dais: the artist's model in perspective.* London, Gentry Books, 1972. Inaccurate and superficial accounts of the lives of famous artists' models.

'Sex and Erotica', entry in *Encyclopedia of World Art.* New York, Toronto, and London, McGraw-Hill, 1966. Short but good articles on 'Sexuality and Art' (Mario Praz), 'Sexual Symbolism in Prehistorical and Primitive Art' (Hermann Baumann), 'Antiquity' (Gennaro Peach), 'The Christian West' (Eugenio Battiste and Francesco Negri Arnoldi) and 'The East' (Robert van Gulik); very academic approach but full of useful information; bibliography; illustrations.

Silvestre, Armand, *Le Nu au Salon.* Paris, Bernard (1880–1900). Annual photographic record of nude salon paintings.

Smith, Bradley, *Erotic Art of the Masters: The 18th, 19th and 20th Centuries.* New York, Lyle Stuart, n.d. (1974). Glossy coffee-table book with some interesting illustrations, though emphasis is on sexual, not artistic, content; text of little value; Introduction by Henry Miller.

Speaight, Robert, *Life of Eric Gill.* London, Methuen, 1966. Touches on erotic aspects of Gill's work and ideas; illustrated.

Spencer: *A Private View of Stanley Spencer* by L. Collis. London, Heinemann, 1972. Contains new information on Spencer's sexual habits and their importance to his work; illustrated.

Stokes, Adrian, *Reflections on the Nude.* London and New York, Tavistock Publications, 1967. Very interesting, personal approach; illustrated.

Straker, Jean, *Nudes of Jean Straker.* London, Charles Skilton, 1958. Selection of nude photographs by one of the pioneers in the search for artistic freedom.

Toth, Karl, *Woman and Rococo in France, seen through the life and works of a contemporary, Charles-Pinot Duclos.* London, George Harrap, 1931. Interesting background information on eighteenth-century France; useful illustrations of erotic engravings and drawings.

Turner: *Turner the Painter: His Hidden Life* by B. Falk. London, Hutchinsons, 1938. Study of Turner as a human being, not merely a painter; interesting ideas about his sexuality.

Van Maele: *The Satyrical Drawings of Martin van Maele.* New York, Cythera Press, 1970. Beautiful reproductions of the erotic prints for *La Grande Danse Macabre des Vifs*; good bibliography.

Vaudoyer, Jean-Louis, *The Female Nude in European Painting.* London, Longmans, Green, 1957. Mainly a picture-book; very brief Introduction.

Vertès: *The Erotic Perceptions of Marcel Vertès,* Introduction by M. Gloser. Los Angeles, Art Editions, 1972. Fair Introduction; nice selection of engravings.

Villeneuve, Roland, *Fétichisme et Amour.* Paris, Editions Azur, 1968. Text thin; includes interesting erotic-art illustrations.

Villeneuve, Roland, *Le Diable: Erotologie de Satan.* Paris, Pauvert, 1963. Interesting discussion of the sexual connotations of devil worship; and the fascination this subject has held for artists; very well illustrated; bibliography.

Villeneuve, Roland, *Le Musée de la Bestialité.* Paris, Editions Azur, 1969. Beautifully illustrated from the art of many civilisations, treating theme of sexual relations between humans and animals; text shows little insight into the subject.

Von Heuenstein, Bettina and **Verrou, Jan Lue,** *Softgirls.* Germany, Zero Press, n.d. (c. 1969). Beautiful collection of explicit sexual photographs.

Waldberg, Patrick, *Eros Modern Style.* Paris, Pauvert, 1964. Translated as *Eros in La Belle Epoque,* New York, Grove Press, 1969. Well-illustrated and informative survey of the flowering of eroticism in France, 1880–1910.

Watteau: *Watteau: A Lady at her Toilet* by D. Posner. London, Allen Lane, 1973. Exemplary study of the painting, including a discussion of the role of eroticism in his work and in eighteenth-century art in general.

Wesselmann: 'Wesselmann: The Honest Nude' by G. R. Swenson, *Art and Artists.* London, May 1966. Fair assessment of Wesselmann's nudes; illustrated.

Whittet, G. S., *Lovers in Art.* London, Studio Vista and Dutton, 1972. Picture-book of polite depictions of lovers with brief text.

Wulffen, Dr Erich, *Die Erotik in der Photographie.* Vienna, Berlin, and Leipzig, Verlag für Kulturforschung, n.d. (*c.* 1930). Well-illustrated pioneering study of nude photography.

Younger, Archibald (Introduction by), *French Engravers of the 18th Century.* Edinburgh, Otto Schultz & Co., n.d. (*c.* 1930). Very useful collection of illustrations of erotic prints.

Zichy: *The Erotic Drawings of Mihály Zichy.* New York, Grove Press, 1969. Reproductions of the forty drawings in the Love series; very brief Introduction.

Zwang, Gerard, *Le Sexe de la Femme.* Paris, La Jeune Parque, 1967. Thematic but unscholarly text; very well illustrated with art works.

SECTION III: LITERATURE

A. Erotic Literature

Allsop, Kenneth and **Pitman, Robert,** *A Question of Obscenity.* Northwood, England, Scorpion Press, 1960. Intelligent arguments for (Pitman) and against (Allsop) censorship of works of erotic literature (*Lolita, Ulysses, Lady Chatterley's Lover,* etc.).

Almansi, G. (ed.), *The Treatment of Sexual Themes in the Modern Novel. 20th Century Studies.* Canterbury, University of Kent, November 1969. Good articles on Lawrence, Joyce, Miller, Genet, Burroughs, Gide.

Anderson, Rachel, *The Purple Heart Throbs: the sub-literature of love.* London, Hodder and Stoughton, 1974. Entertaining survey of popular romantic fiction from 1850s to today.

Anon, *Frank and I.* New York, Grove Press, 1968. First published 1902.

Anon, *A Man With a Maid.* New York, Grove Press, 1968. First published 1890s.

Anon, *The Memoirs of Dolly Morton.* California, Brandon House, 1968. Classic American pornographic novel of turn of the century; Introduction by Jack Hirschmann; illustrated with drawings.

Anon, *The Romance of Lust or Early Experiences.* New York, Grove Press, 1972. First published in four volumes, 1873–76.

Apollinaire, Guillaume, *L'Enfer de la Bibliothèque Nationale.* Paris, Mercure de France, 1913. Independent catalogue of segregated collection of French National Library.

Apollinaire, Guillaume, *Memoirs of a Young Rakehell* and *The Debauched Hospedar.* California, Collectors Publications, 1967.

Apuleius, *The Golden Ass.* London, Bestseller Library, 1950. Introduction by Jack Lindsay.

Aretino, Pietro, *The Ragionamenti.* London, Odyssey Press, 1970. English translation of Italian sixteenth-century classic dialogues about sexual habits; Introduction by Peter Stafford.

Aristophanes, *Lysistrata.* New York, St Martin's Press, and London, Academy Editions, 1973. Translated by Jack Brussell; illustrated with Beardsley's drawings.

Ashbee, Henry Spencer (Pisanus Fraxi), *Forbidden Books of The Victorians.* London, Odyssey Press, 1970. Useful Introduction by Peter Fryer; abridged edition of Ashbee's bibliographies of erotica: *Index Librorum Prohibitorum* (1877), *Centuria Librorum Absconditorum* (1879), *Catena Librorum Tacendorum* (1885); invaluable as bibliographies but not a serious study of erotic literature; see also *Index of Forbidden Books,* London, Sphere Books, 1969.

Atkins, John, *Sex in Literature—the erotic impulse in literature.* New York, Grove Press and London, Panther Books, 1972. Interesting and well annotated compendium of long quotations from wide range of authors; useful though limited bibliography.

Auden, W. H., 'The Gobble Poem', *Suck,* No. 1. Amsterdam, October 1969. Explicit homosexual poem, never acknowledged by Auden; not very good poetry but interesting.

Ayres, Michael, *English Homosexual Poetry of the 19th and 20th Centuries.* London, Michael de Hartington, 1972. Descriptive catalogue of the Timothy d'Arch Smith collection.

Bataille, Georges, *The Story of the Eye.* California, Brandon House, 1968. Translation of *L'Histoire de L'Oeil,* Paris, Pauvert, 1967; Introduction by Jack Hirschmann.

BIBLIOGRAPHY

Baudelaire, Charles, *A Une Courtisane* (*To A Courtesan*). Los Angeles, Avanti Art Editions, 1972. Introduction by Jarved Rutter discusses Baudelaire's relationship with Jeanne Duval and the poems it inspired in *Les Fleurs du Mal*; fair translations; illustrated.

Baudelaire, Charles, *The Flowers of Evil*. London, Routledge & Kegan Paul, 1955. Text in English and French with Baudelaire's three Prefaces; translators include Roy Campbell and Aldous Huxley.

Baudelaire: *Baudelaire* by E. Starkie. England, Pelican, 1971. Includes detailed discussion of *Les Fleurs du Mal* and the obscenity trial; scholarly work; bibliography and full references.

Beardsley, Aubrey, *The Story of Venus and Tannhäuser*. New York, Award Books, and London, Tandem Books, 1967. Complete text of *Under the Hill* of 1897, illustrated with Beardsley's drawings; Introduction by Paul J. Gillette.

Blyth, Henry, *The High Tide of Pleasure: 7 English Rakes*. London, Weidenfeld & Nicolson, 1970. Interesting chapter on John Wilmot, 2nd Earl of Rochester, author of *Sodom*, etc.

Bradshaw, Jon, 'Dog Eateth Dog', *Queen Magazine*. London, 4 January 1967. Long and interesting article on prosecution of *Last Exit To Brooklyn* with opinions of Sam Beckett, Anthony Burgess, Brigid Brophy.

Bretonne, Restif de la, *Monsieur Nicolas*. London, Barrie & Rockliffe, 1964. Memoirs of arch-enemy of de Sade, and author of *L'Anti-Justine* (1798); abridged translation by Robert Baldick.

Brittain, Vera, *Radclyffe Hall: A Case of Obscenity*. London, Femina Books, 1968. Study of obscenity trial of *Well of Loneliness*, 1928.

Burns, Robert, *The Merry Muses of Caledonia*. New York, Capricorn Books, 1965; Edinburgh, MacDonald, 1959. Good Introduction by Sydney Goodsir Smith; texts of erotic poems by Burns and Scottish folk songs.

Cleland, John, *Memoirs of a Woman of Pleasure, Fanny Hill*. London, Mayflower, 1970. Includes *The Trial of Fanny Hill* by Richard Bennett; unexpurgated.

Cleugh, James, *The Marquis and the Chevalier*. London, Melrose, 1951. Interesting study of de Sade and Sacher-Masoch.

Cocteau, Jean (Preface and illustrations by), *The White Paper*. New York, Macauley, 1958. The autobiography of a homosexual, attributed to Cocteau; translated from *Le Livre Blanche*, Paris, Erotika Biblion, 1970.

Coppens, Armand, *Memoirs of An Erotic Bookseller*. New York, Grove Press, 1970. Racy memoirs with little bibliographical interest.

Craig, Alec, *The Banned Books of England and Other Countries*. London, Allen & Unwin, 1962. Very good account of literary obscenity, especially legal aspects; interesting chapter on pornography and what the term means and has meant; good bibliography.

Cray, Ed (ed.), *The Anthology of Restoration Erotic Poetry*. Calfornia, Brandon House, 1965. Poems by Rochester, Sedley, Butler, but mostly anonymous; bibliography.

Cray, Ed (ed.), *Bawdy Ballads: A History of Bawdy Songs*. London, Odyssey Press, 1970.

Cray, Ed (ed.), *The Fifteen Plagues of Maidenhead and other forbidden verse*. California, Brandon House, 1966. Includes Herrick, Rochester, Sedley, Suckling, Wilkes, etc.

Croft-Cooke, Rupert, *The Unrecorded Life of Oscar Wilde*. London and New York, W. H. Allen, 1972. Good recent biography.

Crowley, Aleister, *White Stains*. London, Duckworth, 1973. Reissue of privately printed erotic (and mostly bad) poems of Crowley; Introduction by John Symonds.

d'Arch Smith, Timothy, *Love in Earnest: Some Notes on the Lives and Writings of English Uranian Poets from 1889 to 1930*. London, Routledge & Kegan Paul, 1970. Discussion of a group of English homosexual poets; illustrated; references.

Dawes, Charles Reginald, *A Study of Erotic Literature in England Considered with Special Reference to Social Life*. Cheltenham, England, privately printed, 1943. Very good survey of erotic literature with long quotations; unpublished; a copy is in the British Museum Library.

Deakin, Terence J., *Catalogi Librorum Eroticorum*. London, Wolf, 1964. Very good critical bibliography of bibliographies of erotic literature and book catalogues.

[485]

Desnos, Robert, *L'Erotisme Considéré dans ses Manifestations Ecrites, et du Point de Vue de L'Esprit Moderne.* Paris, Le Cercle des Arts, 1953. Interesting text.

Devereaux, Charles, *Venus in India.* London, Sphere, 1970. Introduction by Ronald Pearsall; first published 1889.

Dictionnaire des Oeuvres Erotiques. Paris, Mercure de France, 1971. Dictionary of French erotic literature; well illustrated.

Duffy, Maureen, *The Erotic World of Faery.* London, Hodder and Stoughton, 1972. Freudian interpretation of fairy tales, everything seen in terms of sexual symbolism; a literary study; illustrated; bibliography.

Duffy, Maureen, 'Sex and Literature', *Man and Woman.* London, Vol. 5, Part 64 (1971). Fair short survey of erotic literature.

Ernst, Morris L. and **Schwartz, Alun U.,** *Censorship: The Search for the Obscene.* New York, Macmillan, 1965. Well-documented account of trials in United States of books for obscenity: *Ulysses, Lady Chatterley's Lover,* etc., by two lawyers; discusses nature of obscenity.

Ernst, Morris L. and **Seagle, William,** *To The Pure—a study of obscenity and the censor.* London, 1929. Interesting though now necessarily outdated; mainly concerned with legal aspects.

Fanny Hill's Bang-Up Reciter. London, Wells Publishing Co., 1965. Collection of bawdy songs; illustrated by eighteenth-century erotic prints; first published 1835.

Farmer, John S. and **Earnest, William,** *The Slang of Venery.* Chicago, Henry N. Carey, 1916. Useful dictionary of sexual slang terms and sexual metaphors, covering various European languages, using information from Farmer and Earnest's *Slang and Its Analogues* (1890–94; 7 volumes) and other sources.

Farmer, John S., *Vocabula Amatoria: French-English Dictionary of Erotica.* New York, University Books, 1966. The classic dictionary of French erotic terms with English translations and quotations from sources, including Rabelais, Voltaire, Molière, Rousseau, Zola, etc.; first published 1896.

Foxon, David Fairweather, *Libertine Literature in England, 1660–1745.* New York, University Books, 1966. Very useful discussion and bibliography.

Fryer, Peter, *Private Case—Public Scandal: Secrets of the British Museum Revealed.* London, Secker & Warburg, 1966. Fascinating record of Fryer's detective work in bringing the Private Case to public attention; discussion of some of the books in the Private Case.

Fryer, Peter, 'To Deprave and Corrupt', *Encounter Magazine.* London, March 1967. Points out anomalies and dangers of Obscene Publications Act in regard to serious works of erotic literature.

Gay, Jules, *Bibliographie des Ouvrages Relatifs à L'Amour aux Femmes, au Marriage, et les Livres Factieux Pantagrueliques, Satyriques, etc.* Paris, 1894–1900 (four volumes). Very important bibliography concerned mainly with French-language erotica.

Ginzburg, Ralph, *An Unhurried View of Erotica.* London, Secker & Warburg, 1959; New York, Helsman Press, 1958. Entertaining rather than scholarly survey of erotic literature from Ovid to Henry Miller; unreliable; bibliography. Translated as *Les Enfants de l'Erotisme, Domaine de Langue Anglaise,* Paris, Pauvert, 1960, with numerous illustrations.

Greenwald, Harold, *The Prostitute in Literature.* New York, Ballantine, 1960. Interesting selection of texts from the Bible, Lucian, Villon, Brantôme, Cleland, Zola, Shaw, Joyce, etc.

Grigson, Geoffrey (ed.), *Faber Book of Love Poems.* London, Faber & Faber, 1973. Anthology concentrating on pre-nineteenth-century poetry.

Haight, Anne Lyon, *Banned Books.* London and New York, Bowker, 1970. Dictionary of authors whose works have been banned, with details; useful appendices—Nazi-banned books, library censorship, freedom of the press, court decisions, etc.; useful bibliography.

Hall, Radclyffe, *The Well Of Loneliness.* London, Corgi Books, 1968. Erotic lesbian novel, first published 1928.

Harris, Frank, *My Life and Loves.* London, Corgi Books, 1967. Autobiography of a friend of Oscar Wilde and journalist; notoriously unreliable; unexpurgated five volumes in one; Introduction by John F. Gallagher.

Hughes, Douglas A. (ed.), *Perspectives on Pornography.* London and New York, Macmillan,

1970. Includes 'What is Pornography?' (Anthony Burgess); 'Eroticism in Literature' (Alberto Moravia); 'Night Words: High Pornography and Human Privacy' (George Steiner); 'Dirty Books Can Stay' (Kenneth Tynan); 'The Pornographic Imagination' (Susan Sontag); critical writing of a high standard, both for and against freedom of expression.

Hurwood, Bernhardt, J., *The Golden Age of Erotica*. London, Tandem, 1968. Well-researched survey of erotic literature, especially of the seventeenth and eighteenth centuries; many quotations; bibliography.

Jenkins, Roy, 'Obscenity, Censorship and the The Law: the story of a bill', *Encounter*. London, October 1959. Account of Obscene Publications Act of 1959 by its instigator.

Joyce, James, *Ulysses*. London, Bodley Head, 1958.

Kingsley: *The Beast and the Monk – a life of Charles Kingsley* by Susan Chitty. London, Hodder and Stoughton, 1974. Biography including interesting hitherto unpublished letters and drawings revealing the sexual frustrations of the clergyman and author of *Water Babies*.

Kronhausen, Drs Phyllis and Eberhard, *Erotic Fantasies: A Study of the Sexual Imagination*. New York, Grove Press, 1970. Useful for its numerous excerpts from erotic literature: Rabelais, Aretino, Rochester, Nerciat; *Teleny, Gamiani, Gynecocracy, Romance of Lust,* etc.

Lautréamont, Comte de (Isidore Ducasse), *Maldoror*. London, Allison & Busby, 1970. (*Les Chants de Maldoror*, Paris, Club Géant, 1967.) One of the most outstanding erotic novels, first published 1867; fair translation and Introduction by Alexis Lykiard.

Lautréamont: *Nightmare Culture: Lautréamont and 'Les Chants de Maldoror'* by A. de Jonge. London, Secker & Warburg, 1973. Scholarly discussion of one of the finest and most fascinating examples of French erotic literature.

Lawrence, D. H., *Lady Chatterley's Lover*. Harmondsworth, Penguin, 1961. Good Introduction by Richard Hoggart; first published 1928.

Lawrence: *The Trial of Lady Chatterley: Regina* v. *Penguin Books* C. H. Rolph (ed.). Harmondsworth, Penguin, 1961. Edited transcript of the trial in London, 1960.

Legman, Gershon, *The Horn Book—Studies in Erotic Folklore and Bibliography*. New York, University Books, 1964. Important, well-researched book; discusses *Rediscovery of Burns' Merry Muses of Caledonia; The Horn Book: a Girl's Guide to the Knowledge of Good and Evil* (published Paris or Brussels, 1899, translated from a French book of sex-instruction); Pisanus Fraxi (Ashbee) and his erotic bibliographies; great collectors of erotica.

Legman, Gershon, *Rationale of the Dirty Joke, an analysis of sexual humour*. London, Panther, 1972. Much researched two-volume anthology which covers many works of erotic literature as well as folklore and hearsay.

Leiris, Michel, *Manhood*. London, Cape, 1968. *L'Age d'Homme*. Paris, Gallimard, 1946. Fascinating sexual and emotional self-revelation; Leiris describes his obsessions with the historical Lucretia and Judith.

Linton, E. R., *The Dirty Song Book*. Los Angeles, Medco Books, 1965. Collection of American bawdy songs.

Loth, David, *The Erotic in Literature* (*a historical survey of pornography as delightful as it is indiscreet*). London, Secker & Warburg, 1961. Survey of historical attitudes to sexual literature rather than analysis of eroticism; confusion between pornography and erotic literature; useful, though at times unreliable; bibliography.

Marchand, Henry L., *The French Pornographers*. New York, Book Awards, 1965. Compendium of French erotic literature from medieval period to nineteenth century; short on insight.

Marcus, Steven, *The Other Victorians*. London, Corgi Books, 1969. Includes excellent studies of Ashbee, the bibliographer of erotica; *My Secret Life*; and of Victorian pornographic novels; also a comparison between pornography and erotic literature.

Marcuse, Ludwig, *Obscene: the History of an Indignation*. London, MacGibbon and Kee, 1965. Discussion of obscenity trials: Schlegel's *Lucinde*, Flaubert's *Madame Bovary*, Baudelaire's *Les Fleurs du Mal*, Lawrence's *Lady Chatterley's Lover*, Miller's *Tropic of Cancer* etc., with a rational argument for literary freedom.

McCarthy, Tony (compiled by), *Bawdy British Folk Songs*. London, Wolfe, 1972. Text and music.

Michelson, Peter, *The Aesthetics of Pornography*. New York, Herder & Herder and England, Fowler Wright Books, Ltd, 1971. Intelligent discussion of erotic realism in literature from *Fanny Hill* to *The Rosy Crucifixion*; especially good on de Sade and Genet; good comparison of *Playboy* and *Screw*; misleading title, for the author terms any sexual writing 'pornography' (the word is used impartially).

Miller, Henry, *Tropic of Capricorn*. London, Panther Books, 1969.

Millot, Michel and **L'Ange, Jean,** *The School of Venus*. London, Panther, 1972. Translation of seventeenth-century French erotic novel, discussed by Pepys in his diary; long Introduction by Donald Thomas on the history of bawdy writing.

Mordell, Albert, *The Erotic Motive in Literature*. New York, Collier Books, 1962. A very psychoanalytical approach to literature.

Musset, Alfred de, *Gamiani or Two Nights of Excess*. New York, Award Books and London, Tandem Books, 1968. Unexpurgated, complete; Introduction by Paul J. Gillette.

Nabokov, Vladimir, *Lolita*. London, Corgi, 1961.

Nelson, Howard, 'Forbidden Treasures', *Penthouse*. London, Vol. 5, No. 12, March 1971. Interesting though not very scholarly review of erotic writing: Ashbee, Hancarville, Ovid, Aretino, Restif de la Bretonne, Nerciat, Wilkes, Burns, Verlaine.

Ovid, *The Art of Love*. London, Bestseller Library, 1959. Introduction by J. Lewis May.

Partridge, Burgo, *A History of Orgies*. London, Bestseller Library, 1962. Interesting background information on John Wilkes, Aleister Crowley; not very scholarly.

The Pearl: A journal of voluptuous reading. New York, Grove Press, 1968. Republication of famous Victorian journal of erotica, 1879–80.

Perceau, Louis, *Bibliographie du Roman Erotique au 19e Siècle*. Paris, Fourdrinier, 1930. Two-volume bibliography of French erotic novels of the nineteenth century; very useful.

Perrin, Noel, *Dr. Bowdler's Legacy—a History of expurgated books in England and America*. London, Macmillan, 1970; New York, Macmillan, 1969. Gives numerous examples of expurgated books; with unexpurgated passages from famous books; scholarly; full references.

Praz, Mario, *The Romantic Agony*. London and New York, Oxford University Press, 1970. After forty years, still an astonishingly readable and instructive critical analysis of the exotic eroticism of nineteenth-century European literature, from Romanticism to Decadence; numerous quotations, discussed with real insight; good Foreword by Frank Kermode.

Reade, Brian (Introduction by), *Sexual Heretics: Male Homosexuality in English Literature from 1850–1900*. London, Routledge & Kegan Paul, 1970. Good introduction to wide selection of authors including Swinburne, Pater, Wilde, Burton, Housman, Crowley; illustrated.

Réage, Pauline, *Story of O*. With note on the *Story of O* by André Pieyre de Mandiargues, New York, Grove Press, 1965; translation of *Histoire d'O*. Paris, Pauvert, 1954.

Rembar, Charles, *The End of Obscenity*. New York, Random House, 1968; London, André Deutsch, 1969. Illuminating accounts of the obscenity trials in America of *Lady Chatterley's Lover*, *Fanny Hill*, and *Tropic of Cancer*, by the lawyer who defended them.

Roche, Peter (ed.), *The New Love Poetry: Love, Love, Love*. London, Corgi Books, 1967. Interesting anthology including McGough, Henri, Horovitz.

Rodgers, Bruce, *The Queen's Vernacular: A Gay Lexicon*. London, Blond & Briggs, and San Francisco, Straight Arrow Books, 1972. Very well-researched dictionary of homosexual slang; bibliography.

Rolph, C. H., *Books in The Dock*. London, André Deutsch, 1969. Interesting and well-documented account of the English obscenity laws and their history; Introduction by Sir John Mortimer.

Rose, Alfred (Rolfe S. Reade), *Register of Erotic Books*. New York, Jack Brussel, 1965. Very important bibliography of mainly English erotica up to 1936 (first published) in spite of omissions and errors; some British Museum Private Case pressmarks given; two volumes.

Routisie, Albert de, *Irène*. New York, Grove Press, 1970 (*Le Con d'Irène*, Paris, L'Or du Temps, 1968). One of the finest Surrealist erotic novels; first published 1928; translation by Lowell Bair; Preface by Jean-Jacques Pauvert discusses clandestine publishing of erotica in France in 1920s and 30s.

Sacher-Masoch, Leopold von, *Venus in Furs*. London, Sphere Books, 1969.

Sade, Marquis de: *Marquis de Sade: Selections from his Writings* by S. de Beauvoir. London, Evergreen, and New York, Grove Press, 1954. Includes 'Must We Burn De Sade?' (*Faut-il brûler de Sade?*) in *Les Temps Modernes*. Paris, December 1951, and January 1952; very good discussion of de Sade; bibliography and selections.

Sade, Marquis de: *The Marquis de Sade's 120 Days of Sodom and the Sex Life of the French Age of Debauchery* by I. Bloch. California, Brandon House, 1966. Interesting discussion of French eighteenth-century life in general, and the Marquis and one of his most important works in particular; bibliography; illustrated by eighteenth-century erotic paintings and drawings.

Sade, Marquis de: *The Life and Ideas of the Marquis de Sade* by G. Gorer. London, Panther, 1964. Very good analysis of de Sade; bibliography and references.

Sade, Marquis de, *Oeuvres Complètes* (fifteen volumes). Paris, Cercle du Livre Précieux, 1963–64. Very useful collection with excellent prefaces by Georges Bataille, Pierre Klossowski, Maurice Heine, Maurice Blanchot.

Sade, Marquis de, *Justine, or The Misfortunes of Virtue*. London, Corgi Books, 1965. Very good Introduction on De Sade's writings and ideas by Alan Hull Walton; complete translation; good critical bibliography; (first published 1791).

Sandford, Derek (collected by), *The Body of Love: Poetry in Praise of Women*. London, Blond, 1965. Selections from Chaucer, Donne, Shakespeare, Herrick, Dryden, Rochester, Swift, Whitman, Rossetti, Swinburne, Lawrence.

Selby, Hubert, Jnr, *Last Exit to Brooklyn*. New York, Grove Press, 1965; London, Calder and Boyars, 1968.

Smith, T. R. (ed.), *Poetica Erotica: a collection of rare and curious amatory verse*. New York, Crown Publishers, 1927. Very large number of erotic poems and verses from earliest times to twentieth century, 'avoiding the merely vulgar and obscene'; useful collection.

Southern, Terry and **Hoffenberg, Mason,** *Candy*. New York, Putnam, 1968; London, New English Library, 1970.

Sparrow, John, 'Regina *v*. Penguin Books, an undisclosed element in the case', *Encounter*. London, February 1962. Important article pointing out Lawrence's advocation of a 'perverted' form of intercourse in *Lady Chatterley's Lover*.

Stallworthy, Jon (ed.), *Penguin Book of Love Poetry*. London, Allen Lane, 1973. Entertaining selection.

Thomas, Donald, *A Long Time Burning: The History of Literary Censorship in England*. London, Routledge & Kegan Paul, 1969. Well-researched account; illustrated; useful bibliography and appendix.

Thomas, Donald, 'Master of Renaissance Erotica', *Penthouse*, Vol. 5, No. 6. London, September 1970. Interesting article on Pietro Aretino, author of sixteenth-century Italian erotica.

Trilling, Lionel, 'The Last Lover', *Encounter*. London, October 1958. Interesting review of *Lolita* with discussion of eroticism in literature.

Verlaine, Paul, *Amies et Femmes*. Los Angeles, Avanti Art Editions, 1972. Introduction by Maurice Glosser discusses Verlaine's affair with Rimbaud and its effect on his poetry; translations very literal; illustrated.

Verlaine, Paul, *Femmes: Hombres*. London, Eric & Joan Stevens, 1972. Fascinating explicit erotic poetry; illustrated by Michael Ayrton.

Vicarion, Palmiro, *Count Palmiro Vicarion's Book of Bawdy Ballads*. Paris, Olympia Press, 1959. Entertaining selection including full texts of *Eskimo Nell*, *The Ball of Kirrimuir*, *Abdul Abulbul Emir*, *The Good Ship Venus* etc.

Vidal, Gore, *Myra Breckinridge*. New York, Bantam Books, 1968, and London, Panther, 1969.

Walter, *My Secret Life*. Eleven volumes in one volume, New Jersey, Castle Books, n.d.;

eleven volumes in two volumes, New York, Grove Press, 1966. Complete and un-expurgated edition, with good Introduction by Gershon Legman, of sexual autobiography first published *c.* 1894.

Walter, The English Casanova, a presentation of his unique memoirs, My Secret Life. London, Polybooks, 1967. Long extracts, annotated by Phyllis and Eberhard Kronhausen from the point of view of the sexual psychology the book shows.

Wedeck, H. E., *Dictionary of Erotic Literature.* London, Peter Owen, 1963; New York, Philosophical Library, 1962. Lists sexual subjects, and also authors, with excerpts from Apuleius, Boccaccio, Casanova, Chaucer, Rochester, Ovid, Villon, Wilde, Zola, etc.

Wicked Victorians: Selections from Victorian Hard Core Erotica. London, Odyssey Press, 1971. Some interesting long quotations.

Wilde, D. Gunther (compiled by), *When Maidens were Deflowered and Knightly Lost Their Heads.* New York, Belmont Books, 1967. Collection of bawdy tales and verses including *Les Cent Nouvelles Nouvelles*; Straporola, Aretino, Boccaccio, Firenzuola, Herrick, Rochester, Villon, etc.; illustrated.

Wilde, Oscar (att. to), *Teleny, or the Reverse of the Medal.* California, Collectors' Publications, 1968 (unexpurgated); London, Icon Books, 1966 (expurgated, with Introduction by H. Montgomery Hyde). First published 1893.

Wilkes, John, *An Essay on Woman, and other pieces.* London, John Hotten, September 1871.

Young, Ian, *The Male Muse.* New York, Crossing Press, 1973. Anthology of homosexual poetry by contemporary authors including Isherwood, Ginsberg, and Tennessee Williams.

SECTION I·I: LITERATURE

B. Pornography and Related Topics

Aratow, Paul, *100 Years of Erotica.* San Francisco, Straight Arrow Books, 1971. Amusing portfolio of pornographic photographs, mainly French and American, 1845–1945.

Barber, D. F., *Pornography and Society.* London, Charles Skilton, 1972. Intelligent discussion of the subject; bibliography.

Barnes, H. J., 'Danish Experiment in Pornography', *Encounter.* London, September 1970. Interesting study of Danish abolition of anti-pornography laws.

Barry, John, *Erotic Variations.* California, Brandon House, 1967, and Hemel Hempstead, England, K & G Publications, 1968. Case-histories of deviated sex practices in con-temporary U.S.A., with pseudo-scientific comment.

Brown, Norman O., *Life Against Death.* London, Routledge & Kegan Paul, and New York, Wesleyan University Press, 1959. Good statement of ideas on sex and politics, etc.

Bugler, Jeremy, 'The Sex Sell', *New Society.* London, 15 May 1969. Good short article on sexual persuasion in advertising; illustrated.

Calder-Marshall, Arthur, *Lewd, Blasphemous and Obscene.* London, Hutchinson, 1972. Accounts of the trials of nineteenth-century forerunners of today's progressive ideas, *e.g.* Havelock Ellis.

Chandos, John (ed.), *To Deprave and Corrupt: original studies in the nature of obscenity.* New York, Association Press, and London, Souvenir Press, 1962. Specially commissioned articles on the nature of obscenity in law and in literature; interesting.

Crumb: Marjorie Alessandrini: *Robert Crumb.* Paris, Albin Michel, 1974. Good text in French; well illustrated; bibliography.

Ellis, Albert, *Sex Without Guilt.* New York, Grove Press, 1965, and London, New English Library, 1967. Pioneering psychologist's sensible attitude to sex-instruction and sexual behaviour; bibliography; first published 1958.

Estren, Mark James, *A History of Underground Comics.* San Francisco, Straight Arrow Books, 1974. Intelligent and well-researched survey from the *Tijuana Bibles* to *Zap* and *Big Ass*; very well illustrated.

Eysenck, H. J., *Psychology is About People.* Harmondsworth, Penguin, 1972. Includes 'The Uses and Abuses of Pornography', presenting contentious idea of objectively measuring amount of pornography in any writing by a rating table referring to number of mentions of sex.

Fleishman, Stanley (Introduction by), *The Supreme Court Obscenity Decisions*. New York, Reed Classic Library, 1973. Text of 1973 rulings on constitutional position of censorship.

Freeman, Gillian, *The Undergrowth of Literature*. London, Panther, 1969. Excellent survey of 'minority interest' sex magazines and pornography; Foreword by David Stafford-Clark; illustrated.

Fryer, Peter, 'A Map of the Underground: The Flower Power Structure and London Scene', *Encounter*, London, October 1967. Attitudes, sexual freedom, hopes, etc., of the underground movement of summer of 1967 in London.

Gabor, Mark, *The Pin-Up—A Modest History*. London, André Deutsch, and New York, Universe Books, 1972. Useful collection of illustrations which errs on the side of modesty; little insight.

Gerber, Albert B., *Sex, Pornography and Justice*. New York, Lyle Stuart, 1965. The law in relation to pornography; illustrated.

Gilmore, Donald H., *Sex, Censorship and Pornography*. San Diego, California, Greenleaf Classics, 1969. An attempt at a serious study of the subject of contemporary pornography; explicit illustrations; two volumes.

Ginzburg, Ralph, 'Eros on Trial', *Fact Magazine*. New York, Volume 2, Issue 3, May–June 1965. Creator of *Eros* Magazine tells story of his trial for obscenity; illustrated with some art work from Eros.

Girodias, Maurice, 'The Erotic Society', *Encounter*. London, February 1966. The publisher of erotica replies to George Steiner's attack on pornography: 'Night Words'.

Goldstein, Michael J. and **Kant, Harold Sanford,** *Pornography and Sexual Deviance*. Berkeley, Los Angeles, and London, University of California Press, 1973. Important report of research carried out by the Legal and Behavioral Institute, Beverly Hills, California; concludes that pornography does not incite criminal or anti-social acts and can lessen such developments.

Greer, Germaine, *The Female Eunuch*. London, MacGibbon & Kee, 1970. Clear and well-researched statement of Women's Liberation philosophy.

Greer, Germaine, 'What Turns Women On?', *Esquire*. London, July 1973. Sensible article on women and sexual titillation; discussion of pin-up magazines for women; illustrated.

Harris, Sarah, *The Puritan Jungle: America's Sexual Underground*. London, Mayflower, 1970. Sensationalised, journalistic view of sexual activities in America in late sixties.

Hegeler, Inge and Stan, *An ABZ of Love*. London, Spearman, 1969. Revised from the Danish by Alex Comfort; sensible dictionary of sexual matters illustrated with drawings.

Holbrook, David (ed.), *The Case Against Pornography*. London, Tom Stacy, 1972. Anthology of essays plus hysterical Introduction by the editor pointing out the deadly dangers of pornography.

Holt, R. G. (Introduction by), *Little Dirty Comics* and *More Little Dirty Comics*. San Diego, California, Socio Library, 1971. Reprints of the 'Tijuana Bibles' of the thirties, featuring the unofficial lives of Flash Gordon, Popeye, Dick Tracey, Dagwood and Blondie, Lil Abner and Daisy Mae, etc.; two volumes of comic strips.

Hunold, Günter, *Sexual Knowledge*. London, H. R. Publications, 1972. Translated from the German; intelligently written; explicitly illustrated.

Kemp, Earl (ed.), *The Illustrated Presidential Report of the Commission on Obscenity and Pornography*. San Diego, California, Greenleaf Classics, 1970. The full text of the enlightened American obscenity report, unofficially published with hundreds of explicit examples of the material described; an invaluable document on all aspects of pornography.

Kilpatrick, James Jackson, *The Smut Peddlers*. London, Paul Elek, 1961. Rather philistine survey of the pornography 'racket' in United States up to 1960; short bibliography.

Kinsey, Alfred, *Sexual Behaviour in the Human Male. Sexual Behaviour in the Human Female*. Philadelphia, W. B. Saunders, 1948; 1953. Pioneering studies in human sexual behaviour; bibliographies and references.

Krafft-Ebing, Richard von, *Psychopathia Sexualis: Aberrations of Sexual Life*. London,

Panther, 1965. Classic study of sexual deviations from medical viewpoint (first published 1886), edited by Alexander Hartwich.

Kronhausen, Drs Phyllis and Eberhard, *Freedom To Love.* New York, Grove Press, 1970. Script, illustrated with stills, of film pleading for sexual freedom; excerpts from McClure's *The Beard* and Weill's *Geese*; interviews with Hugh Hefner, John Trevelyan, Kenneth Tynan, etc.

Kronhausen, Drs Phyllis and Eberhard, *Pornography and the Law: The Psychology of Erotic Realism and Hard Core Pornography.* New York, Ballantine Books, 1970 (first edition 1959, revised); London, New English Library, 1967. Intelligent attempt to distinguish between hard-core pornography and erotic realism; discussions of Pepys, Casanova, Walter, Frank Harris, Henry Miller, Bataille, D. H. Lawrence, Genet, Cleland in relation to pornographic writings, with long quotations; long bibliography; Introduction by Theodor Reik (New York), H. Montgomery Hyde (London).

Kronhausen, Drs Phyllis and Eberhard, *Sexual Response in Women.* London, Corgi Books, 1968. Good account of nature of women's sexuality; long bibliography.

Kuh, Richard H., *Foolish Figleaves: Pornography in and out of court.* New York, Macmillan, 1967. Anti-pornography; by lawyer suggesting legislation to keep pornography off the streets; not hysterical.

Lauret, Jean-Claude, *The Danish Sex Fairs.* London, Jasmine Press, 1970. Interesting account of Copenhagen Fair, 1969, and Odense Fair, 1970; useful document; Foreword by Fernando Henriques; illustrated.

Lawrence, D. H., *A Propos of Lady Chatterley's Lover and other essays.* Harmondsworth, Penguin, 1967. Includes essay 'Pornography and Obscenity' (1929), the best statement of Lawrence's ideas on this topic.

Legman, Gershon, *The Intimate Kiss.* New York, Paperback Library, 1971; published as *Oragenitalism*, London, Duckworth, 1972. Intelligent and unsensational discussion of oral erotic technique.

Levy, William, *The Virgin Sperm Dancer.* The Hague, Bert Bakker, 1972. Erotic adventures of a boy transformed into a girl for one day in Amsterdam; imaginative explicit photographs by Ginger Gordon.

The Little Red Schoolbook, London, Stage One, 1971. (Translation of *Den Lille Rode Bog For Skoleelever*, Copenhagen, Reitzels, 1969.) Very useful little compendium of information usually denied schoolchildren in Britain; sections on sex and drugs; very liberated approach. (Second edition has section on sex removed, as a result of the obscenity trial.)

Lo Duca, G., *De Erotica II: Technique de l'érotisme.* Paris, Pauvert, 1960. Translated by Alan Hull Walton as *The Technique of Eroticism.* London, Rodney Books, 1966. A reasonable study of ad-men's and entertainers' exploitation of man's natural erotic desires; well illustrated.

Mailer, Norman, *The Prisoner of Sex.* London, Weidenfeld & Nicolson, 1971. Discussion of contemporary sexual attitudes, especially in relation to literature; attack on Women's Liberation.

Marcus, Steven, 'Pornotopia', *Encounter.* London, August 1966. Very interesting comparison of pornography and erotic novels; material from *The Other Victorians.*

Marcuse, Herbert, *Eros and Civilisation.* London, Sphere Books, 1969; New York, Beacon Press, 1956. Influential work relating Freud's teachings on sexual instinct to a political view of man at the mercy of the industrial state.

Masters, William and **Johnson, Virginia,** *Human Sexual Response.* Boston, Little, Brown & Company, 1966. Pioneering exploration of human sexuality; bibliography; references.

Matisse, Sylvano, *Pornography Exposé: Eroticism and Pornography Down The Ages.* London, Diamond Star Books, 1972. Scrappily-illustrated soft-pornography posing as serious history.

Millett, Kate, *Sexual Politics.* London, Sphere, 1972. Standard statement of Women's Liberation attitude to the role of women in the modern world.

Mishan, E. J., *Making the World Safe for Pornography.* London, Alcove Press, 1973. Title essay in this collection argues with doubtful logic and faulty history that the permissive revolution is leading us to our doom; curious parallels are made with Nazi Germany.

Nelson, Edward J., Jnr, *Yesterday's Porno: A Pictorial History of Early Stag Photographs.* New York, Nostalgia Classics, 1972. Very brief text; large selection of early pornographic photographs; two volumes.

Neville, Richard, *Playpower.* London, Paladin, 1972. Documentation of the alternative society movement with a section on the sexual revolution, by one of its heroes in England.

North, Maurice, *The Outer Fringe of Sex: A Study in Fetishism.* London, Illustrated Press, 1972. Poor, unscholarly, sensationalised.

'The Nude Business', *Town Magazine.* London, January 1967. Interviews with Bob Guccione, Leslie Bambridge, Harrison Marks, Paul Raymond.

Packard, Vance, *The Sexual Wilderness.* London, Longmans, 1968. Necessarily dated analysis of sexual relationships among the young; full reference notes.

Palmer, Tony (ed.), *The Trials of OZ.* London, Blond & Briggs, 1971. Transcript of OZ trial; drawings by Feliks Topolski.

Peckham, Morris, *Art and Pornography, An Experiment in Explanation.* New York and London, Harper & Row, 1971. Thought-provoking discussion marred by lack of understanding of art and too wide a definition of pornography; illustrated.

Poland, Jefferson F. and **Alison, Valerie,** *The Records of the San Francisco Sexual Freedom League.* New York, Olympia, 1971. Information on West Coast sex-revolution of late sixties.

Polsky, Ned, *Hustlers, Beats and Others.* England, Pelican, 1971; New York, Aldine Publishing Co., 1967. Intelligent book on 'sociology of deviance' in America; Chapter on 'The Sociology of Pornography' suggests that pornography, like prostitution, provides 'antisocial' sex as a necessary complement to the concept of the family; makes no attempt to differentiate between pornography and erotic works of literature; full references.

Pomeroy, Wardell B., *Dr. Kinsey and the Institute for Sex Research.* London, Nelson, 1972. Story of the work of Dr Kinsey on human sexual behaviour.

Pornography: The Longford Report. London, Coronet Books, 1972. Full text of the private report; naive and bigoted.

Reich, Wilhelm, *Function of the Orgasm.* New York, Farrar, Strauss, Giroux, 1961; London, Panther, 1972. Influential work on the vital importance of the role of sex in modern society; controversial ideas about political repression of sex; first published 1942.

Richards, Abe and **Irvine, Robert,** *An Illustrated History of Pornography.* New York, Athena Books, 1968. Pseudo-scholarly work of little merit; illustrated, mainly with soft pornography.

Robinson, Paul A., *The Sexual Radicals.* London, Paladin, 1972. Intelligent studies of Wilhelm Reich, Geza Roheim, Herbert Marcuse; Foreword by Alex Comfort; U.S. title, *The Freudian Left.*

Rolph, C. H. (ed.), *Does Pornography Matter?* London, Routledge and Kegan Paul, 1961. Symposium, including contributions from Sir Herbert Read, Geoffrey Gorer, Dr Donald Soper etc.

Roszak, Theodore, *The Making of a Counter Culture.* London, Faber & Faber, 1970. Brown, Marcuse and their effect on alternative thinking; reasonably useful.

Rund, Jeff, *The Adventures of Sweet Gwendoline.* New York, Belier Press, 1974. Entertaining anthology of drawings and writings by John Willie.

Ryan, Alan, 'The Right To be Left Alone', *Times Literary Supplement.* London 25 February 1972. Balanced and well-reasoned defence of the right to obtain whatever literature people require.

Sadecky, Peter, *Octobriana and The Russian Underground.* New York and London, Harper & Row, 1971. Discussion of the Progressive Political Pornography Group in contemporary Russia and its anti-Soviet publications; illustrated.

Sadoul, Jaques, *L'Enfer des Bulles.* Paris, Pauvert, 1968. Selection of eroticism in openly-published comic strips, especially 1930s and '40s, French and American.

Sex and Culture, issue of *Encounter.* London, March 1972. Includes: 'The Sex Offences Act', Lord Arran; 'Making The World Safe for Pornography', Edward J. Mishan; 'Film Modalities of Sex', John Weightman; 'Onwards from Oz', Michael Beloff; useful.

Sex In The Sixties: a candid look at the age of mini-morals. New York, Time-Life, 1968, by the staff of *Time* magazine. Journalistic, superficial survey; edited by Joe David Brown.

Shrapnel, Norman, 'The Porn Market', *Times Literary Supplement*. London, 11 February 1972. Survey of pornography available in Soho in early 1972.

Simons, G. L., *Pornography Without Prejudice*. London, Abelard-Schuman, 1972. Fair statement of liberal attitude to pornography; discussion of prosecutions (e.g. *Little Red Schoolbook, Oz* etc.).

Smythe, Tony (Introduction by), *Against Censorship*. London, National Council for Civil Liberties, 1972. Good articles on the dangers of obscenity laws being used for political purposes.

Stein, Ralph, *The Pin-Up from 1852 to Now*. London, Hamlyn, 1974. Glossy coffee-table book with some good early photographs; later examples are almost entirely from *Playboy*; poor text.

Steiner, George, 'Night Words: High Pornography and Human Privacy', *Encounter*. London, October 1965. Intelligent attack on pornography as an invasion of privacy and as contemptuous literature.

Storr, Anthony, *Sexual Deviation*. Harmondsworth, Penguin, 1964. Very sound survey of the subject; bibliography.

The Summing up by Mr. Justice Stable: Regina v. *Martin Secker & Warburg: The Philanderer Case*. New York, Knopf, 1954. Very good legal definition of obscenity.

Swan, Peter, 'The Problem of Pornography', *Library Association Record*. London, November 1968. Bigoted, patronising argument for the need for librarians to protect library-users from 'dangerous books'.

Teal, Donn, *The Gay Militants*. New York, Stein & Day, 1971. Serious discussion of Gay Liberation movement in America; detailed footnotes.

Tom: *The Best of Tom of Finland*. Los Angeles, A.M.G. Studios, n.d. (*c.* 1970). Many of Tom's male-nude butch drawings illustrated; appreciation of Tom by Orsen.

Trevelyan, John (Preface by), *The Obscenity Report*. London, Olympia Press, 1971. Includes *Presidential Commission on Pornography*, 1970; *Arts Council Report on Obscenity*, 1969; *Report of Danish Forensic Medicine Council, 1966; important collection of texts.*

Ullerstam, Lars, *The Erotic Minorities*. London, Calder and Boyers, 1964. A Swedish psychiatrist's passionate call for complete sexual freedom for the individual.

Wilson, John, *Logic and Sexual Morality*. Harmondsworth, Penguin, 1967. Intelligent advocation of a public morality based solely on respect for the rights of the individual; very full footnotes.

Wortley, Richard, *Pin-Up's Progress*. London, Panther, 1971. Entertaining collection of illustrations.

Yaffé, Maurice and **Tennent, T. G.,** 'Pornography: A Psychological Appraisal', *British Journal of Hospital Medicine*. London, March 1973. Well-researched survey of psychological studies of pornography; comes to no conclusion as to dangers or benefits.

Zack, David, 'Smut for Love, Art, Society', *Art and Artists*. London, December 1969. Good article on American underground comics; discusses work of Crumb, Wilson, Shelton; illustrated.

SECTION IV: THE PERFORMING ARTS

Alexander, H. M., *Striptease: The Vanished Art of Burlesque*. New York, Knight, 1938. Discussion of American burleque in general and striptease in particular, successfully capturing the atmosphere of the subject; well illustrated; useful glossary of burlesque slang.

Alley, Robert, *Last Tango In Paris*. London, Pan Books, 1973. A novel based on the film; illustrated by stills.

Anger, Kenneth, *Hollywood Babylone*. Paris, Pauvert, 1959. San Francisco, Straight Arrow, 1974. Interesting survey of the great era of Hollywood, especially the stars and the star system, private lives and public images; well illustrated.

Aulnoyes, François des, *Histoire et Philosophie du Striptease: Essai sur l'Erotisme au Music*

Hall. Paris, Pensée Moderne, 1958. Text rather superficial, but interesting illustrations; *Striptease et Erotisme* (1958) has identical text but politer photographs.

Bazin, André, *What is Cinema?* University of California Press, 1971. Two volumes of early essays, including 'Entomology of the Pin-Up Girl' (1946); 'The Outlaw' (1948); 'Eroticism in the Cinema' (1957); rather dated.

Beauvoir, Simone de, *Brigitte Bardot and The Lolita Syndrome.* London, Weidenfeld & Nicolson and André Deutsch, 1960. Very subjective essay on sex symbols; illustrated.

Brusendorff, Ove and **Henningsen, Poul,** *Erotica for The Millions: Love In The Movies.* London, Rodney Books, 1960. Of interest only for a good selection of stills.

Cheshire, David F., *Music Hall in Britain.* Newton Abbot, Devon, David and Charles, 1974. Discusses morality and the music hall, and censorship; illustrated; bibliography.

Chevalier, Denys, *Metaphysique du Striptease.* Paris, Pauvert, 1960. Thoughtful discussion of historical and philosophical aspects of striptease; well illustrated.

Cinema, special issue of *Censorship,* London, No. 2, Spring, 1965. Good articles by N. M. Hunnings, Donald Thomas, and Raymond Durgnat (on 'Horror, Violence and Catharsis').

Cinema and the Nude—a pictorial history. London, Top Sellers, n.d. (*c.* 1970). Collection of stills from exploitation films; text valueless.

Derval, Paul, *Folies Bergère.* Paris, Les Editions de Paris, 1954; London, Methuen, 1955. Entertaining and well-illustrated memoirs of the director of the night club; Preface by Maurice Chevalier.

Durgnat, Raymond, *Eros in the Cinema.* London, Calder and Boyars, 1966. Very interesting series of short articles on various aspects of eroticism in films up to mid-sixties; useful bibliography; well illustrated.

Durgnat, Raymond, *Sexual Alienation in the Cinema.* London, Studio Vista, 1974. Thought-provoking study of the breaking of cinematic taboos in commercial and underground films; well illustrated.

Elsom, John, *Erotic Theatre.* London, Secker & Warburg, 1973. Thought-provoking discussion, though too concerned with history and weak on analysis of recent developments; Introduction by John Trevelyan; well illustrated.

Fagan, Jim, *Sex at the Cinema.* London, Melbourne, and Sydney, Scripts Pty. Ltd., 1967. Discussion of sex films from earliest times to 1960s; some interesting information, but basically very lightweight; illustrated.

Film Censorship: issue of *Screen,* London, vol. 2, no. 3, 1970. Includes 'Film Censorship in Great Britain' (John Trevelyan); 'The Effects of Violence in the Mass Media' (Vicki Eves); 'The Damned: Visconti, Wagner, and the Reinvention of Reality' (Margaret Tarratt); useful material.

Findlater, Richard, *Banned! A Review of Theatrical Censorship in Britain.* London, Panther, 1968. Careful account of theatrical censorship in Britain up to its abolition; bibliography.

Gidal, Peter, *Andy Warhol—Films and Paintings.* London, Studio Vista and Dutton, 1971. Discusses and illustrates *Blow-Job, Chelsea Girls, My Hustler, Couch, Blue Movie (Fuck), Lonesome Cowboys,* etc.

Hamill, Pete (Introduction by), *The Deep Throat Papers.* New York, Manor Books, 1973. Articles on *Deep Throat* plus transcript of the trial; illustrated with stills.

Hanson, Gillian, *Original Skin: Nudity and Sex in Cinema and Theatre.* London, Tom Stacey Ltd, 1970. Interesting survey of eroticism in the Theatre and Cinema in the sixties, but lacking in insight; short bibliography; illustrations.

Houghton, Mick, 'Shock Rock', *The Story of Pop.* London, Part 16, January 1974. Interesting short article on sexual explicitness in stage displays and songs of rock stars—Zappa, Beefheart, Fugs, Alice Cooper.

Hunnings, Neville March, *Film Censors and the Law.* London, Allen & Unwin, 1967. Good legalistic survey; well documented; bibliography.

Koch, Stephen, *Stargazer: Andy Warhol's World and his Films.* New York, Praeger, 1973; London, Calder and Boyers, 1974. Thoughtful and detailed study of Warhol's films up to *Lonesome Cowboys,* especially an analysis of the theme of homosexuality; illustrated; filmography.

Knight, Arthur and **Alpert, Hollis,** *The History of Sex in Cinema.* New York, *Playboy,*

April, May, June, August, September, November 1965; February, April, August, September, October, November, December 1966; January, April, June, November 1967; April, July 1968; January 1969. *Sex in Cinema*, November 1969, 1970, 1971, 1972, 1973, 1974. *Sex Stars*, December 1969, 1970, 1971, 1972, 1973, 1974. Very useful series of long and well-documented articles; fully illustrated and well researched.

Kyrou, Ado, *Amour-Erotisme au Cinéma*. Paris, Eric Losfeld, 1966. Personal view of film eroticism; illustrated.

Lee, Ray, *A Pictorial History of Hollywood Nudity*. Chicago, Merit Books, 1964. Journalistic and superficial account; some interesting photos.

Levy, William (ed.), *Wet Dreams: Films and Adventures*. Amsterdam, Joy Publications, 1973. Account of the festivals of erotic films held in Amsterdam in November 1970 and October 1971; film catalogue includes Genet's *Chant d'Amour*, Bodil's *A Summer's Day*, and the German cartoon version of *Snow-White and the Seven Dwarfs*; explicitly illustrated.

Lo Duca, G., *L'Erotisme au Cinéma*. Paris, Pauvert, 1966. Three volumes; chiefly of interest for the wide selection of stills though necessarily dated as the books were first published 1957–62.

Mailer, Norman, *Marilyn*. New York, Grosset & Dunlap, and London, Hodder & Stoughton, 1973. Rather badly organised and uneven, but interesting text on Marilyn Monroe; beautiful illustrations.

Malina, Judith and **Beck, Julian,** *Paradise Now*. New York, Vintage Books, 1971. Text and philosophy of Living Theatre's most famous project; illustrated.

McCormack, E., 'Hip Smut Baron's Pornographic Film Fest', *Rolling Stone*. San Francisco, 4 January 1973. Discussion of second New York Erotic Film Festival, December 1972.

Miller, Henry, *Quiet Days in Clichy*. New York, Grove Press, 1965. Adapted for the cinema; illustrated with stills from the film.

Milner, Michael, *Sex on Celluloid*. New York, McFadden-Bartell, 1964. Sensationalised and superficial treatment; some interesting illustrations.

Morin, Edgar, *The Stars*. London, Calder & Boyars, 1960. Useful insight into star system, screen goddesses, etc.

Pascall, Jeremy, and **Jeavons, Clyde,** *A Pictorial History of Sex in the Movies*. London, Hamlyn, 1975. Fascinating compendium of information; very well illustrated.

Rabenalt, Arthur Maria, *Mimus Eroticus*: Vol. 1, *Die Erotische Schauszenik in der Antiken Welt* (1965); Vol. 2, *Das Venusische Schauspiel im Mittelalter und in der Renaissance* Part I (1965); Vol. 3, *Das Venusische Schauspiel im Mittelalter und in der Renaissance* Part II (1965); Vol. 4, *Beitrage zur Sittengeschichte der Erotischen Szenik im Zwanzigsten Jahrhundert* Part I (1965); Vol. 5, *Beitrage zur Sittengeschichte der Erotischen Szenik im Zwanzigsten Jahrhundert* Part II (1967). Hamburg, Verlag für Kulturforschung. Well-researched history of eroticism in the theatre from Classical to modern period, plus a discussion of sex in the cinema; good bibliographies; very well illustrated.

Rabenalt, Arthur Maria, *Theater ohne Tabu*. Emsdetten, Verlag Lechte, 1970. Intelligent discussion of eroticism in the recent theatre, mainly concerned with Germany; well illustrated; bibliography of German publications.

Rabenalt, Arthur Maria, *Theatrum Sadicum: Der Marquis de Sade und das Theater*. Emsdetten, Verlag Lechte, 1963. Interesting discussion of de Sade's concern with the theatre, setting his ideas in a historical perspective, with consideration of those influenced by him; bibliography; illustrated by Heim Heckroth.

Rabenalt, Arthur Maria, *Voluptas Ludans: Das Erotische Geheimtheater im 17., 18. and 19. Jahrhundert*. Regensberg, Verlag die Schaubühne, n.d. (*c.* 1964). Interesting discussion of erotic theatre; illustrated; bibliography.

Ragni, Gerome and **Rado, James,** *Hair*. New York, Pocket Books, 1970. The script (complete); illustrated with photographs from New York production.

Renan, Sheldon, *The Underground Film*. London, Studio Vista, 1968. Interesting though now outdated survey; first published as *An Introduction to the American Underground Film*, New York, Dutton, 1967; illustrated.

Rostagno, Aldo with **Beck, Julian,** *We, The Living Theatre*. New York, Ballantine Books, 1970. Pictorial documentation of *Paradise New* and other projects, with commentary.

BIBLIOGRAPHY

Rotsler, William, *Contemporary Erotic Cinema.* New York, Ballantine Books, 1973. On the whole, a worthless guide to pornographic and near pornographic films; illustrated.

Schechner, Richard, *Dionysus in '69.* New York, Farrar, Strauss, Giroux, 1970. Text and photographs from The Performance Group's production of Euripides' *The Bacchae* in New York.

Schechner, Richard, 'Pornography and the New Expression', *The Atlantic Monthly.* Boston, January 1967. Good article on erotic theatre.

'Sex and the Arts: Explosive Scene', *Newsweek.* New York, 14 April 1969. Journalistic survey of increasing freedom in British and American films and plays; illustrated.

Shulman, Irving, *Harlow: An Intimate Biography.* New York and London, Mayflower-Dell, 1964. Full of information, but over-sensationalised; illustrated.

Sjoman, Vilgot, *I Am Curious Yellow.* New York, Grove Press, 1968. Script and stills from the film, with transcript of the trial in New York.

Theatre, special issue of *Censorship,* London, No. 4, Autumn 1965. Good articles by John Mortimer, Donald Thomas, and Edward Bond (on his play *Saved*).

Trevelyan, John, *What The Censor Saw.* London, Michael Joseph, 1973. Entertaining reminiscences of former Secretary to the British Board of Film Censors; surprisingly suggests that censorship is only justifiable for children.

Tyler, Parker, *Homosexuality in the Movies.* New York, Holt, Rinehart & Winston, 1972. Sane plea for sexual freedom, and argument that everyone is basically bisexual; very good critical analysis of homosexuality in films; illustrated.

Tyler, Parker, *Sex Psyche Etcetera in the Film.* New York, Horizon, 1969; Harmondsworth, Penguin, 1971. Important articles on Warhol's *Fuck*; the sex goddess; *I Am Curious Yellow*; Antonioni; Fellini; Bergman.

Tyler, Parker, *Underground Film: A Critical History.* New York, Grove Press, 1970; London, Secker & Warburg, 1971. Useful work; discusses eroticism in Surrealist and underground films; illustrated.

Tynan, Kenneth, *Oh! Calcutta!* New York, Grove Press, 1969. Script and photos of New York production.

Vogel, Amos, *Film as a Subversive Art.* London, Weidenfeld and Nicholson, 1974. Well researched and wide-ranging discussion of taboos in the cinema from Surrealism to the present day; excellent sections on *nudity, erotic and pornographic cinema,* and *homosexuality and other variants*; very well illustrated; film catalogues for each section.

Walker, Alexander, *Sex in the Movies.* Harmondsworth, Penguin, 1968. First published as *The Celluloid Sacrifice,* London, Michael Joseph, 1966; especially good on the screen goddesses and on screen censorship; illustrated.

Warhol, Andy, *Blue Movie.* New York, Grove Press, 1968. Script and stills from the film.

Washington, Irving, 'The Film Censor is Dead, Long Live the Film Censor', *Time Out.* London, Nos. 63 and 64, 30 April–6 May; 7 May–13 May, 1971. Interesting critical review of the role of the film censor, of film clubs, and of TV censorship.

West, Mae, *Goodness Had Nothing To Do With It: The Autobiography of Mae West.* London, W. H. Allen, 1960; revised edition, New York, MacFadden-Bartell, 1970. Fascinating reading; illustrated.

Whitehouse, Mary, *Who Does She Think She Is?* London, New English Library, 1971. Mrs Whitehouse's entertaining, though also disturbing, story behind her campaign to clean up television.

Williamson, Bruce, 'Porno-chic', *Playboy.* New York, August 1973. Well-illustrated investigation of overground hard-core films, *e.g. Deep Throat, Devil in Miss Jones, Behind the Green Door,* etc.

[497]

Index